DOMINION FROM SEA TO SEA

Dominion from Sea to Sea

Pacific Ascendancy and
American Power

BRUCE CUMINGS

Yale University Press
New Haven & London

Published with assistance from the Louis Stern Memorial Fund.

Designed by James J. Johnson and set in Adobe Caslon type by Keystone Typesetting, Inc.
Printed in the United States of America.

The Library of Congress has cataloged the hardcover as follows:

Cumings, Bruce, 1943–
Dominion from sea to sea : Pacific ascendancy and American power / Bruce Cumings.
    p. cm.
Includes bibliographical references and index.
ISBN 978-0-300-11188-0 (cloth : alk. paper)

1. Pacific States—History. 2. Pacific States—Civilization. 3. Pacific States—Economic conditions. 4. United States—Relations—Pacific Area. 5. Pacific Area—Relations—United States. 6. United States—Territorial expansion. 7. United States—Historical geography. 8. United States—Foreign relations. I. Title.
F851.C94 2009
979—dc22
2009018236

ISBN 978-0-300-16800-6 (pbk.)

A catalogue record for this book is available from the British Library.

10 9 8 7 6 5 4 3 2

To Eleanor Sharts Cumings-Hood

He shall have dominion also from sea to sea,
and from the river unto the ends of the earth.

—Psalm 72

Contents

V *A Tipping Point*

Color illustrations follow pages 40 and 264

Preface

This book develops a Pacific perspective on America's relationship to the world, standing in James Polk's Washington a century and a half ago and coming down to the present, drawing a fairly straight line all the way from the origin and development of California and the West ultimately to the heartland of the People's Republic of China. If Walt Whitman and historian Richard Drinnon had not thought of it first, "facing West" would be the title of this book. In other words, this is not a book about the West or about American involvement in the Pacific. It is about both, as a way of erasing the line between domestic and international perspectives. In exploring the contemporary American ascendancy, I attempt to join together what other authors usually treat separately: domestic and international history, international relations and political economy, and both sides of a vigorous Pacific economy. This book is also about technological change, and how sharp leaps forward in economic growth created a bicoastal national economy that has led the world for more than a century, a development that also transformed, undercut, or simply crushed original American conceptions of the continent they first inhabited nearly 400 years ago: a garden, an Eden, Arcadia, someday a Utopia.

Most of the American literature on international affairs remains deeply imbued with Atlanticism, but I will argue for a dual posture: an Atlanticist dimension in our relations with Europe and a Pacific dimension that began with the frontier and mid-nineteenth-century relations with East Asia, but which in the past half-century has come to rival and perhaps surpass our Atlantic relations, giving us a new way to make sense of the American position in the world. The global leader that the United States replaced had the same curiosity as the one that was going to hold sway in the current century: Great Britain and Japan both occupy small islands, set just far enough away from the mainland to breed a solipsistic sense of ineffable superiority (indeed, for the British, "continentalism" connotes European provincialism). Once the United States was also called an "island country," sheltered by two great oceans. It was the only great power that for more than a century was entirely self-sufficient unto itself and therefore invulnerable to external dependencies, and the only power with vast reaches yet to be filled up with people and enterprise (save for Russia's frigid and still-undeveloped frontier in Siberia, or the deserts and mountains of China's Central Asian steppe, still home to tribes and nomads). The American position in the world, however, owes much to its being the first hegemonic power to inhabit an immense land mass: not an island empire like England or Pacific Century–pretender Japan, but a continent open at both ends to the world's two largest oceans. The United States is the only great power with long Atlantic and Pacific coasts, making it simultaneously an Atlantic and a Pacific nation. The historic dominance of Atlanticists, gazing upon a Europe whose civilization gave birth to our own, averts our eyes from this fact (indeed, the continental divide still makes a New Yorker uncomfortable in Los Angeles—and vice versa).

I want to put forth a "Pacificist" interpretation of America's role and position in the world, or for short, a non-Atlanticist text. But "Pacificist" sounds too much like "pacifist" (and is a synonym for it according to the *Oxford English Dictionary*), which is hardly my intent, nor is it to critique or supplant Atlanticism. That is a venerable narrative, kept alive in our time by people like Henry Kissinger, for the world, and the late Samuel Huntington (*Who Are We?*), for the ethnic core that shaped it: Anglo-Saxons. It would be boorish to point out that most Atlanticists seem to know very little about our Pacific involvements, or East Asia itself; Kissinger's multivolume tome is the best memoir of a secretary of state since Dean Acheson's *Present at the Creation,* but when it comes to trying to understand Japan or China, one is a kabuki play and the other is boxes-within-boxes.

My main themes are these, recurring throughout the analysis: (1) the American singularity of a thickly settled and still dynamic Atlantic Coast and Middle Border (the Midwest, as it was long called), and an even more vibrant Pacific Coast that keeps reinventing itself; (2) the expansion of settlers through a continent perceived as empty and unspoiled, a limitless garden—or Eden, or Arcadia—requiring only white settler fertilization to bloom into Utopia, and the absence in the same narrative of any means of comprehending the relentless industrialization that began to transform this garden nearly two centuries ago and has never quit; (3) the white settler encounter with people of color, which was and remains fundamentally different from American interaction with Europeans; (4) American relations with East Asia which, beginning more than 150 years ago with Perry's "opening" of Japan on the heels of Polk's war with Mexico, have never conformed to the Atlanticist narrative and in fact depart dramatically from it; (5) the tipping point that 1941 signified in our interactions with East Asia and the rest of the world, which ultimately became more important and determining than our historical relations with Europe—since Pearl Harbor the United States has operated differently in the Pacific compared to the Atlantic, and this increasingly seems to be the way we operate globally—leading to the deepest divisions with our traditional Atlantic allies since the victory in 1945; (6) the role of the central state in developing the West and especially California; (7) the global archipelago of military bases that arose during the Korean War and the cold war and that has its strongest impact in the Pacific; and (8) a state-funded digital revolution in the past half-century that is a core element of American preeminence. These themes recur in chapters that move both chronologically and back and forth in time from the 1840s to the present.

The Pacific is the world's largest ocean, indeed it is the planet's "biggest single feature," in Colin McEvedy's words; twice the size of the Atlantic, it occupies about one-third of the earth's surface. It also has more islands than any other ocean, about 25,000. Few books with Pacific in the title fail to dwell on the islands—and their romance, exoticism, and freewheeling ways (think of Michener's *South Pacific*). This book isn't about that vast ocean or that romance. The equator marks off the southern boundary of my interest. It isn't that the southern region is unimportant: it's that American interactions with East Asia are much more important. They began with China, Hawaii, Japan, and Korea, then a war with Spain over the Philippines, then the Pacific War; since Pearl Harbor we have fought three major wars in East Asia (one win, one draw, one loss)—and since roughly the same time, the opposite shores of the northern Pacific have had world-historical industrial booms.

The Pacific West has been an engine of growth for more than 150 years. The gold rush touched off the Americanization and multiethnic peopling of California, and industrial agriculture, citrus, the discovery of oil, movies, and real estate booms followed on its heels. The Roaring Twenties was not just an era of flappers and the Charleston, but years of pioneering innovation when Californians first sampled the seductive possibilities of mass consumption and mass culture that the rest of the world now absorbs as part of its lifestyle: automobiles, suburbs, radios, Hollywood films, professional sports, "consumer durables" like refrigerators. And a sharp-eyed Willa Cather noticed: "The whole world broke apart in 1922 or thereabouts"; America "had got ahead wonderfully, but somehow ahead on the wrong road," she thought. At that time American industry perfected both mass production and the means to digest the same goods—en masse. The 1920s capped an amazingly quick

American rise to world preeminence: the United States had 29 percent of global industrial production in the 1880s, 36 percent by 1913 (compared to Britain's 14 percent), and 42 percent in 1929—the highest percentage ever, save for the abnormal period just after World War II when all the advanced industrial economies had suffered extensive war damage, except for the unscathed United States (which temporarily held half of all global production). Southern California occupied the horizon of 1920s-style mass consumption, a new form of pioneering that defined the third industrial revolution (autos, assembly line mass production often called Fordism).[1]

The successive administrations of Franklin D. Roosevelt provided the turning point from continental isolation to global involvement. When he was "Mr. New Deal," an open spigot of federal spending brought the direct involvement of the national government into the extensive development of the Far West, and especially water and power; the New Deal built massive infrastructures (like the Grand Coulee Dam) and managed and developed western farmlands and the immense water works necessary to till them. When Roosevelt was "Mr. Win-the-War," under emergency conditions federal administrators authorized and subsidized hundreds of new war-related industries in Southern California, the Bay Area, Portland, and Seattle, thus accomplishing the industrialization of the Pacific West while the gross national product doubled in five years. The emergence of Los Angeles as a major industrial city in the space of one decade (1940–50) symbolized this continental "market completion," and another huge shot in the arm came via the Korean crisis and permanent cold war defense spending at historically unprecedented levels. The stage was thus set for the American political economy to grow in tandem with both Atlantic and Pacific interests and involvements.

Defense firms like Lockheed failed several times before the war but flourished thereafter, all through the cold war and until its end, when defense contracts began drying up. (In 1996 Disney spent $45 million to turn Lockheed's Stealth aircraft design facility, long known as "the Skunk Works," into an animation studio.)[2] Just as this happened, however, new information-age industries drove America's Pacific economy out of recession and into the longest peacetime boom in American history. Boeing teamed with Microsoft to transform Seattle from a backwater to a major Pacific Rim city in the space of one decade (roughly 1980–90), Intel and Nike brought Portland out of the 1970s–80s doldrums of an old economy based on resource exports (mainly timber), and California recaptured its leading-edge position in the national economy as Silicon Valley made northern California richer even than Southern California. I will argue that the core of California's incessant industrial innovation resides in a peculiar combination of youthful initiative and fulsome state funding, a phenomenon that goes back to the Depression and World War II, and trades on California's salutary *distance* from the dominant institutions of the East. Other parts of the American West will interest us: Texas, an anomalous aspect of the story, is nonetheless part of it. Like the Pacific Coast states, it also fronts on an ocean, but the other western states do not and thus belong to a different narrative.

It might appear that this is a Pacific Rim book. But I never understood this term that came of age in the 1970s and 1980s or the counterpart locution of the 1990s, "the Asia/Pacific"—and I don't think anyone else did either. (Is Guatemala included in the "Pacific Rim"? Is Burma or Bangladesh in "the Asia/Pacific"?)[3] These are inventions and constructions of the powerful, especially America and Japan, and they occupy what Alexander Woodside called a "prophetic culture"—China (or Japan, or the Pacific Rim) is rising, or a miracle, or a menace—and the prophecies tend suddenly to evaporate when history illustrates their obsolescence, as in Japan's bubble economy and subsequent stagnation or the 1997 Asian financial crisis which abolished the rhetoric about "the four tigers." Still, prophetic hoopla doesn't change the fact that Japan began its essential industrial pattern of state-guided bursts of growth in the 1880s and since the 1950s has been East Asia's most formidable industrial state; Korea and Taiwan got off the mark in the 1960s and haven't stopped. Our old antagonist Vietnam is one of the fastest growing nations in the world. But China puts everyone else in the shade, growing by nearly 10 percent annually since Deng Xiaoping's epochal reforms in 1978—a snapshot of a "Great Leap Forward" that will help to shape the rest of this century. All this is true. But the American Pacific states also had great leaps forward after Pearl Harbor, completing a continental industrial economy the likes of which the world has never seen. This is the basic reason why the American share of global GDP has remained steady since 1970, at about 30 percent, as against a nattering flock of Cassandras predicting East Asian advance and American decline—or even oblivion.

I have written much about the East Asian side of this Pacific phenomenon in my earlier work, and like that work, there is a theoretical framework at the basis of this book. I have tried to wear it lightly because it puts off or bores the nonspecialist, but the appendix contains some essential ideas about "late" development, "spurts" of growth, technological innovation, the role of the American state, the curiosities of space and time in expansion and development on a continental scale, and ill-understood words like "empire" and "hegemony." The claims in this book are not theoretical, however. My concern is to unfold an argument about general patterns; figuring out exactly what happened (let's say up on Cripple Creek or in the Southern California citrus boom or in the origins of Silicon Valley) is compelling, the details are fascinating, but I am more interested in what the larger patterns mean for the American role in the world. Where I have failed in grasping a particular history, the reader will find rich sources of correction (not to mention many ideas for further reading) in the bibliography. Meanwhile if I fail at the general level, I have no one to blame but myself.

Historians of the West still experience a sense of distance, even an inferiority complex, around their colleagues who consider their own work (say, on a village in colonial New England) more central and more important. People who work on the West are thought to do regional rather than national history—or maybe their region *is* history (in her first teaching job Patricia Nelson Limerick was told that her courses shouldn't go past the 1890s). This book asserts that the United States cannot be understood without knowing the West; that in the past 150 years the country has been shaped more dramatically *by* the West and American Pacific involvements than by any other region; that one state—California—is a more dramatic shaper of national destiny than any other; and that America's position in the world, the ultimate whole we are trying to understand, is inexplicable without grasping the intertwined power of the coastal states and U.S. dominance across the expansive oceans on which they gaze.

I think this is a story of the past and the present, but many will think it is prophecy—a claim on the future. It doesn't matter, really; paradoxically, the old and timeworn traditions of western history return to us today with a new freshness, as the search for India or a northwest passage to the Orient or Berkeley's westward march of empire or America as the "middle country" linking Asia and Europe acquire a true depth of meaning with an ascendant Pacific trade, and more importantly with the mingling of diverse peoples and cultures, now so casual and unexceptional on the West Coast and in much of the country. American destiny is finally and thoroughly intertwined with Mexico, China, Korea, Japan, Vietnam, and again finally, India.

The emergence of the United States after 1941 as a simultaneous Atlantic and Pacific power, operating at a cutting-edge technological pace on both coasts and at many places in between (Chicago, Houston, Denver) is the central idea of this book, and I believe it is the essential basis of a global hegemony that has reached no more than early middle age in our time, if that. The central problem of the book is how to understand and explain the difference between an Atlantic-facing internationalism and a Pacific-facing expansionism, the twin sides of America's relation to the world. Just in time, as if history relishes an illustrative counterpoint, along came a westerner with the most finely honed example of the expansionist tendency since James Polk, Teddy Roosevelt, or Douglas MacArthur: George W. Bush. But I began working on this book years before he came into office, and I am forced to admit that I thought things were moving in the other direction—toward a new internationalism (called "globalization") in both Europe and East Asia, which Bill Clinton seemed to understand and forward effortlessly.[4] Today it appears that unless extraordinary efforts are made to overcome our historic unilateralism and easy recourse to the use of force in Asia, thus to engage and involve the East Asian countries in a spirit of equality and mutual advantage, this century is going to have prolonged and devastating consequences for world peace.

A Personal Note

My life, if not my career, has been shaped by the Pacific states since I learned how to drive (age ten) and began my prodigious after-school reading: *Hot Rod Magazine, Rod and Custom, Car Craft, Road and Track;* my imaginary adolescent life was shaped by car customizers like the inimitable George Barris and drag racing stars like Don Garlits, and my fondest wish was to cruise down Whittier Boulevard in a '32 Ford Hiboy. (Little did I know that a University of Chicago student had already linked hot rodders to one innovation after another in Detroit—and of course to American ingenuity and individualism.)[5] My parents moved to Palo Alto when I was eighteen, "voting with their wheels" for a new life like so many other Americans, and I learned then about a very different California, the one in the north (the civilized part) that Alfred Hitchcock brilliantly portrayed in *Vertigo*. This was 1962 when the national media "discovered" it again, the occasion being California passing New York as the most populous state, but the perennial text was California's embodiment of the American dream, a window to the future for the rest of the country.[6]

Fifteen years later I got a job in Seattle, still in the backwash of Boeing having laid off tens of thousands of workers in 1969–71; it appeared to be a company town, a sleepy backwater in an exquisite setting facing the contiguous forty-eight's only genuine fjord (Puget Sound), more often facing "back East" (which seemed to mean anywhere over the Cascade Mountains), an Omaha that just happened to be on the Pacific—except that it had a very good coffee shop named Starbucks down at the Pike Street Market. When I

left in 1987, Bill Gates was adding a world-class monopoly to Boeing's oligop-
oly, Starbucks was franchising outward to the world, Asians and Asian-
Americans were pouring in, and the Emerald City had permanently turned
around to face West, a new jewel in America's Pacific crown.

The original germ of my intellectual interest in the West and California,
which took a long time to germinate but stayed always in my mind, came in
December 1974 when I was dawdling around waiting to defend my doctoral
thesis at Columbia and walked into a $2.00 second-run theater on the Upper
West Side to see *Chinatown.* For the first time in my life I stayed on for a
second viewing; the film is enigmatic and difficult to decipher at one sitting
(the producer, Robert Evans, said the script "was pure Chinese" to him)[7] or
even two or three. Ostensibly a crime noir filmed in apricot shades steeped in
nostalgia for the old, vanished Los Angeles, it is the most intelligent film ever
made about the prewar western social milieu, which had its concentrated
essence in the WASP oligarchy that ran Los Angeles and the people of color
who worked for them. The screenwriter, Robert Towne, reversed our optic by
taking the stereotypical view of Chinatowns at the time—inscrutable deviants
mired in tong wars, opium dens, filth, prostitution, incest, omnibus mayhem,
"you could never tell what went on there"—and making it the story of the
oligarchy. He took what scholars call the theory of Oriental despotism (the
satrap above, the masses below, moving rivers to deliver water and create
wealth in an arid climate) and brought it home to the Los Angeles aqueduct,
the San Fernando Valley, the collapsed St. Francis Dam, and the curious,
poignant figure of Hollis Mulwray, director of water and power—otherwise
known as William Mulholland.

The film is entirely typical of a Southern California discourse which
holds the industrialists responsible for fouling the air, the real estate speculators for desecrating the land, cars and freeways for despoiling the Edenic
environment, and the politicians for making it all possible. It is a singular film
bringing China to Southern California and imbedding it in a determining
and largely true municipal history. More broadly, the film symbolizes what
contemporary Americans will face for the rest of their lives: the joining of
enormously productive semi-arid valleys, the ones that Californians watered
with the Owens Lake and the Colorado River, and the Yangze and Yellow
river valleys that China now showers with a billion talents. For the first time
in world history, the Pacific Ocean is joining the Mediterranean and the
Atlantic: the expansive scene of an infinity of human transactions and ultimately a Pacific civilization that we envision but dimly today.

I am still humbled by the history I attempt to interpret and the substantial literature that has been my guide—however badly or wrongly I may have used it. Carey McWilliams once remarked, "All my books represent efforts to relieve my ignorance," and I have had the same feeling since I first directed my ignorance toward the Korean War. I am all too aware of how much more could be said and done, how many omissions remain, how tentative many of my generalizations really are. The best that can be said: this is the book I wanted to read but couldn't find, so I wrote it myself. I offer it to the reader in the spirit of Joseph Schumpeter's aphorism: "We all of us like a sparkling error better than a trivial truth."

Acknowledgments

My academic expertise developed on the opposite side of the North Pacific, East Asia; I know something about Korea, Japan, China, Taiwan, and Vietnam, which is a reasonable definition of "East Asia," and it is that part of the Pacific that has concerned me in my career. To say that I am not an expert in western history is only to begin to express my debt to several generations of scholars who are or were. History in this country usually means American history, and usually the Americanists dominate history departments. That has its demerits from time to time, but it so focuses the historical mind that there seems to be a book for almost any subject, big or small. The literature on the American West is thus overwhelming: but through mostly self-directed reading I learned to rely on the kindness of strangers: fellow historians, most of whom I have never met.

The literature on the West is also overwhelmingly about California—or sometimes just about Los Angeles, a city that must have a larger literature than any other in the past century, even more than New York—and so Kevin Starr has almost become a companion through his work: no other state has been blessed with such an adroit, literate, learned, and indefatigable historian-laureate. Had he not invented himself, I quite doubt that another such person would exist. William Cronon's work on Chicago as the first city of the West deeply influenced my thinking, as did Patricia Nelson Limerick's *Legacy of Conquest* and Donald Worster's *Rivers of Empire.* D. W. Meinig has pioneered a wonderful combination of geography and history in his many books. In an earlier generation, Walter Prescott Webb had a genius for a compelling kind of historical reductionism, and Bernard DeVoto's many books were also a great help, not to mention a delight (some contemporary historians call him a "neo-Romantic," but as Lincoln said about Grant, they should all take whatever he was drinking). No authors have made me think more about the meaning of the West than Richard Slotkin (the *Regeneration Through Violence* trilogy), Richard Drinnon (*Facing West*), and Mike Davis (*City of Quartz* and *Ecology of Fear*). Meanwhile a host of expert books on somewhat lesser subjects proved keenly absorbing. One overwhelming impression gleaned from this literature is that the concerns of western historians come to a creaking halt when they hit the shoreline—they barely get their toes wet in the Pacific. The American West and America in the Pacific are two entirely different literatures (although Drinnon's book is a remarkable exception). Crossing, melding, and erasing that line is a major purpose of this book.

This book was researched and written with the assistance of two fellowships, the first (2000–2001) from the Center for Advanced Study at Stanford with financial support from the Andrew W. Mellon Foundation, and the second (2004–5) from the Abe Fellowship Program, administered by the Social Science Research Council and the Council of Learned Societies, in cooperation with and with funds provided by the Japan Foundation Center for Global Partnership. Several deans at the University of Chicago—Richard Saller, John Boyer, and Mark Hansen—helped me with additional research funds, as did Dali Yang and Ted Foss at the Center for East Asian Studies. I am most grateful for all this support.

My endnotes will not interest the general reader as only rarely do I say anything beyond what is in the main text. They make brief reference to the author and year of publication, corresponding to the listing of the source in the bibliography. The notes are numerous as they must be in a book like this, to give proper credit to the multitude of fine scholars laboring in the vineyards. Like most of them, I use words like "American," "Indian," "Anglo," and "haole" colloquially, as people use them in everyday life.

Ronald Steel was nice enough to suggest to me that a swath of my 1990 Korean War study be extracted and published as a separate book on U.S. foreign relations. Not wanting to repeat myself since the never-ending dilemmas of the Korean peninsula have led me to do quite enough of that already, I decided instead to start from scratch. Harry Harootunian and Tets Najita have supported my work from the day they conspired to hire me in 1987. I was fortunate to occupy the Norman and Edna Freehling Professorship during most of the time that I worked on this book, and I would like to thank their son, Paul Freehling, for his generosity. Graduate students in my international history seminar and undergraduate students in my history and film class provided many insights, and perhaps now—with this book—they will understand what I was talking about. David Gibbs, Akira Iriye, Chalmers Johnson, James Kurth, Walter LaFeber, Charles Maier, Immanuel Wallerstein, and Marilyn Young also deserve thanks for their advice and support. Daniel Chirot provided a most useful commentary on my book for Yale

University Press, as did an anonymous reader. James B. Palais was a great friend and avid reader of my work, and I deeply regret that he passed away in 2006.

A multitude of other people helped me with this book, while indulging my inability or unwillingness to quite explain what I was doing (it is a fact that I don't really know what I think until I sit down and write). At the Center for Advanced Study, the director Robert A. Scott, Nancy Pinkerton, Christine Duignan, and Kathleen Much were most helpful. Herb Leiderman's enthusiasm for my project stimulated me a lot. Among Center fellows who helped my thinking along, I would like to thank David Holloway, Charles Ragin, Michael Doyle, Amy Gutman, and David Nirenberg. My colleague Jim Sparrow was also very helpful, as was Steve Shallhorn of Greenpeace. Two former Ph.D. students, Lisa Anderson and Kornel S. Chang, taught me a lot through their work on the Pacific world. John Hawk was most generous when I worked in the Donohue Rare Book Room of the Gleeson Library at the University of San Francisco library; staff at the Riverside Citrus Museum and the California Oil Museum were also helpful. Bob Graham went out of his way to help me with Charles Frémont memorabilia. I would like to thank Henning Gutman for locating my book with Yale University Press. Eliza Childs provided deft and meticulous editing, for which I am most appreciative. Bill Nelson's maps and Cynthia Crippen's index were also wonderfully done. Melanie Reilly was also generous with her help and time. Chris Rogers and Laura Davulis deserve thanks for putting up with me, and I thank the director of the press, John Donatich, for intervening at a critical moment to keep this project on track. Margaret Otzel was terrific in helping with the final touches on the book. I would also like to thank Meredith Oda and Kelly Therese Pollock for their excellent research assistance.

Professor Nishizawa Yoshitaki kindly arranged for a visiting position at Doshisha University in the summer of 2004, including comfortable housing and a seminar where various Doshisha faculty reacted to my work. Professor Onozawa Toru arranged a similar seminar at Kyoto University. Over several years professors Akita Shigeru and Kan Hideki have kindly included me in their ongoing working groups, and I learned much from presenting my ideas to conferences that they organized in July 2004, July 2005, and July 2006. Frank Baldwin offered respite at his cottage near Lake Nojiri, where my sons were happy to lighten his pockets in poker. Chung Kyungmo, Wada Haruki, and Lim Chul are good friends who always let me know what they are thinking. Watanabe Masahito was also helpful in many ways. Taida Hideya, the executive director of the Center for Global Partnership of the Japan

Foundation, and Diet member Tomon Mitsuko were also very generous with their time. My old friend Professor Sakamoto Yoshikazu offered many helpful ideas. I had a memorable dinner with Masahide Ota, the former governor of Okinawa, who provided me with many materials and taught me much. Among academics in Japan who were also generous in sharing their time and their views with me I would like to thank: Fujimoto Hiroshi, Gabe Masaaki, Hori Kazuo, Igarashi Takeshi, Iguchi Haruo, Inoguchi Takashi, Iwashita Akihiro, Kang Sang Jung, Kobayashi Hideo, Lee Jong Won, Matsuda Takeshi, Nakajima Hiroo, Sugita Yoneyuki, Yamashita Morihasa, Yi Ilcheong, and Yui Daizaburo.

In Korea I have had so many friends and faculty give of their time that I can name only a few who really went out of their way: Kim Dongno, Kim Kwang Woong, Kim Sung-han, Choi Jang Jip, and Paik Nak-chung. I would like to thank former Prime Minister Lee Hong-gu for arranging a large gathering where I presented my Pacific project, and former Foreign Minister Yoon Young Kwon for sharing his views with me. In China, Xue Mouhong was most helpful, as always; I would also like to thank Dr. Zhang Kunsheng of the Ministry of Foreign Affairs and Professor Shen Dingli; and in Taiwan, Professor Cheng-yi Lin.

I learned much from two people who guided me around the Sasebo Fleet Activities Center, Philip D. Eakins and Aramaki Yoko; likewise Captain Michael Chase and Jon N. Nylander provided much useful information on the largest U.S. naval base in Japan at Yokosuka. Captain Dannie Chung and Sue E. Jevning were very helpful in facilitating my visits to several Marine bases on Okinawa. Colonel Adrienne K. Fraser Darling, the commander of Camps Foster and Lester, was very enlightening in the interview I had with her. I also learned much from Lt. Col. James M. Ruvalcaba, Col. H. Stacy Clardy III, and Major Brad S. Bartlet, the director of public affairs for the Third Marine Expeditionary Force. Sheila Smith, Kathy Ferguson, and Phyllis Turnbull gave me excellent guidance on the military in Hawaii, and the visitor staff and excellent bookstore at Pearl Harbor provided much useful information. The U.S. Army also guided me through another visit to Panmunjom; meanwhile the giant Yongsan Garrison in Seoul (with more than 12,000 American personnel in 2006) has been familiar to me since I was a Peace Corps volunteer sneaking through the gates in search of a good cheeseburger.

Meredith Jung-en Woo knows how to manage a career, a household, two teenagers, a recalcitrant husband, and a hundred friendships, which is a marvel. My ability to write this book was completely dependent on her manifold skills. Ian and Ben can attest that I did most of this book while sitting in an armchair or at the desk in my study, a purposeful method given the waning years left to greet them when they came home from school. They also accompanied me during a year of "field work" at the Institute for Advanced Study, an idyllic Silicon Valley sojourn, but all I did there was sit in my office and read books, too, as my sons can attest, and then drive up and down the state on the weekends, reconnoitering the objects of our desire.

PART I

A Frontier of the Mind

To any meditative Magian rover, this serene Pacific, once beheld, must ever after be the sea of his adoption. It rolls the mid-most waters of the world, the Indian Ocean and Atlantic being but its arms. The same waves wash the moles of the new-built California towns, but yesterday planted by the recentest race of men, and lave the faded but still gorgeous skirts of Asiatic lands, older than Abraham; while all between float milky-ways of coral isles, and low-lying, endless, unknown Archipelagoes, and impenetrable Japans. Thus this mysterious, divine Pacific zones the world's whole bulk about; makes all coasts one bay to it; seems the tide-beating heart of earth.

—HERMAN MELVILLE, *Moby-Dick*

CHAPTER ONE

The Machine in the Garden

Locke sank into a swoon;
The Garden died;
God took the spinning-jenny
Out of his side.
—W. B. YEATS, *The Tower*

Where does the West begin? Historians can't agree, but for pioneers it was once the Appalachians, in Daniel Boone's time it was Tennessee, Illinois was called the Northwest (thus Northwestern University), then Chicago and the railroads made a "new West." The Census Bureau counts thirteen Mountain and Pacific states, including Alaska and Hawaii, as part of the West—but not Texas (not Texas?). Probably the most influential definition is the 98th meridian, the dividing line between rainfall adequate for farming and aridity. But half of the Americans living west of that meridian live in California. So is it the real West? Where would the West be in Saul Steinberg's celebrated *New Yorker* cover? The West starts across the Hudson in Jersey and has space, expanse, width; the East has depth—it has civilization. You live in the one and you fly over the other. Steinberg reveals a state of mind, not a place. New England is the fount of Anglo-Saxon civilization, New York the apex of American culture, and the continent might as well still be an untamed wilderness. It dawned on a woman of nineteen who grew up in Seattle, cruising in a rented Toyota through New England, that she had somehow failed to grasp that "the East Coast was American cultural headquarters."[1]

What about the Atlantic's continental opposite? "It rested on a crust of earth at the edge of a sea that ended a world," Frank Fenton wrote in *A Place in the Sun*. But what world ended there? D. H. Lawrence thought that Fenton's city, Los Angeles, was "silly," a queer place that "turned its back on the world and looks into the void Pacific." In his essay titled "Facing the Pacific," Edmund Wilson stared into the same void, kindly remarking that California writers did not seem to carry "a weight proportional to the bulk of their work." No doubt this failing issued from "the strange spell of unreality which seems to make human experience on the Coast as hollow as the life of a trollnest where everything is out in the open instead of being underground," or from the climate ("the empty sun and the incessant rains"), or from the view ("the dry mountains and the void of the vast Pacific"), or from "the surf that rolls up the beach with a beat that seems expressionless and purposeless after the moody assaults of the Atlantic." San Francisco was "the real cultural center" of California for Wilson, but (regrettably) a victim of "arrested development." Meanwhile San Diego had none at all: "a jumping-off place." Then he drew closer to his real intent: "Add to this the remoteness of the East and the farther remoteness from Europe." And then Wilson made his point: "California looks away from Europe, and out upon a wider ocean toward an Orient with which as yet any cultural communication is difficult." (In a similar essay Wilson put it this way: "an Orient with which, for white Americans, the cultural communication is slight.")[2] For Lawrence and Wilson—and in literary criticism it doesn't get much better than that—Southern California was walled in by mountains and facing west toward "the void of the vast Pacific."

The Belated Pacific

If it is hard to imagine a more jaundiced and blinkered view of the Pacific Coast culture and climate ("moody assaults" are available off Bodega Bay if you like them, and the "empty sun" rarely warms Astoria), these are important statements because they are the kind of thing most eastern intellectuals hesitate to say openly, but it's what they really think—California is remote from Europe, it "looks away" toward a vacuous Pacific. It puts intellectuals out of sorts and so they hustle back to New York or Cambridge with relief and a shudder. What about the in-between, the continent from New York to Los Angeles? Well, that truly is flyover territory. Saul Steinberg's poster recapitulates the geography of Edmund Wilson's mind; he wouldn't pause in Peoria to assay the local culture. Fine: but what about a country that from its founding "looked away" from Europe, that turned to face West, unrolling a *novus ordo seclorum* (a new order for the ages, see it on your dollar bill) on a vast continent, an exceptional nation that would negate Europe's monarchies, its despotism, its landlords and peasants, its wars of nation and class? And what about a literary tradition founded in New England that also faced West in spite of itself?[3]

What of the "void of the vast Pacific"? The Pacific looks like a tranquil, gently rolling, infinite plane promising serenity and long life. Wilson's void is the absence of a common civilization ("cultural communication") on both sides of the Pacific. The distances were too far, the cultures too disparate, the peoples too incomprehensible. We see the Atlantic or the Mediterranean as a distinct entity and subject for inquiry, but not the Pacific. We say Atlantic World, but Pacific World is a concept just now gaining traction (unless it connotes the romance of the islands). We say Atlantic civilization but we don't say Pacific civilization. Oliver Wendell Holmes, who coined the term "Boston Brahmin," helped found the *Atlantic Monthly* in 1857 to link America with European culture,[4] and it is still an influential magazine; we don't have a remotely comparable *Pacific Monthly*. Americans and Europeans meet each other as equals, as part of the same cultural realm, however much Europeans may think a ration of error crossed the Atlantic. Americans met Pacific peoples very early, as they were discovering their own territory—Chinese in the gold rush, Japanese, Koreans, and Filipinos at the turn of the last century—and they met them with sharp racial discrimination that did not begin to end until the civil rights movement of the 1960s. They met them in continuous wars from 1941 to 1975. They met them in economic exchange after 1960, and now they meet them in universities, corporations, hospitals, courtrooms, and laboratories, a new and burgeoning professional class. In the twenty-first century a Pacific civilization is slowly emerging, linking all sides of the vast ocean in ongoing, daily life exchange. But today the ocean remains primarily a setting for business exchange or popular culture—and an arena of overwhelming American military might.

For Bernard Bailyn "the idea of Atlantic history" emerged in the postwar period as a way to characterize Britain's imperial Atlantic order and an intertwined British-American, internationalist history—a "transnational, multicultural reality," or as Armitage and Braddick term it, a social system "with permeable boundaries, created by the interaction of migrants, settlers, traders, and a great variety of political systems." The new Atlantic history leads David Armitage to say, speaking for a host of historians, "We are all Atlanticists now." An ocean is a natural fact, Armitage goes on, with a built-in geography; the same, ipso facto, is true of the Pacific. But Bailyn and Armitage trace the origin of Atlantic history to engagement with Europe during World War II and the cold war: "the idea of Western civilization . . . owed more to NATO than to Plato," Armitage wrote. The opponents of the Atlantic idea, they say, were isolationists, otherwise called "Asia firsters" (or maybe Pacificists). Atlantic history became increasingly multicolored—a black Atlantic, a green (Irish) Atlantic, a red (Marxist) Atlantic. Are there Pacific counterparts? Yes there are, as we will see. But these historians, too, are talking about a state of mind, a cultural Atlantic, built around an internationalism that they privilege. For David Armitage "the Pacific is belated" when compared to the Atlantic world and it was Europeans, not natives, who first saw it whole.[5] But it took them forever to grasp the whole—and is it still "belated" in the new century?

The Anglo-Saxon Atlantic

The late Samuel Huntington not only posited a "clash of civilizations" but a clear preference for one of them: "Americans should recommit themselves to the Anglo-Protestant culture, traditions, and values that for three and a half centuries have been embraced by Americans of all races, ethnicities and religions and that have been the source of their liberty, unity, power, prosperity, and moral leadership as a force for good in the world." The United States was not a nation of immigrants for him, but one of *settlers*—people who left in groups to found a new society, often to escape religious intolerance—and those settler societies replicated themselves over two and a half centuries as the frontier expanded. It stopped expanding, according to Huntington, at the same time Frederick Jackson Turner said it did: 1890. Since then a multi-ethnic settler society has been diluted by immigration, he wrote, such that now more than half of the American population has no settler heritage. Huntington wanted us to revitalize "the American Creed" (reminding us of Richard Hofstadter's quip "It has been our fate as a nation not to have ideologies, but to be one").[6] Huntington's image is again cultural: what distinguishes Atlantic civilization are "its values and institutions"—which he lists in the following order: "Christianity, pluralism, individualism, and rule of law," all of which "made it possible for the West to invent modernity." He approvingly quoted Arthur Schlesinger Jr. on Europe as "the source—the *unique* source" of these basic attributes, and the responsibility of American leaders should be "to preserve, protect, and renew the unique qualities of Western civilization." The Atlantic world that Huntington wanted to revive and preserve is the only civilization truly worthy of his respect, and defending it is less a matter of confronting external enemies than husbanding its flagging resources at home and abroad. The home struggle, predictably, is against "multiculturalism" and the "culture wars" that raged in the 1990s.[7]

Against all the hard labor of racial and ethnic enlightenment since the 1940s, Samuel Huntington still pursued "the great historico-transcendental destiny of the Occident," in Foucault's words,[8] more specifically the destiny of the Anglo-Saxon Occident. Here is a long lament for a lost or declining

Atlanticism, an America defined originally and primarily by New England (Huntington came from an old-line Boston family) and a "West" led by white men—and hopefully Protestant ones. Huntington was honest and straightforward about his preferences and betrayed no concern for partisan advantage. But the majority of Americans who differ in color, class, or gender from Boston Brahmins will not find their views and interests represented in his book.

According to Huntington the original settler societies were fully known and realized examples of Puritanism, exemplifying an Anglo-Saxon homogeneity. But did they not encounter difference from the beginning and get transformed by it—by the encounter with Indians, by the introduction of slavery, or by the lack of Turner-like settlements beyond the 98th meridian? Is not a Frederick Douglass or a Malcolm X a central part of American civilization? Are the "blue states" and "red states" of recent elections an example of the clash of civilizations (or "Atlantic culture" vs. multiculturalism) or further testimony to the deeply contested nature of American liberalism? Maybe WASPS are just another minority group? These questions answer themselves and suggest that the attributes of liberalism that Huntington held dear manifest themselves around the world in a heterogeneous democratic civilization available to all peoples, growing stronger all the time.

An Atlanticist's Pacific

The New England worldview may appear to be some quaint relic of a bygone past, and it is surely threatened—why else would Samuel Huntington defend it?—but it structured three important American institutions: the academy, the China trade, and the Foreign Service. Harvard, the self-nominated pinnacle of academe, has always been a redoubt of internationalist doctrines and so are most other elite universities; prominent Harvard scholars like Huntington still routinely supply their students to run central journals, like *Foreign Affairs*. Meanwhile diplomatic service was the wholly-owned subsidiary of graduates from Harvard, Yale, Princeton, and a few other schools from the beginning until the late 1960s—and usually wealthy graduates, since salaries were so low. As an observant man who happens to be English wrote, "To an extent that is quite astonishing to Europeans, who are brought up to think of the U.S. as a great populist democracy with a strong anti-aristocratic bias, the foreign policy of the U.S. as a great world power over the whole seventy years from 1898 to 1968 was a family affair." That foreign affairs "family" had blue running in its veins and proper schooling at Choate or Andover, Harvard or Yale.

After graduation they inhabited institutions like the Council on Foreign Relations, the Atlantic Council, the Carnegie Endowment for International Peace, and the Trilateral Commission and belonged to the Cosmos Club in Washington and the Century Club in New York. Since 1941, Godfrey Hodgson noted, the foreign policy establishment was fully united on these points: prize Atlanticism, support internationalism, oppose isolationism.[9]

Economics had an Atlanticist view, too, coming not simply from one Harvard don after another loving Adam Smith and loathing protectionists, but generations of merchants applauding free trade—and especially the China trade. John Winthrop's "City on a Hill," after all, was overlooking an ocean. Until the acquisition of California, trade with China was mainly the province of New England merchants. After the Revolution, American ships no longer had to worry about the trade monopoly held by the British East India Company, and growing wild in the countryside was a root that meant nothing to Americans but brought a fine price in China: ginseng, believed to be a fillip to male health and virility. The 360-ton *Empress of China* left New York in February 1784 bound for Canton, loaded mostly with ginseng and financed by Robert Morris (who had also directed the financing of the Revolution). The *Empress* was the largest cargo vessel ever to dock at Canton and quickly deepened the China trade. She returned in May 1785 loaded with tea, silk, and porcelains, having made a whopping profit of $30,000, a net gain of 25 percent on the original investment. Soon other American ships—the *Grand Turk,* the *United States*—followed suit, trading ginseng, furs, and sandalwood for tea and silk, and by that pregnant year—1789—as many as fifteen American ships might be tied up at Canton. The golden age of this trade arrived in the 1830s and 1840s, with $6.6 million in tea and fine porcelains arriving from China in 1840, and ginseng and cotton textiles going out. Only France and Great Britain exported more to the United States than China. John Perkins Cushing lived in Canton for three decades as the agent of Thomas Handsyd Perkins and brought with him upon his return to Boston several Chinese servants, built a grand mansion, and surrounded it with a wall of Chinese porcelain. Bostonian Russell Sturgis easily accounted for half of the trade, but Pacific commerce also built great wealth in Boston, New York, and Philadelphia— "Lowells, Girards, Astors, Lows, Griswolds, Copes" named some of the larger fortunes accrued at least in part through the China trade.[10]

John Jacob Astor, Caleb Cushing, Abiel Abbot Low, and other American traders all loved free trade, but they did not scruple to spurn importing opium to China, mostly from Turkey, which helped them to balance their trade just as it did the British; American traders even reaped windfall profits by selling opium *during* the Opium Wars. It hardly hurt their social standing, either: Low was president of the New York Chamber of Commerce from 1856 to 1866, and his son Seth became president of Columbia University, from which we get Low Memorial Library (always the centerpiece of the campus). Only one prominent clipper-ship merchant refused to deal in opium: David Washington Cincinnatus Olyphant of New York, a dedicated Presbyterian who supported many foreign missionary causes.[11] For the China traders, off to the west was an extension of the Atlantic and free trade doctrine that people happened to call the Pacific; it was a large body of water that had no meaning otherwise.

The Genteel Tradition

From the Anglo-Saxon point of view, American culture reached its apogee in the "genteel tradition" of New England and a dominant elite of "Protestant patricians."[12] For two centuries New England had a homogeneity unlike the rest of the country, with as many as 80 percent of its citizens having common English and Protestant origins, and a pronounced class difference not unlike England itself: in Massachusetts in the early nineteenth century, for example, a handful of upper-class white men ran just about everything of importance, controlling all nominations for Congress and operating the state legislature like its handmaiden. This tradition was less specifically European than English: "the true Bostonian," Henry Adams wrote in 1907, "always knelt in self-abasement before the majesty of English standards." By the same token, the true New Englander looked up to England and faced East: here is the cultural origin of Atlanticism. The involvement of many of these same Bostonians in the China trade also made them junior partners to British commerce with palms turned up to London banks, breeding a like-minded free-trade internationalism among New Englanders generally and Harvard dons more particularly, accompanied by the belief that world peace followed in the wake of free trade. Plus Bostonians lived in the core—of America, of the world: Oliver Wendell Holmes considered Boston "the thinking centre of the continent, and therefore of the planet."[13]

New Englanders were also, of course, white—very white, very conscious of being so, and very conscious of the immanent possibility of becoming a white *minority*. Initially they were a white island in a sea of Indians. One might think that after vanquishing them New Englanders were in the comfortable majority for hundreds of years, until inundated by southern and eastern Europeans in the nineteenth century—who appeared to be nonwhite.

But that would be wrong, because to this elite Irish weren't white, Scots were barely white, Germans and French and even Swedes were nonwhite—that is, "swarthy." No one put it better than Benjamin Franklin in 1751: "The Number of purely white People in the World is proportionably [*sic*] very small. All Africa is black or tawny. Asia chiefly tawny. America (exclusive of the new Comers) wholly so. And in Europe, the Spaniards, Italians, French, Russians and Swedes, are generally of what we call a swarthy complexion; as are the Germans also, the Saxons only excepted, who with the English, make the principal Body of White People on the Face of the Earth. I could wish their Numbers were increased. . . . Perhaps I am partial to the Complexion of my Country, for such Kind of Partiality is natural to Mankind."[14] The "Complexion of my Country" is not *white,* according to this founding father, but Anglo-Saxon. We move from race to culture because we must; there is evidently no epidermal distinction between Ben Franklin and, say, his German Mennonite neighbors in Pennsylvania—"Palantine boors" whom he wanted put on the next ship back home. We move from race to culture to Samuel Huntington: we move back to New England and its peculiar Anglophile, Atlanticist predilections—English implants, internal foreigners, taking themselves to be the only true Americans.

Santayana assayed this palpable cultural hegemony from a (continental) European perspective in a series of provocative essays, none more so than the famous one he delivered at Berkeley in 1911, called "The Genteel Tradition." New England patricians had a specialty, and it was called Calvinism. As Santayana put it, the "agonized conscience" of the Calvinist declared that "sin exists, sin is punished, and that it is beautiful that sin should be punished." This doctrine took Nietzsche's excision of the senses to a dramatic extreme: one's own miserable condition ought to be everybody's. Calvinists "feel a fierce pleasure in the existence of misery," their own or anyone else's. Charles Dickens took a trip to Boston in 1842 and noted the denunciation from the pulpit "of all innocent and rational amusements." But modern Americans finally escaped all that, in Santayana's view. He thought an unnumbered mass of Americans would laugh if you told them they were depraved sinners: that kind of American "is convinced that he always has been, and always will be, victorious and blameless." These Americans didn't so much oppose Puritanism or Calvinism, they did something more radical: they ran away from it, or simply forgot it. From his Berkeley podium Santayana urged Californians, also, to liberate themselves from the genteel tradition, and "to salute the wild, indifferent, noncensorious infinity of nature" surrounding them everywhere in the Golden State. (We will see later that they were slow on the uptake.) It followed ineluctably that a child "swaddled in the genteel tradition" named William James should provide a way out for the non-genteel American to settle down happily with his innocent or empty conscience—*pragmatism:* and from there it proved "dangerously easy" to effect a transition "from the principle that truth is to be discovered in the practical consequences of conduct to the notion that whatever works is necessarily truth."[15] Here American philosophy decoupled from Europe.

An Exceptionalism Unaware of Its Roots—and Its Fate

Samuel Huntington was an American exceptionalist. For him the exception took the form of an Anglo-Saxon heritage imposed and reimposed across a virgin continent, planting European roots in new soil. For another Harvard scholar America's exceptionalism derived from its *distance* from Europe. Louis Hartz's learned and deeply reflective books on New World (North and South American) development argued that the absence of feudalism in America created a figurative vacuum in which middle-class fragments spun out their destiny free of lords and peasants, or fascists and communists. For Hartz it was not about what is *there* but about what is *missing* in America, when seen in the light of a comparative contrast: or as Hofstadter put it, "when the political spectrum is laid out against the spectra of European countries, it can be seen in its naked brevity, its simplicity, its lack of range"; when all is said and done American political thought remained "huddled around the Lockean center." Lord and peasant were absent, and so a serious right and a serious left were also absent; but absence "liberates in the end a rich interior development," in Hartz's words: "A part detaches itself from the whole, the whole fails to renew itself, and the part develops without inhibition . . . a North America where the bourgeoisie, having escaped both past and future, unfolds according to interior laws."[16]

The "part," the bourgeoisie or the middle class, escapes both its past and its predicted (European) future and unfolds across the continent according to its own inherent laws and logic. The fragment lacks knowledge of the sources of its freedom, it "cannot see" Europe, and so it can mistake the woodwork for a cause: "they can even attribute their history to the open land of the frontier," Hartz wrote. Turner's theory becomes an uninhibited, freely drawn solipsism, "a splendid collaboration" between an unconscious ahistorical perspective and the psychic needs of the fragment itself—unaware of its roots and unaware of its fate. More broadly, an indigenous nationalism arises which forgets Europe as the prelude to rejecting it.[17]

Readers of my previous work will know how much my own thought is indebted to Hartz, but the ur-text for this line of argument really originated with Karl Marx, whose analysis was grounded not just in the dominance of the American middle class but in the joining of that middle class with the latest technology and a vast continent empty of any but tribal and hunter-gatherer social formations. In a little-known 1857 essay entitled "Bastiat and Carey" (two economists, Frédéric Bastiat being a free trader, and the other—the famous American economist Henry Carey—a protectionist), Marx described the United States as a country "where bourgeois society did not develop on the foundation of the feudal system, but developed rather from itself; where this society appears not as the surviving result of a centuries-old movement, but rather as the starting-point of a new movement; where the state, in contrast to all earlier national formations, was from the beginning subordinate to bourgeois society, to its production, and never could make the pretence of being an end-in-itself; where, finally, bourgeois society itself, linking up the productive forces of an old world with the enormous natural terrain of a new one, has developed to hitherto unheard-of dimensions . . . and where, finally, even the antitheses of bourgeois society itself appear only as vanishing moments." Hartz's elaboration of Marx's analysis is clearest in *The Founding of New Societies,* dealing with the "fragments" of liberalism in North and South America, where he presents a liberalism never fully known or realized, spinning out its *telos* in a vacuum otherwise known as the continent, finding few if any of the "collisions" with nonliberal forms that mark European history or that formed the Latin American amalgam (except in the slave-holding South, and from that we got the grandest American collision, the Civil War).[18]

For Marx, the world economy was the grandest vista of capitalism, and from the mid-nineteenth century forward the United States was on its horizon, adapting the latest technologies to an "enormous natural terrain." This was a new kind of political economy developing "from itself," encountering and mastering problems alien to or absent in Europe. But it was still *in* the world economy, not riding along on an isolated frontier: the whole theme of the essay is (British) free trade and (American) protection as strategies to open and close within the world system, depending on comparative advantage and global timing and competition. Meanwhile the American left and radicalism were "vanishing moments," always needing reinvention (thus the "New Left").

A central state that cannot make a pretense of itself—this stark contrast drew Marx's attention because of his lifelong concern with Hegel and the

Prussian state, both all about pretension. Not so Washington: in the 1850s the capital had no sewers and few paved streets, pigs rooted in the gutters, cows munched on shrubs near the Senate, Zachary Taylor's horse grazed on the White House lawn, and manacled slaves awaited auctions within sight of the Capitol dome. The "federal bureaucracy" was barely visible, let alone anything remotely like, say, the German civil service. A bit over 1,000 federal employees worked in Washington and around 20,000 in the nation, and three-quarters of these "federal bureaucrats" were in the postal service—mailmen running around local neighborhoods. For Tocqueville the federal government was "naturally feeble," and even New York, the commercial and financial capital, paled when compared to European cities: "the United States has no metropolis."[19]

Historians often take Hartz's *Liberal Tradition* to be the grand text of American exceptionalism, but when we place it alongside Marx's ideas we come to two conclusions. First, it is Marx who saw the United States as exceptional, not just Hartz or Turner or Huntington—and maybe even exceptional to his grand theory; there are hints in *Bastiat and Carey* and elsewhere that the abundant continent might negate the otherwise iron necessity to redistribute resources and property to achieve his good society. Second, Hartz was a *European* exceptionalist, that is, a devotee of what neo-conservatives exalt as "the West." European civilization was the only one he really cared about, and he measured America's difference (its exceptionalism) by the degree to which it fell away from European standards. But Hartz—who hailed from Omaha—also knew his country of birth very well. He had the idea that the New World was not Europe, but a fragment of Europe, an implant on the continent which had only a partial understanding of the European liberal project. A Lockean liberalism never fully understood, but believed to be the holy grail of the system: Alasdaire MacIntyre took Hartz's point to a well-thought-out and thoroughly judged conclusion in *After Virtue:* American politics is the fragmented inheritance of a liberalism never fully known or realized—"parts which now lack those contexts from which their significance derived." The roots and the full philosophical development are in Europe, so Americans depart from liberal premises all the while believing that they follow them, leading to a catastrophic divergence (for MacIntyre).[20] The result is the absence of a truly American philosophy or political theory (Hartz: "where life is fixed at the point of origin, how can philosophy flourish?"), or to say the same thing, a national philosophy of pragmatism—something nicely suited to the task of subduing a continent.

Likewise, Henry James and other pragmatists led Americans toward an interest in quantity, not quality—how many miles of pavement in Buffalo, how many telephones in New York. A Harvard president asked Santayana how his classes were going: very well, he responded, whereupon the president said, "I meant *what is the number* of students in your classes."[21] A wag once remarked that if you ask a Frenchman "what is your theory?" he will expound on Rousseau, Sartre, and Foucault; if you ask an American, he will say he rotates his tires every 10,000 miles. Pragmatism and technique allowed people to agree to disagree about morals, religion, philosophy, ultimate reality—or simply to forget all about it. Here was the perfect combination for Americans inventing themselves on the prairies in the midst of incessant technological innovation: what had utility, had beauty (Oscar Wilde believed "there is no country in the world where machinery is as lovely as America").[22]

The Garden of Eden

One thing united New Englanders with Americans of the Middle Border or the West: they saw themselves as special human beings encountering an Edenic wilderness, a new Arcadia.[23] Whether it was Massachusetts in 1630, Ohio in 1820, Oregon in 1840, Kansas in 1870 ("Come to the Garden of the West! Come to Kansas!"),[24] California after the gold rush, South Dakota ("one of the garden spots" to General Custer), or Turner declaring the end of the frontier in 1893, this master mythology went straight back to the Book of Genesis. A discourse of Edens and Arcadias found and lost began the histories of forty-seven states, coming to an end as cities filled up and industries advanced; today we do not expect to find a book titled "Paradise Lost: Nebraska," or "Indiana and the Fictions of Capital," or "Coast of Dreams: New Jersey," or "City of Quartz" about Wichita. Why then does this discourse remain so alive and well in California (and might still describe the most youthful of states, Hawaii and Alaska)? Take a look at some recent titles about California: *Landscapes of Desire, Pacific Arcadia, Paradise Lost, Americans and the California Dream, Endangered Dreams, Farewell Promised Land: Waking from the California Dream*—and this just scratches the surface of a voluminous genre. Other labels for California include Atlantis, Avalon, the Garden of Eden, El Dorado, Land of Milk and Honey, the New Jerusalem, the Promised Land, even the Pleasure Dome of Kublai Khan.

If you come from Chicago—well, it's safe to say that it never occurs to anyone to write about Chicago in this way. But it occurred to many writers to write about a place called America in this way, from the very beginning. "The master symbol of the garden," Henry Nash Smith wrote, "embraced a cluster of metaphors expressing fecundity, growth, increase, and blissful labor on earth."[25] The central problems animating the scholarship and popular commentary on California were all visited before as people and industry migrated westward from New England. This pastoral myth enveloped Jefferson, Thoreau, Whitman, Melville, and any number of other Americans, not least Frederick Jackson Turner; and as it disappeared in the East, people imagined the lost garden, the agrarian ideal, reappearing in the West. The unfolding western garden was the antithesis of the city, burgeoning industry, and the weight of history symbolized by all things European. The horizon was just across the Alleghenies in Jefferson's time, a moving, floating signifier that bathed every place from Ohio to Missouri in the lyrical rhetoric that we associate with California: the Reverend James Smith arrived in northeastern Ohio in 1797 and exclaimed, "What field of delights! What a garden of spices! What a paradise of pleasures!" What the new territories (meaning any place beyond the thirteen colonies) really needed, New Englanders thought, was missionaries, and they needed them as badly as the Sandwich Islands "or the banks of the Ganges." As the Society for the Promotion of Collegiate and Theological Education in the West put it, the basic frontier idea of the genteel tradition was "to plant another New England"—here, there, and everywhere.[26]

The good shepherd of antiquity found himself with an unheard of luxury in America: a virgin continent, an actually-existing Arcadia, a "paradise regained"—shouldn't Utopia be just around the corner? Eden just beyond the ever-receding horizon? The pastoral or Edenic ideal never relinquished its hold on the American mind, whether it was an anticipated future or a golden age retrieved from the past: but one infernal machine after another came along to disrupt or destroy the garden. As the country industrialized, one ideal retreated into an irretrievable past and the other, an unlikely or unreachable future. The back side of Jefferson's rural community was disdain for newly risen industry, a resistance, as Raymond Williams showed, to the newly structured urban order and simultaneous unruly chaos, "a social dissolution in the very process of aggregation."

The recourse to ideas born of a bygone agrarian order ignores not only the impossibility of re-creating them but the inequalities of that order when it existed—the isolation and frequent ignorance of the farms and villages; the slaves held by Jeffersonian Virginians; the oppressions of women, itinerant laborers, and the heterodox of all types; and the huge class of victims claimed by westward expansion. The pastoral ideal, as Williams wrote, is authentic and moving precisely to the degree of its unreality. The rural pastoral and the infernal urban machine dramatize "the great issue of our culture"—the germ, as Henry James put it, "of the most final of all generalizations about America." That generalization is in and of the past for most of the country—but never for California.[27]

Homesteads and Yeomen

The relative ease with which settlers traversed the Appalachians simply by following the Hudson and Mohawk rivers opened up broad swaths of the continent to settlement in the early nineteenth century. The Great Lakes and the Ohio and Mississippi rivers likewise posed few barriers and enhanced every interaction with easy riparian transport. To the north the canoe route from Lake Superior to Lake of the Woods "corresponded exactly to the existing economic systems," making a perfect boundary between two nations. The Rio Grande did the same in the southwest. By the 1840s when Tocqueville traveled the country, Arcadia had already moved to the Mississippi Valley: "the most magnificent dwelling-place prepared by God for man's abode." If nature were similarly accommodating, Americans would have been on the shores of the Pacific in a scant few years. The primary barrier to westward movement was not human, in the form of the Native Americans who long inhabited the continent, but geographical: parched deserts, towering mountain ranges, and yawning, treacherous cataracts that came to be known as the Colorado River and the Grand Canyon.[28] But what we now know as the Middle West filled up quickly.

The westward movement was also a planned and intended replication of New England: every village green should have a church, every 20,000-square-mile plat should have its college, and behind everything in this spreading "New England zone" should be a sharp moral purpose. In the 1780s young people in Connecticut "marched to rude melodies which taught them to dream that toward the setting sun lay an earthly paradise with gates open to welcome them." "The Calvinist Plan of Union" brought forth "cadres of specialists [who] were sent to the front," people trained at Andover, Yale, or Princeton or planned facsimile colleges with names like Oberlin, Marietta, Beloit, and Grinnell. The reality, of course, was different; the midwestern cadres changed as generations passed or as they simply forgot their mission; meanwhile German and Irish Catholics, Jews and free blacks also settled regions like the Western Reserve (Akron and Ravenna were both small cities containing "Little Dublins"), making a simple replication impossible.[29]

The expanding frontier in the Ohio Valley, the Western Reserve, Indiana, Wisconsin, and Illinois provided the template for Frederick Jackson Turner's frontier thesis and turned out to be the region where homesteading as he described it found its best fit. Jefferson's agrarian ideal was inseparable from the people making it happen, yeomen farmers marching as far as the eye could see, constantly pushing and displacing the western horizon. The human carriers of the grand saga of the frontier were families picking up stakes and moving west, seeking a new life and "an independence" or "a competence"—as nineteenth-century Americans defined the virtue that came with family ownership of the land. For many it did: their own private garden. For all too many others, it didn't: dependence on banks for mortgages and farming loans, unyielding soil and catastrophic weather, or simply the backbreaking toil and drudgery required year-round of large extended families to make a living, broke many farmers. East of the 98th meridian (Walter Prescott Webb's chosen point at which the West begins, defined by precipitation falling to less than thirty inches a year) homesteading was reasonably successful, but west of it less than half of the more than one million homesteaders on the Great Plains sustained themselves—most often because of the violent, capricious weather.[30]

The Machine in the Garden

Thomas Jefferson embodied the contradiction between a real-life ideal, the yeoman or homesteading farmer, pillar of the middle class, and rapid American economic development symbolized by the factory and the city. During the War of 1812 Jefferson lamented that the British enemy "has indeed the consolation of Satan on removing our first parents from Paradise: from a peaceable and agricultural nation, he makes us a military and manufacturing one." War drove the machine, and the machine drove war. For Thoreau the whistle of a locomotive breaking the silence of Walden Pond was the machine invading the peace of an enclosed space, a world set apart. Against it an individual recoils and rebels: a retreat to the woods, an escape from the modern, a resolve to go west. And then, sooner or later, a return to the grid of urban, industrial America—typically with a sense of loss and resignation. Thoreau put the punctuation mark on this return: most people lead lives of quiet desperation.

"The pastoral idea has been used to define the meaning of America ever since the age of discovery," Leo Marx wrote in his influential 1964 book *The Machine in the Garden*. For Marx the central American conundrum was not the American pastoral as such but the contrast between it and the technological fetishism that is equally characteristic of our culture, yielding a typical pattern in which an individual withdraws from the technological modern into an encounter with wildness—or simply the wilderness— followed by a return to the modern grid marked by acquiescence if not fatalism. We see this theme as recently as Philip Roth's 1997 novel *American Pastoral*, where, paradoxically, the ingenuity of American industry in Newark (New Jersey) a half-century earlier is the backdrop for an overwhelming sense of things lost and abandoned. D. H. Lawrence's stab at explaining this pattern was to say that "the most idealist nations invent most machines. America simply teems with mechanical inventions." It isn't clear what the relation between ideals and machines is here, and the cause he located is absurd: "Nobody in America ever wants to *do* anything. They are idealists. Let a machine do the thing."[31] Jefferson's lament about the British gets us closer (not the machine as such but war and industry as a deus ex machina), and as we will see at the end of the chapter, Frederick Jackson Turner gets us very close to Leo Marx's conundrum—while wrapping himself up in it.

The American pastoral is a *design*, according to Marx, a "larger structure of thought and feeling in which the *ideal* is a part." The counterforce is a *machine*, preeminently for Thoreau and Whitman the locomotive, or the textile mill materializing in Ishmael's mind as he explores leviathan's skeleton in *Moby-Dick:* "a sudden, shocking intruder upon a fantasy of idyllic satisfaction." The hero of classic American literature takes "a redemptive journey away from society," a withdrawal into nature, a "return to first things" that turns out to be temporary—a renewal or regeneration followed by another return, maybe an equaniminous return (Thoreau on coming back to Concord: "we need the tonic of nature"), more often an acquiescent return to the existing modern, to the mechanized everyday. Thoreau's equanimity, however, did not extend to an America enthralled by technique: "improved means to an unimproved end," he called it, a prophetic and telling observation.[32] Leo Marx's dilemma is not a new one—it is as old as the Greeks. But America raised it to a new, agonizing height because the urban industrial grid that Jefferson hated was just getting started. As the machine grew ever larger, it took corporeal form in a protean city that threatened to gobble up the entire continent.

Chicago: Prairie Apparition

The Second City takes its name from the malodorous vapors rising around the southwestern end of Lake Michigan—not from Gary's steel mills but from the stinky swamp that Pierre Du Sable, a black man, chose to call by the

Indian word for stench: "Chicago." Approaching the sprawling city from Gary, the immense lakefront skyline rises up suddenly like an apparition, oddly unexpected no matter how many times one sees it. That's what the great city did in the mid-nineteenth century, too: rise up instantly as the starkest example of Jefferson's rapacious urban monster operating at a white heat, chewing up the prairies as an early Los Angeles of the Middle Border. Prospering at the confluence of great lakes, broad rivers, westward trails, and soon, railroads, this protean city had a rapid rise unmatched before but a harbinger of instant cities to come in the West and Southwest. Chicago's emergence as the first and quintessential western city was something new under the sun commanding not just the prairies all the way to Denver but everything out to the Pacific coast as well. Then under the combined and awesome powers of the second industrial revolution, it became the core of a regional industrial behemoth, stretching from Pittsburgh through Cleveland and Detroit to St. Louis and Kansas City, which transformed the Middle Border and dashed the hopes and dreams of another Eden, another Arcadia. It brought Turner's slow, evolutionary, amoeba-like path to American development to a creaking halt. The city that works closed the frontier and replaced it with a revolution.

"No other city in America had ever grown so large so quickly," Chicago's historian William Cronon wrote. The size of Toledo in 1840, with about 5,000 residents, it had more than 100,000 by 1860 and was the second most populous American city by 1890. Chicago's rise repositioned the West: it was now everything between the Great Lakes and the coast, that is, everything west of this sudden new meridian. Railroads funneled everything through Chicago, through the eye of a geographic needle, selling all the products of the West in the Midwest, the East, and Europe, from corn and wheat to pigs and cows. Perhaps the broadest meaning of this new city's emergence, though, was its position in the world economy. London and New York constituted the center, and Chicago stood between them and their access to the wealth of the prairies, servicing both financial centers as it processed grain and meat and rail shipments from the continental West and regulated the processes of supply and demand through the ingenious pricing mechanisms of the Board of Trade.[33]

Like Pacific Coast cities in our time, Chicago was also an epicenter of innovation: the grain elevator, the mercantile exchange, and methods of processing that wonderful vehicle for turning corn into meat, the pig. The railroads changed the measure of grain from bushels to "carloads," and the best money came from quickly offloading the grain and dispatching the cars back empty to the West—but that left great piles of grain moldering in the streets of Chicago. The steam-powered grain elevator, invented in Buffalo in 1832, solved that problem: it offloaded the grain to large scales then dropped the grain through rotating chutes into one of many storage bins. Conveyor belts moved rivers of grain, weighing, distributing, and storing them automatically. While St. Louis still used people's backs to move bushels of grain sack by sack from Mississippi River barges to the mills, grain elevators offloaded millions of tons of grain each day. A large grain elevator could empty twelve railroad cars at the rate of 24,000 bushels an hour—and Chicago had twelve elevators. Anthony Trollope called them a mechanism for processing a river of corn, at a time when the corn of the New World produced four times the food value of wheat with about a tenth of the seed.[34] But this same effulgent golden stream created vast supplies that might not find a market, plus what would farmer Jones of Iowa get from selling his corn, as opposed to farmer Smith from Illinois, when the product of their labor was entirely fungible? The Chicago Mercantile Exchange (or Board of Trade) was the answer: let every farmer's ton of corn or wheat have the same, market-set price.

Chicago took on an entirely new character when innovators understood the pig to be the most efficient and lucrative way of moving corn to the market—as meat: now the slaughterhouses were born (so was the abattoir by the lake) and generations of traders wallowed in pork belly contracts and corn futures while rough workers plunged their knives into the throats of wailing beasts ("the animals passed a psychic current back along the overhead trolley," Norman Mailer wrote, "each cut throat released its scream of death into the throat not yet cut and just behind"). Hogs converted grain to meat "with two or three times the efficiency of cattle or sheep," and corn into pig into cured sausage was the solution to making lots of money: "The Hog eats the corn," one man wrote, "and Europe eats the Hog. Corn thus becomes incarnate: for what is a hog, but fifteen or twenty bushels of corn on four legs?" But to make money you also had to move rivers of pigs from the sty to the table. Along came the idea of assembling all the pigs in Chicago and running them through the "disassembly line," and so the bloody, reeking, clanking, rank, and disgusting slaughterhouse became the key forerunner of mass production techniques that swept American industry in the next century (after it was reversed to become Henry Ford's *assembly* line). Once the hog or the cow was fully disassembled, though, there was still the problem of getting the meat rapidly to the market before it spoiled. And so Gustavus J. Swift adapted the refrigerator car (invented by citrus shippers), letting pigs and cows flow to eastern markets as pork chops and T-bone steaks. By the end of the Civil War,

Chicago had snatched the title of Porkopolis from Cincinnati, which once commanded the trade by virtue of its strategic riparian position (in 1850 Cincinnati packed 334,000 hogs and Chicago a mere 20,000; by 1870 Chicago processed more than a million pigs each year).[35] But it wasn't very genteel, this business, and the abattoir by the lake didn't look much like Arcadia.

Chicago's centrality to the revolutionary new-new thing, the railroads, its simultaneous positioning as a huge industrial processing center and a meridian city for the Atlantic and Pacific worlds, made it also the capital of a western empire knit together by singular stretches of iron across the empty prairie and over the Rockies. "The railways which radiate from Lake Michigan and run like lattice-work throughout the West," a railroad magnate said, "gather up business and centering at Chicago pour it by train-loads on to the through lines to the East." The rural West where prairies gave way to cornstalks, wheat fields, and cattle ranches became Chicago's hinterland after midcentury, an agrarian periphery the size of a continent. The city didn't just process nearly every farmer's grain and stock, it also had financial dominance all the way to the coast through its banks and the commodity exchange. Sears Roebuck and Montgomery Wards arose to return farmers' profits to Chicago pockets; both produced catalogs the size of the New York telephone book, which Americans perused with a calculating intensity. But perhaps the critical marker of how Chicago moved the nation's center of gravity westward was the opening in 1903 of U.S. Steel's new plant in Gary, the largest integrated steel mill in the world. By the turn of the new century Frank Norris penned a memorable portrait of Chicago: "The Great Grey City, brooking no rival, imposed its dominion upon a country larger than many a kingdom of the Old World. For thousands of miles beyond its confines was its influence felt. . . . For her and because of her all the central states, all the Great Northwest roared with traffic and industry; sawmills screamed; factories, their smoke blackening the sky, clashed and flamed; wheels turned, pistons leaped in their cylinders; cog gripped cog."[36]

The Middle Border

For another half-century the Midwest remained an industrial powerhouse dominated by Chicago but filled out with a host of other vibrant industrial cities: Cleveland, Buffalo, Pittsburgh, Detroit, Indianapolis, St. Louis, Kansas City, Cincinnati, Akron, Toledo, Canton—the start of a long list indeed. In a fine book that still makes interesting reading, *The American Mind*, Henry Steele Commager wrote in 1950 about the extraordinary dynamism and importance of this "Middle Border"; like the midwestern captains of industry at the time, the book brims with pride and accomplishment. Only a decade later, few again wrote with such confidence about the Middle West, because the dynamism had so clearly moved to the Pacific Coast and the cold war gave Washington and New York a new prominence. Chicago remained preeminent in the region, but all the other cities began a long and mostly irremediable industrial and social decline.

My grandfather liked to train his powerful binoculars across Lake Erie, and when I was a boy he would let me peer through them to watch the elongated oar boats plying the horizon. Iron ore shipped down from the Mesabi Range in Minnesota through Lake Superior and Lake Erie would meet coal coming up from West Virginia by rail; they would converge at the Cayuhoga River, where both poured into the yawning maw of the Cleveland steel industry, a city then known as "the best location in the nation." Today I can visit his grave in Madison, Ohio, a New England town with its "village green" surrounded by white wooden homes, a municipal hall, and one or two churches, and everything is familiar from my youthful memories of half a century vintage; a town of 2,322 people in 1950 and 2,921 in 2000, it is still 98.4 percent white. Likewise when I visit Granville in the rolling hills of southern Ohio, another New England village and home of the college I attended, the changes over decades are so marginal that one has to seek them out (a town of 2,653 in 1950, it had 3,167 people in 2000).[37]

This influence gives the Western Reserve—sometimes called the "Third New England"—and the eastern counties of southern Ohio an ambience different from the midwestern prairies, which begin west of Cleveland and Columbus. (Mrs. Soult held to the firm belief "that Ohio was the western-most point at which a civilized existence could be sustained," McMurtry wrote in *Comanche Moon;* "beyond Ohio, there was only barbarism and bliz-zards.")[38] Granville and Madison still reflect a little-changed pastoral land-scape—precisely because industry barely touched them. But today steel cities like Youngstown are an urban nightmare, and Cleveland has never regained its midcentury vigor. My grandfather was telling me about a powerhouse, integrated political economy that was one of the most productive nodes in the world economy. Neither he nor I knew that we were gazing at the downside of a century-long burst of growth for which there would never again be a comparable upside.[39]

Of what relevance is Chicago's story, so often told, to a book about the Pacific? First, Chicago materialized almost overnight on virgin land—a mud-flat with a few thousand people—just as several western cities would, but just as the settled industrial and commercial cities of the East (Boston, New York, Philadelphia) could *not*. They were filled, and filling them anew ran up against a thousand vested interests. Second, Chicago's history shows how serendipitous geography can interact with incessant innovation to create one new industry after another; if it was the quintessential city of the railway era, it also became an industrial, commercial, financial, and merchandising power-house in one of the most remarkable transformative spurts in the modern world coming "late" in the time of world industry. Third, it emerged as a major city just in time to accommodate and organize the completion of the continent and its business, stretching to the Pacific. Last, the blinding speed of its rise to preeminence as the first city of the West spelled the end of the frontier myth, the Arcadia just over the horizon. Chicago was the machine in the garden, with a vengeance.

The Agrarian Grid

Chicago not only exemplified the industrial grid, it almost invented it—a national and urban network of American rail lines defining a string of new cities along the line from Philadelphia to St. Louis to Denver and San Francisco, and shaping their downtowns into hatch-mark streets, usually spreading outward from great railway stations (Pierre L'Enfant's Washington is one of the only American cities to prefer circles to rectangles). Thomas Jefferson did not like the new industrial cities, but he loved the logic and symmetry of the American pastoral—his kind of modernity. As it happened, the rigid physiognomy of industrial cities that the agrarians disparaged had its exact counterpart in the geometric pattern of land subdivision created by the Ordinance of 1785, an example of American scientific precision just as powerful as the steam engine.

This law "ordered the Northwest Territory surveyed into sections (one mile square, or 640 acres)," Elliott West wrote, "which were to be grouped into townships": 756 of them, each six miles square on the traditional New England model. The strict mathematics made subdivision a breeze; each township could be divided into one-square-mile lots, with four lots reserved for public schools. Two years later the Northwest Ordinance provided for governors in the new territories, a legislature after 5,000 free males had set-tled, and petition for statehood after the population had reached 60,000. With some modifications, both laws came to govern most of the territory of the United States. West draws his conclusion: "The first square inch of the first surveyor's stake was a kind of polestar of national development, the anchored point of reckoning for more than a billion acres. Nowhere else in the world would an area of such size be laid out in a uniform land system." This national mechanism "was an infinitely reproducible pattern, the perfect machine for national expansion." Andro Linklater calls it "the immaculate grid," a ruthless regularity imposed on the land that you can observe on State Route 277 in Indiana, a road running "straight as a surveyor's rule" for mile after mile, but just one mile inside Indiana. The state border running north-south, separating Indiana and Ohio, was surveyor-general Jared Mansfield's "First Principal Meridian," west of which he projected squares "so immaculate that their pattern would be compared to graph paper, checkerboards, and plaid." Route 277 is where Mansfield's gridiron begins, and it doesn't stop until it hits the Rocky Mountains.[40]

Ninety percent of Americans lived on the land in 1800, and land was everything to them. But what appeared to be the rooted, historical farm shared through the generations, a source of primordial attachment, was more often a commodity, and the grid's regularity was a realtor's dream; as an English traveler wrote around 1800, "speaking generally, every farm from Eastport in Maine to Buffalo on Lake Erie, is for sale." The designated price circa 1796 was a minimum of $2 an acre (a formidable sum, almost $2,000 in our time), so in subsequent decades the parcels were sold in lots of 160 acres, then 80 acres, and finally in 1832 the jackpot figure: 40 acres (as in "forty acres and a mule"). An immaculate grid needed immaculate—that is, clear—land titles, and then it was off to the races: a million acres a year sold in the 1820s, a sudden jump to 57 million acres between 1830 and 1837 until prices suddenly collapsed, then the gold rush, and finally by the end of the century more than 250 million acres of the continent had become private property.[41]

On January 1, 1863, Lincoln signed the Emancipation Proclamation, and on the same day the "Act to Secure Homesteads to Actual Settlers on the Public Domain" took effect. The southerners who had opposed this legislation were now well below the Mason-Dixon Line, and so these two epochal measures came into being. The Homestead Act allowed any citizen over twenty-one, man or woman, or any immigrant intending to become a citizen, to claim up to 160 acres of land if they would build a home and a barn, cultivate the land, and stay there for at least five years. At that time they would get full title to the land for a fee of $10.[42] In the five decades after the passage of the Homestead Act, nearly two and a half million people filed for its quarter-section family farms, making for the great heyday of homesteading, "from Texas north across the High Plains to the Canadian prairies," in Nugent's words. Nugent pinpoints the peak of homesteading at 1913, as world war came around the corner and the United States moved toward "a new metropolitan future."

By 1900 two-thirds of homesteaders had given up their farms to banks and real estate speculators, and 35 percent of all American farmers were tenants. The worst problems were west of the 98th meridian. Stegner has a vivid description of the backbreaking labor necessary to build and run a homestead in the arid plains, with failure more likely than success; even with free land, Limerick estimated the cost of a home, draft animals, plow, fences, and seed at $1,000, not a small sum then. Turner's famous 1893 declaration that the frontier had closed was also misleading: more public land went under the plow from 1890 to 1920 than in the three decades following the Homestead Act.[43] Franklin Roosevelt finally ended the program in 1935, after the American farm population had ceased expanding; it remained stable for a few more years, and then began a long, steady and irreversible decline. By the end the act had created homesteads for over 400,000 families, amounting to over 285 million acres of land (the western railroads, to make an interesting comparison, accumulated 183 million acres—an area a bit bigger than Texas—and sold off at least 120 million). But the act did not keep speculators from corralling much of the best land or from filing false claims and piling one 160-acre lot on top of another. Historian Fred Shannon determined that between 1863 and 1900, "nearly half of all homestead entries were fraudulent."[44]

When you fly west from Chicago on a clear day, a perfect quilt of agrarian regularity expands before your eyes all the way to Denver, a thousand miles of rectangular life punctuated at 90-degree angles by a farmhouse, a barn, and a clump of trees, or by a succession of geometric small towns—a pastoral ideal realized with scientific precision. The land, the frontier, the methodical parceling out, the continent, the horizon—a mechanism of calculated modernity was at work in both the country and the city. It all gave to Americans an inherent advantage over Europe, in its geometric expanse but especially in its newness. Modern Europeans did not discover the land they ruled; they just claimed to rule it better than their medieval predecessors. But Americans did claim to have made a discovery and to rule in the name of those who worked the land—and really, in the name of everyman: "The material fact of the North American continent itself," wrote Myra Jehlen, enabled Americans "to declare themselves *incomparable* and the universal representatives of mankind." Wealthy Virginia planters, the American homesteader, the ascendant middle class—they could all argue that they were the universal social solvent and therefore the answer to the world's problems. Lacking a rooted peasantry or an aristocracy based in anything more than premature Atlantic transit

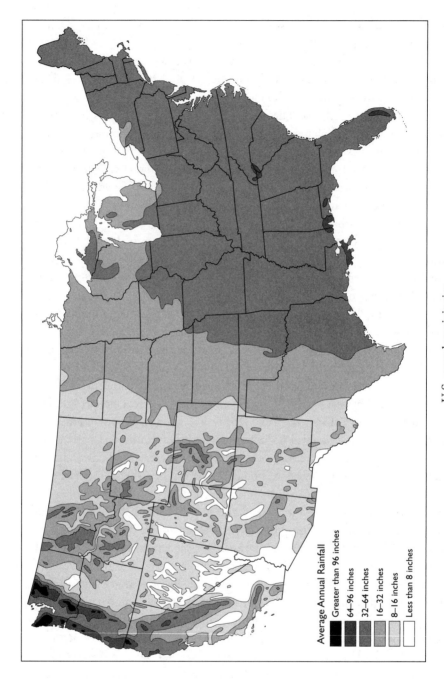

U.S. annual precipitation.

Map by Bill Nelson, based on U.S. Department of Agriculture map, 2008.

Average Annual Rainfall

Greater than 96 inches
64–96 inches
32–64 inches
16–32 inches
8–16 inches
Less than 8 inches

made the story all the more plausible, especially to themselves. The almost miraculous ease with which the continent fell into their laps (as distinct from the arduous difficulties of settling it) seemed providential, a fulfilling of an original plan founded in early seventeenth-century Massachusetts. In this way, to a central figure like Ralph Waldo Emerson, nature, self, and nation were merged: "the meaning of America is in the body of the continent," he wrote, and the horizon was no limit—it kept on going, forever, eventually encompassing the whole world; it is the bright future for the individual and the country.[45] Emerson's all-seeing eye took in everything while ignoring the universal geometric grid (not to mention the original inhabitants), and so did the imagined nation.

The Machine of Conquest

What about the most numerous people on this "vacant" land, Native Americans? As it happened Indians were not so numerous by the time Europeans began to settle North America in the 1600s (as opposed to making forays to explore it after Columbus) because the land had indeed been vacated—by conquest, war, and disease. Europeans did not find a wilderness but soon found ways to create one. The numbers have not been determined with any degree of exactness, but work by historians and archaeologists suggests a figure of slightly over 1 million North America Indians around 1600—a vast decline from Columbus's time when there may have been 7 million, a demographic catastrophe by any definition but still dwarfed by South America where it was far worse: of the roughly 65 million natives alive in Central and South America when Columbus landed, barely one in fifteen survived the onslaught of war, slave labor, and disease—indeed, disease microbes probably thinned large native populations *before* there was extensive or intimate contact with Europeans (traders or small groups of explorers were all it took to spread germs), making counting the native population all the harder. In Mexico the cataclysm was still worse, with 25 million Indians in 1492 reduced to a mere one million by 1600. As Russell Thornton shows, the 70 to 90 million Indians originally populating the Western Hemisphere in 1492 compare to a population in Europe west of Russia of 60 to 70 million people circa 1500, 100 to 150 million in China, 75 to 150 million in South Asia, and 332 million to 542 million in the whole world.[46] A century later somewhere between 12 and 20 percent of all Homo sapiens on the planet had vanished, as if a meteor had struck.

The demise of six out of seven Indians who lived north of Mexico between

1492 and 1600 is impossible to imagine, but the slaughter continued apace after European settlement began. Around this time about half of the North American natives (454,000) lived in the Southwest and another 250,000 to 275,000 lived in California, both regions off the line of westward advance until the 1840s. About 190,000 more inhabited the Great Plains, 115,000 in Colorado and the Great Basin, and perhaps 175,000 along the Northwest coast. Here, too, contact with Europeans since the early explorations had sharply reduced most tribes—the vast majority died through exposure to diseases like smallpox, typhoid fever, measles, cholera, bubonic plague, malaria, and yellow fever, none of which existed in the New World, and accordingly Native American immune systems fell before them, although in South America vast numbers were also murdered or worked to death. (Apparently just one disease transferred the other way, from America to Europe: syphilis.) Most of the time the contagious Europeans spread their microbes involuntarily, but now and then they purposely infected goods transferred to Indians, for example, blankets. Calvinist stalwart Cotton Mather thought this was God's will, but just to make sure he intervened "by sending the Smallpox amongst the Indians." The deterioration was horrific, a Grim Reaper moving inexorably through the continent: 90 percent of Indians along the Massachusetts coast died of smallpox from 1617 to 1619; Huron Indians lost half to two-thirds of their population to epidemics in the 1640s; among various tribes of Plains Indians, some were reduced by 97 or 98 percent, the Crows by 70 percent, Arapahos by 43 percent. Smallpox destroyed the Mandan and decimated the Lakota Sioux. By 1900 Indians numbered between 220,000 and 300,000 across the entire territory of the United States, the surviving remnant of "the greatest demographic calamity in human history."[47]

Congress and the land surveyors assumed that the frontier was not just empty, but that no one owned property. John Winthrop, leader of the Massachusetts Bay Company, had long before declared that Indians were not owners of the land because they hadn't enclosed it or improved it; for their part, the Indian leader Massasoit had asked the Plymouth colonists, "What is this you call property? It cannot be the earth, for the land is our mother, nourishing all her children, beasts, birds, fish and all men"; the earth was "for the use of all," so how can it belong to one man? Massasoit's cogent argument didn't reckon with possessive individualism, soon gobbling up the continent. The third article of the Northwest Ordinance may have stated that "the utmost good faith shall always be observed towards the Indians; their lands and property shall never be taken from them without their consent," but that piece of hypocrisy would be forgotten almost before the ink was dry. As the new agrarian strictures codified the land, they immediately set off an orgy of real estate speculation that would mark every significant new addition of western territory until Los Angeles perfected the process in the 1880s and reinvented it almost every decade thereafter. In 1787 the federal government sold off 5 million acres in southern Ohio to one syndicate, which turned around and sold most of it to another (which included several congressmen) for a nice profit. Eight years later the "thoroughly bribed" Georgia legislature sold 35 million acres west to the Mississippi for a bit over a penny per acre, "probably the most infamous land steal in the nation's history."[48] The logic of rationally surveyed land met the logic of frontier capitalism, and the pastoral ideal waned.

If the land wasn't empty, it was empty of any force capable of resisting an aggressive nation. The simple truth is that Indians and confederations of tribes, some of them sophisticated and others essentially Neolithic, really could do nothing to stop this march to the Pacific; many fought valiantly and desperately, but their inability to coalesce with other tribes—often enemy tribes—vastly weakened the force of their resistance. For the most part they did not really try; Indians were much more welcoming, or less resistant, to whites peopling the continent than most Americans imagine (their imaginings usually driven by Hollywood westerns, but sometimes by tales of real encounters with fearsome Apaches and Comanches). Whites quickly inundated the Indians: in 1788, the average number of people going down the Ohio River on flatboats every month was bigger than the total population of Shawnees; the total for that year "nearly equaled the population of the largest southern group, the Cherokees." On the frontier, Elliott West wrote, "demography was destiny."[49]

Most Indian wars, from Fallen Timbers in 1794 to the last battle at Wounded Knee in 1890, had their origin in white settlers seeking land: making treaties to push the Indians away or westward, breaking the same treaties to expand some more, killing them when they resisted. The butchery and forced relocation of the Cherokee Nation in 1838 under Andrew Jackson's Indian Removal Act exemplified the lengths to which white Americans and their government were willing to go, from the beginning with the Pequots (Puritans burned 800 of them alive in 1637) to the end with the destruction of the California and Nez Percé Indians. When Jackson's barbarity was finished, upwards of 8,000 Cherokees were dead and less than 1,200 Indians lived in the eastern United States. After the Civil War Americans made war on the Indians for the next quarter-century: Ulysses S. Grant and General William Tecumseh Sherman, among others, led the way by calling for their extermination—along with their "commissary," the buffalo. (This strange animal that the Plains Indians lived off was exterminated with an incredible vigor, through disease and a relentless onslaught by skinners, tanners, and the U.S. Army—"every buffalo dead is an Indian gone," one officer said; reduced from a population in the tens of millions, by the 1880s maybe 400 buffalo remained alive in the United States.)[50]

If the general pattern of white violence is clear, there were always Americans who sought common ground with Indians or who cried out against the slaughters. Alan Taylor has a brilliant discussion of the complexities of cultural accommodation and conflict that shaped the settler encounter with Iroquois and other tribes in the late eighteenth century, through a constant back-and-forth negotiation between Indians wanting to preserve their lands but not wanting war, whites who understood this and tried to accommodate Indian demands, followed by a crisis and quick resort to the superior force that the whites could deploy—and then a real estate bonanza. The great Frederick Law Olmsted, a pastoralist who poured his ideals into one magnificent public park after another, called the westward movement a "grand game of assassination," perpetrated by a monstrous racism and the most savage elements of American society. And for him, Arcadian California was the worst—a case of barbarism masquerading as civilization; a minimal estimate is that whites murdered 4,500 California Indians between the gold rush and 1880, and many more thousands fell to disease. In an 1860 report to his superiors, army Major G. J. Raines wrote of "atrocity and horror unparalleled" on Indian Island in Humboldt Bay, where 188 friendly natives were "barbarously" massacred: "babes, with brains oozing out of their skulls, cut and hacked with axes, and squaws exhibiting the most frightful wounds in death."[51]

Whites thus killed far more Indians than vice versa, just as it was more common for Indians to help pioneers than to harm them—nor was it uncommon to pass the entire trip and not see a single Indian. The warlike Shoshones turned out to be among the most cooperative of tribes, saving the lives of many emigrants and returning straying livestock. Highly sophisticated tribes like the Chinook seemed almost to welcome the whites, or at least peaceful and considerate ones like Lewis and Clark. (Limerick wrote that Chinooks greeted whites by saying "Clak-hoh-ah-yah," a pidgin version of "Clark, how are you?") Lewis and Clark wintered with the settled and accomplished Mandan, who welcomed them as friends. It didn't make much difference; soon the Mandan died like flies and essentially disappeared, mainly through smallpox epidemics but also through murder and other depredations.[52]

Savage War

The Apaches and the Comanches, of course, were not hanging around to comfort wayward pioneers—they were the fiercest fighters in resisting the white onslaught. Led by legendary chiefs like Cochise and Geronimo, the Apaches carried on a highly effective mountain guerrilla warfare against white settlers in the Southwest, attacking and then vanishing. The Comanches ruled the southern plains, following the buffalo, and were easily the most feared of Indian braves—indomitable until the 1870s. Walter Prescott Webb had a rare appreciation of the fighting skills of the Apaches and Comanches, who, after Spanish explorers brought horses to the new world, used them to dominate the Great Plains for centuries: "At the end of the Spanish regime the Plains Indians were more powerful, far richer, and in control of more territory than they were at the beginning of it." Carrying a short bow usually made of ash and up to a hundred arrows, "the red knights of the prairie" would descend on their prey at great speed, often hanging to the side of their charging mounts and shooting twenty arrows a minute, keeping as many as eight arrows flying through the air at the same time, arrows unleashed with force great enough to drive the point cleanly through the body of a buffalo—or, of course, a pioneer. The Sioux were brilliant fighters, using "every tactic of guerrilla warfare . . . from simple ambush to complicated confusion." Every tactic indeed; confusion indeed: the legendary fighter Crazy Horse heralded his attacks by sending forth "a hermaphrodite with a black blanket over his head" to ride a zigzag path through the hills. "The He-e-man-eh, as he was called, made four rides," Brown wrote. "Each time he came back to chant a report that he had caught soldiers in his hands. On his fourth ride he shouted that he had a hundred soldiers in his hands," and that signaled to the warriors that the moment for war had arrived.[53]

Whites on horseback with only a single-shot rifle or pistol were easy marks. The soldiers used muzzle-loaders, requiring a halt while the charge was ramrodded into the barrel, which of course became the Indian signal to attack; these rifles weren't much better than rapidly flying arrows. They gained the upper hand only when Colt invented the six-shot revolver in 1835, just in time for the Texas Rangers to use it to pacify their new republic. Later, in the mid-1860s, the cavalry descended upon the Sioux with new breech-loading Springfield rifles, which unleashed center-fire metallic cartridges one after another, with barely a pause; the cavalry was the first in the world to adopt this new technology. With the Springfields in hand the Sioux warriors went down "like grass blades before a blast of wind." A few years later the cavalry had equally effective long-range game rifles and Hotchkiss guns that could unload fifty two-pound shells in a minute.[54] It was a contest of manifest unequals.

It is instructive of the prejudices of the best minds in America before the civil rights movement that this resistance was nearly always cast in words of fear and loathing, like those today who lump any Arab or Iraqi fighter under the encompassing and nullifying label "terrorist." For Bernard DeVoto and generations of Americans before him, the Apaches were "a vigorous and cruel race . . . [until] whiskey and smallpox tamed them"; the Comanches were something else again: "the most terrible savages of the plains," well-practiced "sadists" whose highest aspiration was to visit fiendish tortures upon their victims—tear them limb from limb, skin them alive but slowly, rape white women en masse. "No one has ever exaggerated the Comanche tortures."[55] (It would take a later generation of historians to illustrate that it was also hard to exaggerate white tortures.)

The Indians of the Great Lakes region surely took merciless cruelty to the level of an art form. The Senecas stole children from the Miami tribe and ate them, first lopping off the head before boiling the body in a kettle. When the Miamis got their turn they chopped the heads off Seneca braves and kept them for souvenirs, while sparing one or two to stumble home and tell their tale without benefit of lips, hands, or noses. Peoria Indians caught an enemy warrior and sliced a piece of meat off his thigh, then made him eat it. Then they cut off his calves and threw them in the pot, tore off the rest of his flesh, and finally burned his bones. Yet these were the same Indians who lived together for centuries with French traders and settlers, in relative peace, on the mutually constructed and accommodative pattern of Richard White's "middle ground." Their world was not one of races, intermarriage was natural to them, they had centuries of past practice in adaptation, borrowing from others and accommodating difference. It was the American whites who would not accommodate, because they wanted what the Indians could not give up—the land where they had been living for as long as anyone could remember. The whites' future promised the Indians nothing but "alternative routes to obliteration."[56]

Renewal through Conquest

Richard Slotkin's "regeneration through violence" is at the root of settler expansion, which nonwhites experienced as ostracism or murder; combined with disease, the ultimate result was a genocide that gave pause to few whites.

I am unaware of another historian of America quite as erudite, comprehensively informed, and compassionate; Slotkin's highly imaginative trilogy, begun during the Vietnam War, grows in significance as successive generations revisit and try to comprehend the place of violence in American life, indeed the uniquely American levels of violence that continue to characterize this nation, whether measured at home or meted out to the world.[57] Professor Slotkin begins his first volume with a well-known observation by D. H. Lawrence, the myth of "the essential white America." All the other stuff, he says, "the love, the democracy, the floundering into lust, is a sort of by-play. The essential American soul is hard, isolate, stoic, and a killer. It has never yet melted." (Lawrence's staggering sentence comes after a discussion of Cooper's *Deerslayer*.)[58]

Slotkin argues that as the frontier moved west and south, Jefferson's yeoman Arcadia gave way to Jacksonian democracy, to "the western man-on-the-make," to the slave formation of the South, to national heroes like Davy Crockett who defined national aspirations by "so many bears destroyed, so much land preempted, so many trees hacked down, so many Indians and Mexicans dead in the dust." White settlers renewed themselves in the New World, in the continental wilderness, "wandering outward in space and, apparently, backward in time." Lawrence and Slotkin conjure with a Puritan temperament unleashed on the wilderness, yielding a homegrown nativism. The Puritan conversion experience made them "chosen," God's grace shone upon them; the dark-skinned savages at one with nature were the fallen. So the Indians would be warred upon, removed, or even exterminated. Thereby, "the myth of regeneration through violence became the structuring metaphor of the American experience."[59]

Along Turner's line between savagery and civilization arose the doctrine of "savage war," founded on the idea that certain races "are inherently disposed to cruel and atrocious violence" (in Slotkin's words). Assumed to be about American Indians, the doctrine also worked a stunning reversal: because the enemy was so savage, we could be, too—a rationale for white violence, for Cotton Mather's pleasure at Indians getting "Berbikew'd," ultimately for "wars of extermination." This was nothing unusual in New World experience, of course: the Spanish made similar judgments, equating the Indians with "bestiality, irrationality and barbarism," which then was used to justify European domination. As Tzvetan Todorov aptly put it, the ubiquitous European and American failure was "to admit [Indians] as a subject having the same rights as oneself, but different"; to recognize them as human (which was obvious), but not to grant them human rights: "human alterity is at once revealed and rejected."[60] The Spanish often intermarried with Indians, ultimately dissolving the problem; Americans did not, so the pattern of regenerative violence continued.

It was war and conquest, but it was also something different: a contest of unequals, in which massacre played a prominent role. Indians may massacre, but it is a fact that they rarely did so. Massacre by whites is something else: it happens when modern men displace to the wilderness and are relieved of their civil obligations, of their superegos, and find themselves in "Indian country," deploying abundant power amid diabolical fear. Massacre, Todorov wrote, is thus "intimately linked to colonial wars" waged far from the metropole.[61] A Londoner, F. Trench Townshend, sat around a campfire on Little Beaver Creek in 1868 listening to tales of Indian torture (they had got hold of some American cavalry and pulled their entrails out, he wrote, and "fastened them to a tree, round which they were driven until their whole interior was wound round it") and came to understand the "justice and necessity" of annihilating "every Red Skin we should meet—man, woman, and child." The power of the savage war doctrine is manifest even in the great illustrator of the West, Frederic Remington, who displayed his "cowboy philosophy" in this 1893 outburst: "Jews, Injuns, Chinamen, Huns—the rubbish of the Earth I hate—I've got some Winchesters and when the massacring begins, I can get my share of 'em, and what's more, I will."[62]

Indians were uncivilized at best, savages at worst, so they had no standing, no autonomy, no right to speak, really no right to be *seen* except as objects of curiosity, or when they forced themselves into the white purview—as invaders and warriors. The progressive tendency was to try to assimilate them—the whites would "furnish the grounds of the Other's modification and modernization" and thus launch them from the dark night of prehistory into "civilized time."[63] The savage was a savage, or he was not: the only "was not" is the assimilated savage, the one who had subsumed the ideas of Lockean liberalism and philanthropy: he must "behave himself or die," in the words of the *New York World* in 1874.[64] The mainstream tendency was to remove or exterminate them. Thus Arcadian garden myths went hand-in-hand with xenophobic doctrines that could bring white Americans to a singular pitch of violence, through "the collapse of conceptions of human rights in the face of culturally distant peoples, with resulting civilized atrocities defended as responses to savage atrocities," as Rogin put it. That this reflected a general attitude is evident in a truly unselfconscious usage in a 1973 account of U.S. Navy Lieutenant Charles Caldwell's 1858 chastisement of "savages" in the South Pacific. They were guilty of "foul murder and horrible cannibalism," not to mention rank "insolence," so Caldwell punished them by destroying 110 of the 120 homes in the village of Lomati, killing "14 savages" and then offering their wives the choice of strangulation or being buried alive with their husbands. The 1973 author, Francis X. Holbrook, approvingly quoted Caldwell's appraisal of his men: "The Marines displayed that coolness, courage, and prompt obedience for which their Corps is proverbial."[65]

Another way of thinking about the frontier as a line between savagery and civilization is to ask which was which? The American frontier was not so different from the European frontier in the rest of the world, as the modern world system expanded and projected "an ever-larger number of disease-experienced persons into remote corners of the earth," which "promoted die-offs," in William McNeill's words, which produced yet more frontiers: not an encounter with virgin land but the active or passive slaughter of millions in the *creation* of new wilderness zones where civilizations once existed. Anyone who finds this conception hard to fathom should examine the work of archaeologist Michael Heckenberger on the Amazon jungle, still assumed to be the unscathed home of naked aborigines unevolved from the Stone Age. In fact, a great pre-Columbia civilization existed there and may even have been the fount of the Aztecs and Incas; it vanished under the onslaught of European encroachment and the devouring ravages of the humid jungle.[66] What also links American expansionism to the world is its contemporaneity with all the advanced industrial countries encountering—and often conquering—formerly exotic peoples and places, as a new rush for colonies enveloped the globe.

The Machine in Turner's Garden

Chicago held its grand coming-out party in 1893, a world's fair called the Columbian Exposition, arrayed along the Midway boulevards that now run through the campus of the University of Chicago. It was here that a young man named Frederick Jackson Turner gave the lecture that would make his career, announcing the closing of the frontier. The proximate influence on Turner was the Census Bureau's declaration in 1890 that there was no free land left, but perhaps no historian ever had a more distant relationship between his national eminence and the labor of primary research. Turner did not so much investigate the frontier as invent it and exalt it as a metaphor of a lost Arcadian past—that of the homesteader and his freedom, his "independence." For Turner the West was a line moving across the continent defined by homesteaders carrying and embodying a way of life and, in the process, moving away from Europe and its influences, leaving in its wake monarchy, aristocracy, feudalism, privilege, and wars between nations. His own work, he said simply, left behind "the point of view of the Atlantic coast." Or as Vernon Parrington put it, the frontier thesis uprooted "the lingering prejudice in favor of the pernicious genteel tradition which has come down as a heritage from New England Victorianism"—or "smug Tory culture."[67]

"Up to our own day American history has been in a large degree the history of the colonization of the Great West," Turner wrote—yeoman farmers, homesteading, an amoeba-like spread westward that was not expansionism or imperialism so much as a serial replication of democracy, egalitarianism, and individual liberty. The frontier diffused wealth, provided upward mobility, and became a "release valve" in several senses of the term for the country as a whole—with the yeoman farmer as the hero of the story. The old Northwest had now become the Middle Border, and the frontier had become the new Great West. In 1893 Turner was fully confident in his thesis and in applauding the march of material progress—Americans had a "masterful grasp of material things," but American ideals came from the forest and were the dominant influence. Turner valued everything west of the Alleghenies and had next to no interest in the South. He hated cities and he hated industry. "Facing West" meant facing freedom in a very direct way, and writing a people's fate on the grandest tabula rasa in history. The class structure of Europe that fixed people in their place was abandoned in the American West with an exhilarating relief, and anyone who tried to reimpose it, however marginally through accent or dress or gesture or cutting words, was immediately the subject of mass ridicule; being "lettered" was to fall under suspicion, and "fine arts" were disdained for the fiddle and banjo. Likewise the cathedrals and churches of Europe, simultaneously august and domineering, gave way to a religiosity of equals, where the church was a plain white house and the preacher did not stand above but was merely the most worked-up of the flock, or the catalyst for mass transportation rather than high ritual.

This narrative, so familiar to historians, took an often unremarked turn toward resignation in Turner's later work as the full import of the industrial behemoth rising along the Middle Border gripped him. In "The Middle West" (1901) Turner wrote that a transformation "of deepest import" had been at work: "a huge industrial organism has been created in the province,—an organism of tremendous power, activity, and unity." Iron ore, steel, steam, packing houses, derricks, elevators, and many other "triumphs of mechanical skill" had propelled America to the forefront of the world, the railroads had "gridironed the region" amid a theretofore unprecedented "consolidation of capital." The opening of the Gogebic mines in 1884 followed by the Mesabi Range remade Minnesota and the American iron industry, transplanting it to the Midwest where 80 percent of the pig iron in the United States was now produced, where "the coal of the eastern and southern borders" meets "the iron ores of the north," coursing through a vast water and rail system: the Great Lakes, the Mississippi, the Ohio, and the Missouri. Now it had become "the economic and political center of the republic," with Chicago as the epicenter where "all the forces of the nation intersect." A steel machine in this midwestern garden had completely systematized economic forces in the region: industrialists like James J. Hill, John D. Rockefeller, and Andrew Carnegie now concentrated "economic and social power" in their own hands, radically changing the country—eventualities that threaten "to make political democracy an appearance rather than a reality," while the belching furnaces of Pittsburgh steel mills, surrounded by the congested tenements of immigrant workers, made for "a social tragedy" encountered with "disillusion and shock." "The ideals of the Middle West" came from the forest, Turner wrote, "in the log huts," where rugged individualism, invention, liberty, equality, and democracy flourished. Industry, however, destroyed the forest ("the pine woods of the north") as prelude to giving the battle to the strongest, to "the great forces of modern capitalism." And so "the free lands are gone. The material forces that gave vitality to Western democracy are passing away. It is to the realm of the spirit, to the domain of ideals and legislation" that we must now look. But in the current milieu, he wrote, such a stance required "faith and courage, and creative zeal."[68]

This was Turner's unwavering attempt in 1901 to reiterate that ideals still count—the ideals of the forest, the homesteader, democracy, equality—in the face of overwhelming industrial might. But in this and later essays, Turner treaded perilously close to Henry Adams's resignation before the same forces. His was the perfect Hartzian theory: yeomen replicating themselves across a continent made a middle-class nation, even a classless one, certainly an exceptional nation finally decoupled from Old Europe. No big owners, no massed labor—until the belching furnaces brought a "social tragedy" in Pittsburgh and throughout the Middle Border. Like subsequent historians of the progressive school (particularly William Appleman Williams), Turner always endeavored to say that ideals are still the main thing, the essence of the American people. Industrial might and concentrated capital utterly remade the Middle Border, as an incident to the remaking of the continent—and

Turner's Arcadia, leaving him alone with his thoroughly American subjec-
tivity. For the remainder of his life he preferred the austere simplicity of the
ideal to the tangled woof of fact.[69]

What is left of the Turner thesis? Well, there are all those rectangles
stretching from State Route 277 to the Rockies. American exceptionalism is
still alive and well, if interpreted differently. American idealism sails forward
impervious to any contradictory evidence. Pastoral recourse to Arcadia is still
common.[70] But if we think about the westward march without tears, we can
marvel at how the industrial and real estate machines chewed up the garden
across the "virgin land" out to Los Angeles, recapitulating Chicago's effect
on the Middle Border as it went, and how vaulting economic growth transformed prairies, forests, and wilderness into a modernized continent unmatched elsewhere in the world. It is another way of saying that America
developed late in world time, with abundant, cheap land and a series of
great leaps forward. Opening fresh regions to a development process already
proved in the East also made investors less skittish and their investments less
risky. All this helps to explain why the United States grew more rapidly than
any other industrial country from about 1870 to the eve of World War I, with a
56 percent growth per decade in national product, compared to 49 percent for
Japan, 36 percent for Germany, and 25 percent for the United Kingdom.[71]
Finally, there is the profound directional change that the frontier thesis noticed, reorienting people, getting them to face West—away from Europe and
New England in almost every sense—and to take seriously the fact of a
continent. As Turner put it, "the men of the 'Western world' turned their
backs upon the Atlantic Ocean, and with a grim energy and self-reliance
began to build up a society free from the dominance of ancient forms."

"The Great Rule of Conduct": A Continental Foreign Policy

What would the foreign policy expression of Turner's world view look like?
The frontier thesis was an American artifact, its material base emerging after
the revolution. For 150 years after the Plymouth and Jamestown settlements,
European settlers clung closely to the Atlantic coast with a disinterest in
probing inland that seems inexplicable when compared to the raging expansion of the nineteenth century. But it did not dawn on them that they inhabited a continent until around 1750, and even then they did not know
its immense scope. Then continental expansion finally created an authentic
American worldview that contrasted mightily with New England's anglophile Atlanticism. It was not isolationism, a misleading term that casts the

post-1941 American worldview back upon the nineteenth century. Instead it was a form of exclusive continentalism, appearing autonomously, before direct interaction with the European states. (Isolationism was a reaction *against* that interaction, especially during and after World War I.)

From George Washington's Farewell Address down to the surprise attack at Pearl Harbor—that is, for another chunk of 150 years—the fundamental orientation of this country was toward the West and the Pacific, with Americans turning their backs on Europe to varying and always interesting degrees. If it is almost impossible to fathom this fact in our time, that owes to the heaps of calumny loaded upon anyone who dissents from the Atlanticist (and usually Anglophile) consensus of our relatively tiny foreign policy elite, and the 50 years from 1941 to 1991 when world war and cold war locked Europe and the United States in a tight embrace. But as the years of the new century begin to pass quickly before our eyes, this half-century may turn out to be an anomaly in America's relationship to the world. In any case that is not where American values ran from the founding of this country onward: loathing England was a pastime, a part of the continental soil, it was fun, an amusement indulged in varying degrees of sophistication—from the epithets of the everyday town square to the august judgments of Tom Paine ("It is the true interest of America to steer clear of European contentions") and John Quincy Adams.

Or George Washington: his Farewell Address is always noted but rarely appreciated for the comparative and realistic judgments embodied in it. "Europe has a set of primary interests," he said, "which to us have none, or very remote relation. Hence she must be engaged in frequent controversies, the cause of which are essentially foreign to our concerns." Apart from commercial involvement, there was no need for Americans "to implicate ourselves, by artificial ties, in the ordinary vicissitudes of her politics, or the ordinary combinations and collisions of her friendships, or enmities." The United States could afford to remain distant, detached, disengaged, in a "respectably defensive posture." Given the difficulties and distances in crossing two oceans, aggressors "will not lightly hazard giving us provocation," Washington said. Entangling alliances would hinder American freedom of action, but also draw the United States into European quarrels. "The Great Rule of Conduct" should be to extend commercial relations but "to have with them as little *political* connection as possible" (emphasis in original).[72]

George Washington's rules stood on a par with the Constitution and the Declaration of Independence and guided every administration for the next 150 years (excepting Woodrow Wilson's), persisting through three presidents in the 1920s whose homegrown qualities would not be seen in the Oval Office for another eight decades. They presided over one of the great economic booms in American history, in which California invented the urban and suburban world that the middle class almost everywhere has inhabited since the 1950s. But the Pacific Coast remained fundamentally nonindustrial: it was part of a continental market and had been since the railroads reached the coast, but it was dependent on the East and did not have the stunning quality that it acquired during and after World War II: a new, high-tech industrial base to complement the enormously productive industrial structures of the Northeast and the Midwest. The continuing incompletion of the continental market helps to explain why in the interwar period Americans got isolationism instead of the global prominence that their highly productive economy, in another era, might have demanded; this prolonged the ideal of a self-contained, westward-facing America that cultivated and developed its own garden (the largest national market in the world), kept to itself, and pursued its own interests and ideals. New England, the genteel tradition, and Atlanticism were still a regional and a minority phenomenon before Pearl Harbor.

A New Yorker faces west.
Saul Steinberg, *View of the World from 9th Avenue*, 1976.
Ink, pencil, colored pencil, and watercolor on paper, 28 x 19 in. (71.1 x 48.3 cm).
Private collection, New York. Cover drawing for the *New Yorker*, March 29, 1976.
© The Saul Steinberg Foundation/Artists Rights Society (ARS), New York.

California: island in the sun.
John Speed's map of the Americas, 1626.
Courtesy of the William L. Clements Library, University of Michigan.

John Mix Stanley, *The Last of Their Race*, 1857.
Oil on canvas. Buffalo Bill Historical Center, Cody, Wyoming; 5.75.

A westward empire.
Emanuel Gottlieb Leutze, *Westward the Course of Empire Takes Its Way*, circa 1861.
Mural study. Smithsonian American Art Museum, Bequest of Sara Carr Upton.

Mian Situ, *The Golden Mountain—Arriving San Francisco, 1865*. 2002. Oil on canvas. Courtesy of Mian Situ.

Bencab, *Invaders and Resisters,* 1980. Acrylic on paper. Courtesy of the artist.

Frederic Remington, *Charge of the Rough Riders at San Juan Hill,* 1898. Oil on canvas. Courtesy of the Frederic Remington Art Museum, Ogdensburg, New York.

CHAPTER TWO

"The Remote beyond Compare": Finding California

Not finding islands now proves to him that the land whence he came is a great continent, and that there is the Terrestrial Paradise; 'for all men say,' says he 'that that is the end of the Orient, and that it is,' says he.

—BARTOLOMÉ DE LAS CASAS

Before writers could rhapsodize about California they had to find it. For nearly 250 years nobody could—mistaking it for an island, or a peninsula, or for a worthless but treacherous place inland from the southern desert and the murky shores of the Pacific north of Monterey. To the east, a vast and forbidding territory of mountain ranges, deserts, and grassy plains lay between California and the Middle Border, a thousand miles of rough terrain stretched southward to the Mexican plateau, and across the western shore an imperturbable, infinite ocean vale kept it hidden—because adventurers were looking for treasure in all the wrong places, seeking a northwest passage to the storied trade of the Orient or plying that trade between Boston and Canton without thinking much about what lay in between: a vast continent, essentially unknown until very recent history. When California finally emerged, it did so in a jubilee of gold and rhapsodic discovery and so did the continent, a mere century and a half ago, very late in the time calculated by modernity. This would prove to be a cardinal advantage, because California, once found, occupied the horizon of discovery and invention. But before all that, from the end of the fifteenth to the middle of the nineteenth century, California had a perfect, salutary isolation from the forces making the modern world. When that world "discovered" California in 1849, it was whipped on by a golden lash—and then it remade the place overnight and has never stopped. Unlike any other state, California became a virtual paradigm of unceasing modernity for the nation—and the world.

During the age of exploration California was at the far reaches of the known planet, and so it spent the first few centuries of the modern world as it had for several millennia: a remote environmental paradise with every earthly advantage inhabited by small numbers of sedentary, unwarlike Indians and undiscovered by explorers who had otherwise scoured North and South America after Columbus landed in the West Indies. It is striking to peruse historical atlases of the Pacific: literally for millennia, all the civilized action is happening on the left side, in East and Southeast Asia, and nothing (recorded) happens on the right. California also arrived surprisingly late to our geologic epoch. Like so much else about the state, this fact, too, was the product of a myriad of collisions. Until roughly 100 million years ago there was no Sierra Nevada Range, no Mount Whitney, and big rivers ran across a broad plain to the Pacific; vast fields of granite comprise the High Sierras, but they also contain a rich potpourri of rocks from around the Pacific world thrown up into them as seabed islands erupted and the mountains formed in the late Jurassic period.[1]

An Island on the Land

Europeans first glimpsed the Pacific in 1513 when the Spanish explorer Vasco Núñez de Balboa happened upon what he called the Mar del Sur, the "Southern Sea," a name the ocean retained for almost three centuries. It did not acquire its current conception as "the Pacific" until Captain James Cook's late eighteenth-century voyages, and only acquired it then because northern Europeans were suddenly taking an interest; in other words the Pacific was and is a construct of the modern imagination. The people who lived there had moved east, from Asia, but the new arrivals were moving west, propelled by long-distance trade and the beginnings of the modern world economy. The Spaniards conducted the Manila galleon trade from 1565 onward, linking East Asia to Europe via the Philippines; they exchanged silver drawn from Mexican mines for tea, silks, and other luxury goods.[2] This trade route lasted 300 years and still had influence in the twentieth century (Americans who owned a large gold mine in northern Korea until 1939, for example, paid Korean miners in Mexican pesos), but it was not transformative: just one galleon voyaged off each year, and one returned the other way—for three centuries. (The eastward journey took twice as long, because the Manila galleon rendezvoused each year off Mendocino so it could feel its way along the coast down to Acapulco.)

For Spaniards, California and the American Southwest lay "at the ends of the earth . . . remote beyond compare," in the words of a conquistador in 1592. More than a century later a Spanish colon told the king that for Mexicans, the region to the north was as distant from their consciousness as Constantinople; 1,500 miles separated California from the Mexican capital.[3] Prevailing winds and currents in the Pacific made northward sailing along the coast slow and arduous, just as they made the southward journey a breeze, so to speak. The semi-arid coastline south of San Francisco appeared barren, and navigating northward got more and more difficult as cold, biting winds bore down on sailors.

Columbus, of course, was island hopping through the Caribbean to Cathay, or so he thought. On his third voyage to the New World he traversed the north coast of South America and finally figured out that he had stumbled upon a continent, not a bunch of islands—although he still thought he was reconnoitering the eastern coast of Asia. In the words of Bartolomé de las Casas: "Not finding islands now proves to him that the land whence he came is a great continent, and that there is the Terrestrial Paradise; 'for all men say,' says he 'that that is the end of the Orient, and that it is,' says he."[4] It took Spanish explorers another 250 years, however, to figure out that California was not an island, but likewise part of "a great continent." But they had named it long before: a 1541 map by Domingo del Castillo displays "California" across the peninsula now known as Baja California, a name supposedly derived from the black Amazon Queen Calafia, who, a popular Spanish novel had it, ruled over an island full of gold. A year later the Portuguese navigator Juan Rodriguez Cabrillo left Navidad on the Pacific coast of Mexico in search of the fabled water route to Asia, later known as the Northwest Passage. He sailed his two small ships, *La Victoria* and *San Salvador,* along sandy beaches that he called "California," reconnoitering what is now San Diego (where he spent six days), San Pedro, and Santa Barbara; Chumash Indians piled into their canoes to welcome him. He sailed on northward to Mendocino, but powerful winds kept him from going any farther so he and his crew decided to return south and winter at San Miguel Island. He never left—he died of an infection in January 1543.[5]

Ferdinand Magellan likewise came out of the stormy, tortuous passage through the straits of Tierra del Fuego in 1521, to find himself carried forward by gentle sea breezes on a placid, immeasurable ocean which suggested to him a new name: he wanted to cheer up his crew after it had languished in the harrowing, bitterly cold straits by showing them the "calm and benevolent" ocean on the western side: "I name it the *Mar Pacifico.*" But soon the great navigator died (murdered on a Philippine beach), and it would take three more centuries before that name came into general usage, and even then this ocean, covering nearly a third of the earth's surface, remained inadequately surveyed and charted.[6] Half a century after Magellan, another explorer, Sebastian Vizcaíno, sailed up as far as the Monterey peninsula and quickly discovered its manifold pleasures ("the land is fertile, with a climate and soil like that of Castile," abounding in a rich profusion of wild game); he made reliable charts of the coast which others might well have used—but this was still not enough to make him or just about anyone else want to come back. Indeed, Spaniards did not return for another 167 years and did not build a California settlement until 1769. As Dora Beale Polk put it, "This huge and promising region, the focus of so many dreams, would lie dormant, isolated, untapped, shrouded in mystery, for another century and a half."[7] After staggering around two continents for two centuries in search of gold and silver, the explorers and their masters in Madrid were tired and running short of money; the future Golden State was a mere footnote to an imperial impulse that was slowly petering out.

An imperial impulse that was still vital and growing brought Sir Francis Drake to the California coast in 1579, in the course of a three-year voyage intended to open trade with the Moluccas, to aggravate Madrid by "privateering" in waters patrolled by Spanish ships, and to seek out the Northwest Passage yet again. Drake ended up making the second voyage around the world (after Magellan) in the first English ship to do so. He landed in California by accident, or emergency (his ship, called the *Golden Hinde*, had thirty tons of captured Spanish booty, mostly silver, but was falling apart and needed repair), putting up for five weeks some twenty miles south of Bodega Bay and very near San Francisco, and putting up with the fogs rolling in from the Pacific ("night-fog, thin, clammy, and penetrant").[8] Sir Francis left a brass plate claiming California for the queen ("In the name of Herr Majesty Queen Elizabeth of England and Herr successors forever"), which now sits in the Bancroft Library, but no British settlers ever arrived to put that claim into practice. Drake also journeyed up the Northwest coast, but did not venture inland because of a climate worse than northern California's: "most vile, thicke and stinking fogges." Vitus Bering, a Dane in the employ of Peter the Great, tried to find America by following an easterly route from the Kamchatka Peninsula in 1721; he found the Aleutian Islands but also ran afoul of "perpetual fogs" and turned around somewhere off the Alaskan coast—and told Peter that you couldn't get to America going that way.[9]

The essential reasons for California's long isolation were thus geographic and technological. The Pacific is a vast ocean, with distances far more daunting than the Atlantic (the Atlantic at 41 million square miles covers about 20 percent of the earth's surface; the Pacific at 70 million square miles covers one-third). Navigating it was not the problem: as we saw, Spanish galleons crisscrossed the Pacific from the mid-sixteenth century onward. But direct and frequent sea travel between the American Pacific coast and East Asia did not get going until California was itself a state, in the mid-nineteenth century. To the east was a formidable set of mountain ranges, the Sierra Nevada and the Rockies, to their southwest a forbidding and seemingly endless desert, and to the west was the genuine, not the figurative, void of the Pacific. Nobody could grasp the whole so they ended up grasping for the parts, like a blind man feeling an elephant's tail and thinking he had hold of an ox.

For most of the sixteenth and seventeenth centuries experts said California was an island, even though Spanish explorers had demonstrated to their own satisfaction on a voyage in 1539 that it was clearly a peninsula, an appendage of some body of land. Never mind, the experts declared it to be an island and it would remain so until the middle of the eighteenth century. One of the largest continents in the world thus became an ever-receding horizon, an island just beyond which lay Asia and, especially, the China trade. It was remote and rockbound but also imagined to be a land full of gold and freethinkers: a terrestrial paradise of exotic, free-loving women. Rocky but golden, bare but voluptuous: the natives were said to make love on all fours, and the men had such "virile members" that they wrapped them around their waist four times. California was, in other words, a "dream" from the beginning (if not a hallucination).

Cartographers and geographers are just like everyone else—they copy each other and hate anyone who strays from the consensus—and so for decades, indeed throughout the seventeenth century, a proliferation of island maps ensued. This island got bigger and bigger. John Speed's 1626 map seemed to anticipate the awful aftermath of an erupting San Andreas fault, with the entire state separated from the continent—but it was just another, if better informed, rendering of island California. A French cartographer, Nicholas Sanson, produced a map of island California in 1657 putting "Mar Vermejo" between it and the mainland; this map influenced many other mapmakers for at least fifty years. Guillaume Delisle's 1714 map showed California well fastened to the continent, but the peninsular form of Baja still exaggerated California's actual physiognomy. Delisle was a well-respected expert, but in 1727 another map (by Juan Antonio de Mendoza y Gonzalez) still showed it to be an island. Finally in 1747 a mélange of rough knowledge about an error now two centuries old had accumulated sufficiently to prompt Emperor Ferdinand VI to issue a royal dictum: "California is not an island." Ferdinand's declamation anticipated an explosion of new cartography just around the corner, which would correctly and finally determine that the fabled land was neither an island nor a peninsula but the western shore of a great continent. Still, the first reasonably accurate map of the coast of California did not appear until 1771 (five years before the Revolution), and eight decades passed before S. Augustus Mitchell finally produced an accurate map of California, Texas, and New Mexico—in 1846, just in time for Americans to learn the dimensions of what they were about to appropriate from Mexico.[10]

Spaniards Trickle into a New Continent

In 1778 Captain James Cook directed his ship *Resolution* northward along the Oregon coast, almost 200 years after Sir Francis Drake had made landfall in northern California—making Cook the first Englishman after Drake to visit both coasts of North America. Cook became convinced "that the continent of North America extended farther to the west than from the most reputable charts we had reason to expect." After centuries of captains who set sail without knowing how to calculate longitude, Cook became the first man to begin to gauge just how wide the continent was and thus singlehandedly demolished three hoary myths: island California, the Northwest Passage, and the Southern Continent—but not many were listening.[11] Alaska was indubitably part of this great land mass, he found, and the coast indubitably harbored something of great value—otters with their soft, pliant, fine fur. The Indians virtually gave them away, but the furs commanded a high price across the Pacific, in Canton. Thus was launched the first industry of the West Coast, fur trading, and a great American fortune: John Jacob Astor's, who by 1811 had established Fort Astoria on the Oregon coast.[12]

Now Spaniards also began to trickle into their unknown empire. Father Junípero Serra, the legendary Franciscan pioneer, established one mission after another north from Baja California, each a day's horse ride apart, the first at San Diego in 1769 (and thus the first Spanish settlement in Alta California, 220 years after Juan Rodriguez Cabrillo), the second at Monterey, and eventually another nineteen strung out along the coast. A brief examination of the "Sacred Expedition" illustrates the unimaginable difficulties of migrating the modest distance from Baja to San Diego just a few years before the American Revolution, another hook for the Spanish belief that California was "remote beyond compare"—and another reason why the Spanish impact on California was so late in coming and so brief and inconsequential when it did.

Two land parties and three sailing ships made up the expedition. It departed Baja in early 1769 with an infantry contingent (including twenty-five Catalan soldiers), Indian guides, doctors and surgeons, cooks, blacksmiths, and a cartographer. Three ships left the Baja coast, one after the other: the *San Antonio* had the easiest time of it, arriving in San Diego on April 11 after 54 days at sea; a scurvy epidemic caused the flagship *San Carlos* to take 110 days to get there; the *San José* never made it, foundering at sea and losing all onboard. The two overland groups departed with horse-mounted light cavalry and *vaqueros* driving herds of cattle, mules, and horses; the first contingent left the northernmost Spanish settlement in Baja on March 24 and slogged through desert and wilderness for nearly two months, arriving in San Diego on May 14. Father Serra was in the second land party that departed on May 15, following the trail made by the first group; the great Franciscan did not reach his destination until July 1.

Of some 300 men who began this expedition, fewer than half reached San Diego alive. Many more died of scurvy in the tent hospital that became the first Spanish settlement above Baja. Most of the Indian scouts died or deserted the entourage, and local Indians menaced the Spaniards. "The whole situation was stark and desperate," Bean wrote, with Father Serra caring for more than 50 invalids. Nonetheless in late July he founded the mission of San Diego de Alcalá in a small hut on Presidio Hill. Indians attacked in August, but they were thrown back by Spanish muskets. After many more travails, the mission finally began to flourish, but even then it was like pulling teeth to get more Spaniards to settle in California. The authorities promised to outfit them completely and pay their settlement expenses for years, and still few were willing to come.[13]

The Spanish fathers proceeded up the California coast on a grand road, indeed a royal road: *El Camino Real* (which closely paralleled today's Highway 101). In coming decades they built twenty more missions and four presidios on the Roman empire model of presidial frontier towns (Monterey and San Francisco being the most famous), along with three pueblos; the first one they called Los Angeles. Well, not exactly: this mudflat with no harbor and no reliable river, this virgin site, got the august appellation, *El Pueblo de Nuestra Señora la Reina de los Ángeles del Río de Porciúncula* (The Town of Our Lady the Queen of the Angels by the River of Porciúncula, "Porciúncula" meaning "small portion," and "Nuestra Señora," of course, connoting the Virgin Mary). The first Angelenos, forty-six in all, came from the poorest sections of Baja society (like most California settlers); these pioneers were hoping for a better life at Spanish expense. Arriving in 1781, they included Indians, blacks, and variant admixtures of Spanish blood. By that year a mere

600 settlers had come to live in California. The last mission, San Francisco Solano de Sonoma, appeared in that storied wine region in 1823—just as the Spanish period creaked to a halt. Like the others, it was part of a slender colonization of the coast. (Spaniards never went inland further than Soledad, about thirty miles from the ocean.)[14]

Spain's colonial strategy called for Christianizing Indians, teaching them Spanish, and even intermarrying, thus to assimilate the natives and make them Spaniards—a sharp contrast with British colonial policy "of whom it is said that on arriving on the new shore they fell first upon their knees and then upon the aborigines."[15] But the English and the Spanish fell upon each other, too, in a series of wars from 1796 to 1808; Spain also had to contend with Napoleon, who made his brother king of Spain in 1807 as prelude to invading the next year. It took six years of warfare and guerrilla insurgency finally to expel French forces from Spain, leaving Madrid no time to take an interest in "the remote beyond compare." Even the storied missions were little more than sedentary encampments, a telling remnant of the Spanish imperial impulse—a distant and unplumbed colony running on empty—which would subsequently become the source for a thousand romantic American tales about "old California." An immutable element in California nostalgia (visualize Kim Novak and Jimmy Stewart at San Juan Bautista in *Vertigo*), this mission society had a remarkably short heyday of a couple of decades after 1775, before giving way to another few decades of contestation between Spaniards and Mexicans born in California (and therefore known as Californios), and the Mexican government—itself frequently in turmoil. In 1821 New Spain became independent of Madrid, and Mexican rule over California arrived the next year.

The Mexican government inherited an expensive liability in the missions and so ordered them secularized—the main result of which was that mission Indians (who had done all the hard work) ran away. Many of them had also fallen to disease during the mission period, reducing their numbers from about 72,000 to somewhere between 15,000 and 18,000 by 1834. Mexico City might have done more to enhance its power in California if one government after another had not collapsed, and if fourteen different governors of California had not come and gone in a thrice. Nor did many new immigrants arrive in the lovely coastal enclaves stitched along the coast during the faltering Mexican ascendancy: by the 1830s about 4,000 Hispanics lived in California. (Texas was similarly underpopulated with around 2,500 settlers; by comparison New Mexico had about 30,000 Hispanics.) Soon Mexican authority had almost collapsed, a decline mirrored in San Francisco's breathtaking presidio: two of its four walls had crumbled, and its main residents were not soldiers but dogs, seagulls, and vultures. When it all ended in 1846 maybe 7,000 non-Indians lived in California—less than 1,000 of whom were adult males and perhaps one-tenth of whom were literate. Some of the richest Californios owned thousands of acres but could not write their own name; that hardly bothered them since their horses and cattle (and therefore their wealth) multiplied magically in the California sun. Soon they fell before "a conquering and often wickedly progressive race," in Josiah Royce's words.[16]

Finding the Sierras

If Father Serra plowed through the wilderness, the American pioneers needed six months to trek west to the coast—if they could cross the desert or hoist themselves over the High Sierras. The southwestern deserts and northwestern peaks blocked human purview enough to make it still plausible that California, whether island or peninsula, was separate from the continent—and entirely separate from a modern world running amok with new technologies. So the western passage through the mountains or across the desert also obscured human sight for centuries, leaving California alone beyond a different pale—one made of granite and silicon.

The amazingly peripatetic explorer Cabeza de Vaca got shipwrecked on his way to Florida and wandered around much of the south and southwest in 1528–36. He was the first white man to see the Mississippi, trekking back and forth across the Sacramento Mountains of New Mexico and the Chiricahua Mountains of Arizona and touching the Gulf of Mexico. He lived for years with different bands of Indians, who treated him with unbidden generosity: "The people are well disposed," he wrote, "serving such Christians as are their friends with great good will." He was followed a few years later by Garcia López de Cárdenas, the first European to witness the Grand Canyon, which he christened Tízon. But these intrepid infiltrations soon ended, and 236 years would pass before another white person peered into that magnificent cataract.[17]

The Yankee fur trapper Jedediah Strong Smith, twenty-seven years old, was the first white American to cross the desert west to California, and the first to return again east—via the Sierra passage. From an old New England family removed to Ohio and Illinois, Smith was an upright Calvinist not given to wine or women, unlike the stereotypical "mountain men" of the frontier. He and seventeen other trappers left northern Utah in August 1826 hoping to open "a virgin beaver country" and establish a fur-trading post on the Pacific. They followed the Colorado River and then crossed the Mojave Desert (courtesy of Mojave Indian guides, who treated them well), passing through what is now Needles (often the hottest town on the venerable Route 66), thence through the unimposing San Bernardino Mountains to the San Gabriel Mission by November, where the superb hospitality of the Franciscans led them to remain for several weeks. Smith and his party crossed back over the San Bernardinos in early 1827, then traveled north to the San Joaquin Valley—which turned out to be full of beavers, virgin or not, a fur trapper's dream. They then accomplished the first recorded American crossing of the High Sierra, near the Stanislaus River and Ebbetts Pass—plowing their way through eight-foot-deep snows at the summit in May 1827. The party returned to Utah with hundreds of pelts but only one mule and one horse— privations in the desert had forced them to eat several of their pack animals. In 1831 this fearless adventurer, who had lost tens of his men to Indian attacks, was himself killed by Comanche braves along the Santa Fe Trail.[18]

In spite of Smith's exploits the westward movement of the frontier was still stymied by the "Great American Desert" (the Great Plains before the windmill delivered water), the vast distances, the actual deserts, and the Rocky and Sierra mountain ranges; struggling pioneers overleaped these barriers to reach the Pacific in Oregon territory in the 1840s, but only the gold rush brought thousands to California—and then it was a stampede. The mountain passage forever imbedded in the American mind is not Smith's return but the Donner Party's trek into the High Sierra in 1846, just a bit too fatally late in the autumn. This party of eighty-seven people departed from Springfield, Illinois, and got through Independence, Missouri, by May, the right time to cross the plains and mountains and reach California before the onset of winter. But they diverged from the established route on a southerly course, and by the time they got to the Truckee River and up into the Sierras it was early November. Just short of the summit they pitched their camp to stay overnight. The next morning heavy snows cascaded into the pass and buried them, and they remained buried under deluges of fall and winter snow for many weeks, blizzards then believed to be the heaviest in the world (twenty feet of snow could fall in a few hours). Forty of the original party died and a handful of survivors ended up eating their dead.[19] A cautionary tale about an awesome mountain range was born, at a high price.

The Sierras make up a colossal wedge of the earth's crust, "a rotational granite block" with steep faults and sheer faces rising above 11,000 feet to the east but sloping gently and gradually into the Central Valley on the west. Once submerged under the waters of the Pacific, as we have seen, the Sierras and their cousins to the north (the Cascades) rose from the sea toward the end of the Jurassic period, roughly 135 million years ago. The Sierra chain runs north to the southernmost volcano of the Cascades, Mount Lassen, and south to the Tehachapi Pass where elevations are the highest in the contiguous states, with Mount Whitney the summit at 14,495 feet; even today this region remains a natural barrier to ground transportation (however formidable, at 7,239 feet the Donner Pass is still only half as high as Mount Whitney). Most of the passes over the Sierras lie between Yosemite and Mount Lassen. Like the Rockies, the Sierras are essentially two ranges separated by a *graben* or deep-fault depression. The faultless Lake Tahoe sits in that graben, which also creates two ridges and two summits, one to the east and one to the west. Pioneers following the Truckee River came up against an eastern granite face so steep and forbidding that wagon trains had to be knocked down and pulled over ridges by rope and winch and then reassembled.[20] But slowly they mastered the passage, and Americans soon trickled into California. They found a pristine, almost untouched land.

Nicholas "Cheyenne" Dawson went overland to California in 1841: that is, he got lost several times or waylaid and misled by Indians, his draft animals died or wandered away, and he ended up alone and famished—once he had nothing to eat but a coyote (the worst meat he ever tasted). Finally he stumbled into California expecting to see settled homes and ranches but found instead a primitive life: San Jose was "a sleepy village of perhaps one hundred and fifty inhabitants," with adobe houses and no regular streets; three Americans lived there, each with Mexican wives. But by becoming a Mexican citizen or marrying a Mexican or simply via Catholic baptism, a man "could have granted to him as much land as he wanted"; all he needed was the small recording fee for the deed. The Californios entertained themselves by putting a grizzly bear and a bull in a ring to watch them fight; if the bear got hold of the bull's nose first, he won; if the bull gored the grizzly, he won—and the fight was usually over after the first sally. But when spring came Dawson was overcome by California—"flowers by the acre, of every hue"; every kind of game, huge stocks of fish in the streams; a sheer abundance as far as the eye could see. One day he took his wagon over the hills to Santa Cruz, on the coast: "The climate is delightful, moderately warm and balmy; the atmosphere impregnated with the odours [*sic*] of the different herbs and flowers that we pass. In short, there is everything here to make a country life delightful, and yet the imbecile Mexicans permit a few Apaches to drive them out of as beautiful a country as heaven ever smiled on."[21]

It is a most remarkable fact of modern life: one of the most attractive and productive regions in the world, with a GDP usually making it the fifth largest economy in the world (an Italy all of our own), with a glorious year-round climate south of San Francisco, a bracing and pleasant temperate zone to the north, marked by magnificent mountain ranges to the east and a legendary coastline to the west—great white-capped waves to drive a surfer mad, broad expanses of alabaster sand as far as the eye can see, a lush agricultural paradise and a future industrial colossus—this place was off the beaten track of the modern world until recently, say, the 1848 revolutions or the invention of the telegraph, the extension of railroads, and the growing clouds of civil war in America. Owing to its quite curious and mostly unremarked physical separation from the modern world for centuries, California's "opening" was contemporaneous with China's and Japan's. But it continued a new kind of relative or comparative autonomy within the United States: if not "remote beyond compare," it was distant enough to be unknown or irrelevant to East Coast elites. Oregon, as we will see, is a beautiful garden but a garden-variety state; it's what Maine would look like if it fronted the Pacific. Washington is typical, too, at least until the Emerald City emerged dramatically in our time as a global high-tech emporium. When people finally located California it proved to be different, however, as I will argue throughout this book—a fecund, protean, always changing mother of "the next new thing" since its very inception.

PART II

From Sea to Shining Sea: Manifest Destiny

Facing west from California's shores,
Inquiring, tireless, seeking what is yet unfound,
I, a child, very old, over waves, towards the house of
    maternity, the land of migrations, look afar,
Look off the shores of my Western sea, the circle almost
    circled. . . .
Long having wander'd since, round the earth having wander'd
Now I face home again, very please'd and joyous,
(But where is what I started for so long ago?
And why is it yet unfound?)

    —WALT WHITMAN, Inscription 310, Arch of the Setting Sun
    (east side), Panama-Pacific International Exposition, San Francisco, 1915

CHAPTER THREE

A Continent in Five Easy Pieces

All hail, thou Western world! By heaven design'd
Th' example bright, to renovate mankind.
Soon shall thy sons across the mainland roam;
And claim, on far Pacific shores, their home;
Their rule, religion, manners, arts, convey,
And spread their freedom to the Asian sea. . . .
Proud Commerce' mole the western surges lave;
The long, white spire lie imag'd on the wave;
O'er morn's pellucid main expand their sails,
And the starr'd ensign court Korean gales.
—TIMOTHY DWIGHT, *Greenfield Hill,* 1794

Americans today are uncomfortable with the idea of empire, for a variety of reasons having to do with recent history, but throughout the nineteenth century their leaders were not—either because they believed in the distinctive anti-imperial origins of the country, or because they redefined empire to suit their needs: empire of liberty (Jefferson), empire of destiny (Polk), empire of colonies (Roosevelt), empire of values (Wilson). For most of the century, "empire" was the name of an expanding American realm, used time and again without the connotations we give it today. Europeans look at the American map in 1800 and again in 1900 and see the inexorable expansion and colonization of the continent by whites, followed by a leap across the Pacific to seize Hawaii and the Philippines; most Americans look at the same maps and see the spread of freedom and democracy. Taken for granted by all is the familiar continental dimension of the country; the forty-eight contiguous states arise somehow, come together, and live happily ever after in the grand space below Canada and above the Rio Grande. One grand event recalls an incomplete continent, a division, but not on an East-West basis: the Civil War. Yet the die was cast for a nation linking the Atlantic with the Pacific long before that terrible conflict, and in retrospect, upon close inspection, what stands out is how easy it was to put the continent together, as if divine fate intervened—the hoariest belief of Manifest Destiny.

The thirteen colonies; Jefferson dispatching an emissary to Paris; Polk posting a sentinel above the Rio Grande; Polk again, almost inadvertently as if no one were watching, securing the Pacific Northwest; Seward buying Alaska—and there you have it, five easy pieces to make a continent.

It was the colonists who took their sweet time in fashioning their piece of the puzzle. From Massachusetts they penetrated but slowly beyond the next forest or mountain—which didn't hinder them from claiming everything to the west, all the way to the ocean. Under the seventeenth-century charters of Massachusetts, Connecticut, and Virginia, the writ ran from sea to sea—they just didn't know which sea or how far away it was. But the idea of a two-ocean entity existed from the beginning, and the movement was to the west, toward the setting sun—at least if we believe an inscription on a rock in Monument Bay, near Plymouth Rock: "The Eastern nations sink, their glory ends, And empire rises where the sun descends."[1] In spite of this injunction settlers managed to live under British rule for 150 years and give off few hints of a westering proclivity; posted to a new continent, they had no idea of its dimensions but a healthy appreciation of its perils: to the west was a setting sun, true, but also a dense wilderness and fearsome Indians. Then came the War of Independence, an onerous conflict, let it be said (but not so onerous when compared to other struggles for autonomy around the world). And just as the thirteen colonies became the United States, people were finding an easement through the Alleghenies to new territories. However long it took, however easy or difficult, the first piece was secured.

April in Paris: Empire for the Asking

Thomas Jefferson was an original and celebrated Arcadian, believing that "those who labour in the earth are the chosen people of God." But he was also a possessive individualist (in the best sense that land guaranteed individual independence, and the worst, as a slaveholder), an amateur geographer, and an early "westerner"—that is, an expansionist. He quickly grasped the vast opportunity of a country of transcontinental potentials characterized by cheap land and dear labor (a formula that defines so much of early American political economy). Henry Nash Smith called him "the intellectual father of the American advance to the Pacific"; for Jefferson everything to the west of Virginia constituted "a self-renewing engine that drove the American Republic forward . . . America's fountain of youth."[2] This Garden of Eden was expansive, limitless, and virtually free for the taking, so he thought.

Actually it *was* free for the taking if we are talking about anyone inclined to stand in the way, as Jefferson proved with the Louisiana Purchase. In 1800 none other than Napoleon Bonaparte had wrested from Spain not only Louisiana but the great strategic river of the continent (the Mississippi), yet he proved to be a pushover. Jefferson dispatched Robert R. Livingston in 1803 for perhaps the finest April anybody ever spent in Paris, even if this wasn't clear to Livingston for a time. From a politically powerful and very wealthy family in New York, he was supposed to see if he could buy New Orleans from the French and thus place American power at the strategic mouth of the Mississippi Delta. Napoleon had his hands full elsewhere—especially in Haiti, where independence fighters under Toussaint L'Ouverture and an epidemic of yellow fever had decimated his troops—and might well give the bayoued city up, the Americans thought. But Talleyrand kept toying with Livingston, prevaricating, making him wait, taunting him, ignoring him.

On April 11 Livingston showed up again to receive his due load of abuse (induced also by Livingston's arrogance, irritability, deafness, and inability to speak or understand French), whereupon Talleyrand brought himself upright and asked, almost as an afterthought, what might President Jefferson pay for all of Louisiana? (Say what?) And again, "What will you give for the whole?" *The whole*, Livingston inquired: what might that be? "Whatever it was we took from Spain." Livingston readily agreed to buy it (whatever it was). "I can give you no guidance on how big the parcel is," Talleyrand told him, "but you have made an excellent deal for yourselves." It was the understatement of this new century: the price for "the whole" turned out to be $23,213,567.73, not a small sum if you were buying the port of New Orleans, but a pittance, mere pennies on the dollar, if you were buying a vast wilderness that turned out to be roughly one-third of a continent and a doubling of the existing territory of the United States.[3]

On a continental map "the whole" spread out like a plume of smoke or spilling liquid running northwest of New Orleans, up the Mississippi almost to Duluth, fanning out westward almost to the Columbia River, not failing to touch the headwaters of the Rio Grande, Colorado, and Snake rivers. Forget about yeoman farmers opening up some more land: suddenly an inland empire, fabulously rich in natural resources and unexploited wealth, a territory mostly untouched by European hands, was part of the United States. And it was free for the taking: no one—not Napoleon, not London, not Madrid, nor any other power—was going to assert an interest and stand in the way. Jefferson purchased much of the continent, but more than that: he purchased American freedom in a world of nations, effectively purging the continent of European empires, except for the strongest, the British (who still spelled

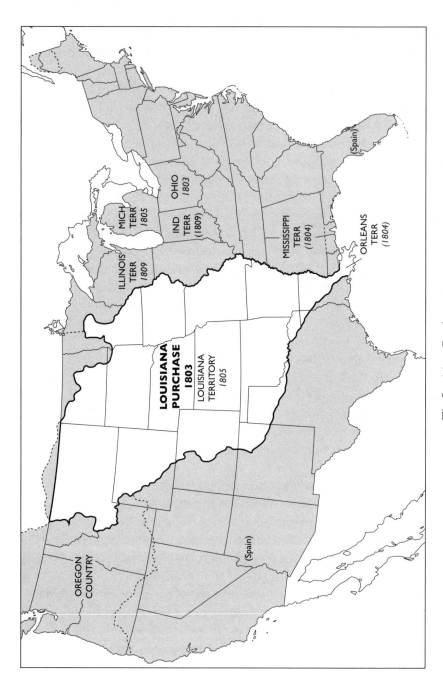

The Louisiana Purchase, 1803.
Map by Bill Nelson.

trouble), and the weakest, Spain—but James Polk would take care of them both soon enough. This was "the decisive step of the United States on an independent career as a world power, free from entangling foreign alliances," Frederick Jackson Turner was right to say (he alluded, of course, to Washington's Farewell Address).[4]

White Americans could be a "westering"[5] people—yeomen could go in search of their homestead, the continentalists could seize a continent—because there was no power capable of standing in their way. In this sense the continent *was* empty, a great-power vacuum with land free for the taking. In 1630 the Reverend John Cotton bade farewell to John Winthrop's Massachusetts Bay Company, saying, "that in a vacant soyle, hee that taketh possession of it, and bestoweth culture and husbandry upon it, his Right it is." Historians down to the recent period have assumed the same thing: the American wilderness was "a fair, blank page," Turner wrote, and Henry Nash Smith titled his formidable book *Virgin Land*—about "the vacant continent beyond the frontier." John Stuart Mill referred to the New World as "the unoccupied portion of the earth's surface," and Tocqueville wrote that even though "many indigenous tribes" lived in the boundless wilderness, it really formed "one great desert" because the Indians "occupied without possessing it"; providence had placed them "amid the riches of the New World only to enjoy them for a season; they were there merely to wait till others came."[6] The continent wasn't unoccupied or empty, of course, but the nations who might seriously resist American westering declined to do so, and ultimately the people for whom the continent was home, Native Americans, couldn't: they faced an overwhelming imbalance of power.

The great powers were no threat additionally because this new nation, just by virtue of its coming into being, posed the greatest threat of all to the European empires in its anticolonial origins—along with the periodic influence of leaders who took that origin seriously enough to make it their task to dismantle those same empires: preeminently John Quincy Adams. He deftly clothed American expansion in the anti-imperial garb of getting Spain out of Florida, challenging imperial trading monopolies and privileges in Latin America through the Monroe Doctrine (it ought to be called the Adams Doctrine), establishing the line that would later become the boundary with Canada in the northwest, and more or less telling the British off whenever he got the chance—as in his memorable exchange with Minister to the United States Stratford Canning in 1821. First he assured Canning that he would never dare to accuse the British of territorial claims on the moon, noted their modesty in claiming merely the entire earth, and finally asserted the American right to expand "to all the shores of the South Sea" (meaning the Pacific), whether England liked it or not: "keep what is yours, but leave the rest of the continent to us."[7]

Winter in Oregon: Empire on the "emence Ocian"

Jefferson's astonishing coup didn't look like much at the time. Americans knew Louisiana, they knew the Mississippi, but they had little idea of the great beyond; the president, like everyone else, could not appreciate the dimensions of the vast space he had bought fair and square (827,192 square miles, not quite doubling the 900,000 square miles of national territory circa 1800), what it contained, and what it might be good for. And so he sent Meriwether Lewis and William Clark running along to reconnoiter "the whole" and perhaps find the "Northwest Passage" (even if Captain Cook had already figured out that there was none). Jefferson instructed them to "find an easy portage from the Missouri to a westward-flowing river" (i.e., flowing toward the Pacific), but also gave them letters of credit should they be required "in the South Seas and the Cape of Good Hope." Like Columbus, they were still on a passage to India; like Columbus, the point was a new route for commerce with the East. What they found was not a quick easement to the fabled trade of the Orient but an unmapped continental wilderness that unfolded ever farther before their eyes.[8]

Comprising a corps of fifty and aided by their seeing-eye Shoshone maiden, Sacagawea, whose main role apart from various legends (that she bore Clark a child, etc.) was to translate Indian tongues, the party eventually stumbled upon a Northwest Passage—but it was by land: the South Pass, a windswept grassy valley between the Platte River flowing to the east and the Snake River flowing to the west (and ultimately northwest into the Columbia River). On a soggy wet Oregonian morning in November 1805, Lewis and Clark finally dipped their toes in the Pacific and completed the most consequential exploration in American history. The confluence of the infinite ocean and the mighty river unloading into it immediately impressed upon Clark the immensity of their discovery: "The waves appear to brake with tremendious force in every direction quite across a large Sand bar. . . . [M]en appear much Satisfied with their trip beholding with estonishment the high waves dashing against the rocks & this emence Ocian [*sic*]."[9]

The coast was less impressive after hunkering down through a dank winter near Astoria. Pelted by incessant rain like Sir Francis Drake in 1579 ("an unnatural congealed substance" making for "vile, thicke and stinking fogges"), Lewis and Clark eventually made their way back home. They were gone so long people thought they were dead; when they finally reappeared to instant acclaim, their most important finding was the continent in its fullness—not that North America was a continent, which was known by then, but the extraordinary breadth and depth of it: rolling, immeasurable plains; towering mountains; broad, unbridled rivers; deep, rich valleys; a pristine land teeming with myriad things new to the eye. Lewis and Clark discovered an America that was much bigger than anyone had realized, chock full of flora and fauna—wild animals in diverse abundance, astonishing, unheard of beasts like the grizzly bear, stunning fish like the Northwest's iridescent salmon, not to mention valued goods—furs, minerals (gold and silver)—and of course the variegated multiplicity of Native Americans. The wide publicity given to their findings made the West "an object of desire," in Goetzmann's words, "a virgin wilderness that formed a thousand-mile vacuum between the great powers of the world and the United States." John Quincy Adams, possessing a supple mind mostly unmatched in American statesmen ever since, quickly determined that the continent "should ultimately be ours" but acknowledged that it was but "very lately that we have distinctly seen this ourselves; very lately that we have avowed the pretension of extending to the South Sea." Still, as late as the 1840s geographers could not accurately place the Rocky Mountains on the continent—atlases showed mountains in Kansas, the Rockies running to 800 miles in width, and phantom rivers coursing to the Pacific.[10]

The Exterminating Havoc

Jefferson believed in "an empire for liberty." He and many others saw the United States as a special country that would inspire other peoples to burst the chains of despotism. But his empire expanded to the west, in the unfolding of the yeomanry ideal; it did not anticipate a foreign expression, nor colonies, nor any "imperative of world redemption." Nor large standing armies, realpolitik, or imperialism: the westering of the yeomanry would move away from those European sins, not toward them. In his 1801 inaugural address Jefferson referred to "the exterminating havoc" of the Old World, from which the United States was separated "by nature and a wide ocean"; to the west was the New World, "the chosen country" with "room enough for our descendants to the thousandth and thousandth generation." Jefferson's empire was based on the consent of the governed, where the governed were white settlers. His conception of empire swept most Americans and most historians before it; indeed, it was the basic theme of Harvard professor Frederick Merk's 1963 account of Manifest Destiny and his colleague Samuel Flagg Bemis's rendering in 1965: "American expansion across a practically empty continent despoiled no nation unjustly."[11] (But despoiled some justly?) Jefferson was implicated in slavery and the clearing away of Native Americans; that made him no different from other Virginians of his class. But we can't call him an imperialist; he paid for his empire in cold cash, to the apparent pleasure of Napoleon. Nor was this "manifest" destiny; it took Lewis and Clark plowing forward to the South Sea and back to reconnoiter the manifest of this purchase.

John Quincy Adams was also a founding father of expansionism, like Jefferson, and a very early continentalist: he wanted it almost as soon as geographers proved its existence, writing in 1811 that the United States was "destined by God and nature" to occupy the land from sea to sea and to be "the most populous and most powerful people ever combined under one social compact." But unlike Jefferson, Adams was the opposite of an agrarian or an Arcadian; a completely worldly man (even by Jeffersonian standards), highly educated, master of five languages, he took close account of the maritime interests of New England traders, trusted Britain not one bit, and wanted a continental nation from Atlantic to Pacific both to secure the national market for Americans and for the United States to take its proper place among the nations—that is, at the forefront. An envoy to the Hague at thirty-one, and later to Holland, Russia, and the Court of St. James before President James Monroe made him secretary of state in 1817 (he became the best of the nineteenth-century secretaries), Adams was an architect of empire.[12]

Adams is best remembered, of course, for the Monroe Doctrine. During the 1820s various Latin American peoples revolted against Spanish colonialism, encouraged by British and American traders, and the United States was quick to recognize their independence. In 1823 Adams urged Monroe to issue a declaration of American disinterest in the politics and wars of Europe (nothing new), and a declaration that any European interference with the politics of Latin America or any attempt to acquire new territory there would be seen as an unfriendly act (very new). The greater purpose of the doctrine was to make clear that no new European colonies would be allowed on the continent.[13] Nothing much happened for two decades to show what Adams and Monroe had in mind with this audacious declaration of American hegemony in the Western Hemisphere. We have the record of Adams's fine mind and some action here and there, but like Jefferson, he was not an expansion-ist by force of arms. All of that changed in the 1840s with the arrival of a novel doctrine.

Manifest Destiny

A man named John L. O'Sullivan coined this phrase in the *Democratic Review* in 1845—"our manifest destiny to overspread the continent allotted by Providence for the free development of our yearly multiplying millions" was his phrase, one of the less florid in a stunning assemblage of rhetoric that soon became par for the course whenever his continental theme got broached:

> The last order of civilization, which is the democratic, received its first permanent existence in this country. . . . A land separated from the influences of ancient arrangement, peculiar in its position, productions, and extent, wide enough to hold a numerous people, admitting, with facility, intercommunication and trade, vigorous and fresh from the hand of God, was requisite for the full and broad manifestation of the free spirit of the new-born democracy.
>
> The far-reaching and boundless future will be the era of American greatness. In its magnificent domain of space and time, the nation of many nations is destined to manifest to mankind the excellence of divine principles . . . her high example shall smite unto death the tyranny of kings, hierarchs, and oligarchs.[14]

The rhetoric engulfing Manifest Destiny soon became so replete with purple prose and gaseous emission that one imagines a venal politician taking lessons in circumlocution while lubricating his throat as if readying for an opera—the great West, the continent, the "far West" (China), the world itself, it seemed, was now an American plaything. At its heart was an ide-alized image of the United States as the preeminent democracy in the world, whose manifest virtues should be spread far and wide to awaken other peoples to the evils of monarchy, despotism, and (undemocratic) empire. But one kingly country took precedence over the others: "Why should not England be republican?" the *Democratic Review* argued; "are her lower classes unfit for the burden of government?"[15] Apart from this democratic impulse, in other words, Manifest Destiny turned its back on and shut the American door to the British.

Manifest Destiny took corporeal form, however, in a man of few words, an unprepossessing man of action. Under his prodding, in another brief moment, another sudden spurt of acquisition, the United States again added on an immense territory—bigger even then the Louisiana Purchase—making it by 1848 an Atlantic and a Pacific power with borders clear for all the world to see, secure from the attentions of any other great power. A year later California would get populated overnight, San Francisco would become a great Pacific city almost as quickly, and a few years on Matthew Perry's "Black Ships" would glide into Edo (later Tokyo) Bay. Emerson observed in 1844 that "the nervous, rocky West is intruding a new and continental element into the national mind, and we shall yet have an American genius."[16] The year 1844 did not produce a genius, but it did elect one of the more interesting, severely underrated, mostly unappreciated (when not completely unknown, which he remains to most Americans), and summarily decisive of American presidents: James K. Polk.

Polk's war of aggression against Mexico, commenced in 1846 with a jerry-rigged incident of enemy attack, was the cutting edge of Manifest Destiny and the technological advances of the decade. Long a "forgotten war" in the United States, "the War of American Intervention" proved much more important to Latin Americans than the fratricidal Civil War that came later; for them—and they were right—it was the birthplace of forcible expansion and intervention by Washington. As in so many of America's wars, the enemy of choice was economically weak and militarily inferior, the war went from victory to victory with the loss of relatively few American lives, and pretty soon the troops found themselves in occupation of Mexico City and much of the country. (And as with other wars, it dragged on to the point of unpopularity; Polk had wanted and expected a quick victory but didn't get it.) Americans had a key technological advantage, too: General Zachary Taylor, war hero later made president (enabling his famous horse, Old Whitey, to graze on the White House lawn), may have been a barely literate, crashing mediocrity ("few men ever had a more comfortable, labor-saving contempt for learning of every kind," General Winfield Scott said), but he had brains enough to promote good young officers, and at the battle of Palo Alto in May 1846 Lieutenant Ulysses S. Grant wheeled up a new-new thing—light artillery used as mass firepower to pound enemy lines. DeVoto saw this as the first success in Grant's distinguished military career and a harbinger of the ultimate defeat of the Confederacy. War victories enflamed American passions, leading many to call General Taylor another Alexander, Napoleon, or . . . George Washington.[17]

Mexico was also the first instance in what subsequently became the American way of going to war, which is either to wait for or to provoke an incident which can then be used to mobilize the people. A nation of superior strength will often find an advantage in letting the weaker side strike first; the reasons can be gleaned from Clausewitz's discussion of "the superiority of the defense over the attack" in *On War,* and also in Mao Zedong's dictum, as related by Zhou Enlai, that "we control others by letting them have the initiative." You structure a situation so that your opponent does what you wish him to, without having to be told—remote control, as it were. Revisionist historians have tried to show that one American war after another began with some inveigling or maneuvering of the enemy: Charles Callan Tansill thought Lincoln tricked the South into bombarding Fort Sumter, controversy surrounded the sinking of the *Maine* and the *Lusitania* and of course Pearl Harbor, where Roosevelt and Henry Stimson expected—and wanted—Japan to fire the first shot. Dean Acheson's Press Club speech six months before the Korean War and the Tonkin Gulf incident in 1964 are other cases in point, but perhaps McGeorge Bundy, close friend to Stimson and brother-in-law to Acheson's daughter, best exemplified this strain of American thinking: when a company of Viet Cong soldiers attacked a Marine base at Pleiku in February 1965, precipitating a rapid escalation of the war, Bundy remarked that "Pleikus are streetcars," that is (in George Kahin's words), "you could expect one to come along presently, and you were ready to board it as soon as it did."[18] It was James K. Polk, though, who inaugurated this business, and Mexico foolishly took the bait.

Polk was the first American president who could reasonably be called an expansionist by force of arms: a short, composed, and self-confident man with flashing gray eyes, known for his brains (he finished first in his class at the University of North Carolina) and his ethical probity—both virtues coalescing into conspicuous self-righteousness—he was a protégé of Andrew Jackson, a former governor of Tennessee, and a two-term Speaker of the House of Representatives. He came into office in March 1845 by the slimmest margin (38,000 out of 2.7 million votes) over Henry Clay but acted as if he had a mandate: he proclaimed to the cabinet his desire to put together Texas, California, and Oregon (a metastasized Oregon, stretching all the way up to what is now the border of Alaska); gain harbors in San Francisco and San Diego; and turn the United States into a continental and Pacific power. If this sounds like an imperial White House, it wasn't: Congress was so niggardly that Polk had to pay for his own secretary. If Polk sounds like an imperial president, he was—working long hours into the night, riding herd on matters big and small, closely monitoring every aspect of the war he launched, hectoring his generals, pushing the boundaries of the use of military force as his instrument for distending the boundaries of the nation (all with an army numbering 7,885 men when he arrived in the White House).[19]

An Immanent State, Lacking Pretense

The federal government and the ostensible army could be so small for 150 years because the greater part of both was in the people's heads—they would get up in the morning as good citizens conscious of their rights and liberties without having to be told, and with the myriad militias around the country they were effective riflemen. Americans were "born free" in Hartz's words, because the Revolution was not about the nature of governance but about casting off colonial masters so that the American government could proceed to model itself on . . . its colonial masters (minus the monarchy). English parentage is evident throughout the familiar founding moments and the entire shape of American governance. A Tudor polity, its strengths were similar to England's.

If most of American life went on as if Washington did not exist, if the bureaucracy and the military were ridiculously small compared to those of European states, that still did not mean this was a weak state. The English state was formidable and entirely capable of running a global empire—not because it mimicked the bigness of continental states but precisely the opposite: a long "war against the state" in the name of liberty, John Brewer wrote, succeeded in making government more open and efficacious, parliamentary oversight made it more accountable, and the libertarian consciousness of the citizenry limited the range of state power. "Too often strength is equated with size," when in fact big bureaucracies and big military organizations may be a sign of weakness.[20] Even the nineteenth-century American military—typically portrayed as tiny, weak, scattered, little more than a militia—proved entirely capable of shutting the British, French, and Spanish out of any significant role on the continent.

Seizing Bagdad

Like California, Texas had never enticed many Spaniards to settle. Spain occupied it in 1716, producing "a thinly settled province of garrisons, missions, and smuggling settlements vulnerable to attack by the Apaches." It never developed much beyond that. Even its fine natural harbors on the Gulf of Mexico were left undeveloped because the perils of smuggling were deemed worse than the benefits of trade; they remained closed until the end of the colonial era. South of Corpus Christi ran a barren strip of land about 120 miles wide which linked the Nueces River in the north and the Rio Grande to the south. Hardly anybody lived there except "prairie pirates," smugglers, and horse rustlers going after the many Mustangs romping around; but if it had few residents and fewer claimants, it had long been a recognized part of Mexico. After declaring independence in 1836, Texans claimed it for themselves nonetheless, and not a few Americans scrutinized the map and thought the great river traced a better southern boundary than the Nueces.[21] Polk sent U.S. troops under Zachary Taylor (who had fought Tecumseh and Black Hawk) to Corpus Christi on the south bank of the Nueces: with orders to treat any Mexican soldiers who might materialize with every courtesy.

Polk's goal was not to seize a bit of wasteland or start a war: it was to get Mexico's attention and get a negotiation going to buy out California. (Texans wouldn't stand for a buy-out of their honestly stolen republic, but Polk was prepared to find a way to compensate Mexico for that, too.) If a war might result, however, Polk could live with that. In November 1845 he sent a former Louisiana congressman who shared his expansionist goals, John Slidell, to Mexico City to assert new American territorial claims on Mexico in Texas and California. Polk offered $25 million to make the Rio Grande the new border from its mouth to El Paso and from there along a line due west to California essentially following the 32nd parallel, plus another $2 million if Mexico recognized Texas's claim south of the Nueces—"the whole Rio Grande from mouth to source," in Horgan's words, a new boundary "from sea to sea," in Meinig's. The Mexican government could not easily back down, since Mexicans had been goaded for years by politicians railing against American and Texan aggression and other Yankee sins. Mexico refused Polk's offer, so the president ordered General Taylor and his 2,300 troops to march through the Nueces to the Rio Grande and plant the flag, which they did on February 4, 1846. Two months later Taylor told Brigadier General William Worth to cross the river and ask to see the American consul residing in Matamoros. He did, and he was refused. "I have now to state," Worth responded, "that a refusal of my demand . . . is regarded as a belligerent act," and should any Mexican officer send his soldiers across the Rio Grande "in hostile array," he would view it as "as an act of war." The Americans busied themselves raising up "Fort Polk" at Point Isabel, just north of the little town of Bagdad, perched on a sandspit in the Rio Grande—which the Mexicans also fortified.[22]

Polk and his cabinet decided that General Worth was right—they decided on war. Before the president could send his war message to Congress, however, on April 24 a reconnaissance party of Mexican troops crossed the river "in hostile array" and fired on American soldiers, killing eleven (who didn't belong there in the first place). Polk then sent his war message to Congress saying that Mexico had "invaded our territory," mixing into it "the self-righteous wrath of the Old Testament with the long-suffering patience of the New," in David Pletcher's words. War was on: presently American troops seized Bagdad, finding it empty save for some smugglers and swimmers.[23] Before long a volunteer army of nearly 75,000 was mustered, and before long American troops were in Mexico City, after a series of easy victories (although in the end this war cost 13,000 American lives and many more Mexicans dead).[24] This war made Zachary Taylor a national hero and, ineluctably, a president—he had "no nerves and nothing recognizable as intelligence"; but he also "was too unimaginative to know when he was being licked, which was fortunate since he did not know how to maneuver troops."[25] The U.S. Navy was the most effective of the services, its fleet fast, its shells destructive; Matthew Perry's ships trained their eight-inch "Paixhan" guns on Ulúa Fortress, destroying it—a key element in the victory at Vera Cruz in early 1847.

The American army at the time did not amount to much—held in contempt by the people, unattractive to young men who could profit more by farming a homestead, and mainly engaged in either fighting Indians or removing them westward. It was staffed "in the upper ranks by oratorical veterans of 1812, some of them approaching senility," DeVoto wrote, but it had fine younger officers trained at West Point. One of them was Lt. Col. Ethan Allen Hitchcock, an excellent fighter who later delivered a dissent that became the consensus of historians: "It looks as if the government sent a small force on purpose to bring on a war, so as to have a pretext for taking California." My heart "is not in this business," he wrote, "I am against it from the bottom of my soul as a most unholy and unrighteous proceeding." Lots of Americans, prominent or otherwise, agreed with Hitchcock. Thoreau thought a Mexico "unjustly overrun" called for "honest men to rebel and revolutionize," while Ulysses S. Grant later called it "one of the most unjust [wars] ever waged by a stronger nation against a weaker nation." Polk had mimicked "the bad example of European monarchies" to unjustly expand the national territory. Many critics pointed to the utter contempt in which Americans held Mexicans, starting with Polk; as Thomas R. Hietala put it, "expansionists believed that race was a fundamental determinant in human history."[26] It appeared that the majority ruled, though; most Americans accepted the idea that their empire was different, resting on consent rather than brute force, and were ecstatic that their nation had just swallowed Texas, the New

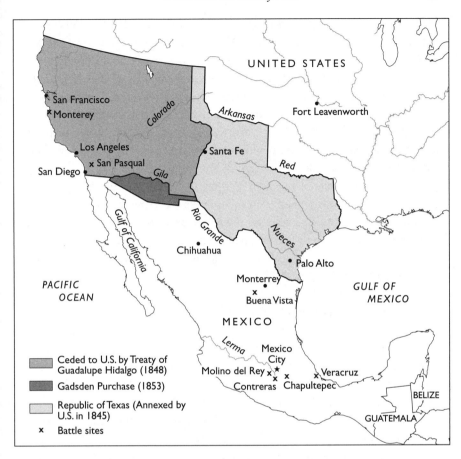

Territory acquired from Mexico, 1845–53.
Map by Bill Nelson.

Mexico territories (taken with barely a shot fired), and a long swath of the Pacific coast. In other words the war was immensely popular, as was the continental completion.

Jefferson doubled American territory by accident when Napoleon handed it to him on a silver platter. Neither had more than a remote idea of the extent of this "purchase," but purchased it was. Polk doubled the national territory, too, expanding north to the 49th parallel and south to the 32nd, but through stealth, subterfuge, force, and massive aggression. Open a history of the period written by Mexicans, and you will read of America's "war of conquest," its "frenzy to usurp and gain control of that which rightfully belongs to its neighbors"; no one ever said that about Jefferson or Adams. Furthermore

Jefferson was a Europhile (more specifically a Francophile), but Polk was a native son, for better or worse, facing West. To him, Democrats were the real Americans, while the opposition Whigs were handmaidens of England; better to charge ahead with no glances over the shoulder to Europe. DeVoto aptly described him as "pompous, suspicious, secretive," not to mention humorless and vindictive, not to mention "rigid, narrow, obstinate," with a second-rate mind in spite of his North Carolina grades. But he was a strong and effective executive who knew what he wanted and how to get it; there wasn't a stronger president between Washington and Lincoln. His election was proof that expansionism was at a "white heat," and so Polk presided over the acquisition of nearly 1.2 million square miles, as America again amplified itself almost twofold—to a colossus ten times larger than France and Britain combined. (Yet the population expanded even faster: 5.3 million Americans in 1800 became more than 23 million by 1850, with immigrants accounting for about one-fifth of the growth.)[27]

Translatio Imperii: "Going to the West"

With astonishing successes coming one after another in the 1840s—victory in war, railroads, the telegraph, California, gold—and Americans pushing deep into Pacific whaling and a China trade long monopolized by the British, it is difficult to exaggerate the hold that the popular rhetoric of Manifest Destiny had on the American people. It was as if someone mouthed the two words and a florid incantation poured forth, usually a theory of world history placing America at the center; however fatuous it may have been, as Kris Fresonke remarked, its practitioners were "untroubled by fatuity." Senator Thomas Hart Benton of Missouri was a leader of towering influence and the best known and loudest of expansionists (but also a devoted Jeffersonian, which he and many others saw as no contradiction), forcing his grandiloquent rhetoric through an ever-willing foghorn throat, giving fond voice to the "circumambulation" of the globe—"the disposition which 'the children of Adam' have always shown 'to follow the sun.'" Americans obey the same impulse, he said, "*that of going to the West;* which, from the beginning of time has been the course of heavenly bodies, of the human race, and of science, civilization, and national power following in their train." President Polk was so fond of Benton and his booming trachea that in the middle of the conflict (which Benton opposed, calling it an "aggressive war on Mexico"), the president gave the senator a new title—lieutenant general of the army, which placed him above all the general officers (Congress later demurred).[28] More than anything else,

Senator Benton leaned in one direction: to the West: "I for one had as lief see American ministers going to the emperors of China and Japan, to the King of Persia, and even to the Grand Turk, as to see them dancing attendance upon those European legitimates who hold everything American in contempt and detestation."[29]

Benton was hardly alone. James DeBow, an editor in New Orleans, announced in 1850, *"We have a destiny to perform,* a 'manifest destiny' over all Mexico, over South America, over the West Indies and Canada." After that "the gates of the Chinese empire" must come down, the same for "the haughty Japanese," then the "eagle of the Republic" will fly over the Urals, the Himalayas, and even the fields of Waterloo, until "a successor of Washington ascend[s] the chair of universal empire!"[30] If DeBow holds some kind of record for expansive hogwash, any number of others proclaimed America's destiny over Mexico and points south, Canada and points north, the Orient, and of course the still dark and little-known continent. "Westward the course of empire takes its way": if orators invoked Bishop Berkeley's 1726 incantation once, they did it a thousand times, not stopping before a great university got his name. (An Englishman, F. Trench Townshend, crossed the continent in 1868: "Everywhere in the hotels large placards may be seen" saying, "Westward the star of empire wends its glorious way," heralding the near-completion of the continental railroad.) A physician in Lyon, Raphael Dubois, argued that the earth's eastward rotation fairly required humans to go west.[31] It was an ancient and comforting idea, *translatio imperii,* empire and civilization moving east to west, rising where the sun sets, and best exampled by its completely unimaginable opposite (until our time): empire and civilization moving eastward across the Pacific.

Blather about the China trade usually came from Americans in the Mississippi Valley, who had never been to China and knew nothing about it, rather than from New England merchants who had traded at the port of Canton for decades. Their alliances were less to midwestern expansionists than to their New England allies, to their British counterparts, and to southern planters, all implicated in a mutually beneficial global business always connoted as "free trade." Benton's attraction to the West, however, was the obverse of his disdain for Europe and New England. For him the Atlantic coast was "the English seaboard," where British traditions stifled the American personality "by imposing deference to precedent and safe usage." The arena of freedom and national destiny, the place of continuing human renewal, was the West—Benton was a firm believer in the westerly direction of empire, civilization, science, even "the heavenly bodies." Never one to shrink from the implications of either his logic or his self-delusions, he thought taking California would be a fitting slap in the face not to Spain—but to England. Benton's overarching idea, however, was to link the "the Central National Highway," the "highway to California" (otherwise known as the railroad), to the commercial blessings of Pacific trade. Here humanity would come full circle, back to the point where trade first started ("the channel of Asiatic commerce . . . has been shifting its bed from the time of Solomon")—a central expansionist theme that lived on for a century (Gen. Douglas MacArthur reiterated it in a 1951 speech). The possessor of that Asian commerce would reach (in Benton's words) "the highest pinnacle of wealth and power."[32]

It was left to William Gilpin, a young friend of Senator Benton's who came from a wealthy family of mill owners in Delaware, to take his elder's aria to a crescendo; or as Wallace Stegner aptly put it, "He saw the West through a blaze of mystical fervor, as part of a grand geopolitical design, the overture to global harmony; and his conception of its resources and its future as a home for millions was as grandiose as his rhetoric, as unlimited as his faith, and as splendid as his capacity for inaccuracy."[33] Gilpin bumped into Charles Frémont, soon to be Benton's son-in-law, on the Oregon Trail in 1843 and accompanied him all the way to Walla Walla. Soon he returned to Washington and became Manifest Destiny's most certain trumpet, counseling Benton, James Buchanan, and especially President Polk. Gilpin authored an unforgettable declamation—"the *untransacted* destiny of the American people is to subdue the continent"—after which the homilies shot forth like bullets:

- to rush over the vast field to the Pacific Ocean
- to animate the many hundreds of millions of its people
- to cheer them upward
- to agitate these herculean masses
- to establish a new order in human affairs
- to regenerate superannuated nations
- to stir up the sleep of a hundred centuries
- to teach old nations a new civilization
- to confirm the destiny of the human race
- to emblazon history with the conquest of peace
- to dissolve the spell of tyranny
- to unite the world in one social family
- Divine task! Immortal mission.[34]

Elsewhere Gilpin fastened on geographer Alexander von Humboldt's "isothermal zodiac," a climatic zone above and below the 40th parallel which

Gilpin decided was the avenue for the westward course of empire (the most vigorous peoples were to be found in this zone, Humboldt opined), consummating itself—where? Well, right where Senator Benton lived: St. Louis and the basin of the Mississippi, which governs the continent "as supremely as the sun among the planets." Here, at this pinnacle, would be built "the Republican Empire of North America." A newly rising city also caught Gilpin's fancy: Denver, where Atlantic and Pacific worlds met—smack on the isothermal axis, as it happened: "We consent to face about! The rear becomes the front! Asia in the front; Europe in the rear." But what was the main point of these exhortations? Or the multitude of others bringing "Golden Cathay" to St. Louis or "twinkling sails" to Canton or reawakening Thebes, Memphis, Palmyra, and Balbee? America needed a transcontinental railroad and the government ought to make the way for it—and pay for it.[35]

Walt Whitman took Benton's program and Gilpin's florid rhetoric and gave it lyrical and sometimes eloquent voice, as the bard of Manifest Destiny. Whitman had not gone beyond the Mississippi when he penned some of his most influential poems, Henry Nash Smith noticed, but Manifest Destiny was about imagining the West and the continent not as a known place, but as the fulfillment of a fundamental departure from the Old World. A new order was rising, untainted by Europe, by wars, by feudalism (by history), and it would carry empire back to its starting point—"the circle almost circled," in Whitman's words. *Leaves of Grass* was for every place west of the Mississippi; he wrote about the entire region as some people still do California: "a free original life there . . . litheness, majestic faces, clear eyes, and perfect physique." In 1860 he was again chanting: "I chant the world on my Western sea . . . I chant the new empire, grander than any before." Other chants were not so glorious: "What has miserable, inefficient Mexico . . . to do with the great mission of peopling the New World with a noble race?" (this at the onset of the 1846 war).[36]

Not all adherents to Manifest Destiny were expansionist windbags. Caleb Cushing, heir to a Massachusetts China clipper fortune, hated Britain not because of its continuing influence in New England but because of its trade depredations; in the early 1840s he was looking westward, but beyond the continent to China. Half a century before John Hay's Open Door notes, Cushing was thinking in similar terms. Britain had forced open five ports and established a colony at Hong Kong as its price for ending the Opium Wars of 1839–42, and Cushing wanted the United States in on the action—not as a colonial power, but with *access* to the fabled China market. In May 1843

President John Tyler made him a special commissioner to China, and a year later under the Wanghsia Treaty the Chinese agreed to open five ports to Americans, too, with full extraterritorial rights.[37]

A Machine for Circumambulating the Globe

Frederick Merk, Turner's successor at Harvard, dutifully carried on the master's obsessions. His magnum opus on Manifest Destiny begins and ends with a paean to "Mission" as the driving force in American history and American foreign policy—but not the force behind the expansion to the Pacific. "Continentalist and imperialist doctrines were never true expressions of the national spirit," he concluded; instead the essence of that spirit was "Mission"—"idealistic, self-denying, hopeful of divine favor for national aspirations, though not sure of it." If Manifest Destiny died in the nineteenth century, in 1963 he thought "Mission" was "still the beacon lighting the way to political and individual freedom."[38] Hardly anything in his long book supports this interpretation, instead it is a coda tacked on at the end to show his fealty to Turner's willful, come-hell-or-high-water idealism. Just as the ideals of the forest were going to motivate Americans even as a Tyrannosaurus Rex named Chicago was tearing up the prairie, so "Mission" was going to be the driving force in American history no matter what the evidence might show.

The machine that built the western garden (or destroyed it, depending on your point of view) was not pioneering idealism or mission, but the iron horse. After unifying continental transportation, railroads went on to structure just about everything else in the country for a century, from central cities ranging across the continent to the physiognomy of a thousand small towns. The China merchant Asa Whitney had lobbied for a transcontinental railway in the 1840s, an "iron path" that would complete the continent and capture the China trade—"which has been the source and foundation of all commerce from the earliest ages." William Gilpin pushed this China angle in a wacky direction, arguing that a railroad to the Pacific would revitalize a degenerate America because China was still in a pure and uncontaminated (by Europe) condition and would thus become America's salvation. Not surprisingly, it was Thomas Hart Benton who found a more convincing way to incorporate railroads into his theory of world history.

Benton rose in the Senate on January 16, 1855, to sing the praises of iron circumambulation. After inveighing against projected northern and southern routes, he touted instead a line running along "the belt of country, about 4 [*sic*] degrees wide," demarcated by the 38th and 39th parallels, from Missouri to

California. This central railway would be "the true and good route for the road which is to unite the Atlantic and the Pacific, and to give a new channel to the commerce of Asia"—"a road of our own to the East Indies." "The great idea of Columbus will be realized, though in a different and a more beneficent form. Eastern Asia is reached by going west . . . and the channel of Asiatic commerce, which has been shifting its bed since the time of Solomon . . . [will] become fixed upon its shortest, safest, best, and quickest route, through the heart of our America, and to revive along its course the Tyres, and Sidons, the Balbecs, Palmyras and Alexandrias, once the seat of commerce and empire."

The final virtue of this great railway would be to make Europe "submissive and tributary to us," as Americans would now "circumambulate" the globe until "the children of Adam" finally returned to their parent: China. Then "the rich commerce of Asia will flow through our centre [*sic*]." If Whitney—whose rhetoric uncannily prefigured Benton's perorations—was a classic New England trader, Senator Benton longed to be free of all European and East Coast interests; his was a classic Pacific worldview. (A Princeton geographer named Arnold Guyot tried valiantly to point out that "life and action" in America will always point toward the Atlantic coast, but that impressed no one amid the clamor for a transcontinental railroad, whatever its ideological justification.)[39] The only question was where the rails would go, and the eventual answer was the one Benton and the Donner party chose: west from St. Louis through Denver, along the Truckee Valley and over the High Sierra. It wouldn't get there for a while, though, and by 1849 something else commanded American attentions.

Yankees Lead the World?

Historian Norman A. Graebner saw in the expansionism of the 1840s a clear commercial motive; indeed, he thought New England mercantile interests in the Pacific "determined the course of empire," with the immediate purpose of gaining ports on the West Coast and long-range goals of deepening or opening trade with China, Japan, and Asia more generally. As we have just seen, there was no shortage of pumped-up cant to this effect from Benton and Gilpin, and Cushing clearly qualifies for Graebner's point, as does the New England firm, Russell and Company, which handled the bulk of American trade with China. Boston ships plying a lucrative trade in hides had rendezvoused for years in San Diego Bay, and its manifold virtues as a port did not escape them. San Francisco was barely formed as a city before a daily paper declared in 1851, "The whole Pacific seas are before us and invite us to occupy them with our trade." So this clear motive was there, but it sits amid an overdetermined causality.

Polk was an expansionist and a continentalist for a host of reasons: he could be another Jefferson, buying another big chunk of territory; if he had to gain Texas and California by force, he could be a war hero; he had a midwestern constituency bent on opening vast new regions for westering settlement; the Jacksonian mission to spread American freedoms was still strong, feeding a burgeoning nationalism; Polk could forward a transcontinental railway, loudly bruited by Benton and Asa Whitney; he could ward off British ambitions; *and* he could get ports on the Pacific and deepen trade. He could do all of the above, square the circle and a bunch of circles, because it was so *easy*—the opportunities were too good to pass up. As ever in the nineteenth century no power stood in the American way, and nothing abhors a vacuum like expansionism. Graebner puts the general point nicely: "Polk's America was as restless as a caged leopard and as charged with latent energy."[40] The full dimensions of the continent had but recently been apprehended, a host of new technologies drove the industrial economy, and completing a continental United States offered an outlet for that energy, with an irresistible sea-to-shining-sea logic to it. Polk did it in 1846–48, but if he hadn't someone else would have no later than the next year, when the gold rush began—even if New England merchants had suddenly called all their ships home.

General Grant's massed artillery was by no means the only new technology crashing through the forests of this new Eden. Instead an industrial revolution, quickening dramatically in the 1840s, gave material life to the exclamations of Manifest Destiny. Until 1860 the manufacturing complex beginning in Boston, Lowell, and other textile towns and extending down through New York to Philadelphia and Wilmington was perhaps the most rapidly growing region in the world. Elsewhere came McCormick's reaper (300 manufactured in 1846); Jackson Roberts's wheat-threshing machine; new cotton looms; iron for the axles of wagons going west hardened by steel through a cold-air process (which just happened to anticipate the coming technology of the Bessemer Converter); the first use of coking coal in blast furnaces to make steel; the discovery of great iron ore sources in upper Michigan and Minnesota; a highly efficient water turbine; the clipper ship *Sea Witch* launched in 1846, faster than any other in the world (it shortened the Boston-Canton run to seventy-nine days, whereas a voyage to China had taken six months in 1800); the rotating printing cylinder that produced 8,000 newspapers in an hour; the telegraph and only two years after it the printing telegraph (later known as a teletype machine); the Colt 45 revolver that revolutionized firearms—all in all, a maturing American industry that was not clearly behind England in anything industrial or technological: "The Yankees led the world" and showed it at the famous Crystal Palace Exhibition in London in 1851. Suddenly British manufacturers began buying American machine tools, rather than vice versa.[41]

The completion of the continent now meant that American industry had at its disposal the largest free trade area or national market in the world. Here was not just a frontier but an arrow of westward development as innovation piled on innovation (but also replication on replication) and huge new swatches of the country came on line, so to speak. But that line rarely ran south of Baltimore or Cincinnati or St. Louis; the Baltimore and Ohio Railroad traced this path—and the fatal exclusion of the South. In one of the few examinations of the frontier thesis by economists, two of them applauded Turner's emphasis on a continental perspective; this is all the more surprising because geography—the concept of space, which is so crucial for American development—is largely absent from the concerns of economists (see appendix). The westward movement brought forward a plethora of "new slabs" of resources, they wrote, affording "broad production possibilities with high marginal productivities of both capital and labor" moving *in sequence,* thus opening up successive frontiers of extensive development. "*Successive* additions of rich natural resources" propelled economic growth, just as technological innovations were applied not once but many times over, creating successive "spurts" of development as the western terrain opened. This sequential process is rarely seen elsewhere in the world, they thought, and thus "*may be important enough to make the American frontier process unique.*" Joseph Schumpeter put the point more simply: with the extension of the American frontier "new land" entered the Euro-American sphere, producing "a vast access of wealth" and making for "a quite exceptional factor," indeed, "a unique one." Or, if not unique, then perhaps the world's most eloquent testimony to Braudel's view that "geography . . . helps us to rediscover the slow unfolding of structural realities, to see things in the perspective of the very long term."[42]

Years later John Gast put oil to canvas to produce an image called *American Progress* that quickly became a ubiquitous advertisement for the westering life—and the new technologies. An ethereal, angelic woman faces west, more or less naked in a flowing white gown, a star on her forehead (the star of empire), a schoolbook in one hand and a coil of telegraph wire in the other; she floats above a procession heading toward the horizon—train, stagecoach, covered wagon, Pony Express, Indian fighters, miners with pickaxes.

"The rising sun illuminates the East; ahead, to the West, the dark clouds of ignorance and barbarism still enshadow the land." Soon, however, the continent will be "bathed in light."[43] At the least, it would be bathed in new technologies.

A Telecommunications Revolution

Railroads and steam engines were the obvious accompaniments for the rhetoric of Manifest Destiny in the 1840s, annihilating space and time, but no technology was as momentous for expansionism as the telegraph, because it conquered an ancient enemy of commerce, distance. It also had immediate commercial and military application, it easily crossed international borders, and it had no competitors (besides semaphore and homing pigeons). Polk was elected in the same year that Samuel F. B. Morse invented this technology. The basic idea was born in France in 1791, but Morse developed the first cheap and effective commercial application, relying upon a soon-famous code of dots and dashes powered by short and long bursts of electric current. Braudel recorded that news traveled at less than 100 kilometers per day in sixteenth-century Europe, and the measure of sea travel was weeks and months (it took as much as two weeks to sail the Mediterranean, north to south, and two or three months to travel from Madrid to Moscow). In 1775 it took five and a half weeks for London to learn that a revolution had broken out in America, and even the news of the British victory at nearby Waterloo took a deliberate three days to reach London in 1815; news traveled little faster than it had when the Romans built Hadrian's Wall in northern England.

The telegraph flashed the news of war breaking out along the Rio Grande in a few minutes, and with new rotary cylinder presses churning out thousands of copies, newspaper readers could follow the course of the war on a daily basis. Polk's announcement of gold found in California ricocheted through the country (east of Denver) in a thrice. The shrinkage of time to the instantaneous moment in the communications revolution of recent decades—fax machines, e-mail, the World Wide Web, global cell phones—is impressive enough, but imagine the difference between dispatching a horseman from Washington to New York and sending a wire, or giving your message to the Pony Express for a lathered ten-day ride from St. Louis to San Francisco, versus getting your stock quotes from Wall Street every few minutes while gazing upon the Pacific. Think of a world without global news services like Associated Press or Reuters—which used the telegraph to establish regional monopolies 150 years ago.[44] We come to understand that the shrinking of the world in our time is a matter of degree, but in the 1840s it was a matter of kind, imparting an entirely new quality to life on this planet.

Tom Standage calls it "the greatest revolution in communications since the development of the printing press," meaning not just the telegraph lines, but the undersea cable that linked London and New York in 1858, or Alexander Graham Bell fiddling with his "harmonic telegraph" in 1875 and stumbling upon the telephone, or the lines hooking up to a teletype machine, a direct forerunner of electronic mail. By 1850 nearly all American cities were connected by telegraph (although San Francisco had to wait for its line until 1861). If the Mexican War was the first in history to be reported by telegraph, it could also thereby be "pictured." Richard Caton Woodville did his famous painting *News From the Mexican War* from his studio in Dusseldorf.[45] Meanwhile Emanuel Gottlieb Leutze, a German painter and the most eminent artist of American themes, sat in his studio (also in Dusseldorf) painting *Washington Crossing the Delaware*—and in 1862 produced *Westward the Course of Empire Takes Its Way*, a 600-square-foot mural.[46]

Now the still unfamiliar continent could be meticulously mapped through an "American System" using simultaneous signals from telegraph stations fifty or more miles from each other, with each river, mountain, and town represented to the American people. Senator Benton may have been a blowhard, but he also had a knack for capturing the moment: in pushing the transcontinental railway in 1848, he correctly observed: "The age is progressive, and utilitarian. It abounds with talent, seeking employment, and with capital seeking investment. The temptation is irresistible. To reach the golden California—to put the people of the Atlantic and the Pacific into direct communication—to connect Europe and Asia through America . . . such is the grandeur of the enterprise!"[47]

Seizing California

Polk knew Texas, which had been independent for a decade, but he had no more idea what he would get from California than Jefferson did the Louisiana Purchase: hardly any American had laid eyes on it in 1845, apart from coastal reconnaissance. Like other midwestern agrarians, Polk was looking beyond the continent to opportunities for new markets, fearful that overproduction on farms and plantations would not find a proper outlet. But the son-in-law of Senator Benton, John Charles Frémont, had seen California. He was already famous for his foray into California with Kit Carson and other "mountain men" in 1845–46—Frémont the explorer, soon to be dubbed "the Pathfinder"—mapping the Oregon and California trails, teaming up with his literary superior (namely his wife Jessie) to produce a book from the exploration that quickly became a best seller. It was a classic Arcadian account—into the wilderness, the wind rustling the leaves of an abundant greenery, Americans chasing after the sun: DeVoto was still under (Jessie) Frémont's spell a century later. Witness this lyrical encomium: "He saw the Western country with eager eyes—saw it under sun, bent and swollen by mirage, stark, terrible, beautiful to the heart's longing, snow on the peaks, infinite green and the night stars." Frémont was one of the first to describe in some detail California's great potential for agriculture; he was, for his time, a scientist and a visionary. But he was also a card-carrying exponent of Manifest Destiny, and a couple of years later he mounted a violent putsch in California to found the "Bear Republic" on the Texas model.[48]

President Polk purposely put American troops in harm's way on the Nueces, figuring something useful might turn up; in California it was only a bit different. Frémont, pretending to have secret orders from Washington, staged an uprising by a few American settlers and assaulted the Spanish absent the slightest provocation. He began by raiding a hacienda on June 10, 1846, making away with a couple hundred horses belonging to the herd of Commandante Don José Castro, thus to force the issue and proclaim a republic as prelude to bringing California into the Union. A kind of expansionist telepathy was at work: unbeknownst to Frémont, Polk had sent a secret message to the U.S. consul in Monterey, Thomas Larkin, urging him to trump up a "revolution" to detach California in case of war with Mexico, and another one to Commodore John Sloat to seize San Francisco in the same event. Meanwhile Larkin, who had become wealthy in the Pacific trade, fed back to Polk every tidbit of evidence, real or fancied, about how much the British coveted California.

Seizing California was child's play. Instead of real colonial rule or a functioning government you had a vacuum of power, into which even a small force might move and end up victorious. Spain and Mexico did not rule the place; instead their northerly extensions went up like curling fingers into the American Southwest, with no lateral connections uniting them. California was tethered to a feeble and squabbling Mexico and a relative handful of mission priests and rancheros who had not bothered to build frontier defenses—or schools, or good roads; they hadn't even bothered to sow seeds in some of the world's most fertile soil (there are more Basques in California today than there were Spaniards in old California). Furthermore, the British weren't coming, Mexico wasn't fighting, and it quickly became clear that many Californios preferred Washington to Mexico City. And so Frémont's forces faced barely any resistance: Sonoma, for example "could have been captured by Tom Sawyer and Huck Finn," in DeVoto's words; when Frémont thundered into town he found the commanding general of the northern frontier, Don Mariano Vallejo, asleep in his baronial estate. (Nor did it matter whether he was or wasn't; Vallejo, perhaps the most respected figure in California, was also an advocate of American annexation.) Military displays by presidio garrisons resembled "dress rehearsals for a comic opera." In the depths of night Frémont intrepidly stormed the fortress above San Francisco Bay, El Castillo de San Joaquin; it hadn't been occupied for a generation. But it wasn't all in vain: when Frémont beheld the morning vista from the presidio he coined the term "golden gate."

Shortly after routing the not-very-resistant enemy (Frémont's bungling led to guerrilla resistance in places that had already surrendered, and there was a months-long stand-off in Santa Barbara), the Yankees declared the "Bear Flag Republic." William Todd, a nephew of Mary Todd Lincoln, used some homespun Mexican cloth and a red strip from his wife's flannel underwear to make the portentous flag; he put a lone star on the upper left of the flag to signify another Texas and in the center, drawn with "berry-juice," a grizzly bear (finally, a fearsome anti-American aggressor had shown his ugly face, except many thought it looked like a hog). Birth-seed of the state of California and a thousand myths, this republic lasted about a month. The weakness of Spain and Mexico in this far periphery of empire, the caution of the British, and the absence of anyone really wanting to fight for it encouraged Polk to acquire this most low-hanging of all fruit: there it is, take it.[49]

DeVoto rightly called Frémont a freebooter (his initial raid being pure thievery, he figured he better call it war) and quite a bit else: "worse than a fool, he was an opportunist, an adventurer, and a blunderer on a truly dangerous scale." Polk was a schemer and an aggressor, too, but a much more sober and calculating one. By hook and crook, almost overnight the two of them created "a new Texas on the golden shore," just what Polk had been looking for; but he wasn't looking for yet another war, and so he flipped aside expansionists who wanted to gobble up Canada ("54°40′ or bust"), and to the surprise of many, settled with the British on the 49th parallel as the dividing line—the one that still separates the United States from Canada. His flip-flopping secretary of state, James Buchanan, finally screwed up enough courage to oppose this deal. But Polk fell all over him and Buchanan "collapsed like a punctured bladder" (in DeVoto's words) and accepted 49 degrees. Many Americans thought Britain had designs on California, Polk above all (another

RAISING THE FLAG ON THE PEAK—HEIGHT, 13,570 FEET.

Frémont plants the Bear Flag.
From "Life of John Charles Frémont," campaign literature for Frémont's 1856 presidential campaign. Artist unknown; publisher Horace Greeley and Thomas McElrath. Courtesy of Robert Graham.

useful rationalization for U.S. expansion), but when Foreign Office papers were declassified half a century later, no such designs could be found—not on California, not on Oregon, of course not on Texas. Instead London figured that the unavoidable consequence of challenging Washington would be war; its hand was also restrained by the dependence of its textile industry on cotton exports from the South—and with Texas added, the United States had a stranglehold on global cotton production.[50] The result was a new line of expansion drawn from Texas through the Southwest around and up the Pacific coast all the way to the Puget Sound and beyond, one of the more astonishing and fateful territorial acquisitions in world history—all in the flash of an eye.

Finding Japan

The completion of the continent instantly suggested a move beyond, conveyed by clipper or steamship and announced by telegraph, to still more unknown places across the Pacific. California was simultaneously a new frontier and prelude to the next one. It was instantly configured and recognized as such, too, because the acquisition of California, a century after the "discovery" that it was part and parcel of the American continent, was followed and punctuated immediately by the gold rush and the global attentions that it drove and by Commodore Matthew Perry's further "discovery" of Japan in 1853. Soon Karl Marx, as we have seen, put California on the horizon not just of the continent but the globe, seizing the grand terrain of the world market. It was gold, then California, then Japan—and suddenly an entirely new vista opened for the long-distance trade that Fernand Braudel thought so critical to rapid growth: except in this case long-distance trade flourished most of all *within* the newly continental boundaries of one tariff-free nation, an ecological windfall[51] of astounding proportions.

During the dynamic and potent 1840s the United States became the global leader in ship design: its clippers were the fastest in the world. These square-rigged sailing ships had their forerunner in the *Anne McKim*, built in 1832 for Isaac McKim, a wealthy China trader who contracted for a 493-ton, 143-foot-long ship (about twice the size of others in the China trade), with "coppered bottom, live oak frames, mahogany deck fittings and twelve brass guns." Within a decade, mammoth, fast-moving ships like the 750-ton *Rainbow* became the norm, making the run from New York to Canton in an unheard-of ninety-two days, the world's fastest pace. The clipper *Oriental* arrived in London in 1850 with a cargo of tea from Hong Kong, and Britons stood around aghast at this ship with a low, lean hull whose tall, raked masts "dwarfed every other ship in sight." At about the same time American traders finally got accurate charts of the American Pacific coast, making San Francisco a key global trading post by the 1850s.[52]

It is a curiosity that Japan should have been "opened" in 1853 and then reopened in 1945 by Americans who closely conformed to the feudal ideal of

the stately, noble individual, with neither of them—Perry or MacArthur—
ever at a loss for imperious self-importance. Commodore Matthew Calbraith
Perry was the younger brother of Oliver Hazard Perry, who had defeated
British forces in the Battle of Lake Erie in 1813 and thus spared the country's
northern frontier a British invasion. Matthew Perry was "an awesome presence" on any quarterdeck, "ruthless, stiff-necked, the embodiment of 'Manifest Destiny.'" Not only a navy man but a diplomat with wide experience,
Perry understood the historic importance of his mission from the beginning
even if much of his nation did not, and in typical midcentury fashion he
linked his enterprise to the thread of westward progress which "broke in the
hands of Columbus," but which he would again tie up to "the ball of destiny,"
rolling it forward until Japan is brought "within the influence of European
civilization." With California in the union and "our territory spreading from
ocean to ocean," Perry thought the United States, midway between Europe
and Asia, was now the real "Middle Kingdom."[53] The Navy Department was
well disposed, too, desiring coaling stations in the far Pacific (the importance
of steam power having been fully demonstrated), but most Americans paid
little attention, before and after (the little towns around the Great Lakes
named "Perry," "Perryville," and the like are named for Matthew's brother).

Although talk of "opening Japan" was not new and other Americans (like
James Biddle) had tried before, President Millard Fillmore responded to the
desires of New England whalers and traders by sending Perry on his mission
to the "far West" (China), by venue of putting a bigger navy in the Pacific and
building coaling stations in Japan. But the devout Perry was no mere agent of
commercial interests: he was taking "the gospel of God to the heathen,"
reconnoitering an important part of the world unsullied by the "unconscion-
able government" residing in London ("our great maritime rival," in his
words). Perry embarked in command of a large Asiatic Squadron comprising
ten ships, but he reconnoitered in Tokyo (then called Edo) Bay with just four
of them: "black ships" consisting of the twenty-gun sloops *Saratoga* and
Plymouth, moving under sail, and two new state-of-the-art vessels, the *Mississippi* and the *Susquehanna*, propelled by steam. Cruising via the Cape of
Good Hope and the Indian Ocean, with many stops en route, including
Hong Kong and Shanghai, the squadron arrived off Okinawa in spring 1853;
American marines landed and marched through the streets of Naha, as marines would a century later—where today the only Marine Expeditionary
Force remains on permanent foreign duty. In early July splendid Mount Fuji
came into view, and on July 8 the four ships anchored near Uraga, at the
entrance to Tokyo Bay.

A week later two columns of well-armed marines stood stiffly as Perry walked slowly into a brand new reception hall and handed over President Fillmore's letter for delivery to the emperor—as if he were an equal, which astonished the assembled officials. The letter opened with an even more pregnant line: "You know that the United States of America now extend from sea to sea." Perry then retreated to his black ships and began a stately "exhibition of seclusion that rivaled that of Japan," in Bryant's words. Perry cloistered himself in his stateroom pending an audience with the emperor and demanded that Millard Fillmore be addressed on the same level, using the same Japanese designation, while his crewmen dazzled the Japanese with a variety of new technologies (the telegraph, the daguerreotype, steam engines, Colt revolvers). After several weeks of fruitless negotiations, during which the Japanese urged him to depart for Nagasaki where foreigners were always received, leading Perry to maneuver his ships closer by the day to Tokyo, he finally weighed anchor for Hong Kong. He returned in February 1854 with eight warships—nearly the entire American Asiatic Squadron—and resumed his practice of cloistering himself and deploying ever closer to the Mikado. "The more unyielding he might be in adhering to his declared intentions," the commodore thought, "the more respect these people of forms and ceremonies" would accord him. But just in case, according to Japanese records, Perry also threatened war: American forces had recently taken the capital of Mexico, he pointed out; "circumstances may lead your country into a similar plight." At length, after much back and forth about Japan having no interest in trade and the United States now being a great Pacific commercial nation (with Japan's leaders painfully aware of their military inferiority), on March 31, 1854, Perry secured the Treaty of Kanagawa, an accord of "friendship and commerce."[54]

Out of it came several coaling stations, the opening of the ports of Shimoda and Hakodate to trade, and another orgasm from Walt Whitman when a return Japanese delegation materialized in New York ("The Originatress comes, Florid with blood," "I chant the new empire," "I chant America, the Mistress"; "I chant commerce opening, the sleep of ages having done its work—races, reborn, refresh'd . . . with the arrival of the American pioneers in the Pacific a glorious millennium begins"). But Perry's visit takes its place in history not for its impact on America, which was negligible at the time, but as the spark detonating Japan's remarkable rise to power, drawing it out of the Tokugawa isolation that had lasted since 1600 and propelling it into fifteen years of internal civil struggle, the outcome of which was the top-down revolution in 1868 known as the Meiji Restoration. These momentous events, linking American expansionism to the birth of East Asian modernity, dawned slowly on the world and especially Americans, who greeted Perry's return with muted enthusiasm. Never a shrinking violet, Perry took a page from Frémont and produced a book-of-the-mission in 1856 that made him—however temporarily—a national hero.[55]

This large book has a particular fascination in recounting American reactions to the various peoples encountered on the voyage—blacks in Capetown, Portuguese and Arabs in Macao, Chinese in Canton and Shanghai—who by and large were seen through the condescending lenses of race. And then come the Japanese, who make a startling and unexpected impression in their impeccably good manners, their decorous rituals, their overweening curiosity in spite of themselves about Americans and the mechanical wizardry they deployed (a miniature train set got all the officials hoping for a ride), and their intelligence and cleanliness. Cleanliness was not next to Godliness in the nineteenth century, with states like Kentucky having to pass laws requiring people to take a bath at least once a year, but it was impressive when located among the nonwhite races who were thought to be unhygienic (unlike Kentuckians). The Japanese scrubbed themselves squeaky clean, albeit in communal baths with both sexes mingling together stark naked. The officials liked to drink rice wine called "saki" and took readily to American whisky, getting quickly inebriated; amid general hilarity they would exclaim, "Nippon and America, all the same heart!" Japan also housed "huge monsters," men "enormously tall in stature and immense in weight" with necks "like the dewlap of a prize ox," who flung their bellies at each other with abandon and called it *sumo*. There were perhaps signs of poverty in the country "but no evidence of public beggary," the men of all classes "were exceedingly courteous," and the women were prim with no hint of "wantonness and license." Japanese homes were plain and simple "but always scrupulously clean and neat." *Plus ça change, plus c'est la même chose.* Perry and his men decided that Japan was "the most moral and refined of all eastern nations," a judgment that would color American perceptions for nearly a century, until a different stereotype arrived in the 1930s.

Finding Alaska—and Korea

William H. Seward wanted to extend Perry's project onward (to China) and upward (to Alaska). He was another first-class expansionist, a true believer in empire and Manifest Destiny and willing to use force if necessary. He urged the Senate in 1853 to "open up a highway through your country from New

York to San Francisco," to put "ten thousand wheels of manufacture in motion, multiply your ships, and send them forth to the East"—the nation that
does so will be "the great power of the earth." Seward wanted a canal across
the Central American isthmus and to annex Hawaii and to keep on going to
seize the China trade. But by the time he became secretary of state, the
wounds of the Civil War were unhealed, and the best he could do was acquire
Brooks Island (later called Midway) and Alaska, both in 1867, and both not by
force but in the Jeffersonian manner: he bought them (Alaska, at least; Midway was uninhabited). Hardly any Americans could (can?) locate Midway on
a map, a scant speck in the vast Pacific about 1,200 miles west of Hawaii, but
the navy wanted coaling stations and Midway became a permanent naval base
down to the present. Alaska they could find and the $7 million purchase they
could name: "Seward's folly," "Frigidia," "Walrussia." Seward wasn't a man of
great personal force: "a slouching, slender figure; a head like a wise macaw; a
beaked nose; shaggy eyebrows; unorderly hair and clothes; hoarse voice; offhand manner . . . no one could tell which was the mask and which the
features." But he was the right man in the right place—at the wrong time.
Nonetheless with the barest expenditure of effort he added another 586,000-
square-mile piece to the American continent, a place 250 percent bigger than
Texas.[56] Eventually it would find its destiny as the strategic cap of a North
Pacific dominated by American power.

The United States also tried its hand at opening up Korea as a follow-on
to beginning trade with Japan, when the merchant schooner *General Sherman*
sailed up the Taedong River toward Pyongyang in 1866. A heavily armed ship
with a mixed crew of Americans, British, and Chinese, it received the message that foreign commerce contravened Korean law. Undaunted, the *Sherman* forged ahead. Shortly a hostile crowd gathered on the shore, into which
the frightened sailors unloaded their muskets. After that volley the provincial
governor, a much-respected and temperate official named Pak Kyu-su (who
later negotiated Korea's first treaty with Japan), ordered the *General Sherman*
destroyed. The tide obligingly receded, grounding the vessel. The Koreans
killed all its crew in battle and burned the ship.[57]

It was a dastardly act, the authorities in Washington declared; what an
outrageous affront to a peaceable bunch of people who just happened to be
sailing a man-o'-war up the river to Pyongyang. Seward proposed a joint
expedition with the French to punish the Koreans, and Commodore Robert
W. Shufeldt (who fancied himself Korea's Commodore Perry) determined to
"go up the 'Ping yang' river at the proper season and inflict proportionate
punishment." But it did not happen until 1871, and by then the United States

had decided to open Korea's ports by force. The American minister to China, Frederick F. Low, was put in charge of the American expedition. The invading forces embarked from Nagasaki and entered Korean waters on May 19, 1871; they included the Asiatic Squadron warships *Monocacy* and *Palos*, plus "four steam launches, and twenty boats, conveying a landing force of six hundred and fifty-one men, of whom one hundred and five were marines." Low, as it happened, also saw himself as another Commodore Perry and mimicked his methods: steaming right into strategic islands near the capital as if he owned them, he refused to meet with lower-level officials and announced that he would keep deploying closer to Seoul. After Korean entreaties to go no farther lest a calamity result, the ships soon breached "the gateway to the capital"—and Korean cannons opened up.[58]

In this "Little War with the Heathen," as the *New York Herald* called it, the Americans killed a lot of Koreans but also paid a stiff enough price to get scared off. Marines hit the beaches of Kanghwa Island and sought to capture several strategic Korean forts. These were filled with Korean tiger fighters renowned for their courage, who fought ferociously; when their weapons were empty they threw sand in the Americans' eyes and fought to the last man in hand-to-hand combat. In the end about 650 Koreans died, according to William Griffis: "Two hundred and forty-three corpses in their white garments lay in and around the citadel. Many of them were clothed in a thick cotton armor, wadded to nine thicknesses, which now smouldered away. A sickening stench of roasted flesh filled the air. . . . Some of the wounded, fearing their captors worse than their torture, slowly burned to death." Commander Low thought the Koreans fought back with a courage "rarely equalled and never excelled by any people." After some desultory and fruitless negotiations, the Americans withdrew and did not come back. King Kojong later reflected that the Americans betrayed "utter contempt" for Korea, as if it were "a country without anybody to take care of it."[59]

The "Little War with the Heathen" was the largest American battle between the Civil War and the war with Spain, but it was little noted nor long remembered in the United States. More than a century later, however, my North Korean hosts were pleased to show me the stone monument that still marks the spot where the *General Sherman* burned. It is not far from Kim Il Sung's birthplace, and my hosts assured me that his great-grandfather had led the charge. In 1882, Commodore Shufeldt and Chinese leader Li Hung-chang got together in Tientsin and secretly negotiated the first American treaty with Korea, to the point of choosing Korea's new national flag (and still the flag of South Korea). As Frederick Drake aptly put it, Shufeldt "was discussing the treaty with the viceroy of Chihli . . . writing it in Tientsin in the Chinese language, and arranging it through the agency of China's diplomats for a Korean official he had never formally met and had seldom seen!"[60]

A perfect example of the unequal treaties of the era, the deal nonetheless duly impressed the commodore: he had accomplished, he later wrote, "the feat of bringing the last of the exclusive countries within the pale of Western Civilization."[61] Indeed, Shufeldt was proud to the point of prurience with his climactic feat: he now hoped that Korea and China would come to look beyond Japan for the source of the rising sun, and then (mixing metaphors) come together on the bridal couch with a new American empire of the Pacific:

> As everything that is bright comes from the East—even as the sun rises in the East & as still the Star of Empire westward takes its way—so China must look to the shores of America for a new Civilization & a more vigorous regeneration. This is the natural course of events, the true march of human progress, the irresistible flow of the human tide. . . . The pacific [*sic*] is the ocean bride of America—China & Japan & Corea—with their innumerable islands, hanging like necklaces about them, are the bridesmaids, California is the nuptial couch, the bridal chamber, where all the wealth of the Orient will be brought to celebrate the wedding. Let us as Americans—see to it that the "bridegroom cometh" . . . let us determine while yet in our power, that no commercial rival or hostile flag can float with impunity over the long swell of the Pacific sea. . . . It is on this ocean that the East & the West have thus come together, reaching the point where search for Empire ceases & human power attains its climax.[62]

Back home barely anyone paid attention to Shufeldt, but he demonstrated that the rhetoric of Manifest Destiny was still alive and well in at least one randy commodore.

The Un-manifest Destiny of a Complicated Nation

An ocean of historians' ink spilled forth to link the 1840s couplet "manifest destiny" to a rising American nationalism, to imperialism, to the westward-displacing frontier, to spreading democracy and liberty, to settler expansionism, to "mission."[63] But this was not a simple moment: the 1840s went to the heart of what kind of a country Americans had founded. Clearly continentalism was something everyone could agree on—a beeline for the Pacific coast. This line of march was not only immensely popular, it drew in the finest American minds: Thoreau hated the passions of the time ("the nation may go their way to their manifest destiny which I trust is not mine"), but he also wrote, "I must walk toward Oregon, and not toward Europe." This, he thought, was "the prevailing tendency" of Americans: "Westward I go free, Eastward I go only by force." In 1846 Walt Whitman waxed lyrical on Santa Fe and California: "How long a time will elapse before *they* shine as two new stars in our mighty firmament?"[64] And, of course, there is the poem that began this section, "Facing West from California's Shores": "the circle almost circled" (*translatio imperii* again), but with the dangling thought, "why is it yet unfound?" What remains unfound? Whatever they were looking for in the westward march (but what was that?). A question like this might have been on the lips of John Quincy Adams, who, on the day the treaty ending the war with Mexico arrived on the Senate floor for ratification, rose to speak, crumpled back to his desk, and died two years later at the age of eighty.

If this was the birth of the expansionist impulse, it was also an ending for a different United States. What was dying had something to do with Thoreau's Arcadia, and the new had something to do with industry and empire, the Old World aggression that the Founding Fathers had decried. Linus P. Brockett, author of a biography for Grant's presidential campaign, wrote in 1882 that in the thirteen colonies "lay the germ of the grandest empire this world has ever seen—an empire designed to realize . . . the dictum of the great Roman orator,—*Imperium et Libertas.*" But for Brockett, like Jefferson, this empire of liberty was an agricultural garden.[65] The year 1846 marked the birth of a new kind of expansionism, a westward-bound movement that would not be blocked for more than a century. But it would be mightily interrupted, as fratricidal war consumed the nation and Manifest Destiny's highway to the Pacific and Asia would disappear, not to be revived for a quarter century.

Changing, also, was the encounter with nonwhite peoples to the west increasingly seen as numerous, an obstacle to expansion, and alien to a new nationalist conception of what it meant to be an American. The alien was the Other, his culture was the antithesis of the Anglo-Saxon creed, assimilation was out of the question given the stain of race, and so this garden-cum-empire was fueled from one end to the other by a virulent racism. Blacks in the South, Indians on the frontier, Mexicans in California, eventually Filipinos, Chinese, Japanese and Koreans—all suffered outrageous abuses and indignities. Still, D. H. Lawrence's acidic judgment that democracy is mere by-play compared to the essential American soul ("hard, isolate, stoic, and a killer") has as much bile and prejudice in it as the racial bombast of "Manifest Destiny." There are people who fit his description—Cotton Mather, for example. Was he an American, or was he English, like Lawrence?

The important distinction is between an "East," Europe and New England, that was thickly settled, imbedded in history, the origin of American civilization, and assumed to be the wind at one's back; and an imagined "West" that was vacant, inhabited by people without history, fated to disappear or dissolve in an ineluctable civilizing mission. It is between aggressors like Napoleon who seized whatever they wanted, Josiah Royce thought, and the American who "wants to persuade not only the world but himself that he is doing God service in a peaceable spirit, even when he violently takes what he has determined to get." It is between a prehistory in which frontier people of various races and nationalities experienced the West and a turning point in 1846 after which the whole nation began to take part, as Paul Horgan put it, in the life of a West now tied "to all the United States by longing, and letters, and hope."[66]

If Manifest Destiny lived primarily in the florid rhetoric of its proponents, it caught the direction of American ambition at midcentury and offered a vocabulary for westering self-justification well into the next century. It was not just fatuous blowhards like William Gilpin who characterized the era, but the best American civilization had to offer in the achievements of Emerson, Hawthorne, Melville, Whitman, and Thoreau. A great scholar, F. O. Mathiessen, located an American renaissance in the 1840s, a moment when American arts and letters left Europe and proclaimed their distinction and their independence. If Thoreau or Emerson or especially Whitman voiced a naïve and lyrical optimism, or even when they were "dangerously expansive" like Benton or Gilpin, here was also the finest American voice, and the finest art, the nation had yet produced.[67]

Expansion across the Pacific to Japan or China remained much less important than the intensive "deepening" of the opportunities that expansion brought at home (the story of California's life since 1848). Fifty years later James Bryce wrote, "Western America is one of the most interesting subjects of study the modern world has seen. There has been nothing in the past resembling its growth, and probably there will be nothing in the future." His list of attributes was common—natural resources, benign climate, fertile soil, and "trackless forests"—but his next point was uncommon: a vigorous people bringing "all the appliances and contrivances of modern science at its command" to populate the West which made for "phenomena absolutely without precedent in history, and which cannot recur elsewhere, because our planet contains no such other favoured tract of country."

Bryce saw virtually everything in America through a comparative lens; so was he right—no such "tract" elsewhere on the planet? The ancient silk route might make the reader think of China's vast western territory, but it is mostly desert and mountain ranges with few vast forests, and if somehow water, people, and development could be brought, it would still open into Central Asia and not the Pacific Ocean. Brazil's westward plunge into the jungle keeps finding more jungle. Russia's Far East does have endless timber and Vladivostok on the Pacific, but sustained efforts to develop it under the tsars, Stalin (who studied the American westward movement for pointers), and Russia's current leaders haven't begun to erode Bryce's prescient argument, because most of this tract is under permafrost. But perhaps a Germany with neither an Atlantic nor a Pacific coast might grasp the point best: it is said that German prisoners of war understood that Hitler could never win the war "after five days of continuous rail travel had failed to deliver them from east coast to west coast."[68]

The lasting meaning of Manifest Destiny was not conquest, even if Polk dismantled half of Mexico, but inhered in his single consistent goal, which was to join California to the Union. That completed the continent and opened a grand vista onto the Pacific. It got rid of great power conflict in this hemisphere, as Spain retreated and Britain settled with Polk on Oregon and never again challenged American power on the North American continent. In a thrice California unleashed a never known or imagined river of gold into the economy, as if by magic. But the grandest meaning of the incorporation of California is what it did for the creation of a new kind of country: if it completed the continent, it also capped the vast interior for further development. As Charles F. Lummis put it so well in 1900,

> Our real West dates from California. It is not enough to remember that Minnesota, Oregon, Kansas, Nevada, Nebraska, Colorado, the two Dakotas, Montana, Washington, Idaho, Wyoming, Utah, have been admitted as States, and New Mexico, Arizona, Oklahoma, and Alaska organized as Territories, since California came into the Union. *The pertinent question is how many of them we should have if there had been no California.* . . . The United States was mostly content to remain a narrow huddle of provinces when California, suddenly and almost empirically, unrolled our trivial halfway map to another ocean and gave us a national span, and pulled along population enough to vindicate the map. To this day there are many excellent people who never reflect what Uncle Sam's stature would have been if he had slept on with Canada as his head, Mexico for a foot-board, and his back against a British wall somewhere about the Platte.[69]

California's conquest happened almost simultaneously with the discovery of gold, which instantly transfigured it into what it still is: a singularly productive economy that arrived "late" in world time but remains a kind of heady pump for the rest of the American economy—a gift that keeps on giving—and a dream that perpetuated the themes of the Garden of Eden and Arcadia into the present. It brought a cascade of new-new things: virgin gold, a polyglot town named San Francisco, railroads, our own private Mediterranean, amber waves of grain gathered up by giant machines, fragrant orange and lemon groves, canned fruit, you name it, America now had its special version of long-distance trade within and around the boundaries of the country, to augment its trade with the world at large. But standing above everything else was the physical unification of the continent—because, elementary fact, nowhere else in the world, then or now, was a continent united under one flag from sea to shining sea.

CHAPTER FOUR

Manifest Destiny's Offspring:
Gold, the Continental Railroad, Texas

The signs of exchange, because they satisfy desire, are sustained by the dark, dangerous, and accursed glitter of metal. An equivocal glitter, for it reproduces in the depths of the earth that other glitter that sings at the far end of the night: it resides there like an inverted promise of happiness, and, because metal resembles the stars, the knowledge of all these perilous treasures is at the same time knowledge of the world.

—MICHEL FOUCAULT, *The Order of Things*

If the American space broadened by 60 percent under Polk's aggressive ministrations, two gargantuan territorial fruits of the war with Mexico grabbed everyone's attentions: they are called California and Texas. The one jumped to the forefront of this nation's destiny and never dismounted; the other mounted a horse and created a legend that never died. For California it began with gold and never ended; for Texas it began with longhorns and leapt forward with the other dark, dangerous, equivocal treasure nature buried in the depths—black gold. It is a minor irony that the word "California" turned up in an early sixteenth-century novel by García Ordóñez de Montalvo called *Las Sergas de Esplandián* (The Exploits of Esplandián), as the name of a mythical island "at the right hand of the Indies" where the only metal to be found was—gold.[1] It is a crushing irony that the Spanish never found gold in California (they barely looked for it), only to have it cascade out of the mountains just as they signed the place over to America.

The United States closed the war with Mexico and acquired Texas and California for $15 million in the Treaty of Guadalupe Hidalgo, signed on February 2, 1848—nine days after James Wilson Marshall found his nugget the size of a small pea. The news was slow to travel (Marshall and his employer John Sutter took their sweet time weighing, hammering, and scrutinizing the glittering pea behind a firmly locked door, even if it would soon ricochet around the world with the speed of light), and the treaty makers knew nothing of it—perhaps a peculiar case of Montezuma's revenge. In any case, by the time the gold began flowing out, Mexico had no claim on it. Even if it had—even if Polk's war had never happened—the discovery of gold would have brought California into the Union almost as quickly, by whatever means necessary.

Thou Common Whore of Mankind

James Marshall was a versatile carpenter and mechanic who went up to a valley ringed by canyons and sugar pines along the American River to find a good site for a sawmill. The riverbanks were also a favorite spot of the Yalesumni Indians, who were happy to help Marshall with his carpentry. By the time the mill was nearly finished, its water wheel was too low, however, puddling water around it. So the Indians helped him pound the tailrace ("a sluice cut through a sandbar") down through gravel to bedrock, giving the rig more stability and making the tailrace function as it should—as a sluice. As they dug deeper in the early morning hours on January 24, a small iridescent object in the riverbed, a flash glinting off some metal chips, caught Marshal's eye—he had been noticing a lot of "blossom" or quartz, but this equivocal glitter looked like either "*sulphuret of iron,* very bright and brittle" in his words, or "*gold,* bright yet malleable." Marshall pounded some of the metal on a rock; it was soft and did not break. In the next few days he and his men picked up an ounce or two more, and then he grabbed a pouch of the metal and galloped back to New Helvetia, forty-five miles away.[2]

That was where John Sutter lived, a blond-haired, blue-eyed German-Swiss originally named Johann August Suter who fled Switzerland for America in 1874 rather than face debtors' prison after his dry goods business went belly up. He spent some time working in St. Louis and fur trapping in Oregon, until at the age of thirty-six he arrived at Monterey on the good ship *Clementine,* in 1839, with an Indian boy he bought from Kit Carson for a hundred dollars. The Swiss gendarmes being sufficiently distant, he now felt free to call himself Captain Sutter, lately of "the Royal Swiss Guard of France." He must have charmed the pants off the Mexican governor because soon the captain got Mexican citizenship, a grant of a hundred thousand acres of nice land where the American and Sacramento rivers converge, and an appointment as a regional official in "New Helvetia," another Mexican moniker for their fading California realm. Sutter even resurfaced as a good credit risk: a loan of $30,000 got him Fort Ross, a Russian fur-trading post. It was a real fort, too, with cannons and three-foot-thick walls; but quickly, as we might guess, it was renamed Sutter's Fort and soon became a required stop for every American coming down the long slope of the High Sierra into the Sacramento Valley.[3]

Captain Sutter, who had sent Marshall looking for the sawmill site, cracked open his *Encyclopedia Americana* and perused the entry for "gold." They put Marshall's nuggets on one side of an apothecary's scale, silver on the other, and lowered the scales into water, since the specific gravity of gold exceeds that of silver. The side with the gold dipped low. They took out a pellet and pounded it with a hammer: it filigreed out, but didn't break. Sutter judged it to be gold of a high quality—twenty-three carats or higher. That sent Marshall charging back to the site on his horse in the middle of a rainy night, the first but hardly the last Californian bitten by the gold bug. Sutter knew he should keep the discovery quiet, but given his nature he couldn't help boasting about it. He even sent six ounces of gold to the military governor of Monterey, Col. Richard B. Mason. Desultory and querulous notices appeared in a couple of San Francisco newspapers, attracting little attention. So nothing much happened until May 12, 1848, when a Mormon elder, real estate speculator, and all-around loudmouth named Samuel Brannan went down to San Francisco and waved around a bottle of gold dust, yelling, "Gold! Gold! Gold from the American River!"[4] Brannan ran a store at Sutter's Fort and had been accused by none other than Brigham Young of using "the Lord's money," Mormon tithes, for his own profit (Brannan retorted that he would give the money back when he got a receipt from the Lord). He learned about the gold in March, and in a speculative brainstorm that set the pattern for an entire way of life in California, Brannan bought up every conceivable item that miners might need before traveling down to San Francisco for his fateful announcement.

The American westward movement so far had been amoeba-like, spreading from one homestead or town to another; if trappers and Indian fighters ranged far and wide, the replicating frontier advanced with the family farm and quickly took on a settled character. When gold was discovered, the western edge of the agricultural frontier was still 2,000 miles from the Sierra Nevada, with vast plains, deserts, and the Rocky Mountains in between. It took about six months to cross the continent by wagon train, and five or six months to get to California from New York by ship; crossing the Isthmus of Panama was quicker but opened the traveler to dread diseases (especially malaria). So what? Now pioneering became a stampede as tens of thousands of people from the rest of the country and around the world fell all over themselves to get to the gold fields. Cities and towns emptied all over California, of course, but the news was also a shot heard round the world. By 1851

Londoners were using "California" to mean money—got any California in your pocket?

The next year Engels told Marx that California and Australia (where gold was also discovered) should send them back to the drawing board; here were "two cases not provided for in the *Manifesto:* the creation of large new markets out of nothing. We shall have to allow for this." Marx was so stimulated by the gold discoveries and their effect on the world economy that he decided to begin his studies over, as he says in the preface to the *Contribution to the Critique of Political Economy,* a decision culminating in *Das Kapital.* So fascinating was the glittering metal that he interrupted his theorizing to offer a little textbook entry on placer mining, presented with childlike fascination: gold is found in nature "in its metallic state . . . curious by its yellow colour," Marx wrote; "it finds its way into the sand of rivers" and "the *debris* of mountains;" because of its specific gravity, "even the tiniest pieces can be extracted by stirring gold-bearing sand in water," just using a small pan. Then he draws his conclusion, that the search for this accursed glitter brought distant continents "into the metabolism of circulation," achieving gold's true or final generality in the creation of the world economy.[5] Ultimately, however, it would take a Schumpeter to appreciate the full effects of this explosion because Marx was fixated on the weight of history bearing down on the living ("like an Alp"), whereas the aristocratic Schumpeter, like Tocqueville before him, could appreciate a completely non-European setting where social forces did not combine to preserve the status quo. Why? Because there was none.

Erosion from a flow of molten gold produced when the Sierra Nevada Range first erupted out of the Pacific had slowly leached into the riverbed, creating a "mother lode" of gold-bearing quartz veins that ran continuously for 150 miles from Sutter's Fort up to the North Fork of the Feather River and down south to Mariposa, spreading as much as 2 miles wide in some places; the lode reached an apotheosis at Carson Hill, where someone found a boulder of pure gold weighing just under 200 pounds—the largest ever found in California. (Some say it was only 120 pounds—but so what?) The wide dispersal of the mother lode reinforced the "American" character of this find; relatively few conflicts over claims occurred, mostly it was one miner for one claim amid rough democracy and rough law, fortified by pistols—and when everyone packs a firearm, sober people do the right thing. ("I never lived among a more honest and, apparently, honorable set of men," Nicholas Dawson wrote.) Around six thousand people sought out gold by the end of 1848, but the rush was just beginning: in his message to Congress on December 5 President Polk spoke of "an abundance of gold" in California, and that also set the '49ers in motion. The War Department put 230 ounces of California gold on display, and the Philadelphia Mint declared it to be of equal quality with its own gold coins. The United States had produced a total of 43,000 ounces of gold in 1847; two years later it yielded 1,935,000 ounces—all the addition coming courtesy of Marshall and Sutter. America produced more than 3 million ounces by 1853, almost all of it from California. The yield tapered off in succeeding years, but California continued to be the biggest gold producer in the nation (including Alaska) well into the twentieth century.[6]

The simple technology—puddling river bottom mud and sand in a metal pan and swishing it around looking for "pay dirt"—had been known at least since the Romans. Georgius Agricola explained it in *De Re Metallica* (1556): "The gold particles settle in the back part of the bowl because they are heavy, and the sand in the front part because it is light." This mundane method was a great goad to any adventurer, and for a couple of years it worked to make many people rich, even if doing it all day long was very tiring; $1,000 in a week was not unusual and $40 a day was average, this at a time when an ounce of gold brought $20.66, ordinary clerks made $50 a month, and an upper-middle-class family required an income of around $5,000 a year. By 1852, the peak year, some $80 million in gold had been found (or something over $2 billion in current dollars), mostly by individuals or small operations—a few men in a team operating a mining cradle.[7]

At first all you needed was a sheath knife to pry golf-ball-sized nuggets out of crevices (like finding Easter eggs under the hedges), then a tin pan (placer mining, Agricola's method), later a rocker, "long tom" and sluice—simple and cheap technology, all of it within reach of ordinary individuals: "One man's chance of making a strike [was] about as good as the next man's." Two Germans got started by pushing a boulder to the side and finding a beautiful lump of gold underneath; two men dug out $30,000 in gold from Iowa Hill in one day; God even smiled on a man named Job (Job Dye) who used fifty Indians to retrieve 273 pounds of gold in two months flat. Mc-Williams estimated the average yield in 1849 among four hundred men working the American River at $30,000 to $50,000 a day—while '49ers were still clamoring to get there from all corners of the globe. Long the talisman for the "rugged individualism" of the Anglo frontier, the early days of the gold rush were a study in multiethnic avarice—several thousand from Chile; hundreds from Portugal, Germany, India and Hawaii; free blacks; many Mexicans; and many more Indians than most accounts acknowledge. The biggest foreign group was probably also the best at finding gold: the Chinese lived on rice and dried fish, maneuvered around with small packs, relaxed by smoking opium instead of drinking (thus avoiding whiskey-induced gold swindles), and stayed in place long after the others bolted for new (and often imagined) claims.[8] San Francisco is called *jiu jin-shan* in Chinese, Old Gold Mountain, but that mountain was really up in the High Sierras.

Hardly any of the wealth wound up in tax coffers because the state barely existed and there was no federal income tax. Government was so distant, the gold so dispersed in the mountains, and previous economic development so minimal that big firms and monopolies did not control it—"a democracy in production" made this a "poor man's gold rush." Because so much of the gold stayed in remote California, a virgin market, as currency or investment, the new supply didn't cause prices to implode (gold was $21 an ounce in 1845 and $21 in 1855). Out of the ground came the wealth for innumerable small and large investments in farms, homes, businesses, banks, new industries, and of course field days for swindlers, saloons, and whorehouses. Antonio Coronel, a poor schoolteacher, dug out enough gold in three days to transform his life and get himself elected mayor of Los Angeles four years later; soon he was treasurer of California. Mary Ellen Pleasant, a black woman, found gold in her famed cooking skills, parlaying her restaurant into mining stock and gold speculation, eventually yielding three laundries and several other properties in San Francisco. An Irish ox-cart driver, John Sullivan, pulled out $28,000 in gold all by himself and went on to found the Hibernian Bank. There were many similar stories. Nor did the Civil War disrupt California's growth— quite to the contrary; the state's remoteness meant that it was hardly touched by the war, except as a lucrative source of supplies that provided yet another propulsion forward. Californians kept the war at bay by conjuring with seces- sion should the South win—or even if it didn't; the state was largely self- sufficient and might (again) declare its own republic, or join with Oregon, Washington, Utah, and New Mexico in a "vigorous Caesarian Republic on the Pacific," in the audacious words of one politician.[9]

When Abraham Lincoln signed the bill for a transcontinental railroad in 1862, it was done in part to keep California in the Union. His magnificent second message to Congress, delivered in the midst of war on December 1, 1862, was as much about the continent as the country: he found "no line straight or crooked, suitable for a national boundary upon which to divide" the American "national homestead." Our people find "their way to Europe by New York, to South America and Africa by New Orleans, and to Asia by San Francisco. . . . These outlets, east, west, and south, are indispensable to the well-being of the people inhabiting and to inhabit this vast interior region." In this light, Henry Nash Smith was right to say that for Lincoln, the Civil

War "was but an incident" happening on one part of a spacious continent that brought its own imperatives of unity and integrity upon the nation. Anyway, California had little involvement in the war: Lincoln never extended the draft west of Kansas, and had he mobilized it for the war, California might have seceded from the Union, too. Only one outcome could have impeded the inevitable continental unity: England's constant intrigue to divide (and thus mortally weaken) its up-and-coming American rival into two nations, under the guise of peacemaking.[10]

The population of California was about 15,000 in 1840 and 25,000 in 1848; it had doubled by the summer of 1849, and soared to 165,000 in 1850. Yerba Buena Cove had no more than six buildings in 1840 and exactly 459 people in 1847, when its name changed to San Francisco; it had 35,000 in 1851, but the city doubled or tripled its population every few weeks. Ships choked the harbor and were routinely abandoned, leaving listing hulks years later. A man named John Freaner wrote in October 1849, "It is utterly impossible for any person to keep pace with the onward march of general melioration in all things. . . . I came thither about three months ago, and since that time the town has more than quadrupled in size." The state population grew to 380,000 in 1860 and 865,000 by 1880, by which time its per capita wealth was the highest in the country. Whites would later pride themselves on Los Angeles' seemingly unbroken Anglo-Saxon leadership and preternatural destiny, but California as a state and San Francisco as a city began with a remarkable racial and ethnic diversity. A quarter of the 1850 population was foreign-born, including Europeans (Germans, French, Irish), Mexicans, and especially Chinese. A decade after gold was found almost 40 percent of Californians were foreign-born, compared to 13 percent for the country as a whole. Chinese and Irish were the largest single groups until the twentieth century, and at around 34,000 in 1860, nearly identical in size. Then came Germans (about 20,000), Scots (17,000), French (8,000), blacks (5,000), and Italians (3,000). People born in Mexico counted 9,150, added to several more thousand natives of California. So many Scots, Welsh, English, and Canadians were there that visitors from Britain felt quite at home.[11]

Overnight San Francisco was the effective urban capital of the Far West and the American Pacific, far and away the most diverse city in the Union and soon a great city to rival New York, Boston, and Philadelphia; indeed, California is the only "frontier" state to have begun as an urbanized (or quickly urbanized) society, yet another of its "late"-coming characteristics. "Like the magic seed of the Indian juggler, which grew, blossomed and bore fruit before the eyes of his spectators," Bayard Taylor wrote, "San Francisco seemed to have accomplished in a day the growth of half a century."[12] But it wasn't just any city that the gold rush built: yes, it was a "City on a Hill"—but it was the Sodom and Gomorra of John Winthrop's nightmares. Your average everyman came down from the American River with his pockets bulging; why couldn't anyone do that? Single men came running from all corners of the earth; could a cavalcade of prostitutes be far behind? And what enterprising con artist wouldn't like to relieve the young man of a bit of that "found" wealth? If hustlers stood on every street corner, what would you call the hustle that the Big Four soon pulled off, moving from "dry goods" to world-historical railroad and real estate fortunes in the wink of an eye? Arcadia might be a bit far off (although you wouldn't know it from the breathtaking vantage point of Nob Hill), but so what? As Kenneth Rexroth put it, "nobody cared what you did as long as you didn't commit any gross public crimes" (a city dweller's favorite stipulation), and a singular virtue lay hidden amid the city's overflowing vices: San Francisco was "the only city in the United States not settled overland by the spreading puritan tradition." The residents of the city by the bay had their faults, to be sure, but at least "they were not influenced by Cotton Mather."[13]

In other words, the denizens of this unique American city, then and now, never seemed troubled by the machine in the garden, in total contrast to Los Angeles—probably because they figured it wasn't a garden in the first place. They don't "face East;" they are not humbled by New York City, or by London or Paris, let alone the genteel tradition. To Lord Bryce this was "a New York which has got no Boston on one side of it, and no shrewd and orderly rural population on the other, to keep it in order."[14] Here is easily the most Asian-influenced city in America for the past century and a half, but it doesn't face West either. The Golden Gate forms a magnificent visual barrier to the cold and treacherous waters of the Pacific, and the capacious bay is sufficient in itself. In fact San Francisco's history depicts a naturally occurring phenomenon that defines the rise of the modern city; it could just as easily be somewhere else, were it not for the discovery of gold in 1848. It is a stretch to call it a frontier city, or an artifact of expansionism, or even a city that shares much with the Golden State and its "dream." An infinitely varied human traffic followed in the wake of the "accursed glitter" to make San Francisco a city unto itself.

The folks who made real money, of course, were the gold brokers and the mining suppliers, like John Studebaker who built wheelbarrows, or Levi Strauss, a New Yorker who made rough denim pants favored by miners and founded a blue-jean fortune, or Darius Ogden Mills who was a bank clerk in

New York when he got word of the gold strike. After trying his hand at placer mining he set up a supply shop in Sacramento. Buying his first stock of goods with a mere $40, he turned a $40,000 profit in one year. In the winter of 1849–50 he had a sturdy vault shipped out from New York sufficient to open the "Bank of D. O. Mills." Later he returned to New York and built an early skyscraper at Wall and Broad streets, across from the New York Stock Exchange. With his California grubstake, in other words, Mills founded one of America's great fortunes, and his family went on to own (along with Hearst interests), gold, silver, and copper mines in the Dakotas, Peru, and northern Korea; ultimately his grandson became Herbert Hoover's secretary of the treasury.[15]

George Hearst arrived in California in 1850, tried placer and quartz mining, began trading claims, then when the Comstock news came in 1859 he sold everything and plowed every penny into the Ophir mine near Virginia City, Nevada. The Comstock Lode consisted of some sixty mines a bit east of Lake Tahoe, yielding an astounding $292,726,130 between 1859 and 1882. This silver became the core of the fabulous Hearst fortune. But mining silver in Comstock or copper in Montana required large investments that only big firms and banks could muster, so it did not have the multiplying effect that California gold did: in the century after 1848, Montana, Utah, Idaho, and Arizona produced about $10 billion of copper compared to $2 billion in gold, without this wealth having "anything like the stimulating effect that the discovery of gold produced in California." Later came the Homestake gold mine in the Black Hills, Anaconda Copper in Montana, and by the turn of the century the Cerro de Pasco copper mine in Peru—long a symbol of American imperialism in Latin America. The latter company, like the others, "enjoyed a vertical monopoly controlling fuel, water, and transportation, as well as a company store that served to rapidly ensnare Indian [or American] miners into the system of debt peonage known as *enganche* (hooking)." James Ben Ali Haggin, an associate of William Randolph Hearst, put up $3 million in initial capitalization, Hearst $1 million, D. O. Mills $1 million, J. P. Morgan $1 million, and steel baron Henry Frick put up still another million. Soon the same core group—Hearst, Haggin, and Mills—would own the Oriental Consolidated Mining Company in northern Korea, the largest gold mine in East Asia. Donald H. McLaughlin, chairman of the Atomic Energy Commission's Advisory Committee on Raw Materials from 1947 to 1952, was concurrently president of Homestake Mining and a close associate of the Hearst family; he aggressively moved Homestake out of gold and into uranium production for the government, thus linking the '49ers with the atomic era.

The Mills and Hearst families were a classic example of American expansionism in action, building fortunes and political influence lasting well over a century.[16]

When the easy finds ran out along the mother lode, big companies arrived to dismantle the hills with high-powered hoses called "dictators," pushing thousand of gallons of water per minute through nozzles sixteen feet long and taking 1,500 tons of rock off the side of a mountain in twelve hours ("hydraulic mining," more like hydraulic artillery). The mountainous terrain was pillaged as nearly 50 million cubic yards of sludge went into the rivers every year—and the little fellow was out of luck. But lots more gold flowed out. Ultimately people extracted 106 million ounces of gold from the Sierra, a third of all the gold ever produced in the United States.[17]

California gold and Comstock silver fueled an economic boom that lasted a quarter-century, until the Panic of 1873. It made extractive mining the most valuable industry for decades in the West and bred a mentality of easy riches and zero-sum games. But the Comstock Lode unlocked the full rapaciousness of nineteenth-century capitalism. Like Cronon's harrowing narration of the destruction of Minnesota white pine to build Chicago and its industries, silver mining likewise demolished the pine forests of the High Sierras: every year "not less than eighty million feet of timber and lumber are annually consumed on the Comstock lode," Dan De Quille wrote at the time. "For a distance of fifty or sixty miles all the hills of the eastern slope of the Sierras have been to a great extent denuded of trees of every kind."[18] Entire mountainsides collapsed into rivers, bringing tons of sludge laced with corrosive chemicals cascading all the way to San Francisco. Californians discovered gold, and the machine discovered them.

A Small Matter of Genocide

The gold and silver mania brought on the effective destruction of Indians who resided anywhere near mining claims. On the eve of the American takeover, perhaps 7,000 non-Indians lived in California. Most Indians were "Diggers," food gatherers rather than growers, migrating seasonally; their shelters were "crude huts of sticks, reeds, and mud," their skimpy clothes were mere woven grass, their tools the most rudimentary. They made nice woven baskets but had no pottery and no knowledge of how to make fire. Mark Twain was particularly nauseated by them, but he was hardly alone: "Theirs was the most miserable life lived in North America since the ice retreated," DeVoto wrote. Archaeological evidence has indicated that their culture had been relatively unchanging for several thousand years; "it was probably the simplest culture in all aboriginal North America." The Chumash, who lived along the coast, were mildly elevated by comparison—with a similarly primitive culture but beautiful canoes that plied back and forth to the Channel Islands. They had mostly become "modernized" as indentured servants or slaves of the missions, and few resisted the Americans. Others, like the Modoc who lived along the northern California coast, were peaceful and settled, with a more advanced culture.[19]

Thousands of Indians were murdered in these years in what some scholars believe to be "the clearest case of genocide in the history of the American frontier." Of some 150,000 Indians in California in 1848, only 30,000 remained by 1860. Anthropologist Theodora Kroeber wrote that the Ibero-American invasion of California may have been disastrous, but the Anglo-American was worse because at least the Spanish and the Mexicans did not frown on intermarriage, whereas the Anglos could not countenance differences of color and saw race-mixing as contemptible when it wasn't a sin. That did not stop them from raping and enslaving hundreds of women and children in the Sacramento Valley. Miners murdered Indians and pillaged their settlements with impunity—when pogroms weren't openly sponsored by government officials. In 1851 several federal treaties with California tribes established scattered reservations, but state officials opposed them; in an 1851 message to the legislature, California Governor Peter Burnett remarked with apparent equanimity that "a war of extermination will continue to be waged between the races until the Indian race becomes extinct."[20]

One terrible massacre somehow bequeathed a trope for California's self-image. Some Yahi Indians stole a cow or two in 1853, and whites killed twenty-five Indians in revenge—and so began the extermination of Yahi and Yana Indians, men, women, and children alike; whites liked to hang their scalps outside their homes for fun. Of some three thousand Yana Indians, ten years later only a scattered few bands remained. This remnant began "the Long Concealment," hiding away from whites as best they could. In 1868 thirty-three of them were caught and massacred in a cave north of Mill Creek. A survivor named Ishi hid out in the wilderness, to emerge in 1911 like Rip Van Winkle and then find himself the object of friendly and anthropological curiosity. Theodora Kroeber wrote a book called *Ishi in Two Worlds*, asking if the last of the first Californians might not be a guide to a better future for the state: "respect for nature on its own terms, the need for culture and identity, avoidance of war, the struggle for peace and harmonious patterns of life," in Starr's words.[21]

The Big Four

Levi Strauss may have made a fortune selling his blue jeans to miners, but that was nothing compared to how four other forty-niners parlayed their gold rush earnings into world-historical fortunes. Each has a name instantly associated with contemporary California: Mark Hopkins (the venerable Nob Hill hotel), Leland Stanford (the university), Charles Crocker (Crocker National Bank), and Collis P. Huntington (as in Huntington Beach and any number of other places and monuments named for him or his nephew Henry); a century later their descendants still dominated San Francisco's *Social Register.* They were dubbed the "Big Four," and not just because of their robber baron notoriety: together they weighed in at nearly 900 pounds.

Huntington was born in Connecticut to a poor family, left school at fourteen to work as a peddler, ran a hardware store in Oneonta, New York, and headed west in search of gold. He spent exactly one day trying his hand at mining and ended up "prospering in dry goods" in Sacramento (like the gunfighter William Munny in Clint Eastwood's brilliant western, *Unforgiven*). Specializing in mining supplies, Huntington cornered the market for shovels—but the Big Four all did dry goods. Crocker, a red-bearded blacksmith, crossed the continent in 1850 carrying his worldly belongings "tied up in a cotton handkerchief" and also opened a general store; he became the general boss and overseer of the railroad workers. Hopkins, a cranky workaholic and dry goods proprietor, added little to the Big Four's girth (he was a lean vegetarian) but a lot to their effort: he was a master accountant and money man. Stanford was a master lobbyist—but he also got going as a store owner, together with his brothers on L Street in Sacramento. Unlike most dry goods proprietors, they lent no credit: everything had to be paid in gold. And then, as John McPhee put it, "Cretaceous gold . . . virtually conjured a transcontinental railroad."[22]

The four men gathered on the second floor of the Huntington and Hopkins hardware store on K Street in Sacramento in November 1860 to listen to the real father of the western railway lay out his plans, a construction engineer aged twenty-eight named Theodore Judah. Shortly after he graduated from Rensselaer Polytechnic Institute, Judah built a cantilevered railway through the heights of the Niagara Falls Gorge, convincing many of his engineering genius. He also convinced the Big Four to buy stock in his railway company; used their money to complete a thorough engineering survey in 1861 of the grades, tunnels, curves, and bridges needed for the western line; had a bad falling out with them; and then proceeded to die—of yellow fever, contracted in Panama. The Big Four inherited his plans. Stanford probably helped the project most by getting himself elected governor of California (in 1861); he, Huntington, and Hopkins were all important figures in the state's fledgling Republican Party. Crocker supervised railway construction, that is to say, he drove his workers relentlessly with a fearsome energy, in spite of his imposing bulk. The shrewd and exacting Hopkins kept the books, and Huntington brought in supplies from back East—and especially politicians. "Tigerish and irrational in his ravenous pursuit," Huntington did not wait for American politicians to do the right thing after exhausting all the other alternatives (in Winston Churchill's phrase), he bought and paid for them: sometimes a man "won't do right until he is bribed to do it," Huntington thought. In 1860 the combined assets of these four men numbered about $100,000, but they ventured only some $7,000 of their own money on the railroad while getting the people of Sacramento to provide $400,000; Los Angeles anted up $602,000, and the people of the state, $2.1 million. Eventually the railroad project brought them an estimated $200 million profit, a geometrically mushrooming sum off the original capital—and the money went to them, not to the railroad. In due time the Southern Pacific Railroad (which absorbed the Central Pacific) dominated "the whole region south of the Columbia River and west of the Colorado and Great Salt Lake," in Earl Pomeroy's words. It would be 1910 before anybody else ran a train east from San Francisco, and 1931 before another line ran north from the city by the bay.[23]

The race to build from the east and build from the west began in 1865, just in time to distract Americans from the carnage of the Civil War and to make Lincoln's second message to Congress prophetic—giving everyone a new future to dream about along the meridians of the West, not the latitudes of civil conflict. The Big Four had no trouble getting land through the government, but they had a huge problem finding the necessary labor in the sparsely populated West. They found a solution in China: its laborers were very good and they worked for two-thirds of the wages of whites, saving the Big Four an estimated $5.5 million. "They built the Great Wall of China, didn't they?" Crocker liked to say. The two converging railways raced to the finish line with the whole nation watching, Chinese laborers in the west against Irish in the east; Crocker drove his men with a fiendish intensity. One reporter witnessed Chinese laborers swarm over a sixteen-car supply train, unloading tons of rails, spikes, and bolts in eight minutes flat. They then laid tracks at 144 feet per minute, fastening down a pair of rails every twelve seconds. The rails finally joined at Promontory, Utah (near Ogden), on May 10, 1869. Leland Stanford set down an eighteen-ounce gold spike with a large gold nugget on top; he swung his sledge hammer . . . and missed—an appropriate denouement, since the people who really laid his rails, the Chinese, had been shooed away lest they spoil the commemorative photographs. But the portly dry goods salesman had made his mark, too, a life memorialized in the sandstone porticos reminiscent of Bologna that still distinguish the architecture of Stanford University.[24]

The Big Four now constituted the commanding heights of San Francisco's elite. Crocker, Stanford, and Hopkins all built massive, ornate mansions atop Nob Hill, filling them with European art and the city's social climbers; they ran cable cars up the sheer heights to that panoramic point so they wouldn't have to walk—a necessity, since Crocker crested 300 pounds and Stanford was less than svelte. The abstemious, slender Hopkins lived more frugally, reigning as treasurer of the Central Pacific while living in a rented cottage and resisting his wife's desire to build an enormous turreted mansion—also on Nob Hill. Finally he relented, but the home wasn't finished before he died (in 1878, in a director's car on a railway siding in Arizona).[25]

If Leland Stanford endowed a great university, Collis Huntington lived long enough to endow an empire. In the 1880s he was the lone survivor of the Big Four and one of America's wealthiest men, building grand estates in California and New York and a summer colony for plutocrats in the Adirondack Mountains. Foiling a congressional investigation into the Central Pacific's stupendous corruption by burning fifteen volumes of company books in 1873 was one far-sighted step, and another was to bring his nephew, Henry Huntington, into the railroad business. They drove the Southern Pacific down south, again with thousands of Chinese workers who strung the rails through and across the Tehachapi Mountains with consummate skill; the golden spike broke the earth in September 1876, and a few months later the first carload of California oranges, packed by citrus pioneer William Wolfskill, rolled over the High Sierras and on to St. Louis. Soon hardly any freight moved if the "Pacific Associates"—another name for the Big Four—didn't approve it. Collis, who aged "like a barnacle-encrusted old tortoise," in Bain's words, died in 1900 at his Adirondack retreat while Henry was building a new and even more lucrative empire around his trains and electric trolleys in Southern California. Henry E. Huntington believed that Los Angeles was "destined to become the most important city in this country, if not the world. It can extend in any direction as far as you like; its front door opens on the Pacific, the ocean of the future. The Atlantic is the ocean of the past. Europe can supply her own wants. We will supply the wants of Asia."[26]

Machines to Unify a Continent: The Railroads

American industry came roaring out of the Civil War mobilization to dominate many sectors. In the 1870s pig iron production doubled, coal went up
600 percent, and soon the United States produced more steel than Britain.
Shortly American industry ranked second in the world; Germany may have
had a faster growth rate, but that was because the United States combined
early (textiles) with late development; America was the wave of the future,
pioneering in electrification and communications and a host of other new
technologies.[27] With California in the Union, the conditions were perfect for
laying a railway network across the entire continent.

England and the United States were "early" industrial developers also in
that both relied mostly on the private sector to sustain even the grandest nineteenth-century projects, like railroads (otherwise the United States
exemplified many characteristics of late development). Elsewhere—France,
Japan—the state built the railways and by and large still runs them. The
American state had a distinct role to play, however: supportive adjunct to the
amassing of the greatest capitalist fortunes the world had ever seen. Railroads
were the dominant economic and social force in the decades between the
Civil War and World War II, transforming the country; a truly radical force,
they knit the continent together but also sketched Benton's "geothermic" line
of development. Soon mimetic villages and towns sprouted along the rail
lines, each oriented around the railway and the passenger station and showing
little concern for replicating New England models. A panorama of great cities
emerged, symbolized by architecturally magnificent union stations on a line
running from New York, Washington, and Philadelphia through Pittsburgh,
Indianapolis, St. Louis, Kansas City, Denver, and finally California where the
rails met the City by the Bay and the City of Angels. American railroad
technology was the world's best. Its steel rails were valued all over Europe and
later in Japan, holding up under ten times the tonnage of iron rails; so were
American locomotives, whose traction power increased 100 percent from 1870
to 1910. The grand era of railroads made kingpins like Jay Gould and Jim Fisk
not just fabulously wealthy, but poster boys for a new era of unbridled capitalism: the robber barons wanted the government in when they needed it
(most often to regulate competition and stabilize the industry)[28] and out
when they didn't.

In a manner typical of the expansionist view of what government is good
for, the central state provided huge subsidies and absorbed the risks but left
the enormous projected profits alone. Congress passed the Pacific Railroad

Bill of 1862 creating two corporations to build the transcontinental route, the Union Pacific and the Central Pacific. It authorized the federal government to loan the two companies $16,000 for each mile of level track and up to $48,000 for each mile of mountain track, repayable over thirty years at 6 percent interest. The bill gave the companies a right-of-way that amounted to ten square miles for each linear mile of railroad track. The Union Pacific ended up getting 19 million acres from the government (spending nearly half a million dollars to bribe congressmen helped), the Central Pacific about 7.3 million, and the Great Northern a whopping 40 million acres (but then it didn't get any government loans). Still, the two companies dragged their feet and lobbied for more help: so in 1864 Congress upped the ante to twenty square miles per linear foot and changed the 6 percent bonds into a financial vehicle enabling the companies to issue bonds themselves. Now there was next to no risk for the builders—and so they began their work. The state's largess and particularly the vast land grants "turned the railroad companies into 'empire builders,' landlords on a par with the federal land office itself"—except that unlike Washington, they could charge whatever real estate prices the new, railroad-enhanced markets would bear. Meanwhile the cavalry would control the Indians and immigration officials would look the other way as tens of thousands of Chinese flooded in to build the western system.[29]

Thoreau famously located the train's whistle as the arch despoiler of Arcadia, but Walt Whitman was much more representative in singing of "the metrical, now swelling pant and roar" of the engine, while Emerson embodied the stance of most Americans to this new, earth-shaking technology: once absorbed, it would make a continental Eden accessible to all, not destroy it; it would speed American development by fifty years or more, he thought, and push Americans westward toward a new, intimate relation to the continent—to face West, away from Europe, the right orientation for the country (Emerson thought). For Americans at midcentury the machine came out of the garden, rather than ruining it; however dramatic and transformative the cascading number of American inventions and contrivances might be, they were thought to originate not from great corporations and monopolies but with hardy tinkerers and the "useful arts" cultivated by agrarian mechanics and artisans—pragmatism at work. Even a machine so unmistakably urban and industrial as a steam locomotive was magically encased in polished brass and "German silver" (an amalgam of copper, nickel, and zinc) and trimmed with beautifully burnished woods—ash, black walnut, cherry, and mahogany—that might decorate a drawing room. An American locomotive was a thing of beauty, with an unquestioned usefulness in tying up and shrinking the nation: "I see over my own continent the Pacific railroad surmounting every barrier," Whitman wrote; "I hear the echoes reverberate through the grandest scenery in the world." The railways were the perfect machine to unite East and West, George Ripley said in 1846: "A railroad between the Atlantic and Pacific" would be a continental colossus, "connect[ing] ocean with ocean by iron and granite bands." New England products could now reach China in thirty days by rail and ship, cutting the time by 60 percent.[30]

We are accustomed to hearing in our time that the ubiquity of cell phones, beepers, pocket organizers, electronic mail, and a wireless world have warp-speeded our lives beyond imagination. But the telegraph's shrinkage of communications time, as we have seen, was world-historical—and so was the train's shrinkage of time and space. Andrew Jackson needed a month to travel by horse-drawn coach from Nashville to Washington for his inauguration in 1829; the first trains reduced the trip to three days. Heinrich Heine poetically expressed his feelings upon riding on a train for the first time (from Paris to Rouen) in 1843: "What changes must now occur, in our way of looking at things, in our notions! Even the elementary concepts of time and space have begun to vacillate. Space is killed by the railways, and we are left with time alone. . . . I feel as if the mountains and forests of all countries were advancing on Paris. Even now, I can smell the German linden trees; the North Sea's breakers are rolling against my door."[31]

"Annihilation of space and time" was the ubiquitous phrase accompanying the railway age, compressing Europe to a small, crowded peninsula with cities suddenly just a day train away from each other. Europeans often experienced the rails as a destructive blow to a highly developed artisanal culture and a venerable horse-drawn and riparian travel network.[32] But in America this creation-and-destruction anxiety was felt mostly in thickly settled New England (and thus Thoreau's lament). Otherwise the rails became the first effective means to navigate a continent, to convey anyone with a ticket across the flat prairies and through a mountain wilderness. They brought the Atlantic and Pacific scale of the country, so recently acquired, to immediate fruition as an economic fact and, more important, as something palpable that could be experienced and *seen*. No other country came close to this expanse of useful land, and compared to Germany, which still had to contend with all kinds of internal barriers—taxes, principalities, duchies, Junkers—America was a veritable blank slate; the rails effortlessly created a national market the size of China and a continental garden that the rails ran to and through, revealing it rather than destroying it.

Sea routes and roads had long connected eastern cities, but in the Middle Border most traffic coursed through an extensive riverine system—steamboats, paddle wheelers, long industrial barges. Whereas British railcars resembled carriages with declining appointments, depending on the ticket class (and a third-class seat in France meant an open cattle car), American rail cars were long and broad, with four seats across separated by an aisle—like a steamboat, showing the influence of a great age of river traffic, but also embodying an egalitarian mode of travel: "the classless open car" was another expression of American democracy and yet another reason to welcome this radically new form of transport.[33]

The rails transformed the continent itself into a grid and put Americans on a uniform time schedule. Until the railroads divided the country into four time zones, when it was noon in Chicago it was 11:50 in St. Louis, and 11:27 in Omaha; Illinois had twenty-seven local times, Wisconsin thirty-eight.[34] The railroads, though, finally got Americans looking at their watches and arriving on time to work and everyplace else; indeed the rails put all the industrial world onto a new-new thing: a timetable. The extension of the rails accompanied and stimulated both an industrial and an agricultural revolution, with an enormous leap forward by the turn of the new century when several trunk lines crossed the continent to the Pacific Coast—getting products like wheat, citrus, and heavy-volume minerals (iron ore, coal, copper) out to the national and world markets, boosting real estate values, and knitting the country together: the Acheson, Topeka and Santa Fe in the Southwest, running along the Santa Fe Trail; the Southern Pacific from Los Angeles to New Orleans and thence to a dense, interlaced rail network; the Northern Pacific linking Chicago with the Columbia River—culminating in James J. Hill's Great Northern, which reached Seattle from St. Paul in 1893. When Abraham Lincoln found "no line straight or crooked, suitable for a national boundary" to divide the national homestead, he anticipated a redirection of the determining national axis from north-south to east-west, the manifest destiny of a continent unified by the Promethean industry of the era.

Untimely Texas

Texas, like California, is a large state (second only to Alaska) that also came into the Union courtesy of James K. Polk. It likewise grew out of an imperial past characterized mainly by Spanish indifference, it is arid (west of the 98th meridian), it has big farms, and like California it emerged on the continent "late" in world time. But its peculiarity was very different, a determining untimeliness: late Indian fighting, late plantations, late slavery, late extractive commodities, late to lay down the traditions of the frontier or the cruelties of Jim Crow. So Texas is also a very different state, something noticeable in its population following the war with Mexico: when San Francisco had more than 100,000 residents, Texas's biggest cities were Galveston (13,818) and San Antonio (12,256); Houston was under 10,000, and Dallas was a village of about 3,000 people. The largest city in 1900, when Los Angeles was explod-ing, was San Antonio with about 53,000 people.

Unlike California, until recent history Texas was dominated by a handful of commodities, like cotton or oil, and its rural traditions were strong and lasting—while California had none. Lyndon Johnson grew up in the hill country without running water or electricity; Larry McMurtry witnessed the passing of "the rural, pastoral way of life" and a general poverty in his West Texas teens in the 1940s—and only after that did the words "Texas" and "affluent" go together. Before that there wasn't the time or the money "for much to happen, in social or cultural terms." Texas didn't get a hint of its populous future—or its status today—until the 1933 Chicago World's Fair, where Frigidaire exhibited a fully air-conditioned home.[35] Why? Because Texas is so infernally *hot.* It isn't uncommon for Houston or Dallas to have three-figure temperatures for much of the summer, nor is it a dry heat like Phoenix. Postwar air-conditioning was as determining for Texas's large popu-lation as gold and a temperate climate were for California.

Texas is a microcosm of the continent itself: the 98th meridian divides the state in two: fertile east and arid west. As it happened, Lyndon Johnson's family lived just beyond this meridian in a "dog-run" cabin. It was "a remote and dangerous frontier" in the early 1800s, with most of the dangers coming from fearsome Comanches who ruled Texas until new weaponry arrived to match their horseback fighting skills.[36] But it was cotton and slaves that first populated the territory. Early American arrivals like those accompanying Stephen F. Austin in 1821 were like pioneers on the Oregon Trail a few years later; they sought a fecund, well-wooded and -watered terrain and so they settled down near the rivers, stopping just short of the 98th meridian. They were illegal aliens, but Mexico initially welcomed them with land grants proffered at minimal fees, and about 3,000 of them had settled by 1823. A little over a decade later, 30,000 Anglos resided in East Texas, along with some 3,000 black slaves; Mexicans were now a minority.

Pitched battles between Anglo settlers and Mexicans in 1836 led to mu-tual slaughter and the declaration of the Lone Star Republic on March 2, the heroic symbol of which, of course, was the resistance at the Alamo by 188

Texans—who held off 3,000 Mexican troops for twelve days in San Antonio until they finally perished. Antonio López de Santa Anna had won a great victory at the Alamo, it seemed, until Sam Houston's forces trapped 1,500 of his men along the San Jacinto River a few weeks later and demolished them. A day later Houston captured Santa Anna, negotiated an end to the fighting, stuck a ball and chain on his leg, and threw the Mexican president in jail. It was the first of several American sequences of violence-putsch/revolution-republic-annexation, a settler conquest of another's sovereign territory that California soon imitated. The Texas republic was now independent and like California it had "huge tracts of land free for the taking," but it remained outside the Union because opponents disdained bringing in another slave state (statehood finally came a decade later). It was also a republic with imperial pretensions, claiming dominion south to the Rio Grande, northwest to Santa Fe, and even into present-day Wyoming. Finally, it was a republic that would join the Union but would long hold to the view that this was a union of sovereign states, brooking no outside interference.[37]

A Southern State

The American narrative of Texas is about the Alamo, gunfighters, Comanches, cowboys, longhorns on the Chisholm Trail, big oil, big hair, and colorful politicians. It rarely accommodates Texas's central place in southern history as a slave and cotton state of the Confederacy. Yet cotton and slavery drove the populating of Texas and helped make the American South the source of almost two out of every three cotton bales sold in the world by 1840. Around the time Texas declared independence (1836), perhaps 3,500 Spanish settlers lived there, most of them raising cattle. A rush of immigration by white settlers quickly overwhelmed them in the 1830s and 1840s. Indian numbers were similar or perhaps even smaller, mainly a few thousand Apaches and Comanches. A thinly settled region rich in resources with a wonderful coastline, it was child's play (except for the Alamo and a few other glitches) for settlers to declare the Lone Star Republic and then petition for membership in the Union. But many of the newcomers were slave owners (when Austin led 300 families into Texas, this colony was supposed to be slave-free, but soon about 400 slaves lived among a white settler population numbering around 2,000), and so Texas came into the union in 1845 as a slave state. On the eve of the Civil War, Texas had over 182,000 slaves living amid a white population of about 430,000, just over 40 percent. Like the South, it was a good place to raise cotton—so long as labor cost was kept at slave-reproduction rates. After the Civil War, Texas was a Jim Crow state for black sharecroppers (and also for Mexicans), who lived in segregated housing and were denied service in restaurants and at lunch counters. Well into the 1940s a town proudly displayed a sign reading: "Greenville Texas: the blackest land, the whitest people." It is striking that Simone de Beauvoir's first—and nauseating—glimpse of Jim Crow during her travels in 1947 happens soon after her Greyhound Bus crosses into Texas from New Mexico.[38]

Alongside big plantations sat small family farms. Eli Whitney's "gin" was essentially a cylinder fitted with wire teeth that pulled cotton through a screen, separating the seed from lint; a worker who before might clean one pound of cotton a day could now clean fifty. Instead of dozens of slave gangs on the plantations, now a small farmer could raise cotton and get it ginned in town. Moreover, as poor southern whites moved west, small farmers and slaveholders alike worked the cotton fields. But as Oscar Lewis nicely put it, cotton and the Civil War made Texas appear "too southern, hence Confederate, defeated, poor, and prosaic."[39] Nor could an aristocracy of planters romanticize life here—the planters and the cotton were both too new. Better to go with cowboy boots, Stetson hats, and a Colt 45.

A Western State

The Nueces Valley at the southern tip of Texas, where Mexico, the Rio Grande, and the Gulf Coast come together, and the starting point for the Mexican War, also became the starting point for a new kind of American society: the kind most Americans still associate with their imaginings of Texas. Large-scale cattle production for eastern markets produced a sharp increase in wealth and a culture formed around cattlemen, cowboys, and horse riding that soon spread across the plains; it didn't last that long as a social formation, but long enough to produce several great fortunes (the vast King Ranch still occupies large portions of the Nueces Valley) and the central, archetypical figures and myths of American expansionism.

Cattle have stomachs with four chambers that process grass into food and its byproduct, gas—literally methane; amazingly, their flatulent exhaust makes a large contribution to greenhouse gases. What Walter Prescott Webb called the "empire of grass" stretched from southern Texas well northward and westward into the plains, a vast, open environment of mild climate, sufficient water, and feed (grass) free for the taking as far as the eye could see. Cattlemen ran independent kingdoms in this empire, doing things their own way and dismissing with any kind of government—unless they needed its help with water or rights of way, of course. After the Civil War settled the issue of slavery and Texan loyalties, the state had about 5 million cattle, worth $4 apiece there but $40 in Kansas City or Chicago. Whoever got them to the railhead would make a fortune: take an initial capital of $8,000 ($4 a head), drive 2,000 head of cattle to Abilene, and turn over $80,000, minus the cost of supplies and the mere dozen cowboys needed to do the job.

Over the next fifteen years 5 million head got heaved to market, primarily over thousand-mile-long trails to railheads like Sedalia in Missouri or Abilene in Kansas, for movement to the Chicago gallows as cattle and (after the "disassembly line") to eastern cities as steaks. Economically Texas divided into arid cattle territory west of Dallas and Austin, where in a thousand square miles less than one hundred people lived, and the fertile East Texas, with one person for every square mile. But that was only Texas: a new way of life spread across almost the entirety of the Great Plains from 1865 to about 1885, and then faded out almost as quickly when barbed wire and windmill-drawn water made homesteading and stock raising feasible in the same region, and when railroads arrived through most of the West to pick up the cattle. (Texas led all other states in laying down rails, and by 1904 it ranked first in railroad mileage.)[40] But this economic and social formation never faded from the American mind: the free, open range, the ranch and the cattle baron, a handful of men on horseback wrestling thousands of longhorns up to the railhead became the essence of a new, romantic legend, another lost past like the closing of the frontier or the mechanized gobbling up of the garden, but a drama with far more compelling characters set against the matchless natural panorama of the West.

The Benighted but Manly West

Most Americans find it impossible to separate what they know or don't know about the West from the Hollywood westerns they have seen. It is our only regional drama. We don't have "easterns" or "northerns"—and our only real "southern" is *Gone with the Wind*. The primary concern of southern literature, fiction and nonfiction, is race, a subject not for John Ford myths but for the depths of a Faulkner. The primary concern of the western is the lone, taciturn individual riding into town to set things straight: Alan Ladd dueling in the mud with Jack Palance in *Shane*; Gary Cooper defending the town while the good citizens cower in *High Noon*; Clint Eastwood tearing up the saloon in *Unforgiven* to avenge the murder of his friend, who happened to be black (like many cowboys); and the apotheosis—Marion Morrison of Glendale, otherwise known as John Wayne, a "perfect mold" through which to pour "the inarticulate longings of a nation wondering at just what pass the trail had been lost." Even so rock-ribbed an Atlanticist as Henry Kissinger confessed that he liked to think of himself as "the cowboy who rides all alone into the town." (Henry playing the Lone Ranger is less difficult to imagine than Henry on a horse.) The final proof of Hollywood's saturation of the western imaginary, however, is Jane Kramer's "last cowboy"—Henry Blanton, foreman of a large ranch in the Texas panhandle, who learned cowpuncher lore by watching Chill Wills, examined *High Noon* and *The Virginian* for pointers, wore black because Gary Cooper did, and paraded in front of the mirror to get his stance just right: "his eyes narrowed and his right hand poised over an imaginary holster."[41]

Red River was the first movie I ever saw (1948), Howard Hawks's tour de force starring John Wayne in one of his best performances. Cattle rancher Tom Dunston embodied all the virtues of the cowboy: adventurous, strong, courageous, direct, silent (a man of few but telling words), a self-reliant individual not just home on the range but free as a bird, a stoic living by a rough code of honor (never shoot a man in the back, never tolerate a coward), deploying self-contained coercive power: a Colt 45 and a Winchester repeating rifle. (The diminutive Oklahoma outlaw Al Jennings amended the Declaration of Independence when he memorably remarked that "a Colt's 45 makes all men equal.") The Winchester was just as famous as the Colt: a lever-action breech rifle that fired several shots without reloading, John Wayne memorialized it in his films: "Get me my Winchester." (The Winchester factory in New Haven displayed a bronze statue of Wayne in its lobby; it finally closed in January 2006.)[42]

Most of *Red River* consists of Wayne and his crew driving 10,000 head of cattle a thousand miles up the Chisholm Trail to Abilene. Less evident is a fleeting parable on Polk and Mexico: at the beginning Wayne rides down to the Rio Grande and claims a huge swath of land; a Mexican shows up to say the estate is owned by one "Don Diego" living 400 miles to the south. Wayne scoffs at him and moments later shoots the man off his horse. (Later in the film a sidekick remarks that Wayne "took empty land.") Even more fleeting is Hawks's temerity in invoking *Brokeback Mountain* half a century before its time: the gay actor Montgomery Clift prefigures his role in *From Here to Eternity*, an accomplished but reluctant gunfighter whom Wayne punches around to the point where Clift finally fights back, whereupon another character says, "You two love each other"—for the second time in the film.

A hardy lone man, a rough-hewn but fair individualist, laconic, stoic, unburdened by history, bringing a violent justice to the frontier: John Wayne again. His talent was not acting; he couldn't act, or rather, he had but one act: cowboy. Either Marion Morrison looked like a cowboy when he was spotted on a Glendale tennis court, or Hollywood made cowboys look like him. Wayne didn't always play a cowboy, but when he was a soldier or a cop or hunting Reds for HUAC he recapitulated the same character in a different place—and if and when he didn't, no one remembered. The singular role that he embodied projected strength, determination, and courage in a powerful physique of feline carriage. An actor projects character through his movements, Garry Wills and others have written, and Wayne became the graceful celluloid fulfillment of an apparently unconflicted masculinity (so maybe Wayne was an actor?). In *Red River* he walks among a multitude of Texas longhorns in his Stetson cowboy hat, leather chaps, boots clinking with spurs, moving easily through their midst, as if he commanded the cattle and they followed him. It proved to be an archetypal role, and Gerald Mast thought no one else could have played it. Wayne wasn't just a cowboy, he was an American cowboy: he was an American: he was "Manifest Destiny on the hoof," in Garry Wills's words. Americans ranked John Wayne number three among favorite movie stars—not in 1948, but in 2006, twenty-seven years after his death. Of course, Wayne wasn't always loved: when he put on his Stetson, six-guns, and spurs and strode onto the stage at the Aiea Heights Naval Hospital in Hawaii in 1945, marines wounded in the Okinawa campaign booed him off the stage.[43]

No one escapes the cowboy legend. I have seen a picture of Bill Clinton as a boy, dressed head to toe in a Hopalong Cassidy outfit with pearl-handled revolvers at each hand. I got the same head-to-toe wardrobe on my seventh birthday. Former Joint Chiefs chairman John Shalikashvili learned English by watching John Wayne movies. Sherwood Anderson played cowboy-and-Indian games when growing up, but by the time he was an adult he could hardly believe he had done so.[44] Ronald Reagan and George W. Bush donned cowboy attire and went out to the back forty to chop wood or clear underbrush, as a centerpiece of their political imagery. If Bush seemed to force himself into the macho image, hunching his shoulders and trying to look tough,[45] Reagan learned in Hollywood that you do it with aplomb, not with sweat and beady brow.

No Duty to Retreat

Violence attended every step of the cowboy myth and remains permanently connected to the state of Texas. "Murder was too harsh a word to apply to his performance," Webb wrote of the western gunman, the death of an enemy was "a mere incident, as it were." The code only demanded that the gunman "must give notice of his intention" even if the action—murder—followed on the notice like "a lightning strike."[46] The code developed in the absence of law, because the range was lawless; an offender was not a criminal but an "outlaw." This was incomprehensible to the easterner accustomed to the rule of law and therefore strange, exotic, fascinating. Central to the code was the "no duty to retreat" doctrine, that a person was legally justified "in standing one's ground to kill in self-defense." This was purely American, having no English common law background, and instead grew out of ideals of mas-culine bravery on the frontier. Although this doctrine by no means applied just to Texas (the Supreme Court upheld it in 1921), it seems to have had greater application there, entering and never leaving the culture. When law came it was in the form of the Texas Rangers, who began as a mounted militia trying to keep Indians at bay and protect settlers from raids and evolved into a legendary force that combined vigilante justice with professional and (by 1840) legal armed force. They ended up, along with many cowboys, small ranchers, and Klansmen, forming the Border Patrol, where many of the rough rules of the Wild West became institutionalized—like being "a little quick on the trigger."[47]

Few things are more satisfying to the viscera than retributive violence, a bad guy getting what he deserves. Texas-style violence is deeply human be-cause everyone, at least at the first spasm, loves the instant gratification of a wrong righted, revenge on the wing, the good triumphing over the bad. John Wayne embodied this American catharsis: someone mouths off to you, well, don't say a word, just punch him out. Recently a British parliamentarian, George Galloway, came before our Senate and unleashed a withering tirade at a committee supposedly investigating him, accusing his accusers of lying, chicanery, and aggressive war, while remaining coolly in control of himself. It was artful and convincing parliamentary behavior, perhaps typical for Britain, but in many state legislatures he would have been punched or thrown out of the building before getting to his third sentence. But think what Texas pio-neers faced: in 1840 a combined force of 700 Comanches and Kiowas roared through towns like Victoria and Linnville, killing everyone in sight and capturing fully 1,500 horses. This scourge was the Indians' salutary (and no doubt deeply satisfying) revenge for the pioneers having lured their headmen into a trap where thirty warriors and a number of their women and children died. And then the vigilantes-cum-police named the Rangers took more revenge against the Indians in a continuous cycle, yielding tales and sagas that frightened people for generations, even though most Comanches were on the reservation by 1875.[48] Texas in these years recalls Martin Sheen's remark in *Apocalypse Now:* "Charging a man with murder in these circumstances is like handing out speeding tickets at the Indy 500."

The code of retributive justice and immediate satisfaction still lives in Texas, of course, even under the rule of law; until recently men who killed their wife's lover were routinely acquitted of murder. But Hollywood did more than any other force to keep this code before the American people, long after it had run its course in the West. The cowboy is a killer, but only in a fair fight—and he kills the people who need killing (just like American soldiers abroad). He doesn't shoot a man who is not part of the code (like, say, an effete eastern dandy). He is chivalrous to the ladies and supremely loyal to his friends. In the climactic scene of *Unforgiven,* Clint Eastwood slides into a barroom and empties his shotgun into the owner: "Why you yellow-bellied coward," Little Bill says, "You just shot an unarmed man!" "He should'a armed himself" is Eastwood's retort, which seems to violate the code until we understand that two values are in conflict: the owner was indeed unarmed, but he allowed Eastwood's murdered friend to be displayed in a coffin out front of the saloon—so he got what he deserved. After Eastwood cleans out the place, the eastern pantywaist, who had fainted during the gun battle, asks him how he single-handedly took down so many men. It was lucky, he said; "I've always been lucky when it comes to killin' folks."

Lyndon Baines Johnson was a native son of the Pedernales, of central Texas and the 98th meridian, and couldn't hide it from anyone if he tried. Richard Maxwell Brown sought to link the endemic violence of this region to Johnson's prosecution of the Vietnam War.[49] No doubt others do the same for George W. Bush and Iraq. But central Texas was an extreme version of a general problem, the extraordinary violence with which white Americans confronted people of color everywhere, while determining to ignore it, forget it, or pretend that it never happened. Which is more difficult to understand: how Johnson's Texas upbringing explains his championing of civil rights for blacks, or how a Boston Brahmin like McGeorge Bundy should have had so much more to do with catastrophic violence in Vietnam than President Johnson? In Texas the American strain of violence which Brown depicts so well persisted because of slavery, the necessities of Jim Crow, its location next to Mexico and the interior presence of so many Mexicans, the encounter with ferociously effective horse-mounted Indians, and a prolonged dilation of the frontier mentality in the form of Texas Rangers and the cowboy as myth and reality (remnant cowboys still corral longhorns today). "Comanche County" might be the best example of this survival; known for its night-riding

Committee of 100 and endemic mob violence in the 1880s, in the 1940s it still had a reputation for lawlessness.[50]

White Studies

If cotton culture came in the east, cattle in the northwest, and eventually petroleum everywhere, south Texas departed from the slave and Confederacy or *latifundia* narrative. It was and is a classic borderland region mingling Anglo, Mexican, Spanish, African, and later English, Polish, German, and Czech influences, yielding extraordinary "social heterogeneity and hybridity." Particularly it yielded lots of Mexicans and still does, leading to high rates of intermarriage and sharp difference with the Confederate South. Central Texas had yet a different mix, being the "west" of the cotton belt and the "north" of the cattle-breeding south, bringing together blacks and whites from the slave states with Mexicans and Anglos from the Southwest, and putting industrialized cotton alongside the small farms of poor people— plantations met haciendas and they both met picayune tenant farms. (Texas had 300,000 sharecroppers and tenants in 1930.) Amid this diversity, once again a social and cultural definition of white skin animated elite pretensions.

In the center of the Lone Star State Neil Foley found *white* whites, and whites who weren't quite white: "white trash," "scrubs and runts," "worthless human silt," "cotton-mill swill"—people at risk of losing their white-skin privilege. And always, there was a scientist who could lend these invidious distinctions some kind of validity: "poor white trash" became "cacogenic" (bad gened) whites; "race scientists" like Lothrop Stoddard warned "Nordics" that "defective" whites were screwing up the gene pool, and even the president agreed (Calvin Coolidge, so. . . .). Maybe these degraded white people needed to be sterilized, the experts said—including Boston Brahmin Oliver Wendell Homes, whose most notorious Supreme Court opinion supported a Virginia case in which a retarded young white woman was sterilized: "cutting the Fallopian tubes" of those who "sap the strength of the State" may be necessary, Holmes wrote, lest the country be "swamped with incompetence" (so?). The (low) wages of whiteness were smuggling in class difference, and for anyone with eyes to see, demolishing racism itself. Central Texas was "highly miscegenated" from the word go: German farmers, Czech dairy men, poor Irish Catholics ("niggers inside out"), and pea pickers from the piney woods of Alabama were polluting whiteness itself. Germans established many orderly communities in and between San Antonio and Houston, with German-language newspapers in their towns, but they were still Ben

Franklin's "Palantine boors" to wealthy whites. Of course, all the whites—high and low—thought they knew a black when they saw one. But blacks, too, had intermarried (or copulated, or got raped) with whites, Indians, and Mexicans for generations. Hardy men of whatever "race" worked the fields, and the women—well, a lot of women did too, as it happened. One of William Faulkner's tenant farmers tells a landlord he can put "six hands" into the field—four of them women.[51]

In the South you were either white or black, judged by as little as a drop of blood. That was the past. Central Texas turns out to be another microcosm for the country, in the here and now, of all the race, class, and gender myths Americans live by—underlining Richard Walker's point that "racism is not an unalloyed quality of whiteness but a nerve that can be agitated or calmed depending on circumstances and leadership (as we can see in our own time)." Texas differed completely from California, however, in having almost no Asians until the last few decades. When tens of thousands of Chinese lived in California in the 1870s and constituted 30 percent of the population in Idaho, there were 25 such individuals in Texas. When California's Chinese population reached its pre–World War II height in 1890 of 107,488, Texas had 710 Chinese. Other Asians were equally scarce. A few hundred Japanese came to Texas to grow rice after Saibara Seito (a graduate of Doshisha University in Kyoto and former parliamentarian) opened a rice plantation near Webster in 1903 and succeeded in producing two to three times more rice per acre than local farmers. Their good business reputations did not keep some 450 Japanese-American Texans from getting interned in one of three concentration camps opened in the state during the war. The Asian-American population remained small until after the 1965 immigration law, when it grew into the tens of thousands. But as late as 2000 there were barely more than 650,000 Asian-Americans in Texas, less than the number in Chicago and several other big cities.[52]

Texas is thus a diverse state that the dominant narratives—cowboy or cotton or oil man—typically elide. One film doesn't, though: Terrence Malick's *Days of Heaven* (1978), which presents a gorgeous panorama of the Texas panhandle in the days just after World War I. Sam Shepard is a wheat farmer presiding over a large Victorian home in the middle of nowhere, with giant combines coursing through his mammoth estate. Texas had fields of one's wildest dreams, just like California: Henrietta Chamberlain King of Corpus Christi had 1.4 million acres, C. W. Post of "Post Toasties" fame had 200,000 acres, and the marriage of vast tracts for cotton or cattle created a highly concentrated and powerful landed oligarchy.[53] The seasonal workforce was as varied as California's, too, and in Malick's film, field hands—Mexican, black, German, Polish, Chinese, perhaps Ukrainian and Russian, maybe Native American—don't talk to each other, indeed they can't, they converse in their own languages, so the soundtrack is a record of murmured unknown tongues. The high technologies of the early twentieth century accumulate at odd moments, like the birds in Hitchcock's film by that name: Model Ts, a motorcycle, a small airplane. Great open spaces, vast fields of wheat and cattle, the transforming effects of technique, a polyglot population doing the hard work but internally divided, the myth of wealth springing from the head of a single charismatic individual. For my money it is the best Texas film Hollywood has produced (and it produced many-many).

Black Gold

For decades Spindletop Hill was thought to be a worthless heap of salt, pullulating with sulphur and stinky water, but a one-armed man named Pattillo Higgins wanted to stick a drill through it anyway. He hit several dry holes until it blew out one fine morning—and a glistening slick black column 6 inches wide and 125 feet tall towered above. Spindletop erupted on January 10, 1901, just outside Beaumont, spewing 100,000 barrels a day over the earth until it was finally capped (back then successful wells pumped a hundred barrels a day). Derricks sprouted like mushrooms after a hard rain, and Beaumont grew from less than 10,000 to 30,000 in a few weeks; land prices went from $40 to $100,000 an acre, and farmers would sell out for $20,000, only to watch a speculator unload their land twenty minutes later for $50,000. Four years later another huge strike, called the Glenn Pool, came in near a small village called Tulsey Town; it became Tulsa, "Oil Capital of the World." Both strikes set off explosive growth and fevered speculation throughout Texas and Oklahoma: "Petrolia in 1904, Electra in 1911, the Ranger field in 1917," they just kept coming until "petroleum was found under the majority of Texas counties." The state eclipsed California in oil production by 1928, but just two years later came a fantastic strike in East Texas, and many more in far west Texas after World War II.[54] The nation's largest petrochemical industry grew out of these finds, usually producing four-fifths of total American output—but this industry wasn't labor intensive. The popularity of television soap operas about the Dallas superrich and their "ostentatious vulgarity" reflected the reality of a vast but still peripheral state with no authentic middle-class narrative, a working class nothing like the midwestern industrial states, and a highly diverse but scattered and weak underclass.

The newer discoveries were by independents, and they fought off Standard Oil's attempts to bring them under its control. Populists and the state government backed Texas "little oil" against big oil, setting up a conflict between nationally based independent firms and integrated multinational conglomerates that would last for decades. Texas regulated the independents and got most of the tax revenue, and the government plowed money back into the state—for example, founding the University of Texas. California oil firms, too, like Union Oil and Southern Pacific, were independent of the majors, thus establishing the conditions for major industrial conflict that spilled over into politics—most obviously with H. L. Hunt of Hunt Oil, who loathed the Rockefellers and routinely accused them of trying to control the world, a split that deeply affected the postwar Republican Party.

If Hunt became notorious for bankrolling the John Birch Society and for his conspiracy theories involving the Rockefellers (not surprising), communists (?), and the United Nations, Sid Richardson and Clint Murchison were more representative of wealthy oil men. In fact Richardson was the real Texas thing, a wildcatter who borrowed $40 from a friend's mother in Wichita Falls during the Depression and hit black gold in the Keystone and Slaughter fields in West Texas. Soon hugely wealthy and devoted to the industry, he was a lifelong bachelor who conducted his business from a drugstore in Fort Worth (while buying up huge chunks of the downtown). He gave away most of his fortune when he died in 1959 but reserved $11 million in oil assets for that generous friend: his nephew, Perry R. Bass. Perry had learned the business at Sid's knee, and prospered beyond anyone's dreams in 1930s Wichita Falls: the Basses sold Sid Richardson Energy Services for $1.6 billion in 2005, a mere fraction of a family fortune estimated in recent years at $9 to $11 billion by Forbes; much of this growth owed to the efforts of Perry Bass's oldest son: called Sid. Like the Bechtels in San Francisco or the Wrigleys in Chicago, the secretive Bass family shuns publicity and rarely talks to the press. Like the Bushes, they send their sons to Yale.[55]

Clint Murchison made his vast fortune not from drilling oil wells—although he drilled many—but from sitting at the nexus of the industry and how it was run and regulated in Texas and Washington: leasing oil rights, running pipelines, and drilling wells using other people's money, with his main eye on tax advantages—especially the oil depletion allowance. Oil exists naturally, of course; it isn't as if people grow it. They find it and lay claim to it. But after intense lobbying and the exchange of unknown sums of cash, oil came to be treated as if it were the personal property of the finder, an asset the depletion of which would entitle him to a tax deduction: the notorious oil depletion allowance enabled owners to exempt 27.5 percent of their oil-derived income from taxation.[56] Texas Democrats like Sam Rayburn and Lyndon Johnson became diehard defenders of the oil industry and the breathtaking depletion subsidy. Here was just another example of freedom Texas style, where the state was useful when compliant—and any government infringement on whatever an oil man wanted to do was an outrage, bordering on communism. Perhaps that is why Murchison, Richardson, H. L. Hunt, and other oil men loved Senator Joseph McCarthy, bringing him down to their ranches so often that he was called "the third senator from Texas."

Between the Nueces and the Rio Grande, prairie pirates and horse rustlers are long gone, but two of the most powerful political families in the state reside there, on the mammoth King and Armstrong ranches. When Vice President Dick Cheney rose from a crouch looking for grouse and shot his friend Harry Whittington's face full of buckshot, he was hunting on the Armstrong Ranch; Katherine Armstrong divulged this news many hours after the fact by calling a friendly local newspaper. The Armstrong family is one of the most effective clusters of political power in the Republican Party, a kind of Hyannisport south of Corpus Christi. Over a half-century Tobin and Anne Armstrong raised thousands of cattle and perhaps hundreds of politicians: they counseled Presidents Nixon, Ford, Reagan, and both Bushes, raising oodles of campaign funds for all of them. Gerald Ford made Anne Armstrong ambassador to the Court of St. James, and when he was governor George W. Bush appointed both her and her daughter Katherine to prestigious posts in Texas. When Bush's political consigliere Karl Rove opened his first consulting firm, Tobin Armstrong provided much of the financing. Anne Armstrong is also a powerful lobbyist whose clients included James Baker's law firm; she made $760,000 in lobbying fees in 2004 and 2005 alone. She and her husband were "pioneers" in the 2000 election, defined as people who raised at least $100,000 for George W. Bush.[57]

Conclusion: The Lights Come On All at Once

In the literature on California, Carey McWilliams is almost alone in grasping the spurts and surges, the herky-jerky movement, and the telescoping of change that characterized the state's development over the past century and a half. For him it was the key to California's exceptionalism: "California has not grown or evolved so much as it has been hurtled forward, rocket-fashion, by a series of chain-reaction explosions." If he indulged metaphors from the leading technologies of his time, he had also just experienced the shock of explosive, transformative growth and change since Pearl Harbor. McWilliams was not theorizing but observing a century of California history—the 1949 centennial of the gold rush when "the lights came on all at once, in a blaze, and they have never dimmed."[58]

But California's pattern of growth was more than just spurts and lunges forward: it was combined, compressed, concatenated, synchronized development across multiple force fields of wealth, technology, energy, and people. It was recent—everything since 1849—meaning that it was "late" in world time; it also occurred in a vacuum of previous development because California was truly virgin land. Rooted interests did not have to be shoved aside or deconstructed or disestablished or transformed as new ones emerged. Growth generated enormous momentum, not only catching up quickly but surpassing other parts of the country and the world, thus locking in advantages that accumulated systematically over time. The technology behind the discovery of gold in 1849 was as simple as it could be, but it coincided with a great burst of industry in America and the world—in applications of the steam engine, new technologies and machines set to work in the wheat fields, the extension of railroads, the nearly instant communications of the telegraph, widely spreading print media, with a corresponding shrinking of the world that made the movement of masses of people possible. The gold rush set off a mass migration that for the first time gave California a significant population, but it would not have been possible without the new technologies of mass transportation and communication. Had this pattern ended in a typical boom and bust fashion, like Texas, it would not hold our attention; but California has had one spurt after another: gold, wheat, citrus, oil, real estate, canned citrus, automobiles, lettuce (called "green gold"), Hollywood films, aircraft, wartime industrial production, cold war defense contracts, intercontinental ballistic missiles, real estate (again and again), the microprocessor, the Internet boom. Often they have combined together, as in the water, electricity, oil, citrus, tourism, autos, films, and housing boom in Southern California in the first three decades of the twentieth century. If the American River was the gift that kept on giving to a multitude of '49ers, California is the gift and that never stops giving—a Cripple Creek all of our own.

CHAPTER FIVE

Abroad in Search of Monsters to Destroy

Practically we own more than half the coast on this side, dominate the rest, and have midway stations in the Sandwich and Aleutian Islands. To extend now the authority of the United States over the great Philippine Archipelago is to fence in the China Sea and secure an almost equally commanding position on the other side of the Pacific—doubling our control of it and of the fabulous trade the Twentieth Century will see it bear. Rightly used, it enables the United States to convert the Pacific Ocean almost into an American lake.

—Whitelaw Reid

Manifest Destiny had a second run half a century later, half a world later really, because of the turmoil driven by an entirely different geographic axis: the North-South Civil War. The drive to the Pacific hardly ceased, but it was a people's movement and not dependent on events in Washington or elsewhere. The gold rush populated California overnight. Pioneers kept arriving in the western states, and two new ones emerged on the shores of the Pacific: Oregon and Washington. But the continent nearly broke in two in the 1860s, concentrating minds on the grand themes of the South that barely touch upon the concerns of this book—or the untransacted destiny of the West. Destiny arrived, however, in a confrontation with the oldest American empire.

The war with Spain began with the sinking of the *Maine* in Havana Harbor on February 15, 1898, a massive explosion that took the lives of 266 men—and an explosion which every American believed to have been determined by Madrid. President McKinley had dispatched this ungainly battleship, sporting four ten-inch guns, to Havana in case American citizens might need evacuation amid the sporadic war ongoing in Cuba since 1895, when some 30,000 armed insurgents launched an insurrection against Spanish rule to the cheers of many Americans. But war between the United States and Spain was avoidable until the *Maine* exploded and the famed "yellow press" kicked up an incessant racket. (William Randolph Hearst offered $50,000 to find the criminals who used a "secret infernal machine" to demolish the warship.) And so a reluctant, sleepless, and haggard William McKinley authorized the strike that Teddy Roosevelt, Henry Cabot Lodge, Whitelaw Reid, and their friends had long anticipated. The army was a mere 27,865 strong in 1898, but volunteers quickly swelled its ranks, this time to over 200,000 men, and it was soon reorganized into a modern fighting force by Secretary of War Elihu Root. It was the newly enlarged and competent navy, however, that struck the first and hardest blows.[1] Admiral George Dewey's decisive attack on the fleet at Manila provided a large mass of American patriots with another lightning victory and dealt a quick death blow to the Spanish empire in the Pacific. Of course it was hard to tell here (and in much of the war) whether Dewey was brilliant or the Spanish incompetent. In any case, he outgunned them two-to-one, with the Spanish guns ranging from antiques to brand new cannons that somehow they had forgotten to mount. In Cuba an opera bouffe ensued "in which an enfeebled Spain," in Robert Dallek's words, "outdid the United States in military ineptitude."

Easy initial victories in Manila and Havana cost the lives of a mere 770 Americans, but as with Korea, Vietnam, and Iraq, the easy initial victories gave way to years of bloody and inconclusive warfare, this in spite of commanding officers skilled in Indian fighting: Walter L. Williams discovered that 87 percent of the generals who fought Filipino rebels had also fought Indians, but the most illustrious was Brigadier General Arthur MacArthur, who at the age of eighteen had distinguished himself at Missionary Ridge in the Civil War, who fathered Douglas MacArthur, and who commanded 5,000 soldiers—all of them "totally ignorant" of the Philippines.[2]

Soon they put their ignorance into action in a dirty war that lasted nearly three years. Men, women, and children were slaughtered; captured guerrillas were tortured with the "water cure" (forcing water down the throat) among other techniques; one town after another was put to the torch, destroying food stocks (1 million tons of rice and 6,000 homes destroyed in just one week in 1901), ultimately forcing masses of Filipinos into "protected zones." One soldier remarked, "This business of fighting and civilizing and educating at the same time doesn't mix very well," an understatement but evincing more brains than his superiors: General William Shafter thought it might be necessary "to kill half of the Filipinos in order that the remaining half of the population may be advanced to a higher plane of life than their present semibarbarous state affords," and Secretary of War Elihu Root recommended using "methods which have proved successful in our Indian campaigns." It goes without saying that not all American soldiers and officers indulged in massacres; indeed, many decried the indiscriminate violence, but a ubiquitous turn-of-the-century racism made everything worse. White soldiers almost always called Filipinos "niggers" or "goo-goos" (the origin of the term "gook"), and officers disparaged Filipinos time and again. Perhaps as a result some 500 African-American troops decided to stay in the Philippines, and most intermarried with Filipinas. All this after Aguinaldo had "desperately wanted an alliance with the United States" from the beginning and, of course, recognition of the Philippine Republic he and his allies established in January 1899. The war began a month later and lasted until July 1902.[3]

The war occasioned America's first extensive colonial acquisitions, ending continentalism with a leap into the Caribbean and across the Pacific: the United States seized Cuba, Puerto Rico, and three strategic positions in the Pacific: Guam and Wake Island along the line to Manila, and the Philippines itself. Cuba got its independence in 1901, but not before the navy got a base on Guantánamo Bay, and under the Platt Amendment Cuba remained a virtual American protectorate until 1959, an adjunct to American-owned sugar plantations, nickel mines, and casinos, as Washington reserved to itself a "right to intervene" to protect "life, property, and individual liberty." Panama was more or less the same. Puerto Rico was a protectorate, modeled on the British colony of Hong Kong, and it remains so today; it was joined by the informal protectorates of the Dominican Republic, Haiti, and Nicaragua.[4] The United States had carved out an empire in the Caribbean, and with Pearl Harbor and Manila, Guam (1,500 miles south of Japan), Wake (2,000 miles west of Hawaii), and Midway (2,200 miles east of Japan), stepping stones across the Pacific to a boundless maritime empire.

Less conspicuous was the simultaneous development of a Japanese empire in the Pacific, beginning with the colonization of Taiwan in 1895 and the emergence of its first-rate navy; suddenly the "West" was not empty of anyone who could effectively resist, the vast ocean was not a void, "natives" had arisen who were formidable. Akira Iriye's life work has taught us how half a century of cooperation and rivalry, trust and distrust, friendship and secret war plans, accommodation and racism played out across the plain of the North Pacific as prelude to that "sneak attack" at Pearl Harbor.[5] Commodore Perry had awakened a sleeping giant that unaccountably gave off surprise after surprise: here were Orientals who were "clean" and vigorous instead of "torpid and slow," leaping forward instead of vegetating in the teeth of time. After a "sudden revolution," the most isolated, exclusive, rigid, and conservative nation in Asia overnight had become "the most active and enterprising."[6] This was an American, Henry M. Field, commenting in 1877, but this became the consensual American judgment after Perry: the Japanese are different, they give surprise, they are special, they are formidable—they are dangerous.

If the United States now had an empire resisted by tens of thousands of guerrillas in the new century, Americans would still claim it for the anti-imperialist side, a war of liberation in the interest of Filipinos against a decrepit Spain that should have been ashamed of itself for not vacating the historical stage sooner. The previous pattern of "savage war," in which barbarity by the enemy justified even greater barbarity by God-fearing whites, now sanctified empire in the guise of self-determination. Equal measures of self-righteousness, ambition to be not just a stronger power than others but a better one (a special one), zeal to remake the world in the American image, and ignorance of that world to be remade mingled with a characteristic lack of introspection or reflection and the predictable mundane material interests (the China trade, Philippine mahogany and coconuts) to convince American leaders that right made might, and might made right—Santayana's American in a repeat performance: victorious and blameless. It proved to be a pattern repeated in every big war down to the present, with the singular exception of the one conflagration that truly threatened America's vital interests: World War II.

Empire?

McKinley's war with Spain and Roosevelt's presidency add up to a self-conscious policy of empire on the territorial European model: colonies and protectorates. Before 1898 Polk, Cushing, Perry, Seward, and many others rarely missed an opportunity to expand, and especially to extend, the realm of American trade. Likewise the literature abounds with attributions of single purpose and imperial ambition to Jefferson, Adams, Monroe, and Seward. If the issue was expansion across the continent or new opportunities for trade, yes. But they didn't want colonies, and they didn't have a country behind them that wanted such things—they didn't even have a State Department behind them, Foggy Bottom specializing in prevarication, caution, and passivity; the Foreign Service never approximated a diplomatic service like those in Europe until the 1920s. Expansionism was westward bound, away from Europe, toward regions thought to be empty both of people who could resist and powerful nations who might want to try. New territory came through serendipitous, entirely unexpected windfalls, like the Louisiana Purchase, and through conscious intent, like Polk's acquisition of Texas and California. But there was no conscious follow-on to these events, no continuity, no systematic policy of expansion or empire that followed ineluctably from one president to the next, and no daily calculation of how any of this played into the European balance of power. Perry's Black Ships continued the pattern of westward movement into places not occupied by other empires, yet shortly after "opening" Japan, the United States was consumed by civil war and three decades passed before the United States and Japan came into close contact again. After the vast expansion of armies in the interior cataclysm, the U.S. Army fell back to a skeleton crew of roughly 25,000 men—this for a continent still contested by hostile Indians—and the navy dropped from 600 ships to 60. When Washington thought about chastising Chile for some infraction in 1881, it discovered that Chile's navy was larger than its own.

A great power signifies a central state, large standing armies, and a capital: London does this, Paris and Berlin do that. Washington was a sweltering, muddy place where mangy dogs and greasy pigs ran through the streets, the muggy headquarters of a state that could not make a pretense of itself, as Marx said, in a country still preoccupied with local affairs, local autonomy, and self-government. Likewise an empire is not constituted by grandiloquent rhetoric, far-reaching schemes, or distant outposts that can't be defended: empires have structures like war industries, blue-ocean navies, forward-based troops, a civil service schooled in colonial administration. Westward expansion had a sporadic, patchy, intermittent quality of sudden spasms forward, and except for California gold, the new acquisitions did not have strong refractory effect on Washington or really on the nation itself. People lived where they lived, and if California or Alaska was acquired it did not change the lives of those in Maine or Ohio, or force a new worldview on them—or their president.

Even near the end of the century Josiah Royce was still so impressed with the vastness of the unplumbed continent that he illustrated how the United States was a world all in itself. He prepared a map showing how England, Germany, France, Italy, Greece, Turkey, and Palestine—really everything from Edinburgh to Baghdad—could easily fit inside the United States with enough room left over to accommodate Japan (which he draped over two-thirds of California) and "China proper" (which he centered over the Great Plains). (The area of the contiguous forty-eight states is 7.8 million square kilometers, of Western Europe, 2.9 million.) Missionary that he was, he ran this map under a line from the Song of Solomon: "He shall have dominion also from sea to sea, and from the river unto the ends of the earth." Royce thought the West would fall back upon and dominate the eastern United

States soon enough, since Berkeley's westward course of empire would termi-
nate at the Pacific—and "there is no further West; beyond is the Orient."[7]
Traders always wanted new frontiers at home and abroad, of course, but they
didn't dominate foreign policy and generally abhorred the use of force. (Wall
Street opposed the conflict with Spain until a critical point in March 1898,
when it turned and urged McKinley to war.) As Robert H. Wiebe wrote,
"Foreign relations were composed of incidents, not policies—a number of
distinct events, not sequences that moved from a source toward a conclusion."[8] The normal state of the nation was a comfortable and unthreatened
isolation from world affairs, in the natural shelter of two great oceans—and
that remained the normal state, minus a couple of intermissions, until Pearl
Harbor. As we will see, however, McKinley's new empire set several high-
level Americans to thinking about how the broader world might be made to
conform to new American rules.

A Continent Pregnant with Energy

Amid this isolation and indifference, American industry continued to lengthen
its lead over everyone else. Professor Turner may have made Chicago's 1893
Columbian Exposition famous by declaring the end of the frontier, but few
recall that he was surrounded by an astonishing plethora of new products and
technologies, most of them invented by Americans: General Electric's three-
ton searchlight and its Edison Tower of Light, a shaft nearly eighty feet tall
worthy of Albert Speer; the company town of Pullman, providing for the
worker's every need (housing, stores, health, culture); Transportation Hall
full of mighty, polished locomotives of all types and finely appointed dining
and sleeping cars; Machinery Hall, with Westinghouse's incandescent lighting system and oil-fired dynamos to drive it, making for the largest central
power station in the country (with Standard Oil's experimental forty-mile
pipeline bringing in the petroleum); Electricity Hall, with long-distance
phones, trolley cars, washing machines, sewing machines (hugely important
to the textile industry), typewriters (already creating a revolution in the office), even early dishwashing machines; Agricultural Hall, with threshers and
reapers towering over a lesser-known aspect of American commercial dominance: food processing, as in California pears, Armour bacon, Swift beef
roasts, and Borden condensed milk. Here was the American dream of high
technology and mass consumption spread out for a world that barely knew
what either one was, as Emily Rosenberg said, but was eager to try; in the
two decades after the exposition American exports rose 240 percent as the

world sampled Colgate tooth powder, Heinz ketchup, Kodak cameras, Columbia gramophones, and Fords and Oldsmobiles powered by Rockefeller's gasoline.[9]

Henry Adams took it all in and decided that even Harvard dons would be reduced to the level of "retarded minds" trying to fathom "a *watt* or an *ampere* or an *erg*" (just as they are today with *terabytes* and *nanobots* and *googols*). Barely was the Columbian fair a memory before X-rays came along, also radium and atoms—"absolute, supersensual, occult" discoveries. Chicago was "the first expression of American thought as a unity," Adams wrote, a protean unity beyond measure—but the unity was pragmatic, mechanical, and capitalistic and he didn't like it anymore than he could resist it: a crawling infant in 1838, by 1904 Adams had himself become "a howling, steaming, exploding, Marconing, radiumating, automobiling maniac."[10] As in the 1840s, this bursting energy found a foreign outlet.

"Fire When Ready": Seizing Manila

No one has ever quite explained how the battleship *Maine* found itself at the bottom of Havana Harbor, setting Washington on a course of war with Spain: the experts think it was an accidental explosion internal to the ship. But Spain was instantly blamed, and that set in motion the American way of going to war: behold, an unprovoked attack, prelude to a howling throng of outraged congressmen, newspaper pundits, and other demagogues. After weeks of clamor and agitation, Congress declared war on April 25, 1898, and provided $50 million to President McKinley, who had finally been shaken into momentary action by Henry Cabot Lodge. Fighting began a week later with Admiral Dewey's spectacular dawn attack on the Spanish fleet.

Dewey's ships were pre-positioned in Japan: why? Because on a Friday afternoon in February when his boss had gone home early and he was momentarily "acting secretary" of the navy, Theodore Roosevelt had sent Dewey a secret dispatch ordering him to attack if war was declared with Spain. Dewey, commander of the Asiatic Squadron at the port of Nagasaki, left for Hong Kong in February 1898 aboard the gleaming white flagship *Olympia*, accompanied by the small cruiser *Boston*, a gunboat named *Petrel*, and an ancient paddle-wheel steamer called the *Monocacy* which had taken part in the "Little War with the Heathen" in Korea back in 1871. Around midnight on April 30 Dewey maneuvered his warships in the bright moonlight past Corregidor and several batteries of Spain's sleeping sentinels into Manila Bay, and at dawn the next morning issued through a brass speaking tube his memorable order: "You may fire when you are ready, Gridley." Soon the Spanish fleet, which returned fire with uncanny inaccuracy (a five-hour barrage hit nothing of substance), was on the bottom of the bay at the cost of about 380 Spanish casualties and a mere 8 Americans wounded (slightly). With no armor to speak of, antique muzzle-loading guns with much less range than Dewey's eight-inch cannons, and the hare-brained placement of the defending ships outside the protection of shore batteries, defeat was almost instant. Americans hailed it as the greatest naval victory in history. Meanwhile, the Spanish commander in Manila, fearing Aguinaldo and his insurgents much more than the Americans, beseeched Dewey to mount a small, face-saving exchange of gunfire before imposing the surrender. After that and quick campaigns in Cuba and Puerto Rico (a young Charles Beard soldiered in Cuba), Spain capitulated—ending nearly four centuries of rule in the Philippines. John Hay's "splendid little war" was almost as easy as taking California, if 345 combat deaths and 2,565 soldiers dead from disease can be called splendid.[11]

McKinley announced that the United States was sovereign throughout the Philippines on December 21, 1899. The president didn't know what to do with the islands when they fell into his lap and couldn't find them on a map when Dewey reported his victory. But it would be wrong, he surmised, to let Spain keep them; taking Manila would be sufficient for this purpose. But taking the capital required taking all of Luzon, the military said, plus there was a new republic seeking independence—and so presently McKinley discovered that Filipinos were "unfit for self-government." At length, while lying awake one night, the president prayed for divine guidance, and it came to him that the only decent mission would be to "uplift and civilize and Christianize" the Filipinos—"benevolent assimilation" as it came to be known. But the real movers and shakers were Roosevelt, Hay, Lodge, and Whitelaw Reid (the latter was instrumental in convincing the president to take it all). So the United States found itself in occupation of Manila and little else in this sprawling archipelago, now an American colony but also a tinderbox. Not for the first time, the United States had won the battle but not the war. Independence forces under the leadership of Aguinaldo controlled Luzon (where about half of the 7 million Filipinos lived) and several other main islands in the archipelago, and it took 126,648 American soldiers and three years of counterinsurgency to defeat them, at the cost of somewhere between 200,000 and 700,000 civilians, 16,000 to 20,000 insurgents, and 4,165 American soldiers dead of all causes.[12] This counterinsurgency campaign is mostly unknown in the United States, but it is well remembered in the Philippines. It took the form of subsequent conflicts in Korea, Vietnam, and Iraq: stumbling into an unknown political and cultural thicket with widespread expectations of easy victory and messianic deliverance only to get bogged down, lose popular support, and ultimately find no way out short of defeat or indefinite occupation.

McKinley stumbled along into empire with "no more backbone than a chocolate eclair" [*sic*] in Roosevelt's view. The president wanted to avoid war with Spain but the *Maine* forced his hand; after Dewey's victory he reckoned ground troops better go to Manila, then he decided Luzon should be ours, too; then it turned out the natives "appear unable to govern" (in Dewey's words), so finally the president sanctioned colonization of all the islands. "There is a very general feeling," he said in October 1898, "that the United States, whatever it might prefer as to the Philippines, is in a situation where it can not let go."[13] When a sailor sees that his heading is disastrous he changes course, but imperial armies sink their boots in quicksand and keep marching, if only in a circle, while the politicians plumb the phrase book of American ideals.

Savage War Again

The war offered Major General Arthur MacArthur a chance finally to implement his 1883 "Chinese Memorandum": as he told the Senate in 1902, the Philippines provided a way station toward the China market and "a commanding position" against any enemy; furthermore the Filipinos would become missionaries for the American cause of commerce and republican institutions throughout Asia. Major General Elwell S. Otis assured McKinley that Filipinos did not support Aguinaldo but preferred the president's strategy of benevolent assimilation, and just in case they didn't, in February 1899 he launched his forces against Aguinaldo. The campaigns "quickly assumed a numbing similarity," in Brian Linn's words: "Otis would dispatch a column . . . the soldiers would deploy and attack; the Filipinos would withdraw." Then the column would push on after them for a few days, until dehydration and exhaustion in the hot and humid jungle took their toll—and then the column would withdraw. Aguinaldo's forces would return and punish collaborators. It was "like passing a finger through water," one veteran said. A year later things were not better, with endless skirmishes and ambushes yielding little result. Aguinaldo was finally captured in March 1901 and many of his followers capitulated, but fierce resistance continued in southwestern Luzon and the island of Samar. The war petered out in 1902, but now the United States had its first formal colony to administer; if Dewey had his way it would also have a naval base at Subic Bay, and it was fighting *insurrectos* in south-western Luzon and Moro Province—and a century later Americans were still fighting Moro's Muslim insurgents, who were never completely pacified.[14]

American atrocities were indulged liberally, like previous attacks on Indians—and not a few made that comparison, including General "Howlin' Jake" Smith, who fought the insurgency like an Indian war: "Kill and burn, kill and burn. The more you kill and burn, the more you please me." He wanted to turn the island of Samar into "a howling wilderness" but drew the line at killing children: his men were authorized only to kill men and women above the age of ten. When President Roosevelt got wind of Howlin' Jake's statements he called a cabinet meeting and instantly demanded all the facts of the situation, punishment of those guilty of "cruelty or brutality," and the court-martial of General Smith. Elihu Root, however, justified Smith's actions via the brutality of the *insurrectos* and the "half-devil and half-child" nature of the Filipinos, while Governor William Howard Taft thought Filipinos inferior to "the most ignorant negro" and completely unfit for self-government.[15]

Mark Twain's "To the Person Sitting in Darkness" (1901) may be the best anti-imperial polemic among the many penned by Americans at the time. Unsparing in its account of American atrocities and racism, it also penetrated into a peculiar propensity to combine pitiless violence with idealism:

> There have been lies; yes, but they were told in a good cause. We have been treacherous; but that was only in order that real good might come out of apparent evil. True, we have crushed a deceived and confiding people; we have turned against the weak and the friendless who trusted us; we have stamped out a just and intelligent and well-ordered republic; we have stabbed an ally in the back and slapped the face of a guest; we have bought a Shadow from an enemy that hadn't it to sell; we have robbed a trusting friend of his land and his liberty; we have invited our clean young men to shoulder a discredited musket and do bandit's work under a flag which bandits have been accustomed to fear, not to follow; we have debauched America's honor and blackened her face before the world; but each detail was for the best.

Twain was merely the most brilliant of a broad swath of Americans—politicians, philosophers, writers, labor leaders, academics—who condemned this war and the empire that resulted. Some saw in American actions a crucial victory for Europe and its doctrine of power politics and "entanglements." Others opposed expansion because it might bring more nonwhites into the

Union. Opposition to the war was not necessarily opposition to empire; William Jennings Bryan opposed the Philippine adventure but wanted to annex Puerto Rico and get coaling stations in Cuba and the Philippines. Other anti-imperialists desired merely a hemispheric empire, not a global one, and opposed expansion into areas where the "ignorance and inferiority" of the people made the American Constitution inapplicable. Steel magnate Andrew Carnegie made it simple: he offered $20 million to buy Filipino independence. The mass of Americans may or may not have agreed, but often repeated a line that would become formulaic for more than a century: it might have been wrong to invade the Philippines in the first place, but now that we have them we can't let them go. William James, a vociferous, top-to-bottom critic of the whole enterprise, had this riposte: "The truth of an idea was found in the bright light of its consequences."[16]

Readers will not have trouble intuiting the relevance of these judgments a century later. What then do we make of the even more cogent remarks by E. L. Godkin, three years before the war with Spain began? "An immense democracy, mostly ignorant, and completely secluded from foreign influence . . . with great contempt for history and experience, finds itself in possession of enormous power and is eager to use it in brutal fashion against anyone who comes along, *without knowing how to do it,* and is therefore constantly on the brink of some frightful catastrophe."[17] With contempt for history and experience, and *without knowing how to do it:* which is worse? The one begets the other, Louis Hartz would say.

Grasping for an American Global System

At the turn of the new century affairs again shifted out of plumb, as a new and clear direction came to a handful of critically placed Americans. An assassination brought Roosevelt to power, famously an "exploding, radiumating" force in his own right. But he was also a man of the world who believed in power politics and whose tenure coincided with the rise of a core of people who began to form a distinctively American disposition toward the world: John Hay (a protégé of Seward), Elihu Root, Henry Cabot Lodge, naval strategist Alfred T. Mahan, Whitelaw Reid (son-in-law of gold rush millionaire Darius Ogden Mills and publisher of the *New York Tribune*), and an academic named Woodrow Wilson. They remained true to the nineteenth-century dictum that expansion should be away from Europe, toward Asia and Central America (toward perceived vacuums), but they brought a considered new logic to America's place in the world: not only was the United States the embodiment of the new and Europe the personification of the old, but the affairs of the world itself should now be conducted on a new basis.

Others knew Roosevelt was president before he did, because he was vacationing in the Adirondacks when an assassin shot William McKinley. Telegrams on September 13, 1901, told the vice president that McKinley was "critically ill," his prognosis grave, which brought Roosevelt "bouncing in a buckboard down the rain swept slopes of Mount Marcy" just after midnight; even on a good day it took him seven hours to reach the North Creek rail station.[18] But it wouldn't take him long to master the Oval Office: he would prove to be the strongest executive since Lincoln. The new president embodied and expressed the bumptious, combustible energy of the age. Aristocrat, cowboy, historian, widely read author, popular politician, well-traveled Harvard man, leader of men and man of the people, soldier on horseback, and frank imperialist—this all goes without saying. Roosevelt was a perfect American mixture, in Howard Beale's words, of "aristocratic distinction and democratic disregard of caste, a blending of simplicity in taste and regard for proprieties, and an amalgamation of his own love of all sorts of humankind and his wife's concern about good breeding."[19] First in line to be the undertaker of the Spanish Empire, he also wanted the isthmian canal, Hawaii, the Philippines, of course a big navy, and he coveted and enjoyed rivalry with the European powers and with Japan in the Pacific.

Roosevelt was an American nationalist in pure form, a patriot to the core who believed in the inherent goodness of his country (for him the conflict with Spain was "the most absolutely righteous foreign war" of the nineteenth century). He was an imperialist, but in the American grain (doing it our way, not the European way), indeed, he was the premier imperialist of his era and a direct link back to the 1840s ("I am a bit of a believer in the manifest destiny doctrine," he wrote in 1893).[20] He shared the racial prejudices of his time and a belief in the superiority of Anglo-Saxons but did not let bias get in the way of his thorough admiration for the Japanese, and he often denounced crude racial bigotry. Roosevelt believed in the judicious use of force and the balance of power, making him a rare realist among American presidents. There wasn't a better statesman going back to John Quincy Adams and forward to his cousin, Franklin Delano Roosevelt. Nor was he merely an Atlanticist, although he was that, by tutoring and travel if not temperament; he was the first president to have a clear sense of the United States as both an Atlantic and a Pacific power, and to plan for a grand navy on that basis; more than that, he was the first to see the Pacific as an arena in which the United States could emerge as a great power in its own right. "I wish to see the United States the dominant power on the shores of the Pacific," he wrote in October 1900, "at the dawn of a new century we wish this giant of the West, the greatest republic upon which the sun has ever shone, to start fair in the race of national greatness." A few years later during a visit to San Francisco, Roosevelt proclaimed himself an "expansionist" (as if anyone doubted it), but even more of an expansionist now that he had toured the Pacific Slope—in the new century "the commerce and command of the Pacific will be factors of incalculable moment in the world's history."[21]

Teddy Roosevelt was also the incarnation of the myth of regeneration through an encounter with wildness and violence. After the tragic deaths of his wife and mother in 1882, he took off for his cattle ranch and served as a deputy sheriff, hunted big game, and later, wrote a biography of Thomas Hart Benton. In the war with Spain, of course, his "Rough Riders" charged up San Juan Hill and smashed the enemy; "I killed a Spaniard with my own hand," he boasted. He loved Turner's frontier thesis, but his own worldview mingled the notion that America occupied the pinnacle of civilization together with social Darwinism and the ubiquitous but unfortunate turn-of-the-century tendency to see humanity through the lenses of race.[22] Such a perspective, of course, can explain everything: if the United States was the most productive power in the world (which by then it was), then the Anglo-Saxon race and its virile qualities must explain it. If Japan is ascending and China is the sick man of Asia, well then the Japanese are a progressive and virile people and the Chinese are the opposite, vegetating in the teeth of time (and thus Roosevelt happily embraced Japan's protectorate over Korea as a civilizing mission, and made the United States a kind of hidden signatory to the 1902 Anglo-Japanese Alliance). If Indians and Filipinos go down before American power, then they must be identical: "Everything that could be said for Aguinaldo was said for Sitting Bull." Only foolish idealists would fail to understand that if you left the continent to the Indians, it would remain "nothing but a game preserve for squalid savages." American intervention in the Boxer Rebellion in 1900 extended the analogy to China: the Boxers were just so many more Indians. Roosevelt was preeminent in pushing Manifest Destiny beyond the continent, linking Indian fighting to imperial adventure and the westering of the American people, and Anglo-Saxons to the "great fighting races." Jefferson's empire of liberty had turned into Roosevelt's imperialism—"we but pitch the tents of liberty farther westward."[23]

For Roosevelt and especially his close friends like Hay and Lodge, America's new possessions were not only stepping stones to the fabled Orient, but the closed regions of the Far East were now to be *opened:* in effect they

announced the end of territorial colonialism. In place of colonies came the
Open Door, the logical strategy of a rising power since colonies were another
name for closed economic zones and the United States thought it could
compete against anybody, anywhere (even if it protected American sugar
producers with a tightly closed door in Hawaii). In place of nasty power
politics came a call to follow an enlightened program of democracy and
human rights, as the United States sought to fashion a world in its image (or
at least the image of its capacious middle class). The extension of the realm of
freedom, something present from the country's founding, now got redefined:
the realm was the world. The Open Door also nicely avoided administrative,
military, or enforcement responsibilities, a drain on the treasuries of the
colonial powers. Perhaps most important, these leaders began the task of
bringing Great Britain, singular global hegemon but entering incipient decline, into the American system. Hay helped that inevitable process along by
declaring American support for China's unity and gaining London's assent, as
against a dumbstruck group of powers trying by all means to carve it up.
France, Russia, Germany, and Japan wanted China trussed up like a turkey
and permanently divided; the Open Door was designed both to get the
American foot solidly into a market always fantasized as unfathomable and to
hold China together "at that critical level between competence and impo-
tence."[24] China needed to be strong enough to ensure some level of stability
but not strong enough to resist imperial encroachment—exactly where it
remained for the first half of the twentieth century.

The Open Door was a master stroke not because of China—it did not signal a new stage of American involvement with the Middle Kingdom, and the
Chinese barely noticed it amid a general scramble for imperial privilege[25]—
but because it expressed concretely and metaphorically an American way of
looking at the world, a weltanschauung, instantly relegating old world imperialism to a place in and of the past. If Great Britain was reaching out to the
United States in the interests of partnership and cooperation (this rapproche-
ment had been going on for a long time, but intensively in the 1890s), something entirely predictable for a declining and threatened (by Germany) power,
the United States was reaching toward a new conception of global leadership,
a new diplomacy for a new century that the United States would dominate,
making Old World power politics seem as obsolescent as it was cruel. To keep
on the good side of the most powerful industrial nation in the world was
absolutely essential for Great Britain now, for if American trade with China
was still miniscule, Britain controlled 70 percent of the China trade which
was, in turn, one-sixth of Britain's commerce.[26] It also needed American high

technology. It would take half a century, two world wars would intervene and punctuate everything appalling about European squabbles, but the grand task of making England America's junior partner and guiding the world along American lines had finally begun.

This was still, however, an Atlanticist perspective: the truly important powers were European, imperialism was not so much outmoded as needing a new direction (international law, an organization like the League of Nations, mandates for the colonies), America would do the same things they did, but differently—and above all, better. If Roosevelt admired one Pacific power, Japan, it was because of its military prowess and the "virility" of its samurai, as the overcompensating president never tired of saying. Others paid it much less attention. A Bostonian like Henry Cabot Lodge was saturated with every British virtue and prejudice, "English to the last fiber of his thought" in the eyes of his close friend Henry Adams; in 1891 Lodge had taken it upon himself to examine 14,000 "men of ability" and claimed that they almost all came from New England or the "Middle" states (he found some statesmen and soldiers in the South). The main virtue of taking Hawaii and the Philippines, in Lodge's opinion, was to lay down a trans-Pacific cable "with only four relays" to London: after all, "commerce follows the cables." (Lodge could face East by facing West.) All of them were learning at England's knee, thus to replace her; the formative experiences in world affairs of John Hay and Henry Adams had been at the Court of St. James. Hay wrote that "a sanction like that of religion" bound the United States and England "to a sort of partnership in the beneficent work of the world"; for him and for Elihu Root, "the rule of law" in the world was synonymous with British and American law (although Hay acknowledged that this writ had little purchase in most of the country because of "a mad-dog hatred of England"). Even as worldly a man as Adams found almost nothing to say in his *Education* about the non-Atlantic world, the American West, the Pacific, China, or Japan; the instant completion of the continent via Polk's war with Mexico gets bare mention, likewise the seizure of the Philippines.[27]

Many prominent Americans brought forth stentorian nonsense about the significance of the Philippines for the China market, of course, but among this core group of imperialists and internationalists, only Whitelaw Reid argued for the strategic significance of Spain's defeat in putting the Pacific Ocean "in our hands": "Practically we own more than half the coast on this side, dominate the rest, and have midway stations in the Sandwich and Aleutian Islands. To extend now the authority of the United States over the great Philippine Archipelago is to fence in the China Sea and secure an almost equally commanding position on the other side of the Pacific—doubling our control of it and of the fabulous trade the Twentieth Century will see it bear. Rightly used, it enables the United States to convert the Pacific Ocean almost into an American lake."[28] Put Reid back together with his Atlanticist friends, and an American global ambition had been born that knew no limits. But this was a handful of people holding temporary power, an infinitesimal minority of Anglophile sophisticates in the sea of self-contained American indifference; the fatal gap between these cosmopolites and ordinary people anywhere outside New England expressed the slim base of the internationalists in the national body politic that would dog them down to our time.

A Lesser American Lake: The Caribbean

There was no rift or distance, however, between American leaders when it came to the Western Hemisphere. Should any foreign power or tinhorn dictator try to confront the United States in Latin America, and especially Central America, they would find marines in their midst. No one was really interested in the region, of course, unless some other power was. At the turn of the century Great Britain did more or less what it had always done since the War of 1812: it got out of the way of rising American power, quickly relinquishing most of its interests in Central America (in the 1901 Hay-Pauncefote Treaty). Colombia was not enthused about an American canal coursing through its isthmus in Panama, so Roosevelt supported yet another putsch masquerading as a "revolution" (with three American gunboats idling offshore); in came the marines "to protect American lives and property," Panama got its independence, and the United States got unilateral control of an autonomous military zone five miles deep on both sides of the canal (not opened for business, of course, until 1914, the first through cargo being a heavy load of Hawaiian sugar) that it did not relinquish for eight decades. Cuba also got its independence so long as it didn't interfere with American sugar barons, which Washington assured by arrogating to itself a right to intervene in Cuba should disorders materialize. Subsequent interventions followed in the Dominican Republic, Honduras, Nicaragua, and Haiti. Woodrow Wilson was particularly active in sending the marines around this barely concealed informal empire: they landed in Haiti in 1915 and occupied it until 1934; the next year the marines invaded the Dominican Republic in the midst of a civil war and did not leave until 1924; Wilson sent 7,000 soldiers commanded by General John J. Pershing on a punitive expedition throughout northern Mexico, searching for Pancho Villa.[29]

Woodrow Wilson, champion of self-determination, remembered as the father of the idealist strain in American foreign relations, epitomized the strange way in which stern Calvinism (he was a preacher's son) and corresponding self-righteousness, missionary zeal, high intelligence, expansive virtues, racial condescension, and the aggressive use of force could mingle uneasily in the same American person (by no means for the first or last time). But if Roosevelt, Lodge, Hay, and Mahan represented something new to the country, the assertive power politics of a newly risen nation and a desire for independent American action in the world, by his time Wilson represented something newer: international cooperation and a world under progressive rules (self-determination, the League of Nations), with Washington making the rules; it was like drawing out the lines, laws, and implications of Hay's Open Door world. From Wilson's presidency onward American foreign relations would oscillate between the long tradition of nationalism, facing-west expansion, independent action, unilateralism, and a pox on the house of Europe, and the new direction of Atlanticism, internationalism, multilateralism, and a world ruled by progressive (British and American) ideas and laws. The first tendency was the oldest and dominated the interwar period, and the second would last through two wars: World War II and the cold war.

The Great White Navy

Naval theorist Alfred Thayer Mahan had argued as early as 1890 that the United States needed a two-ocean navy that could patrol both coastlines and the Pacific out to a radius of 3,000 miles (he put forth this idea in an article in the *Atlantic*),[30] and until World War II naval power seemed to be the ideal defensive force for a bicoastal nation. But if American clipper ships were nonpareil, the United States was far behind Britain and France in steam-powered ships—and navy leaders didn't like steam. Furthermore, the Civil War and the preoccupation of Americans with filling the continent led to a sharp decline in the efficacy of American sailing ships; Perry's mission to Japan was probably the high point of United States shipbuilding in the nineteenth century. The most famous naval innovation before the Great War, of course, was the dreadnought, a fast-moving twenty-one-knot battleship powered by new turbine engines, protected by eleven-inch Krupp-style face-hardened armor and carrying huge twelve-inch-bore "all-big-gun" armaments that would blow just about anything else—well, out of the water. Pioneered by the British Admiralty, they displaced almost all other big ships in the Royal Navy by the time of World War I. They came onstream in 1905 but were easily copied. By 1910 Germany had ten, America six, and Japan five; when the war broke out, Germany had twenty-three and America had eleven (to Britain's thirty-four); these were advanced *Dreadnoughts*, moving at twenty-eight knots with fifteen-inch guns and armor-piercing shells accurate at twelve miles.[31]

In December 1907 Theodore Roosevelt sent the Atlantic battleship fleet down the coast and around Cape Horn to the Pacific, amid alarms about a brewing crisis with Tokyo. Japan's stunning defeat of the Russians in 1905 had raised the specter of a threat to the West Coast, just as it impressed Roosevelt with Japanese manliness; not for the last time would Japanese success be greeted with American ambivalence. "Japan Sounds Our Coast," Hearst's *San Francisco Examiner* blared in 1905; "Brown Men Have Maps and Could Land Easily" read another headline. What was really upsetting whites, though, was the success of Japanese businesses in California, leading to various anti-Japanese protests and assaults and an extraordinary intervention by Roosevelt to ask Congress for a law naturalizing Japanese-Americans. He probably wasn't serious, but he was sincerely outraged by the depredations of white Californians and authorized the use of federal armed force to protect Japanese throughout the country.[32]

"The Great White Fleet" showed the flag on the longest cruise ever taken by any naval power. It appeared to augur a two-ocean navy, even if the United States had ships enough to defend only one. The sixteen battleships received huge welcomes all along their route—Rio, Buenos Aires, Punta Arenas in Chile—but got their wildest reception in San Diego, where they rested at anchor shadowing the magnificent Hotel Del Coronado. San Diegans had lost many battles to Los Angeles (the railroad, the port, water delivery), so they didn't want to lose this one: hankering to be the navy town of the Pacific Coast, they showered the sailors with oranges (3,300 of them) and bouquets of flowers. Local leaders staged a grand ball at the Coronado for junior officers, inaugurating the city's practice of integrating the navy and the wealthy (which, of course, happened everywhere; the navy's connections to the wealthy classes always gave it more prestige than the army). San Franciscans gave the sailors an enthusiastic welcome, too, but in Seattle nearly half a million people turned out to watch the ships parade through Puget Sound, the eventual home to a major naval base at Bremerton. By the time the fleet got to Hawaii the wonderful natural port at Pearl Harbor was still undeveloped, although Congress had fortuitously appropriated $1 million to make it the navy's main Pacific base. But that, in turn, rendered the strategic significance of the Philippines moot: Subic Bay and other points were fortified, but no naval base emerged, and American strategists "despaired of defending the islands" against Japan right down to the attacks that came on December 7, 1941 (a few hours after Pearl Harbor).[33]

In spite of some trepidation about visiting Japan because of attacks on Japanese-Americans in California, the sixteen white ships cut through a dense fog to anchor in Yokohama and found a grand reception that the Japanese had worked on for months. Local citizens fell all over each other to show the sailors a fabulous time. One thousand English-speaking college students guided them around while tens of thousands of school children sang American songs; meanwhile the high officers got a rare treat, an audience with the emperor. The extraordinary hospitality of the Japanese pleased Roosevelt no end because he so admired the country's leaders; Admiral Tōgō Heihachirō's surprise attack on the Russian fleet at Port Arthur was already the stuff of legend for the president. In keeping with his idea that "the just man with a gun" best exemplified power, Roosevelt also knew the fleet would impress the Japanese with America's new-found potency. Japan was by then a formidable maritime nation; here were just the kind of people to appreciate this display of American naval prowess. By the time the ships returned to Hampton Roads in February 1909, a few days before he left office, Roosevelt could be justly proud of his accomplishments. He had done much more for the navy than any previous president: it was now the dominant American fighting force and the second largest navy in the world with 1,096 officers and 44,500 enlisted men.[34]

Unbeknownst to the open and hospitable publics in the United States and Japan, however, both navies were now planning on the assumption that they might one day be Pacific enemies—and the navy was also Japan's most formidable service. Probably nothing energized the Japanese more after Perry's visit than modern naval technology; by 1866 they had built their first steam warship and five years later Admiral Tōgō had embarked for studies in Britain along with eleven other naval trainees. For the next half-century Japan modeled its navy on British experience and acquired many battleships from British yards; naval officers learned their techniques, their attitudes, and even the style of their uniforms at the British knee. By 1907 Yamagata Aritomo, a leader of the Meiji Restoration and the father of the Imperial Army, had formulated a Basic Plan for National Defense calling for twenty-five standing army divisions and two battle fleets in an "eight-eight" configuration (eight battleships and eight heavy cruisers), one of which would monitor "the other shore of the Pacific Ocean." Japan sat out World War I but still built fourteen capital ships between 1911 and 1923, compared with America's seventeen. This arms race came to an end in the Harding administration, when it convened the Washington Naval Conference in 1922 and succeeded in imposing unequal limits on Japan: it was left with a 315,000-ton navy while the United States and Britain each got 525,000 tons. This sorely discomfited Japan's military leaders, who had decided at roughly the same time that eventual war with the United States in the Pacific was inevitable.[35] Japan's alliance with England also came to an end at this time, leaving it to navigate a second-rate, junior-partner status with both Washington and London; it did just that in the 1920s, uninterested in upsetting the status quo. This pattern—Japan as number two—began in 1902 and continued long into the 1930s, until it ruptured and Japan sought unilateral dominance in the Pacific; after World War II Japanese and American leaders again returned to it, except that well into the twenty-first century Japan's number two status was economic, not military.[36]

Roosevelt's successor, William Howard Taft, lacked his predecessor's brain power and much else, leaving tracks on Pacific history that were ephemeral when they weren't ridiculous. Taft was less enamored of Japan than China (he visited Japan in 1905 and decided that "a Jap is first of all a Jap and would be glad to aggrandize himself at the expense of anybody"). He was also enamored of "dollar diplomacy" (by which he meant "modern diplomacy is commercial") and sought an American sphere of influence in Manchuria. Taft's secretary of state, Frank Knox, and the classic American expansionist Willard Straight (a longtime advisor to E. H. Harriman, who hoped to build railways across Manchuria as part of his dream to circumnavigate the globe by train) developed a "grandiose vision," in Charles Neu's words, for an "economic, scientific, and impartial administration of Manchuria" (in Knox's words), a joint supervision by the great powers—but especially Britain and the United States, and especially over the railways. The goal of the plan was to create "an immense commercial neutral zone"—an open door—from which all the powers would benefit. To underline the importance of these events, in 1909 U.S. Navy planners finally decided on Pearl Harbor as the chief American base in the Pacific (where a fleet could be stationed that "would control the Pacific"), and Taft's General Board "began systematic consideration of war with Japan." By March 1911 it had worked out a detailed "Orange Plan." Taft thus inaugurated a pattern that has lasted down to the present, in which American diplomacy occasionally flirts with a "China first" policy (Taft, Franklin Roosevelt, and Richard Nixon are good examples), only to be called back to the hard reality that Japan, with its high technology and advanced industrial base, is the more important power in East Asia. Maybe Taft understood that fact by 1910, when his plans to develop a Manchurian great power trusteeship under British-American auspices (not to mention Harriman's railways) lay in ruins, his major accomplishment having been to alienate Japan.[37]

A Decided Predilection to the West

The most important Pacific moment after Woodrow Wilson replaced Taft in the White House was the much-vaunted opening of the Panama Canal in August 1914—just a few days after the outbreak of World War I. The canal vastly shortened global shipping distances, cutting the mileage from San Francisco to New York by nearly 8,000 (13,107 miles dropped to 5,289), and knocking more than 5,500 miles off the voyage to London. London was now 8,059 miles from Panama, and Yokohama 7,702—the canal being almost equidistant between Europe and Japan. The American Pacific coast was a good bit closer: "The Canal has given San Francisco a new position on the planet" —a position the city's leaders quickly sought to promote. World War I raged across Europe in 1915, but San Franciscans barely noticed it as they opened the Panama-Pacific International Exposition, perhaps the city's most determined effort to "face West," amid a sprawling panorama of artifacts rivaling Chicago's 1893 Columbian Exposition. Like many others associated with the exposition, the official historian Frank Martin Todd saw the war as more testimony to Europe's depravity, whereas the new canal would mark "the shift of world interest into the Pacific." The goal of this entire, ambitious effort, Todd wrote, was "to produce in San Francisco a microcosm so nearly complete that if all the world were destroyed except the 635 acres of land within the Exposition gates, the material base of life today could have been reproduced . . . an outline sketch of civilization at the end of the prosperous era preceding the German war."[38]

Visitors walked through two enormous arches, recalling the Arc de Triomphe in Paris, united by long colonnades and a profusion of sparkling rhododendrons. On the east side of the Arch of the Setting Sun Walt Whitman's paean to facing West was inscribed, and the western side bore a prescient observation by Goethe in 1827 of America's "decided predilection to the West": "It may be foreseen that this young state, with its decided predilection to the West, will in thirty or forty years, have occupied and peopled the large tract of land beyond the Rocky Mountains. It may furthermore be foreseen that along the whole coast of the Pacific Ocean, where nature has already formed the most capacious and secure harbors, important commercial towns will gradually arise, for the furtherance of a great intercourse between China and the United States." Goethe went on to say that all this would be vastly facilitated should Americans "effect a passage from the Mexican Gulf to the Pacific Ocean; and I am certain that they will do it." Meanwhile exhibition scribes commented that the Aryan race, originated in Asia, had now finally reached "the western edge of the American continent" by virtue of its "spirit of conquest."[39]

A sculpture titled "The Nations of the East" sat atop the Arch of the Rising Sun. The exhibition *Blue Book* listed its figures: "Arab warrior, negro servitor bearing baskets of fruit, camel and rider, Falconer, elephant, . . . a figure embodying the spirit of the East and attended by Oriental mystics, . . . camel and rider (Mahometan), negro servitor, Mongolian warrior." Fastened to the top of the Arch of the Setting Sun was another sculpture, "The Nations of the West." According to the *Blue Book* it depicted "the colonizing nations" of the Americas: "Enterprise, the Mother of Tomorrow" stands in front of a covered wagon, and atop the wagon, a voluptuous nude sculpted by A. Stirling Calder; additionally one found "an Alaskan," a "squaw," and an American Indian. James Earl Fraser sculpted "The End of the Trail," showing a dejected, drooping horse with an Indian mounted on it, symbolizing "the end of the race which was once a mighty people" (an Iroquois Indian, "Chief American-Big-Tree," posed for six months for Fraser).[40]

The Arch of the Rising Sun was not about progressive Japan, Todd wrote, but an Oriental procession of "those old, sad, hopeless parts of the planet" plodding along on "an endless, fateful march" (although not without a certain "gloomy grandeur"). Meanwhile the Arch of the Setting Sun, the Occidental nations, represented "the aspiring and achieving races" and thus was "hopeful, buoyant, and progressive." Here could be seen "the thrusting heave of western ambition and progress"—the latter being perhaps the dominant theme of the exposition.[41] (All this while "the civilized nations" were tearing each other limb from limb.) Throughout his five official volumes Todd sprinkled the words "Manifest Destiny" liberally, as if it were still 1846. When Teddy Roosevelt spoke of "peace and war" at the exposition, Todd thought he spoke with eloquence and "great vehemence," and as he finished each sheet of his speech he crumpled it and threw it angrily to the floor, "as though he therewith flung from him every loathed Chinaficationist and mollycoddle in the country."[42]

Apart from the conquering frontier imagery, the exhibition showcased the best American manufacturers. Ford had an assembly line turning out eighteen autos a day; the Southern Pacific Railroad had an entire marble,

Arch of the Setting Sun. Panama-Pacific International Exposition, 1915.
Courtesy of Donohue Rare Book Room, Gleeson Library, University of San Francisco.

columned building with locomotives and sleeping cars inside; Westinghouse and U.S. Steel both mounted huge manufacturing exhibits. *The Gateway of Nations,* a mural by Wm. De Leftwich Dodge, depicted a muscular naked man leaping forward on a white charger, with an angel watching over him; this was "the winged horseman of Imagination or purpose"; behind him languished an exhausted Indian, while a white conqueror pointed into the distance—and a steam shovel arced above both. France was busily at war, but it reproduced the Palace of the Legion of Honor (an enormous building). Japan, sitting out the war, built a huge exhibit called "Japan Beautiful," recreating various facets of Japanese life, environment, society, and commerce; it hoped to convince visitors that Japan was no longer of the vegetative Orient but had joined "the progressive nations."[43]

Japan brought along its master landscape architect, H. Izawa (who had done the Japanese Gardens in London), lugging 257 rocks weighing a ton or more apiece from his home country. With "meticulous care" he placed the rocks and assorted flora, seeking to reproduce the beauty and harmony of nature. Japanese carpenters built a replica of the magnificent *Kinkakuji* or Golden Pavilion in Kyoto. Continuous presentations of the tea ceremony achieved "the infinitely rarified atmosphere of reason and the spirit," Todd decided. He swooned even more over the reproduction of the shrines of Nikko and concluded that Japan's contributions were among "the most brilliant events of the year"; all in all it was an "exquisite revelation of herself to her neighbors of the Pacific." Also on display was an "Imperial Japanese war fan" with 800 inlaid pearls—a fine piece of Korean war booty, stolen in the 1590s by the warlord Hideyoshi. Left unstated was any hint of how Japan had transcended the "old, sad, hopeless" part of the planet that it hailed from. But Todd had a ready answer for the successes of the Philippines: its steady progress and increasingly high standing were "the fruits of fifteen years of colonial administration for the benefit of the colony instead of the suzerain" and thus a symbol of "the moral dignity of the United States."[44]

An Indifferent Pacificism

Ultimately Roosevelt's glorious world tour, Taft's machinations, and even the burgeoning transit through the Panama Canal did not amount to much. The gleaming white ships returned home to the Atlantic only to get reclad a drab ancient mariner's gray (to make them less visible on the horizon); the fleet remained at Hampton Roads until World War I erupted, still oriented toward Europe and its silent partnership with the British navy. The dream of the China market also faded. Exports to China had more than tripled to $35 million in the period 1895–1905, led by cotton producers in the South, helping convince the venerable Li Hung Chang to tour the United States in 1896. Welcomed everywhere by government and business, he wasn't quite up to the hard work of impressing Americans: he didn't feel like reviewing the Great White Fleet, declined to come ashore at West Point because it was raining, cancelled an entire day of events after catching his finger in a carriage door, and missed a shipyard visit because his servants feared waking him from his afternoon nap. (Vaunted Sinophile diplomat William Rockhill had already anticipated difficulties: "I don't like dancing attendance on any kind of a dirty Chinaman, on Li more than on any other.") The basic problem, though, was that most American investors weren't interested in China. By 1912 exports to China had faded back to $24 million, less than 1 percent of total American trade.

There was talk of an American base in the Philippines, but the army and navy couldn't get together on it, and in spite of the 1909 plans for Pearl Harbor, not much was accomplished. Plan Orange got redrafted in 1913, emphasizing a defensive rather than expansionist strategy. Along came World War I and all Colonial Army troops were redirected to the European theater —thus wiping the slate clean: "the U.S. Army had all but vanished" from the Pacific. (Meanwhile, after the war Japan had potential control of the entire western Pacific, its naval realm stretching down from the Kuriles to Taiwan and more.) What counted was not the American military, but the world-beating industrial strength of the United States: in the early years of the new century the country produced 14 million tons of pig iron, to the combined total of the United Kingdom and Germany of 16.5 million, and twice the amount of steel as the British. The output of Germany, France, and Britain together barely equaled the total value of American manufactures.[45]

Various international conferences in the 1920s not only limited armaments but appeared to raise the prospect that wars had ended forever, a pacifism exemplified in the 1928 Kellogg-Briand Pact outlawing war, which drew upon and reinforced traditional American distrust of standing armies. And so for two more decades Hawaii, Guam, and the Philippines remained weakly defended, and army strength never went above 25,000 for Hawaii and the Philippines combined (since 1945 the United States has had about 100,000 troops in South Korea and Japan alone). Russell Weigley thought the army was less well trained and combat-ready in the early 1930s than it was during the Indian campaigns.[46]

This hardly mattered in the 1920s and 1930s, but perhaps it did a few weeks before Pearl Harbor when the American commander in the Philippines, General Douglas MacArthur, granted an audience to Brigadier General Bradford Chynoweth during his inspection visit to Manila: the latter found MacArthur "in [a] complete fog about his Army and his subordinates"; to Chynoweth "an air of almost surrealistic lassitude pervaded the army" (in Linn's words). Manila Bay was barely defended, training was intermittent if not optional, ammunition stocks were low. In other words, it was a typical day in the life of the Pacific Army—the soldiers trained in the morning, played sports in the afternoon, and just played in the evening. The officers had servants at home, played polo with the local *cacique* elite (the army had eight polo teams in the 1920s), wined and dined at the splendid Army and Navy Club in Manila, took a month of vacation every year at the military's "Camp John Hay" resort in Baguio, and retired to the boards of major export corporations. The enlisted men frequented movie theaters, bowling alleys, and swimming pools on the base, and waiting outside the gates were saloons, whorehouses, tattoo parlors, and shops that would tailor them a new suit. Brigadier General Jonathan M. Wainwright, notable for his emaciated appearance on the deck of the USS *Missouri* in Tokyo Bay on September 2, 1945, had a workday in the tense summer of 1941 that began with a horseback ride, then a hearty breakfast, observations of the troops, a stop by the office, then luncheon followed by eighteen holes of golf.[47]

The truth is that from Perry's mission in 1853 down to the late 1930s, the United States was not really a Pacific power. If its navy became formidable under Roosevelt, its military forces as a whole and its inattention to Pacific bases made it a lesser power in the region than Great Britain or Japan, perhaps even less than France or Germany. China was not being enlightened by American missionaries, the Open Door did not save China from disintegration or make America into China's special friend, and American behavior in the Philippines, during the intervention in the Boxer Rebellion, and in many other ways distinguished it but marginally from the other imperial powers—in spite of what generations of Americans liked to think or believe. One could just as easily argue that the United States was the handmaiden of its imperial friends, serving as a silent partner in the Anglo-Japanese Alliance, which gave Japan a free hand in Korea, and then helping to deliver Korea to Japanese imperialism at the Portsmouth negotiations that ended the Russo-Japanese War (for which Roosevelt won the Nobel Peace Prize), or using imperial privileges to further the interests of American business and seek concessions—like the 1866 contract given to a Philadelphia banker to build long-distance phone lines between China's treaty ports or the railway, gold mine, and electricity concessions wrung from the Korean monarchy in the late 1890s.[48] Woodrow Wilson was the first American president to shake East Asia with his strategies—but then he shook the world, too, together with a rather different man named Lenin, both of whom announced novel and lasting global visions for the world in the aftermath of the war to end all wars.

Conclusion: An Empire of "Masterly Inactivity"

Individuals who came to awareness in the 1840s, like Henry Adams, experienced that decade as a definitive rupture with the past—the new machines, the American people pressing to the shores of the Pacific, a country turned into a continent: "The old universe was thrown into the ash-heap and a new one created. He and his eighteenth-century, troglodytic Boston were suddenly cut apart—separated forever." As it happened, Adams had the same sense of being cut adrift yet again, in the "Indian summer" of his life, when a thousand new machines appeared, the *Maine* capsized in Havana Harbor, and McKinley conjured up a new empire. Here indeed was "a new world," one well beyond his previous understandings of his own country (and few understood it better than he).[49] Reading Adams a century after his *Education* appeared is not to encounter a person jolted of place and time, though, so much as an entirely modern man jolted into sardonic awareness of the unstoppable momentum of a country that did not so much grow as palpitate or gyrate, propelled forward incessantly—but toward what? To empire, to a precipice, to ever greater triumphs, to an abyss? Like Whitman, Adams didn't know—what the country was looking for was "yet unfound." But he had a sensibility that feels entirely contemporary about a nation roaring ahead into the future with no one (least of all a passive, distracted and vacillating president named McKinley) in charge.

The acquisitions of expansionism accumulated, sometimes with and sometimes without a plan—but they were never reversed. Expansionism accreted, but it didn't recede. Now the United States had potential forward bases across the Pacific: Alaska and Midway Island were acquired in 1867 thanks to Seward, and in 1872 the commander of the U.S. Pacific squadron, Richard W. Meade, arranged with a local chief to establish an American naval station in Pago Pago, with its fine, landlocked port—a smaller version of Pearl Harbor; in 1878 the United States established a naval base there in return for assurances of American protection. Hawaii and the Philippines were annexed during the war with Spain, and in 1899 the United States took possession of Samoa from Australia, partitioned it with Germany but retained the base in Pago Pago, and annexed Wake Island (uninhabited). But Congress was not inclined to appropriate money for these acquisitions or the military bases some wanted, and soon the American people, in Lodge's words, had "lost all interest" in colonial expansion. By the time of the Russo-Japanese War the United States still had no naval base in the eastern Pacific: the Asiatic Squadron depended on Japan and Britain for dockyards in Nagasaki and Hong Kong. By the end of his second term even Roosevelt was wondering if keeping the Philippines was a good idea. It was again a pattern of war, leaps forward, relapse, forgetting, indifference. Still, if the United States may have acquired a small and poorly serviced empire with little more than halfhearted support for it at home, Brooks Adams correctly took the measure of its potential in 1903: "The Union forms a gigantic and growing empire which stretches halfway round the globe, an empire possessing the greatest mass of accumulated wealth, the most perfect means of transportation, and the most delicate yet powerful industrial system which has ever been developed."[50]

It is entirely possible that after the fact a particular administration might not have ratified the distant actions of expansionists, or might even have undone them, but no one ever did. Expansionism worked because of the forward momentum of those in the field, so to speak, but more importantly because there was nothing standing in the way, no one capable of saying no, this far and no farther. Fighting a weak Mexican army, scattered and highly diverse bands of Indians, or a nearly comatose empire like Spain's was easy; the victories came quickly and the costs were either light or easily hidden, followed by huge territorial acquisition and a quick return to normalcy. Wordsworth's famous lines (paraphrasing Thucydides) captured the essential truth of American expansion: "That they should take, who have the power, And they should keep who can."

Frederick Jackson Turner wanted to take and keep. After the war with Spain this champion of pioneer democracy embraced the new "imperial republic" because it had one undeniable virtue: it faced West. Indeed, Turner outdid his contemporaries in celebrating the new westering empire: "The dreams of Benton and of Seward of a regenerated Orient, when the long march of westward civilization should complete its circle, seem almost to be in process of realization. The age of the Pacific Ocean begins, mysterious and unfathomable in its meaning for our own future."[51] Turner turned Americans around to face West and, in essence, forget about the rest.

McKinley's adventures posed starkly the problem of the *methods* used to attain national ends: as William Appleman Williams put it, "What counts is how the game is played." A man like William Henry Seward, Lincoln's secretary of state, might opine that Americans should expand all over the continent, including Canada and even Central America, and he believed the Pacific Ocean would be the key to American global power. But he rejected war and conquest (if not the judicious application of military force) as an appropriate vehicle for expansion. "I want no war," he said when the conflict with Mexico neared in 1846, "I want no enlargement of territory, sooner than it would come if we were contented with a 'masterly inactivity.'" The only empire he thought worth having was the commercial dominance of the world. John Hay thought much the same thing.[52] Likewise territorial control was not the point for John Hay. Colonies were in and of the Old World and outmoded in the new century; like Seward he was interested in commercial hegemony and in replacing Britain by bringing it into an American system. The American military was entirely subordinate and tangential to these leaders—military officers were neither consulted nor taken seriously. Naval strategy had a place in their thinking, but it was people like Mahan, not naval officers, who informed their ideas.

The larger meaning of this second coming of Manifest Destiny was the beginning of the end of America's isolation in the world and its distinction from Europe. That distinction was based on an exceptionalism that was bedrock belief throughout the nineteenth century, that America constituted a new order for the ages, an anti-imperial challenge to the powers and a beacon to those they oppressed, and that its destiny faced West, away from the Old World. John Hay, Elihu Root, Henry Cabot Lodge, and Theodore Roosevelt wanted to join that Old World and reconstitute it on American principles, just as leaders in London sought to bring America into partnership, as insurance against their own decline. In a few short years Woodrow Wilson would harness their high-minded ideals to more foreign ventures, but neither he nor any other president could again speak with the conviction and clean conscience of John Quincy Adams in his celebrated Independence Day address in 1821: about the revolutionary nature of the United States, its independence, its principles—tenets which were simultaneously the undoing of the rest of the world: "It was the first solemn declaration by a nation of the only *legitimate* foundation of civil government. It was the cornerstone of a new fabric, destined to cover the surface of the globe. It demolished at a stroke the lawfulness of all governments founded on conquest. It swept away all the rubbish of accumulated centuries of servitude." Adams went on to say that America had always respected the independence of other countries and abstained from interference in their affairs "even when conflict has been for principles to which she clings." And then this indelible promise: "Wherever the standard of freedom and independence has been or shall be unfurled," he said, the United States will welcome it. "But she goes not abroad in search of monsters to destroy. She is the well-wisher to the freedom and independence of all. She is the champion and vindicator only of her own."[53]

PART III

Pacific States, New England Peoples

It may be foreseen that this young state, with its decided predilection to the West, will in thirty or forty years, have occupied and peopled the large tract of land beyond the Rocky Mountains. It may furthermore be foreseen that along the whole coast of the Pacific Ocean, where nature has already formed the most capacious and secure harbors, important commercial towns will gradually arise, for the furtherance of a great intercourse between China and the United States.

—JOHANN WOLFGANG VON GOETHE, 1827

CHAPTER SIX

East of Eden: The Pacific Northwest

Here, as throughout America, one is struck not only with the wonderful variety
of form and colour, the beautiful combination of wood, water, and mountain,
but, with the immensity, the grandeur of scale. . . . The rivers are actually wider,
the mountains are actually higher, the pines are taller, the colours are brighter,
than the eyes of a European are accustomed to look upon in his own country.

—HENRY J. COKE, near The Dalles, Oregon, in 1850

Elementary geographic distance and an immense ocean vale shrouded
the Northwest until the 1840s, just like California. It was nearly as
isolated, developing a scant few years before the gold rush. British
and Russian ships occasionally reconnoitered the Pacific coast above California, mainly for the fur trade, but the weather was often terrible, and it got very
cold to the north. Sir Francis Drake sailed up the northern Pacific coast in
1579, along the Oregon shores and perhaps as far as present-day Vancouver.
He named the region "New Albion," cursed the "stinking fogges," and never
returned—and neither did anyone else for the next two centuries. Russian and
Spanish explorers came along the same coast in the middle of the eighteenth
century, and Captain James Cook pushed his two ships, the *Resolution* and
the *Discovery*, northward all the way to the Arctic Ocean in 1778—but missed
the Columbia River and the strait that would have taken him to Puget Sound.
A Greek explorer named Apostolos Valerianos claimed to have found the
same strait in 1592; he was known as Juan de Fuca. Whether he did or not, his
name graces the body of water lying between Washington and British Columbia. Exactly two centuries later Captain George Vancouver again located
this strait and Puget Sound, which he reconnoitered for two months, providing names to several islands (Whidbey, Vashon). Meanwhile Boston clipper
ships had their eye on China, not a west coast that had barely been surveyed;
anyway Canton was closer: in 1800 a sea captain setting out from Boston for
the fur post at Astoria had 40,000 miles to cover and three years of sailing.[1]

Had Sir Francis Drake (or Lewis and Clark) journeyed along the Oregon coast in less foul weather they would have discovered another earthly paradise, but a much different one than the placid Pacific vistas of Southern California: a panoply of craggy rocks, gritty reefs, dark headlands, and shadowy beauty: "river mouths, bay-mouth spits, sheared-off headlands, beaches, dunes, rock islets and stacks, arches and caverns," in Don Kelley's words, stretching well into northern California's "Lost Coast," an austere wonderland that remains isolated and remote even today. (The genuinely "conservative" Oregonian temperament also led to an astounding triumph in 1913: the shoreline belongs to everyone, with open access to all but twenty-three miles of the outer coast; meanwhile around 65 percent of the California coast is privately owned.)[2]

Because explorers didn't get very far or stay very long, they missed the most breathtaking river in America. The vast Columbia River basin, opening into the Pacific between what is now Oregon and Washington and opening at such breadth (six miles) and such volatility (waves could reach 100 feet high), remained virgin territory until an American claimed it, very late in world time—1792, Columbus's tricentennial. In May of that year Boston sea captain Robert Gray guided his sloop *Columbia Rediva* upstream, amazed by huge salmon cavorting in the river, by trees that climbed as high as 300 feet along the banks, and by the free-trading Chinook Indians from whom he bought the fur of 150 otters and 300 beavers. When this river tumbles into the Pacific tides it is a wonder to behold and a terror for seamen. In 1840 Captain Charles Wilkes of the U.S. Exploring Expedition encountered "a white foaming sheet for many miles, both south and north of the mouth of the river, and threatening with instant destruction everything that comes near it." But Wilkes also loved the many harbors on quiescent Puget Sound and urged that they never be surrendered to the British. Gray's visit essentially assured that they never would; international law, such as it was at the time, gave sovereignty over the nearby coast, the river valley, and the watershed to the discovering nation.[3]

The Cascade mountain range divides both states, Washington and Oregon, into an eastern farming region of typical midwestern-style population, a coastal region with one great city, and a host of excellent year-round harbors along the placid Puget Sound or near the roaring Columbia River. Oregon's Willamette Valley got settled quickly in the 1840s; Washington's Walla Walla Valley came along a bit later but had a stronger development: some 2 million acres came under the plow in the Columbia Valley and southeastern Washington: "Population exploded at a typical frontier 400 percent rate during the 1870s, trees tumbled and wheat flourished, and the area soon began calling itself the Inland Empire."[4] By the time the first settlers' children were mature (the 1880s), Portland was linked by Pacific coast railways to San Francisco, and the Great Northern stretched out to Minneapolis and St. Paul. Seattle hooked into the railway network in the early 1890s, and from that point onward became the most dynamic city in the Pacific Northwest (including Vancouver). With the irrigation of the Yakima Valley, apple orchards spread widely, the 1890s peopling of the rich farmlands of the eastern part of the state led to large winter wheat crops and the emergence of the lumber industry, and Washington became in the early part of the twentieth century "a demographic success story" second only to California.[5]

Seattle is blessed on one side by the Puget Sound and on another by Mount Rainier. With a peak just a few tens of feet below Mount Whitney and a sheer rise from sea level, it has a rounded, perfect symmetry superior even to Mount Fuji. Captain George Vancouver named it after a friend in the British Admiralty and waxed Arcadian about the region it commanded: "The serenity of the climate, the innumerable pleasing landscapes, and the abundant fertility that unassisted nature puts forth, require only to be enriched by the industry of man."[6] But to one of Bill Gates's (many) detractors, Seattle's weather was simply Sir Francis Drake-stinky: "sky soupy gray, the roads slick with rain, the landscape draped in a fog thick as porridge"; Microsoft's Redmond campus was "a mushroom colony—a damp, leafy mulchpile [*sic*] where spongy-beige coders multiplied in the dark."[7]

In fact Seattle's climate is sublime in every season but the dead of winter, when it gets but eight hours of sunlight (it is about 47°30′ north latitude, very northerly for the United States), a lot of rain, and a clammy, overcast cold that you feel in the marrow of your bones. But even then it isn't unusual to have a 60-degree sunny day—called "sunbreaks"—and freezes are quite rare. The summers are often glorious, with little rain from April to October, an eternal sun (it sets after 10 p.m. in June), and barely a trace of humidity. Seattle gets less rain than most East Coast cities, it just comes down more slowly—no umbrella needed; the local weather reporters have fifteen different ways to describe it (mist, fog, sprinkles, sprays, showers). You know you've become a native when you enjoy the soft, sweet rains as much as the sunny days. With a mix of evergreen and deciduous trees you get four seasons, even snow now and then. Cherry blossoms, azaleas, and rhododendrons sprout all over the city in late February. Then there are the two lakes, the Sound, the mountains, the Olmsted Brothers' genius with parks and beaches, the bike and hiking paths that go on for miles and were far more developed twenty-five years ago than they are in most cities today. People at the University of

Washington like to walk across the campus through Japanese cherry trees to Rainier Vista and stand by a fountain surrounded by flowers, gazing at Mount Rainier in the distance—a mountain that is either "out" or not depending on the weather, but when it is out, it is a miracle of ever-changing atmospheric hues; as the sun sets it gradually reddens, but in a myriad of shades. Of all America's cities that dispose of world-class industries, Seattle lives most comfortably with the crushing beauty of its environment (even if it doesn't live well enough).

Here in the Pacific Northwest was another of Thoreau's gardens, instantly reminiscent of a Massachusetts setting except for the volcanic peaks, and it didn't require nature-remaking aqueducts or hordes of cheap labor: it could be transformed overnight into another New England, one that resisted the intrusive machine for a very long time. It just happened to be across the continent from Concord. Until recently the Northwest always stood in the shadow of California's breathtaking growth and dynamism, but since World War II a strong pace of development marked the Northwest as well: it's just that the machines have been high-tech, allowing intellectuals in Seattle and Portland to hope that they remain subordinate to the environment and human artifice.

Maine Once Removed

If Arcadia had not existed by the time white settlers began to flow into the Willamette Valley, with its green prairies, bountiful earth, life-giving rains, warm days and cool evenings, lush woods and dramatic forest openings sheltered by shimmering mountains, someone would quickly have been inspired to invent it.[8] Lying between the Cascade Range and the coastal foothills, this abundant river basin runs from Portland down through Salem and Corvallis to Eugene, gets three times the annual rainfall that drops on the eastern side of the Cascades, and has much more temperate weather (in winter Portland is often 50 degrees warmer than eastern Oregon). This valley quickly yielded to early pioneers who claimed homesteads more bountiful than those in Ohio or Missouri, and unlike the plains, they didn't have to pray for rain: Oregonians got all they wanted, and then some. (Like Lewis and Clark, in 1858 C. H. Crawford suffered through a dank winter when it rained for forty days and forty nights; come spring he was ecstatic to escape to California.)[9] In contrast to the Middle Border, moreover, this valley stood in awe of Mount Hood, which shadows Portland like Mount Fuji sets off Tokyo; several other round snowcapped mountains, extinct volcanoes and ones that now and then roar to life, run in a chain of symmetrical white cones up to Canada and down across the California border. If the Pacific Northwest claims a different beauty than California and has no claim on the Golden State's superb weather, it always has its grand mountain peaks.

"Oregon" is supposed to be an Indian word, even if no one is certain what it means. But it wasn't long after Lewis and Clark returned home that Oregon connoted a new "City on a Hill" or another Massachusetts Bay Colony—according to Hall Jackson Kelley, an eccentric Boston schoolteacher whose many publications (based mostly on Lewis and Clark's findings) made Oregon familiar to Americans in the 1820s. Shortly (1834) some Methodist missionaries arrived in the Willamette Valley to minister to the remnant natives (epidemics had mostly eliminated local Indians). They determined that they had found the "Garden of Eden" and opened up churches for incoming white settlers.[10]

The trek to Oregon leapfrogged the trailing edge of the frontier by 2,000 miles, a difficult and often harrowing journey taking six or seven months that nonetheless sought familiarity: a lot of Oregon looked a lot like New England. John Fiske called it "the New England of the Pacific," and the settlers lost no time in making it so, as pioneers arrived and facsimiles of New England towns cropped up one after another. The state of Maine symbolically guided the replication of New England here—why not let Portland be Portland? For decades the social event of the year was the annual "New England dinner" held a week before Christmas in Portland, and travelers remarked on how "the industry, the thrift, the briskness of business" was so reminiscent of Maine. The terrain and environs resembled New England even more than the Western Reserve in Ohio, and industry was already rising there. Until the gold rush, Oregon was a superior destination to California, the pioneers choosing it by a ratio of ten to one; the first showed up in 1840, and a decade later about 11,500 settlers had arrived, compared to 2,735 for California before the gold rush. The always improving route called the Oregon Trail remained the major path to the Pacific Northwest until railways came along in the 1880s. This early settlement shaped the Oregon that we still encounter today: as D. W. Meinig noted, young families seeking order and tranquility in an agrarian, small town life, "homogenous and provincial" people representative of "classical republicanism," took the north fork at Pacific Springs; young, impulsive, footloose men took the south fork, seeking fortunes in gold, commerce, the city, or just seeking a warm sea—a heterogeneous, cosmopolitan, exuberant, dynamic population promising "turbulence and conflict." Oregonians liked to say a sign pointed to Oregon and a pile of quartz to California, and all the illiterates turned south.[11] In fact, the one replicated New England and the other replicated nothing, inscribing an unknown future.

In 1843 the Oregon Country provisional government offered to any white settler 640 acres of choice land per married couple, free for the taking. These generous land grants, offered in a package that could make a farmer prosperous, tended to discourage the hyperactive real estate speculation that marked much of the frontier. Nearly all of the farms were in the Willamette Valley, with family heads presiding over large homesteads. Nearly all of the pioneers came from midwestern farming families, and many of them were related, beckoned by brothers and cousins, yielding an ethnic and social homogeneity that would indelibly mark this state and provide a sheer contrast with California. Later came town and city builders from New England and Upstate New York, but they carried in their minds the civic culture of Puritanism and Jeffersonian democracy instead of the newborn thrust toward industry and empire.

More than most Americans, Oregonians shared egalitarian ideals; beliefs in independence, self-reliance, and sacrifice for the common good; and a radical antipathy toward the financial and industrial forces that were transforming the country. Nothing matched plunging one's hands into the soil to make it bloom: "Of all the occupations . . . none is more honorable or enviable than that of Farming," an Oregonian wrote (paraphrasing Jefferson). Something less than country squires in spite of their large farms, Oregonians prized hard work and a republican equality. Politically they saw themselves replicating the best wisdom of the Midwest—indeed, the Indiana state constitution ("gold refined," one writer called it) provided the model for their own, as they moved toward statehood in 1857, and Washington drew on Oregon's example for its constitution in 1889.

Both the virtue and the agrarian largesse went to white males—Oregonian values were no different than those of the rest of the country when it came to people of color. In 1845 early residents turned away a column of eighty covered wagons because one free Negro rode with them: his name was George W. Bush. The state constitutional convention in 1857 founded a "liberal commonwealth" which nonetheless denied civil and property rights to blacks, Chinese, and Native Americans. Delegate George H. Williams, a key founder of the new state, wanted to "consecrate Oregon to the use of the white man, and exclude the negro, Chinaman, and every race of that character." The constitutional convention outlawed slavery but also proscribed "the idea of racial equality"—and one delegate wanted simply to exclude from the state "Chinamen, Kanakas [Hawaiians], and even Indians," in spite of thousands of the latter having more or less welcomed the whites to their land. In the 1860s Chinese established a small community in Portland, but it wasn't long before the mayor wanted all Chinese quarantined, amid general disdain for them; a law requiring "a census of the sanitary and thrift habits of Orientals" remained on the books until 1949. Segregated restaurants lasted until 1951, when Mark Hatfield pushed a civil rights bill through the legislature.[12]

Oregonians were often more tolerant than the letter of the law indicated. A young black woman named Marie Smith was happy to leave Paris for Oregon in 1910—Paris, Texas; she joined her father, who was a coal miner. The granddaughter of slaves, she ultimately became the first woman president of the NAACP branch in Portland. Blacks "lived all over the city," another NAACP leader said; blacks and Asians could not own homes before 1926, but white lawyers would find ways to buy homes for blacks, and in this manner a strong black middle class emerged.[13] And if Chinese were disdained, the Orient was not. From the time of the earliest settlers the lure of Pacific trade brought people to Oregon and fond hopes to chambers of commerce. "I have almost caught a glimpse of the Oriental world over the tranquil and alluring surface of the great ocean," a traveler wrote in 1844. Many thought statehood would help Oregon open up the China trade.[14]

Indian groups stretched up and down the Northwest coast, including Chinooks, Kwakiutls, and Athabascans (who spoke the same language as some Alaskan Indians). Here, too, visits by Cook and other explorers brought diseases that caused a quick decline after the 1780s, and sometimes tribes to the east, like the Nez Percé, carried smallpox to the Northwest. A hundred thousand Indians may have once lived in the region, even two or three times that number, but pioneers found a mere remnant when they arrived in the 1840s. White settlers in Oregon and what became Washington touched off a virtual war with Indians in 1855, after the Yakimas accused miners of raping the daughter of a leading chieftain. Joined by the Walla Walla tribe, they retaliated with a few small-scale raids against the whites. Oregon volunteers got hold of "the dignified and much respected leader" of the Walla Wallas, murdered him, and, according to a witness, "skinned him from head to foot" and drank toasts from glasses containing his ears—while making razor-straps from his skin. This war was never fought to a conclusion, it just dwindled away. Then the Modoc War erupted in 1872 as white settlers pressed upon Indian lands, and other skirmishes continued until the U.S. Army defeated a band of Shoshones known as Sheepeaters in 1879. Most Indians were on reservations by then, many of them isolated along the coast where they remain today, including the Makahs and the Nootkas of the Olympic Peninsula, famed for their skill at killing whales in long wooden canoes seating eight or ten hunters.[15]

Yankee Conservatism on the Pacific

For more than a century after the establishment of the Oregon Trail, Americans crossing from California to Oregon crossed from a vibrant commercial culture to something else, something different that people nonetheless had trouble putting their finger on: "There is a distinctively Oregonian look about all the natives and old residents which is hard to describe," noted a writer in 1873. "Certainly they are not an enterprising people," but they care about "a good easy life."[16] Less uncertain travelers spoke of a phlegmatic mood, ennui and melancholia, perhaps brought on by the winter rains (Lewis and Clark suffered eleven straight days of rain in 1805: "The rainey weather continued without a longer intermition than 2 hours at a time," Clark wrote; it was "the most disagreeable time I have experienced confined on a tempiest coast wet, where I can neither git out to hunt, return to a better situation, or proceed on." Christmas Day was no better: "The day proved Showerey wet and disagreeable"—sun shone on a mere six days of their long winter.) A British tourist in 1879 found the Pacific Northwest "cold and sedate" by contrast to California's "electric buoyancy" and also attributed the difference to the inclement weather. Almost a century later, in 1972, a historian wrote that "one looks in vain for flashes of brilliance." And a few years after that another sojourner put the point squarely, if unkindly: the Maharaj Ji, who set up a large (and cursed and loathed) commune which he reconnoitered in his fleet of Rolls-Royces, opined when he was forced out of the state, "I have been all over the world. I have seen the Pakistani idiot, the Bengali idiot, and the European idiot. But nothing prepared me for the Oregonian idiot."[17]

Portland was named after its counterpart in Maine, but not without a spirited campaign by Amos Lovejoy, who wanted to call it Boston; a coin toss with Francis Pettygrove of Maine decided the issue in 1845. (Portland "would have been Boston except that the coin fell tails," DeVoto wrote.) The city sits on the Willamette River, about twenty miles south of the Columbia—as far inland as seagoing vessels could travel. It looked like an eastern city from the beginning, and soon it looked like a wealthy one. The business elite of Portland, like its counterpart in Los Angeles, was white, male, wealthy, atop the social heap, and convinced that "private enterprise could do anything better than government."[18] It was even more likely to be Protestant, however, Catholics being a small minority in the state—and highly unlikely to be Jewish. (When asked why his firm had hired no Jews in seventy-five years, a lawyer responded that they "never found a Jewish fellow that fit.") But they were settled and conservative people rather than movers and shakers, content to rule the roost in a comparative backwater.

An eastern visitor to Portland remarked in 1903 that the traveler expects a crude western town and discovers instead "a fine old city, a bit, as it might be, of central New York . . . [with all] the signs of conservatism and solid respectability." Maybe too old? "Portland had seemed old even when it was young," Earl Pomeroy wrote, "respectable when it was still crude." For two historians, "Portland moved in 1965 as slowly and deliberately as it did in 1865," and a Time-Life survey two years later found that the old guard "fended off sophistication as inherently suspect." Perhaps Freeman Tilden got off the best line, apparently with a straight face: "To know how Portland, Oregon, would act under the stress of any given circumstances, it is only necessary to imagine how Calvin Coolidge would act."[19]

Oregon was the exception proving the rule of the West: together with the coast of Washington, here was the only place west of the Rockies that looked like a replication of New England. Elsewhere—the Southwest, California, Nevada—Anglophile mimicry had little relevance to the arid climate, or to towns and cities settled by miners and their hangers-on, or to the multitude of new railroad towns. In politics, Oregon resembled New Hampshire: from 1896 to 1988 Oregonians went Republican in every presidential election but two (1912 and 1964), except for a straight-flush FDR-Truman hegemony from 1932 through 1948. The state's solid Republican status did not prevent progressives from passing initiative and referendum legislation in 1902, however; known as "the Oregon System," it engendered engaged and litigious citizens ever since.

Eventually the railroad disrupted the Willamette Valley's tranquil Eden, and it was the same old Southern Pacific—but it wasn't the Big Four who pushed it through. Instead Henry Villard, a Bavarian émigré who became a renowned journalist during the Civil War and married the daughter of abolitionist William Lloyd Garrison, came to control that Pacific coast line (it later became the Northern Pacific), which ran from Portland through various Columbia River towns, and then on to Idaho and Montana and into Canada. By 1882 more than 500 miles of rails ran through the state, and quickly the Oregon lines connected up to the entire transcontinental rail network. But Villard soon went bankrupt (although not too soon to endow the University of Oregon), and by 1887 the Oregon rail system was controlled by either the Big Four or capitalists in New York and Boston. Rail and coastal trade brought a rapid population increase in the last part of the nineteenth century; by 1900 the state's population topped 400,000, eight times what it was in 1860, and the newcomers included for the first time a significant minority—more than 10,000 Chinese who took jobs at the low end of the workforce, with 4,000 skilled cutters working in the fish canning industry, using heavy knives to chop salmon into pieces small enough to can. (But they weren't allowed to fish: an unwritten law stipulated that they could be shot on sight if they dared try, the result of the Chinese having dominated the California fishing industry in the 1860s.) Along came a high-tech machine cutter in 1903, considerably dubbed the "iron chink," and the Chinese were thrown out. The 1900 census counted 10,397 Chinese in Oregon, but after anti-Chinese agitation Oregon had but 3,000 Chinese-Americans by 1920. At the turn of the new century the state was little changed, especially compared to its southern neighbor: it was "as much a backwater as it had been in 1849." Portland, however, had become the center of Pacific Northwest banking and trade, with an "economic dominion over the Pacific Northwest," and its residents liked to tell visitors that it was the richest city in America. It commanded not only the Pacific and riparian terminus of the Willamette Valley, but the nearby forests which quickly turned to lumbering, and the Great Columbia Plain with its abundant fields of wheat.[20]

Portland, the Willamette Valley, and much of coastal Oregon built their settlements "facing East," and in some ways have never stopped. There are many reasons for this, but the principal one is simply the pioneer preference for Oregon over California and the highly developed sense of civic culture that the settlers of the Willamette Valley brought with them. The Pacific coast, so serene and placid in Southern California, is rocky and inclement much of the year in Oregon, and its great beauty shrouded rather than encouraged the gaze across the Pacific. To say this was not a Mediterranean climate is only to begin to understand Oregon's four seasons: evergreens may be permanent, but deciduous trees abound and a palm tree would be very lonely, if indeed it survived.

A newly wed New Yorker who arrived in Portland in 1925, Edith Feldenheimer, told a historian that the city had "a sort of semi-New England background and I felt that having gone to Smith College, I was very much aware of what New England had to offer in the way of culture."[21] You can walk down leafy residential streets in Eugene, Oregon's main university town, and feel the same ambience. Like the Ohio towns of Madison or Granville, Oregon is New England once removed.

The Emerald City

Seattle was founded in the years immediately after the gold rush, but it lacked the hothouse, late-arriving dynamism of Los Angeles. It had boomlets in the 1880s and around the turn of the century, and another modest wave of growth in World War II, but the driving force of its contemporary vigor really did not arrive until the 1980s, when Microsoft, Starbucks, and later Amazon and Nintendo put the city on the map. At the same time its history was short—it began in 1852; one of the original pioneers of the Denny family lived until 1939, when Boston Brahmins could count three hundred years of American lineage. When truly big fortunes were made the money was held elsewhere, exemplified by the Hills and the Weyerhausers in St. Paul. Seattle therefore had no aristocracy to speak of, just lineages from the first handful of pioneers; the enormous influx of Scandinavians carried its own egalitarian values, and the working class in and around the city tended to be more skilled, working in cutting-edge industries like aircraft. The Emerald City therefore grew with perhaps the least obvious class distance in the nation, social and cultural difference was also modest, values were not just civic-oriented but egalitarian, and in spite of the treatment of Chinese in the 1880s and blacks during the war, by and large minorities have found it less oppressive than eastern and midwestern cities.

The first white settlement in Washington was Spokane House, established in the 1830s to trap beavers for the fur trade. Wagon trains began arriving in the 1840s, including the eighty-wagon caravan that left Missouri in 1844 and after eight months and 2,000 miles, found itself excluded from Oregon because it harbored a black man. This man was George Washington Bush, and he kept on going. Part of the first organized pioneer party to reach Puget Sound, Bush had made a fortune in cattle trading in Missouri, erected the obligatory sawmill in Seattle, and kept on prospering. Another famous namesake, George Washington, the son of a slave father and white mother, founded the town of Centralia and later was renowned for his philanthropy in building churches, cemeteries, and helping poor people. Meanwhile famous city fathers Arthur A. Denny (thirty years old), Charles D. Boren, William Bell, and David S. Maynard had gone looking for the Willamette Valley but in 1852 wound up staking claims to land on the east side of Elliot Bay, which would become the core of the city named for Chief Sealth of the Duwamp Indians and (later) home to one of its key attractions, the Pike Street Market. For many years the focal point of city life was Yesler's sawmill, an avatar of the Sawdust Empire and the many lumbering communities that dominated the regional economy into the 1980s. Still largely unexploited, however, was the Puget Sound itself, easily the finest inland sea in the contiguous forty-eight states, protected from storms and running coolly and calmly from the San Juan Islands down through Everett and Seattle to Tacoma. Chief Sealth and his tribe knew all about it, and when the whites banished them to the Kitsap Peninsula after some minor fighting in 1855, the chief left this for posterity: "A few more moons. A few more winters—and not one of the descendants of the mighty hosts that once moved over this broad land or lived in happy homes, protected by the Great Spirit, will remain to mourn over the graves of a people—once more powerful and hopeful than yours. . . . Every part of the soil is sacred in the estimation of my people. Every hillside, every valley, every plain and grove, has been hallowed by some sad or happy event in days long vanished. . . . At night when the streets of your cities and villages are silent and you think them deserted, they will throng with the returning hosts that once filled and still love this beautiful land. The White Man will never be alone. Let him be just and deal kindly with my people, for the dead are not power-less. Dead, did I say? There is no death, only change of worlds."[22]

For decades Seattle was little more than a collection of homes, shops, sawmills, saloons, and streets scattered with sawdust, arrayed on a hill over-looking the bay. By the end of the Civil War it had but 300 residents, com-pared to 5,000 in the rapidly growing city to the south, Portland. But the Northern Pacific Railroad extended to the shores of the Puget Sound in the 1880s, and both Tacoma and Seattle took off; the latter's population quadru-pled to 50,000 in that decade. The railway instantly become the largest land-owner in Seattle, but as always, the manifold virtues of the pioneers assured good fortune, too: in this case the virtue of getting there first and beating oth-ers to the punch. In 1884 the Northern Pacific's land was valued at $592,345, but Arthur and David Denny held land worth a total of $472,661, somewhere around $12 million in today's dollars.[23]

The Olmsted Brothers report of 1903 opened many miles of public parks along the shores of Lake Washington and around Green Lake; Ravenna Park and an arboretum were also part of the original plan, which the city generally followed. After decades of labor a ship canal and the "Montlake cut" finally linked the Puget Sound with Lake Union and Lake Washington, thereby creating a first-rate fresh water harbor, and the diggings were employed to create a downtown waterfront district. Three beautiful bodies of water now surrounded the city. The Olmsteds also worked their Arcadian magic on the design for the 250-acre campus of the University of Washington for the 1909 Alaska-Yukon-Pacific Exposition, its centerpiece fountain and gardens arrayed to take in Lake Washington (a twenty-two-mile-long mountain spring–fed body of water) and a breathtaking vista of Mount Rainier. The newly developing university also surpassed Stanford University's interest in East Asia by founding one of the nation's earliest and best Far Eastern institutes. But in both Washington and Oregon the state universities divided into general and agricultural schools (Washington State at Pullman, Oregon State at Corvallis) much like the midwestern pattern, and this proved to be a long-term weakness in competing with Berkeley for West Coast preeminence; Berkeley was never divided up (it was added onto, with the establishment of UCLA and many other state campuses), and for decades it remained the premier research institution on the West Coast.[24]

Empire Builder to the Orient

When I taught at the University of Washington I enjoyed asking my classes, sometimes three hundred strong, if anyone knew who was depicted in the large statue near the "Hub," the student union. They never did, but James J. Hill was a builder of the Pacific Northwest every bit as important as the Big Four in California. With controlling interests in railroads, land, and politicians, Hill dominated the Northwest from his Romanesque Summit Avenue mansion in St. Paul, on a line running from the Twin Cities through to Seattle and down to Tacoma. Brooks Adams wrote that he exploited the Northwest "precisely as a Roman proconsul might have plundered a conquered province," neglecting to mention that Hill's friend and neighbor Frederick Weyerhauser and many other business barons did the same. Hill was born in Ontario in 1838, to a Quaker family and to Quaker schooling. After losing an eye in a boyhood accident, he moved to St. Paul in 1856 and began working in steamboat transportation, then coal, then local railways. He developed a reputation for meticulous attention to detail, for centralizing all affairs in his own hands, and for tyrannical leadership.[25]

These qualities made him difficult to deal with, need it be said, which hardly distinguished him from the other industrial titans of his era. Moreover there was virtue in this empire: Hill built his rail system without loans from the federal government and ran it so well that it quickly paid dividends to shareholders, and he was more than a match for Seattle bigwigs with fond dreams of Pacific commerce. He liked to point out that Seattle was equidistant from London and Tokyo. When the railway celebrated its arrival in Tacoma, Hill spread out wheat cookbooks written in Chinese and Japanese, and President Grover Cleveland said Hill knew more about East Asia than any man he had met (that might be because Hill sent employees to gather information about China and Japan on a budget bigger than the government's for the same purpose). The last spike was driven on the Great Northern in the snowy depths of the Cascade Mountains in January 1893; six months later the first through train for the coast departed St. Paul as the city celebrated Hill's achievement at a grand banquet attended by George M. Pullman, Marshall Field, and various other magnates. The Northern Pacific was about making Seattle dependent on California, but when James J. Hill drove the Great Northern to its new terminus at Seattle in 1893, this east-west artery opened up both the continent and East Asian trade to the Emerald City, and the city fathers fell all over themselves to reward the domineering Empire Builder— with sixty feet of right-of-way along the waterfront and a new union terminal on King Street (the railroad ran from Grand Forks to Burlington in northern Washington, then flared north and south to link up Vancouver and Seattle). Meanwhile Hill and his partner J. P. Morgan seized on the 1893 panic to buy out the bankrupt Northern Pacific.

This railroad had enormous stimulative effects: quickly the Pacific Northwest gained half a million new residents, amid a fourfold increase in the value of real estate. Meanwhile Hill, Harriman, and the Big Four in California "ruled as probably only the Du Ponts have ruled in Delaware or the copper magnates in Montana." Tacoma was a company town of the Northern Pacific, which controlled the Light and Water Company, the gas works, and the streetcars. Hill followed through on his dreams of Asian trade by building two big ships, the *Minnesota* and the *Dakota,* to connect Pacific commerce to the Asia-Europe "land bridge" of his railway, and named his top express train the "Oriental Limited"; it steamed by Pier 89 in Seattle, where the ships tied up. But not much came of this: both ships went out of service in 1905, and by 1910 Hill lamented a peculiar conception "lingering grotesquely" in many minds: the illusion of "Oriental trade."[26]

Sawdust Empire

When Hill took over the Northern Pacific railway in 1893, he got with it some 1.5 million acres of land, much of it forests full of Douglas fir (the Northern Pacific had received the largest land grant ever awarded by Congress, sixty sections of 25,600 acres each). In 1900 he sold 900,000 acres of land at six dollars an acre to his good friend and next-door neighbor in St. Paul, Frederick Weyerhauser, in "one of the largest private land transfers in American history"; Hill also promised his friend the lowest eastbound freight rates in the country. Soon Weyerhauser had 2 million acres all of his own (the size of Delaware and Rhode Island combined), and through share holdings and dummy companies, he ended up controlling about one-quarter of all American commercial timber and lumber—and he did so mostly from St. Paul; he rarely visited the Pacific Northwest. Weyerhauser mechanized production with the latest technology, especially the "donkey engine" (a steam winch that hauled and stacked huge logs for shipment by rail), wielding it against great firs that can grow 200 feet tall and last a thousand years; lumber cutting quadrupled to 4 billion board-feet annually. Other important discoveries (plywood in 1904, sulfate processes to make paper pulp out of worthless wood in 1909) drove the industry to the forefront in the Northwest, with big paper mills in Everett and Tacoma among other places. Weyerhauser processed nearly 8 billion board-feet of lumber in 1913 alone, but the firm was so dominant (with its companion, the Great Northern, it owned nearly half of all the privately owned timber in Washington) that the "Sawdust Empire" connoted an extraordinary dependency on the timber industry throughout the region. For most of the twentieth century Oregon ranked first in the nation and Washington second in sawtimber. This business also helped to structure the ethnicity of the Pacific Northwest, as thousands of loggers emigrated from Sweden, Finland, Norway, and Denmark. They established communities in northern and western Seattle, especially the Ballard neighborhood that stretches for miles from the university district out to Puget Sound. But James J. Hill did not live to see much of this; he passed away in 1916 after a nasty hemorrhoid got infected and sent gangrene coursing down his leg.[27]

If Seattle and Portland were similar cities in the 1890s, both stars in the empire of sawdust and neither with large industries, James J. Hill's choice of Seattle as the terminus for his railroad (over Portland's spirited objection) made a big difference. Along came the Klondike gold rush of 1897, and Seattle got a permanent leg up over Portland, making for a mini San Francisco of bankers, merchants, and suppliers as the city became the base of goods and services for the northern mining trade. By the end of 1900 some $18 million in Klondike gold had arrived at the Seattle Assay Office and stimulated business throughout the region; not only miners but all Alaskans remained dependent on Seattle for almost everything for many more decades. Seattle boomed for the next twenty years, its population growing six times over, with wealth bursting out everywhere—"all the fine old neighborhoods" were built then, Roger Sale wrote, along with one of America's best park and boulevard networks. Historian Earl Pomeroy is one of the few to link Seattle with Los Angeles, from an early point onward: "probably no two cities owed more to their chambers of commerce, their railroad builders, and the city engineers who planned their water supplies."[28] Still, both northwestern cities were regional capitals in the first half of the twentieth century, no more important to the nation than Indianapolis or Des Moines and way off the beaten track for most Americans.

Washington State still remained primarily agricultural, with wheat the dominant crop. Because the Cascade Range blocks most Pacific rains, the atmosphere moves from humid to arid in a thrice; the Snoqualmie summit gets one hundred inches of rain a year, and the valley eighty miles to the east gets no more than ten, dropping quickly to six inches further onward. But volcanic ash blowing eastward across the land from the Cascades gave a high-alkaline content of loam to the soil, perfect for wheat. Like California, early wheat farms were mammoth (averaging 384 acres) and worked with the latest machines. By 1910 Asian markets were already taking in a lot of Washington wheat, an export market that would reach major proportions after World War II. Otherwise the Great Columbia Plain, or Inland Empire as it was also called, resembled nothing so much as a transplanted Midwest—"in its town and country architecture, in its general agrarian character and attitudes and organizations, in its solid republicanism" (in Meinig's words).[29]

A Klavern or a Soviet in the Northwest?

Oregonians have long prided themselves on their progressivism and toler-ance, so its status as a Ku Klux Klan stronghold on the West Coast in the 1920s is surprising—and it wasn't the "bad people" joining up but "the good people—the *very* good people," a journalist wrote. Klansman Walter Pierce won the governor's race in 1922 by a large margin. Part of it was hostility to the Wobblies, the Industrial Workers of the World (IWW), who had made strong inroads in organizing the lumber industry; part of it was a vicarious fear brought on by the Wilson administration's postwar witch hunt; part of it was disgust for radicals next door in "the soviet of Washington." But little of it had to do with racial conflict, since so few Asians, blacks, Jews, and other minorities lived in the state; instead most of the Klan's animus was directed at the Catholic Church, vastly disliked by small-town and rural Protestants (Klansmen said the KKK stood for battling "Koons, Kikes, and Katholics").[30] Labor unions were less developed in Oregon than in other Pacific states during the Depression, but Oregonians mobilized themselves as if they were, with a state syndicalism law and the "Citizens Emergency League," a self-described "voluntary association of able-bodied, patriotic American Citizens" to protect property and maintain law and order. A major dock strike occurred in 1934, and strikes became frequent in the late 1930s; Governor Charles H. Martin, a former army general (and Democrat), got a "Weekly Report of Communist Activities" from the Portland police Red Squad, the better to stop "labor goons" in their tracks. The Works Progress Administration (WPA) worked its magic in Oregon, however, sponsoring post office murals and building courthouses, low-income housing, and the masterpiece Timberline Lodge, halfway up Mount Hood. With hand-hewn logs and carved wood designs gotten from Northwest Indians, it is still a favorite of tourists—even after Stanley Kubrick used it for his singular horror film *The Shining*.[31]

The Pacific Northwest wrote several stirring pages in the annals of labor history after the Wobblies arrived in Washington. They organized some 3,000 lumber workers and, with the American Federation of Labor, mounted a strike in 1917 that shut down nearly all the mills. Woodrow Wilson sent in the "Spruce Division" (army soldiers) to run the industry, a combination of wartime strikebreaking and progressive reform: the army demanded and got the eight-hour workday that the Wobblies had advocated. Once the war ended, the IWW and the AFL built up such strength that they were able to close down Seattle on February 6, 1919, in a four-day general strike that idled just about everything—factories, restaurants, streetcars—while making Anna Louise Strong (an organizer and pamphleteer) famous, further inciting the "Red scare" then sweeping the country and leaving James Farley's quip—"the 47 states and the soviet of Washington"—to rankle in the minds of civic leaders for decades. Soon, however, the radicals' success was punctuated by an appalling vigilante reaction: on Armistice Day in 1919 American Legion thugs marched on an IWW hall in Centralia, shots rang out (who fired first was never determined), and four legionnaires and two Wobblies soon lay dead. The mob grabbed hold of Wesley Everest, an ex-serviceman and Wobbly, emasculated him, and hanged him from a railroad bridge; a local jury subsequently convicted seven Wobblies of murder, sentences that were not pardoned or commuted until the 1930s. If Wobblies then seemed to disappear, they and other radical organizers left a legacy of social protection that made Washington a progressive state well before the New Deal. In Seattle the Wobbly legacy combined with a spirited and idealistic kind of middle-class radicalism; building again during the Depression and through the 1960s, it remains a strong force today.[32]

After the general strike, Seattle settled into a long, benign, more or less uninteresting life as a provincial city run by nice white folks. Blacks and

Asians were few, Mexicans almost nonexistent, and the ethnic whites were mostly Swedes, Finns, and Norwegians. While New York and Chicago filled up with Irish, Italians, blacks, and immigrants from Eastern Europe, the west side (Ballard) filled up with Scandinavians. Seattle remained a backwater, run in a distracted way by a white oligarchy that could afford to be benign and inattentive because it did not have to run a white police force into black or Mexican parts of town, or move rivers of water to anoint a desert (Seattle had all the water it could ever want). The culture was also predictably tame and uninspiring, sounding a slow pulse—but one that gave Vernon Parrington time to write his masterpiece, *Main Currents in American Thought*, while teaching at the University of Washington: "still the best book to come out of this city," Roger Sale thought half a century later.[33] As in California, World War II changed all that.

CHAPTER SEVEN

Edens Lush and Frigid

The Eastern nations sink, their glory ends,
And empire rises where the sun descends.
—seventeenth-century inscription on a rock in Monument Bay

In 1820 the American Board of Foreign Missions put six earnest missionaries from small towns in Maine aboard a ship named *Thaddeus*. They traveled halfway around the world to find themselves standing on a mountain top—an unaccountably verdant, even Edenic mountain top, swept by cooling trade winds under eternally blue skies. They were atop a volcanic rock pile jutting upward from the floor of the Pacific Ocean formed by lava erupting from the depths, called the Sandwich Islands. Captain James Cook had named them in honor of the fourth Earl of Sandwich, his patron John Montagu.[1] Here, in this Pacific paradise more remote from the terra firma of the continents than any other place on earth, the missionaries founded the purest American colony in the world.

Captain Cook had gone looking for the legendary Northwest Passage, like everyone else, but stumbled upon Hawaii instead and thus became the first white man to "discover" these islands (people from central and eastern Polynesia who mastered long ocean voyages populated them no later than AD 750, ranging more than 2,000 miles from their home islands). A master captain who pioneered chronometry and "lunar distances" and finally began the era of exact navigation, Cook stopped at the "Big Island" now known as Hawai'i (Hawaii refers to all the islands) in 1778, where the natives welcomed him as the long-anticipated god named *Lono*. On a return voyage the next year things didn't go so well: the natives took umbrage at Cook's murder of one of their number, got hold of him, killed him, cooked Cook—and ate him. Or maybe they just hacked his body into pieces (some say no parts were eaten). Cook then exacted his posthumous revenge: his men killed five chiefs and twenty-five other Hawaiians and mounted their severed heads aboard ship. This massacre was a mere beginning; nearly half a million Hawaiians died of disease in the twenty-five years after their first encounter with the good captain, the most famous navigator of his day, highly respected in his native England, where he was elected a fellow of the Royal Academy for the ingenious remedy he invented for scurvy, a disease afflicting men at sea for lengthy journeys (sucking on limes does the trick—and thus "Limeys"). But what Captain Cook really invented was the Pacific—the concept of the Pacific, a Euro-American construction—which acquired its now-familiar dimensions only after his epochal voyages, and which struck people at the time as a "second new world," a sudden expansion of the known world by half. Soon British and American ships were calling regularly at Hawaiian ports, which became the center of American whaling in the Pacific; by the peak in 1852, 131 whalers and 18 merchant ships called the port of Honolulu home. There was also a brief heyday of sandalwood exports to China.[2]

This really was Eden, it wasn't a case of mistaken identity in this Kansas prairie or that Oregon valley. Herman Melville, Jack London, Isabella Bird Bishop—they all sang the praises of these idyllic islands. Even grumpy Mark Twain was impressed ("no other land could longingly and so beseechingly haunt me, sleeping and waking"), and the air was so uniformly lovely and warm (75 degrees the year around, give or take 6 degrees) that the natives had no word for "weather." Where Seattle TV weathervanes struggle to find novel ways to say "it's raining," weather reports in Hawaii are hilarious for their innovative variations on "perfect." The historic low temperature recorded at Honolulu International Airport was 53 degrees; the high, 95. True, earthquakes, volcanic eruptions, tsunamis, and hurricanes lash the islands—so *rarely* that people have trouble remembering the last one (a tsunami killed 159 in 1946, a hurricane killed 8 in 1992). There is no rain in Honolulu for 265 days of the year, and when it rains it doesn't pour (thunderstorms appear 7 days each year on average)—you just need it for the brilliant rainbows. Normal humidity is 68 percent, and 2 of every 3 days are clear or partly cloudy. Tropical birds (the red-footed booby, the red-vented bulbul) abound and flowers come in a thousand shapes and colors, all year round. Maui is a special corner of this paradise, lava craters and stark moonscapes alternating with lush jungle, the Haleakala volcano rising majestically, shimmering white sand beaches, offshore islands glowing in the distance.[3] How unfortunate that the last people in the world who might take naturally to the place were a constricted bunch of Calvinists from Maine.

Hawaii's American history can be put alongside California's in the destruction of native populations (mostly by disease rather than the American hand) and the latifundia-like colonization by a small elite holding huge parcels of real estate—except that in Hawaii they were out-and-out plantations, raising sugar or pineapples for export. Five big firms, held or managed by thirty or forty strategically intermarried families with hereditary succession, controlled the banks, hotels, utilities, and above all the land—nearly 50 percent of which was still held by big landowners as late as the 1960s. The WASP oligarchy dominated the islands for well over a century, Governor John Burns wrote, "as a closed shop, and their policies and opinions had the force and effect of law." Just about everyone else worked for them: in the heyday of big sugar a century ago, one-third of the population (around 50,000 people) labored in the fields and mills.[4]

The critical differences from California were two: Hawaii became central to the American strategic position in the Pacific long before the West Coast did and continued to grow in importance as American power expanded in the world. Since 1940 it has been the headquarters of the commander-in-chief for the Pacific (CINCPAC), base of a great armada of naval, land, and air forces, and the unrivaled core of American power in the Pacific. No other nation has seriously threatened U.S. command of this vast ocean realm since Japan's defeat: Hawaii is the earthly foundation for a truly awesome power projection across some 100 million square miles of land and sea, just about half of the planet's entire surface.

The second difference arose in the perceptions of the early missionaries: Hawaii was in the Orient (or at least *their* Orient). The natives were therefore Orientals, they were strange and even savage in their eyes, but docile and amenable, quickly educable, and quickly convertible to Christianity—that is what the missionaries believed. The native leaders, and especially Hawaiian royalty, were cooperative, malleable, even congenial, sufficiently to intermarry at surprisingly high rates. This all began very early in the American extension to the Pacific, two decades before pioneers set off on the Oregon Trail, three decades before the gold rush. They were small specks in the ocean, these islands, but they gathered up overriding importance in missionary eyes because they were stepping stones halfway to China—halfway to the *conversion* of China. Missionaries were almost always at the forefront of the Pacific expansionism pack, and here was the perfect microcosm and testing ground for all of Asia. If it went well with the natives (and they almost always thought it did), Hawaii bid fare to be the first of many serial conquests for Christ in the Orient. The islands thus provide a riveting example of New England liberal doctrines of natural rights warring with "an absolutist theology that conceived of human nature as inherently evil . . . and projected caste distinctions into eternity," in Vernon Parrington's words, in a modern setting that recalled the first encounters with American natives in the 1620s. But the next generation fell away from mission and into filthy lucre: instead of converting heathen they converted fallow fields to sugar production, establishing by the time of Polk's war with Mexico the purest example of American imperialism, the tightest little colony of any nineteenth-century pioneer experience (not to mention great commercial wealth). But in commerce, too, Hawaii was half-way to China—and maybe halfway to God: "The world is to be Christianized and civilized," Josiah Royce proclaimed, "and what is the process of civilizing but *the creating of more and higher wants? Commerce follows the missionary."[5]

Adam and Eve

The problem was that the missionaries had stumbled not into the Orient, but into an earthly Garden of Eden where the natives sampled way too much forbidden fruit. They ran around half-clothed, surfed the waves buck naked, danced the hula and sang ribald songs, appeared to do no gainful labor, and worst of all, seemed to be having a great time. "Each heathen would paddle three or four hundred yards out to sea (taking a short board with him)," Mark Twain wrote, "then face the shore and wait for a particularly prodigious billow to come along; at the right moment he would fling his board upon its foamy crest and himself upon the board, and here he would come whizzing by like a bombshell!" Two royal "chiefesses" went swimming, then stopped by to say hello to missionaries at Kailua—in the nude. The locals thought it odd that in this tropical paradise the missionaries went around in layer upon layer of clothes, often woolens, usually black. Sailors might call on Pacific islands like Tahiti with overweening anticipation (the women were mostly naked there, too, and even more ravishing in their fragrant palm oil and love of sex), but it didn't take long for the missionaries to arrive at certain unshakeable conclusions: these were "naked savages" who desperately needed God's word, not to mention a decent set of clothes (they shrouded willing native girls in "Mother Hubbards," neck-to-toe cotton gowns). Sarah Lyman let the natives have it in 1832: "The majority of them are more filthy than the swine. Their houses are wretched hovels and the abode of vermin, and the inhabitants covered with sores from head to foot. Some are afflicted with boils, some with sore eyes and a variety of diseases unheard of in our country, arising no doubt from a want of cleanliness. . . . Like brutes they live, like brutes they die." Another missionary, Charles S. Stewart, observed "their naked figures and wild expressions of countenance, their black hair streaming in the wind as they hurried over the water," and decided that they were "half man and half beast."[6] The Puritan penchant for the excision of the senses blanched before the natives' easy relations between the sexes—their thorough knowledge of how to have a good time.

If scholars may quibble about the meaning of Cook's visits (was he taken for a god or not, was he really eaten),[7] missionary founding father Hiram Bingham decided that England's finest navigator deserved exactly what he got: he died because he violated God's will. "How vain, rebellious, and at the same time contemptible, for a worm to presume to receive religious homage and sacrifices from the stupid and polluted worshippers of demons and of the vilest visible objects of creation . . . to encourage self-indulgence, revenge, injustice, and disgusting lewdness as the business of the highest order of beings known to them, without one note of remonstrance on account of the dishonor cast on the Almighty Creator!"[8] Twenty years later Bingham was still complaining (this time to the House Foreign Affairs Committee) about "the lowest debasement of idolatry" among Hawaiians.

The reader may have gathered that Mr. Bingham was less than impressed with the ways of the natives, but what gave ultimate offense to those in the missionary position was the joyful, effulgent abandon of Hawaiian love-making; what Bingham and his ilk took to be a repugnant, unavoidable necessity, the uninhibited natives—and particularly the women—regarded as one of life's sublime pleasures. For centuries their mores had smiled on men and women taking several mates, sometimes sitting around in circles trying to locate a good one for the night, if not for every night; men and women appeared to have sex whenever they wanted, even if they had rigid rules about other matters of gender (men and women were forbidden to eat together, women couldn't eat coconut or pork, and so on). "No women I ever met were more ready to bestow their favors," said Captain Cook. What were a handful of bleached-out Calvinists going to do about all that—were they going to try and abolish human desire, as Walter Lippmann once put it, "with a law or an axe"?[9] Even with missionary boys succumbing to the temptations of the flesh and marrying Hawaiian girls?

The racism so central to the missionary vision was quickly diluted by intermarriage, as first families with prominent names like Bishop and Wilcox acquired Hawaiian in-laws, usually from royal lines: a sugar baron, magistrate, and haole lawgiver of the 1850s, Benjamin Pitman, married Chiefess Kino'ole-o-Liliha; two-thirds of haole men outside Honolulu had taken Hawaiian wives by the 1850s, and that was before major Asian immigration. Soon the elite included District Court Judge George Washington Akao Hapai of white, Hawaiian, and Chinese extraction, who married Harriet Rebecca

Kamakanoenoe Sniffen in 1870, a union that produced seven children of indeterminate ethnicity. Hawaii's current status as the most diverse of American states thus has a long pedigree, forwarded in the first instance by Hawaiians themselves who had no taboos or proscriptions regarding "miscegenation" (indeed, they had no word for it). By 2000 only 39 percent of the population claimed to be all or partially white, 21 percent had two or more ethnicities in their background, and the majority (58 percent) were of Asian ancestry.[10]

The missionaries were moral people doing good works by their own lights, and a little over a decade after their arrival they had 53,000 students in their schools, and by 1846, 80 percent of the population could read. The missionaries developed an alphabet for the Hawaiian language, pushed the monarchy toward constitutional government, and admitted so many natives into their churches that Reverend Titus Coan used a whisk broom dipped in water to baptize more than 5,000 converts. The general absence of armed resistance reinforced the missionary idea that this was a marriage made in heaven, except for the troubling tendency of Hawaiians to die—of mild illnesses like diarrhea and the common cold, or dread diseases like smallpox that killed more than 10,000 in 1853; four more smallpox epidemics came along one after another. Other natives got drunk and stayed that way until their livers gave out, and still others seemed to die simply by virtue of lacking the will to live. Observers spoke of an "overwhelming despair" as Hawaiians watched their civilization evaporate, and as the population withered from 300,000 at the time of Cook's first visit to less than 60,000 by the 1850s, some wondered if the natives would eventually disappear. In fact they nearly did: only 24,000 remained by 1920.[11]

Nearer My God to Sugar

Hawaiians abjured land ownership but the haoles from Maine had no deficiency in the acquisitive instinct, and within a short few years had acquired huge tracts of land. Reverend Richard Armstrong had 1,800 acres by 1850, and sixteen other missionaries had an average of almost 500 acres apiece. Second-generation missionaries were even more likely to shed their mission and turn into capitalists, usually sugar barons. Reverend William Shipman's son got most of his land on the Big Island from the estate of King Lunalillo, who died in 1874, and soon the Olaa Sugar Plantation was among the largest in Hawaii. Sugar prices doubled from the 1840s to the 1860s, by which time haoles owned nearly all the important sugar plantations and the majority of merchant ships visiting the islands; they controlled about 80 percent of all Hawaiian trade. Three million pounds of sugar were raised in Hawaii by 1860, 24 million pounds a decade later, and for the next half-century sugar dominated the economy.

Sixty-three sugar plantations operated in Hawaii by 1880, but real power rested in the hands of a tiny oligarchy of "factors." These were the sugar agents—the companies that hired the laborers; stored, shipped, and marketed the sugar; kept the accounts; husbanded the commissions; banked the profits and provided the lawyers to protect their monopolies. Castle and Cooke, Alexander and Baldwin, Brewer and Company, American Factors, and Davies and Company were the "Big Five," and they were involved in everything important to the economy: banks, insurance, utilities, railways, department stores, hotels; Matson steamships carried whatever they exported, Bishop First National Bank loaned out their money, they suppressed competition even in minor industries like cigars. Like Noah Cross in *Chinatown*, Richard A. Cooke owned the telephone exchange and the electric company. The Big Five were mostly run by the second generation of missionaries, but they still called each other father, mother, cousin: "Father Cooke, Brother Castle, Sister Bishop." Their kids all attended the elite Punahou School, they all intermarried, and they interlarded their boards of directors with each other. Father and mother may have come to convert the heathen, but they ended up running a tight little plantation oligarchy with two overriding interests: no tariffs on sugar exports to the mainland, and "cheap servile labor" to work the fields.[12]

The owners quickly ran out of useful laborers among the natives, since they preferred fishing or surfing or raising taro (shiftless natives "doing nothing" in the planter argot) to the backbreaking toil of the sugar plantations, and most were now literate—whereas the owners preferred illiterate labor. Whites also shrank from the work: "you cannot get a man with white blood" into the fields, a plantation spokesman told a congressional committee; "it is most arduous work. Cane grows very thickly, there is hardly a breath of air in the dense growth." So they began importing labor—Chinese, Japanese, Portuguese. By the end of the nineteenth century nearly 50,000 Chinese and 15,000 Japanese had come to work in the plantations, along with 13,000 Portuguese (many in supervisory roles) and nearly 2,000 Germans and Scandinavians, most of whom were employed as draconian field bosses called "lunas," famous for cracking their black snake whips.

The Japanese, especially, became ever more numerous—after all, this was their outpost in the middle of the Pacific, too. Numbering 43 percent of the population by 1920, most of them had emigrated from Hiroshima, Fukuoka, and Kumamoto. A carefully calculated racial division of labor allocated $1.09 per day to a Japanese doing the same work as a Portuguese ($1.54) or a part-Hawaiian ($1.73). But if people of "white blood" ran away from the harsh work in the fields, so did everyone else. Chinese were 50 percent of plantation labor in 1882 and only 10 percent two decades later, as they virtually monopolized the restaurant business, while Japanese left sugar cane for dry goods shops and truck farming (and later on they all hustled into real estate).[13]

Ananus Comosus: Strange Fruit

It is true: rich people are different from us. They can be childlike in trying to convince us that they rose to great wealth or high position through dint of their own efforts. James Dole arrived in Hawaii at the age of twenty-four with "no money," according to his grandson, and "no business connections." Yet somehow he single-handedly built the largest pineapple operation in the world.[14] His cousin Sanford Dole may have been governor of the territory, he may have been a Harvard graduate with a degree in horticulture, he may have had instant entrée to top status in a place wholly owned and controlled by a tiny elite of odd propensities—rigid Calvinism, Maine stubbornness, sugar plantations—running a banana republic masquerading under the "rule of law": but he did it all on his own. As it happened, James Dole arrived in Honolulu in 1899 with $1,500 in his pocket (about $40,000 today) and quickly came under the wing of Castle and Cooke, who pointed out the virtues of the Ewa Plantation, which Dole plowed cash into for a 21 percent return on his money in a short four months. Governor Dole then called his attention to 200 acres of *Ananus comosus*, the prickly big apple that Guarani Indians had first cultivated in Paraguay, the *halakahiki* or "foreign fruit" to the Hawaiians, long considered a rare delicacy (eaten by the rich)—and soon he owned them. Beyond that nice head start, James Dole was an effective entrepreneur. He was a close student of the natural habits of the pineapple and horticulture more generally; he learned to raise pineapples commercially where others in Hawaii had failed going back to the 1850s; he made one innovation after another in the virgin field of mass production and consumption of this strange fruit, especially the Ginaca machine that automatically removed the tough outer shell; like orange growers in California, he joined the fledgling canning industry just in time for new technologies that would keep the fruit edible long after it reached mainland markets; he convinced investors to buy stock in his fledgling company, including fifty shares bought by William R. Castle Jr., son of William Castle and later ambassador to Japan (in the late 1940s he was a key player in bringing Japan back under the American wing). By 1903 Dole had his company, his plantation, and his fortune. Finally Dole just outright bought the entire island of Lanai and gave it over to pineapple production.[15]

Soon Americans learned all about Hawaiian pineapples through ad campaigns in the major magazines, or via wahinis in grass skirts slicing them up at the 1909 Alaska-Yukon Exposition, or through popular ditties about the pineapple's virtues in keeping people regular. By 1930 Hawaii produced 90 percent of all the canned pineapple in the world, and Dole held about a third of that market. The Big Five never acquired the stranglehold on pineapples that they had on sugar, and in 1931 Dole infuriated them by switching his shipments away from the Matson line (which monopolized Hawaiian exports and was mostly owned by Castle and Cooke) to another company which offered cheaper rates. He had no choice because it was the Depression and Dole Pineapple wasn't doing well, but soon Mr. Dole found himself unable to secure loans from the banks. The next year the directors unceremoniously put him out to pasture—while appropriating the famous Dole name for the brand—and reorganized the company, replacing Dole with a Castle and Cooke executive named Atherton Richards. It was a telling measure of the oligarchy's continuing power.[16]

James Dole was never a team player with the oligarchy—even though he was a charter member by birth. Otherwise the Doles differed but little from the Bishops and the Baldwins. Like the original missionaries they lived a life of extraordinary tropical privilege, courtesy of an ethnic division of labor analogous to Evelyn Mulwray's estate in Beverly Hills. The main plantation was managed by Dole and an indispensable man named Ah Wo, who dedicated his working life to the firm. Ah Kui and two helpers kept the gardens and grounds of their Green Street mansion on the hillsides of the Punchbowl. An unnamed cook handled the kitchen and his wife was the downstairs maid, while Ah Kyau handled the upstairs duties. Howard Ho chauffeured the children back and forth to the Punahou School. The entourage spent their summers on Kahala Beach next to the Cookes and the Athertons. In 2004 Dole's daughter summed up their quotidian existence: "Jim had adequate means, but none of the children grew up thinking they were wealthy."[17]

This equable complacency, incomprehensible to anyone unused to a phalanx of servants, nicely illustrates the ineffable blindness through which the haoles ran their splendid little colony and exemplifies the incapacity of God-fearing white Americans in the West and the Pacific to hold their actions to any realistic mirror, given ideals of liberal and Christian mission that were beyond reproach (plus they did it all on their own . . .). Meanwhile under the blazing sun and amid the backbreaking labor, the workers always seemed happy—at least that's what the pineapple ads and posters always portrayed. When I chugged around the Dole Plantation on a little choo-choo train in 2005, that's what I saw: here a worker, there a worker, strategically placed to grin and wave at the tourists. (Just to make sure I went around twice.) The companies also inserted publicity shots of smiling Caucasians among the women of color laboring in the canneries.[18]

"Handy at Honolulu": The Annexation

By the late nineteenth century Hawaii had acquired a peculiar character merging Atlantic and Pacific experience: the American towns had a distinct New England feel, but the missionaries were pioneers in the tryptic of American expansion in the Pacific—missions, diplomacy, and capitalism went hand in hand, often in the same person, and all were of one mind about any natives they encountered: they should be civilized, that is, "modernized." As Martin Sklar aptly put it, "'Missionary diplomacy was the very essence of rationalism in the strict sense of modernization theory. It was the other side of the same coin occupied by 'dollar diplomacy' and struck in the name of the Open Door." The haoles' imperfect appreciation of native culture led to a quick resort to the use of force, but that hardly marked a departure from the liberal doctrine of the time. No less an authority than John Stuart Mill had sanctified despotism as "a legitimate mode of government in dealing with barbarians" if the goal was their improvement, the elevation of "backward peoples"; liberalism achieved its universality precisely through a kind of missionary dictatorship.[19] In Hawaii the pioneers plunked down New England villages amid a classic tropical, monocultural plantation economy; the two cultures merged in the fabulous mansions that the planters raised up in the hills overlooking Honolulu or Pearl Harbor and in the exclusive clubs renowned for their extravagant society balls. Navy officers were quickly welcomed into this elite; when the Great White Fleet rounded Diamond Head and docked off Waikiki in 1908, "wealthy pineapple and sugar growers entertained the officers royally."[20]

American white settlers—planters, missionaries, freebooters—followed the California model by overthrowing the Hawaiian monarch, Queen Liliuokalani, in January 1893. A "Committee of Public Safety" drawn from the white oligarchy and compliant natives called in 162 sailors and marines from the USS *Boston*, which happened to be sitting in the harbor (the marines were "handy at Honolulu" in Frederick Merk's words), told the queen to abdicate, and elected Sanford Ballard Dole (the son of Maine missionaries, he was running the Punahou School) president of a provisional government. For good measure marines surrounded government buildings and someone declared martial law.[21] Instead of declaring another "Bear Republic," however, the conspirators petitioned Washington for annexation, with sugar planters William R. Castle and Claus Spreckels in the lead (their export interests had been undermined by the McKinley Tariff of 1890). But they also fretted about whether they could sustain their contract labor system under American law.

In any event, newly elected President Grover Cleveland turned them down (and even had the audacity to demand the return to power of the queen, and even said the proposed acquisition violated republican traditions), so they had to form an ersatz lone-star state after all, called the Republic of Hawaii. Seventy percent of its officers were from missionary-related families; it aptly represented planter interests by collecting "very large powers in the hands of the few," in the words of one constitutional delegate (or powers concentrated "in the hands of the Teutons," as a professor put it). Queen Liliuokalani, a strong leader determined to take back the islands and run them on behalf of the natives, continued to resist this usurpation—and so in early 1895 the Teutons knocked on the door of her fine mansion on Washington Place, said "aloha," and clapped her in jail. Remanded to trial, she was given a large fine and duly sentenced to five years hard labor. A limited pardon followed, but she remained under house arrest and later "island arrest" in perpetuity (she couldn't leave O'ahu). In the middle of war with Spain and amid a huge patriotic fervor, President McKinley finally granted the haoles their wish: "We need Hawaii just as much and a good deal more than we did California," McKinley said incredibly; "It is manifest destiny." The haole elites were now Republicans, not a vigilante Committee of Public Safety, and that party dominated the islands through World War II, providing one governor after another (usually of Maine genealogy) and a majority of five or six to one in the state house, patiently legislating in favor of the Big Five, big sugar, and the lowest real estate taxes in the country.[22]

Hawaii's new destiny hadn't seemed very manifest to Grover Cleveland, but McKinley was a Republican who never liked to see a business interest go unpromoted, and here was the stepping stone or "half-way house" to the China market (not to mention those sugar planatations); furthermore the upstart Japanese had made an audacious move on the new Pacific chessboard after Samuel Dole had blocked anymore Japanese immigration to the islands. (Japanese had grown to one-quarter of the Hawaii population, and writers like Nagasawa Setsu had already promoted the islands for Japanese expansion.) A month after McKinley's inauguration, Tokyo sent the heavy battle cruiser *Naniwa* into Honolulu Harbor and let it sit there—agitating Assistant Secretary of the Navy Teddy Roosevelt to announce the "very real present danger of war." He and his president considered dispatching the USS *Maine*—but it was needed in Havana. After several months the *Naniwa* took its leave and the episode was over—except that Congress finally appropriated $100,000 to dredge Pearl Harbor, the Naval War College drew up the first "Plan Orange" for war with Japan (the first of many), and McKinley moved quickly to annex Hawaii. It was now a "territory," not just a bunch of islands, and all its residents were U.S. citizens—that is, Americans—including the overly amorous wahinis. And as if history had a sense of humor, "President" Dole was instantly rechristened "Governor" Dole.[23] Most Americans had little idea what they were getting, but Teddy Roosevelt, Henry Cabot Lodge, and Alfred T. Mahan had brought continuous pressure upon the president to seize this strategic outpost because they thought American Pacific power could take a big leap forward—from a point just north of Honolulu.

A Pearl Worth Its Weight in Sugar

It is difficult to find any place in the world where significant American influence came before that of the other great powers, but Hawaii was one of them—the ill-fated Captain Cook notwithstanding. It was like California, remote and essentially undiscovered. A stepping stone across the Pacific and a stopping point, Hawaii quickly gained a place in American naval strategy. In 1840 the U.S. Exploring Expedition had stumbled upon "the best and most capacious harbor in the Pacific" right where the Pearl River, known for its succulent oysters concealing tiny pearls, spilled into the ocean: Pearl Harbor. The British and the French took an interest, too, of course, but the island power elite was mostly American, and they began to tempt Washington with Pearl's strategic virtues in the 1860s, as a means toward annexing the islands to the United States. The 1875 reciprocity treaty between Washington and the islands was mainly a gift to sugar interests (sugar exports to the mainland would now come in free of tariff), but the treaty had a deeper significance because it "excluded foreign competition and at the same time protected the islands from conquest by any third power" (a protectorate, in other words) and transferred Pearl Harbor to the U.S. Navy for use as a coaling station. This treaty was only good for seven years and then had to be renewed annually, so in 1887 Washington got King Kalakaua to give Pearl Harbor (where the royal family maintained fish ponds) over to the exclusive uses of the navy—but it didn't become a naval base for two more decades.[24]

The strategic visionary who first recommended Pearl Harbor as the centerpiece of American power in the Pacific was a Medal of Honor recipient from the Civil War, Major General John M. Schofield. Unlike any other port in the islands, he wrote in 1873, Pearl was "deep enough for the largest vessels of war" and "spacious enough for a large number of vessels to ride at anchor, in perfect security against storms." The narrow channel to the sea was good for naval defense (when the harbor is looked at from its Pacific mouth, it resembles a narrow colon opening out to a uterus, or kidneys); it would have to be widened and dredged at an estimated cost of $250,000—but little else needed to be done. America would then have a base of critical strategic importance, "the key to the Central Pacific Ocean." His study was done for the secretary of war, but it soon got printed in a local magazine, carrying a perfect oligarch's title: "Worth Its Weight in Sugar—Pearl Harbor." Along came the Panic of 1873 and General Schofield's prescient report rotted on the shelf.[25]

The navy declined precipitately after the Civil War, slashed from 600 to 60 ships, and its leaders, such as they were, preferred sail to steam—even though the United States held the world lead in steam-driven ocean speed (sails dominated long-distance seafaring until the end of the nineteenth century). So Pearl wasn't even much of a coaling station for the next quarter-century, and more dithering followed annexation of the islands. In spite of congressional appropriations, the navy did nothing in the matter of cutting and dredging a usable path to the sea, so Congress anted up more money in 1901, and finally a narrow channel good for small gunboats was dug: but thirty years after the first American accession, the United States was still crawling along on "its slow, bumbling path toward creating a Naval Base."[26]

Hawaii was a colony masquerading as a territory, but it didn't look much like an imperial outpost, let alone an artifact of urgent and manifest destiny. President Roosevelt felt some urgency after Japan smashed Russia in lightning naval strikes in 1904–5, however. In 1907 the Asiatic and Pacific Squadrons merged into the Pacific Fleet, and a year later Congress appropriated real money for Pearl Harbor: $1 million for dredging, dry docks, machine shops, and the like, which soon amounted to more than $2 million. By the end of 1911 a big ship finally could negotiate the narrow channel into Pearl: the cruiser USS *California*, as it happened, carrying on its flying bridge the newly cordial Sanford Dole and Queen Liliuokalani (no longer under "island arrest," it would appear). During World War I the United States built a submarine base inside Pearl, but the war drew American subs to Europe and after the war when the subtender USS *Beaver* returned, the sailors found the base to be "a swamp covered with cactus." Meanwhile the dredging continued —and continued, as if it would never end. Japan's aggression against China in the 1930s concentrated minds, however, and by 1939—but only by 1939—Pearl was capacious enough to harbor the Pacific Fleet, and the navy had developed a sense of style to match Pearl's strategic value: the great ships would turn at Diamond Head and parade past Honolulu "mounting lights on every mast and line of every ship and sweeping the skies with searchlights" before traversing the channel into Pearl and lining up alongside Ford Island. Franklin Roosevelt took a close interest in Pearl, believing its strategic mid-Pacific placement had a huge deterrent effect on Japan; he named it a Defensive Sea Area in 1939, forbidden to all aircraft except Pan Am Clippers, and ordered the fleet to remain at Pearl after sea maneuvers in 1940. In May 1941 FDR declared a state of national emergency and jumped Rear Admiral Chester Nimitz over fifty senior officers to become CINCPAC—commander in chief, Pacific Fleet (it had been CINCUS, but that rhymed with "sink us"). Except that Nimitz thought it unseemly to jump that far, so the command went to Admiral Husband E. Kimmel, who liked to dock the entire fleet at Pearl over weekends to give his men a pleasant Saturday night shore leave.[27]

When viewed from the air, Ford Island sits at the center with a narrow channel leading into the ocean—widened many times to accommodate larger and larger ships. Today Hickam Air Force Base is to the side of the channel, but in 1941 the air force didn't exist: the army air forces were at Hickam, and so were B-17 heavy bombers. Ford Island harbored the Naval Air Station, and to its eastern side was "Battleship Row" where much of the Pacific Fleet sat on December 7, 1941—the battleship *Arizona* (flagship of the Pacific Fleet, it was two football fields long with twelve 18-inch guns in four triple turrets), the *Nevada*, the *Maryland*, the *West Virginia*, and several others, but not (to subsequent Japanese regret) the carriers: the *Enterprise* was returning from Wake, the *Saratoga* was docked in San Diego, the *Lexington* was heading for Midway. Wheeler Air Field, in the middle of the island next to the Schofield Barracks, deployed P-40, P-36, and P-26 fighter planes all nicely gathered together (to prevent sabotage).[28]

The End of Haole Hegemony

The small haole elite still dominated just about everything up to Pearl Harbor and acted politically through a Republican Party that merged white and Hawaiian native power as against the immigrants of color. As a sugar planter's agent, Royal M. Mead, told a congressional committee in 1920, "the white race, the white people, the Americans in Hawaii are going to dominate and will continue to dominate—there is no question about it." Plantation *luna*s stood by the polling offices as workers came to vote (and told them how to vote). Haole elites still went about the islands in morning coats and vests, even on the warmest days, peering at the natives through pince-nez, according to proper genteel tradition.[29] And then came the war and their colonial idyll in the sun abruptly ended.

Hawaii posed a special security problem in the minds of the authorities after Pearl Harbor since so many Japanese-Americans lived there (160,000 or 40 percent of the population, with 38,000 of them foreign-born), with, they thought, questionable loyalties to the United States. Upwards of a thousand Japanese aliens were immediately interned and hundreds of Nisei (second-generation Japanese) were thrown in with them, as security risks. But you couldn't put 160,000 people into concentration camps[30] without demolishing the economy. Thus the mainland solution—guilt by ethnicity, through the internment of 120,000 Americans of Japanese ancestry—was infeasible in Hawaii. And so they ran free, free enough to commit nary a single act of sabotage during the entire war, and free enough to form the 100th Battalion and the 442nd Regimental Combat Team, the latter being the most decorated single combat unit in the war. (In a curious and glorious episode that recalled the Alamo, after weeks of draining and intense combat in Italy the 442nd was ordered into southern France to save the Lost Battalion, infantry troops made up mostly of Texans who were bereft of food and supplies and surrounded by Germans. Through hand-to-hand combat and firing at point-blank range, the Nisei liberated the Texans in what "may have been the most heroic battle of the war," according to Leonard Fuchs—and so when Hawaii wanted statehood, the entire Texas congressional delegation championed the cause.) In the end more than half of the 7,500 soldiers in the 442nd were wounded, 700 died, and 700 were maimed.[31]

The New Deal did not have the determining effect in Hawaii that it had elsewhere, but there were important strikes. Well before the Depression, labor struggles (Japanese launched a mass strike in 1909 and a sugar plantation walk-out in 1920, and Filipino workers walked off their plantation jobs in April 1937) had pushed many plantations toward paternal, company-town measures to placate their workforce, providing housing, health care, shops, various subsidized services, and above all, credit. Long and bitter strikes transformed labor relations in the sugar and pineapple fields, whose 30,000 workers eventually earned the highest paid agricultural wages in the country (field laborers in Hawaii were generally better off than Mexicans in the California fields or textile workers in New England). Hawaiian unions were the first to operate on an interracial basis, against much opposition from big labor leaders. Hawaii also had its Harry Bridges: Jack Hall, a former communist who brought industrial democracy to the islands when he began organizing dockworkers in 1935, broke the plantation barons in the 1958 sugar strike and had nearly 24,000 workers in his union by 1969 despite two attempts on his life. Within another generation, however, mechanization had reduced the number of field workers to a fraction of their former size.[32]

Asian-Americans eventually came to influence Hawaiian politics to a degree unmatched elsewhere in the United States, and the roots of this were in the 1920s. The missionaries were zealots for education (at least those not running sugar plantations), and they established schools all over the islands—which would eventually be their undoing. Public education was a primary route to upward mobility, and McKinley High School, sometimes called "Tokyo High," was the central educational institution on O'ahu, even though it educated the majority of students on the islands. There Nisei children were taught to be Americans, through assimilationist doctrines that quickly created young football players and bobby-soxers but also taught liberalism in the classic sense, ideals like the self-evident truths of the Declaration of Independence that, when long ignored, motivate people to fulfill them: all men are created equal. McKinley High's famous class of 1924 contained politician Hiram Fong, multimillionaire Chinn Ho, Hawaii Supreme Court Justice Masaji Marumoto, and a host of future doctors, lawyers, and professors—almost all of them sons and daughters of plantation workers. Of 2,339 students in 1929, 43 percent were of Japanese ancestry, 20 percent were Chinese, and less than one in ten were haoles. Ultimately nonwhites in Hawaii founded one fortune after another (Chinn Ho's real estate and automobile distributors, Hiram Fong's politics-and-business conglomerate, Larry Kagawa's insurance, Hung Wo Ching's Aloha Airlines)[33]—and then the endlessly burgeoning tourist trade, the real estate industry-cum-cornucopia, and apparently bottomless investment emanating from Japan allowed nearly everyone to live happily ever after (assuming real estate prices didn't tank), under a liberal political regime that the tourist trade floated.

For most Americans and the millions of tourists who visit every year, Hawaii's American history begins with the "sneak attack" at Pearl Harbor, and not a few who saw *From Here to Eternity* believe they actually witnessed the assault on that sudden Sunday, even if from the relatively unscathed confines of the Schofield Barracks where much of the movie was filmed—and where a scared teenager named James Jones was an office clerk in the 27th Infantry Regiment. Or they believe they know the beaches of O'ahu by watching Burt Lancaster and Deborah Kerr roll around in the surf below the Halona Blowhole Lookout. This in a paradise where a cadre of American pioneers had landed on an inexplicably sublime mountaintop and called it home for 120 years.

Edenic Wilderness

One frontier did not close in 1890, indeed, it never closed: Alaska remains the singular American state where rugged individuals still hunt fur, dig gold, fell timber, fend off grizzly bears, and reel in sparkling salmon, and where they still confront the loneliness and isolation of the wilderness. Here Indians still imitate Marx's pastoral idyll—fishing in the morning, hunting in the afternoon, and writing (to their congressman) in the evening. Here Washington still appears as the capital of a distant colony with an Indian name ("Alaska" is an Aleut word meaning "great land"), given over almost completely to the extraction and export of raw materials. "Great Land" names an enormous expanse more than ten times the size of New York State; three Californias can fit inside Alaska's boundaries with New York and Pennsylvania thrown in. Three waves of settlers arrived during the Klondike gold rush, World War II, and the long cold war during which Alaska was a front-line state, yet in that broad land live barely more people than in the District of Columbia. Alaska also takes western history to another extreme: the federal government was, is, and will be the dominant force in this state, giving, taking, protecting, and legislating the lifeblood of daily affairs for 600,000 people who depend on Washington as much as they resent its interference.[34]

Alaska is washed by the Pacific more than any other West Coast state, with a coastline 31,246 miles long. It's just not a very hospitable Pacific, dropping torrential rains and blizzards and never warming above 50 degrees in the summer. But then Alaskans are supposed to live in snow drifts at 40 degrees below zero for most of the winter, aren't they? In fact the southeastern panhandle, "knuckled to the main body of Alaska by a glacier the size of Rhode Island" (in John McPhee's words) and home to Juneau, is warmed by the Japanese current and has an inclement maritime climate much like Seattle's, with lows of 20 degrees in the winter, mild 60s or 70s in the summer, and as much as 200 inches of rainfall annually (it rains about 220 days a year; some residents say Juneau ought to be domed). The Aleutian Islands are similarly foggy and wet, but cooler. Fairbanks has the best (or worst?) of both worlds, with summer temperatures that reach 90 degrees, but then frost arrives in late August, and by January it's minus 60 degrees. Much of the state is green much of the year—and greening all the more with global warming.

The northern tundra steppe does not disappoint Alaska's frosty image, however. It is arid, with something close to permafrost: the ground rarely thaws below a few inches, even in July. Some sixty-five mountains crest over 10,000 feet, and America's highest peak, Mt. McKinley, rises to 20,302 feet; Alaskans argue that in sheer vertical rise—18,000 feet from foot to crest—it is the world's tallest mountain. Indians worshipped this awesome rock pile, which still seems close when viewed from fifty miles away. They liked to call it Denali, but on his trek out of the mountains in 1896 a young Princeton graduate heard the news that William McKinley got the Republican nomination, and named the great peak for posterity. From an airliner window the largest American state appears to be an unbroken icy labyrinth of sharp peaks and glaciers, but it has at least sixty active volcanoes, 10 percent of the world's total. Russians watched an island being born out of a fiery volcanic eruption in 1796, and on Good Friday in 1964 an earthquake registering between 8.7 and 9.2 on the Richter scale erupted under Prince William Sound, sending a mammoth tsunami crashing into (and destroying) Valdez and demolishing many buildings in Anchorage. Alaska contains "most of the nation's designated wilderness," William L. Lang wrote, "the greatest expanse of roadless areas, the largest national forest . . . the largest known oil reserves, and a physical isolation that ranks second only to Hawaii . . . a place of wilderness dreams and experiences."[35]

A Frosty Cripple Creek

Whites showed up in numbers not too long after Seward's folly, when modest amounts of gold were discovered on Douglas Island in 1880 and homes, hotels, and shops sprouted in Juneau, across a narrow channel from the mines. Along came more strikes at Fortymile in the Yukon, also Mammoth Creek, Mastodon Creek, and Birch Creek; by 1900 the Treadwell Mines had the largest gold stamp mills in the country, and Juneau had twenty-two saloons swamping its three churches in a river of alcohol. Eventually the Gastineau Channel overflowed the mines (in 1917), ruining them, but the rough-hewn citizens of Juneau persisted through rain and flood, thick and thin, and one day found themselves residing in Alaska's capital. Meanwhile people came clambering up to the Klondike after four oddballs out of the western imaginary—George

Washington Carmack (aka "Lying George"), his Indian common-law wife Kate, and two other Indians calling themselves Skookum Jim (Skookum is an Indian word for "strong") and Tagish Charlie—found huge deposits of gold in 1896 at Rabbit Creek, a Yukon River tributary, and announced it in Big Bill McPhee's Caribou Saloon at Fortymile. Soon it was called Bonanza Creek, the richest placer stream ever known to the world.

Argonauts had to thrust and drag themselves over the nasty terrain and the heights of Chilkoot Pass, but as many as 40,000 did so, and by 1898, 20,000 of them lived in the instantly legendary town of Dawson. The vast majority were Americans who couldn't be bothered about poaching on foreign territory (the Klondike happened to be in Canada, where the Yukon Territory triangle almost reaches the Gulf of Alaska and almost divides Juneau from Anchorage), most came up empty-handed, and so did Dawson—not even a thousand people lived there by 1901. But $150 million in gold came out of the Klondike, and elsewhere there was copper; the Guggenheim Corporation mined rich deposits with funds underwritten by J. P. Morgan, and Alaska got America's only national railroad courtesy of the federal government. Even E. H. Harriman showed up (in 1899), bringing a big research crew of scientists and a retinue of servants (120 people in all) along on a 250-foot-long yacht, to reconnoiter Alaska and see if his dreams of a railway through the Aleutians to Asia had merit. Harriman brought along chickens, pigs, and cows to feed everyone, but he also bagged a brown bear on Kodiak Island—after his men had beaten the bushes for three days to flush out his quarry: "an old sow with cubs." Then he sailed away—but the good federal bureaucrats stepped in and declared Kodiak's bears a protected species, and they still are: so it takes about three hours, not three days, to find one today.[36]

Alaska was no different than Hawaii in the transformation that Pearl Harbor wrought in government spending, as World War II and the cold war provided most of the investment and growth in Alaska for fifty years until the Trans-Alaska Pipeline boom. Before 1941 most big business was absentee, dealing in gold, salmon canning, and copper. From the turn of the century until the war the settler population was steady at about 30,000, with Indians about an equal number. New Deal agencies built bridges and breakwaters, municipal buildings and roads during the Depression, but Pearl Harbor sent federal spending skyrocketing. The U.S. Army built the Alaska Highway and army and army air bases in Anchorage, which became headquarters of the Alaska Defense Command at a time when fears of a nearby Japanese invasion were not fantasies like they were in California. Indeed, in June 1942 Japanese

forces captured the islands of Kiska and Attu at the western tag end of the
Aleutians (Attu is the closest Aleutian island to the Kuriles, about 650 miles
away from where Yamamoto's strike force assembled at the end of November
1941). The army's Seventh Division together with Canadian units took Attu
back in bitter fighting in May 1943, with 600 American dead and more than
1,000 Japanese killed or suicides, save for 28 POWs. Around 6,000 Japanese
were still holding Kiska, but they evacuated the island—first by submarine
(losing three of them to U.S. attacks), and then in July some 5,000 soldiers
crept away in heavy fog aboard the cruiser *Tama* and several other ships. A-20
light attack bombers flew from Ladd Field in Fairbanks to Siberia, delivering
Lend-Lease aid to the Russians, and by the end of the war nearly 8,000 flights
had departed Fairbanks on this "Red Star Line." A southern racist, General
Simon Bolivar Buckner, ran the Anchorage Defense Command and much
else as Jim Crow territory—except the "crows" were usually Indians. Restaurants posted signs saying "no dogs or Indians allowed," and the military
operated segregated movie theaters. Buckner's command removed nearly 900
Aleut villagers from the Aleutians and interned them in four abandoned fish
canneries, leaving them to fend for themselves the rest of the war with no
doctors and skimpy provisions. Military personnel occupied—and looted—
their homes, and the navy burned several villages, presumably to deny them
to invading Japanese. The Aleuts returned to their homes after the war, minus
the 40 children and elderly who had died during internment.[37]

Seward's Savvy

It took a while, but "Seward's folly" turned out to have been a master stroke:
his offhand acquisition permanently removed the Russians from the continent, pushing them back just far enough to pose no strategic threat (until
ICBMs made them a threat everywhere). More important, Alaska capped
the ceiling of the Pacific with its twin panhandles, running southwest to
Unalaska Island and the Aleutians, back through Anchorage and then southeast to the sliver of temperate land containing Juneau and Ketchikan and
Prince of Wales Island, thereby mimicking the shape of the North Pacific
itself—like the silhouette of Commodore Perry's "fore and aft" cocked hat.
Now a comprehensive American Pacific Rim began in San Diego, ran north
along the coast for more than 2,000 miles and then northwest to the Bering
Strait and the Aleutians, arced down along the Asian coast by the Kamchatka
Peninsula, Japan, and Korea, and then on to the Philippines, potentially
gathering in everything Pacific north of the equator. Isolated Hawaii now sat

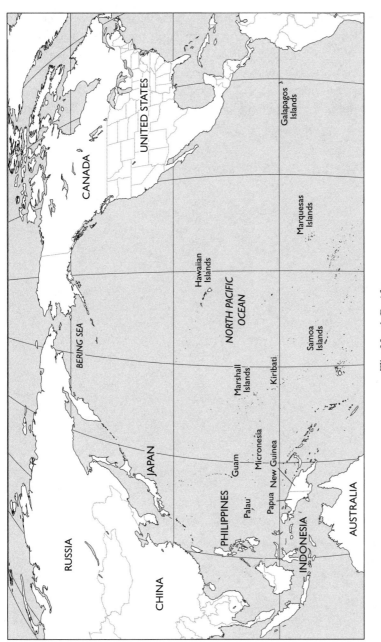

The North Pacific.
Map by Bill Nelson.

in the middle, looking suddenly like a strategic centerpiece rather than a bunch of Polynesian islands almost equidistantly remote from Los Angeles or Shanghai. By 1900 Manila and Pearl Harbor were in American hands, and by 1945 American forces would garrison every valuable strategic point (Japan, South Korea, Taiwan, the Philippines, Okinawa, Guam, Midway, Wake Island), turning the seemingly limitless North Pacific into an American lake.

CHAPTER EIGHT

Pacific Crossings:
Asians in the New States

The first generation passed away, the next de-Chinaized, Americanized and educated, would soon become absorbed in the national life, and known only as model artisans and workers. As the ocean receives all rains and rivers . . . so America receives the Saxon and the Celt, the Protestant and the Catholic, and can yet receive Sambo and John, and absorb them all.

— GENERAL JAMES F. RUSLING, 1866

From the very moment that Americans welcomed California into the Union, the westward march of empire ran into people going the other way—"eastering" across the Pacific. This ocean crossing eventually brought millions of Asians to the Pacific states, but for more than a century after the gold rush these early pioneers endured an appalling racism that barely distinguished the West from the abusive treatment of blacks in the South. If slavery was not widespread (it did exist from time to time), various kinds of indentured servitude often began an Asian pioneer's life, lynchings were frequent, and many massacres stained the soil. This sorry record culminated in the forced removal to ten concentration camps of 120,000 Americans of Japanese descent after Pearl Harbor. Opportunities for everyone abounded after the war ended, but public spaces remained segregated in the Pacific states, real estate covenants kept cities divided, antimiscegenation laws were still on the books, and Asian immigration remained sharply restricted until 1965. The dramatic change that year—a new immigration law that was also a strong expression of the civil rights movement—opened floodgates that brought millions of new Asian-Americans to Los Angeles, San Francisco, Portland, and Seattle.

Longtime Californ'

Tens of thousands of Chinese '49ers crossed the Pacific, and no significant group of pioneer Californians was any earlier. The pull of the gold rush and the push of the massive Taip'ing Rebellion brought Chinese streaming to the

West, as many as 25,000 by 1852, and in some states, like Idaho, they came to constitute as much as 30 percent of the population. They were unquestionably pioneers, but their passage and arrival evoked the experience of other Americans—those from Africa: workers ubiquitously known as "coolies" were sold or indentured to European and American agents for transit across the Pacific. In 1852 a British report described the scene in Amoy: "The coolies were penned up in numbers from 10 to 12 in a wooden shed, like a slave barracoon, nearly naked, very filthy, and room only sufficient to lie [down]; the space 120 by 24 feet [held] . . . the number in all about 500." Each one's destination was scrawled on his chest—C for California, S for Sandwich Islands—and then they were shoved onboard and into the hold where they were confined for the ocean voyage, often in cages and chains. One load in 1855 led to the suffocation of nearly 300 people; about 30 percent of coolies shipped to Peru over a three-year period died during the passage. California's Ellis Island had a wholesome name: Angel Island. But the Pacific immigrant passage was not like that of the European: the Guantánamo prison camps of the second Bush administration would be a closer comparison. For three decades after 1910, some 175,000 Chinese were detained on Angel Island in appalling, overcrowded conditions; they spent weeks, months, and even years trying to show that they should be admitted to the United States. In the end, the vast majority (about 90 percent) were, but many others were deported for any kind of infraction, however minor. For decades Chinese could not return to China to see relatives without fearing that they would not be allowed back in.[1]

A grand total of seven Chinese residents lived in California in 1848, a decade later there were 35,000, and by 1860 every tenth Californian was Chinese; they were present at the creation of this state and present for the creation of long-lasting Anglo stereotypes. The *Shasta Courier* reported the arrival of Chinese miners in April 1852: "An immense number of the uncouth visaged [*sic*] and picturesquely dressed sons of the Orient passed through this place . . . enroute [*sic*] for the Trinity mines. . . . How these little, weakly looking hombres manage to carry such loads over such mountains . . . we cannot possibly comprehend. However, we suppose it is done by some sort of legerdemain, as it is well known that the Chinese can do almost anything through the instrumentality of certain mystic sciences."[2] But there was nothing surprising, let alone "mystical," about it: southern China had a long tradition of sending adventurous young males throughout Southeast Asia— Singapore, Indonesia, Malaya. Now they were just extending the domain of their Pacific.

Chinese workers on the railroad were often highly skilled, and unlike

many others they didn't pass the nonlaboring hours with whiskey and women
—mostly they sipped life-giving green tea or took daily baths or laundered
and pressed their clothes (astonishing the slovenly whites), while the white
workers reinvented the gold rush days: the railroad brought "a brawling,
whoring, drunken civilization" to the West (yet again). Upwards of 12,000
Chinese built the western line, fully 90 percent of the workforce. They were
hardworking and fearless—dangling from long ropes in wicker baskets, a
venerable Yangze River technique for canyon labor; poking dynamite holes
into the face of granite mountains (Summit Tunnel was drilled through a
quarter mile of granite); laboring through the howling Sierra winter; learning
how to deploy nitroglycerin without blowing themselves up (which nonetheless happened all too often); or facing a blank wall of prejudice that led to
frequent murders and lynchings: the western railroad was the handiwork of
thousands of nameless and faceless individuals, most of whom embarked
from a few counties near Canton. From this point onward, big business
favored Chinese immigration, and organized labor became its biggest and
most powerful opponent.[3]

In 1854 the *California Farmer* wrote that growers were tired of the "bindle
stiffs" and "fruit tramps" representing the flotsam and jetsam of failed '49ers;
they wanted instead to bring in the Chinese: "The Chinese! . . . educated,
schooled and drilled in the cultivation of these products are to be to California what the African has been to the South. This is the decree of the
Almighty, and man cannot stop it." Chinese immigrants were particularly
important in the Central Valley: they built dykes, dug irrigation canals, and
showed whites how to farm intensively, whether they were raising rice, potatoes, strawberries, or apple orchards. They were "the first farmers in the
West to produce and market" a host of commercial crops, "leading the way in
the transformation of California's wheat fields and cattle ranges."[4]

By 1880 one-third of all farm laborers were Chinese. Giant producers like
Miller and Lux liked Chinese labor because it was low cost, disciplined, and
self-sufficient—the workers fed and housed themselves. The owners contracted with the Six Companies (Chinese firms or "tongs") in San Francisco
to bring labor gangs to the fields, giving the brokers $27 a month per worker
in the 1870s, from which the broker took his cut and then used the rest to pay
off the debts incurred in shipping the laborer from China (no Chinese could
return to his home village without a clearance from the Six Companies). The
growers loved the system. As Alice Prescott Smith put it, the Chinese labor
boss would provide fifty replicas of himself, carrying their own food and
bedding: "They lived in the field, worked as locusts, cleared the crop, and

melted away." In return the companies provided social protection, insurance, and banking services, even armed force through the "specials" that roamed through the Chinese ghetto. And as Jake Gittes could have told you, "For many years the Six Companies kept a special Chinatown contingent of San Francisco policemen on their payroll." Jack Manion spent twenty-five years running "the Chinatown Squad" from 1921 into the World War II era; an Irishman like most of the city police force, he was "really the law" in Chinatown—well, either he was or the Six Companies were. Actually these companies were above the law, enforcing their own rules somewhat like the Mafia to sponsor illegal gambling, extort protection money, and traffic in women and drugs. (It seems that they still do, at least in New York.)[5]

Chinese males probably constituted about one-fifth of the gainfully employed in California by the 1870s, and among wage workers it was more like one-quarter. Where Chinese were not excluded—in mining, agriculture, and trades like cigars and tailoring—they almost took them over: of about 8,700 people in the cigar industry in the 1880s, 8,500 were Chinese; of 8,510 tailors, 7,510 were Chinese. Many of them were Californians much longer than whites, but they had to live in their own hermetic Chinatown world. Chinese were excluded from San Francisco business clubs, law firms, brokerage houses, and the ranks of judges and city supervisors. Large sections of the city would not sell or rent to them; they quickly ran into trouble if they dared cross the perimeters of Powell Street, Broadway, or Kearny by themselves. Thus they had to live cheek-by-jowl in sections of the city open to them, which in turn became objects of Anglo curiosity—people liked to gather and watch Chinese laundrymen "distend their cheeks with water and then sprinkle the undergarments of ladies and gentlemen there from."[6]

Others drew a truer picture of people of color in the new West. General James F. Rusling wrote a fascinating account of his military inspection mission in 1866, full of insight and wise observation. In Portland he encountered "John Chinaman" and decided that "as a class [they] were doing more hearty honest work by far, than most of their bigoted defamers. We could not refrain from wishing them well, they were so sober, industrious, and orderly." By the time he got to San Francisco he concluded that without the Chinese, the industry of the Pacific Coast "would soon come to a stand-still." On New Year's Eve 1866, General Rusling gathered at the grand Occidental Hotel in San Francisco with assorted city fathers and many of the wealthiest Chinese merchants to celebrate the launching of the *Colorado*—the first steamer on the new monthly route to Hong Kong. Representatives of the big Chinese companies were there, too, and they all seemed to get along amiably with the San

Francisco elite. "Here, surely," General Rusling wrote, "is evidence of fine talent for organization and management—the best tests of human intellect and capacity . . . [that] imply a genius for affairs, that not even the Anglo-Saxon can afford to despise."[7]

General Rusling was appalled by the whorehouses in Chinatown—but mainly by the white men who frequented them: "the brutality and bestiality of Saxon and Celt here all comes suddenly to the surface, as if we were fiends incarnate." This and other "shameful spectacle[s]" that he observed led him to think that "justice will not sleep forever" when confronted by "a strong race trampling a weaker one remorselessly in the mud." He went on to urge that millions more Chinese be enticed to emigrate; they will do all the hard work and slowly assimilate: "The first generation passed away, the next de-Chinaized, Americanized and educated, would soon become absorbed in the national life, and known only as model artisans and workers. As the ocean receives all rains and rivers . . . so America receives the Saxon and the Celt, the Protestant and the Catholic, and can yet receive Sambo and John, and absorb them all." Rusling thought this was what Jefferson meant by the preamble to the Declaration of Independence—his was an early call for assimilation and multiculturalism.[8]

Outside the relative sanctuary of San Francisco, whites could do with Chinese whatever they wanted. In Rock Springs, Wyoming, whites demolished the Chinese community in 1885: they massacred twenty-eight people and drove some six hundred more from their homes, which they then put to the torch at a total loss of $150,000; the authorities sided with the whites. Two years later renegade "cowboys" murdered thirty-one Chinese miners working along the Snake River, mutilated their bodies, and looted their belongings. A white jury later refused to convict anyone for the crime ("none of the jury knew the Chinamen," a local rancher explained). Meanwhile Indians were equal-opportunity marauders: Paiutes slaughtered forty to sixty Chinese miners in 1866, and lesser massacres of Chinese by Indians were commonplace in the West.[9]

Relatively few Chinese lived in Washington's cities and towns in the late nineteenth century compared to California or Oregon, but that did not stop the proper citizens (especially the police) of Seattle and Tacoma from abusing and ultimately banishing them. In 1885 the mayor and the police chief of Tacoma spearheaded a movement to expel several hundred Chinese from their homes and buildings, and a year later the Seattle police chief led an angry mob of whites into Chinatown under the guise of examining sanitary conditions, whereupon the mob broke into homes, loaded belongings and furniture onto wagons, and forced the Chinese to march to the dock and get onboard the *Queen of the Pacific,* bound for San Francisco. The rule of law resurfaced momentarily when a federal judge kindly informed the Chinese that no law required them to go, but most of them had the good sense to clamber aboard—especially since teamsters had already loaded their furniture and belongings. Trouble was, there were too many of them. So 196 left and 200 remained, as the threatening crowd closed in on them—"raving, howling, angry men." Whites grabbed rifles from the police and fired into the crowd, killing two Chinese. The governor declared martial law and began summary arrests; the next day President Grover Cleveland ordered in federal troops. The remnant got out as best they could, and Chinese did not return to Seattle for many years. Similar efforts to drive the Chinese out occurred all over the West in the 1880s and particularly in California—except for San Francisco, to which the Chinese typically fled; newspapers once estimated that the city's Chinese population grew by 20,000 in a few months. Labor unions didn't like that, so they organized a Pacific Coast anti-Chinese congress given over to nauseating racial invective. Within a few years, all the anti-Chinese agitation culminated in the 1902 law permanently excluding Chinese immigrants.[10]

In both Los Angeles and San Francisco new Chinatowns replaced old Chinatowns, like a palimpsest burying history. The first Chinatown in Los Angeles was legendary—an underground city, "a nest of catacombs where inscrutable sins were committed," in Norman Klein's words. For paleface sinning there was also an aboveboard city: all legalized prostitution was situated in Chinatown until 1909. The whores and the opium dens were mostly for whites, and it was all fine until the city fathers decided to demolish Chinatown to make way for the Southern Pacific train depot (the Union Station that still sits as a monument to 1930s art deco, Mission Revival style); here was a multiple palimpsest, because Union Station and the old Chinatown stood on the site of the first orange grove ever laid out in California (by a Kentucky trapper in 1841). City fathers burned the brothels, opium dens, and cribs to the ground in fear of bugs and germs that might carry bubonic plague.[11] A new Chinatown emerged a few blocks away, a spiffed up Potemkin Village attractive to tourists instead of the slumming whites who patronized the cribs. In San Francisco the great earthquake and fire destroyed a Chinese ghetto that traced its roots back to the gold rush, so the city replaced it with a red-and-gold simulacrum for tourists. (The 1906 fire also burned up city records on Chinese immigration, enabling thousands to make up genealogies attaching them to Chinese families already resident in the city.)

A German photographer, Arnold Genthe, recorded the old Chinatown and then tried to reconnoiter the lost past of his own camera images in the new one. All the grime and dirt, the inclement density of people forced to live on top of each other, the fascinating human panorama—it had all washed away, he wrote in 1913: "On brilliantly illuminated streets, smoothly asphalted, filled with crowds in American clothes, stand imposing bazaars of an architecture that never was, blazing in myriads of electric lights. Costly silk embroideries in gaudy colors, porcelains of florid design, bronzes with hand-made patina, and a host of gay Chinese and Japanese wares which the wise Oriental manufactures for us barbarians, tempt the tourist to enter." Some tourists were taken in, while others saw more: Oscar Wilde called San Francisco's Chinatown "the most artistic city I have ever come across." Will Irwin, in a book containing Arnold Genthe's photographs of Chinatown, exemplified the interchangeability of Oriental stereotypes in California. He offers a paean to the Chinese cook (found in every California mansion according to him): "He was the consoler and fairy-teller of childhood. He passed on to the babies his own wonder tales of flowered princesses and golden dragons . . . he saved his frugal nickels to buy them quaint little gifts. . . . The Chinaman was an ideal servant." But now, "the insolent and altogether less admirable Japanese" were taking their places by the cook stoves, and so "your San Francisco housewife will never cease lamenting for the old order."[12]

American Stoics

Throughout the United States and much of American history Chinese individuals and families have lived in isolation, running a restaurant or a laundry in a small place, often as the only Chinese-Americans in town. It is a largely unnoticed diaspora, taken for granted by other Americans as a fact of life—but not a very interesting one. In 1953 Paul Chan Pang Siu completed a dissertation at the University of Chicago entitled "The Chinese Laundry-man: A Study of Social Isolation." (People on the Pacific Coast had sent laundry to be done in Canton before many Chinese came to America, believe it or not, which began the association of Chinese with washing clothes.) Siu called the laundryman neither a marginal man nor a person interested in assimilation; he was instead "a sojourner." Not that he expected to return to China (although Americans liked to ask when he was planning to go back)—the sensibility of the sojourner was a response to discrimination. Likewise he worked as a laundryman out of necessity, not choice; none of the subjects Siu studied ever said their ambition was to be a laundryman. Most of them were single, social contact with customers was perfunctory, the hours were long;

they led miserable workdays waiting for a few hours of "frantic release" on Sundays to gamble or visit a prostitute. They passed the time in the laundry thinking up new Cantonese insults to mock unsuspecting customers who came and went.[13] Racial oppression cannot destroy the curious phenomenon that it creates, namely, W. E. B. DuBois's famous "gift of second-sight," which takes the measure of the oppressor.

When Jack Nicholson comes looking for Faye Dunaway in *Chinatown*, a Chinese maid greets him at the door: "Mrs. Mulwray no home." That was the only line Beulah Ong Kwoh spoke in the film—an English literature major at Berkeley with a master's degree from the University of Chicago who spoke perfect English. The writer Frank Chin, a fifth-generation American, still bumps into whites who congratulate him on his fluent English and ask what part of China he's from: "You dumb bitch, I'm not from China," he wants to say. When he worked in a bar as a student they called him "the Indian"; drunks would apologize to him for nuking Hiroshima. Blacks feel that they have been emasculated by whites, Chin wrote, but "the genius of white racism in regard to the Chinese is that they never granted them balls in the first place. They convinced them that it's so. That it was a virtue to be passive, to keep your place." His own father was example number one—yet he was president of the Six Companies. "I look at the way he tunes the television set, it's all wrong. The people look like they're dead. They come on looking dingy, gray, the color of Roquefort cheese. But that's the way he sees the world."[14]

A "New Japan" in California

Chinatown in Los Angeles was much smaller and less influential than its northern counterpart. The City of Angels was instead a mecca for Japanese. Also pioneers in an easterly direction, early migrants hoped to find open land that they could develop, thus "to create the second, new Japan" in the American West (as an 1887 guide for emigrants put it). Between 1895 and 1908 about 130,000 Japanese migrated to the United States and Hawaii, most of them males from better-off rural households looking for bigger earnings. By 1935 around 32,000 Japanese lived in Los Angeles County, 13,000 in the city itself, and almost all of them lived in Little Tokyo spreading out from First and San Pedro streets. At least half were born in the United States but almost all of these were kids—perhaps three-quarters were under twenty-one. The Japanese cornered the produce business, supplying from some 5,135 farms three-fourths of the fresh vegetables—cauliflower, strawberries, spinach, tomatoes, celery—that the great city consumed. More than 500 Japanese fishermen plied the nearby coastal waters. Subject to continuous prejudice and restrictive housing covenants, Japanese-American aspirations were nonetheless thoroughly American and middle class—"home-owning, church-oriented" (even if Buddhist and Shinto congregations sat alongside Christian churches)—and dedicated to the American pastime that took hold so readily in Japan: baseball. A third of their children went on to college.[15] Teenage boys with their letter sweaters and cheerleading girls in bobby sox crowded into hamburger joints and movie drive-ins.

The Nisei desire to Americanize and settle down did little to stop the racial hatred that had denied them home and farm ownership, and that kept them penned up in segregated housing—which of course meant segregated schools (and for good measure, in 1906 the San Francisco school board ordered all Oriental students into a single segregated school in Chinatown). Carey McWilliams gave a name to this sorry experience—the California-Japanese War of 1900–1941—that aptly reflected how white Californians had contaminated United States–Japan relations long before Pearl Harbor, and how American expansion, especially the acquisition of Hawaii, had brought tension to the relationship with Japan. This was race- *and* class-based antagonism; Japanese farmers were too good, they threatened their white counterparts. At the peak in 1909, 42 percent of the farm labor supply in California was Japanese, rising to 66 percent in sugar beets and 86 percent in berries. In Los Angeles alone, Japanese-farmed acres grew from 6,173 in 1910 to 30,820 in 1940, with much of the acreage along the lovely coastline of the Palos Verdes peninsula, thought by Anglo farmers to be too arid. Soon these lands drew the highest truck farm rents in the state. If anti-Chinese fervor was strongest among labor unions, anti-Japanese agitation came from middle- and lower-middle-class whites threatened by their success.[16]

Japanese-Americans tried to fit in. K. K. Kawakami, secretary of the Japanese Association of America and a writer on United States–Japan relations, published several books from 1903 to 1920 arguing that the rise of Japan as a modern nation-state posed no threat to the United States but would complement America's own power in the Pacific (this is China's line today); he also sought to downplay white racism against Japanese-Americans. Baron Gōtō Shimpei, a veteran of the architectonic colonialism the Japanese built in Taiwan and Korea, wrote in 1921: "Thirty years ago when the stream of the Japanese immigrants began to pour into the Golden Gate, Americans welcomed it with a true Walt Whitman spirit, 'I am large, I contain multitudes.' The process has since been reversed." Other Japanese leaders pointed out that racist campaigns like "Keep California White!" violated the commitment to racial equality in the charter of the League of Nations; a famous journalist, Kayahara Kazan, said Americans, unlike Europeans, still regard Japanese as children. For Washington these campaigns were not idle matters but central to the health of the United States–Japan relationship, but the discussion effectively ended with the Oriental Exclusion Act of 1924. In Congress a coalition of western anti-Asian constituencies combined with southern racist votes to push through exclusionary legislation for the nation as a whole; during the debates racist caricatures of Asians sometimes were drawn to make them look like blacks.[17] Emigration across the Pacific to America essentially ceased for the next forty years.

In these years racism provided a vocabulary and a grammar to understand the world. Books like Lothrop Stoddard's *The Rising Tide of Colour against White World Supremacy* (1920) took it for granted that world politics revolved around an axis of race relations. For this Harvard Ph.D. and the biologist who introduced the book (Madison Grant, chairman of the New York Zoological Society), "science" had proved the superiority of whites and the inferiority of the red, yellow, brown, and black peoples. Dr. Grant did not stop just at colors: there were also evil "Semites," and the "Mediterranean race"—"swarthy-skinned" and "long-skulled." True, their skull shape had an inexplicable affinity with the head shape of "the great Nordic race," but most other races were round-skulled (technically the "brachycephalic" skull type, found among "the Asiatic Mongols" among others). The just-concluded Great War, Grant thought, was mere prelude to the coming assault on Western Europe by "Bolshevism with Semitic leadership and Chinese executioners." Stoddard, however, was more worried about the pollution of white America by immigrants. The white world—which, we remember, still controlled most of Asia and Africa—stood "at the crossroads of life and death" because of the global march of colored peoples: "Fifty millions of our race wherewith to conquer and possess the earth! . . . China is our steed! Far shall we ride upon her!"[18]

These were not crackpot views but representative of American leaders from Benjamin Franklin to Woodrow Wilson's well-known racism to Berkeley professor R. L. Adams, who in 1921 classified various ethnicities into "an absurdly retentive, racialized bestiary" that ranked their suitability for agricultural labor in California, and to Jack London, who thought "the menace to the Western world" lay in "the little brown man" (the Japanese) undertaking to manage "the four hundred millions of yellow men." London's writings were tremendously influential, imparting an image of an intelligent, efficient, clean, but dangerous Japan and a dirty slumbering Chinese giant, hardworking under proper leadership and therefore also dangerous (but otherwise indolent). London's paranoid fears of organized Orientals are all too evident in "The Unparalleled Invasion" (1907), which imagines China's teeming population spilling over into white colonies in Southeast Asia, whereupon Western armies cordon off all escape from China and then bombard it with deadly germ projectiles cooked up by an American scientist. China, now happily empty of the Chinese, is fumigated and then resettled by people of other nationalities under a "democratic American program."[19] It is as if China were forcibly returned to the condition of the New World after smallpox and other European diseases had run their course.

The 1924 exclusion of "Orientals" marked a change, however, from the harebrained science of race, focusing on head shape and the like, to an official racism emphasizing "cultural, national, and physical *difference*," in Mae Ngai's words. For the first time numerical limits were placed on immigrants, and for the first time the United States established "a *global* racial and national hierarchy that favored some immigrants over others." The disfavored were those thought to be *unassimilable*—"that our white race will readily intermix with the yellow strains of Asia," California governor William Stephens wrote in 1920, "And that out of this interrelationship shall be born a new composite human being is manifestly impossible." Likewise the Asiatic Exclusion League of North America argued that Asians were "incongruous and non-assimilable"; between the white American and the Asian, "there is no common tie whatever. There is no community of thought, nor of feeling, nor of sympathy," just a Pacific void. A genuine Caucasian, Bhagat Singh Thind, argued that he was white and should be naturalized, but the Supreme Court ruled that whites were those deemed white by the common man—and so South Asians were not white. The American Federation of Labor's *Clarion* backed Asian exclusion, while sounding like the ladies of the *Social Register:* "This great Caucasian club of ours must vote out people who are not clubbable." Unfortunately dictums about the unassimilability of Asians were widespread, long lasting, and convincing, even to progressive historians like Charles Beard.[20]

Our little brown brothers in the Philippines fared little better. In 1934 Franklin Roosevelt pushed through Congress the Tydings-McDuffie Act, transforming the Philippine colony into a semi-autonomous commonwealth, pending independence that was scheduled for 1946. This gift from one hand was instantly nulled by the other: the bill deprived Filipinos of American citizenship and cut their immigration quota back to fifty per year. Dr. George Clements, a publicist for big agriculture, wrote in the *Pacific Rural Press* in

1936 that the Filipino was "the most worthless, unscrupulous, shiftless, diseased, semi-barbarian that has ever come to our shores."[21] (Clearly the *latifundistas* had no more need for Filipino labor, as whites emptied Oklahoma.)

The Coming War with Japan

A stock article in the expansionist lexicon was the invasion of California that Japan was stealthily preparing. An odd hunchback named Homer Lea argued in *The Valor of Ignorance* (1909) that a conflagration between the United States and Japan was inevitable: Lea outlined a complex logic by which growing economic competition would ultimately lead to war. Once it started the Japanese navy would deposit a million invaders at three spots: Chehalis in Washington, Goat Island in San Francisco Bay, and Los Angeles. His book, complete with detailed maps and replete with nonsense, sold very well. The American general staff paid close attention to *Valor*; General MacArthur's intelligence chief, Charles Willoughby, was still quoting Homer Lea in 1941. The Hearst press frequently trumpeted alleged Japanese threats to the Pacific Coast and even provided a plan of how war would happen in a September 1915 article: photographs depicted Japanese soldiers training for an amphibious landing on the shores of California (later they proved to be doctored photos from the Sino-Japanese War). Los Angeles newspapers imagined that once the war began Japanese railway workers would seize Henry Huntington's "Red Car" system to move their divisions around Los Angeles County; Americans who ridiculed this discourse were called "white Japs." A novel titled *Invasion* conjured the ultimate Angeleno nightmare: Japanese planes set the city ablaze with firebombs and then hordes of paratroopers "fiendishly gorge on oranges."[22]

The most famous scenario for United States–Japan war was Hector Bywater's 1925 book, *Sea Power in the Pacific: A Study of the American-Japanese Naval Problem.* War would begin with a Japanese attack on the American Pacific Fleet, he claimed, gaining him a retrospective fame (he anticipated some aspects of Japan's attack on the Philippines and Guam in 1941, if not Pearl Harbor). The only way to contain Japan, Bywater thought, was to establish naval bases in the Philippines and Midway and Wake islands—and that really was prophetic of the war and its aftermath. Admiral Yamamoto Isoroku, architect of the attack at Pearl Harbor, carefully studied Bywater's book as a young naval attaché in Washington, sending reports on it back to Tokyo. Needless to say, this was going to be a "race war," whites against yellows, Anglo-Saxons against Japanese samurai; Field Marshal Yamagata Aritomo was particularly taken with the idea of an apocalyptic clash between the races.[23]

Not Quite Belonging

An eighteen-year-old Japanese youth named Noguchi Yonejirō had arrived in the United States in 1893, or as he later wrote, "a sudden turning" had thrown him into "the strange streets of San Francisco." The English he learned in Japan was of little avail, he couldn't understand a thing; he chose to remain silent, as if a deaf mute, but he began reading. He walked all the way to Palo Alto to pick strawberries and read Victor Hugo in his spare time while holed up in the Menlo Park Hotel. He hiked to "the heights," a secluded enclave in the hills above Oakland (that is, Piedmont), washed dishes, delivered newspapers, gardened, working quietly the while. He befriended poet Joaquin Miller and began to write his own poetry. Soon he published a book of poems: *Seen and Unseen; Or, the Monologues of a Homeless Snail.* His silence was eloquent, a memento for the multitudes of Asian-Americans who labored on the railroads or in the mines, fields, and gardens, saying nothing but taking everything in. Later on Noguchi left California for Chicago, New York, and London. He fathered a child with a white woman in 1904 and took the baby back with him to Japan. That child was Isamu Noguchi, subsequently an artist and sculptor of extraordinary range and talent—from great murals to sets for Martha Graham and her dancers, to geometric hanging lamps and giant stainless steel sculptures.

One Sunday morning Isamu Noguchi set off in his "woody" station wagon along the coast south of L.A. to pick up some stones for his work from a supplier: it was December 7, 1941. Soon after Americans of Japanese descent were incarcerated, he voluntarily went to live for six months in the camp at Poston, Colorado (the Poston camp was built inside the Colorado Indian Reservation and run by the Bureau of Indian Affairs). As he later recalled: "Pearl Harbor was an unmitigated shock. . . . With a flash I realized that I was no longer a sculptor alone. I was not just American but Nisei." This remarkable act of courage and witness—to join a camp of 17,000 where every inmate had a serial number, not a name—grew out of the "haunting sense of unreality" that had marked his first four decades, a feeling "of not quite belonging." Noguchi later said he wanted to get to know his fellow Nisei, but to them (as to white Americans) he was racially "mixed"—that curious term we ought to apply to all humans, with our DNA as the proof, but applies only to people like Noguchi. He was a hybrid, and he wrote prophetically in

1942, "To be hybrid anticipates the future. This is America, the nation of all nationalities."[24]

In spite of restrictive legislation going back half a century, in 1941 Japanese still ran 5,000 farms in California and marketed more than 40 percent of its truck crops. War hysteria after Pearl Harbor led to many attacks on Japanese-Americans and panic by official agencies: FBI agents, for example, wasted little time in arresting 100 leaders of the Japanese community in Seattle on the very "date that will live in infamy," December 7. They had done no wrong, of course (and city newspapers had applauded their patriotism), but political leaders weren't listening; in early 1942 Idaho's governor, Chase Clark, urged that they all be sent back to Japan—and after that, "sink the island [*sic*]." "They live like rats, breed like rats, and act like rats. We don't want them." The University of California wanted at least one, though, at its graduation in the spring of 1942: Harvey Akio Itano, a premedical student who was the valedictorian of his class; he had been removed to a resettlement center in April. Ironically, Japanese-Americans found welcome in the Owens Valley, where the infamous Manzanar camp was established—not at first, but after local businesses began to prosper by supplying the needs of the nearly 10,000 Japanese-Americans incarcerated there.[25]

The Japanese relocations were hardly unprecedented, and not just because of massive Indian removals: when millions of jobs disappeared after the 1929 crash, powerful Americans decided to get rid of Mexicans, too. From 1929 to 1935 public authorities from the federal level on down expelled between half a million and a million Mexicans, of whom only some 100,000 had arrived in the United States illegally. Mexicans and anyone who "looked Mexican" (in the Southwest the U.S. immigration service was notorious for lumping various peoples of color as Mexican) were picked up in widespread sweeps, and if they didn't have proper papers on them, they were packed onto long trains and shipped from Los Angeles to the El Paso border. In 1931, the worst year, 138,519 people were deported, but the total was always above 70,000 a year during the Hoover administration. After Roosevelt came in the deportations lessened considerably—only three trains departed after April 1933.[26] This disgraceful ethnic relocation, worthy of Stalin, was abruptly reversed when the war started and massive labor shortages developed; now came the "Bracero Program" to bring cheap Mexican labor pouring back across the border as fast as possible; 200,000 came in during the war, with the government paying their transportation costs. The number of braceros peaked at 450,000 in 1956, when they made up more than half the labor force in lettuce, tomatoes, sugar beets, and cotton. Richard A. Walker calls this "a kind of indentured labor: contracted by the government, housed in closed camps, bused to the fields, and sent home to Mexico once the season was over." During the Bracero Program the authorities still launched assaults against illegal Mexican aliens; "Operation Wetback" in 1954 mounted "a direct attack . . . upon the hordes of aliens facing us across the border," in the words of General Joseph Swing, who commanded this massive assault in Texas and Southern California. Cesar Chavez lodged one of his first big victories when the Bracero Program finally ended in 1964.[27]

Concentration Camps East of Eden

After the Chinese were driven away from Seattle in the 1880s, Japanese-Americans slowly arrived until they were the city's largest minority by 1941, numbering nearly 7,000. They lived on "Skid Road" (made famous in Murray Morgan's wonderful book by that title), or the south side of First Hill, or up Beacon Hill—older and usually dilapidated parts of the city. Kazuko Itoi's father ran the Carrollton Hotel on Skid Road, a flophouse like many others, but he kept it clean and safe. Born just after the Great War, Kazuko had a wonderful child's life growing up in the middle of the city; if her parents spoke Japanese and kept to the old ways, she was a budding American, a Seattleite who tended to forget her Asian heritage until some white reminded her (when are you going back to China?). She was like her much more numerous counterparts in Los Angeles, a bobby-soxer running off to the soda shop or the movies—until 1941.[28]

The first relocations took place on nearby Bainbridge Island in March 1942, when fifty-four families were carted off to camps; soon the entire community was eliminated. Kazuko and her friends were shocked and flabbergasted, but off they went to the camps. Local newspapers reported on all this matter-of-factly, as if it were of little moment. Seattle took notice of the deportations only when a senior at the University of Washington, Gordon Hirabayashi, refused to go along, or even to obey the army's nightly curfew. A conscientious objector born to Quaker parents, he turned himself in after Seattle had been emptied of his kind, in the middle of 1942. After being sentenced to three months in prison, he appealed his case all the way to the Supreme Court—which upheld his conviction. A young William O. Douglas argued that no racial discrimination was involved; in his dissent Robert Jackson eloquently argued that it most certainly was. A bit later this precedent was cited when the Court decided *Korematsu v. United States,* a California case that is much better known. After he got out of prison Hirabayashi worked with the American Friends Service Committee in Spokane and refused to fill out a questionnaire designed to test Japanese-American loyalties. Back to jail he went for another year. Later he got a Ph.D. at the University of Washington and became a hero among his people—and among many whites who had remained silent during his incarceration.[29]

The Japanese Garden

Until the recent period, Asian influence in the West, apart from migrating Asian-American laborers in various trades, has primarily been architectural, aesthetic, and gastronomical—Japanese gardens in Beverly Hills, Asian motifs in residential design, art collections in the museums and homes of the wealthy, dinner out at a Chinese restaurant—a kind of patrician Orientalism, to borrow Jack Tchen's apt term, with roots in the China trade of the early Republic. The genteel tradition in the Pacific states was rarely overtly racist, but like Teddy Roosevelt, overtly Japanophile: admiring of Japan's modern prowess (when it didn't threaten the United States) and awed by its aesthetic taste and spiritual sensibility. Before 1965, of course, this was all surface, exterior influence, merely epidermal rather than cultural or civilizational; Asians still lived in their communities and went to the back door.

Charles Augustus Keeler, a Berkeley poet whom Kevin Starr nominated as the author of "a garden ideology" for California, wanted to bring the Mediterranean and East Asia together in gardens designed to "exhilarate our souls by the harmony and glory of pure and brilliant color . . . in the shadow of the palm and . . . the whisper of rustling bamboo," while William Hammond Hall figured out how to build a thousand-acre park and woodland atop shifting sand dunes in the 1870s, thus creating Golden Gate Park in San Francisco, with its famous Japanese tea garden. The Bernheimer Japanese Gardens in Los Angeles also attracted many tourists.[30] The Pacific Coast Highway opened in 1937 and coursed through perhaps the most impressive wilderness in America, the Big Sur running along the shore from San Luis Obispo to Carmel, with great cliffs rising above the sparkling surf, capping mountains and foothills that extend back into the interior through unspoiled forests[31] and truly natural gardens—Arcadia unveiled.

Big Sur would not reach its apotheosis as the epicenter of transcendent mind-body experience and all-round therapeutic curative for the well-heeled and the hippie alike until the 1960s, but an itinerant Tibetan lama already signified this telos as early as 1915. On a pilgrimage to Monterey he told reporters that the Point Lobos cypress groves arose from seeds planted a thousand years ago by wandering monks who got there via China and Japan (he might have had a point, because they grow nowhere else in America). How the monks did that he chose not to reveal, but he vouched that the trees came from a monastery in Lhasa. This auspicious beginning did not last much past the opening of the coast highway, however, as the local literati, firmly facing East, determined that Big Sur really resembled the western Irish coast, and thus they beheld "the second Celtic Twilight."[32]

In San Diego, though, Orientalism had a kind of heyday even before the Tibetan's pilgrimage. Katherine Tingley brought Theosophy to the city in 1897, more particularly to Point Loma overlooking the Pacific; this religion made eclecticism into a fetish, taking guidance from Buddhas and Brahmins, Cabalists and Gnostics, neo-Platonists and "Swedenborgian teachings" (a liberal doctrine of the nineteenth century involving, not surprisingly, the interplay of nature and spirit). Her smorgasbord of religious quackery found not a few takers (this being Southern California): "Wisdom of the Ancients," "World Soul," meditation, reincarnation, escape from tarnation—there was something for everybody. Tingley built her national headquarters at the Point (right next to the navy), and by 1910 three hundred students were enrolled at her Raja Yoga School. Some raved about it, others put out rumors of "forced labor and nighttime lockups." Strange midnight processions of people in pajamas added to the fun. But lots of English and American artists and freethinkers showed up, and in the end, at least according to one observer, Point Loma did as much as any other institution to bring culture and the arts to San Diego.[33]

Meanwhile the formidable Huntington Library dedicated itself to "the origin and progress of the civilization of the English-speaking peoples with special reference to their intellectual development," and the bulk of its original collection was steeped in British culture and civilization. In this Henry Huntington merely expressed in philanthropy "the Anglophilia of establishment culture" in Southern California.[34] If that made them no different from their establishment peers in New York or Boston, the latter were not peering East from a distance of 3,000 miles, backs turned to the Pacific. Maybe one elite college makes the point best: there it is, situated in an idyllic natural setting five miles from Pasadena, founded in 1914 by "Protestant oligarchs" as "a more refined alternative to rah-rah U.S.C." Myron Hunt designed the campus in "opulent Mediterranean Revival."[35] Its name is Occidental College. One wouldn't have expected it to be called Oriental College, of course, but can we say that the City of Angels, perched on the Pacific, was merely part of the Occident?

Bad for the Glass

The legion of Japanese gardeners in Southern California had the deepest aesthetic influence, transforming one arid setting after another into a new, nature-conforming aesthetic—except that most of the "nature" was either imported or worked carefully at the Japanese hand to make a pine tree or moss-covered rock look natural (much as in Japan, except the plastic, transformative effect was much greater in California because Japan is not arid). Here was the deepest penetration of any East Asian influence into the life and culture of the Pacific Coast before the war, satisfying Californians' Arcadian desires for harmony and order, serenity and balance in life. Falling water, strategically placed stones, cherry and peach blossoms, a lily pond with multi-colored goldfish (otherwise known as carp) swimming under a spare wooden foot bridge, artful arrangements of small pine trees (the pine is worshipped in Japan and used in a thousand ways)—this became a formula replicated in one garden or home or public space after another by some 2,500 Japanese gardeners. Add a Greene and Greene Craftsman bungalow (an architecture also absorbing Japanese technique and design), and you have "the temporarily unassimilable metaphor of Japan as a conscious model for imitation and usage by white California."[36] The Issei and Nisei themselves, of course, were to be seen in the garden and not elsewhere, they were not assimilable; instead a wall of exclusion kept them just as confined in Little Tokyo as blacks were in Bronzeville. I may mistake Kevin Starr's meaning, but does "temporarily unassimilable" mean there was a later point where Japanese metaphors and influence, or Japanese-Americans themselves, were assimilable, beyond home and garden or sushi restaurant? I don't think so; Larry Ellison's secluded estate in Woodside (called "Sanbashi" or Three Bridges) is a thorough paean to the way extremely wealthy Japanese live: but apart from its absurd extravagance, how does it differ from the teahouse in Golden Gate Park or Mrs. Mulwray's backyard pond?

Conclusion: Not Quite Belonging

World War II did not end state discrimination against Asian-Americans. During the cold war the FBI harbored deep suspicions about the various Chinese and Korean communities, engaging in its own close surveillance while allowing the dictatorships in Taipei and Seoul to spy on and often terrify local communities. Both regimes funded newspapers, held gala celebrations on this anniversary or that, acted in loco parentis for college students, and sought to intimidate any and all critics of the dictators. Then everything began to change, thanks to the civil rights movement: "eastering" turned into an avalanche. A mere 7 percent of immigrants in 1965, Asian-Americans accounted for a quarter of all immigration in 1970 and more than a third by 1975. Koreans poured into Los Angeles, which quickly surpassed Japan as the primary location of the Korean diaspora.[37] By the 1990s boom in Silicon Valley, one-quarter of the population was Asian-American, and soon Berkeley, UCLA, and other California universities welcomed freshman classes in which Asian-Americans were nearly the majority.[38] Orange County, almost uniformly white until 1965, sprouted Chinese, Vietnamese, and Korean communities in Monterey Park (now 63 percent Asian), Westminster, and Garden Grove. At long last "eastering" Asians had a fighting chance for equality —and still, a sense of not quite belonging.

PART IV

"A Crust of the Earth"
Protean California

California is a place in which a boom mentality and a sense of Chekhovian loss meet in uneasy suspension; in which the mind is troubled by some buried but ineradicable suspicion that things had better work out here, because here, beneath that immense bleached sky, is where we run out of continent.

—JOAN DIDION

CHAPTER NINE

A Garden Cornucopia

In the full spring on the banks of a river—
Two big gardens planted with thousands of orange trees.
Their thick leaves are putting the clouds to shame.

—Du Fu (Chinese poet, 712–770)

The road was asphalt now; it shimmered in the heat, and whenever it fell away before you, a mirage made it look like water. It was lined with orange-groves; dark green shiny trees, golden with a part of last year's crop, and snowy white with the new year's blossoms. Now and then a puff of breeze blew out, and you got a ravishing sweet odor. . . . There were hedges of roses, extending for long distances, eight or ten feet high, and covered with blossoms. There were windbreaks of towering thin eucalyptus trees, with long wavy leaves and bark that scales off and leaves them naked.

—Upton Sinclair, *Oil!*

"I am not exactly pleased with the Atlantic," Oscar Wilde declared upon arriving in New York; the ocean was not "so majestic, or even as large, as I expected." An ocean should be there to please the man—and when he got to the Pacific, it did: the Pacific coast reminded him of the Mediterranean, and San Francisco of Genoa. And it was suitably large: the American Pacific coast runs to nearly 8,000 miles when measured by the "Detailed Tidal Shoreline" methods of the U.S. Coast and Geodetic Survey; add Alaska, and the length is 39,246 miles. For most of those 8,000 miles, it is blessed with one of the nicest climates in the world.

The *kuroshio* or black current comes up from the tropics to warm Japan, then cools in the North Pacific—but not too much, so it can move south and become the source of the year-round temperate climate along the continental edge. Around Vancouver Island the *kuroshio* gets rechristened the California Current, pushing North Pacific waters southward—cool waters in the summer and warm in the winter. Storms begin in the Gulf of Alaska and then sweep south and east across the Pacific Northwest, but most miss

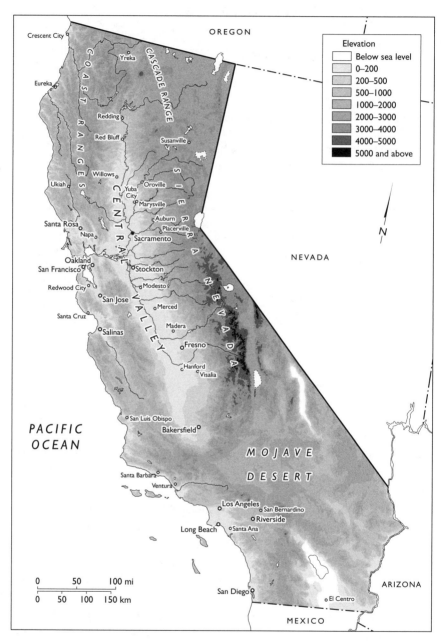

Elevation
Below sea level
0–200
200–500
500–1000
1000–2000
2000–3000
3000–4000
4000–5000
5000 and above

OREGON

NEVADA

ARIZONA

MEXICO

PACIFIC
OCEAN

MOJAVE
DESERT

CASCADE RANGE

COAST RANGES

CENTRAL VALLEY

SIERRA NEVADA

Crescent City
Yreka
Eureka
Redding
Red Bluff
Susanville
Willows
Ukiah
Oroville
Yuba City
Marysville
Auburn
Placerville
Santa Rosa
Napa
Sacramento
Oakland
San Francisco
Stockton
Redwood City
Modesto
San Jose
Santa Cruz
Merced
Salinas
Madera
Fresno
Hanford
Visalia
San Luis Obispo
Bakersfield
Santa Barbara
Ventura
Los Angeles
San Bernardino
Riverside
Long Beach
Santa Ana
San Diego
El Centro

N

0   50   100 mi
0   50   100   150 km

California's Central Valley.
Map by Bill Nelson.

California because of "the Pacific high," an air pressure front that keeps nearly all precipitation to the north; when California gets hit, it is the periphery or skirt of larger storms in Oregon or Washington. The Pacific High sits northeast of Hawaii for months on end, "like a policeman in a traffic island, directing the winds and mobile low-pressure systems" to moderate the climate. This massive zone of air pressure sends wind currents and ocean squalls all across the North American continent: for half the year, beginning in April, it pushes storms northward, over British Columbia and onward to the Great Plains; for the other half of the year, starting in November, it drives them into California where the Sierra Nevada and the coastal ranges trap the moisture, creating a "rain shadow" on the western side of the Great Central Valley. Coastal mountain ridges allocate the rain, Steven Stoll wrote, leaving the coast moist in the winter and the interior dry, but also sending "ghost clouds" east to the "retaining wall" of the High Sierra, where they cool off and shower rain in the valleys and snow on the peaks. Pacific Ocean water is cool from Alaska down to well south of San Francisco because of "upwellings" of cold currents from the depths; when things get too hot, more upwellings off Baja California act as a moderating thermostat.[1] Nature seems to have put one, two, many moderators in place to make this region remarkably pleasant for human beings: Arcadia with its own air-conditioning.

California neatly separates into four geographic parts. The Sierra Nevada Range rises sharply in the east; indeed, it rises higher than any mountain range in the continental United States, "like an airfoil, or a woodshed" with a sheer front facing east and "a long, sloping back" down to the second region, the Great Central Valley. The coastal mountains don't rise very high but high enough to hold the valley and desert winds at bay most of the time. The Central Valley sits more or less at sea level, is flatter than the plains states, and accumulates what is probably the most fertile soil on the planet. Bigger than Denmark, the Central Valley runs 500 miles north to south in a rough oblong shape, with an average width of 125 miles; inside is an alluvial plane 400 miles long with an average width of 45 miles, surrounded by mountains and drained by the Sacramento River to the north and the San Joaquin River to the south. As fast as the valley seems to sink, it gets filled up with alluvium; drillings have to go to 3,000 feet in some places to hit bedrock.[2] The deserts to the south constitute the third region and the temperate coast, of course, is the last.

California offered nature's definition of Arcadia to the pastoral idealist—a land of milk and honey with a year-round temperate climate, promising a life of ease within a halcyon, untouched (until 1849) environment. The pastoral dream and the Garden of Eden were centerpieces of European imaginings of the New World, and once it was possible to talk about the Cuyahoga River or Indiana in these terms. But belching smokestacks and fleeing populations purged the pastoral imagery from the city and the prairie. California is the singular massively populated industrial state where the pastoral dream has never died, has never left the state, because it is still not possible to say that the vision is untrue. But because California's "late" development took place entirely within range of the photographer's eye, we are made aware of our losses—and today it is the losses that hold our attention. Whole shelves of literature attest to the death of "the dream." For Joan Didion, "All that is constant about the California of my childhood is the rate at which it disappears." Raymond F. Dasmann writes of "places we have lost," places taken away: "filled in, paved over, drained, torn down, burned out—inevitably crowded out."[3] If we are talking about Los Angeles, yes: flying into its airport is to behold a vast basin of gray pavement. But drive 20 miles to the north, and you encounter an Elysian stretch of natural beauty all the way to San Francisco. It isn't the death of the garden that defines the state but the unparalleled dynamism of the machine within the garden: Italy with an attitude.

John Charles Frémont's literary touch—that is, his wife's—did not fly away with his California putsch. He became an early and eloquent advocate of twinning California and Italy, a prescient concept since the state's gross domestic product rivaled Italy's for decades (although now it's bigger). But Frémont wasn't thinking of something so coarse as GDP: Italy's length and breadth resembled California's, so did its climate and the products of its soil (fruit, wine); mountains, valleys, and plains intermingled with large rivers, spilling into bays that mimicked Genoa or Naples. Italianizing California would be a good start toward loosening up Yankees, toning down Puritans, and softening up Calvinists, thawing their frozen souls out in the sun. California was "a sort of prepared but unconscious and inexperienced Italy, the primitive *plate*, in perfect condition," Henry James wrote, "but with the impression of History all yet to be made."[4] It never quite worked, of course; Italians have had centuries to bring their humanity and their religion to terms with modernity. Anglos quickly removed to the coast were more likely to go fundamentalist or run amok than to turn Italian in the sun.

The Los Angeles Basin's difference from Italy and from northern California is not just in the layers of concrete sprawling across it, but in its volatility, which is mostly absent elsewhere in California—because the counterpart of its aridity is fire, a devil riding in on the wings of desert sciroccos. Fire and water are essential life forces, so some ancients taught us, while others spoke of earth, wind, and fire. Water is smooth, supple, slippery, a flow that in its natural state exemplifies the archaic ideal of the golden mean. It upsets nature and humanity only at the extremes of drought and deluge. Fire is always volatile, always extreme, always ready to flare. It knows no balance or neutrality except before its victims, which it annihilates with a perfect equanimity. Even its smallest quantities can awaken a holocaust, like the homespun blue flame under a stewing kettle on a stove, or the errant match tossed into the ground-cover chaparral, periodically igniting fires all around Southern California. That is why the fire's trace—the "spark"—has no linguistic counterpart for water: in its scant volume the water's trace, the "drop," still has beauty and can still save a life. Baptisms come by fire and water, but according to time-honored mythology humans are tried and judged only by fire. Los Angeles has always had too much of the capricious elements, fire and wind, and not enough of the propitiating other: water. And so it sits poised on catastrophe, violating the Confucian middle way, the composed balance that regulates life. Southern California's survivors, those best adapted to its nature, are the fireplants: the dense chaparral covering the ground and warming up in the sun, heating to the point that the plant reaches an infernal equinox, whereupon it germinates. This is the evil genius of the chaparral: Southern California needs it for watershed, to hold back the overflow; but it's so combustible that fire consumes it, overwhelms it, and then brings along in its absent wake, the flood.[5]

Lords without Peasants

Charles Lummis stumbled westward into Southern California in 1885, after walking across the continent from Chillicothe, Ohio: immediately he determined that he had found "God's country." It was January, yet "the ground was carpeted with myriad wild flowers, birds filled the air with song, and clouds of butterflies fluttered past me. I waded clear, icy trout brooks, startled innumerable flocks of quail, and ate fruit from the gold-laden trees of the first orange orchards I had ever seen." (Lummis wasn't a homeless hobo or a manic-depressive on the loose: editor of the *Scioto Gazette* in Chillicothe, he was asked by Harrison Gray Otis, owner of the *Los Angeles Times*, for a weekly column as he trekked toward the promised land. Soon he was a stalwart member of the Los Angeles elite.)[6] An embarrassment of riches defines the state of California, but the bounty from its land is almost implausibly abundant.

California's world-leading industry marches hand in hand with the most prosperous and productive agrarian system on earth. When Americans sit down to the table, one-third of what they eat is grown in California, which ranks first in the country in seventy-six crops from alfalfa to carrots to garlic to pomegranates to spinach and walnuts. This cornucopia reaches a kind of zenith with rice: while Asian farmers still do the backbreaking work of planting and then transplanting rice seedlings, in California the seeds are casually thrown from airplanes and have been since the 1930s. Farms for rice, a latecomer among the state's many crops, exceeded half a million acres by 1980, with nearly half of the crop exported (mostly to Japan and Korea). The number one farm state since 1960, it has had a steady, steep upward graph line of ever-increasing production that began a century earlier, in the heyday of the gold rush. In 2000 the value of the state's farm output was nearly $25 billion, compared to Iowa's $11 billion; California is even more dominant in processed food, shipping five times as much as the second-ranking state, Illinois. If most Americans know about California lettuce, grapes, and oranges, they probably don't know that dairy products and cattle rank first in their annual value of farm production and have for a century (today California produces almost as much cheese as Wisconsin). Even the dangerously flatulent cattle came along late: new breeds from Europe, the East Coast, and Texas joined fine-bred dairy cows driven out to California in the 1850s, and because of the great distances they weren't huge herds—just the best specimens.[7] This striking agrarian achievement is another instance—and one of the most telling—in California's "late" development.

The Central Valley was the first great source of California's wealth, richer by far than the gold rush for Americans who turned it, almost overnight, into one of the earliest regions of industrial agriculture. A modern agriculture could arise in the 1870s across the grand, fertile spaces that California possessed because the land had never been farmed to any important degree before, no extant social or agrarian formation had to be overcome, and everything could start fresh, from a clean state. You see amber waves of grain stretching as far as the eye can see elsewhere, but only in places like the former East Germany where collectivization got rid of estates and family farms and knocked down field-margin barriers to mechanized agriculture. But you didn't need communists to do this in California: here was a stunning example of Hartzian America "born free," a stark departure from most of the world's history of sharp struggles between landlord and peasant. But it seems hard for people to grasp this simple fact; as recently as 1996 Victor Davis Hanson lamented the decline of the democratic culture of "small, independent yeomen on the land, who make their own laws, fight their own battles, and create a community of tough like-minded individuals."[8] Hanson is both a scholar and a fifth-generation farmer: in California, a place where yeomen barely made a dent. In Ohio an 1820s Madison homestead might look little changed today; the self-conscious civic planning of settlers in the Willamette Valley a few years later might still describe rural Oregon. But California agriculture differed dramatically from the Jeffersonian ideal from the beginning—in its industrial scope, its high-tech machines, and its employment of masses of cheaply paid labor in a milieu of rank exploitation (always poor people of color until the Depression).

A good example of a lord with no peasants would be Agoston Haraszthy. Born into an aristocratic landowning family in Hungary, he left the family estate and its peasants for America in 1840 when he was twenty-eight and shortly found himself "the darling of the Washington social season" with his "heavily gold braided and richly trimmed" Hungarian Guard uniform. But he continued his journey west, pausing to set up a transportation system in San Diego with Don Juan Bandini; by 1850 he was the sheriff of San Diego County and then the first city marshall. When he wasn't cleaning up the waterfront and jailing drunken sailors, he would entertain the tiny San Diego elite, playing Bach and Beethoven on the piano. Not long after that Haraszthy removed himself again to an inexplicably (to a Hungarian noble-man) empty Sonoma and established the Buena Vista Winery. While Americans bloodied each other in the Civil War, he was off touring Europe for months on end, purchasing 100,000 grapevines and planting stock for olives, almonds, pomegranates, and chestnuts—not to mention oranges and lemons. He returned to introduce the zinfandel grape while offering some of his imported vines to his European friends Charles Krug and Jacob Grundlach. Two years later Haraszthy crowned his merger with the California aristoc-racy, such as it was, by marrying his sons Attila and Arpad off to the twin daughters of General Don Mariano Vallejo (the somnolent commander of the northern frontier). From time to time Haraszthy liked to retreat to his estate called Hacienda San Antonio in Corinto, Nicaragua; that is where we find him on July 6, 1869, fording a river and then vanishing forever—presumably into the belly of an alligator. From this entirely improbable career Don Agoston Haraszthy is recalled as the father of California wine.[9]

During the Spanish and Mexican era, a small number of rancheros held vast tracts of California land, living in sprawling haciendas—the supply of land dwarfing the demand. In just one decade, 1836–46, the Mexican govern-ment doled out about 600 land grants. Around 800 ranchos with a land area greater than 10,000 acres existed shortly before statehood (some had more than 300,000 acres), out of a total of about 11 million acres of land grants.

Most of the land was given over to cattle grazing, the owners living in rambling haciendas with their extended families amid fields, gardens, and vineyards. The extent and limits of these estates were usually indistinct, or unknown: Mexican documents indicated that the entire Pomona Valley was Rancho San José, for example, located "distant some six leagues, more or less," from Mission San Gabriel, and "vacant" (again, *más o menos*).[10] For their real estate "surveys" Californios used a rawhide lariat rope tied to stakes at both ends; cowboys hammered a stake into the ground, galloped on ahead to run out the length, hammered another and then repeated the process. Huge herds of cattle grazed these lands, requiring little attention because only their hides were sold, enabling a life of luxury, ease, and comfort for the big owners—who had their daily cares provided for by indentured Indian servants and various other *pobladores*. This carefree, charming, fun-loving existence was despised by uptight Yankees who saw only indolence and squandered opportunity, and as they began flowing in they quickly substituted themselves for the Californio elite.[11]

The virtually instant transfer from remote imperial periphery to statehood caused many of these haciendas to pass into American hands, often at ridiculously cheap prices. Land surveyors were absent, real estate lawyers even more so, and ranchos often conveyed with a mere handshake: "a thousand acres *más o menos*," what difference did it make when land was so abundant? It was child's play for Anglos to get control of these mostly uncharted domains. A Land Commission in 1851 did what colonizers do everywhere: it demanded of the existing owners contracts, deeds, and proof of title; usually there were none. Although some say the process was reasonably fair,[12] large tracts quickly passed into the hands of Anglos. General George S. Patton of World War II fame was the grandson of a man who arrived in California in 1866 and bought 2,200 acres of land in and around the towns subsequently named San Bernadino and Riverside; he paid $2.20 an acre. That grubstake soon made the Pattons part of the Los Angeles aristocracy. The Lankershim Hotel once was one of L.A.'s finest, and today Van Nuys is a thriving and well-known town: in 1869 Isaac Lankershim purchased half of the San Fernando Valley for $2.00 an acre from two Californio ranchers (one of whom was the famous Pio Pico), sowed wheat, and got another Isaac with the family name of Van Nuys to run the operation. The latter married up (the boss's daughter), and when Isaac Lankershim died Van Nuys inherited everything. James Ben Ali Haggin acquired 413,000 acres along the Kern River—making him "Grand Khan of the Kern." But James Irvine got more: he left Ireland to join the gold rush, purchased a large ranch, and ended up owning much of what is now called Orange County. Then the Southern Pacific railway out-did everyone else in its wholesale purchases, forced ousters (of pioneer home-steaders—called "squatters" in California), and legal legerdemain giving it title to vast holdings of land. What it couldn't buy or force out of someone's hands, it got through federal largesse—Washington doled out more than 20 million acres in grants directly to railway companies or to the state for building railways.[13]

Henry Miller and Charles Lux, two of the most famous agrarian moguls, owned enough of the San Joaquin Valley to create a second Belgium. Miller, formerly a butcher, spent $1.25 an acre for "swampland" and got the state to reimburse his purchase price on Miller's word that a like amount of money would be spent to reclaim the swamps. What looks like a swamp in the rainy season might be rich land, but so what: dry land, too, could be called a swamp. During the drought of 1862–63, Miller surveyed many dessicated acres on a horse-drawn wagon and then swore he crossed them in a boat. Soon he owned a 100-mile-long strip including both banks of the San Joaquin River. Miller and Lux, both of them from southwestern Germany, both of them starting off in America as butchers, owned 1.25 million acres of land by 1900 and dominated Pacific Coast meat markets.[14]

Midwestern Machines in the California Garden

Most of the great landowners chose to raise wheat, which grows easily in most climates and requires little care; farmers could seed in the winter and harvest throughout the summer. Amber waves of grain covered the whole valley in the 1870s. The result was a clear pattern of latifundia agriculture that concentrated immense domains in the hands of a tiny elite, beginning in the 1860s and lasting down to the present. As in the movie *Chinatown*, the people responsible to the public for essential services were often the first and biggest speculators: government land surveyors, for example, became some of California's richest land brokers. California's almost immediate leap into industrial agriculture was similarly free of the tedious business of buying out small farmers to consolidate large-scale production or having to contend with the pastoral ideal and its democratic forms and pressures (the history of much of the Midwest in the twentieth century). This was not agriculture so much as highly developed and lucrative industry; it is the machine in the garden with a particular vengeance, an industrial dystopia that just happened to be capable of feeding much of the world. California immediately occupied the fore-front of mechanized agriculture and stayed there ever since—McWilliams's "factories in the field" collapsing and leapfrogging centuries of evolutionary agrarian development in Europe.[15] Here the soil was not farmed so much as mined, and market calculations (as opposed to subsistence farming, or house-holding for one's family) drove production from the beginning.

California was a pioneer in a new sense: the unusual marrying of the latest technologies to a latifundia-like land system where the hard labor was always done by disadvantaged groups (Mexicans, Chinese, blacks, "Okies"), thus creating a harshly exploitative but highly productive agriculture that quickly became a major American comparative advantage in world markets. Californians made some of their own innovations, but most of the machines in the field were invented elsewhere—they were just adopted in California very quickly, with no stodgy traditions to overcome and every incentive to mechanize. California's alluvial soils are easy to break, so single plows quickly gave way to multiple, horse-drawn "gang plows" that could prepare a field for harvest in one operation. In 1854 a Kalamazoo combine, a revolutionary device invented in 1836 that enabled twelve horses and five men to do the work of scores of farm laborers, was shipped from Michigan around Cape Horn to San Francisco; people came from miles around to watch it in action. A man driving a Stockton rig with five blades cutting ten inches down, pulled by eight horses, could plow up the earth and sow seeds across eight acres in a single day, using a mechanical seeder and a spring-tooth harrow running behind the gang plow; mechanics in Stockton produced about 20,000 of these rigs between 1852 and 1886. By 1880 combines were in general use throughout California, a generation before farmers elsewhere got them. A wheat ranch in San Joaquin County had a field 17 miles long for a total of 36,000 acres, deploying multiple combines and cutting labor time per kilogram of wheat to less than thirty seconds; by contrast, farmers in New England put in seven minutes of work per kilogram. By the 1880s large-scale industrial-capitalist agriculture blanketed California, producing high-quality hard, dry wheat kernels that would keep while being shipped all the way to England or China; harvests averaged forty bushels an acre, compared to twenty in the East. The state produced 20 million bushels in 1870 and 40 million in the late 1880s, when wheat peaked. It was easily the most mechanized agriculture in the nation, if not the world.[16]

The captains of wheat and railroads constituted an oligarchy that was the real power in California, aided almost every step of the way by federal and local government. The character that emerges here is not the yeoman farmer or the master of the orange and lemon grove in cravat and bowler but a secretive, ruthless, tyrannical mogul subduing the soil and bringing in the harvest with the latest technology for delivering water, the latest machinery for sowing and harvesting the crop, while keeping the politicians happy in Sacramento or Washington. Nor is this mere history—the land barons in their Stetsons still bestride the (irrigated) earth. One of them is James Griffin Boswell II, one of the richest men in America. His uncle, Lieutenant Colonel J. G. Boswell, founded a cotton company in 1921 and married into Los Angeles' first family, the Chandlers. Colonel Boswell established a tradition of secrecy, hoping never to attract attention: "As long as the whale never surfaces, it is never harpooned." It obviously hasn't surfaced very often; most Americans have never heard of the Boswells. The nephew now controls 200,000 acres in the Central Valley, running "the most highly industrialized cotton operation in the world." An absentee owner, he flies in on his jet four or five times a year to check on the company's operations. A self-described "rugged individualist" who doesn't like the federal government or the "enviros" who sometimes inhabit its agencies (if lightly), he gets as much as $20 million per year in federal agricultural subsidies. Senator Gaylord Nelson dared to bark out in 1979 that "Boswell's cotton farm is five times as large" as the next biggest one in the United States, and that his well-lobbied and greased legislative exemptions were worth "millions and millions and millions of dollars." (In 1983, for example, Boswell got $3.7 million in return for keeping 14,000 acres of farmland unplanted.) Whereupon his fellow liberal senator, Alan Cranston of California, rose to speak: and there ended Nelson's attempt to rein in the river of federal largesse flowing into Boswell's pockets.[17]

Wheat ranching became so highly mechanized and efficient that it led to massive overproduction, causing national and global prices to plummet. If California wheat had the virtue of surviving long distance shipment to markets, it also had the vice of exhausting the soil quickly when planted year after year. The annual returns on wheat thus slowed in the 1880s to an average of 4 percent. Just in time (1888) the refrigerator car enabled a massive switch from wheat to fruit.[18] As the mining and wheat bonanza tapered off a new-new thing came booming along, in a pattern that would repeat itself for the next century: in this case fruit—grapes, apples, pears, and plums, and above all citrus.

Translatio Imperii: Thin Skins and Thick Albedos

If mechanized wheat production was the antithesis of Turner's Arcadia, the next cascade of development reinvented homesteading: Calvinist flatlanders producing oranges and lemons in the Mediterranean sun. This, too, was wildly successful (if forwarded serendipitously by the refrigerated railway car), and it created a pageant of urban beauty that fills the nostalgic imaginings of Southern California and still punctuates, if rarely, the freeway concrete. A panorama of citrus and fruit towns stretched south from Santa Barbara to San Diego and westward to Pasadena, Whittier, Riverside, San Bernardino, and out to the desert towns—all the way to Palm Springs (lemons and oranges) and Indio (figs and dates), whereupon it evaporated in the white heat of desert towns called Mecca and Thermal. The Southern Pacific Railroad and its offspring *Sunset Magazine* promoted the irrigated homestead throughout the country; by 1900, 5.6 million orange trees grew in California and by 1920, 9 million, along with a myriad of other orchards. Citrus contributed mightily to the average California farm tripling in value from 1900 to 1920.[19]

California has a myriad of agrarian microregions suitable for cultivating most of the world's produce, from acorns to zucchinis. The coast below San Francisco, with its intermittent rolling fog and its utterly reliable sunshine, was perfect for orchards—apples, cherries, plums, and the apricot that symbolized California (*apricus* from the Latin meaning "to love the sun"). European vintners planted grape vines in Sonoma, a valley that needs no introduction today as one of the world's premier wine-producing regions, but the vineyards also mingled grapes with new crops of walnuts and almonds. Armenian and Turkish immigrants raised dates, figs, raisins, and prunes in the interior, alongside vast estates that, later on, produced mountains of lettuce, lima beans, alfalfa, barley, artichokes, and garlic. Franciscans brought the olive tree to California, planting the best groves around San Jose. By the turn of the last century, the state had 1.5 million olive trees.[20] Almost any crop seemed to grow better in California; only in corn did the Midwest remain dominant (you can grow corn in California, of course, but other crops were more valuable). In the vast middle reaches of the state, between the foothills and the mountains, as we have seen, an incredibly productive agriculture arose on America's only latifundia pattern. But in Southern California, fruit and citrus cultivation developed on a small, family-based scale, begetting an entire mode of production that bred both a substantial middle class and a longstanding tendency toward political conservatism.

Citrus trees migrated around the world searching for such climates, on a westerly pattern like Berkeley's course of empire. They originated in southern China, moved to Southeast Asia and then to the Mediterranean, Europe, and the New World. Citrus seeds are incestuously productive: plant an orange seed and you might get a grapefruit; sow a seed from that grapefruit and you might reap a lemon. Most lemon trees in California have orange roots; it's the other way around in Florida. California's aridity makes for a thin skin but a thick albedo—the inner white layer between the rind and the fruit. (Florida's humidity gives the orange a thick skin and a thin albedo.) The Washington navel orange—thin skin, thick albedo—was perfectly suited to an arid climate. It got its name from the navel-like blossom end, and it just happened to have the most beautiful hew, according to John McPhee—"a deep, flaring cadmium orange."[21]

Mrs. Luther C. Tibbets planted a couple of navel trees in Riverside in 1873, and as they proliferated she—or they—became the matriarch of nearly all navel oranges grown anywhere in the world. It and the Valencia (the other main type of orange) were both perfect for California: the navel ripens in the fall and winter, the Valencia in the spring and summer, so the industry produces all year long. Meanwhile lemons, originating in the hills of northeastern India and migrating to the Mediterranean, thence to Spain and finally arriving with Father Serra in California, were thick skinned and thin albedoed, favoring "thermal slopes" where frosty air drains away on cold nights. Early growers discovered that lemons could be stored for several months of "curing," wherein the outer rind slowly thins and the flesh becomes juicier. Another Luther—the artful Luther Burbank—diversified the Golden State's cornucopia by grafting different seeds together to form thornless blackberries, Santa Rosa plums, the Russett Burbank potato (mother of all fast-food French fries), and many, many other varieties; he was "the Edison of the plant world." From the 1880s into the 1920s, the citrus industry was the main armature of the Southern California growth machine.[22]

The fortuitous timing of this new leap forward, coinciding with the great railroad age, nonetheless had a high-tech base: a refrigerated railroad car, achieved by venting icy air over the cargo. Just as Gustavus Swift's new cars transformed Chicago into the hog butcher for the world, cold continental transit made California the fruit capital of the nation—and even the world. Although attempts to ice down fruit for transcontinental shipment began as early as 1870, much of it spoiled before reaching the East. Swift's trains were state of the art, however, with big scoops on the top that drew in a whoosh of fresh air and fanned it over blocks of salted ice. By the late 1880s freight trains laden with cherries, plums, oranges, apricots, lemons, and grapes were arriving in eastern markets. In 1892 the ice cars and the cool storage hold of an Atlantic steamer brought tons of oranges all the way to London (where Queen Victoria declared herself mildly pleased with the taste). By then more than 20,000 train cars of fruit shipped out of California every year, and by 1906 nearly 82,000; eastbound trains often convoyed 20 fruit cars and just 1 or

2 passenger cars. Intensive fruit crops accounted for 4 percent of the total value of California agriculture in 1879 but almost four-fifths of the total by 1929; 6 million boxes shipped out in 1899 and 20 million by 1920. Just before Pearl Harbor, Sunkist was still shipping 65,610 railcars of oranges and 16,148 cars of lemons annually.[23]

At its height the California fruit belt was 800 miles long and 200 miles wide, encompassing most of Southern California between the Tehachapi Range in the north and San Juan Capistrano to the south, running out well into the desert and then north to two other pockets of production, in Tulare County surrounding Porterville, and in Butte County above Sacramento. As early as 1870 orange production earned a thousand dollars an acre, and the region's many sheep ranchers quickly traded wool and mutton for oranges and lemons. More than half a million orange trees dotted Los Angeles County in the early 1880s, and Hollywood overflowed with orange groves (and Beverly Hills overflowed with lima beans).[24] A nearly ideal nighttime temperature for oranges—40 degrees—wafted in from the snow-capped mountains, making freezes much rarer than in Florida: Arcadia with its own air-conditioning.

Bourgeois Flatlanders

Californians were increasingly middle westerners once removed, "flatlanders" as they were often called, although that was just the mildest of the epithets that intellectuals attached to the displacement en masse of the Babbitry of the Middle Border. Sometimes they were pretty smart Babbitts—or maybe just pretty early: in 1873 some wealthy people in Indianapolis formed the "California Colony of Indiana" and sent an agent named Daniel Berry off to look for a nice place to develop. The agent located a 2,800-acre parcel shaded by the San Gabriel Mountains a bit east of a wooded canyon. He thought just harvesting the fruit would recoup the cost of investment in three years; if that didn't work, the tract would pay for itself by selling surplus water to arid places to the south. The price was $10 an acre, rather high, except that fruit could be grown throughout the parcel. The Indiana colony thus founded "the key of the valley"—or "Pasadena" in an Indian tongue. Within a year the Hoosiers had constructed Orange Grove Avenue, shaded on both sides by orange blossoms and soon, stunning mansions. Pasadena staged the first "Tournament of Roses" in 1890, which, it is worth remembering, was only fourteen years after Custer's "last stand" against Crazy Horse. By 1910 it was the Fifth Avenue of the richest town in America, and the Rose Bowl was permanently ensconced in the nearby "wooded canyon." Pasadena became the epicenter of an imported genteel tradition which gave a New England or "Bostonian" atmosphere to the upper middle class.[25]

Most flatlanders were less wealthy and often elderly, having sold the farm and retired to Long Beach—sometimes called the main seaport of Iowa. Teetotaling Methodists went to Compton, Quakers to Whittier, New Englanders to Claremont—citrus towns all. But just as often they were farmers moving upscale, to apply their tender mercies to an intensive kind of cultivation that might well make them rich, and if not, at least comfortable. No more Keokuk cyclones, Kankakee tornadoes, Kitzville blizzards, Kiowa dust storms, or Kansas grasshopper invasions (like the one in 1874 that gobbled up whole cornfields in a single day). In a climate that offered perfection the year around, they busied themselves with Mediterranean or Brazilian orange cuttings, Persian lemon seeds, and apricot trees imported from the Levant, through an initial planting that often did not bear fruit for several years—a significant amount of initial capital long preceded any quick return, breeding virtues of savings, patience, self-reliance, husbandry. Initial investments for land, water, vines, a house, tools, horses, and the like were high, upwards of $2,500 a year for three years until the first harvest, but credit was available in the citrus colonies and the yield was remarkable: a producing grove might soon be worth as much as $30,000 (in the 1880s the price of farm land increased fourfold), and in a good year the annual profit could pay off the initial cost of the land. If orange trees take four or five years to become productive, they produce for decades—or even centuries (an orange tree planted in 1421, called Le Grande Bourbon, lived 473 years).[26]

Building an orchard meant arranging a suitable pattern for the trees (usually in double square rows), budding and grafting the fruit, planting, irrigating, fertilizing, weeding, pruning, above all crafting a golden mean of sun and water so that the trees would grow to fruition (so to speak). While the seedlings spread their roots into the ground, growers planted eucalyptus trees on the perimeter of the grove, thus to break the "red wind" siroccos roaring in from the desert and to direct and muffle breezes that might otherwise throw the fruit to the ground prematurely. (The lissome eucalyptus, casting a lovely whiter shade of pale throughout California, quickly became a symbol of the state's Edenic claims. But like everything else these trees were imports—in this case from another arid climate, Australia.)[27] A grower raised a couple of Doberman pinschers to be ready, a few years hence, to deal with any thieves who might ignore the "no trespassing" signs to pilfer fruit while it ripened on the vine.

Each acre could hold hundreds of trees, and each tree not only bore lots of fruit but kept on bearing it practically forever. Once the trees finally flowered, and apart from the annual frenzy of the harvest, a person could watch the fruit ripen and live a life of profound leisure. Indeed an early manual of "orange culture" instructed the grower to inspect his orchard "attired in suit, vest, cravat, and homburg hat," the very essence of the gentleman farmer. A traveler from Indiana observed that "the aristocracy here work and raise fruit."[28] If not aristocrats, at least artisans; Californians were not farmers so much as the tenders of lemon and orange groves, strawberry fields, almonds, avocadoes, figs, or raisins. And they were doing God's work, in the Garden of Eden: the successful citrus towns like Pasadena, Anaheim (a German colony), Redlands ("the Chicago colony"), Riverside, and Pomona all vied with each other for the title of "earthly paradise" and "garden spot of the earth."[29]

Many Englishmen hearkened to the cultivator-aristocrat claims of booster pamphlets in the 1880s, but a Keokuk farmer might also hope to blossom into a Riverside peer of the realm. Or, an incompetent slob from New Jersey might inherit his uncle's cruddy farm, useless for growing much but great for a racetrack. So Harold Bissonette arrived and sold out to the horsemen, bought an orange grove, and sipped whiskey on his porch as Bissonette's Blue Bird Oranges flew out to market. W. C. Fields played Bissonette in the 1934 film *It's a Gift*, but he might have been talking about Charles Collins Teague (who looked a bit like Fields). Born in Caribou, Maine, he moved to Kansas with his family when he was eight; his father promptly went bankrupt, so they migrated to Ventura County—where Teague latched onto a job with his uncle on the Limoneira Ranch, cultivating 400 acres of lemon groves. He was general manager by the age of twenty-five and then president of the ranch for the next half-century. For good measure he became president of two banks, owned water companies, and helped found the California Fruit Grower's Exchange—the very "archetype for a bourgeois planter class."[30]

The imperatives of fruit cultivation bred a like-mindedness that structured almost everything: here was the Protestant ethic cloning itself in the Garden of Eden. Churches grew at an algorithm analogous to the spread of the orange groves. A 1922 study found that schools and churches helped maintain a high moral tone in Orange County; the main denominations were Methodist, Episcopal, Presbyterian, and Baptist, with many evangelical congregations—about one-sixth of all Protestant churches were evangelical.[31] Citrus imperatives also encouraged cooperative endeavors with one's peers, a civil union designed first of all to get sufficient water to the fields, leading to irrigation cooperatives; the second requirement was to get the ripe crops picked, packed, and off to market on a merciless time schedule before the fruit rotted—the great terror of the business. Sunkist, the contraction of a sun-kissed orange marketing cooperative founded in Riverside (otherwise known as the Southern California Fruit Growers' Exchange), came close to a monopoly in packing, shipping, and selling.

The local Sunkist subsidiary packed, crated, and loaded fruit, and the district and central exchanges sold it; in 1922 some 11,000 producers were contracted to the central exchange for a twenty-year period. Sunkist also aided orchard owners (many of whom had failed to turn a profit before), by supplying seeds, fertilizers, insecticides, tools, and know-how and brought a seamless uniformity to the industry that was as amazing as it was lucrative. The growers waved good-bye to their oranges once they went off to the packing houses, where a host of innovative machines (invented mostly in Southern California) washed the fruit, weighed it, and moved it by conveyer belt to female graders who recorded the size and quality of each lot for the growers. The oranges then went to automatic sizing machines that pooled the fruit into common grades, sizes, and weights; next the oranges were pre-cooled and loaded onto railcars, whereupon district exchanges pointed the cars to cities where they would fetch the best price. In other words, if Chicago was glutted, the railcars traveled on to Detroit. Telegraph and telephone communications kept conditions in the national market at the fingertips of district managers. Within five days of a sale in eastern markets, the growers got a check for the proceeds. Meanwhile at the consuming end, elaborate Sunkist rules guided advertisers and supermarket window displays. California growers also mastered the art of preserving fruits and vegetables at the same time that refrigerated cars made possible the mass shipment of fresh produce; the value of canned fruits and vegetables grew from $6 million in 1889 to $220 million in 1920, by which time canneries were the second-ranking industry in the state (after oil).[32] By 1920 California had 9 million orange trees and oranges were the most valuable of the state's crops.

Citrus had miraculously recreated a Jeffersonian civic culture on the opposite side of the continent. Civic virtue extended from the churches and cooperatives to the founding of one fragrant citrus town after another, each with new churches, schools, movie theaters, boulevards, and parks.[33] Soon the golden apple of Greek mythology came to symbolize California, lending its name to everything: Orange Grove Avenue in Pasadena, redolent of a fabulous new bourgeois lifestyle ("Pasadena was a liberal Protestant upper-middle-class daydream"),[34] and above all Orange County, heartland not just of citrus groves but of a concentrated form of Republican politics.

One town and one place seemed to crystallize this marriage of citrus and politics: Riverside, with its long miles of concrete-lined irrigation canals; Magnolia Avenue flush with magnolias (and palm trees) extending through the orange groves "as an almost ceremonial boulevard"; and the Mission Inn, the town centerpiece—Riverside just didn't happen to be in Orange County (just as Riverside never happened to have had a Spanish mission). Judge John Wesley North, a prominent Minnesota Republican and close friend of Abraham Lincoln, had founded Riverside in 1870. Once the groves began producing—Valencia and navel oranges, Lisbon and Eureka lemons— it was an affluent community; the owners sat on their verandas reading philosophy, one writer said in 1879, waiting for the fruit to grow. For William Ellsworth Smythe, a patron saint of arid lands who believed water delivered growth, community, and democracy, Riverside was "a product of irrigation" and a dream come true for "comparatively poor men" who sought out the West. Nearly all homes fronted on boulevards, "presenting to the passer an almost unbroken view of well-kept lawns, opulent flower-beds, and delicate shrubbery." This endlessly idealized life, a bounteous garden, was also intensively wealthy: sheep pasture bought for seventy-five cents an acre sold for twenty-five dollars an acre in the 1870s; a few years later the same unimproved land brought five hundred dollars an acre; if orange trees were on it, the price was one to two thousand dollars an acre.[35]

Frank Miller, owner and developer of the Mission Inn, spent a quarter of a century (beginning in the late 1890s) building a massive Spanish revival resort, "a neo-Franciscan fantasy of courts, patios, halls, archways, and domes," designed by architect Myron Hunt and fitted out with stained glass, statues of saints, southern European domes and arches: "It was as if the Midwest Protestant American imagination, disordered with suppressed longing," Starr wrote, "now indulged itself in an orgy of aesthetic hyperdulia."[36] Dick and Pat Nixon got married the first time at the Mission Inn, and Ron and Nancy Reagan for his second time; Teddy Roosevelt visited in 1903, and the lobby still sports the widened and reinforced chair that the hotel built specially for the arrival of William Howard Taft, who visited his 320-pound bulk on Riverside in 1909.

The halcyon heyday of California's citrus culture (1880–1941) is a central theme in the romance of the state's past and recently got a lyrical benediction from Kevin Starr: "Rarely, if ever . . . has such beauty and civility, such luxuriance and orderly repose been achieved on an American landscape as that brought about by citrus on the landscape of Southern California. . . . Groves such as these, broken intermittently by gingerbread cottages or Spanish-style haciendas, conferred on parts of Southern California an ambience of Mediterranean idyll, a visual poetry of leaf, blossom, or fruit."[37] Here was orange-crate pastoralism, a form of agrarian civic culture that seemed to realize the Jeffersonian ideal of the rural (or the modestly urban), the urbane and the profitable, a mannered wealthy existence open to that classic American arche-type, the God-fearing individual willing to rely on himself, work hard, be thrifty, and find his just reward down the pike. Starr's eulogy for a California that mostly disappeared in the recent past is not unusual—citrus civility is the essential template of nostalgia for a lost Arcadia. Almost any intellectual, writer, or filmmaker lamenting the ravenous sprawl of California pavement, the greedy realtors, the foul air, the craven billionaire moguls—that person imagines a sunbathed Riverside boulevard circa 1925, a Stutz-Bearcat cruising by amid the overwhelming spring fragrance of the orange blossoms. Conservatives and progressives alike rhapsodized about this orange grove paradise; it is remarkable to see, in his best book (among many fine ones), how much Carey McWilliams loved the old Southern California.[38]

Jim Crow Lemon Groves

Arcadia looked a bit different if you weren't a WASP orchard-tender. Mexicans or Asians were to be seen at harvest time, in the great multitudes required, and then hustled out of town as fast as possible. The citrus belt was almost as segregated as any southern town until the civil rights movement broke down the barriers: segregated schools, whites-only real estate covenants, the balcony for any Mexican who wanted to watch a movie, and one day a week reserved for people of color at the swimming pool—the day before it got drained and cleaned. Discrimination just wasn't as obvious in California; the absence of "colored" drinking fountains or waiting rooms made it less visible. The placid civility of the citrus towns disappeared at the hint of a strike: 2,500 Mexican workers launched a big one in 1936, seeking forty cents an hour instead of twenty-five, and vigilantes instantly emerged—400 armed men deputized by the sheriff, summary arrests of hundreds of people, shadowy night riders, assaults with impunity. Carey McWilliams encountered former classmates from the University of Southern California, "famous athletes" armed with revolvers and clubs, "ordering Mexicans around as though they were prisoners in a Nazi concentration camp."[39]

Picking oranges is extremely hard work—combining "the agility of a monkey and the stamina of a horse." A picker has to shinny up into the branches, clip the root, and pick every tree clean as fast as he can because he is paid by piece-rate. An average picker can do about eighty boxes of oranges over a long day, which brought him $20 in 1966 and far less in the nineteenth century. The boxes weighed about 70 pounds, and "rustlers" at the packing houses typically carried 500 to 700 a day. A young investigator for the state named Frederick Mills worked from dawn until 9:00 p.m. hoisting these boxes for just one day in 1914 and went home with huge blisters, torn hands, and "a red hot sear" rubbed into his thighs by the edges of the boxes. "I no longer wonder why there are so many I.W.W.s," he remarked.[40] The owners liked their workers gendered, too: men, usually organized by race (Chinese, Mexicans) worked in the fields, women in the packing houses.

Chinese-American agriculturists came as early to citrus as the flatlanders, migrating into it after the gold mines and railroad jobs dried up. They constituted upwards of 90 percent of the agricultural labor in California by 1870, and they dominated citrus work into the 1890s (when they were violently driven out). Chinese workers did much more than pick fruit. They brought a tradition of intensive farming and specifically citrus cultivation, since southeastern Guangdong, where most immigrants to the Pacific Coast came from, was one of China's oldest orange-growing regions—back well before poet Du Fu rhapsodized about their thick green leaves. They also originated the "China pack," wrapping each orange in its own tissue paper ("every wrapper smooth, not a wrinkle") and then carefully arranging the fruit in the crates so that they would travel unblemished to the East, where a grocer could open them and instantly create a store window display. Chinese also worked cheaply and docilely—because they faced remorseless oppression if they got out of line. The California Supreme Court decided in 1854 that Chinese were to be treated like blacks or as "a variety of Indian." And so like blacks in the South, they could be killed with impunity: in 1862 alone eighty-eight Chinese were murdered. After the turn to citrus in the 1880s, every citrus community had its "Chinatown" nearby, the workers of course living in terrible conditions; when the season ended they dutifully disappeared into San Francisco. The growers had a grudging admiration for their skills and hard work—according to the *Pacific Rural Press* in 1893, they "are the mainstay of the orchardist," expert in garden work and superb packers. This stinting praise left quite a bit out, McWilliams observed: "The Chinese actually taught their overlords how to plant, cultivate, and harvest orchard and garden crops." But by the 1890s they were driven from the fields by anti-Chinese attacks and riots (over the protests of large growers, of course).[41]

After the turn of the century Japanese laborers replaced many of the beaten, scorned, or deported Chinese. By 1910 some 30,000 Japanese farm laborers worked in California; most of them were already experienced farmers before emigrating, they were knowledgeable and industrious and particularly adept at intensive, specialized agriculture. Like the Chinese before them, the vast majority were single men, and they dutifully vanished when the season ended. No one claimed to know where they lived during the season (in fact they camped out), relieving the growers of providing what they euphemistically called "housing." "The Japs and Chinks just drift," J. H. Nagle of the California Fruit Growers' Exchange said: "We don't have to look out for them. White laborers with families, if we could get them, would be liabilities."[42]

Actually Japanese-Americans didn't "drift": their communities in America quickly developed cooperative associations known as *kyowakai* (just as they did in their subsequent colony in Manchuria). Every member of the community, whether Christian or Buddhist, would join and make the *kyowakai* the center of social life. Like Chinese in the ostensibly tapped-out gold mines, Japanese farmers took over some of the worst land; through careful "soil preparation, crop and seed selection, planting, cultivation, irrigation and spraying," they made the soil remarkably fertile. Japanese farmers quickly converted uncultivated and "waste" land to rice production, working 25,000 acres of rice fields by 1918 and producing nearly 10 billion bushels of rice annually, which grew to a $20 million business by the late 1930s. Wataru Tomosaburo Donashi arrived in Yorba Linda (Richard Nixon's birthplace) in 1907, bought twenty acres, and planted citrus trees, sticking tomato and pea seeds between the rows to live on while the trees slowly grew. He and his family packed up the ripened tomatoes and peas and drove into Los Angeles to sell them, "truck farming" as it was called, in which the Japanese soon were dominant. Japanese farmers specialized in sugar beets, flowers and nursery products, and above all potatoes: George Shima, the "potato king," controlled 85 percent of potato production in California when he died in 1926. In the Newcastle fruit belt, Japanese farmers owned or leased 14,000 out of 18,000 acres of its orchard land, producing as many as 2,500 carloads of fruit annually in the 1920s and 1930s. (Wartime internment ruined that effort; the Newcastle orchards never recovered after 1945, and in 1958 "Newcastle's Japantown was leveled to make way for Highway 40." Today Interstate 80 passes by the empty shipping houses of "fruit house row.") Through legendary thrift and long hours of hard work that employed the whole family, they were easily the most competitive farmers in California.[43]

Mexicans replaced Chinese and Japanese farm laborers in the 1920s, mostly after the Oriental Exclusion Act of 1924. The growers loved them because they could be trucked in from Mexico for the harvest (an average of 58,000 per year from 1924 to 1930) and trucked back out just as quickly: "When we want you, we'll call you," a ranch foreman said. "When we don't—git." They were good, unorganized, docile workers—and when they weren't, they could be shoved back over the border: deported. That's exactly what happened during the Depression, as we have seen, when tens of thousands were deported "to get them off the relief rolls." This was also, of course, a recognition that the Depression had whitened the migrant work force: upwards of 50 percent of the workers were native whites by 1934, and the proportion continued to increase.[44]

Orange Politics

As late as 1960 Los Angeles County was nearly 90 percent white. Still, white hegemony was by no means as seamless as it was in the South: ask any African-American who grew up in California. There was always Los Angeles, where a southern black migrant might live segregated in Watts but find lots of opportunity; or San Francisco, the equal of any eastern city in its (always relative, always qualified, never less than discriminatory) openness to people of color. But in the ambience of the Orange or Riverside County citrus town, the conservative habits of fruit cultivation and white racism got married to the imperatives of bringing in the crop as quickly as possible at the cheapest labor cost possible, creating a toxic and long-lasting mix.

Citrus towns were not really made up of family farms, where the adults and children helped bring in the harvest. Even 20 acres was too large for a family to cultivate; besides, this was a business, not subsistence agriculture: better to live in town, along the fragrant boulevards. Leland Stanford represented the ideal to which owners aspired—his colossal 3,900-acre vineyard required 70 workers year-round, twice that number for some tasks, and about 700 at harvest time.[45] A single fact thus brought the intensive agriculture of citrus together with the extensive farming of the Central Valley: both saw any combination among the workers, any hint of regulation, any government interference (excluding their subsidies) as rank communism. The big owners and the citrus crowd basically won the California lottery—where those who arrived first claimed the lion's share—but they bathed themselves in American virtues of self-reliance, thrift, and optimism. Orange County thus became the fount and epicenter of a special kind of American politics.

Raymond Cyrus Hoiles owned the dominant Orange County newspaper, the *Santa Ana Register:* Robert A. Taft was too liberal for his taste, he wanted taxes and public schools abolished (education taxes were compulsory robbery), along with the post office, taxpayer-supported police, and of course the League of Nations and later the United Nations.[46] Hoiles was an extreme version of the general conservatism of the county, born in the orange groves, tied to religious fundamentalism, and deeply hostile to eastern elites whether Democratic or Republican—an attitude partly born out of California's dependency on eastern banks and markets until World War II, which cut particularly deep among the middle class and the wealthy. Orange grove owners detested any kind of government influence, basing themselves on ideals of individualism, strong religiosity, and the belief that when a community needed cooperative endeavor, they should do it themselves (as with Sunkist). Local government was the exception when it mobilized police to help growers control migrant laborers, and the federal government was the exception when it bore the costs of delivering water to the Southern California desert: but government became the eternal enemy when it materialized in the form of FDR's New Deal.

Religion was just as important to the orange growers as it was for New England Puritans or Oregon Trail pioneers. But it had a different displacement, coming from the plains of the Middle West rather than the genteel tradition which, we recall, had Harvard at its core. Southern California WASPs had Indiana or Nebraska at their core, and to the degree that they attained the bourgeois heights of gentleman farming, they had more time to nurture their assets and more time for the church. No orange grove town lacked a church at the center of the community, and that church was likely to be fundamentalist. Indeed, this is where the *Fundamentals* were published between 1910 and 1915, pamphlets now taken to be the origin of the Christian fundamentalist movement, just as Reverend Bob Shuler pioneered fire-and-brimstone preaching to a congregation numbering 42,000 by the 1920s.[47] Of course there is no way to separate Orange County from Los Angeles in this regard, except that the sprawling city provided something amorphously religious for everybody, from Aimee Semple McPherson to yogis and Sufis; religion was a moneymaker as predictable as the movies or real estate. No one has ever fully explained the Southern California penchant for religiosity in crackpot or fundamental form, even if everyone likes to try; it has something to do with displacement and anomie, or maybe just the perpetual human recoil and attraction in beholding history evaporating in the wake of the next new thing. In the citrus belt, however, a relatively seamless fundamentalism united the town churches, making a Boston Unitarian as alien as an atheist.

Walter Knott was born in San Bernardino in 1889, to a father who was both an evangelical preacher and a wealthy rancher. The son grew even richer with his renowned berry farm—long a combination theme park and church. Knott was an innovator (he introduced the boysenberry) and jelly-jar packer, but his biggest impact was his entrepreneurial role in spreading the right-wing political gospel. From the John Birch Society to the Billy James Hargis Crusade to Fred Schwartz's Christian Anti-Communist Crusade and his "School of Anti-Communism" (located at the berry farm), Knott's hand was visible. Unlike them, however, he also moved in the Southern California mainstream. He was a member of Ronald Reagan's campaign finance committee in 1966 and promoted right-wing politics with large corporations like Fluor and Shick Razor; Hollywood legends like Roy and Dale Rogers, John Wayne, and Pat Boone; and Southern California Baptist preachers who differed little from their southern counterparts, frequently spilling their politics over into racism and anti-Semitism. Knott was a one-man distributor of political tracts, preeminently John Stormer's *None Dare Call It Treason;* one of his organizations gave away half a million copies.[48] (Sometimes called *None Dare Call It Reason,* the book had the Rockefellers and Foggy Bottom blue bloods in bed with the United Nations and the Kremlin in a fiendish plot to take over the world.) Stormer's book became the bible of the New Right's worldview, showing up in recent guise, for example, in Phyllis Schlafly's 1998 mouthful to the effect that "global treaties and conferences are a direct threat to every American citizen," the Senate should reject any and all U.N. treaties out of hand, so the nation can remain pure: "We Americans have a constitutional republic so unique, so precious, so successful that it would be total folly to put our necks in a yoke with any other nation"—not to mention heretics (she also cited St. Paul: "Be ye not unequally yoked together with unbelievers").[49]

Conclusion

In the year that Hitler invaded Poland, California packed 75 million boxes of oranges and millions more of lemons, limes, and grapefruits. But after the war the orange empire died, inundated by an onrushing deluge of wet concrete (roughly 250 pounds per capita) that just about paved over this sylvan Garden of the West. By 1970 land devoted to agriculture in Los Angeles County had dropped by 96 percent.[50] Today you can drive through Whittier, Pomona, Riverside, and San Bernardino and see mere remnants of this lost past. If Frederick Jackson Turner had lived to take the same trip, he might have concluded that the ideals of the frontier had again been trampled by "such a consolidation of capital and so complete a systematization of economic processes" as the world had ever seen. Luckily for him, though, he spent his elder years at 23 Oak Knoll Gardens in "the key of the valley," Pasadena, when it was still in its Arcadian heyday—drinking three glasses of fresh orange juice every day and, one imagines, relishing his own garden at the end of the frontier's rainbow.[51]

CHAPTER TEN

"There It Is. Take It": Water and Power

"LET'S START DRAINING QUAIL AT 12:00" was the 10:51 a.m. entry . . . "OK" was the response recorded in the log. I knew at that moment that I had missed the only vocation for which I had any instinctive affinity: I wanted to drain Quail myself.

—JOAN DIDION

Quail is a reservoir near Los Angeles which holds 1,636,018,000 gallons of water. What Didion wanted was the autonomy to control it—water and power. That's what the movie *Chinatown* is about. It is rare for a Hollywood crime drama to spawn a literature and unrelenting controversy, but by now this film inhabits one book after another about water and power in California and the origins of Los Angeles. It has become part of that history—of the aqueduct that enabled the founding of a great city, the founders themselves, and their hopes, plans, dreams, and crimes. One writer condemns the film for inaccuracy, another acclaims its insight, and a third frames an entire chapter through this film's eye; in 2006 a new water-and-power book appeared titled *Beyond Chinatown.* Somehow a two-hour noir got stuck deeply under the skin ("Los Angeles authorities are livid on the subject of Chinatown").[1] This film didn't tell a quintessentially American story; it told a California story. By probing the story itself and the history behind it, however, we may find a much more general narrative of how the West was won and subdued.

In the preface I wrote that *Chinatown* achieved a brilliant inversion of popular imaginings of the West: home to the autonomous cowboy riding the free range, the rugged individualist, the intrepid pioneer, the courageous homesteader, the minimal state—the region epitomized the open promises and freedoms of the frontier, or American freedom itself. Nonwhites that got in the way could be pushed aside or penned up, in reservations and urban ghettoes like Los Angeles' Chinatown—and in those places, American virtue was stood on its head and all the vices came into play. The film takes the classic stereotypes of Chinatown and folds them into the daily life and be-havior of the city oligarchs; it takes American conceits about freedom and liberty and replaces them with the Asiatic mode of production: autocratic WASP satraps who deploy water in search of unbounded wealth and power.

Hollis Mulwray was right to believe that life begins in the tide pools. Water is everything: the human body is two-thirds water, the surface of our planet is two-thirds water, and the Pacific is two-thirds of all that water. But we take it for granted—we open the spigot and drink, turn on the shower and bathe, dive into a pool and swim. Southern California never could take it for granted. Instead water brought it to life and made just about everything that people take for granted into a human contrivance (the Los Angeles aqueduct) or a transplant (the palm tree) or a simulacrum of nature (Japanese gardens in Beverly Hills). Water is not just life-giving in Southern California, it is wealth, it is power, it is the future—an ever-expanding future so long as a huge supply of semi-arid land can be irrigated into profitable real estate.

Reconnoitering the Future on a Buckboard

Fred Eaton was the chief engineer of the privately owned Los Angeles Water Company from 1877 to 1886, when he became the city engineer. A handsome, even charismatic figure born to one of the city's "top drawer" pioneer families, he was elected mayor in 1898 as a strong advocate of municipalizing the water supply. In 1901 a bond issue passed, and the city bought out Eaton's water company for $2 million. It had been a lucrative private business, earning an estimated annual return of 10 to 35 percent, but the preponderance of opinion was that the city should own and manage its own water supply. Soon Eaton sought public funding for an aqueduct that would bring water—Owens River water—to Los Angeles; that is, half would go to the city, and half would go to him, for distribution to irrigation districts along the south coast. Eaton then quietly bought up land and water rights in Long Valley, which sits above the Owens Valley. As the author of the standard account, William Kahrl, put it, "He never conceived of the [aqueduct] as anything other than a private scheme that would work to his personal profit."[2]

Then Eaton convinced William Mulholland, chief engineer of the De-partment of Water and Power, to take a buckboard ride across the desert to map out the aqueduct's route. What they talked about as they emptied one whiskey bottle after another over nightly campfires, nobody knows. But when Eaton showed him the Owens River and the Owens Valley (the river runs for 125 miles from the High Sierras into Owens Lake), Mulholland saw enough water to support 2 million people (even if Los Angeles only had 200,000).

This valley sits behind the southern Sierra Madre Range, about 240 miles north of Los Angeles; from the highest point in the forty-eight states, Mount Whitney, you can see across Owens Valley all the way to Death Valley—the lowest point in the United States. Mulholland and Eaton wanted Owens Valley water conveyed by the aqueduct to the city through the San Fernando Valley, where any water showered on the earth would end up in the sizable aquifer of the Los Angeles River, a natural reservoir where it could sit without evaporating—giving the city "free storage" in the late Marc Reisner's words.[3]

After returning to the city Mulholland met quietly with the Board of Water Commissioners, a central organ of the Anglo oligarchy, and laid out Eaton's plan for the aqueduct. Well impressed, the board was also well versed in how to keep a secret. Nothing broke into the newspapers as Eaton, Mulholland, and their friends secretly prepared a bond issue to get citizens to fund the aqueduct and spread rumors that a drought was threatening the city (it wasn't); some claimed that Water and Power was draining its reservoirs into the Pacific at night to make the drought seem real (it may have been). Meanwhile former mayor Eaton and a colleague, J. B. Lippincott, bought up options on land in the Owens Valley, hoping to get cashed out later by the city. Eaton laid out about $15,000; the city later bought him out for $450,000, and he made another $100,000 on options in the valley. Meanwhile he retained control of another 23,000 acres.[4]

In *Chinatown*, Noah (water) Cross (Christ) is the epitome of WASP evil: water and power, vast wealth, some friends downtown ("he *owns* the police!"), an intricate real estate conspiracy punctuated by a murder, finally a bid to control L.A.'s entire future—and he's an incestuous child molester to boot; and he murdered his own son-in-law to boot. (One Water and Power official complained that the film was "totally inaccurate" as to the real facts; when asked to name one, he said, "There was never any incest.")[5] Perhaps no incest at the department, but they did have a conspiracy—both in the film and in the history of the city: Kevin Starr wrote, "The water destiny of Los Angeles was unfolding as a conspiracy in which public ambition and private self-interest mingled murkily."[6] Not a minor or trifling observation, this, because the story of Owens Valley water is also the foundational narrative of Los Angeles.

He Made This City

It isn't clear which historical figure Noah Cross represents in the film. He might be Harrison Gray Otis, if Otis had his brains (he didn't). Cross is meant to encompass and embody the syndicate that bought up the San Fernando Valley and the Anglo oligarchy that ran the city. In the film, however the director of Water and Power, Hollis Mulwray, clearly recalls William Mulholland.[7] Most Americans who don't live in Los Angeles have probably never heard of him; they might have heard of Mulholland Drive or at least the film by the same name. To those who do know him he's an enormously controversial figure—to the historians, the city fathers, and even distant progeny who still seek to rectify his good name. But when John Huston tells Jack Nicholson that Hollis Mulwray "made this city," he could only have been talking about one man: William Mulholland.

Mulholland was born in Dublin in 1855, and before he was twenty he hired on as a merchant seaman and arrived in the United States. After knocking around the Great Lakes taking odd jobs for a couple of years, he sailed for Panama and then San Francisco. In the summer of 1877 he rode down through the Big Sur and into Los Angeles on a horse—a lean, tanned, rugged, and highly intelligent Irishman. Mullholland caught on with the water company, tending ditches and sloughs to keep them free and flowing, and slowly got to know the Los Angeles River and its odd and erratic ways with a rare and deeply felt intimacy; he often said he was happiest when walking along the riverside—"a beautiful, limpid little stream with willows on its banks." In the evenings Mulholland taught himself water engineering and hydraulics, botany and history; by 1886 he was superintendent of the entire water system, and he still was when the city took it over in 1902. Like Mulwray in the film, Mullholland avoided the wealthy circuit and their clubs in the city (even though he became rich himself) and lived modestly.[8] He was a remarkable example of that American hero, the self-taught and self-made man.

After his success with the aqueduct Mulholland was a public figure of towering prestige in the city, its "indispensable citizen," and well enough known in the country to bring his influence to bear in Washington on one of the great engineering projects in world history, the Hoover Dam. Admiring citizens often urged him to run for mayor, prompting Mulholland to retort, "I would rather give birth to a porcupine backwards than become the mayor of Los Angeles."[9] (Like Robert Moses in New York, he preferred to run a more powerful entity.) In 1926 Water and Power began to build yet another dam, this time in the San Francisquito Canyon north of the city, on a site that Mulholland had picked out and following a design that he had approved; it was his fourteenth dam. He completed it in early 1928 and as the water in the vast reservoir filled to the brim (a height of 1,832 feet) for the first time on March 12, just short of midnight, the dam collapsed and sent a tsunami as much as 100 feet high cascading toward the Pacific, 55 miles in the distance. It took a little over an hour to get there, gushing through Simi Valley toward the sea with 10,000-ton chunks of concrete borne along like rowboats, leaving smashed towns, houses, and cars in its wake and nearly 500 people dead, a majority of them Mexican citrus workers. This, of course, is the tragedy that Robert Towne alluded to in *Chinatown*, except that it's called the Vanderlip Dam and after it Hollis Mulwray is still in full command of Water and Power. The broken St. Francis, however, also broke Mulholland: "Founder of the city . . . Goethals of the West . . . builder of the aqueduct," he never recovered from a debacle that traced directly to him—and he was the first to admit it. He had overruled experts who warned him about the geological fragility of the site as early as 1911; he even visited the St. Francis Dam on the morning of the disaster, to examine leakage—and then dismissed it as inconsequential. He died a broken man in 1935 at the age of eighty.[10]

William Mulholland was a rugged individual out of mythic Americana, muscular, competitive, and self-reliant; and that's what the Los Angeles Aqueduct's legacy was, too—"muscular, competitive and self-reliant," in William Kahrl's words, a monument to private enterprise in the private and public interest and a contrast with water development elsewhere in the West, almost always accomplished under the aegis of the federal Bureau of Reclamation.[11] This fit the vision of the city's founders, its "private sector"—oligarchs who hated government (unless it was working for them), despised combination at the workplace, and who knew "how to get things done." Perhaps the proof of this pudding is in the words of Mulholland's most fervent defender, his granddaughter Catherine: "The whole thrust of the Los Angeles enterprise looked to the future. Just as Caesar did not look back to Alexander for his model of a Roman empire but anticipated as a model a kind of city-state existing in Rome's own peripheries and provinces, so leaders of an expanding Los Angeles looked to extend boundaries in order to create a new kind of city."[12] She must not realize how much she sounds like Noah Cross.

Everybody Makes Money

Mulholland was not a man to profit mightily from public service. Fred Eaton did do well by himself: he made a small fortune for the time. But he was a piker compared to the wealthy oligarchs who set up a syndicate to purchase land in the San Fernando Valley—arid land of course, obtained for thirty-five dollars an acre—pending the arrival of Owens Valley water: Henry Huntington, Harrison Gray Otis, Edwin T. Earl (publisher of the *Express*), banker

Joseph Sartori, and E. H. Harriman (owner of the Southern Pacific) were some of the businessmen in the group. For good measure this syndicate also included a member of the Board of Water Commissioners, Moses Sherman; a very wealthy man for whom the town of Sherman Oaks is named, he had merged several trolley lines into the Consolidated Electric Railway and later purchased the Pacific Railway, thus dominating Los Angeles transportation in the 1890s. Five days after Lippincott met secretly with city officials to discuss the aqueduct, they founded their syndicate, the San Fernando Mission Land Company. Soon they owned a vast tract that today includes the towns of Canoga Park, Reseda, Sherman Oaks, Van Nuys, and Woodland Hills. This was just one facet of a host of real estate deals involving millions of acres modeled on the San Fernando Valley operation, the point of origin for the syndicate's influence over Los Angeles and the South Coast. By 1914 Otis's son-in-law Harry Chandler "headed the largest real estate network in California" and later bequeathed an estate estimated as high as half a billion dollars; as for the syndicate, its holdings of land purchased at an average of $20 an acre now fetched $2,000 per acre, yielding a profit on the San Fernando Valley alone of $100 million.[13]

It seems to confound reason that this deal should also have brought public ownership of electricity so early to Los Angeles, in a town run by oligarchs fanatically committed to private enterprise and blaring about it every day in the *Times,* whereas in cosmopolitan San Francisco, the privately held Pacific Gas and Electric had a virtual monopoly over power and electricity. It happened because public ownership hardly threatened the oligarchy's control; its representatives sat on the Board of Water Commissioners, which supervised the Department of Water and Power and insulated it from public scrutiny— thus making it "the second government of Los Angeles." And now the people would pay the bills. When the decision was taken to use the aqueduct water not just to fill reservoirs but to generate electricity, the board centralized even more power in its hands.

This is municipal chicanery of a deft and high order, and this being a rough and tumble democracy, it eventually burst out into the newspapers and caused an uproar. But this was also a democracy that could do little to hinder the schemes of wealthy and powerful men, so the bond issue soon passed (on June 12, 1907) by a nine-to-one margin and William Mulholland was ready to build "the longest aqueduct in the Western Hemisphere" and the fourth largest engineering project that Americans had ever undertaken.[14] Big city corruption works best when everybody makes money (as a convicted and jailed Seattle public official said in the 1980s), and everyone wanted a taste of the real estate bonanza that the displaced Owens Valley water would soon create—oligarch and good citizen alike.

It isn't as if the oligarchy just built the aqueduct: they built everything—they built the city: water and power, the highways, the port, newsprint, the downtown (which was really a downtown by the 1920s), the Miracle Mile on Wilshire, the wealthy subdivisions (Beverly Hills, Palos Verdes). They laid out many fine parks (the 1927 Citizen's Committee on Parks included Edward Doheny, Van Nuys, Lippincott, George Getty, the O'Melveny brothers, and Cecil B. DeMille). They built the hotels, like the Biltmore across from Mac-Arthur Park; a big syndicate organized by Joseph Sartori, including Harry Chandler, Henry M. Robinson, and many others, developed this magnificent hotel, which opened in 1923 a block away from the splendid art deco city library (probably they built that, too). An elite that numbered less than a hundred did everything—politics, media, public works, banking, business—and pioneered the subdivisions of the modern home-building industry, precursor of the suburban sprawl now surrounding every big city. They built upon Southern California's most abundant resource—virgin land, otherwise known as real estate, where the lion's share of the money was made.[15]

When I sit in the Biltmore eating breakfast in the high-ceilinged, Italian marble–tiled restaurant, I wonder if anything ever got done in Los Angeles without their approval. But I also wonder if this oligarchy did not do great things. Would a hotel of such enduring beauty exist without Mr. Sartori and his friends? Is a robber baron like Henry Huntington necessary to a certain result, namely the Huntington Library, set in his San Marino estate with glorious architecture, matchless gardens, priceless antiquities, and a library of 600,000 books and 2.5 million manuscripts—and those were just the holdings when it opened in 1919. In the end it isn't surprising that they thought so little of government, because Washington was so far away—and they *were* the government. Their monopolies and oligopolies hardly resembled the free market, but the private sector built this city more than any other, with an added virtue: it was *their* private sector, a market all of their own. But none of it was possible without water.

Water Running into Money

While Mulholland stayed out in the field and drove his men relentlessly through six years of construction, living and working with them, Lippincott became an assistant chief engineer for the city and Eaton was still hoping to get a million dollars for 12,000 acres of the land he bought up in Long Valley, along the line of the 235-mile aqueduct. Mulholland simply refused to meet his price, marking the end of their close friendship. Finally the moment came: November 5, 1913: the invitations to the celebration likened the project to "Caesar and his Roman Aqueduct," a huge crowd gathered, cannon boomed, and Mulholland had his men lift the gates that finally brought the Owens River to the city. As the water crashed out of the long spillway, Mulholland remarked, "There it is. Take it."[16] He and the oligarchs, like Roman and Chinese emperors, had deployed water and earth into the power to found a great city, enough for a tenfold increase in population; they had built the future. The future was yet to come, however. The enormous surplus water (eight times what the city needed in 1913) had to go somewhere—and so it did: into a vast expansion of nearby towns and cities. Mulholland was happy to sell cheap water to any community, so long as it was willing to join the city—you "bring the water to L.A. and L.A. to the water," as Noah Cross put it. Los Angeles annexed the San Fernando Valley in 1915, doubling its size to 285 square miles (the city's "Louisiana Purchase"); by 1930 it had 442 square miles, "the largest metropolitan territory under a single government in the United States," big enough to plunk down Boston, San Francisco, and the five boroughs of New York, a kind of city-state dominating all of Southern California.[17] The Panama Canal opened a year later, which favored L.A. compared to San Francisco and finally prompted it to build a deepwater harbor, at San Pedro; just 70 miles off the great circle route between Panama and Asia,[18] the port flourished, and by 1924 it was the leading port in tonnage on the Pacific Coast. Water again: it was everywhere.

If Robert Towne's narrative of Mulholland's aqueducts and dams collapses history, it doesn't violate the essential truth of what happened. But it does suggest that the skullduggery central to turning the San Fernando Valley into a real estate bonanza was somehow unique to Los Angeles, when it was merely grander in scale than the speculation all along the westering frontier— and almost standard operating procedure in California. George Chaffey, for example, developed plans in the 1890s to bring Colorado River water to the barren Imperial Valley, through a rudimentary 50-mile-long ditch capable of irrigating a million acres of public land. Then mostly a desert, this valley in the southeastern corner of the state is about 45 miles long and 30 miles wide. It has the longest growing season in the United States (300 days), twice as much cotton per acre grows there compared to the rest of the country, and farmers can harvest six crops of alfalfa annually. Chaffey used the Homestead Act and the Desert Land Act of 1877 to get a lot of that public land free or for the modest sum of $1.25 an acre, which could be reclaimed once irrigation was

Mulholland's aqueduct snakes across the desert toward Los Angeles.
Lippincott Collection, Water Resources Center Archives,
University of California–Berkeley.

completed; the water of the Colorado River, of course, was also free for the taking. After the ditch started filling, he and his associates established the Imperial Land Company and began selling off real estate at huge multiples of what they paid for it (if they paid anything). They took settlers through the necessary procedures to get their land bought and irrigated, providing 6 percent mortgages and long-term water contracts that locked in permanent profits far beyond what was realized in the initial sales. The Mediterranean metaphors of Southern California real estate boosters didn't work so well in this desert, however, so Egypt came to mind: the Colorado was the Nile, the Imperial Valley was the Delta, behold the biblical lands and the desert coming to life, even the Pharaohs. But Chaffey was the real Pharaoh of this scheme, Starr wrote, "a massive use of public resources for private profit."[19]

Wasn't San Francisco thirsty, too? The Hetch Hetchy Valley sits about

20 miles northwest of Yosemite, about half its size but its equal in beauty—although much more remote and inaccessible. John Muir, the great environmentalist who had been instrumental in getting Congress to make a national park of Yosemite, and his Sierra Club friends were among the few people to have seen it. Through the valley ran the Tuolumne River, and San Franciscans wanted its water—delivered through a 150-mile-long aqueduct. Bringing the water to the city paralleled the story of the Los Angeles aqueduct: a city engineer in San Francisco, Michael O'Shaugnessy, drove the endeavor like Mulholland in Los Angeles, and he also joined together with a former mayor, James Duval Phelan, the Fred Eaton of this project.[20] Otherwise the drama was rather different: only one man really profited by putting arid land aside to wait for the oncoming, nourishing water, the San Francisco elite did not intrigue and scheme, the water was brought to the city and for the city—not for real estate fortunes or for the imperial city to incorporate hundreds of square miles of nearby valley. Instead this symbolizes a different California theme: the Arcadian delights of the untouched wilderness versus the mundane needs of the big city; inundating Hetch Hetchy was entirely an "act of desecration" for Muir, the Sierra Club, and the genteel academics in Stanford and Berkeley who populated the club.[21] Muir had seen it and knew its awesome beauty, but after 1923 only the fish had the privilege: the valley disappeared when the O'Shaughnessy Dam raised a reservoir 86 feet high that drowned its cliffs, forests, and trout streams. John Muir's struggle to save Hetch Hetchy and his remorse at failing contributed to his death in 1914.

William Hammond Hall, the creator of Golden Gate Park who went on to be California's first state engineer and also the first person to think systematically about the state's water needs and its hydraulic architecture, was a charter member of the Sierra Club. He quickly came to understand that the immense capital outlay required for the hydraulic restructuring of California could only come from government, from the public treasury; private firms would not be able to do it. In 1891 Hall headed the California division of the U.S. Geological Survey and recommended Hetch Hetchy as the best site for a long-lasting source of water for San Francisco. Meanwhile this public servant spent his spare time investing in barren land before the delivery of water turned it into a real estate bonanza. Professor Charles Marx of Stanford, also a charter member of the Sierra Club, became chief spokesman for the aqueduct, and Woodrow Wilson, arch-progressive, signed the law authorizing the aqueduct in December 1913. J. B. Lippincott of Los Angeles notoriety was involved, too, after Mayor Phelan detailed him to investigate Hetch Hetchy's value for the city. It was equal-opportunity hypocrisy in search of water.

Unlike the Los Angeles oligarchy, however, Hall was about the only one who got rich off Hetch Hetchy. Mayor Phelan was a progressive Democrat who wanted municipal water for the city. Lippincott chose not to buy land this time. San Francisco got a bond issue passed in 1910, built the aqueduct for about $100 million, took the water it needed when it was finished in 1934, and then sold the rest to independent communities on the peninsula down south to San Jose. Capable of watering 4 million people, this was not an aqueduct to lubricate a metastisizing city or build an oligarchy's future.[22] If it were, San Francisco would have annexed Oakland as prelude to bringing the entire Bay Area and a good part of the peninsula under its aegis: then it might be something like Los Angeles. Still, the water remained under private control: for half a century the city got its water supply from the Spring Valley Water Works, which built several reservoirs in San Mateo County and had a monopoly on the delivery of water to the city. The city finally acquired it in 1929.[23]

Utopia or Empire?

Two decades after seeing *Chinatown* I read Donald Worster's *Rivers of Empire*, a definitive reinterpretation of western history that only makes the film seem more brilliant and telling. In this book, the "land of untrammeled freedom" inverts into "a land of authority and restraint, of class and exploitation, and ultimately imperial power," with the empire resting on the federal government, managerial statecraft and expertise, state-developed technologies, and "abstracted Water, rigidly separated from the earth and firmly directed to raise food, fill pipes, and make money." The water is abstracted by dams, aqueducts, canals, tunnels, concrete-lined ditches, and finally becomes a water of "accumulated expertise," state and technically controlled if still life-giving water, separated from human beings by chain-link fences with signs warning people to "stay alive by staying out."[24] Worster's account achieves the same shock of recognition that Jake Gittes got when a wall of rushing water splayed him against a chain-link fence which he barely clambered over before drowning, losing a new Florsheim shoe in the process.

For Worster, the American West is "a modern *hydraulic society*," a social and techno-economic order "imposed for the purpose of mastering a difficult environment" and ruled by a power elite "based on the ownership of capital and expertise."[25] It differs from Asian hydraulic societies not in any American preference for the private sector—the state is active and often dominant at all levels, with large mandarinates, otherwise known as federal, state, and local bureaucrats—or in being a federation of states rather than an empire, but in the state's role in creating an artificial water-driven environment and economy from which the private sector benefits, and the biggest beneficiaries are the biggest owners, first of all California agribusiness. The state dominates nature in the interest of private enterprise but otherwise leaves business alone—or should. Instead of seeing the West as a colony of the East, a venerable interpretation developed by great historians like Walter Prescott Webb and Bernard DeVoto, Worster sees the West as a new kind of empire, and after Pearl Harbor "a principal seat of the world-circling American Empire." But this is not a determinist account—Worster is a learned and thoughtful historian. As he rightly says, historical truth is not about strict cause and effect but rather "an imaginative grasp of subtly interacting relationships."[26]

Other scholars, like Richard Walker, call Worster's book "the most ambitious theoretical work on California's countryside ever undertaken" but declare him to be "magnificently wrong." He puts irrigation first in explaining the state's prodigious agricultural output, Walker writes, but it was really a laggard, trailing the spread of agriculture by half a century. Yet Walker's evidence doesn't seem to make his point; his own data show steep increases in harvested land that correspond to the opening of the Los Angeles Aqueduct and the Hoover and Shasta dams, and anyway agrarian output is not really Worster's point. Walker also says urban capitalists were the ones sending rivers of investment into the fields, well before the federal government got involved.[27] This is a more telling criticism, but it needn't detain us; he might be talking about William Mulholland and other Los Angeles elites who made little distinction between public and private—they might own the city water supply or they might not, depending on their interests.

Washington was, for most Americans and especially Californians, a distant abstraction. But sometimes it was useful: Mulholland and his friends, or cotton king Boswell, went to the federal government for the same reason that Willy Sutton robbed banks: that's where the money was. Worster presents a narrative and a theory of heavy state involvement in the remaking of the western environment, and as we will see, that involvement was even greater in the origins of western industry. However distant Washington may seem, strong state involvement has characterized this region more than any other. But the water empire of the West is controlled and driven by local leaders, and the broader American empire has little to do with irrigation in the West. Worster's analysis generalizes this water empire as a model for American involvement in the world but says little about the *contribution* of the West to the American role and position in the world; the West may be "a principal seat" of empire, but this empire is not made up of dams and public works, but of defense industries and military bases constituting an archipelago of armed force, which still falls well short of constituting the whole of American hegemony. With nary a dam built in the West you would still have the Atlanticist East, with a worldview originating in New England, taking guidance from England, looking after the whole and governing most of American diplomacy since 1900, and a Pacific-facing, western-directed expansionism that does not look after the whole but accumulates and subordinates the parts. But you wouldn't have Southern California—and that's what the empire of water built.

A New Form of State and Corporate Power

Hydraulic societies do not have to be centrally concentrated and managed, as Holland's dense irrigation network illustrates. In the early days, before Worster's empire, others offered an alternative vision of water and power in California, like the irrigation colony in San Bernardino that the Mormons founded, or the cooperative approach to urban planning and water delivery that the Ontario colony pioneered under the scientific tutelage of George Chaffee (not the Imperial Valley's George Chaffey). He and his associates first built a capacious highway, 200 feet wide and running 8 miles into the foothills, planted magnificent trees on both sides, and ran a trolley car along the parkway in the middle of the road. Then they tapped the underground water table to irrigate orange groves, already carefully plotted, and banned the sale of alcohol to attract churchgoers. This Ontario model was copied widely, and for the 1904 World's Fair in St. Louis, American government engineers erected a scale model of Ontario to exhibit Californian social innovation and public ingenuity.[28] William Ellsworth Smythe, building on the ideas of John Wesley Powell, had a fully developed vision in *The Conquest of Arid America* (1900) for a social-democratic commonwealth in California based on the rational and planned application of water. Aridity was a blessing, not a curse, Smythe thought, because it enabled scientific control of the delivery of water to the earth; farmers did not have to pray for rain but could make their own. They would also have to cooperate with each other to irrigate the fields, and as this cooperation spread, so would social democracy.[29]

While Smythe was cogitating and Mulholland was reconnoitering the aqueduct, the federal government came into the picture under Theodore Roosevelt—who, in his first message to Congress in 1901, opined that "in the arid region it is water, not land, which measures production." Water and power moguls like Mulholland found a new willing ear in Washington through Roosevelt's vision combining progressivism and conservation with a strong role for the central state. Roosevelt delivered exactly what the Los Angeles oligarchy wanted. In 1902 he got the National Reclamation Act through Congress, which funded 600 civil engineers, gave Washington the primary responsibility for irrigation throughout the country, and began thinking about a network of dams and aqueducts that would, he said, "spread prosperity for centuries." The Interior Department could now lend taxpayers' dollars to irrigate homesteads up to 160 acres, a limit that remained in the law for decades but was rarely enforced in California. The new Reclamation Service, with maximum authority over the irrigation of public lands, quickly became a vast lever of central power to transform the West. Teddy Roosevelt traveled often to California and, like his cousin Franklin, believed strongly in massive public works managed and financed by the federal government as a means to develop the West, and especially Southern California; he gave his personal imprimatur to the transfer of Owens Valley water to a newly flourishing Los Angeles.[30]

These measures were every bit as significant as the Homestead Act of 1862, perhaps more so: now the way was open to harness the great rivers of the West, like the Colorado or the Columbia (which drains a watershed the size of Texas, and carries ten times more water to the sea than the Colorado),[31] to the entire future development of the Pacific states—to channel and control the rich abundance of water in the Pacific Northwest and to deliver life-giving water to the semi-arid California south. Thus water took its place alongside gold, silver, wheat, citrus, oil, electricity, and land (real estate) as a huge early boost to California and the West more generally, a series of incalculable "leading sectors" and multipliers of its comparative advantages. By 1900, however, it wasn't one leading sector following another (silver follows gold, wheat follows silver), but several combining together all at once.

Of these commodities, water came first—and still comes first. The Colorado River unites the center of the continent with the Pacific: it runs for 1,400 miles from the Continental Divide to the Gulf of California, a "unified drainage and watershed region" encompassing 260,000 square miles, including seven western states. Not as majestic as the Mississippi or the Columbia, muddy and dark most of the time, it found its American telos in giving life to Southern California, slaking its thirst and making it bloom. If the Colorado River were suddenly to run dry, millions of people would have to "evacuate most of Southern California and Arizona and a good portion of Colorado,

New Mexico, Utah, and Wyoming," in Marc Reisner's words. "The river system provides over half the water of greater Los Angeles, San Diego, and Phoenix; it grows much of America's domestic production of fresh winter vegetables; it illuminates the neon city of Las Vegas, whose annual income is one-fourth the entire gross national product of Egypt—the only other place on earth where so many people are so helplessly dependent on one river's flow."[32] The Owens River was one thing, giving Los Angeles ten times the water it needed, but bringing the Colorado to California was a world-historical undertaking: and that is what the federal government decided to do under Herbert Hoover. The Hoover Dam signified a new role for the federal government in grand public works, mostly in the West, something that President Hoover enthusiastically began but that Franklin Delano Roosevelt took hold of like no previous president; it also represented the beginning of a new assemblage of western private power in the form of the six firms who built the dam.

In the same month as the stock market crash, President Hoover got his Stanford classmate, Ray Lyman Wilbur (by then secretary of the interior), to look over various applications (twenty-seven in all) for the water and power that the dam project would generate. Wilbur made sure his native California got more than its share: 36 percent of the water and power to the Metropolitan Water District of Southern California, 13 percent of the hydro-electric power to Los Angeles, another 15 percent of the electricity to Southern California Edison and some other companies and cities. Nevada and Arizona got 18 percent of the output, with rights to transfer what they didn't need to California. In other words the "greatest dam in human history" was going to deliver nearly all of its water and power to the empire of California—once a canyon was plugged with 4.5 billion cubic feet of concrete.[33]

This great dam was all about California in more ways than one. The low bid came from the "Six Companies," a consortium named for the Six Tongs of San Francisco's Chinatown. They included the little-known Bechtel Corporation; a fledgling cement contractor named Henry J. Kaiser; a firm run by Marriner Eccles and other Mormons (the Utah Construction Company, which had already built the Hetch Hetchy Dam); Morrison-Knudson from Boise (who brought in Frank Crowe, widely thought to be the best dam builder in the United States); the J. F. Shea Company of Portland, a tunnel and sewer builder; and the MacDonald and Kahn Company of San Francisco, which specialized in steel construction. All the firms profited from their work on the Hoover project, of course, but Bechtel and Kaiser, which had started off in cement and construction, got propelled upward to something like "corporate nation-states" by the end of World War II—not bad for two men who were paving roads in the late 1920s.[34] Kaiser had a progressive paternalism at heart and epitomized FDR's idea of the New Deal industrialist. His companies had mostly disappeared a generation later, but Bechtel remains today among the world's most powerful firms, global in scope and local in its politics—for example in Washington, where its officers routinely fill powerful cabinet positions. (Caspar Weinberger, George Shultz; John McCone got his early start with Bechtel and later ran the CIA during the height of the cold war.)

These new captains of industry drove their workers mercilessly around the clock, with one of three shifts laboring at all times in miserable working conditions. Ultimately nearly a hundred workers died, the majority from heat prostration but many others from industrial accidents. Conditions improved when Roosevelt came in and Harold Ickes became secretary of the interior, but no unions ever operated at the dam; when Wobblies protested lousy wages, terrible working conditions, and living quarters unfit for animals in 1931, company thugs and federal marshals shooed them away. Starr is right to link this project to an "iron fist" of rightward-leaning laissez-faire industrialism, similar to the industrial cultures of Germany and Japan, "a subtle triumph of the industrial Right."[35] But Hoover Dam was just the first prominent example of the state-directed and state-funded industrialization of the Pacific states that would reach a crescendo during World War II, bringing the Far West much closer to the industrial policy of pre- and postwar Japan and rather distant from "the natural workings of the market."

"Laissez-faire" was the cry when business was asked to pay taxes, or provide decent working conditions, or bargain with unions, or succumb to regulation by "the federal government," or attend to the environmental damage of which they were heedless. But it evaporated when that same government dangled construction contracts worth billions of dollars. Indeed, no company can possibly have benefited more from its connection to Washington than Bechtel, which later built U.S. military bases all over the world and erected cities in the Saudi desert. If the New Deal conformed more to the postwar German and Japanese model of corporate politics—business, labor, and the state working together, with a safety net for all—Bechtel resembled the prewar *zaibatsu* model: all-powerful, privately held conglomerates, shielded from public scrutiny, thriving on support from the state. Hoover Dam was the birthplace of a particular corporate propensity that was dominant in the Republican Party—condemning the federal government, taxes, unions, and regulations while fattening off public works and defense contracts. But this is a retrospective view; at the time the whole nation watched the great dam rise on the Colorado, and the novelty of this new form of state power made it difficult to separate right from left: the English novelist J. B. Priestley visited Hoover Dam and got "a first glimpse" of what collective planning can accomplish—"here is the soul of America under socialism."[36] (Socialists like Herbert Hoover and John McCone, perhaps.)

Los Angeles got its Colorado River water from a 242-mile aqueduct running from Lake Havasu (created by the Hoover Dam) through a complicated network of tunnels, canals, covered conduits, siphons, dams, and reservoirs that took eight years to finish and kept thousands of people working during the Depression. In 1928 eleven cities in Los Angeles and Orange counties founded the Southern California Metropolitan Water District, and like Water and Power, the board was all-powerful. In the postwar period it was led with an iron hand by Joseph Jensen, a Getty Oil executive who was the chairman for two decades. He and the fifty other board members essentially held their positions for life, with the average age of each usually pushing seventy. Often called "Water Buffaloes" for their devotion to bending the rivers of the West to their interests, they operated outside of public scrutiny in spite of their extraordinary power—for example to impose property taxes throughout the region. They were L.A.'s mandarins, holding their positions forever as they move water this way and that. A century after the aqueduct the water and power story does not stop: the Southern California Metropolitan Water District finished the Eastside Reservoir in 1999: 80 miles outside of Los Angeles, it cost $2 billion. It is a 6-square-mile vat, "one of the largest bathtubs in human history" into which 1,700 Rose Bowls could go and, like Mulholland's aqueduct, designed to secure the region's future. But no oligarchy put this deal together—and it is so environmentally correct that even the environmentalists like it.[37]

"As Little as Possible"

Owens Valley water sits at the juncture of past and present, between a pristine Southern California Arcadia and the great, proliferating city that the aqueduct built. This is the founding story of Los Angeles, and it sits uneasily on the city's mind because of the means employed to get the water—the movers and shakers' favorite metaphor, "you need to break some eggs to make an omelet," doesn't quite work when one entire valley got sucked dry and the cooks ate so much of the omelet, in the form of the other valley (the San Fernando). The best historian of the episode, William Kahrl, sees in the events a merger of private interests with the greater public good of bringing water to the city; "no conspiracy was necessary; their objectives were the same." William Alexander McClung, however, suggests the problem was not just the means but the end—by bringing the water to L.A. and L.A. to the water, the act of irrigating the garden becomes a kind of fall, a "primal error"; it creates an artificial Arcadia, breaking with the natural past and putting Utopia beyond reach. Tampering with the natural environment to get water begets the complete reconfiguration of the earth (through endless real estate platting): to get there you need a car, which smothered the same environment in subdivisions and freeways (250 pounds of concrete per person), which befouls the other human essential, oxygen, air—the "cloudless days and gentle sunshine," "the glorious climate" in the words of a booster in 1890. We immediately imagine L.A.'s gift to the English language, smog, but McClung points out that Los Angeles had bad air and smoky inversions long before automobile exhaust befouled the skies; in 1912 an observer described "a gray-brown veil hanging over the city," and Cabrillo named the Los Angeles Bay "de los fumos."[38] Maybe there never was an Arcadian, crystal city—just a mudflat with bad air days. But millions of automobiles made it a lot worse, and the Owens Valley episode married corrupted means to the transformative end of the Los Angeles we see today—and whatever else we may say about it, it isn't Utopia and it isn't ever going to be.

To most people, from ordinary Americans to farmers to agribusiness moguls to communitarian idealists like William Smythe, irrigation was a godsend to be applauded. Smythe called the application of Colorado River water to the Imperial Valley "the most dramatic transformation ever seen in the United States," and irrigation in central and eastern Washington, he thought, liberated a rich volcanic soil. In the 1930s Lewis Mumford called for a Columbia River Valley authority akin to the Tennessee Valley Authority, and President Roosevelt said he would like "to see the Columbia Basin devoted to the care of the 500,000 people represented in 'Grapes of Wrath'"; a generation later two scholars were still raving about how much Grand Coulee Dam had done for the Pacific Northwest. (Where in the literature is a critical analysis of irrigation in the Tennessee Valley or the Columbia Basin?) Others, like folk singer Woody Guthrie, showed that when it's about cheap electricity, popular opposition to dams melts away: the 1,200-mile-long Columbia was "a river just goin' to waste," he sang in "Walking Columbia," while people need "houses and stuff to eat"; "folks need water and power dams." Perhaps another American essayist enjoys watching engineers open and close dams and wishes she could do it, too, but if so, I don't know who it is. Joan Didion longed to man the Project Operations Control Center in Sacramento and "put some over the hill" to Los Angeles—that is, put several million gallons over the Tehachapi Mountains, the highest pump-rise of any dam system in the world. Or she might push a button and drain Quail: "I knew at that moment that I had missed the only vocation for which I had any instinctive affinity. I wanted to drain Quail myself."[39]

Richard Walker tosses down some kind of gauntlet to the critics of California's irrigated empire by ending his book on this note: the production system "has grown up big and strong and healthy in the summer sun, achieving a degree of bronzed, agrarian perfection that is hard to find anywhere else on earth in the three hundred years after the English revolution set loose the beast upon the globe." Worster's rivers of empire reemerge as Walker's "world's largest plumbing system": if it exploits workers, drains and poisons the waters, extinguishes plant and animal species, and transforms the landscape, how exactly is it different from any other form of advanced capitalism in our time, Walker asks—a capitalism "without restraint, without a cold war antagonist, without antipode or opposition in an age of market absolutism"? Have the rivers of empire done more to hurt the landscape than the highways we are all happy to use, not to mention the cities and suburbs? It is like William McClung's comment about Mike Davis's work: are we talking about Los Angeles, or are we talking about capitalism? If it's the latter, well, we have a different order of problem. For McClung, too, this is not a watery nightmare but "utopian planning" through hydraulic systems "on the vastest of scales," which "dictate the rhythm of life throughout California and the West"—but who's complaining?[40]

Chinatown is a film inextricably related to the time it was made, when a radical cultural abundance nurtured in the 1960s burst forth, and when a failed war and an unfolding conspiracy named Watergate shook the nation (the name might suggest water and power in California, but it merely referred to an ugly hotel on the Potomac); Nixon resigned shortly after the film was released. This new cultural expression wanted to probe first causes, to get to the bottom of things, to unravel the ways and means of power, after hearing forever that "you may think you know what you're dealing with, but believe me, you don't" (Noah Cross to Jake Gittes). It is to the everlasting credit of Roman Polanski that he refused to end the film well, a Hollywood happy ending; instead the denouement is brute, shocking testimony to power doing what it wants and getting away with it, and to the solace of amnesia: "Forget it, Jake; it's *Chinatown.*"

Robert Towne's achievement was to render the telescoped history of water and power through Jake Gittes, the film's optic. He's up late at night following them everywhere, he's spying through binoculars, he's peering down from rooftops, he secretly photographs Mulwray with his "pretty in a cheap kind of way" girlfriend, he's bending over to examine puddles in the Los Angeles riverbed, he's idling for hours on a cliff until secretly diverted water cascades into the Pacific—the point is, he's going to nail the big boys. But throughout the film his vision is clouded, even occluded. At one point his sunglasses are missing a lens, just as Mrs. Mulwray dies with a bullet that gouges out her eye. Gittes can't quite figure out what he's seeing, what he's uncovered, what still lies behind, and what it all means; he's back on the Chinatown police detail. The more he sees the more trouble he gets into, and in the end he can't do anything about what he learned ("as little as possible" he murmurs as his eyes take in Mrs. Mulwray's corpse—that's what the cops did in Chinatown). But he has seen enough to know in his bones that this is the way unrestrained power works.

Follow the money—or in this case the water—and power will be unveiled, perhaps even undone: that's Towne's principle. Do that and you'll get yourself killed, that's Polanski's principle. Towne's sensibility is entirely American: the truth will set us free—or at least put the crooks and murderers in jail. The sun-dappled sense of lost possibilities that inhabits the film (where did all the lemon groves go?) intimates that it did not have to happen that way. A holocaust survivor, Roman Polanski knows in his bones that Noah Cross was right—"You see, Mr. Gitts [*sic*], most people don't have to face the fact, at the right time and the right place, they're capable of *anything.*" The tension between Towne and Polanski is never resolved, it is just left hanging in the counterpoint of hope for the future (for California) and a tragic European sensibility of inevitable loss and unavoidable truth (power always wins). *Chinatown* is a metaphor for the history of Los Angeles, for American history, for the difference between a European and a Pacific sensibility, and for those who tried to say something new and illuminating in the 1970s.

The rivers of empire and a glacier of corruption still cannot extinguish American optimism. California's attraction was seductive enough to draw Frederick Jackson Turner away from Cambridge to Pasadena, as we have seen, where he demonstrated that his frontier thesis could truly explain anything, including the state's phalanx of water and power. To him this was just another example of pioneer pluck, intrepid self-reliance, shiny optimism, and the progressive good sense of government and business joining hands for the commonweal: "The daring initiative and community spirit of the Pacific coast cities," he wrote in 1926, "notably Los Angeles and Seattle in developing harbours and water fronts, in bringing mountain water supplies and power by long distance electric transmission, and the Los Angeles suburbs in becoming the center of the moving picture production, are indications of the Western spirit in municipal life."[41]

CHAPTER ELEVEN

Southern California: Island on the Pacific

There was a desert wind blowing that night. It was one of those hot dry Santa Anas that come down through the mountain passes and curl your hair and make your nerves jump and your skin itch. On nights like that every booze party ends in a fight. Meek little wives feel the edge of the carving knife and study their husband's necks.

—RAYMOND CHANDLER, opening lines of *Red Wind*

The Monterey cypress groves mark the onset of aridity that character-izes Southern California, where lots of sunshine gets little enhance-ment from rain and the cypress gives way to eucalyptus and chaparral, and eventually to desert. These rare trees (*Cupressus macrocarpa*), haunt-ing in their chalky gray limbs bent in warped, fanciful shapes before the ocean storms (Robert Louis Stevenson called them "ghosts fleeing before the wind") and reminiscent of similarly knotty and twisted trees all over tidal Japan, exist naturally in only two magnificent settings—Point Lobos and nearby Pebble Beach. Hitchcock chose this dramatic environment of "steep, rugged cliffs, sweeping views, and exotic flora" for several scenes in his 1940 movie, *Rebecca* (the only one of his films to win the Oscar for best picture). Landscape artist Francis McComas called Point Lobos "the greatest meeting of land and sea in the world."[1] The gnarled, wind-kinked trees are the perfect, singular point of transition for the joining of two different Californias: the north and the south. These ghosts symbolize two dissimilar and often anti-thetical regions divided culturally, socially, politically, economically, and even religiously.

All human beings coming upon the Monterey peninsula for the first time have a right to say that it ranks among the great, beautiful sites in the world, thrilling in its exquisite interplay of earth, wind, tree, and ocean; nothing really prepares a person for its grandeur, instead we all discover it for our-selves. Here is J. Smeaton Chase, an English author, writing about the Pacific

Albert Bierstadt, *The Oregon Trail*, 1869. Color mural.
The Butler Museum of American Art, Youngstown, Ohio.

The Great Northern Railway's
"Empire Builder." Courtesy of
Carlos Schwantes.

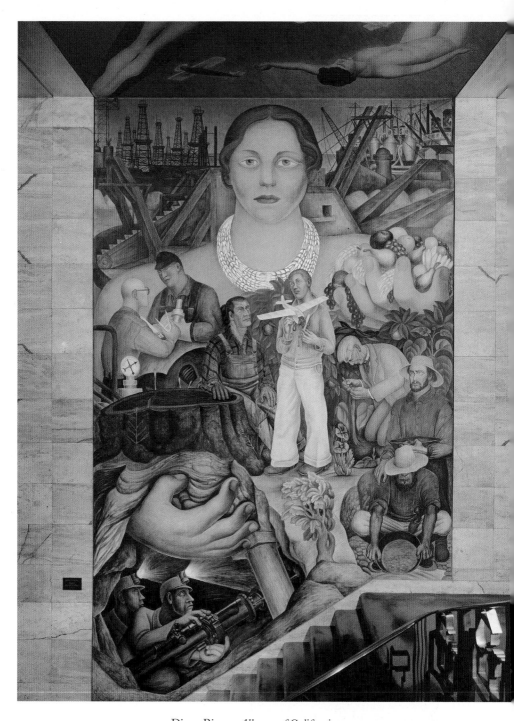

Diego Rivera, *Allegory of California*, 1931.
The City Club. Photograph © 1986 The Detroit Institute of the Arts. D.R. © 2008
Banco de México, "Fiduciario" en el Fideicomiso relativo a los Museos Diego Rivera y
Frida Kahlo. Av. Cinco de Mayo no. 2, Col. Centro, Del Cuauhtémoc 06059,
México, D.F.

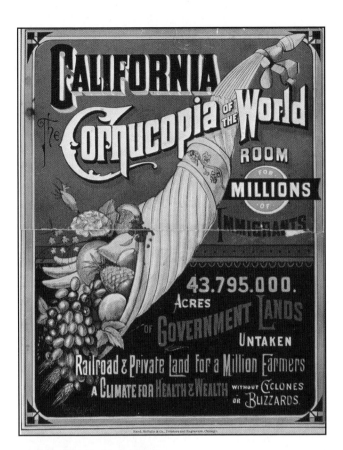

California Cornucopia of the World, a railroad advertisement. Lithographic poster. Rand McNally & Co., c. 1870; negative #41800. Collection of the New-York Historical Society.

Lemon cornucopia.
Fruit crate label. Polychrome lithograph, 12 x 9 in. *Splendid Brand*, June 1938.
Collection of the Oakland Museum of California, Gift of Old Promises.

Lynn E. Coleman, *A Valley Cowboy's Last Stand at Sepulveda Pass*, 1975.
Collection of the artist.

below Point Lobos and its serenity and power: "The sea was a splendor of deep Mediterranean blue, and broke in such dazzling freshness of white that one might have thought it had been that day created. How amazing it is, that the ancient ocean, with its age-long stain of cities and traffic, toil and blood, can still be so bright, so uncontaminated, so heavenly pure! It seems an intentional parable of Divinity, knowing and receiving all, evil as well as good, yet through some deathless principle itself remaining forever right, strong, and pure, the Unchanging Good."[2]

Southern California's encapsulated geography also encouraged people to think that it was a world unto itself. Just below the Big Sur fastness the coast runs almost due east from Point Conception and into the Tehachapi Mountains, a transverse range forming the northern limit of this geographical unit and the lower boundary of the Great Central Valley. The Pacific itself changes: it is warmer, calmer, you can even swim in it. The coast then tapers diagonally down to Los Angeles, and by the time you get there you are east of Reno, Nevada. The border with Mexico is the southern extremity, and to the east the San Jacinto and San Bernardino mountains protect this great basin from the desert heat (if not its winds). If California was thought to be an island for centuries, Southern California is "an island on the land," in Helen Hunt Jackson's famous rendering; geography and climate (if not culture or human direction) lead it resolutely to face West, toward the Pacific, and the ocean returns the favor by sending cooling winds across the land, a gift of "air-conditioned equability" that bequeathed "a freak of nature—a cool and semi-moist desert." Here is a Mediterranean coast without humid summers or malarial mosquitos, "the fertility of Egypt without its fellaheen; the fruits and wild flowers of Sicily without its lazzaroni . . . the sunshine of Persia without its oppressions."[3]

Arcadia, Utopia, or Nightmare?

"Anglophone Los Angeles sought to reconcile two contradictory visions of ideal space and place: an acquired Arcadia, a found natural paradise; and an invented Utopia, an empty space inviting development." This is William Alexander McClung, from his recent book, *Landscapes of Desire*. It is quite a good book, but its theme is not only centuries old in California mythology, but as American as apple pie. He is particularly good at showing how the critical literature that abounds in the library draws on Arcadian mythologies about a lost past—usually a quite recent past—that never really existed. Southern California's history is wrapped up in episodes of original sin, muffed chances, evil deeds, lost Edenic moments. Its Utopias lie waiting in the future, in the recovery of lost innocence—a "desperately sought" future in McClung's words, when everything will be put right. As for the nightmare so many others see in the remains of the Los Angeles day, preeminently Mike Davis, McClung asks if this is a critique of the city or a critique of modern capitalism?

Do people complain about New York or Chicago the way they do about Los Angeles? Of course not: what was Chicago's Arcadian past? New York's Utopian future? People are comfortable with a materialist explanation for Chicago, the city with big shoulders, but that will never do in L.A. The more telling comparison is San Francisco: a long list of adjectives often precedes its name, but they aren't tropes of Arcadia or Utopia—instead it's a city where you leave your heart. But in Southern California this is the discourse that never dies: it is their version of the end of the frontier. Just like Turner, their fond hopes and dreams are confounded time and again by infernal machines grinding Eden under and calling it progress, technologies that seduce them in the moment of their newness, until they find out that for every new world gained another, more precious one, has been lost. It is a way of looking back to compensate for an inability to resist the onslaught of the new; it is a way of facing East, back across the mythologies of American history, that avoids the truly new possibilities and perils of the Pacific and the influx of Pacific peoples who have always crowded the state with enormous drive and talent, but who do not fit any comfortable narrative. Southern California recuperates and preserves the original garden myth of the American people, perhaps because letting it go leaves us adrift in a new world all too resistant to our hopes and dreams.

City of Angels, City of Consumers

California's most productive city, Los Angeles, had a very "late" arrival as an American city, in the 1880s. When it was founded in 1781 it was a nondescript mudflat, and it was "still a mere village" to David Starr Jordan in 1879, a mostly Mexican town surrounded by a desert of cactus and sagebrush. The first American census in 1850 located only 8,329 Angelenos, "half of whom were Indian and most of whom were illiterate." People bathed in open ditches when they weren't relieving themselves in the same place. It was a wild frontier town with a murder rate like L.A.'s today: about one murder for each day in 1850. Not much changed in the next couple of decades, until 1871 when an orgy of mob violence against local Chinese shocked the proper whites into doing something about the murderous public sphere. Upwards of a thousand whites cascaded into Chinatown, beating, shooting, and lynching any Chinese they found; victims dangled by the neck from gateways, awnings, and thrown-together gallows; the mob looted homes, stores, even the pockets of lynched men. Nineteen were hanged (the rope broke on one, so he was strung up again), and most were tortured first. A grand jury indicted 150 men but sentenced only 6 to jail, and soon they were free—after all, members of the police force were at the head of the mob. Finally by the 1880s Los Angeles established a modicum of law and order and was poised to become what it is, a city that does in ten years what other cities do in a lifetime. It grew by 500 percent in that decade, reaching a population of 50,000 by 1889, when more than 130,000 people lived in Southern California, most of them arriving after the Santa Fe railway reached L.A. in 1885. By 1910 the city had nearly 320,000 residents—already embarking on the American dream that would later encompass the entire century: mass production and mass consumption.[4]

The Santa Fe and the Southern Pacific railways competed for passengers, touching off a rate war that at one point dropped the fare from Kansas City to L.A. to $5; prices went up a bit, but for years it was common to get a $25 or $30 fare from Chicago or St. Louis. Los Angeles didn't invent real estate boosters—they followed the westering frontier like flocks of geese—but it took boosterism to an art form, defining its built landscape more than any other city. The first boom took the mudflat and built America's newest metropolis. Total real estate sales in L.A. the year the railroad arrived were about $1 million, $3 million a year later, and $12 million by the middle of 1887: "Developers platted dozens of new towns . . . Riverside beginning in 1886, Hollywood in 1887, then Inglewood, Redondo Beach, Long Beach"; by the time Walter Nugent is done listing them (throw in Claremont, Glendale, Burbank, and Ontario), an entire physiognomy of metropolitan Los Angeles materialized overnight. Touts sold home lots in restaurants, saloons, at curbsides, and even in churches (a newly arrived easterner went to services at a Methodist church, and when the preacher finished his sermon he sold the man a lot in a new subdivision); later on, ducks, midgets, and giants walked the streets with sandwich signs trumpeting new homes, giving L.A. its well-deserved reputation: "a great circus without a tent." Los Angeles "did not grow," McClung wrote, "as sell itself into existence." The great green hope of every homeowner, then as now, was to have his own detached house, a few citrus trees, and to watch his property appreciate—preferably take off like a rocket. L.A. paid off on both propositions more often than not, and especially on the promise of "my home": by 1950 two-thirds of all dwelling units were detached, compared to less than 30 percent in New York and Chicago.[5]

The budding elite of Los Angeles arose through speculation in land.

Henry Edwards Huntington became a billionaire in contemporary dollars (our dollars) by building a state-of-the-art trolley car system for the city, with the help of Frank J. Sprague, an assistant to Thomas Edison. The Pacific Electric Railway Company was sparkling new and remarkably convenient, and as it spread through the valley around the turn of the century (ultimately with more than 1,000 miles of track), it created the urban sprawl that so many subsequently blamed on the automobile, linking forty-two incorporated cities within a thirty-five-mile radius of Los Angeles—it brought L.A. to the valley, too. The trolleys might run at a loss now and then, but that wasn't the point: Huntington and his oligarchic friends bought up undeveloped real estate at rock bottom prices, extended a new trolley line connecting virgin territory to the downtown, named the new town (Newport, Venice, Redondo Beach), plumped the new home plots in the pages of the *Times,* and reaped windfall profits. His Huntington Land and Improvement Company bought up much of the western San Gabriel Valley, he pushed the Red Line through it and then subdivided and sold thousands of land parcels. By 1910 some fifty communities in four counties were served by the railroad, and Huntington was among the richest men in America.[6]

The city's first attraction, widely promoted by the Santa Fe line, was climate and its supposed tonic effect on health. Tuberculosis, arthritis, depression, consumption, rheumatism, lumbago, a bad sacroiliac, a bent frame, and a host of other ill-understood chronic illnesses could be washed away in the California sunshine. So the early population was unusually elderly: the old and infirm seeking the climate, the air, and the sunshine. It worked for many but not for all, and anyway, no one lives forever: so the bright dawn of Southern California's modern history also had the aura of the mortuary, prelude to Forest Lawn with its microphones to talk to the dear departed, drive-in funeral homes with the late beloved ensconced in a window, and the apotheosis of Southern California morbidity, the pet cemetery. "In Los Angeles during these years, death seemed everywhere, and a mood of death, strange and sinister, like flowers rotting from too much sunshine, remained with the city."[7]

Living Better with Petroleum

Just as the 1880s population boom tapered off momentarily, another boom came along: not real estate, but the gusher of oil that Edward Doheny found on the corner of Glendale Boulevard and West Second Street, just in time to fuel the automobiles that would soon saturate L.A. like no other city. Doheny just found it, too; you didn't have to be a crack geologist or a fearless wild-catter when sticky petroleum oozed out of the surface soil. Indians had used it for centuries to waterproof canoes, and federal surveys in the 1850s located hundreds of exposures or "tar springs" in Southern California. The son of an Irish immigrant fleeing the potato famine, Doheny was a mule driver and singing waiter before landing in L.A. almost penniless in 1892. One day he peered out his boarding house window and noticed Mexicans ferrying chunks of tar around. So he and a partner leased a promising lot, got out their picks and shovels, drove a shaft 150 feet into the ground, and with the sharpened tip of a eucalyptus log, detonated one of America's grandest gushers. Within a decade he controlled nearly all of California's oil production.[8]

By the turn of the nineteenth century some 2,300 wells spouted over 9 million barrels a year and California was the leading oil producer in the world. Most of it was used for home and business fuel until Henry Ford made the personal automobile ubiquitous; as early as 1905, L.A. had more cars than any other big city, riding on 350 miles of graded streets. With huge strikes at Maricopa (1910), Huntington Beach (1920), and the Signal Hill bonanza in Long Beach (1921), Southern California inaugurated the mass automobile age with an ocean of fuel at the ready. It seems almost forgotten that California was the biggest oil producer a century ago and the leading American producer in the mid-1920s (263 million barrels in 1923), even though oil wells still litter the landscape in Long Beach. Tony Beverly Hills went from lima beans to oil speculation (a string of dry wells, but so what, this was California; the inves-tors soon subdivided the bean fields and put up mansions for the wealthy).

In most Americans' minds Spindletop (1901), Tulsa, and West Texas still stand for the oil boom of this era (1892 into the 1930s), partly because Texas and Oklahoma took so long to diversify their economies, and after the East Texas boom in 1931 dethroned California as the leading producer, the latter never again boomed quite like it once did. But oil had a differential effect on these states: it got them off coal very quickly and very early compared to other places; the big industrial countries relied on coal for more than a century before World War II, reducing their dependence only as oceans of Middle Eastern oil sloshed into world markets (global usage of oil outstripped coal only around 1960). But unlike Texas, where oil supplemented cotton and thus deepened its dependency on primary products, in California oil was just another boom industry, dovetailing with innovations across several fronts. Oil, natural gas, and hydroelectricity were the modern alternatives to coal— they're generally much cheaper and much cleaner—and California got all of them very early. Its peak coal usage came in 1900, soon it was using less than a

The intersection of Court and Toluca streets in Los Angeles, circa 1900.
Reproduced by permission of The Huntington Library, San Marino, California.

half-ton a year per capita compared to the nation's 5.3 tons, and by 1925 coal made up less than 5 percent of its energy regime and never again went higher. The newness of the oil industry also meant that California had the most technologically advanced facilities.[9]

Living Even Better with Electricity

California moved quickly toward an all-electric life that matched its pioneering of a gasoline-based modern culture, cascading forward from Edison's invention of the lightbulb in 1879. Electricity gives pause to even the most resolute and determined environmentalist or naturalist because it is so clean and so invisible. You can't see it unless it sparks; you can't smell it unless something's wrong; you can't hear it unless it shorts out; you can generate it naturally, with wind or falling water; and it powers almost anything. California's lack of a settled population hooked onto some earlier form of energy (like coal, which still powered furnaces in nearly 60 percent of American homes in 1940) made adopting this new-new technology easy—and it just happened to bring forth huge advances in productivity. Nationally it increased worker productivity in the 1920s by 22 percent, and from 1910 (when electrification was fairly common in business firms) to 1940 American productivity grew 300 percent. The Westinghouse power line from Niagara Falls to Buffalo is often said to be the first great delivery system, but it was preceded by an 11,000-volt line from Livermore to Sacramento, opened in 1895. By the time the lights went on in Buffalo, Sacramento residents had nearly 13,000 incandescent lamps and 35 electric streetcars. By 1923 California had the highest density in the nation of 220,000-, 110,000-, and 55,000-volt transmission lines. If in 1895 L.A. was merely the third-ranking city in telephones per capita, by 1911 it ranked first—not in the nation, but in *the world* (New York was sixth). By 1930 California produced 10 percent of the nation's hydroelectricity for 3.5 percent of its population, it consumed this clean energy at 2.5 times the national rate, and it got fully 83 percent of this electricity from falling water.[10]

Because California remained dependent on eastern industry until World War II, much of the state's prodigious electric capacity was used for homes, farms, cities, and novel industries. Nearly 80 percent of homes were wired for electricity by 1920, compared to 35 percent in the rest of the country (and less than 10 percent for the nation's farms). California boosters immediately grasped its potential to advertise contemporary high-tech living; electricity ran all the 1920s goodies in department store windows that made housework a breeze—it kept baby's milk warm and cow's milk cold; it soothed granny's lumbago with heating pads and cooled grandpa's rocker with fans; it warmed the bath water and burned waffles; for a time it ran your car; it even curled your hair (24 percent of California homes had curling irons in 1925), washed your clothes (36 percent had a washing machine by 1925, compared to 16 percent in the country), and given the mild climate, you could even heat your home with it—and many did. The Panama-Pacific Exposition in 1915 was festooned with the latest lighting technology. Searchlights shot great white spires into the sky, to symbolize through illumination "a measure of the traditions of both the Orient and the Occident." Oriental blue was a particular hit, with nighttime illumination bringing out the Celestials' "absolute values." Twenty years later Stanford's longstanding joint research with the electric power industry yielded perhaps the most magical electricity of all: the microwave.[11]

What distinguished California was its "lateness"—or its perfect timing—

Sacramento's electric extravaganza.
Brochure for the Sacramento Electrical Carnival, 1895.
Sacramento Archives and Museum.

so that every new technology could instantly be applied or adapted without disrupting previous investments, inventory, installations, and existing energy sources and technologies, yielding world-beating gains in productivity. Gas lines had barely been strung in the state when electricity came along. Riverine, canal, and horse-and-buggy routes were nonexistent or served such a small population that railroads, electric trolleys (the Red Line), and above all automobiles could quickly replace them. By 1910 no state could match California in its use of these modern conveyances or in its almost instant electrification. This critical source of cheap energy and the discovery of huge pools of oil fueled the state's very rapid growth up to the Depression. Gasoline and electricity produced a worldwide revolution, but they produced it first in California, where streetcars and automobiles shaped a dispersed, suburban pattern of living in the 1920s, two decades before the 1939 New York World's Fair introduced the concept of "suburb," and three decades before it became a national pattern. Southern California showed the future to the country and to the world after 1920, epitomizing the quality that would turn out to be America's greatest strength: what Victoria de Grazia called its "Market Empire," that is, "the rise of a great imperium with the outlook of a great emporium."[12]

Pioneering Suburban Life

In the first three decades of the twentieth century, Southern California combined an expanding greensward of lovely and affordable land with millions of productive new immigrants and the invention that would remake the physiognomy of the nation and American individuality—my car, my space. By the time of the 1929 crash, Southern Californians had reached levels of home and automobile ownership that most other parts of the country would not match until the 1950s, and that Europe and Japan would not reach until the 1960s and 1970s. All across the country, but especially in Southern California, the old Puritan-republican creed met its match in what Warren Susman called the American "culture of abundance."[13] Spending and consuming (increasingly on credit) outstripped stern rectitude, self-restraint, moral character, and saving: and the primary consumer durable was a private, personal abode that traveled, in which you could increasingly do almost anything you wanted.

By World War I, Los Angeles had everything necessary for a prolonged boom: cheap water, cheap energy, abundant land, infant industries (autos, films), and new technologies (aircraft, radio): it just needed people. We saw earlier the spectacle of Chicago exploding into the dynamo of the prairies, almost overnight. Los Angeles and its surrounding counties and towns have done that four or five times—in the 1880s; 1900–29; the postwar boom after 1945; and the post-1965 immigration boom that is still ongoing, punctuated by a downturn after the cold war ended; and then another boom starting around 1995. Its population quadrupled in the 1880s, doubled in the 1890s, and tripled again in the succeeding decade, to a 1910 figure of 319,000. But that was mere prelude to the real boom; nobody had seen anything like it. Between 1910 and 1930 the American population grew by a lot—one-third, a 33.5 percent increase. New York's population doubled, Chicago's and Philadelphia's nearly did, and San Francisco's tripled. Other Pacific cities like Seattle and Portland grew at 16 or 17 percent, less than the national average. But in those same two decades the population of Los Angeles exploded to 2,319,000, a 727 percent increase. Small towns in 1910, like Glendale (population 2,700), grew to 63,000 by 1930. Southern California had major population upsurges every couple of decades, with peaks in 1887, 1906, 1923, and of course the war years; McWilliams likened it to a "continuous boom" punctuated by major explosions. During the Depression several large American cities lost population, and only two cities grew by double-digit rates during the decade of the 1930s: Los Angeles and Denver.[14]

Another great migration, this time by car more than by train, brought 2 million new Californians—often in "rattletrap automobiles, their fenders tied with string, and curtains flapping in the breeze, loaded with babies, bedding, bundles," in Mildred Adams's words. More than half of the newcomers wound up in Los Angeles County, and more than a third settled in the city. The aqueduct, we remember, had enough water for 2 million people; the city had 200,000 when Mulholland got the idea and nearly 1.5 million by 1930. The city's population doubled in five years from 1920 to 1925; real estate contractors not only built prodigiously for the new migrants but subdivided the city in such a manic way that 7 million people could live there, if all the lots were built and sold. From 1921 to 1928 50,000 acres were chopped up into 3,233 subdivisions and 246,612 building lots. People bought their future, and the future uncannily kept paying them back: land values in downtown Los Angeles rose 800 percent in the twenty years after 1907. Near the end of the decade Los Angeles had almost 400,000 separate residences, a third of them occupied by the owner, giving it a physiognomy unlike any other city. Small-town streets and neighborhoods stretched as far as the eye could see in every direction, and they called it a city. A fine observer named Bruce Bliven said that this booming growth "creates an easy optimism, a lazy prosperity which dominates people's lives. Anything seems possible; the future is yours, and the past?—there isn't any." It sounds like a cliché circa 1955, but the year was 1927—

giving Bliven a prescience not unlike the city itself, which was showing the rest of the country its future, what the "American dream" of my home and my car would look like—"a melting-pot in which the civilization of the future may be seen, bubbling darkly up in a foreshadowing brew," in his words.[15]

By 1930 Los Angeles' population density, measuring the city against the outlying towns, was 3 to 1. New York's was 26 to 1, San Francisco's 30 to 1. At the same time 88 percent of all new retail businesses were locating in suburbs. Wags liked to say that Los Angeles built Long Island without Manhattan, but Fogelson argued frankly that the dispersed quality of the city and its early adoption of the suburban model (he dates it from 1887) was a reaction *against* big city life, especially a city like Chicago with "teeming tenements and crowded ghettoes" of East European and black residents. The residential suburb was "spacious, affluent, clean, decent, permanent, predictable, and homogeneous," whereas the industrial metropolis "was the receptacle for all European evils and the source of all American sins." Amid a multitude of suburbs, Palos Verdes was the quintessential model. Designed by Frederick Law Olmsted and Charles H. Cheney, it had 800 acres of parkland, expensive homes on ocean view sites, flowing residential streets, a few carefully circumscribed commercial areas, in short, "a garden suburb"—Arcadia. The less wealthy found suburbs of a lesser kind, but still on the model of a garden town, pursuing a semi-rural communality that recalled the midwestern farm roots of so much of the population, re-created and updated in a suburban setting (homesteaders once removed to Los Angeles). The dispersed city was a quilt of many squares, each a self-contained community reached by car— and in the eyes of its residents, not a city at all. Even industry was suburban: films in Hollywood, airplanes along the coast, autos and tires in the lowlands. But in this respect and many others, L.A.'s sprawl was pioneering; the city was zoned beginning in 1909, very early by American standards, and its undulating distention, well advanced by the 1920s, anticipated the malling of America and the spread of "edge cities" in the late twentieth century, just as intricately planned suburbs like Palos Verdes Estates anticipated—in 1921— the ubiquitous gated communities of our time. In the early decades, though, many thought Palos Verdes was the jewel in a crown of suburbs, meeting Lewis Mumford's ideal of a garden metropolis "with small, balanced communities serving as stars in a metropolitan constellation."[16]

Los Angeles did not pioneer mass production and mass consumption, as historians Lizabeth Cohen and William Leach have shown, but it took this endeavor—"a vision of the good life" defined by ever more buying—and deepened it beyond anything yet imagined, projecting it to the country both as an urbane cityscape to visit and the primary locus of Hollywood films. It wasn't hard work to transform an ahistorical people into a ritual clamoring for *the new*, the latest and best, the new and improved, stretching into a consumptive paradise called the future. Here was a vision of an affluent, comfortable, exciting life, open to a flatlander from Iowa or anyone else; Los Angeles, New York, Chicago, and a couple of other cities defined a new urban culture that became synonymous with "the *heart* of American life."[17] Frugal farmers accustomed to saving every penny got to L.A. and gave themselves over to easy credit: department store charge cards, Chevies on the installment plan, a bank loan for the home—"the future" under comprehensive mortgage, ultimately creating the early twenty-first-century peculiarity of an entire nation with negative savings, maxed-out credit cards, and an economy two-thirds dependent on consumer spending—and spending, and more spending. Department stores emerged in every city, large and medium, to transform "dry goods" into an American dream, to house the surfeit of things of all types under one roof thus to mesmerize the consumer, and soon it was a family—or at least feminine—ritual to organize an entire day around a visit to Marshall Field's or Macy's. Utopian reformer Edward Bellamy put the new American stores at the center of his futuristic schemes, and even got Wobbly leader Big Bill Haywood to bite.[18]

The department store is an integral part of the American dream, and no one did it better than the art deco behemoth on Wilshire Boulevard called Bullock's. The Roaring Twenties produced a cornucopia of next-new-things, called "consumer durables" by economists: radios, refrigerators, toasters, vacuum cleaners, electric ovens, electric irons, washing machines, and many more; all of them could be surveyed at one's leisure in Bullock's. In case anyone missed them, Bullock's had strategically placed billboards all over Los Angeles County, with one humongous word—"Happiness," "Hospitality," "Imagination"—under a pretty picture of all the *things* you could buy at the store. Three decades later, only 12 percent of West German homes had refrigerators.[19] And three decades later in an iconic cold war encounter in Moscow, Californian Richard Nixon lectured Nikita Khrushchev about the American way of life while standing in front of a Maytag washing machine with a box of SOS pads sitting on top.

The Automobile: Reinventing the Frontier

Los Angeles is the preeminent city of the automobile, shaped by the automobile, at the mercy of the automobile, a Mediterranean paradise wrecked by the automobile—take your pick. If now there are many, L.A. was the first city where *not* having access to a car made life impossible, instantly casting a person out of the middle class and into the (small) crowd of poor wretches who had to use public transportation. There followed traffic jams, spectacular crashes, gridlock, and a thick yellow haze permanently centered over the entire valley. But, as with almost all new technologies and conveniences, there was no turning back because at its inception, the auto instantly trampled on all the alternative forms of human transport. And unlike the ubiquitous train, it was individual, personal, self-directed, the vehicle for a Sunday-drive return to nature: it might have spewed out of the industrial maw like hotcakes, but it appeared to Americans (in this case to Gatsby) as "the spontaneous fruit of an Edenic tree."[20]

Its speed was determined by "horsepower," but it didn't rear up and throw you off, or balk, or leave "piles of steaming waste" in its wake. Trains were just as fast, but train travel forfeited "one's right of self determination," resembled "a transport of prisoners" more than a convenience, and worst of all, could be missed—and then what? Did trains have "the flow of fresh air," the smooth ride with "pneumatics and springs," the "light and gentle floating motion," the sporting position and sense of control of the driver, the "freedom, self-possession, self-discipline, and ease" of going where one would, the choice and autonomy offered the individual, the joy of leaving mere mortals behind in your wake? The auto also took you back to the elegant pre-railroad era of personal coaches and carriages where taste and class could be expressed through your vehicle, with none of the low-tech drawbacks: "The meaning of the automobile is freedom, self-possession, self-discipline, and ease. In it the traveling coach is revived in all its poetic plenitude, but in a form endlessly enriched by the former's exquisite potential for intensified and simultaneously expanded gratification."[21]

All these praises were sung in the first decade of the twentieth century, not by Americans but by Germans—who in my humble view have better cars, better highways, and far better drivers than this country. Of course there were drawbacks to this form of travel—"wordless curses, shaking fists, stuck-out tongues, bared behinds"—road rage, 1902-style. But everyone loves cars, no matter how much they complain about them: academics and vegetarians (Volvos), intellectuals and gourmands (Citroëns), red state farmers (pickup trucks), day-traders and software engineers (Porsches), red state blue-collar workers (pickup trucks), bankers and lawyers (BMWs), red state cacogenic whites (pickup trucks), upscale-mall ladies (gargantuan SUVs), wealthy widows (Lexuses), little old ladies from Pasadena ('32 Ford Hiboy), ghetto hipsters (pimpmobiles), Hispanics (Chevies), hip Hispanics (low-riding Chevies), superannuated hippies (broken-down, high-polluting VW buses). Autos are like Adorno's acidic take on the Hollywood culture industry: something for everyone so no one can escape.

There never was a more seductive or diabolical machine in the garden than this one: it captures everybody. A Chinese friend accompanied my wife and me to Yanan, the legendary base where Mao and his cave-dwelling comrades accumulated enough power in the 1940s to conquer the country. We met the vice president of Yanan University, who turned out to have a master's degree from Northern Illinois University. "I love your country," he said, especially the highways. "My friends and I bought a Toyota for $900, and every school vacation we would take off in one direction or another—Seattle, Los Angeles, Miami, Boston." I have an old friend, a political theorist steeped in the Frankfurt School who lives in Berlin; he was a visiting scholar for several years at Northwestern University. I saw the broad, four-door Chrysler sedan that he quickly acquired and asked him why: "Ever since I was a kid I wanted to get in a big car and drive from coast to coast on your highways." And indeed that's what he and his family did during vacations: drive off in every direction. Another friend, one of our best historians of China, revealed in a recent book his passion—indeed his "compulsion"—to drive back and forth across the country when he was a graduate student. Born in Turkey and raised on Hollywood movies, he had long viewed the American West "as the ultimate in exotic places."[22]

Los Angeles was the epicenter of the automobile revolution in the 1920s. Thirty percent of all cars in the state were registered in Los Angeles County in 1920, when the city had one car for every 5 people, compared to one car for every 13 people in the country. Meanwhile there was an auto for every 228 people in Britain, one for 247 in France, one for 1,017 in Germany. Five years later L.A. had one car for every 2 people—actually for every 1.8. The figure for the nation was one car for every 6.6 people in 1925, in Chicago it was one for every 11, at a time when Ford factories were building 6 cars per minute and 9,000 per day. In other words, the Los Angeles car market was already completely saturated; compare its 1.8 people per car in 1925 to Britain's 2.23, France's 2.24, and Germany's 1.98: *when?* (in 1997). More than 300,000 cars entered the city every day in 1924, higher than the total number of cars registered in New York State.[23]

An automobile civilization was also well advanced by the 1920s. The Automobile Club of Southern California, still residing in its original Hispanic Revival building on Figueroa Street, pioneered a new civic culture built around the auto—a multitude of cars and models for new individual lifestyles, cruising the roads and highways on Sunday drives, heading out to Riverside or Palm Springs, or just driving up and down Wilshire Boulevard, the first commercial avenue built for the automobile, with its best blocks dubbed "the Miracle Mile" in 1928 (it runs fifteen miles from downtown L.A. to the coast, about the length of Manhattan Island). Flatlanders took to the roads with a passion; as a writer noted in 1932: "To the casual observer he may look like a vulgar Babbitt, defacing the landscape with his very presence. But to himself, unconfessed, he is Daniel Boone, he is Kit Carson, he is Frémont, hunting for the road to India."[24]

Fordism for the World

Henry Ford was born in 1863 to a prosperous Scotch-Irish farming family in Dearborn, Michigan. A self-taught mechanic and tinkerer, Henry had little use for education and none for books. His only real hero was Thomas Edison, whom he first met in 1895. Two Germans named Daimler and Benz built a viable internal combustion engine burning gasoline, just as Rudolph Diesel invented the . . . diesel, but Ford showed how to make the new-new thing saleable—a commercial *wunderkind.* He built his first automobile in 1896 and began his famous company in 1903. Four years later he announced his vision, which became an American dream—a pastoral one at that: "I will build a motor car for the great multitude. It will be large enough for the family but small enough for the individual . . . it will be so low in price that no man making a good salary will be unable to own one—and enjoy with his family the blessing of hours of pleasure in God's great open spaces." Henry Ford thus "predicted a new social order," in Warren Susman's words, and a new egalitarianism that made every worker simultaneously a customer. No less than Joseph Schumpeter called the Model T "the great new thing": it made the growing oil industry its virtual subsidiary; speeded the rapid growth of steel, glass, rubber, cotton (for seats); and created "a cement age" through nationwide road construction, while proliferating a thousand new services—from gas stations to motels to hamburger joints to drive-in movies. More than all that, Schumpeter thought, Ford changed "the style of life and the outlook on life probably more than any prophet ever did."[25]

Automobiles were the driving force in American manufacturing after 1910: in one calculation by the National Economic Committee, among eighteen new industries creating 1.1 million new jobs since 1879, by 1929 more than half of these jobs were in automobiles, auto parts, rubber tires, and gasoline. By 1929 the United States also exported prodigious numbers of cars—almost twice as many as Britain *manufactured,* about 350,000 vehicles that could be found not just in European streets, but in Tokyo, Harbin, Johannesburg, and Buenos Aires.[26] The world-shaking force of the automobile can be seen in its sectoral characteristics: it is an industry that pioneered the assembly line and brought mass production and mass consumption to the market (Henry Ford); as it developed it came to symbolize upward mobility and prestige (Alfred Sloan's styling and graduated models—Chevrolet to Cadillac); it deeply reinforced the 1920s tendency toward consumption rather than savings (installment buying from the General Motors Acceptance Corporation); the industry had backward and forward linkages to oil, steel (about one-third of the cost of a car), rubber (tires), cement (highways), chemicals (especially DuPont paint) and plastics, hotels, drive-in restaurants and movies; the industry spawned a host of new lifestyles (nearly all of them pioneered in Southern California); and it became a symbol of national pride because it personified progress.

The world riveted its attention on this exploding American industry, but Germans typically took a no-nonsense approach to it: "(a) technological development cannot be stopped; (b) escape is not an option, so Germany must take the lead; (c) therefore, we are called upon to support the automobile and its industry with all the means at the state's disposal"—a paraphrase of what Hitler said at the Berlin International Automobile Show a few days after taking power in 1933. "Just as horse-drawn vehicles once had to create paths and the railroad had to build rail lines, so must motorized transportation be granted the streets it needs." Seven months later, he turned up in "brightly polished knee boots . . . and begins shoveling like the devil," as the opening shot in the construction of the first autobahn. Later came a Henry Ford–style car for every man, the Volkswagen—literally so, in that the "people's automobile" was to be a Ford, not as a design but as a conception for daily life. But the leading edge of this revolution was in Southern California, not Detroit or Berlin. (Hamburg got its first gas pump in 1923, at a time when Los Angeles already had a culture of service stations.)[27]

The French are like self-aware Angelenos, Kristin Ross pointed out: they experience modernization "as highly destructive, obliterating a well-developed artisanal culture," not to mention a grassroots communitarian ethos; they shudder at the rapidity of American change. But that did not stop them from doing the same thing in the 1960s that Angelenos had done in the 1920s, embracing the automobile and an entirely new world: "France-at-the-wheel enacted a revolution . . . that permeated every aspect of everyday life" and ended up dismantling "all earlier spatial arrangements." It might mean driving off in "a vanilla colored toad with four wheels, whose head was exactly the same as its tail," but it was *my car.* Soon, only food stood ahead of autos in daily French discourse, and the nouvelle vogue in one film after another required action in and around the automobile—often a gargantuan Cadillac convertible, but sometimes Jean-Luc Godard's field of ruined Renaults. Only one in eight French owned a car in 1961 (Los Angeles' average in 1920), and most of them were nearly small enough to fit in a Cadillac's trunk.[28]

Perhaps the most interesting foreign reaction to the mass consumption that Los Angeles typified was across the Pacific, in Japan—the nation that now makes automobiles more efficiently and profitably than anybody else. Japan's interwar leaders used "Americanism" to sum up consumerism in all its forms—cars, movies, radios, advertising, cafes, bars, department stores, and perhaps most noticeably there, clothing—an irruption of Fords and Frigidaires that was simultaneously threatening, seductive, and uncontrollable. The urban masses quickly appropriated these new-new things and made them their own apart from any foreign provenance, but the leadership was shocked because it sought to maintain its dominance through the construction and reinforcing of an essential and exceptional culture that they hoped would be capable of resisting historical change—trying to produce "tradition" as if it, too, were not a product of the present. Their solution was an overcoming of Americanism through a corporate state and organic ideologies which, of course, worked no better in Japan than they did in Italy or Germany to vanquish the American specter.[29] And after the war "Americanism" in this sense won a more complete victory in Japan than anywhere else, both in the production of an endless array of consumer goods and in the raging consumerism in Japan's major cities; Tokyo is a twenty-four-hour-a-day testimony to the spectacle of mass consumption in all its manifold forms, with teenagers cruising around in bull-nosed and lowered Toyotas while their mothers scrutinize skirt hems at Takashimaya Department Store.

A Machine for Every Garden

If the homestead was "an independence" in the nineteenth-century Jeffersonian mold, and the train was divided into classes, the car was egalitarian in its first mass incarnation (the Model T), and it defined a new autonomy. The car also vastly increased privacy, as Americans took to doing everything in the car (including conceiving yet more Americans). What the toilet was to generations of immigrants living in tenements, the car became: a place to be alone, to get away from relatives and everyone else. Autos vastly increased the curious American mode of mobility, which is lateral and geographic much more than it is Horatio Alger climbing the greasy pole (in any given year one in four Americans move)—pile everything into the Cadillac or the jalopy and take off. Jean Baudrillard (another European intellectual in love with our highways) thought the ahistoricity of the American people was vastly aided by the rearview mirror: a former life recedes into the horizon at 70 mph, with the Pacific on the horizon.

This is the real story behind the erasure of the Red Line in Los Angeles, the streetcars and therefore public transportation. They were harbingers of the decentralization of the city that the auto took to its apotheosis, but the main point is, cars were more fun: they were private, your world, a place to be yourself. Like Colt 45s, freeways are great equalizers: "There's no other place in America where social stratification is so little marked," a writer in 1927 noted, "where all classes do so nearly the same thing at the same time."[30] If an automobile dystopia soon came to define Los Angeles—the world-historical traffic jam—it had its upside: Reyner Banham calls the Angelenos' daily commute "the two calmest and most rewarding hours of their daily lives."[31]

Back in the day, though, in the 1920s, one place had a concatenation of fortuitous events: cheap energy (oil), a new leading sector (autos), and plenty of space to drive them around in, all day and all night and, indeed, all year long, since it never snowed—California. The machine may have been in the garden, but it also took you to the garden: Sunday drives, picnics, camping, wilderness tours. The auto united the Arcadian and the Utopian with a new technology. You could escape the grid and return to it without the usual tension. What you could do in your car, moving or stationary, taxed only human ingenuity and imagination. Take the imagination of Frank Lloyd Wright, who designed carports for his Usonian homes (as if everyone would soon own a car), drive-up windows for banks that shocked staid bankers, and "Broadacre City," which integrated the auto with homes, streets, parks, and workplaces. Wright thought automobiles liberated the masses and ended the isolation of rural life, and he loved traveling American highways in his Mercedes. If he isn't good enough for you, how about filmmaker David Lynch, who meditates in the morning, meditates in the evening, and takes a daily break from work to drive over to Bob's Big Boy in the valley and pick up a chocolate milkshake—every day for seven years?[32]

Taking California by storm inevitably meant that the automobile would outrage moralists: "boys and girls together, stimulated by the feeling that they were by themselves" and even "laughing and attracting attention," one prude said, just would not do. As early as 1921 a motorcycle cop decried "the practice of making love on the highways": people parked their cars along country boulevards, turned out the lights, "and indulged in orgies." A flinty Anglo-Saxon asked, "Why not go whirling off for joy-rides, boys and girls? Why not be divorced at pleasure?" A measure of California's influence in the Roaring Twenties may be that this remark came from a Scottish missionary observing young people in 1925—in Korea.[33]

Consumption on Wheels

Dallas invented the drive-in restaurant in 1921 (Royce Hailey's Pig Stand), but California readily adapted to drive-in everything—movies, laundries, banks, churches, mortuaries—and transformed the way commerce was practiced in the United States and the landscape of cities and suburbs. As Richard Longstreth put it, "The important early innovations took place during a short period of time, most intensely during the 1920s and 1930s . . . [and] most of these innovations occurred in a single metropolitan area, Los Angeles." Just about every commercial practice catering to the lone driver/shopper—a force that would remake American urban physiognomy in the postwar period—was functioning in Los Angeles by 1930. What was a filling station in 1910 became the architecturally challenged (a temple here, a minaret there) multi-service "super" gas station by 1920, and soon, the drive-in food store: mother of all supermarkets. Self-service grocery stores were invented in 1912 in Los Angeles (not by Piggly-Wiggly in the South as some claim), and by the 1920s jumping in the car and going to the supermarket—Von's, Ralph's, Seelig, the Parque-n-Shoppe—to stroll up and down the aisles filling a cart had become part of daily life. Meanwhile, as if supermarkets followed the car (indeed they did), Europe was decades behind here, too: the Netherlands had 7 supermarkets in 1961 and 520 a decade later; France had 49 in 1961 and 1,833 by 1970.[34]

California's first drive-in movie opened in 1933, some months after the foundational one in Camden, New Jersey, but the weather meant it could be patronized year-round, and young people quickly pioneered a teenage way of life for consuming Hollywood's output via acrobatic rear-seat positions. The first motel in America opened in December 1925, the Milestone Motel outside of San Luis Obispo, a bungalow court with "the near-mandatory Mission Revival Bell Tower"; it soon metastasized into hundreds more. Tire companies like Goodyear and Firestone pioneered street-side auto emporiums where you could get gas, a battery, or tires. As the Depression began to end, the drive-in concept was off to the races: the first drive-in chain, A&W

Root Beer, got going in Sacramento before the war. In 1955 the Reverend Robert Schuller rented the Orange Drive-In movie theater in Garden Grove to deliver Sunday morning sermons while standing on top of the concession stand; within fifteen years he had 60,000 members and architect Richard Neutra had designed his gigantic drive-in church called the "Tower of Power" along the Santa Ana Freeway just past Disneyland—sometimes called "a shopping center for Jesus."[35]

The final ur-moment arrived in 1954 when a salesman trekked out to a hamburger stand in San Bernardino to see if it was true that the joint had eight of his five-spindle Multimixer milkshake machines all whirring at once, making forty milkshakes at a time. It not only had the eight Multimixers, it was eight-sided and many-peopled at lunchtime, as customers streamed in and out with burgers and shakes. The salesman ogled a strawberry blonde sitting in a yellow convertible who was happily munching away: "It was not her sex appeal but the obvious relish with which she devoured the hamburger that made my pulse begin to hammer with excitement." Customers particularly liked the French fries, "crispy on the outside and buttery soft inside." The salesman was Ray Kroc from Chicago, and the owners of the hamburger joint were Mac and Dick McDonald.[36] Kroc got the franchise rights and the rest is history; indeed, it is the history of Americans (who eat an average of thirty pounds of French fries each year), many of whom *are* history because of their stopped-up arteries.

Others found less to admire. Jeremy Pordage, Aldous Huxley's priggish and British stand-in for himself in *After Many a Summer Dies the Swan* (1939), motors into Los Angeles on a brilliant, cloudless day and sees only DRIVE IN FOR NUTBURGERS. He spies a restaurant shaped like an English bulldog and an Egyptian sphinx that turns out to be a real estate office. SPIRITUAL HEALING AND COLONIC IRRIGATION. "Science proves," a billboard claims, "that 83 per cent of all adults have halitosis." BLOCK-LONG HOTDOGS. A pet cemetery appears, with marble carvings "after Landseer's Dignity and Impudence." IN TIME OF SORROW LET BEVERLY PANTHEON BE YOUR FRIEND. Pordage spies a young woman out shopping—"in a hydrangea-blue strapless bathing suit, platinum curls and a black fur jacket." EATS. He thought he glimpsed a Tibetan lamasery in Beverly Hills, but it was only Ginger Rogers's estate. CASH LOANS IN FIFTEEN MINUTES. And long before *Chinatown*, Jeremy Pordage understood the nexus of water and power: "They've decided to pipe the water into it," Mr. Tittlebaum of the City Engineer's Department secretly reported, "enough to irrigate the whole valley." The unimproved land runs for twelve dollars an acre: "Buy all you can," a man says. "What's Tittlebaum going to cost?" another man says. "Oh, I'll give him four or five hundred bucks."[37] We can all laugh—but this was typically premonitory: who can say Mr. Pordage would be at a loss to locate similar sights today in Houston or Tampa or Kansas City?

Car Dreams, Then and Now

If you were going to be on the freeway all the time, you needed a ride that expressed yourself. The 1920s phenomenon of the glamorous movie star, known the world over, was joined to the perfected automobile; thus Valentino with his crystal white limousines, or Erich von Stroheim dusting off Norma Desmond's Hispano-Suiza in *Sunset Boulevard*. A mass base merged when teenagers took '32 Ford V-8s (the engine John Dillinger loved), stripped the fenders off, and began racing them along the highways—a modest prewar phenomenon that took off after 1945. Within the decade, adolescent rebellion, sex, rock and roll, and customized cars defined the American teenager. Two films symbolized these trends, both set in Southern California: Marlon Brando on the even more rebellious Harley-Davidson in *The Wild One* ("What are you rebelling against? Whaddya ya got?"), and James Dean hanging out the window of his bull-nosed and decked '49 Mercury as the new kid on the block in *Rebel Without a Cause*. A few years later the Beach Boys wrote one hit after another about custom cars ("Little Deuce Coupe," "409"). Thus was born an amazing car culture that entranced young people from Azerbaijan to Zambia. Hitchcock loved exotic cars: Tippi Hedren pilots her Aston-Martin roadster through Bodega Bay, unaware that the birds accumulating on telephone poles will soon swoop down on the schoolchildren. When you're on Nob Hill it's easy to imagine Kim Novak exiting the Brocklebank apartments, white coat setting off her platinum hair, driving her jade green Jaguar Mark VIII sedan past the Fairmont Hotel, turning left on California Street and then motoring off down the peninsula to Monterey.

Meanwhile in Los Angeles there is "Big Slice" and his main customer, the rapper Snoop Doggy-Dog. Otherwise known as Michel Rich, Big Slice (six feet, six inches tall and 295 pounds) grew up in Watts: "You didn't have a whole bunch of stuff to do. It was either sell dope, gang bang or just hang out or do nothing, and I did 'em all." But then he got into hydraulic systems, not the Mulholland kind but the ones that make low riders hop up and down, a phenomenon pioneered by Chicano hot-rodders—a kind of automotive Zoot Suit. Now Big Slice does designer cars for Snoop Dogg: the "Snoop Deville" and the "Laker Car," a 1967 Pontiac Parisienne (one of Detroit's nicest convertible designs) painted in L.A. Laker heliotropic purple and gold. A stoplight, a flick of a dashboard switch, and the frame is scraping the pavement: cool. Big Slice explains: "I'm not a car builder—I'm an artist. One thing I learned with Snoop: if people, when they see the car when you're driving down the street, if they don't do the neck snap, somethin' wrong." In parts and accessories alone, aftermarket sales in the United States run to $30 billion annually. Drag racing is still so big that the U.S. Army enters its 6,000-horsepower nitromethane dragster (0 to 200 mph in 2.2 seconds) in many events to help recruit adolescents.[38]

Dream Merchants

Thomas Edison's "kinetoscope" came to Manhattan in April 1894: you put a nickel in and peeped into a cabinet to see the show (still a New York pastime in certain circles), thus bringing into being the nickelodeon. Thomas Armat's "vitascope" arrived two years later, the first modern screen projector. In 1902 Thomas L. Tally opened his Electric Theater in Los Angeles, taking the projector out of penny arcades and merging the movies with theater for the first time; the next year a rail line opened to Hollywood (a town of 500 people with lemon groves, pea and lima bean fields, and the Stritchley Ostrich Farm). By 1903 Edwin S. Porter, a mechanic and projectionist for Thomas Edison, had produced a famous short called *The Great Train Robbery,* and "pictures" were off and running. Then D. W. Griffith's *Birth of a Nation* accumulated unheard-of box office records while applauding the Ku Klux Klan for its patriotism, among other things.[39]

That film launched the industry and also established Hollywood as the place to make pictures. France had been the clear leader, taking 40 percent of total film receipts in the United States in 1907, but soon Hollywood was the epicenter of movies. Its yearly payroll reached $20 million by 1915, and Charlie Chaplin was making $10,000 a week; a decade later it was the fifth-largest industry in the United States, the fourth largest exporter, and the top industry in California, making the vast majority of all films seen in the world and grossing $1.5 billion a year. In the late 1920s weekly movie attendance was 75 million, and this industry flourished right through the Depression as people relieved their misery with Hollywood fantasies, even if it only expanded marginally (80 million tickets were sold every week in 1939). By Pearl Harbor there were more movie theaters (15,115) than banks in the United States.[40] A handful of young moguls, most of them Jews who came up the hard way in the face of discrimination and ostracism, created the business and changed the face of American entertainment—from what people did on Saturday nights, to the magazines they bought, the clothes they liked, to the downtowns of every city and town where movie theaters recentered the community with architectural marvels—palaces of dreams. William Fox was born in Hungary and worked as a cloth sponger in New York; Jesse L. Lasky was a vaudeville cornet player in San Francisco; his brother-in-law, Samuel Goldfish, was born in Poland and booked steerage to New York at age thirteen, making his living selling gloves; Louis B. Mayer, born in Russia, collected rags in New Brunswick as a kid; Lewis J. Selznick remembered beatings from policemen in Kiev. This made them no different from Harrison Gray Otis or Edward Doheny, who likewise came from nothing: but they could pass for WASP. This city's elite was much more "porous" than New York or Boston, but you still had to be white and Christian. The film moguls dragged themselves up to great wealth, but the Los Angeles oligarchy found a thousand ways to remind them that they were doubly and triply suspect: they were Jews, they had no class, and they were from Hollywood. Discrimination extended even to Episcopalian Cecil B. DeMille, who couldn't join the elite California Club. So wealthy Jews constructed a parallel world of clubs, schools, golf courses—even a parallel universe of fine neighborhoods on the West Side. Perhaps most off-putting and obnoxious, the Jews were pro-union, antifascist, and liberal; the "leftward tendency of the Hollywoodians" was attenuated by McCarthyism, but is obviously still alive and well today.[41]

If Hollywood indulged every belief, hope, dream, and myth of American culture on the screen, it was an industry run like an industry. Henry Ford's assembly line worked here, turning out one formulaic picture after another, with actors, writers, and a myriad of specialists and technicians in this new art and industrial form housed (and often treated) like horses in a stable. (The great Coen brothers' film, *Barton Fink,* is scarcely an exaggeration of the prewar Hollywood milieu with Fink, a Broadway playwright stuck in Wallace Beary "wrestling pictures," William Faulkner stumbling out of his writer's hut stone drunk, the cringing but totally cynical underling working on his latest ulcer, and the boorish mogul reminding Barton that he owns what's inside Barton's head.) But this created a culture industry that still makes nearly all the films seen across the country and the world, lacks any serious competitor (as it always has), and remains a central foundation of America's global position—and especially, how the world views Americans. If it became "the major arbiter of taste," in Kevin Starr's words, it also transformed American culture in Adorno's sense: "something for everyone so that no one can escape."

Hollywood's international reach was so great that in the twenties all but 5 percent of films shown in Great Britain were American, 80 percent were American in South America, and 70 percent in France. Eighteen thousand movie theaters dotted the United States by 1930, compared to 2,400 in France and 3,000 in Britain. Meanwhile, Kodak made 75 percent of the movie film used in the world, International Telephone and Telegraph monopolized sound equipment, and Fox Movietone News interpreted daily events to much of the planet. When the Department of Commerce established a Motion Picture Section, the first report was on the China market. World War II made clear how important Hollywood was to public opinion and what a magnificent propaganda weapon it could be. The Office of War Information worked closely with Hollywood producers in putting patriotically bracing films before the American public and writing themes reflecting the New Deal and its goals. The military services supplied warplanes, ships, bases, and various other services to give verisimilitude to war films. In so doing, "the bloodiest catastrophe in world history," in Béla Balázs's words, was portrayed "like an amusing raw-humored manly adventure." The French critic Paul Virilio wrote that what was most unbearable about the Nazi occupation of France for his wife was "the feeling of being cut off" from Hollywood movies, from the epicenter of popular culture. The unnoticed insensitivity of this remark (I suffered: the Nazis wouldn't let me see Hollywood films) makes it all the more interesting.[42]

Because lowbrow cinema pitched to the masses was the Hollywood studio system's bread and butter, critics (usually on the East Coast) not only didn't like it, but vastly underestimated its influence and appeal. Cinema was both commodity and cultural artifact, Victoria de Grazia wrote, flowing over, around, and through the human world: it "overrode national boundaries, eluded political controls, infiltrated local community, insinuated itself into private lives, and was suspected even of penetrating into the unconscious, especially of the most vulnerable individuals, namely women, young people, and children." As cinema saturated the world market, it carried with it an American way of life that captured or threatened (usually both) every mind in its theoretically unlimited audience, establishing a permanent dialogue between film and viewer—"a new vernacular of universal currency whose grammar was always being renegotiated." In 2007 I visited the former Soviet Union and took the train from Moscow to St. Petersburg: Tom and Jerry cartoons played on the flat screen TV for the first two hours of the journey—just another example of "Donald Duck as world diplomat."[43]

It seems incredible in retrospect, but émigré intellectuals and critics also flocked to Hollywood in the 1940s, whether from Germany or Mississippi—which is hardly to say they all liked it. A kind of minimum winning coalition of European intellects found their way to Southern California: Theodor Adorno, Bertolt Brecht, Leon Feuchtwanger, Heinrich Mann, Thomas Mann, and Erich Maria Remarque. Brecht escaped Nazi Germany at the end of 1940 by crossing the Soviet Union on the trans-Siberian railway to Vladivostok, where he caught a small Swedish freighter that eventually docked at San Pedro Harbor; he and his wife took up residence at 1954 Argyle Avenue in Hollywood. In spite of his narrow escape, he was less than impressed with his new sanctuary: Los Angeles was "Tahiti in metropolitan form," and he felt like "Francis of Assisi in an aquarium" or "a chrysanthemum in a coal mine." Meanwhile Theodor Wisengrund, who preferred the name (Adorno) of his mother (a Corsican singer), also wound up in Los Angeles during the war and sat in this sun-dappled paradise scribbling one of the darkest meditations ever written on the modern world, *Dialectic of Enlightenment*, tracing a direct line from the Enlightenment to Hitler and the Holocaust. But Thomas Mann did not denigrate California's natural garden: "I was enchanted by the light, by the special fragrance of the air, by the blue of the sky, the sun, the exhilarating ocean breeze, the spruceness and cleanness of the Southland . . . all these paradisical scenes and colors enraptured me."[44]

Television put a big dent in Hollywood's cultural power from the 1950s onward, and today various new technologies are said to threaten it even more: pirated CDs, iPod videos, cable movies-on-demand, wireless transmission of films. I wouldn't bet on it: I was in Taiwan in 2006 and perused the local movie scene in the capital, Taipei: according to local ads, of some 150 films playing at multiplexes (16 of them, some with 18 screens) and smaller theaters (both of them), by my count 95 percent were American, another 1 or 2 percent were Japanese or Filipino, and the tiny remainder were Chinese.[45] The multiplexes ran no more than one or two films that might not appear locally near my home. A century after Hollywood began making films, this is an astonishing index of hegemonic culture and the American reach.

White Studies: The Los Angeles Oligarchy

The names found on the Board of Water Commissioners and the big-time real estate syndicates around the turn of the century—Huntington, Otis, Doheny, Harriman (the only easterner), and Sartori—were the core of an oligarchy that ran the city well into the post–World War II era. They didn't just make money on real estate, or railroads and trollies, or oil and cars. They made money on everything from irrigation schemes to newsprint to tourism to the platting of new cities. They had varied beginnings, some rich, most hard-scrabble, but they all were cultural white Anglo-Saxon protestants—WASPs, who spread a remarkable, almost Jim Crow-like intolerance throughout the city and the region, again well into the 1940s and 1950s.

Harrison Gray Otis was born poor in a log cabin in Marietta, Ohio. After working for a time as an itinerant printer, he fought bravely and well with the Ohio regiments in the Civil War, spending four years in the field, getting wounded several times, and acquiring the sobriquet, "Captain Otis." He arrived in Santa Barbara in 1876 with nothing in his pockets. After failing in the town's newspaper business, he got appointed to a Treasury Department post in Alaska. He got back to Southern California in 1881 just in time for the boom, and soon he was editor of the *Los Angeles Times*. Beneath his gruff exterior and his enormous moustache, which made him look like a walrus, beat a heart of solid rock.[46]

Harry Chandler grew up in New Hampshire, developed tuberculosis during a harsh New England winter while attending Dartmouth, dropped out, and sought a cure in the Southern California sunshine. Languishing in a boarding house, worrying he might die, he bumped into a tubercular doctor and fruit rancher who offered him a job and a healthy way to beat his illness. He slept in a tent in the orange groves at night, doffed his shirt in the day to work under the sun, and soon had a mahogany tan (Kevin Starr asks if Chandler pioneered the California suntan). Peddling fruit to Mexicans on the side, he earned some money and invested it in newspaper routes. Soon he was circulation manager for the *Los Angeles Times* and such a favorite of Harrison Gray Otis that he married the boss's daughter. In 1917 Chandler took over the paper and used it to further a host of projects (hydroelectricity, zoning) that added up to the newspaper being the best friend the real estate industry ever had.[47] It's hard not to see Chandler as a self-made man, a Horatio Alger—but he also relied on the kindness of two well-placed strangers. Harry begat Norman, who begat Otis Chandler, who finally broke with the *Los Angeles Times*'s right-wing Republican roots in the 1960s and turned it into one of the best newspapers in the country.

What we now know as "the federal government" was distant from the concerns of anyone in Southern California a century ago. It was distant for most Americans, too; it bore little resemblance to the capital of a nation-state, but none were farther away than the Los Angeles elite. They embodied the state in their private persons. A fundamental difference between the late-developing western United States and the continental European or Japanese experience is that these titans could do everything—build a railroad, an aqueduct, a city—by themselves. They needed the state, of course, but they wanted the state to follow their dictate—the opposite of "state-directed" development. The Los Angeles elite lived out the grand myths of American politics, that individuals are the core, the market rules, the private sector always does better than government, taxes are a bane, combination in the workplace is an abomination, hardy pioneering men may get very rich, but ultimately what they have, they deserve—and those that don't have, don't deserve. Harrison Gray Otis took this paradigm to an unusual extreme, of course, ranting and raving in the newspaper that he ran as if it were an army division and he were the commanding general, going to battle against anything that departed from his narrow worldview or stood in the way of him making more money. A person of deep Calvinist belief, he was also a person of stunning ruthlessness. If the workers weren't organizing or striking, he would cut their pay 20 percent so they would and then bring in vigilantes to crush the union and hire scabs. For him, the open shop meant cheap labor, the best way for a newly rising city to compete with San Francisco and New York, where unions were strong. Keeping unions out of L.A. was "a holy crusade," to be fought like a military campaign, lest the Republic be subverted by foreign radicals.[48] With all this, the WASP elite established an unbroken hegemony lasting well into the postwar period.

During the mayoralty election of 1911, featuring candidate Job Harriman of the Socialists, Harrison Gray Otis "patrolled the streets in his private limousine with a cannon mounted on the hood and held forth daily against the 'anarchic scum' who challenged his Campaign to Save Los Angeles."[49] Harriman, an early and consistent critic of the Owens Valley aqueduct who had won a surprising primary victory, got buried in the election—but not before reform-minded Governor Hiram Johnson took the measure of the publisher of the *Times* in these impromptu remarks: "In the city of San Francisco we have drunk to the very dregs of infamy. We have had vile officials, we have had rotten newspapers. But we have had nothing so vile, nothing so low, nothing so debased, nothing so infamous in San Francisco as Harrison Gray Otis. He sits there in senile dementia with gangrene heart and rotting brain, grimacing at every reform, chattering impotently at all the things that are decent, frothing, fuming, violently gibbering, going down to his grave in snarling infamy."[50]

What is a white person? Central Texas showed us that white skin is not quite enough; Irish and Germans are white; many Asians are equally white; and in Japan and Korea, many women are very white because they never venture out in the sun without an umbrella. "Caucasian" is a term with no scientific meaning, and "Anglo-Saxon" is another mostly fictive category. An Irish immigrant could quickly pass for Anglo-Saxon, often with a mere name change; so could an Italian (more Italians emigrated to the United States between 1820 and 1970 than did Englishmen). Germans were the largest immigrant group in that period (15 percent);[51] they could easily pass, and anyway, "Teutonic" had almost as much cachet as Anglo-Saxon. But then many Americans developed micrometer-like gradations between ethnicities; to "the true Pennsylvanian," Henry Adams wrote, "none but Pennsylvanians were white. Chinaman, negro, dago, Italian, Englishman, Yankee—all was one in the depths of Pennsylvanian consciousness." In early Los Angeles, though, where mixed ethnicity was a constant and probably a majority, becoming white was a way of pretending to the elite. So the son of a destitute Irish immigrant, Edward Doheny, arriving penniless in L.A., could strike oil, become a city father and a ruling-class "white" all in the space of a decade: a walrus moustache, British tailoring, and a foothill of cash did the trick. Being white, in short, meant meeting the qualification of more or less white skin, professing a Protestant religion even if a person rarely darkened the doorstep of a church or was born to Irish Catholics, and a claim to Anglo-Saxon background.

The absence of anything resembling an aristocracy meant that the gap between the oligarchy and the mass of white settlers was not big; it was a question of who got there first and who got rich. Culturally they were almost indistinguishable. Jackson A. Graves, president of the Farmers and Merchants National Bank of Los Angeles, wrote in 1930 that he had lived in California since 1857, after his father moved the family from an Iowa farm to a ranch near Marysville. In late middle age, residing at his estate in San Marino containing an orange grove "laid out with mathematical precision," he was the soul of Los Angeles elite probity: short white hair and moustache, prominent aquiline nose, strong chin, patrician blue eyes. "I never bought a piece of realty in Los Angeles City or County that did not pay me handsomely," he proudly wrote. All would be for the best in the best of all possible worlds, he thought, if only the people trusted in the city's leadership, beginning with Harrison Gray Otis and Harry Chandler, instead of hearkening to "the tyrannies and infamies of rabid labor unionism" (which he thought were far worse than those of the Ku Klux Klan). Witness the great Mussolini: "By vigorous, even arbitrary, measures he abolished Communism and labor union terrorism." Meanwhile labor was agitating every day in San Francisco and Chicago: "All such demonstrations should be repressed at the beginning." By contrast the "Chinaman" who ran his family ranch, "Chew Pack," never complained and was just a good, hard worker—and in his spare time he could do whatever he wanted: "I get on street car, go out Main Street see my flend washee house."[52]

This august Los Angeles establishment was mostly constituted by undereducated businessmen who made good—Otis, Chandler, Doheny, and much later Homes Tuttle (a big Reagan supporter who owned five Ford-Lincoln-Mercury dealerships) and oil mogul Henry Salvatori, an early backer of Goldwater and later a confidant of Richard Nixon who was a big contributor to right-wing groups like the Christian Anti-Communism Crusade. (And he led "an almost religious crusade" against the Eastern Establishment Republicans, and especially its standard-bearer in the 1960s, Nelson Rockefeller.) Tuttle, Salvatori, Hollywood's Jack Warner, Justin Dart (of Dart Drugs), and Walter Knott of boysenberry fame were the core of a group of businessmen who "decided to run [Ronald Reagan] for governor of California," in Salvatori's words. Unlike eastern elites, they had long abandoned "the genteel tradition," intellectual pursuits or opera and the symphony, for a life of movies, sports, shopping, and country clubs. Ron and Nancy Reagan fit right in and indeed were at the core of L.A.'s social life before entering the White House in 1981.[53]

City boosters disliked the film *Chinatown* mainly because of its accuracies. Robert Towne and Roman Polanski depicted a seamless web of Anglo power. Every touch is right: Mrs. Mulwray sitting by the pond at her estate, filing her nails while a bent Japanese gardener pulls weeds ("bad for glass"); a black porter polishes her canary-yellow Packard convertible; Mr. Gittes arrives at the door to be greeted icily by the Chinese butler, whose wife dusts the furniture in her maid's uniform. We don't see the cook, but usually he was Chinese, too; here is the complete ethnic formula for running a mansion in Beverly Hills. Arch-WASP Noah Cross effects a wardrobe drawn from the good old days of the Californios: Stetson, Mexican vest, high boots, silver belt buckle, a cowboy with a Hispanic tinge. Meanwhile the Italian cop has made detective, a vantage point from which to look down his nose at Gittes.

White Studies: The Folks

Anglo dominance masked one of the most diverse urban populations in America. Hugely varied and energetic peoples flooded into California after 1849, as we have seen; Irish, free blacks, Mexicans, Chinese, Japanese, Germans, French, Filipinos, Punjabi Sikhs, Italian vintners, Basque shepherds,

Armenian fig growers, Lebanese merchants—and that hardly exhausts the list. Los Angeles was less diverse than San Francisco but quickly became a major Jewish city (70,000 in 1930, 130,000 by Pearl Harbor) and a favorite mecca for blacks (30,983 by 1930 and 75,209 a decade later, the majority from Texas). A generation later novelist Walter Mosely wrote in *Devil in a Blue Dress* that L.A. was "like heaven for the southern Negro," even if you could work all day and "still find yourself on the bottom." Los Angeles never had the Chinese population of San Francisco (4,424 in 1890, only 2,591 in 1920, and 4,736 in 1940), and Japanese were the dominant Asian group until Pearl Harbor (25,597 in 1920, 44,554 in 1940); Little Tokyo in Los Angeles was the center of Japanese life on the West Coast. In the 1920s, 95 percent of housing in the city was proscribed for racial minorities, a situation courts did not strike down until 1948, in spite of many lawsuits (even then, restricted covenants operated informally into the 1960s); in the 1930s many restaurants posted signs reading "No Mexicans or Negroes Allowed." Here, too, the differences between San Francisco and Los Angeles recapitulated themselves. German-Jews of middle and upper classes preferred San Francisco, whereas the domi-nant tone in Los Angeles was "secular, socialistic, and Yiddish—Hester Street in the sunshine." As for San Diego, there weren't too many Jews, but the city had one with a special distinction: Wyatt Earp retired there to raise thor-oughbred horses after a gunfighting career almost terminated at the OK Corral—and Wyatt Earp was Jewish.[54]

Still, no other American city of comparable size was as lily-white as Los Angeles in the 1920s. Thirty thousand Asians, a similar number of blacks, and 45,000 Hispanics, nearly all of them living in ethnic enclaves, added only a little color to a population of 1.3 million, the vast majority of whom were Anglo-Saxon Protestants (the city had about 300,000 Catholics). In other words the Anglo elite had a mass base: flatlanders who made good, who prospered by the Pacific but still wanted to honor their roots. So Buckeyes flocked together while Hawkeyes held not one but two "Iowa State Picnics," the most famous in Lincoln Park on the last Saturday of every February, plus another one in the summer. Folks from Cedar Rapids would gather in one part of the park, those from Des Moines or Ames in another. Los Angeles was just Iowa minus the snow, Kansas minus the cyclones—that's the way they saw it, and all too many observers agreed. Critics, though, spoke of a loss of community in the remove to California, yielding nostalgia for an irretriev-able past, and an "acute loneliness that haunted the region."[55]

Retired farmers, Ford salesmen, hardware merchants, shoe store clerks, rural and small town folks flocked to Los Angeles from the Middle Border, "thousands and tens of thousands of them," Louis Adamic wrote in 1932; they herd into the city "toil broken and bleached out," fugitives from "hard labor and drudgery, from cold winters and blistering summers." The rural pietists imparted "a glacial dullness" to the region, Carey McWilliams wrote, and Willard Huntington Wright listed reasons why—"honorary pall-bearers from Emmetsburg; Good Templars from Sedalia; honest spinsters from Grundy Center," they had spread hypocrisy across the city "like a vast fungus": the place was "overrun with militant moralists, connoisseurs of sin, experts of biological purity."[56] More recently Christopher Rand likened them to "squares from the North European countries of the rectilinear flags"; back in the Midwest "they planted their squareness on the landscape: gridirons on the settlements; rectangular fields, farms, towns, counties. . . . And coming to L.A. they have planted it wherever possible," in a multiplicity of concrete rectangles ("tennis courts, highways, and swimming pools").[57] These generalizations tumble forth easily, perhaps reflecting the obverse face of an inner fear about one's own background, especially in California where so many hailed from the "flyover states," one or two generations removed. (And it isn't as if "the folks" created the rectangles; as we have seen, the entire frontier was a state-plotted rectangle from Ohio to Denver.)

The distilled essence of folkishness was Long Beach, where elderly pensioners lived in tiny homes, going to bingo on Saturday, church on Sunday, picnics in the park with fried chicken and macaroni and cheese, jumping in the Chevrolet sedan for a slow crawl down the highway. Usually pinched for money, the folks would go to the Boos Brothers Cafeteria (a restaurant style pioneered in L.A. in 1905), eating ham loaf with mashed potatoes and apple pie. They were turning the city into "Double Dubuque," according to H. L. Mencken, who never saw a Bible-thumping flatlander he didn't loathe. Even a sympathetic observer found them "incredibly unaesthetic," and to an acute observer, Louis Adamic, the folks were "simple, credulous souls . . . they are unimaginative and their cultural horizons are sadly limited—and as such they are perfect soil to sprout and nourish all kinds of medical, religious and cultural quackery." Trouble was, you couldn't get away from them—"they are everywhere."[58]

Conclusions: The Machine Ate the Garden

Conservatives in America—and sometimes radical critics as well—are usually angry about something from their childhood that got lost along the way, instead of inhabiting what Europeans would call a conservative worldview

(Newt Gingrich once nominated 1955 as the apotheosis of the American Dream). In Los Angeles, Joan Didion's "Chekhovian loss" takes the form of endless railing about unrecoverable pasts—oxygen not smog, citrus pastorals not realtors, fluid freeways instead of six-lane parking lots—as shorthand for the downfall of the entire community. This famously unplanned city was laid out by the private sector on a perfectly coherent logic, so long as you understand the logic: cheap land, cheap water, electricity, and oil; verdant towns platted and grouped within city boundaries, a convenient vehicle to get around—and everybody makes money. When smog filled the Los Angeles basin in July 1943, it seemed to spell the end of an era; no one knew where it came from but everyone suspected the new war industries. This time it *was* the automobile's fault—along with the California sun: a Cal Tech biochemist, A. J. Haagen-Smit, discovered in 1950 that smog was caused by sunlight reacting photochemically with exhaust gas. But there was a silver lining: ever since its first antismog law in 1959, California has led the nation in pioneering methods of cutting down automobile pollution; against every expectation, it became the epicenter of the automobile-environmental movement. Still, the people are wedded to their cars: as Joanne Jacobs put it, "no degree of enviro-sadism will get Californians to take the bus."[59] (Same goes for good, red-blooded Americans.)

A taciturn WASP named George Frost Kennan left a perfect epitaph for what easterners and Atlanticists think about the Southern California lifestyle, and especially its sturdy mount, the automobile, upon which depends "practically every process of life from birth through shopping, education, work, and recreation, even [*sic*!] courtship, to the final function of burial." This dependency on "mechanical legs," Kennan thought, had made "a clean sweep of all other patterns of living" and anesthetized people into "a sort of paralysis of the faculty of reflection." The individual is thus rendered childlike: "fun-loving, quick to laughter and enthusiasm, unanalytical, unintellectual . . . preoccupied with physical beauty and prowess." Southern California, he wrote, was "childhood without the promise of maturity."[60] Maybe so, but it was all there in the twenties, when a leisurely drive through a pastoral, blossomed Eden was still possible. World-historical change was just around the corner, but not because of cars or oil moguls or realtors. It happened when Franklin Delano Roosevelt got ready to fight a war.

PART V

A Tipping Point

Oedipus: What is this region into which I've come?
Stranger: Whatever I can tell you, I will tell.
       This country, all of it, is blessed ground;
       The god of the sea loves it; in it the firecarrier
       Prometheus has his influence. . . .
       That is this country, stranger: honored less
       In histories than in the hearts of the people.

—SOPHOCLES, *Oedipus at Colonus*

CHAPTER TWELVE

The State as Pretense of Itself:
Developing the West

[In America] the state, in contrast to all earlier national formations, was from
the beginning subordinate to bourgeois society, to its production, and never
could make the pretense of being an end-in-itself . . . [and] bourgeois society
itself, linking up the productive forces of an old world with the enormous
natural terrain of a new one, has developed to hitherto unheard-of dimensions.

—KARL MARX, 1857

World War II propelled the United States finally toward the global
leadership role that its productive economy could have supported
at any point after 1890, when it became the leading industrial
power in the world. It retains that leadership today, indeed, it is almost taken
for granted, as is the continental and Atlantic and Pacific reach of the country.
But it was revolutionary when Dean Acheson mounted a podium at Yale
University shortly after Germany invaded Poland in September 1939 and gave
an address entitled "An American Attitude toward Foreign Affairs." "Our
vital interests do not permit us to be indifferent to the outcome" of the wars in
Europe and Asia, Acheson said; nor was it possible for Americans to remain
isolated from them—unless they wished a kind of eternal "internment on this
continent" (only an Anglophile like Acheson would liken North America to a
concentration camp). Reconstruction of the foundations of peace would require new ways to make capital available for industrial production, the removal of tariffs, "a broader market for goods made under decent standards,"
"a stable international monetary system," and an end to "exclusive or prefer-
ential trade arrangements." Acheson later had the opportunity to implement
these ideas, first at Bretton Woods in 1944, then with the Marshall Plan and
the Truman Doctrine, and finally with NSC-68; he is the person who comes
closest to being the singular architect of American strategy from 1944 to 1953.
In 1939 he embodied the fullness of American ambition and expressed it
concisely; as he later put it in reflecting back on this speech, he had really

sought at the time to "begin work on a new postwar world system." But Acheson also called for the immediate creation of "a navy and air force adequate to secure us in both oceans simultaneously and with striking power sufficient to reach to the other side of each of them."[1]

As America quickly developed that capacity and fought a global war on Atlantic and Pacific fronts, the economy doubled in size and soon deployed fully half of the industrial production of the world. Most of the new, advanced-technology sectors of that economy were now in the West, mainly in the Pacific Coast states, as the central government reached across the continent to found an unprecedented industrial system ranging from Liberty ships to B-29 bombers to the atomic bomb. For the first time in American history—indeed the history of the world—productive and advanced industrial bases now fronted both the Atlantic and the Pacific, linked together with the century-old but still robust Chicago-centered industries of the second industrial revolution.

The state took on an utterly unprecedented role in American life—a *developmental* role that was deep, penetrating, and much stronger than most analysts appear to recognize. The New Deal and World War II showered money on the West,[2] beginning a long-term refashioning of the industrial map of America, greatly benefiting the Pacific states and Texas but doing little for the industrial heartland of the Midwest (which retooled existing industries for war but built few new ones). During and after the war new, usually high-tech industries proliferated from Seattle down through California and around to the Southwest states, especially Texas. Here was a complete contrast with the other industrial nations, who built defense industries on top of their existing industrial base. The United States did that, too, in the Middle West and Northeast, but the continental dimensions of the United States enabled a seemingly limitless building campaign located far from the original industrial centers—and war in the Pacific required it. This regional pattern became pronounced again in the 1970s, as the decline of the rust belt went hand in hand with enormous state investment pouring into defense and high-tech industries in the Pacific states and the Southwest.[3]

If the federal government's role during the Depression grew out of Keynesian pump-priming deficit spending—a conservative's nightmare of big government and make-work jobs (although the right wing preferred to call it socialism or communism)—when Roosevelt turned from Mr. New Deal to Mr. Win the War, Washington departed much more dramatically from what had been the presumed American model of political economy, always driven forward by the market and private enterprise. Instead the state took on a central role in remaking the industrial and infrastructural face of the United States: funding, directing, and locating a host of new industries, with the lion's share of the investment going to the Pacific states. Alexander Gerschenkron's analysis tells us that "late" development involved the central state stepping in to accumulate investment capital or to build systems that were too expensive for the private sector to handle, like railroads. But in this profound, telescoped, state-directed jump start, it was as if "Japan, Inc." had been fathered in the American West instead of Tokyo. The Pacific Coast had a late development that paralleled the industrial take-offs in East Asia; it just got there a few years earlier. This would prove to be the deepest transformation in American history since the North's victory in the Civil War.

The transformation was greatest in Southern California. When Hitler invaded Poland, Los Angeles County ranked first in industrial production in five categories: motion pictures, food products, sportswear, oil well equipment, and aircraft. But only two of these products are conventionally called industrial—oil and aircraft, maybe also fruit canning if not citrus; plus beachwear and other fun stuff, and the stuff of dreams. Even then a mere 5 percent of county labor was in manufacturing; in thirty-two other American cities it was 15 percent or higher. To be sure, there was a Studebaker factory on Loma Vista Avenue, Chrysler built cars at Slauson and Eastern, and Goodyear Tire and Rubber was on South Central—all before the war; but this was regional industry tied to South Bend, Detroit, and Akron. As world war beckoned, L.A. was simply nothing remotely like an industrial city.

A New (Western) Deal

The Depression hit Pacific Coast cities hard. From 1929 to 1931 manufacturing declined nearly 40 percent in Los Angeles, 34 percent in San Francisco, and just over 40 percent in Portland and Seattle. The region recovered a bit faster than most other parts of the country, with California and Oregon returning to their 1929 levels of employment by 1937, making Roosevelt enormously popular with voters, including many who had previously voted Republican (like those in Oregon). In his four runs for the presidency, FDR carried every western state in 1932, and won every Pacific state by large margins in the next three contests. One reason for this electoral prowess was the river of cash flowing across the continent from Washington.

The Bureau of Reclamation, founded during Teddy Roosevelt's tenure, exploded with projects during the New Deal—dozens of dams, canals, irrigation projects that remade the West—"a man-made transformation the likes of which no desert civilization had ever seen." If the Hoover Dam initiated this remaking, the arrival of FDR in the White House vastly quickened it; the bureau was the epitome of Keynesian economics: spend government money like water, create jobs like topsy, get consumers buying again. It came under the aegis of the Interior Department, which also housed the Civilian Conservation Corps (CCC), the National Park Service, and the Public Works Administration (PWA). Most important, it came under the tough-minded and indefatigable department director, Harold Ickes—"a stolid, round, owlish, combative ex-newspaperman" whom FDR called Donald Duck because of his "high-pitched squawk of a voice," and others called the "minister of western affairs without portfolio."[4] If the New Deal state initiated innumerable projects—highways, parks, tunnels (like the Lincoln Tunnel), bridges (like the Triborough Bridge), dams (like the colossal Central Valley Project in California, which the Bureau of Reclamation took over in 1935)—the contracts went to private firms, and in the West, they often went to Bechtel, Kaiser, Morrison-Knudsen, those "present at the creation" of the Hoover Dam.

The bureau put up the capital and with other agencies supplied the "hydraulic expertise," while working closely with local officials. "There is no pharaoh" in this hydraulic society, according to Donald Worster, but relatively faceless and impersonal mandarins who deal with people who understand water management and industrial agriculture, and share a common ideology of controlling and dominating water delivery. This was technocratic, instrumental reason oriented toward building and maintaining western water systems, tinged with fanaticism now and then (build more and more dams), afflicted with bureaucratic conflicts (Reclamation against the Army Corps of Engineers), and lubricated by oceans of a different kind—water-interest political money, perhaps the most powerful lobby in Washington. This is a monster, but it isn't sighted to ask questions about whether subduing another river is a good idea or not: "an epidemic of blindness" was the result, particularly about the impact of all this on the earth, the human environment.[5]

The Columbia River runs for more than 1,000 miles through four mountain ranges and drains 250,000 square miles in the United States and Canada (an area larger than France, Belgium, and the Netherlands combined). It draws its water from Canadian glaciers and contains unusual declines along its 1,270-mile cascade to the Pacific—abrupt drops and plummeting rapids that make it perfect for generating electricity; if its power potential had been fully harnessed in the early 1930s, it could have generated enough power to light every home west of the Mississippi. In the Pleistocene epoch a glacier blocked the river's flow so it created a new path for itself, namely Grand

Coulee canyon, 50 miles long, 4 miles wide, and up to 1,000 feet deep. Filling it up required a "concrete plug" 550 feet high and 4,200 feet long, three times the mass of the Hoover Dam and the largest concrete structure ever built. Surrounding Grand Coulee, about 90 miles northwest of Spokane, were more than a million acres with a natural storage reservoir beneath the soil. But a colossal dam for what? Only 3 million people lived in the region and the great majority had no electricity.

Roosevelt's answer in 1933 was the same as William Mulholland's: bring the water and the people and the enterprises will follow; failing that (at least for FDR), you'll get thousands of jobs to keep people busy and put money in their pockets. As early as 1933 visionaries like Stuart Chase saw in these great dams a mechanism to shift population westward by the millions and create a continental economy "like one unified machine, one organic whole." Grand Coulee Dam got started with $14 million from the WPA in late 1933, but three years later "the four largest concrete dams ever built—Hoover, Shasta, Bonneville, and Grand Coulee—were being erected at breakneck speed, all at the same time," and all of them except Shasta were built by recombinations of the Six Companies. Six thousand men worked night and day to build Grand Coulee, finally completing it three months before Pearl Harbor at a cost of $70 million. Subsequently it furnished the vast amounts of power necessary for the new wartime aluminum plants in the Pacific Northwest, but above all for the eight graphite-moderated plutonium reactors on a 670-square-mile reservation—half the size of Rhode Island—called Hanford. (Aluminum requires twelve times the energy needed to make iron. How many kilowatts are required to produce plutonium remains classified.) Six months into the war, 92 percent of the electricity from Grand Coulee and Bonneville was going into war production—aluminum, plutonium, shipbuilding, and especially aircraft production. And of course the people came, by the hundreds of thousands, happy to have jobs and the cheapest home electricity in the country.[6]

During the Depression the Public Works Administration and Works Progress Administration built 140 new schools and 221 government buildings (like post offices) in California, including Hollywood High School, the Lou Henry Hoover School in Whittier, South Pasadena High School—most in a pleasing Streamline Moderne, and most still serve their communities. Many of the new buildings housed carefully crafted murals, an abundant use of expensive stones like marble and granite, and a variety of California styles by then almost "traditional" (like Mission Revival). The federal agencies completed Union Station in Los Angeles and built a handsome Federal Reserve Bank in the downtown. On March 21, 1938, Rose Bowl Queen Cheryl Walker pulled a lever on a steam shovel, and the construction of the Arroyo Seco Parkway began (also assisted by the WPA and PWA). The highway engineers had made a careful study of the autobahns being built in Hitler's Germany, and to good effect: "tunnels and overpasses were designed in monumental Moderne, with Art Deco and WPA Moderne bas-reliefs electric with triumphant national symbolism." Arroyo Seco opened two months after the Pennsylvania Turnpike: both foretold the postwar freeway future for Americans.[7]

The Pacific Coast states were by no means the only western beneficiaries of federal largesse. During the New Deal years Nevada ranked first among western states in per capita federal investment (hardly anyone lived there, of course), gaining new highways, fifty bridges, and well over one hundred schools, hospitals, and other public buildings. In Idaho, which ranked eighth, the CCC built roads, trails bridges, and campgrounds all over the state; the WPA built twenty-five airports, more than a hundred public buildings, seventy-eight schools and other educational buildings, sewer systems and waterworks; and various other agencies spread rural electrification and built and financed homes. A stretch of cities running from Houston and Fort Worth to Wichita joined five Pacific cities in gaining at least $1 billion in defense contracts, and this gave a huge boost to their subsequent growth.[8]

It seems incredible in retrospect, but the United States was still a military shrimp in the late 1930s, after a decade of sharp and ever-growing international crises. When the war began in Europe the U.S. Army ranked sixteenth in the world—between Spain and Bulgaria. An armaments industry barely existed, and aviation ranked thirty-six in the nation in number of wage earners, behind candy and confectioners, and forty-fourth in the value of its products. Franklin Roosevelt won his first term in 1933 and so did Adolph Hitler; Japan withdrew from the League of Nations and the Washington and London naval limitation agreements, and both Japan and Germany rearmed rapidly in the next five years. Roosevelt provided a mere $17 million for the army in 1938, a small force most of whose troops were scattered among 130 posts in the United States, as if the Indians still needed chastisement. Development of military aviation had almost ceased in the 1920s, and it was 1938 before Roosevelt began to worry about airpower. After the war began FDR ordered up a study of how large the army needed to be should the United States enter the war. The answer was a mind-boggling 8.8 million soldiers. But that turned out to be close to the mark: in May 1945 the army totaled 8,291,336 officers and GIs—with the navy and air force and a host of high-technology armaments, the mightiest armed force the world had ever seen.[9]

The navy did better under President Roosevelt, long a navy man. It was the most powerful service, but its mission was entirely defensive. It lost few of its ships in World War I, and for that reason and the isolationism of three Republican administrations, it languished through the 1920s. Less and less money was available, more and more ships went into mothballs; the 1922 Washington Naval Conference proscribed building new capital ships for a decade and led the United States to scrap 845,740 tons of naval shipping, among them fifteen obsolescent battleships. Warren Harding was happy to seize upon the idea of naval limitations, since he had so few others, and where Coolidge was cool, Hoover was positively hostile to the navy. But once Roosevelt took over a virtual "naval renaissance" began. He allocated $238 million to the navy in June 1933, and behind a new technology of high-pressure and high-temperature steam propulsion, American industry built ships that were 25 percent more efficient than those in any other navy. By 1939 the navy had nearly 450 ships of all kinds, built or building: battleships, aircraft carriers, cruisers, destroyers, and submarines; it was the most formidable navy in the world, but because of the 1935 Neutrality Act it could not be deployed in warfare unless attacked[10]—and no one thought there was a nation in the world foolish enough to attack the United States.

France's surrender to the Nazis, however, led the General Board of the navy to ask Roosevelt in June 1940 for a genuine two-ocean navy, requiring Congress to fund 1.3 million tons of new shipping. In April 1940 the Pacific Fleet deployed to Hawaii for maneuvers, 2,500 miles away from its usual base in San Diego, and FDR ordered it to remain at Pearl Harbor. This alarmed the Japanese, of course, but in that same year Japan launched the greatest fighting ships the world had ever seen, the *Yamato* and the *Musashi;* nearly twice the size of any other battleship with a speed of twenty-seven knots, each had nine eighteen-inch guns weighing 162 tons apiece, which could fire off three 1.5-ton shells every two minutes. The *Yamato* served as Fleet Admiral Yamamoto Isoroku's flagship and was the last Japanese battleship still afloat in April 1945 when American carrier aircraft caught her southwest of Kyushu and blew up her magazines in a spectacular explosion. (The *Musashi* went down off Leyte in October 1944.)[11]

A Tipping Point

Japan's strike force assembled off Etorofu Island in the Kurile chain on November 22, 1941, and four days later set off in thick fog and tumultuous North Pacific winter seas: only then were the high command's secret orders opened and read. For the next two weeks the fleet maintained radio silence, kept its lights off, and even avoided dumping garbage or soiled petroleum trails. It was an awesome formation: two battleships, three cruisers, six aircraft carriers (including the mammoth flagship *Akage*, nearly three football fields long), eleven destroyers, and some twenty-three submarines riding with it or forging ahead; the carriers had 423 fighters and bombers lashed to their decks. Japan's navy was first class and its naval aviation, world class; its Zero fighters and Kate-class medium bombers ranked among the best in the world. The Mitsubishi Zero had a high-tech aluminum monocoque shell and a 500-horsepower radial engine; with an amazing range of 1,000 miles, it could also climb to 5,000 meters faster than any other fighter and had an unmatched top speed of 332 miles an hour. The Kate did 230 miles an hour carrying an 800-kilogram (1,764-pound) bomb, and was the world's best torpedo bomber. (Nonetheless the engines for the Zero and the Kate still had to be imported in the 1930s—usually from the United States.)

This massive fleet, grinding and heaving through the seas in silence, moved undetected across more than 5,000 miles of ocean until it entered the tropical waters west of Hawaii. Christmas lights dimmed in Honolulu after midnight, Admiral Kimmel's carousing sailors returned to their ships, and eight hours later the first wave of Kate bombers came in over the northern tip of O'ahu, across the Waianae Mountains, into the valley, and down the west coast, their flanks guarded by Zero fighters. They hit Pearl at 7:55 a.m., achieving complete surprise beyond their commanders' wildest dreams. Some forty planes carrying torpedo bombs were pivotal in the success of the attack, because American commanders thought it impossible to use airborne torpedoes effectively in the spare and shallow confines of Pearl Harbor. But after much trial and error in Kagoshima Bay from 1939 onward, Japanese pilots had perfected techniques of shallow-water launches, and the torpedoes dropped into the South Loch were mainly responsible for destroying the fleet, especially the big battleships *Arizona, West Virginia*, and *Nevada*. The full toll: 12 ships sunk, 9 more with moderate to severe damage, in addition to 171 aircraft destroyed at Hickam, Wheeler, and other bases. Everyone was caught with their pants down, not just Kimmel. But he was a convenient scapegoat, so FDR ordered Nimitz "to get the hell out to Pearl and stay there till the war is won."[12]

Pearl Harbor was a case of unprovoked aggression and has since been condemned not only by Americans—that goes without saying—but by the best Japanese historians. As Professor Ienaga Saburo wrote decades ago, Japan's militarists "charge[d] recklessly into an unwinnable war and continue[d] to the point of national destruction." But it was no *more* than military aggression, of a kind the world had experienced many times before; aggression across international borders for reasons of state was as common to history before 1941 as it was rare after 1945. Furthermore Japan's attack targeted purely military objectives: total American casualties in the Pearl raid were 2,335 navy, army, and marine personnel dead (nearly half of whom were entombed in the *Arizona*) and 1,143 wounded. Total civilians killed: 49. Of those deaths, the majority came from "friendly fire"—anti-aircraft shells falling back to the ground. The stunning (if Pyrrhic) success of Japan's strategic operation is frequently mentioned, but few recall the precision with which the attack separated soldier and civilian. A counterforce strike against the American fleet, it had a soldier-to-civilian kill ratio of about 48 to 1.[13]

If an attack on the Pacific Fleet was unexpected, it still came decades after the first thoughts of war with Japan emerged in Washington, as we have seen, after several years of what Akira Iriye has called a United States–Japan cold war, after three years in which Washington kept a slipknot around Japan's neck, after FDR's embargoes of scrap iron and oil (Japan was still depending on American oil imports in the spring of 1941), and after weeks of expecting Japan to strike at American interests somewhere in the Pacific. About ten days before Pearl Harbor, Secretary of War Henry Stimson entered in his diary a famous and much-argued statement—that he had met with President Franklin D. Roosevelt to discuss the evidence of impending hostilities with Japan, and the question was "how we should maneuver them [the Japanese] into the position of firing the first shot without allowing too much danger to ourselves." Stimson later told a congressional inquiry that it is dangerous to wait until the enemy "gets the jump on you by taking the initiative"; nonetheless, "in letting the Japanese fire the first shot, we realized that in order to have the full support of the American people it was desirable . . . that there should remain no doubt in anyone's mind as to who were the aggressors."[14]

It is not my purpose to argue that Stimson (or Roosevelt) "maneuvered" Japan (or the United States) into the war, but it is noteworthy that since 1846 most American wars have begun when the other side fired the first shot. The strategy of passive defense is not innocent of considerations of power, as any psychologist knows; a nation of superior strength will often find advantage in letting the weaker side strike first. Americans also conveniently forget that the United States was still sitting this global war out, more than two years after Hitler invaded Poland and quickly unified continental Europe under his control—thus to transform the balance of power in the world. Japan's cardinal error was not the "sneak attack" at Pearl, which did what it was supposed to do, but the indescribable senselessness and self-defeating futility of rousing the premier industrial power in the world to unprecedented feats of sacrifice and production. Its architect, the great naval leader Yamamoto Isoroku, thought Pearl Harbor had to be made to ring with shock and awe—"America must be so overawed from the start as to cause them to shrink from continuing the war."[15]

That idea didn't work any better then than it did in March 2003. Japan carried off more stunning victories right after Pearl Harbor—in the Philippines, Singapore, Malaya, Borneo, Guam, and Wake; it soon reigned supreme throughout maritime East and Southeast Asia. But within six months, four of the six aircraft carriers that made the Pearl attack—the *Akagi, Kaga, Soryu,* and *Hiryu*—were at the bottom of the Pacific. The battle of Midway settled that score and foretold the final outcome on the sea, just as the ferocious battles on Guadalcanal signaled the beginning of Japan's demise on land. By 1943 everyone but the Tokyo militarists themselves knew that Japan was heading toward defeat: the only question was when, and how much sacrifice it would require. For Americans, their great victory in the world war would mask a different kind of loss: the end of a preindustrial Pacific Coast, the end of letting others run the world, the end of isolation in the best sense: the worldly innocence provided by the continent and two oceans.

Mr. Win the War

New Deal programs spent some $7,582,434,000 in the West between 1933 and 1939, but wartime spending dwarfed that: in four years, the West got about $70 billion, as the federal government accounted for 90 percent of the available investment capital. From 1940 to 1946 federal spending amounted to $360 billion in the nation; the West got about one-fifth, but California got almost half of that, or 10 percent of every federal dollar spent during the war. Compare that to a single year, 1930, when the federal budget totaled $3 billion—or simply 1933, when the entire gross national product was $55 billion. Total personal income in California was $5 billion in 1930 and did not go higher than that again until 1940; by 1945 personal income in the state had tripled to $15 billion. During the war the manufacturing economy of the state increased by 250 percent.[16] New York and Michigan got more federal money than California, but they had been industrial states for decades. Furthermore, they mostly converted existing factories to wartime production (Ford made B-24s, General Motors made tanks), whereas California founded entirely new industries with the latest technologies—a clear advantage of "late" development. It was open to experimentation and to new industries, like aerospace and electronics, and the new firms did not have to contend with entrenched competitors but could develop autonomously.

Federal funds flowed through the U.S. Army Corps of Engineers and the Bureau of Reclamation, but also through brand new agencies: the Reconstruction Finance Corporation (RFC), which funded factory expansion, and a subsidiary called the Defense Plant Corporation (DPC), established by Congress on August 22, 1940, and which ultimately invested nearly $7 billion in state-owned, war-related industries. Together they supplied capital for nearly all the new rubber plants, 58 percent of aluminum factories, and 71 percent of aircraft factories. Conservatives like Senator Robert A. Taft railed against the RFC when it first surfaced ("the most outrageous legislative proposal" he had ever seen) and complained that now the federal government "could go into just any business it chooses," competing with private enterprise.[17] Taft had a point; Roosevelt deployed state power and finance to found or advance one industry after another, as a completely new American political economy emerged.

Washington funded everything from Kaiser's Fontana steel mill to Studebaker trucks to Howard Hughes's "Spruce Goose" cargo plane. Planners located the Fontana plant, capitalized by the RFC at $100 million (100 percent of the cost), forty-five miles inland in case the Japanese invaded, not a likely prospect—but no one knew that in 1941. Kaiser bought up 2,000 acres of hog farms set amid orange groves and built a state-of-the-art integrated steel mill—the first mill that side of the Rocky Mountains, Kaiser noted in his speech inaugurating the facility in December 1942. In good Kaiser fashion, he added this flourish: "The day of the West is at hand[;] 'Westward the course of Empire takes its way.'" By now steel mills and massive dams were child's play for this arid-lands titan who, in the wink of an eye, had gone from paving roads to building the Hoover Dam and, in another wink, to being FDR's favorite New Deal industrialist. Kaiser destroyed the old "Pittsburgh-plus" formula by which westerners paid a steel price including the cost of shipment from Pittsburgh. Bernard DeVoto had long seen such measures as an index of the West's dependency—"a plundered province"—but by 1946 he celebrated "the ancient Western dream of an advanced industrial economy, controlled at home and able to compete nationally." Independent financial power emerged, too, as A. P. Giannini's Bank of America surpassed Chase Manhattan by the end of the war to become the largest bank in the world.[18]

If Kaiser was emblematic, the Defense Plant Corporation's investments encompassed virtually all the great industrial firms: Alcoa ($509 million, roughly $6 billion in today's dollars), General Motors ($471 million), U.S.

Steel ($372 million), Chrysler ($181 million), Ford Motor ($173 million), General Electric ($137 million). In the first six months of 1942, Washington gave out $100 billion in military contracts, more than the entire gross national product of 1940. The DPC got into anything related to the war effort: steel and machine tools, aluminum and magnesium, alcohol and acetylene, air fields and aviation gasoline, synthetic rubber and jewel bearings. It provided $200 million to build another high-technology integrated steel mill in Geneva, Utah. (Along with Fontana, Geneva also helped to end western dependency on midwestern steel.) The first aluminum plant west of the Mississippi was up and running in Vancouver, Washington, by 1940, and by the end of the war around 40 percent of the nation's aluminum came from the Pacific Northwest.

The DPC's biggest role was to jump-start the aircraft industry. It funded three-quarters of the industry's wartime expansion, and fourteen of the fifteen biggest airplane engine plants. DPC capital was distributed around the country (Michigan got twice as much as California, for example), but in the Midwest this reflected expansion or retooling of existing industries, which quickly returned to automobile production after the war. Packard made Rolls-Royce engines for British planes, Ford built B-24 bombers at Willow Run, and Chrysler operated a mammoth 476-acre engine factory on Chicago's South Side (which later was home to the Tucker cyclops-eye sedan). In the West, however, new industries were founded one after another (steel, aluminum, magnesium; 129 new plants in California, 108 in Texas), and the aircraft industry exploded from virtually nothing to the world's leader in a high-tech sector that would dominate the postwar era—and even with the extant assembly lines back east, West Coast firms still built 46 percent of all warplanes. Four billion dollars went into the aviation industry during the war, one-sixth of all wartime investment in manufacturing, and Washington provided 89 percent of it.[19]

When Hitler invaded Poland about 60 percent of airframe manufacturers and one-third of aircraft employment were located in Southern California, but by early 1941 the regional aircraft industry already had a $1 billion backlog in military orders, a figure greater than the assessed value of Los Angeles; six months after Pearl Harbor, this city was already the country's second most productive industrial base, measured by the size and number of government contracts. By 1944 some 4,000 "war plants" operated in Los Angeles, most of them in the aircraft industry (which employed 228,000 people); the city received nearly half of all federal contracts in California, as managers in Washington came to look upon it as their company town. Shipbuilding took off, too. It had been two decades since the existing yards in the Los Angeles area had built any big ships, but after Kaiser (with much governmental help) established the California Shipbuilding Corporation (Calship) on Terminal Island, L.A. broke the previous record by delivering 15 Liberty ships in June 1942 and ultimately built 467 ships by the time the war ended. Todd Shipyards, Bethlehem Shipbuilding, and the Consolidated Steel Corporation (which launched more than 500 vessels) filled out this new industry that employed 90,000 workers and received more than $1.5 billion in war contracts.[20]

A Kaiser, Not a Pharaoh

Henry J. Kaiser, the epitome of a New Deal industrialist and easily FDR's favorite corporate partner, constructed the integrated steel mill at Fontana and lined the shores of the Bay Area, Portland, and Puget Sound with ship-yards. A huge man with huge appetites—thick steaks, fine scotch, Cuban cigars—he looked the part of the swashbuckling industrialist in his great double-breasted suits. Kaiser lived for his work and thought nothing of call-ing his underlings at four in the morning. But this unlikely package wrapped around one of America's great industrial progressives. Kaiser's major innova-tion was his most lasting: like another "late" developer, Bismarck, Kaiser preempted labor discontent by fashioning a corporate welfare system that was truly innovative in the 1940s. The best-known outcome of this is Kaiser Permanente, now one of the largest health maintenance organizations in the United States. Beginning in 1942, paycheck deductions financed his Perma-nente Health Plan (fifty cents a week in the beginning); the program paid for itself quickly in "healthier workers, less absenteeism, and increased produc-tivity." Each shipyard had counselors who helped newcomers adjust, usually a woman for new women workers, a black for new black workers, and the like. Berkeley child welfare experts helped set up round-the-clock day-care centers for shipyard families; Richmond's had over seven hundred children toward the end of the war, with attention paid to good nutrition and healthy habits. Kaiser's paternalism was reciprocated by his employees, who regarded him as a fatherly leader ("Pop" Kaiser)—and each social innovation seemed to boost productivity.[21] Kaiser also worked closely with unions and brought black workers into his factories from the beginning. Here was a progressive kind of American corporatism—and it made him a national hero.

Oakland was the only Pacific Coast city with substantial industry before the war, and it liked to style itself the Glasgow of America or the Marseilles of the Pacific, but few were buying—then or since. The city was mainly the result of railroad decisions not to push on to San Francisco. Train passengers disembarked in Oakland and took ferries to San Francisco; most freight coming over the rails or by ship was unloaded at the Oakland docks. The transportation network encouraged a proliferation of industries in the neighborhood, like Standard Oil's big refinery in Richmond. A spurt of shipbuilding came and went with World War I, and small auto factories opened in the 1920s. It was another city run by WASP oligarchs, the most famous of whom were William Knowland and Earl Warren. But like Kaiser, they ran it well—Oakland was one of the best-planned cities in the country and one of the first "to exploit fully the possibilities of greenbelts and public transit." But the Depression hit the East Bay hard, it still could not be called industrialized before World War II, and eastern interests owned much of the existing manufacturing. As in Los Angeles, great firms like Standard Oil dominated labor and the local government, supplying many of Richmond's mayors and council members.[22]

The Bay Area got a grand total of almost $4 billion in war contracts, $364 million in new industries financed by Washington, and nearly half a billion dollars worth of new military bases and facilities. Lend-Lease shipping for Britain brought Henry Kaiser's first federal contracts in December 1940, to build Yard One in Richmond across the bay from San Quentin Prison, but after Pearl Harbor he cornered huge contracts to manufacture liberty ships—in Oakland, Richmond, Sausalito, Portland, Vancouver (Washington), and other places; Richmond alone built 20 percent of all Liberty ships (727 ships in all), employing 90,364 people at the peak. Mare Island had the largest naval repair facility in the country, with "row upon row of cruisers, destroyers, corvettes, submarines and submarine tenders" getting fixed up or waiting to ship out again. Along with other nearby towns like Vallejo and Sausalito, the Bay Area got three-fourths of the nearly $5 billion that Washington spent for building ships on the Pacific Coast. Kaiser paid the highest wages in the country and employed the most women, so people came flocking, living in company barracks at $13 a week. Ultimately Kaiser ended up employing nearly 200,000 workers in his various shipyards and built some 1,500 ships with $4 billion in federal money, including 821 Liberty ships, 219 Victory ships (large versions of the Liberties)—30 percent of all American wartime shipping. Although Pacific Coast shipyards at their peak never employed as many people as Atlantic Coast yards—497,000 to 513,000—they got more than half of all contracts while the East Coast yards got less than a third (and the Midwest the rest). The key difference: virtually all the West Coast yards were new and much more efficient with the latest technologies.[23]

By mid-1942 Kaiser had cut the time for making a 10,000-ton ship from 355 to 48 days. He built Liberty ships with prefabrication techniques learned from making dams: as Marilynn Johnson put it, "whole sections of a ship's superstructure—boilers, double bottoms, forepeaks, afterpeaks and deck-houses—were preassembled" and then brought to the shipyard. Prefabrication created new specialties for craftsmen, but the skills could be learned quickly and within a couple of months apprentice workers could advance to journeymen—or journey woman, since women were widely employed in these shipyards (40 percent of welders were women, for example).[24] It was a good thing that Kaiser could adapt his dam construction skills to Liberty ships, since he had absolutely no experience in shipbuilding. He bid on his first contract in 1940 after sending an employee to a library to bone up on the industry's techniques and terminology. His formula was big projects, big government contracts and capital, low bids, and let's get to work—even if he didn't know what he was doing. It was similar to the great Korean industrialist Chong Ju-yong, who got the formidable Korean shipbuilding industry off the ground by securing contracts in Greece and then hiring Scottish technicians to tell him how to build a tanker.[25]

After meeting with an Austrian refugee, F. J. Hansgirg, Kaiser also figured out how to build a magnesium factory, an extremely light metal vital for aircraft. Hansgirg had worked with the Japanese to produce magnesium at a plant in northern Korea, using a new "Carbothermic" method. The Reconstruction Finance Corporation granted Kaiser $9,250,000 to build his plant near San Francisco, and the first magnesium ingot—something absolutely central to the war effort—rolled off the line about two months before Pearl Harbor; before the war ended, the plant produced 10,000 tons of magnesium. His factories also produced an infernal fuel for incendiary bombs out of magnesium dust: called "goop" at the time, Kaiser's 41,000 tons were part of the arsenal that burned out one Japanese city after another in the late stages of the war. Kaiser also helped found a new aluminum industry in the Pacific Northwest—nine new West Coast plants emerged, run by Kaiser, Alcoa, and Reynolds Aluminum.[26]

One of Kaiser's odd moves was to team with Howard Hughes to build the largest transport plane in the world, a flying boat otherwise known as the "Spruce Goose." Hughes, a famously eccentric figure, had arrived in California in the late 1920s with his prematurely dead father's patent on a state-of-the-art oil drilling bit, a monopoly that gushed cash for many more years. With that Texas provenance he combined two of California's great industries —planes and pictures—to become the most flamboyant industrialist of his time. The two titans rarely did more than talk occasionally on the phone, but at one point Kaiser, a workaholic straight arrow with a staid wife, met with Hughes at the Shoreham Hotel in Washington, "a blonde on his arm, this time with long hair over one eye. . . . Mother Kaiser almost died."[27] The awe-inspiring seaplane, built of birch wood and designed for heavy military transport with a wingspan half again the size of a Boeing 747, powered by eight Pratt and Whitney 3,000-horsepower engines, flew just once (after the war, with Hughes at the controls).

A Pharaoh, Not a Kaiser

Another industrial firm working closely with the government, but much less flamboyant—indeed, obsessively secretive—was the Bechtel group. One of the world's great construction firms, its revenues more than doubled after 9/11 from $11 billion in 2002 to nearly $25 billion in 2007, but it remains privately held. Its Republican proclivities should not hide how close this firm has been to government, beginning with its participation in the Hoover Dam project. The firm's founder, W. A. "Dad" Bechtel, began much like Kaiser, in general construction and then road building; he died suddenly in 1933 while on a visit to the Soviet Union, and his sons took over the firm. Almost immediately they got a federal contract to build the Broadway Tunnel through the hills between Berkeley and Oakland. Stephen and Kenneth Bechtel, along with one of their executives, John McCone, formed the Bechtel-McCone Company in 1937 and began constructing oil refineries and chemical plants in Southern California and eventually almost everything—all over the world. Bechtel became in effect a "private" arm of the U.S. government in building oil rigs and refineries, military bases, water systems, air and sea ports, and, famously, entire cities in the deserts of Saudi Arabia (at $30 billion the Jubail industrial complex was the largest construction project in the world in the 1970s)—always with very little public knowledge, let alone scrutiny. Bechtel covets privacy, in that it built enormous projects like nuclear power stations in India, the excellent subway system in Washington, D.C., and the "Big Dig" in Boston while remaining privately held, with a penchant for closed-lip secrecy.[28] During the cold war this Pharaohnic firm ended up privatizing a good chunk of the American empire.

Bechtel, like Kaiser, got a critical boost from the war: it quickly grew tenfold, to revenues of $50 million by 1943. It built and ran Marinship in Sausalito, the idyllic port just across the bay from San Francisco, with a little help from some friends: the firm's board of directors "looked like a Six Companies reunion," according to company historian Robert Ingram. Developed on the tidal marshes of Richardson Bay in the shadow of the Golden Gate Bridge, Marin City grew up overnight to house thousands of working families; unlike many other mushrooming towns, it was carefully planned by Bechtel and federal officials, with pleasant redwood houses situated on rolling meadows, new schools, churches, a brand new shopping center—another example of American corporatism, and a good one: homes, schools, and the workplace were racially integrated, probably more so than any other wartime project. Using Kaiser's prefabrication techniques, Marinship lined up a gargantuan, mile-long assembly line, where two-ton steel slabs stacked in racks were welded into subassemblies and then moved off to one of six shipways where they were cobbled together to complete the vessel. "Flying squads" of specialists moved up and down the line, deploying particular skills as needed and checking up on ship assembly. With a relatively small work force of 20,000, Marinship completed 93 Liberty ships and tankers. Bechtel had long been hostile to unions, but wartime exigencies required it to work effectively with organized labor at Marinship. More important, the Saudi royal family visited Marinship just as Washington was coming to appreciate how much oil it sat on, giving Bechtel a huge leg up on postwar contracts as Middle Eastern petroleum began to flood into world markets.[29]

Pearl of the Navy: San Diego

San Diego is truly one of the sublime garden spots of the world, with a near-perfect ambient temperature the year round, and the best example in California of an open Mediterranean city (at least after architect John Nolen took hold of it in 1908). It has been mostly absent from our narrative so far because it long sat in the shadow of Los Angeles, San Francisco, and Seattle (eastern railroads didn't reach it until 1919, forty years after L.A.) and had no clear identity before World War II—or if it had any, it was supplied by the navy. A Connecticut Yankee named Alonzo Erastus Horton arrived in San Diego in 1867 aboard the paddle-wheel steamer *Pacific,* and in a classic California story, he convinced some local officials to sell him 960 acres of property for a total of $265; the parcel happened to include the harbor and what became San Diego's downtown. Horton was prescient in other ways, too: he "envisioned San Diego as a coastal metropolis connected to great cities on either side of the Pacific in maritime travel and trade." But his counterpart in founding the city, William Ellsworth Smythe, still faced East: an avid irrigationist (as we have seen), he wanted San Diego to be the capital of a surrounding region

of irrigated farms and communities. Smythe won. Until the war, San Diego
was a sleepy port city surveying not the Pacific vista, but groves of lemons,
oranges, and olives. Meanwhile, Kate Sessions, an energetic horticulturalist,
planted thousands of trees all over the city—torrey pines (as in the golf course
by that name overlooking the Pacific), eucalyptus, Monterey cypress, acacia,
pepper, even kuki trees from Hawaii and banyans from Fiji. The Olmsted
brothers came and left quickly, but the city developed great parks (Balboa)
and lovely public spaces.[30]

The basic idea was like Portland's—to avoid Californication, or what they
called "Los Angelesization," through "a Progressive program of planned and
orderly development." As it happened, the U.S. Navy offered the best solution to the problem. In January 1911 a pilot employed by aviation pioneer
Glenn Curtiss took off from the wooden deck of the USS *Pennsylvania,*
demonstrating that an airplane could take wing from a ship, and a week later
Curtiss skimmed along San Diego Bay in a pontoon-equipped plane, landing
and taking off in the water. The navy was duly impressed but remained
unconvinced that San Diego would make a good base. Then Congressman
William Kettner got a $249-million appropriation to dredge San Diego har-
bor and enlisted Assistant Secretary of the Navy Franklin Delano Roosevelt
to come out to San Diego and see the port for himself. Navy man Roosevelt
loved San Diego from that point forward. In 1915 the Japanese cruiser *Asama*
ran aground in uncharted waters off Baja California; it had been trying to
intercept German shipping on behalf of the British. Tokyo sent a squadron
to rescue the *Asama* and somehow managed to spend two months fooling
around off the coast to do it; this predictably set off a Yellow Peril scare about
how the Japanese must be reconnoitering the entire coastline. When Woodrow Wilson took the United States into the war in April 1917, Navy Secretary
Josephus Daniels recommended "the creation of major Navy, Marine, and
Army aviation facilities throughout greater San Diego." Soon there were
naval air stations at North Island, Point Loma, Chollas Heights, and Mira-
mar, a naval amphibious base on Coronado Island, a Marine Corps aviation
base at El Toro—the list goes on, as San Diego and the surrounding region
began to call itself "the Gibraltar of the Pacific" (or a "military theme park,"
depending on one's point of view). Actually it became a navy and marine
town, with the admirals and generals showing up for almost every ceremonial gathering, and cadets and corpsmen squiring the local elite's daughters
around in their dress whites.[31]

Shortly after World War I ended and with the Panama Canal flourishing,
Woodrow Wilson finally approved the American Pacific Fleet that Teddy

Roosevelt had set in motion—thirty-two ships including the battleships *Mississippi* and *New Mexico*, the cruiser *Birmingham*, plus six destroyers. They visited Los Angeles and Long Beach in August 1919 for a huge extravaganza, before the ships dispersed to the ports of San Diego, Pearl Harbor, and Long Beach. Soon thereafter San Diego got two more bases, including a submarine base at Ballast Point and "an unusual concentration of the Navy's infant, cutting-edge technologies," in Mike Davis's words: "long-distance radio transmission, carrier aviation, and, later, undersea and amphibious warfare." San Diego dredged its harbor again in 1931 to create a turning basin for the largest ships; soon new aircraft carriers of the Saratoga and Lexington class resided there, and during the San Diego California–Pacific International Exposition in 1935 the "Harbor of the Sun" hosted the entire battle fleet: 48 battleships, cruisers, and carriers; 400 naval aircraft; 58,000 officers and sailors. If the navy faced West, however, San Diego was still facing East—or facing elsewhere: the 1935 exposition brought forth the anachronism that San Diego was the capital of Mexico and the Spanish Southwest. But now it was a navy town for life, wrapping itself in the flag and imparting a conservative, lily-white, even southern cast to the city (southerners dominated the navy), thus bringing it politically into step with its northern neighbor, Orange County—except that citrus never developed in a big way around San Diego (it had far less underground water than L.A. and lacked the clout to bring in aqueducts).[32]

The city fathers, like their Los Angeles and citrus belt counterparts, thought private business was king and big government was the enemy (not counting the navy). Certainly one businessman might as well have been a king, John D. Spreckles, son of sugar magnate Claus Spreckels whose Big-Four-class wealth was garnered through California sugar beets and Hawaiian sugarcane plantations (at one point he controlled half of all sugar production there). John Spreckles, aged thirty-four, arrived in San Diego in 1887 on his yacht *Lurline* and more or less bought it: he acquired the *San Diego Union*, the main city reservoir turned into his Mountain Water Company, and his San Diego Electric Railroad mined real estate wealth along its urban tracks. He singlehandedly paid 10 percent of all county taxes.[33] In other words, John Spreckles was Harrison Gray Otis and Henry Huntington combined, on only a marginally smaller scale.

If San Diego seems an unlikely victor in the West Coast naval competition, Los Angeles wasn't really interested in the navy, and even if San Francisco was, it had drawbacks: the weather wasn't as good and the San Francisco Bay sea currents were treacherous. Thirty percent of San Diego's annual payroll came from military spending by 1930, and the city fathers were over-joyed to have it. By Pearl Harbor San Diego had one of the two largest naval bases in the country, housing the Eleventh District Naval Headquarters, the destroyer fleet, the Naval Radio Station, and many other facilities.

San Diego could not compare to Los Angeles in aircraft production, but it still built many warplanes. In 1935 the Consolidated Aircraft Corporation brought 800 workers and $9 million in existing orders from Buffalo and proceeded to build a fleet of PBY Catalinas for the navy, "graceful flying boats capable of great speed and distance." Soon Consolidated employed 3,000 workers. The most elegant craft were the flying boats like the Catalina and the Coronado of Consolidated-Vultee; during the war this firm, later called Convair, came to employ 48,000 workers along the shoreline in San Diego, in a mile-long complex shrouded in camouflage.[34]

The war turned San Diego into a port that surveilled the entire North Pacific and a huge staging area for the Pacific campaigns, leading to enormous population growth; 190,000 newcomers arrived (not counting transient military personnel) to nearly double the 1940 population of 202,000. The city-scape was refashioned—"scraped, leveled and built"—to meet the demands of the armed forces (all of them, not just the navy). Engineers didn't have enough waterfront to work with, so they simply pushed it out a mile with landfill and constructed airports and parade grounds. North of the city, Camp Pendleton, named in honor of Joseph H. Pendleton (a marine general who died in the first months of the war), arose on the former grounds of the Rancho Santa Margarita y Las Flores, a 122,798-acre swatch of land running seventeen miles up the coast from Oceanside to San Clemente and inland for more than fifteen miles to the Santa Margarita Mountains. The govern-ment commandeered it in 1942, and 5,000 laborers worked round-the-clock for months in the spring to ready this training camp, which trained three combat-ready marine divisions before the war ended.

If Southern California was mostly navy and marine territory, the army had northern California. Camp Stoneman, for example, 40 miles northeast of San Francisco, was the key nerve center for the movement of troops out to the Pacific fighting. It processed a million soldiers during the war, with 30,000 servicemen there on any give day, residing in endless rows of olive-colored barracks. The Bay Area had the Presidio, the Twelfth District Naval Head-quarters, Hamilton Field Air Force Base, Sunnyvale Naval Air Base, and the Alameda Naval Air Station. Beale Air Force Base was built just outside Marysville in 1941, a town that had been home to many Chinese since the gold rush. Alameda Naval Air Station in the East Bay was hastily thrown together but soon became one of the largest airfields in the world, training thousands of airmen and shuttling them off to duty in the Pacific. California's capital, Sacramento, was an agricultural backwater until Mather, McClellan, and Travis air bases were built nearby. Edwards, Beale, McLellan, Travis, Vandenberg—these familiar air force bases are all in California, and Vandenberg, near Santa Maria, was the third largest air force base in the world, at 154 square miles. The air force operated out of a myriad of airbases in the West and the Pacific, locating new ones in the southern third of the country ("wherever you can grow cotton you can grow aviators," an officer said); almost every city south of the 41st parallel got new or expanded air bases.[35]

Rivers of People: Lateral and Upward Mobility during the War

Americans came running out of the Depression into wartime industries like '49ers—we can call them '41ers. Twenty-five million people, 21 percent of the total population, migrated to another state or county between 1940 and 1947. Some 8 million migrated to states west of the Mississippi, and the vast majority stayed (perhaps 1 million returned home after the war). Newcomers arrived from all over the country to work in the wartime plants (250,000 to San Francisco and the Bay Area alone, another 230,000 to Los Angeles County), including for the first time massive numbers of African-Americans (during the war some 279,000 blacks exited the South to work in the West; by 1950, 600,000 blacks lived in California). California gained 3 million new residents as a result of the war, Washington got 752,000, and Oregon 536,000—about equal to the total number of migrants to Oregon since the first settlers arrived.[36]

Richmond's population quadrupled in just three years, from 1940 to 1943. Its population explosion meant that "nobody knows anybody," *Fortune* reported; "Children go to overcrowded schools in two shifts. The jail is jammed. Streets crack under heavy traffic. . . . The twelve movie houses can't keep everyone amused, even though four of them are open all night." Blacks also gravitated to the East Bay, almost tripling Oakland's black population by 1944; Alameda had 249 blacks in 1940, 4,082 in 1944; Richmond had 270 in 1940, 5,673 in 1944 and well over double that number by 1950. Washington financed a million temporary housing units during the war, ranging from flimsy apartments in Richmond to the suburban-style homes of Los Alamos. In 1944 during particularly heavy troop transfers to the Pacific fighting, churches, synagogues, and high school gyms provided beds for the soldiers; the marines even used Bing Crosby's Del Mar racetrack to set up camp.[37]

"White Man in the Lead"

Southern blacks migrated on a South-North basis before Pearl Harbor: Texas or Arkansas or Mississippi blacks riding the City of New Orleans to Chicago or Detroit, blacks from Florida or Georgia heading to Harlem. When war factories opened on the West Coast, however, a massive exodus began along the western lines of the Southern Pacific and Santa Fe railroads or by car along Route 66, bringing nearly 340,000 African-Americans to Pacific industry, and the favored location was Los Angeles—more specifically, Bronzeville sitting cheek by jowl with Little Tokyo, a stone's throw from downtown. Restricted housing covenants led to huge overcrowding in Los Angeles, but Little Tokyo had "opened up," so to speak, when the evacuations began, and blacks moved in—by 1944 some 80,000 blacks lived where about 30,000 Japanese-Americans had been in 1941; multiple families crowded into several Buddhist temples. (When the concentration camps ended and the evacuees returned—many formers residents chose not to return, of course, going to other cities and Chicago in particular—a remarkably conflict-free negotiation under black, Japanese-American, and white leadership got the returnees back into their homes.) Los Angeles had an influx of 125,000 blacks during the war, but all the Pacific cities diversified: Portland had 1,800 blacks in 1940 and around 15,000 by 1945, the majority from Texas, Arkansas, and Oklahoma; Seattle had 3,789 in 1940 and nearly 30,000 by the end of the war.

Kevin Starr called Los Angeles "a Jim Crow town," and it certainly was in housing, hotels, restaurants, movies, and other services. But discrimination and housing restrictions were rife all along the Pacific Coast. Portland "rigidly excluded" blacks from public amusements and recreations, and most lived in segregated housing. Still, the jobs and the money were good and it wasn't the Jim Crow South, even if it often felt like it: a National Urban League official called Portland "the most prejudiced [city] in the west." In *The Quality of Hurt,* Chester Himes wrote: "Los Angeles hurt me racially as much as any city I have ever known, much more than any city I remember from the South. It was the lying hypocrisy that hurt me. Black people were treated much the same as they were in any industrial city of the South." But the prejudice was more wounding, because it was both virulent and unexpected. The hugely successful singer Nat King Cole, the first black to have his own weekly TV show, was continuously wounded by the discrimination he faced in L.A. Still, during the war blacks in Los Angeles were living the American dream (good job, house, school, car) like other Angelenos—but for them it was a far cry from a sharecropper's shack in Alabama. In the

1940s L.A. was also one of the first cities to employ blacks as policemen and firemen.[38]

Watts and nearby communities are still called "the ghetto," but if so it is a ghetto consisting of row upon row of single-family homes and a few scattered apartment buildings, with the warm California sun shining there like everywhere else. Most of Walter Mosely's wonderful novels are set in this period of the war and the postwar boom, when Central Avenue was a vibrant core of black life. The terrible events of 1965 have blotted all that out, as if constant oppression was the lot of minorities all along. It could just as easily be argued that African-Americans, in spite of daily indignities, lived better in Pacific Coast cities than anywhere else in America. Horace Cayton coauthored with St. Clair Drake the famous book *Black Metropolis* (1947); elsewhere Cayton listed the top ten cities for black living: Seattle (where Cayton was born), Los Angeles, and San Francisco were at the top, with Portland and San Diego excluded for other reasons. Black living wasn't easy anywhere in America, but for the black population to increase nearly ten times in Seattle between 1940 and 1950, and for around 50,000 in 1940 to explode to 600,000 in California in one decade without major social unrest (the Zoot Suit riots of 1943 excepted), the Pacific Coast was giving the country and the world a lesson in tolerance and diversity—just as San Francisco has done throughout its history.[39]

Horace Cayton was the grandson of a black U.S. senator from Mississippi who served after the Civil War and the son of a well-known newspaper publisher in Seattle. His family was well-off, living on Capitol Hill in one of the city's best neighborhoods and employing a Japanese servant; light skinned and well spoken, Cayton sometimes forgot he was black until a white reminded him. In his autobiography he looked back on a pleasant childhood with few racial problems. But when he took a summer job with black fishermen, he sampled the fiery loathing that most blacks harbor for whites at some point in their lives. One man hoped for an army of blacks to rise up, so he could join it and kill whites—all of them. Two older men, resigned to their place in segregated society, had a ritual greeting: "What's new?" said the first; "White man still in the lead," said the other.[40]

The Rise of an Arcadian Industry: Pacific Airpower

Airpower found a home on the Pacific Coast within a few years of the Wright brothers' 1903 flight, first of all because Southern California offered year-round flying (which, of course, wouldn't explain Boeing in Seattle). The industry and major firms like Boeing and Douglas got going during World War I, languished after it, got a boost in the mid-1930s with the fledgling emergence of commercial air travel, and then when the war began in Europe they found their long-term partner and lifeline: the Pentagon budget. The state subsidized aircraft and what later came to be called the aerospace industry from the late 1930s onward, and it still does. And as with Silicon Valley to the north, a major university provided the third part of this triangle: research, development, and the prospect of spinning off a private company for equally private enrichment. Aircraft production was clean, even antiseptic, and highly skilled—an early "high-tech" cutting-edge sector, where the assembly line almost resembled a huge, brightly lit indoor movie set.

Donald Douglas got MIT's first-ever degree in aeronautical engineering in 1914, and after service with the Aviation Section of the army in World War I, he came out to Los Angeles in 1920 with $1,000 in his pocket and launched an airplane company by renting out not the archetypal California garage, but the back room of a barbershop. Harry Chandler and Bill Henry of the *Los Angeles Times* helped him raise enough money to begin manufacturing planes, and later the U.S. Navy provided $40,000 for three aircraft capable of launching torpedoes. Soon Douglas was building a plane every week in a former movie studio on Wilshire Boulevard in Santa Monica. Together with Jack Northrop and T. Claude Ryan, Douglas developed Ryan's M-1 design, a monoplane that quickly became a favorite vehicle for long-distance mail hauling. Along came an improvement, the M-2, the first production monoplane in the United States. Charles Lindbergh then made some more modifications to this design—and the *Spirit of St. Louis* took off in 1927 from Long Island and landed at Paris's Orly field the next day: the first solo transatlantic flight. But Douglas's real coup was in developing the DC-3 in 1935, a twenty-one-passenger plane with two radial air-cooled engines rated at 1,000 horsepower each, enabling a cruising speed of 190 mph. It was the first commercially viable airliner, carrying 95 percent of civil air traffic in the late 1930s, and you've seen it—on the tarmac in the climactic scene of the film *Casablanca*. By that time some twenty-five aviation companies had made Southern California the epicenter of a brand new industry, worth more than $1 billion.[41]

If Donald Douglas started in a barber shop, Victor Loughead and his two half-brothers, Allen and Malcolm, started in the proverbial garage. They grew up in Santa Barbara and loved tinkering with bicycles and automobiles, which left them perfectly placed as teenagers to throw themselves into an infant industry like no other—in that human beings had never found a way to fly. More or less self-taught, they were quick studies: Victor published *Aero-*

plane Designing for Amateurs in 1909. The next year they learned to fly and built the "Model G," a thirty-foot contraption that weighed 2,000 pounds but was airworthy. Soon they brought in a twenty-one-year-old designer named John Northrop and together they constructed a cutting-edge plane, the F-1: "a ten-passenger flying boat with triple tail fins and a 74-foot wingspread." By 1918 the Loughead factory employed eighty-five people, and the navy gave it a contract to build the seaplane HS2L (designed by another air pioneer, Glenn Curtiss). The next year they changed their name to Lockheed and moved the factory to Burbank. The firm had many ups and downs until 1937, when the Army Air Force asked them to bid on a fighter plane, out of which came the famous P-38 Lightning, so useful in the war. Defense contracts enabled Lockheed to go from 1,200 employees to 53,000 just before Pearl Harbor, and then the firm expanded wildly during the war.[42]

Harry Chandler was the leading booster of airpower in Los Angeles, and a powerful one; he not only helped Donald Douglas get started but pulled off a bigger coup when he helped convince Robert A. Millikan to come out to Cal Tech in 1921. Douglas urged him to build airpower laboratory facilities, then completely lacking in Southern California; Millikan soon raised funds to establish the Guggenheim Aeronautical Laboratory of the California Institute of Technology (GALCIT, 1926), and then he won his biggest victory, perhaps, in getting pioneer astrophysicist Theodore von Kármán to relocate from Germany. Cal Tech opened a wind tunnel in 1929 that could test the behavior of plane configurations at up to 200 miles an hour and quickly became a leading center of aviation research. The next year von Kármán arrived; Millikan attracted him to Cal Tech with the prescient argument that Southern California would become the center of the air industry—and Cal Tech the pinnacle of aeronautics. Events proved him right, as the Los Angeles Chamber of Commerce quickly decided that airports were "growth poles," and "airmindedness" became yet another trope of Los Angeles boosters.[43]

A Hungarian who spoke English with a thick accent, von Kármán became famous for explaining the violent oscillations and wind sheer turbulence that brought down the Tacoma Narrows Bridge in November 1940, through his "vortex street"—which had direct relevance to flying. This was a mathematical analysis of how to get wind vortices to oscillate predictably and stably, instead of wildly. The problem with aircraft was the drag formed by the airstream failing to stick to the shape of the wing and breaking off behind it in its wake—in a turbulent series of rotations or vortices. Vortices occurred above, behind, and below the wing; von Kármán thought they would stabilize with a definite geometric arrangement of the vortices: when the vortices were staggered, like lampposts along both sides of the street, they would interact stably and smoothly. It was a fundamental discovery for American airpower. Cal Tech also pioneered a pattern of interaction between universities, corporations, and the federal government that would long characterize the California high-tech industrial scene. Millikan and von Kármán had a wide array of contacts in government and business, especially General Henry H. "Hap" Arnold of the air force. Perhaps their most influential innovation, as we will see, was the spinning off of state-sponsored academic research into corporate profit.

Donald Douglas provided expertise from his firm to the university, and got a just reward: von Kármán's wind tunnel experimentation was instrumental in crucial innovations to the design of one of the most reliable airplanes in history, the prototype DC-1 that led to the DC-2 and finally to regular production of the DC-3 (Douglas sold 803 DC-3s in the first two years of production). Soon von Kármán and Frank Malina, an associate, got going on rocket science, aided by a 1939 military contract to examine jet propulsion. During the war Cal Tech was the most important center for research on rockets, centered at the famed Jet Propulsion Laboratory, which von Kármán, Malina, and a young Chinese physicist named Tsien Hsüeh-shen organized; it would design the first American rockets to penetrate outer space and later become a critical arm of the space program. General Arnold also got von Kármán to head the Scientific Advisory Group for the air force, which, with help from Douglas Aircraft, turned into Project RAND in the summer of 1945 and subsequently the RAND Corporation in Santa Monica—early avatar of that now-ubiquitous thing, the think tank.[44]

Of course, Southern California was not the only place the air force loved: it loved Arizona, too, which also had perfect flying weather the year around, and it loved Boeing in rainy Seattle. During the war and after the Phoenix area got Luke Air Force Base, Williams Air Force Base, Falcon Field, and Thunderbird Field; after the war it helped that the leading Phoenix politician was Barry Goldwater, scion of a department store fortune but more importantly a big fan of airpower. Boeing had become permanently solvent through its invention of the long-range bomber in the mid 1930s, a four-engine prototype of the famous B-17 Flying Fortresses of World War II. Needless to say, the seed money came from the Army Air Corps, but the ideas came from Boeing engineer Claire Egtvedt; ultimately Boeing risked $275,000 without knowing if his design would work. The first design got off the ground successfully in 1935, and soon the Air Corps ordered thirteen of them. By then the industrial production of aircraft was both very new and very complicated.

Detroit assembly lines didn't work, instead you needed highly skilled workers arrayed in entirely unprecedented teams and work groups. Start-up costs also had become enormous, so entry into the industry was difficult. But with war on the horizon in 1939, Northrop and McDonnell Aircraft were both formed because the American government was buying and so were foreigners. The British ordered 200 military aircraft from Lockheed in 1938, for a total price of $25 million; Vultee in Glendale developed an attack bomber called the V-11 in 1936 and everyone came running: Turkey bought forty, Brazil bought twenty-six, and even Stalin ordered nine of them for $2 million. After Hitler's invasion of Poland, the government rapidly stepped up production: Douglas was already working three shifts a day, North American two shifts, and Lockheed—the largest firm with more than 10,000 employees—ran out of space and had to do some of its work outdoors.[45]

Still, in 1939 the aircraft industry ranked only forty-first in the country, with 64,000 workers and a total value of $280 million. Its lowly status ended abruptly on May 16, 1940, when Roosevelt amazed everyone by publicly calling for the production of 50,000 warplanes a year, more than the total of American aircraft built since the Wright brothers first flew in 1903. But by 1943 the United States had built 100,000 warplanes, and 1.3 million Americans now worked in the industry. Every able-bodied man and woman—and many not so able-bodied—flooded into the new plants: the halt (deaf workers were often the best), the blind (Lockheed pioneered in hiring many, so Seeing Eye dogs were everywhere), the lame (disabled veterans from World War I), "morticians and midgets, schoolboys and housewives" (so Lockheed described its workers), they all supplied their skills for three shifts a day, seven days a week. Boeing prospered mightily, too, but got its biggest wartime boost from George Schairer, an employee who was on the Scientific Advisory Group mission to Germany in March 1945 that examined German rocket and aircraft development. Schairer microfilmed German designs of swept-wing planes, then "rushed back to Seattle" to set in motion the XB-47, the first swept-wing American bomber, soon to be the B-47 and then the B-52—with eight jet engines under its swept-back wings, this air force workhorse had a sensuous beauty that Stanley Kubrick brilliantly exploited in *Dr. Strangelove.*[46]

War contracts made Southern California the leading aircraft manufacturing center in the country and Cal Tech the center of aeronautical research. The famous "Big Six" airplane companies (Douglas, Lockheed, Vultee, North American, Vega, and Northrop) were all located there, most of them along a coastal strip near the Los Angeles Airport. In 1940 Westchester, near the airport, had large fields of lima beans and a grand total of seventeen homes; its mushrooming development was unplanned during the war, a matter of emergency housing, yet a short few years later it was a pleasant community: "trim and neat and painfully, incredibly new." By 1948, 30,000 people lived there—mostly young, mostly workers in the skilled trades, with three-quarters of the men war veterans. Ninety percent of the residents owned their own homes or had mortgages.[47]

Southern California aircraft plants had industrial welfare systems like those identified with Henry Kaiser. Lockheed's many programs "made Southern California aviation seem like an industrial utopia," with a full range of social services. All the aircraft factories in Los Angeles County provided medical coverage and preventive health care, optometry and dental care, round-the-clock day care, psychological counseling, and food services capable of providing 60,000 meals a day. Lockheed was also a pioneer in hiring blacks, running free buses into black neighborhoods to pick up the workers, and later set up a new housing complex named for heavyweight champ Joe Louis; at a time when Northrop had no blacks in its working ranks and Douglas had 1,800, Lockheed employed 7,186.[48] Lockheed's critical contribution to American airpower, however, wasn't known for years because it was so secret: building jet planes that have been the envy of the world ever since.

The war also made clear to the nation and the world that scientific talent in California took a backseat to no one: Oppenheimer's direction of the Manhattan Project is the obvious example, but there were many others from Cal Tech, Berkeley, and Stanford. During the war Washington poured money into security-related science and technology all along the Pacific Coast. The Pentagon subvened the Jet Propulsion Laboratory in Pasadena, which not only studied rockets but produced them by the thousands for the war effort. The Scripps Institute of Oceanography in La Jolla proved invaluable to the navy through its work on ocean currents and ocean floor topography. Roosevelt created the Office of Scientific Research and Development in 1941 and got Vannevar Bush to run it. This office provided nearly $100 million in research contracts to western universities, but the government put much larger sums, well into the billions, into Manhattan Project facilities at Los Alamos and the plutonium factory at Hanford, Washington—building entirely new cities, not just reactors and bombs. Los Alamos materialized in 1943 on a remote 7,300-foot plateau across the Rio Grande from the Sangre de Cristo Mountains, a closed town of about 6,500 that was isolated enough to build atomic bombs in total secrecy but near enough to Albuquerque to transport in a myriad of equipment; the most expensive government project in history, it had the most impact on the world—and because of its remoteness and secrecy, the least impact on New Mexico. Likewise most people in Washington had no idea that eight reactors cooked plutonium night and day at Hanford.[49]

War Remakes the Pacific Coast

If Southern California was awash in defense contracts, the Bay Area, Seattle, and Portland weren't far behind—relatively speaking. Manufacturing employment and value-added had actually fallen by an amazing 50 percent in Seattle from 1919 to 1939, a result of the Depression hitting particularly harshly there, but even in the Roaring Twenties when Los Angeles was booming, Seattle grew by less than 50,000. There were more wage earners in Seattle in 1920 than in both Seattle and Tacoma by 1940, so war industry had a correspondingly dramatic impact. By late 1943 when war production peaked, defense employment stood at 385,000—greater than Seattle's entire population in 1940. The city ranked third in per capita war contracts, and eventually its orders totaled nearly $6 billion; manufacturing leaped forward by 265 per cent. (When the war began in 1939, the total value of all industry in Seattle was $70 million.)

Boeing had about 4,000 workers in 1939 and sales under $10 million a year, about 14 percent of total Seattle manufacturing. Then the Royal Air Force learned about the B-17 Flying Fortress, and 10,000 people were working at Boeing by Pearl Harbor. Like Southern California firms, Boeing got the capital from Washington for its costs and an additional fixed fee of profit, and then threw itself into a totally new endeavor—mass production. No one had mass produced aircraft before, but Boeing had a head start in manufacturing very large planes. It built giant enclosed fields to house dozens of B-17s or B-29s at a time and perfected new methods of rapid assembly—not an assembly line so much as a series of platforms and lifts enabling skilled workers and engineers to reach to the top of these huge bombers and into their innards, putting them together, testing them, painting them, swarming around them—the planes were stationary and the workers moved, unlike Ford's assembly line. The B-29 was "a revolutionary aircraft, the first intercontinental bomber" in Richard Rhodes's words; four 18-cylinder engines rated at 2,200 horsepower each lifted a bomb-loaded B-29 weighing 135,000 pounds into the air, propelled it to a top speed of 350 miles per hour, and kept it going for 4,000-mile missions. At the peak of production Boeing had 55,000 workers (nearly half of whom were women) and sold $600 million worth of warplanes; it was able to turn out one bomber every ninety minutes.

"5,000th B-17 Flying Fortress Rolls Out," 1942.
Copyright © Boeing.

Tens of thousands more worked at its factories in Everett, Renton, Belling-ham, Chehalis, and Aberdeen. Seattle accumulated $5.6 billion in war con-tracts, or nearly ten times the level of all Seattle manufacturing in 1939. When the war ended, the Washington economy did not tank, as many predicted; veterans and war workers bought cars, homes, and a new suburban life with their savings and their war-ballooned wages.[50]

Portland had about 200,000 residents in 1940, nearly 360,000 five years later, with about a third of them working in shipyards. Just to the north of the city was Vanport, an empty mudflat in 1940, which became "the world's largest war housing city" by 1943, with 40,000 people—most of them working in Kaiser shipyards. Women came pouring out of the house and into the factories, with 40,000 working in shipyards in Portland and nearby Van-couver, Washington. Henry Kaiser hired more tens of thousands to work in Portland shipyards, brought by the trainload from "back East." Brand new, high-tech aluminum factories in Tacoma and Spokane, using cheap hydro-electricity from the Grand Coulee and Bonneville dams, provided the base metal for Boeing fuselages.[51]

Electricity for a different industry, also requiring enormous amounts, went to the factories at Hanford, Washington—the secret plutonium capital of America, located downriver from the Grand Coulee Dam and the town of Wenatchee. With arms merchant DuPont in charge (its armaments contracts went back to the Revolutionary War, but at Hanford it took only a dollar of profit over costs to avoid the "Merchants of Death" label), specialists built eight water-cooled graphite reactors to cook plutonium in aluminum tubes; three chemical separation plants went up nearby to handle reprocessing— called "Queen Marys" because they were nearly as long as this passenger liner. Enrico Fermi supervised the loading of the reactors in September 1944, and early in 1945 Colonel Franklin T. Matthias hand-carried the first flask of weapons-grade plutonium to show a group from Los Alamos Laboratory. It didn't even weigh 100 grams, but it was just about the world's total supply. In subsequent months heavily guarded convoys of ambulances moved more and more plutonium to Los Alamos, over country highways and usually under cover of darkness. The plutonium core for the first bomb left Hanford for Los Alamos by car on July 11, and it exploded at Alamogordo five days later. (After the war Richland, near Hanford, was proud to call itself "Atomic City," with a high school football team called "Bombers" and a mushroom cloud for the school's emblem.)[52]

Conclusion: A Continental Behemoth

At the end of the war, American industry and weaponry was the best in the world, but it was a world with hardly any rivals left. The sole superpower, this continental behemoth now could dominate in any direction—the Atlantic, the Pacific, and North and South, where Canada and Latin America were essentially American dependencies—and it had no rivals. The British ran their empire from small islands, as had Japan; one empire was gone and the other was going. The Axis powers were in ashes. The Soviet Union was a continental power, but almost all its weight was concentrated west of Moscow, a region mostly demolished by the Nazis; it had suffered more grievously than any other country (27 million dead), and its massive land armies found their critical postwar purpose in maintaining domination in Eastern Europe. Stalin used to read books about the gold rush to figure out how Siberia and the Soviet Far East might be transformed on the American model. But as it happened, there was just one American model, a hegemony unlike any the world had ever seen emanating from a productive continental homeland, a compelling set of ideas (the Four Freedoms were the latest expression), a seductive lifestyle born in Southern California and channeled to the world by Hollywood, and an integrated industrial base from sea to sea.

Putting all war supply contracts for combat equipment and "other" together with wartime projects for industrial and military facilities, California led all other states in the West with $35 billion, Washington came next, while Oregon got a mere margin above $2 billion. No other western state was even close, except for Texas: it got nearly $8 billion in contracts and projects, helping manufacturing output to double between 1940 and 1950 and saving firms like Brown & Root from bankruptcy; with early contracts to build naval air stations, by the end of the war this company bought two surplus pipelines and set up Texas Eastern, later a *Fortune* 500 firm that operated much like Bechtel—building infrastructure at home and military bases abroad.[53] The following table shows the extraordinary leaps forward in manufacturing from 1939 to 1947, with California and Washington more than tripling their value-added figure, while Oregon's quadrupled.

Value-Added by Manufacture (in thousands of dollars)

	1939	1947
California:	1,122,545	3,994,981
Washington:	267,716	874,036
Oregon:	156,696	675,017[54]

In early 1945 industrial production in Los Angeles County exceeded the entire industrial value of Detroit before the war and stood second only to Detroit in total war production. More than 4,000 defense plants had sprung up, but the older textile industry had also grown remarkably, by 475 percent—supplying fabric for military uniforms being the major reason.[55] Everyone feared that industry would not last in California after the war ended, perhaps causing another depression, because so much of the work was war-related—and indeed by 1946 three out of four aircraft workers in Southern California were out of work. At the time automobiles and the continental network of trains remained the primary means of travel, and few understood the potential of the commercial air business. The aircraft companies were in the doldrums for years after 1945, but the Korean War instantly revived the industry, and after that war ended they quickly switched to civilian aircraft production, doing well with the Lockheed Constellation, the Douglas DC-7, and especially Boeing's 707.

Private industrial investment was also intensive during the war, around

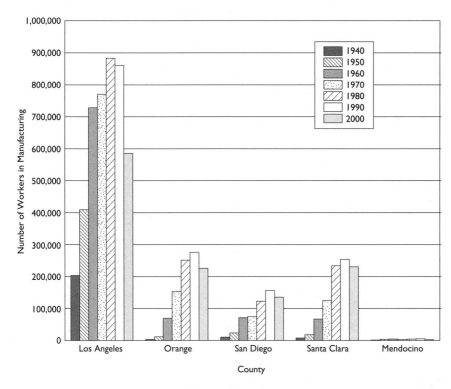

Manufacturing in five California counties, 1940–2000.
United States Census Bureau, California Department of Finance.

$400 million in toto, and these industries were also able to retool quickly once the conflict ended. Los Angeles had four auto factories producing 154,000 cars in 1941; they produced 650,000 in 1948. Kaiser also adapted quickly, moving into automobile production (Kaiser, Kaiser-Frazer, and the innovative Henry J compact car) and into home production on an industrial scale: he built 2,000 new homes on the Panorama Ranch between Van Nuys and San Fernando, about fifteen miles from Los Angeles. Kaiser Community Homes combined everything he had learned about industry and people: he charged $4,000 to $5,000 with a down payment of $150, and he put new amenities into each home: garages, washing machines, dishwashers, backyards for barbecues, with the GI Bill being the new Kaiser connection to the federal government. Kaiser was, of course, a piker when it came to mass-produced housing—in Lakewood, near Long Beach, it was eight homes to an acre, 1,100 square feet per home, $7,575 for two bedrooms, $8,525 for three, and on Palm Sunday 1950, 25,000 people lined up to buy one.[56]

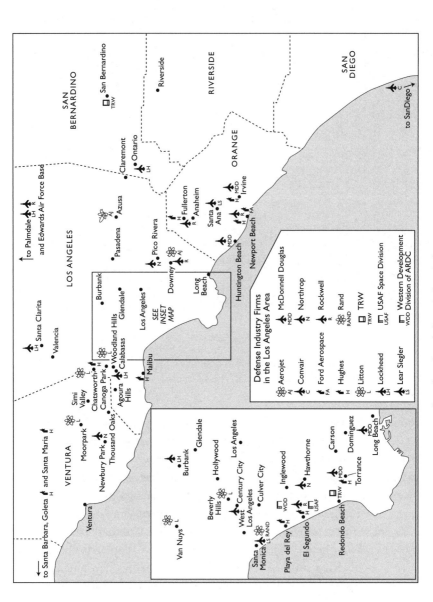

Los Angeles: defense industry firms, 1991.

Map by Bill Nelson, based on figure in Markusen, Campbell, Hall, and Dietrick (1991), 85.

Courtesy of Ann Markusen.

Among American historians Gerald D. Nash stands out for his work on the industrial transformation of the West in the 1940s, and like any important historian he has his detractors; the basic issue is whether World War II was a revolutionary transformation of California, like the gold rush, or just a large but still incremental upsurge in industry. Roger Lotchin argued that New York created more jobs during the war than Los Angeles had in toto when the war ended, and Chicago nearly did as well; of course extraordinary changes took place in the West, he wrote, but rapid transformation is the norm in California.[57] He is right on both counts, but the first point is spurious because New York and Chicago were industrial cities for a century, and new wartime jobs have to be registered against the lost jobs of the Depression, whereas Los Angeles and other Pacific Coast cities barely had factory labor and got industrialized for the first time during the war, usually with the latest equipment and mostly in high-tech manufactures (even Kaiser's shipyards were high-tech, with entirely new methods of prefabrication), a base from which a fully sustained transformation would unfold continuously (after some remarkably minor regress and disruption in the two or three years after the war ended).

Lotchin's second point is valid, at least in California: the war brought abrupt change to a state that had thrived on it for a century. But that is what I have been arguing all along. What is missed in this criticism is (1) the breathtaking completion of a national market across the continent with multiple nodes of Pacific industry, commerce, and finance, breaking any dependency that the West might previously have had on eastern industry and capital; (2) the opening of entirely new possibilities for intensive development in the Pacific states and linking enterprises on both sides of the great ocean; (3) the telescoping into four years of what would ordinarily have taken a quarter-century or more to achieve; (4) the colossal expansion of American military power in the Pacific, the West, and especially along the coast—army, navy, marines, air force, but also jets, rockets, and atomic energy; and (5) the unprecedented role that the central state played in stimulating, organizing, and financing one industry after another—which marks a complete break with any previous episode of industrialization in American history.

Nash's emphasis is on social change, but from the standpoint of political economy (or a Gerschenkron or a Schumpeter), the 1940s constituted an astonishing departure in American history. Not only was the West industrialized overnight and fitted out with world-class high-tech firms (like Lockheed and Boeing), state-of-the art laboratories and research centers (like the Cal Tech labs or Los Alamos), and a huge new flow of human capital (millions of men and women with factory skills, and later, millions of veterans with college educations, thanks to the GI Bill), but the war created for the first time in world history a continental nation with a combined, integral industrial economy from the Atlantic to the Pacific, an "organic whole" that emerged from the war unscathed, now constituting fully 50 percent of global industrial production. And for the first time in American history the Pacific states and much of the West were independent: in oil, steel, factories, and investment capital. Things had not shifted out of plumb: instead the plumb suspended between the Atlantic and the Pacific had disappeared, as the United States now had three formidable industrial bases in the Northeast, the Midwest and the Pacific.

CHAPTER THIRTEEN

Postwar California and the Rise of Western Republicanism

For the first time in its history California now feels that it is definitely a part of
that fantastic world around the rim of the Pacific . . . the great world of the future.
—CAREY McWILLIAMS

Los Angeles had reached a level of development in 50 years that took
New York 175 years to accomplish, Carey McWilliams wrote, as
the war "completely revolutionized the economy of California" and
brought to a conclusion the "insular phase" of the state's development—the
sense of detachment from the continent and the Pacific Ocean. He went on to
link all this to the mantras of the 1980s: the "fantastic world" around the
Pacific Rim. But he said it in 1946 (and he was right).[1] California had several
insular phases in its history: its eruption out of the ocean, the millennia of
cat's-paw imprints made by Native Americans, a salutary 350 years of "island"
isolation after the conquest of the New World, and a century of nonindustrial,
even pastoral, existence as the pot of gold at the end of a very lengthy train
ride. World War II ended all of that.

The Pacific states were now fully integrated with the national market and
industrial complex, tens of millions of new migrants arrived to transform
one town after another into small cities or big suburbs, and rapid economic
growth propelled California toward its current position—a powerhouse that
would rank second only to Germany if it were in Europe. Aviation, aerospace,
aluminum, electricity, industrial agriculture, Hollywood, television, the universities—all these were cutting edge and expanding dramatically. They were
all in place by 1950, and they have all moved and developed within existing
tracks since that time. To put it another way, the West Coast that we see today
would have been unimaginable in 1940 but quite predictable by 1950. The
dramatic wartime industrial and military transformations in the Pacific states,
and especially California, created an infrastructure that enabled, shaped, and
constrained subsequent development. This all amounted to a tectonic shift
that remade the United States and its relationship to the world.

The reader has been asked to think about various aspects of western and Pacific development from the 1840s through World War II. The next period of Pacific history, however, hurries up to the present and is more or less familiar to most Americans. After 1945 the Pacific states inhabited a structure of action that unfolded along the lines of a predictable logic. Instead of a host of new-new things, we mostly have elaborations of existing tendencies and potentials. California's suburban lifestyle plastered the state and increasingly the nation, but it had been invented in the 1920s, just as Californians had taken Ford's utilitarian automobile and turned it into a personal statement. Water and power ran along grooves established in the first half of the century. Great firms like Lockheed and Boeing burst forth in the 1940s, which only makes their prominence today all the more predictable. California's university system expanded beyond imagination, but the same three schools still dominate it: Berkeley, Stanford, and Cal Tech. Agribusiness went from strength to strength—just as it had before the Depression. (By the 1960s California produced *all* the artichokes, figs, almonds, nectarines, and olives in the country; nearly all the lemons, dates, and walnuts; and a third of the nation's fruit. It was also first in beef cattle, turkeys, tomatoes, and beet sugar, second in cotton, third in milk.)[2] The vast garden of oranges and lemons mostly disappeared, however, an erasure that was a direct consequence of the industrial and populations boom during the war. Hollywood has retained all of its national and global dominance, but it is no more dominant today than it was in the 1950s, or perhaps even the 1920s. What passed, if glacially, was the white dominance that had marked the Pacific states for the previous century.

The war also brought smog, ugly subdivisions, metastasizing traffic, and a variety of other daily aggravations, but California (and all the western states) remained vastly underpopulated, a virgin land still—a marvelous comparative advantage owing to the Pacific Coast's "late" arrival to the modern world. Simone de Beauvoir was one of many European intellectuals to visit or live in California in the 1940s and come away disconcerted—and impressed. More adventuresome than her New York intellectual friends (none of whom "had ever set foot in California"), she motored along the Pacific coast in 1947 and later wrote: "Despite its sprawling cities, its factories, its mechanized civilization, this country remains the most unspoiled in the world. Man with all his works is a new and sporadic phenomenon here, whose laborious efforts merely scratch the surface of the earth's crust." (About 9 million people lived in California then; today there are 35 million.) She also noted California's "economic autonomy" (although not how recent it was) and found a "heart-stopping" difference between Los Angeles and the city by the bay: San Francisco was "a city that hasn't just capriciously risen from the ground but has been built and whose architecture is part of a great natural design."[3] A multitude of Americans continued to seek these open spaces, and California just kept on adding people, growing at many times the national rate.

The number of migrants "voting with their wheels" during and after the war is simply staggering. California grew from 6,907,000 in 1940 to 10,586,000 in 1950 and nearly doubled again by 1962, when for the first time it topped New York as the most populous state. Obvious to any attentive demographer, this growth still came as a stunning surprise to specialists "back East."[4] During the 1950s the country's population increased by 26 percent; Los Angeles grew by 54 percent, San Diego by 86 percent, Sacramento by 81 percent, and San Jose by a whopping 121 percent. Meanwhile San Francisco remained below the national average growth of 26 percent, Portland was well below it (17 percent), and Seattle was only a bit above it, fueled mainly by Boeing which reached a peak of employment in 1958 at 73,000 (before B-52 bomber production got sent to Wichita for defense "dispersal"). Lakewood, the sprawling tract of 17,500 homes and a 250-acre shopping mall that pictured the American future, opened next to the McDonnell Douglas plant built during World War II; the first homes got gobbled up just as NSC-68 went to Truman for his signature in April 1950. Bigger in scale even than Levittown on Long Island, it was the combined product of state-funded mortgages through the GI Bill, jobs created by vast new increases in defense spending, and multitudes of incoming migrants. From the era of citrus, lima beans, and tent revivals circa 1941, with a mere 114,000 people, Orange County grew almost 1,000 percent by 1970 and then simply continued, adding another million residents between 1970 and 1990. It's never really had a city, but five urban-suburban agglomerations dominate it: with around 100,000 people each in 1970, they have grown rapidly: Anaheim (332,361 in 2003), Santa Ana (342,510), Garden Grove (167,029), Huntington Beach (194,248), plus the Irvine ranch, which became the planned community of Irvine, with more than 100,000 residents today. All over Southern California real estate developers rolled up the orange groves like a tattered and worn carpet, but this protean county dwarfed any other comparison.[5]

Only one new cutting-edge industry emerged in the postwar period with no clear relationship to federal spending: television was invented in San Francisco in the 1920s but did not catch on until after the war—and it caught on first in Los Angeles. It grew on Hollywood's shoulders, but it grew much too fast, terrifying the industry. With three decades of movie industry experience behind it, Los Angeles was poised to capture this new industry, but at

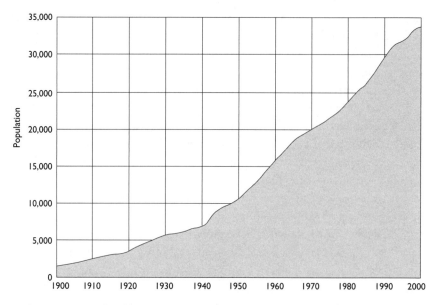

California population, 1900–2000 (in thousands).
United States Census Bureau, California Department of Finance.

the potential price of destroying Hollywood cinema. There were 6,500 television sets in 1945, more than a million in 1948, more than 11 million by 1950—
and then the industry quickly expanded over the next decade to inhabit
almost every home. Movie attendance dropped from 80 million a week in
1946 (only a bit higher than the 1929 figure) to 60 million in 1950 and kept
dropping. While New York pioneered first-rate drama (*Playhouse 90*), highbrow talk shows (Edward R. Murrow), cultural programming (*Omnibus*) and
live, intelligent comedy (*The Sid Caesar Show*), Los Angeles plastered the
market with low-brow game shows, sitcoms, westerns (*Gunsmoke*), family
soap operas (*The Adventures of Ozzie and Harriet*) and kiddy shows (*Howdy
Doody*), many of them produced in Hollywood studios with classic "B-
movie" haste and mediocrity.

The mythic West may have disappeared, but it had a rapid recrudescence
on TV. By the late 1950s Hollywood turned out a western every week and
fully thirty prime-time TV shows were westerns, including eight of the ten
most popular. Pollsters found that Hollywood cowboy and war films made
many Americans believe that John Wayne really drove longhorns and fought
at Iwo Jima, that Frank Sinatra got strafed at Pearl Harbor, and that Humphrey Bogart was a reluctant resistance fighter. Ronald Reagan flourished in

this milieu, selling 20 Mule-Team Borax and General Electric, helping to build and solidify a "conservative cultural hegemony."[6] That the vintage New York programming now seems lost in the Pleistocene era of television merely underlines the massive victory that Los Angeles won. And now the mythic West entered everyone's living room, every evening.

The one economic phenomenon that would amaze a Californian in 1950 is Silicon Valley, which merits a separate chapter. But even the valley had its origins in the government-business-university nexus, and its most cherished conceit—the brilliant inventor puttering around his garage—has its counterpart in Jack Parsons's "suicide squad" and Lockheed's Skunk Works (see below). The one political phenomenon that would flabbergast a Carey McWilliams was a minority fundamentalist and conservative tendency, homegrown in the orange groves, that grew systematically until 1980, when it became a major national movement. Two other postwar tendencies are noteworthy and underappreciated: first, the incalculable importance of federal spending in the Pacific states, and second, the rise of western Republican leaders. If the state sponsored great waterworks in the 1930s and a worldbeating military machine in the 1940s, both forces shaped the postwar Pacific —but defense dollars far more than the empire of water. The early 1950s also saw the transformation of the historic foreign policy stance of the Republican Party and the rise of western politicians who could win national office. As westerners transformed this party, they slowly transformed the country as a whole, and its relationship to the world.

The Transformative Korean War

The industrial explosion during World War II prompted widespread fears of a depression after it ended: what was to be done with the millions of workers and newcomers? Who would buy all the goods and services that the war had geared up? All through the Pacific states, V-J Day signified a great victory and the sound of factory gates closing. In 1943, 65,000 people, 40 percent of them women, worked for Convair. Within a month of Hirohito's capitulation, it had 8,500 workers. The aircraft industry, so important to Southern California and Seattle, was particularly threatened because it got so big during the war but lacked a clear purpose after it, with commercial air travel still in its infancy. "In 1949 the Los Angeles export economy was probably at its nadir," Jane Jacobs wrote, "perhaps lower than at any time since the Great Depression." Harry Truman presided over a vast demobilization of the military and the wartime military-industrial complex. In 1945 the navy, favored under

Roosevelt for four terms, had 3.4 million officers and men and nearly 1,000 ships of all kinds; fifteen months later it had 491,663 men and just over 300 ships.[7] It was as if the country were returning to the normalcy of a small standing army and hemispheric isolation. The Truman Doctrine and the Marshall Plan ended that idle dream in 1947, but Truman and his advisors still did not have the money to fund a far-flung defense effort. Until 1950 the containment doctrine approximated what its author, George F. Kennan, wanted it to be: a limited, focused, sober effort relying mostly on diplomatic and economic measures to revive Western European and Japanese industry and keep the Russians at bay. The defense budget was steady-state in the late 1940s, hovering around $13 billion.

A young and unknown man named Kim Il Sung ended all that by sending several infantry divisions plunging across the 38th parallel in June 1950, a line drawn by Dean Rusk and a colleague the day after Nagasaki was obliterated. They heedlessly divided a country that had been united for more than a millennium, but few people outside Korea cared about that and barely a single American, in the CIA or anywhere else, knew much about General Kim. All through the 1930s he had led guerrillas in Manchuria, fighting against troops led by General Tōjō Hideki among others, but this was a remote and unknown pocket of the struggle against Japanese imperialism. Likewise Kim had never been farther west than Moscow and could not have known that his attack would solve a huge problem for Dean Acheson, Truman's secretary of state: how to get Congress to fund NSC-68, which called for a tripling of defense expenditures. The Korean War was a blind clash of armies ignorant of each other, fighting for murky and incommensurable goals, but it set the United States on a path of permanent armament. Six months into the war authorized defense spending had gone from $13 billion to $54 billion (over $650 billion in current dollars), the highest figure during the entire cold war. "Korea came along and saved us" was Acheson's epitaph for this war. A conflict that remains mostly forgotten or unknown in the United States, embodying an obscure Korean struggle that began in the 1930s and continues today, it was not the cause but the occasion for a new relationship between America and the world.[8]

California's defense industries hardly knew that Kim Il Sung would come along and save them either, but he inadvertently rescued a bunch of big-ticket projects in Southern California: "strategic bombers, supercarriers, and . . . a previously cancelled Convair contract to develop an intercontinental rocket for the Air Force," in Mike Davis's words. By 1952 the aircraft industry was booming again. Los Angeles County had 160,000 people employed in

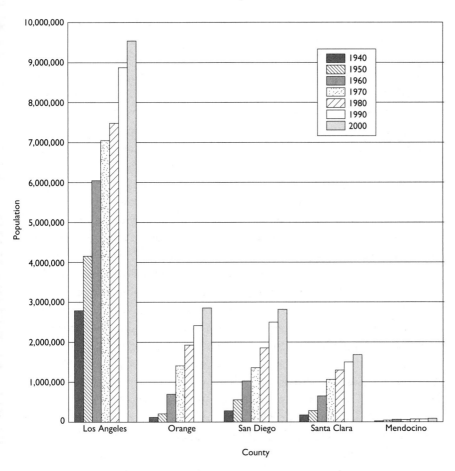

Population change in five California counties, 1940–2000.
United States Census Bureau, California Department of Finance.

aircraft production, compared to 31,000 in Hollywood. In the mid-fifties defense and aerospace accounted directly or indirectly for 55 percent of employment in the county, and almost as much in San Diego (where nearly 80 percent of all manufacturing was related to national defense). "Airmindedness" was again a slogan: planes migrated through "an ocean of air" in every direction, and Los Angeles sat at the center.[9] Center of what? Whatever you might come up with: the coast, the nation, the continent, the Pacific Rim, the Orient, the world. California was always the land of classic high-tech, "late" industries, but airpower had myriad spinoffs and forward linkages to commercial aviation (just getting off the ground in the 1950s), rocketry, satellites, electronics and electronic warfare, light metal production (aluminum, magnesium), computer software, and ultimately the Silicon Valley boom of the 1990s. By the 1970s fully 10,000 Southern California factories serviced the aerospace industry, suggesting that aerospace is something of a misnomer: many firms got into every kind of civic and social problem, from transportation systems (North American) to information systems (Lockheed), waste management (Aerojet General), air pollution, health care, and crime (TRW). The prototype for this is of course the RAND Corporation, the think tank set up by the air force in Santa Monica that studies anything and everything, from war gaming to school desegregation to urban housing.[10]

Since 1950 the Pacific states and the Southwest have consistently outstripped the rest of the country in defense contracts, including New York and New England, the only other seriously competing region. During World War II and Korea, California ranked third in prime contracts after New York and Michigan, but by 1958 it was first, with 21.4 percent of all contracts; New York had 11.6 percent, but when Texas (6.9 percent) and Washington (5.8 percent) are added, the Pacific states and Texas had more than a third of all prime contracts. They still had 32 percent in 1977, until the Reagan buildup directed some spending to Connecticut (5.7 percent) and Massachusetts (5.1 percent); still, in per capita terms the Pacific states got more than three times the national average. Both coasts get the lion's share of all defense dollars, as if the Pentagon had a spending pattern that mimicked its Atlantic and Pacific strategies. California got $5.8 billion in defense contracts in 1963 and $26 billion two decades later; Texas got $1.2 billion in 1963 and $8.2 billion two decades later; Washington went from $1 billion to nearly $4 billion; only bucolic Oregon dropped off the map, with a mere $181 million in 1983. During the years of apparent American decline from 1972 to 1986, manufacturing jobs fell by 28 percent in Illinois, 27 percent in Pennsylvania, and 18 percent in Ohio; they expanded by 34 percent in California, 35 percent in Washington, and 30 percent in Texas, helped along by defense spending. In research and development California got an amazing 41 percent of all contracts issued between the Cuban Missile Crisis and the Reagan buildup, not a minor matter since more than two-thirds of American research and development (R & D) is subsidized by the government, thus perpetuating "the conditions of a youthful, innovative industry" because costs and market competition are much less important than developing the latest technologies, which of course means small-volume production.[11]

In short, since 1941 the federal government has never stopped subsidizing and stimulating the high-tech industries of the Pacific Coast. They seem to be everywhere, from the epicenter of Silicon Valley to Berkeley and Livermore Laboratory, down through "Aerospace Alley" ("the greatest concentration of ultra-high-tech weapon-making capacity in the world") stretching from the site of the original World War II aircraft firms near Los Angeles Airport south through Inglewood, Torrance, Long Beach, and into Orange County—great firms like Lockheed, TRW, Hughes, McDonnell Douglas, and Rockwell powered a continuous military-industrial complex from the Korean War down to the end of the cold war (and Lockheed Martin remained the world's largest arms manufacturer in 2002).[12]

The war with Japan and the revolutions in China, Korea, and Vietnam that followed it muted West Coast perceptions of the China market and Pacific trade for a generation. After the onset of export-led development in Japan, South Korea, and Taiwan, however, politicians and businessmen dusted off the discourse that began in the days of Manifest Destiny a century earlier: "The center for economic and cultural activity used to be Europe," a San Diego banker and advisor to Governor Jerry Brown announced in 1976, "but now the center of gravity is changing. You have masses of people in China; the industrial power of Japan. There are new markets, powerful nations there." Jerry Brown went him one better: even the sun, he thought, was now rising in the west (economically speaking). Meanwhile the oracular governor made a virtue of his eccentricities by visiting a Zen monastery during a trip to Japan in 1977, proclaiming himself enthralled with Japanese culture and industrial prowess; his principal trade advisor, Dick King, said he wanted to sign California up with other Pacific "nations" in a new, Japan-led Co-Prosperity Sphere.[13] By 1980 two-thirds of California's exports went to Asian destinations, and American trade with Asia eclipsed that with Europe. But that was just a beginning; today East Asian and Pacific nations, and especially China and the United States, are the prime movers of the world economy.

Still, this was a predictable follow-on to the wartime transformations on the West Coast. Equally predictable and obvious on the face of it, but rarely given its due, was the materialization of national leaders out of the West. Entirely unexpected, however, was the emergence—in the midst of the postwar boom, with the orange groves fading into memory—of a new Republicanism and a conservative American creed that eventually created a "red state" coalition that hoped to dominate the early decades of the twenty-first century.

The Rise of Western Republicanism

Richard Milhous Nixon was the first western Republican to become a national leader and to bridge the differences between eastern and western Republicanism. He was born, raised, educated, and buried in Orange County, under the "haze of sun leaf-sieved into lemons on Leffingwell's ranch, oranges on the Murphy ranch, and—between the two . . . the Nixon grocery store" (in Garry Wills's words).[14] From the pinched Protestant lower middle class (in his case pinched Quaker shopkeepers), he came up on his own: a scholarship at Whittier College, law school at Duke, and no wealth beyond his (substantial) poker winnings in the navy. Some Orange County millionaires picked him to run against Jerry Voorhis in 1946 (a New Deal liberal and the very model for *Mr. Smith Goes to Washington*), and Nixon won; two years later he became a national figure in the investigation of Alger Hiss, and then defeated Helen Gahagan Douglas for an open Senate seat in 1950 to become Eisenhower's choice for vice president at the 1952 convention. A Connecticut Yankee like George H. W. Bush in H. L. Hunt's court was clearly an imposter, but a Nixon who could bring in the enormous electoral clout of California was something else. (The Bush dynasty, of course, had something Nixon never had—and never would have: central standing in the eastern wing of the party and its epicenters, Wall Street, Yale, and Greenwich.)

Nixon was young and ambitious just when the Republicans deployed an ideological bugaboo to hide their basic nature as the party of business: anticommunism. This was nothing new, of course; Republicans assailed Roosevelt throughout the Depression as a socialist or crypto-communist, and a conservative publication like the *National Republic* (neither the *National Review* nor the *New Republic*), founded in 1928 on principles of anticommunism and unrestrained American nationalism, illustrated this. What was new was the vast power of the Soviet Union, ostensibly exercised from Murmansk to Tirana and from Berlin to Beijing. Furthermore, in the 1930s the United States was not the Hartzian "born free" country of its dreams. The Depression created a strong Left and sharp class conflict, and labor conquered the open shop almost everywhere except the South—and even in Los Angeles. The full employment and unprecedented prosperity of the 1940s left labor much less militant than in the 1930s, however, and cut the slats out from under one progressive party or movement after another. Nixon thus rose up in 1948, in the inquisition of Alger Hiss, to slay a dragon that was already faltering—which made his task all the easier. More than anyone else, including Joe McCarthy, Nixon showed how to climb to power by clubbing the American Left and its serial "vanishing moments."

Jerry Voorhis was a sublime individual who represented a fading politics: the genteel, orange-grove-shaded, high-minded progressivism of Santa Barbara, Palo Alto, and Pasadena. He had also challenged big business (as every liberal activist did in the 1930s), especially the oil firms who enjoyed a free field in California for their exploitation of nature's inheritance. Richard Nixon was set in motion in 1946 by the same people whom Voorhis attacked—oil men, insurance bigwigs, bankers. Nixon charged Voorhis with a "Socialistic and Communistic" voting record in Congress, and in the days before the election voters got anonymous phone calls: "Did you know that Jerry Voorhis is a Communist?" In this way Nixon defeated one of the most popular politicians in California, who never knew what hit him; a year later he was still reeling from Nixon's campaign blitzkrieg.[15]

Helen Gahagan Douglas combined everything that the right wing hated about Hollywood: She was a stunning beauty. She was well born. She was rich. She was cultured and highly intelligent. She was articulate and effective, with patrician carriage and voice. She was liberal. At her hillside home on Senalda Road above the Hollywood Bowl, Los Angeles spreading out below, she lived a lifestyle like Evelyn Mulwray in *Chinatown*—cooks, servants, swimming pool, two Cadillacs. This formidable woman frightened men: or at least she scared Prescott Bush, grandfather of George W., who in a moment of singular candor admitted that he was "afraid of women who are pithy and sharp and sarcastic at times." Ms. Douglas made the mistake of caring about people less fortunate than herself; a principled liberal and early feminist, her role model was Eleanor Roosevelt. She won her congressional seat in 1944 by renting an apartment in South Central L.A. so she could represent blacks, Hispanics, Little Tokyo, Chinatown, poor people in slums. She was the first white congressperson to hire a black secretary. The obvious conclusion: she must be a Red, a "pink lady," an uppity woman who needed a real man "to slap her around a bit" (according to the leading political writer of the *Los Angeles Times*).[16]

Douglas had a permanent lock on her congressional seat, but in 1950 she chose to run for the Senate: so did Nixon. His campaign relied on Murray Chotiner, a ruthless but effective political operative; Herb Klein, a reporter; John Erlichman, a recent graduate of UCLA; and H. R. "Bob" Haldeman, heir to a substantial fortune. Behind Nixon stood a full panoply of Southern California wealth. A "Committee of Twenty" businessmen created a secret political fund for his use; a river of oil money sloshed into his campaign, since Douglas had opposed bills favoring big oil; Rexall Drug president Justin Dart (later a big backer of Ronald Reagan) also funded his campaign, as did Dean Witter (stockbroker), W. W. Crocker (banker), Harry Haldeman (millionaire car dealer), Robert Di Georgio (from California's "fruit king" family), and Hollywood mogul Louis B. Mayer. The oil barons of the Texas right wing also kicked into the campaign—H. L. Hunt, Hugh Roy Cullen, Clint Murchison.

Nixon toured up and down the state in a yellow 1949 Mercury station wagon (a "woody") and his campaign brought to bear every political smear yet invented, plus some new ones. Chotiner cribbed and cut Douglas's public statements to put slanders in her mouth and scripted editorials against her for the use of a host of newspapers: Helen Gahagan Douglas was plotting to overthrow the government. She was responsible for the war in Korea. She wanted to give away atomic secrets. She liked Negroes too much. She was pink, "Red hot," procommunist, maybe a communist ("Don't vote the Red ticket! Vote the red, white and blue ticket!"). On the eve of the election, the anonymous phone calls came again: "Did you know Douglas is a Communist?" It was a savage, vicious political campaign but it worked: Nixon won an overwhelming victory—nearly 60 percent of the vote to her 40 percent. What he lost was the possibility that any future opponent would ever respect him. A few days after his victory Nixon was dining at columnist Joseph Alsop's home: in walked Averell Harriman, who had campaigned for Douglas: "I will not break bread with that man," he said, and walked out the door.[17] All this proved to be a grand success throughout his career and a gift to many other Republican candidates, until he immolated himself in the Watergate scandal.

Apart from Joe McCarthy, no politician was more excoriated in the liberal press and the liberal establishment. The great cartoonist Herblock spilled lots of black ink sketching in the bucket of mud Nixon swung around, and his swarthy five o'clock shadow (merely one of the shadows that famously undid him in the first televised presidential debates in the 1960 campaign). John F. Kennedy was the very embodiment of the genteel tradition (never mind that he was an Irish Catholic)—suave, handsome, rich, slim, athletic, a Harvard degree, an intelligent, articulate, and humorous politician whom the camera loved—and the TV camera was now the dominant media force in American politics. So it is hard to remember that Nixon nearly won the election. Afterward he retreated to California, ran for governor in 1962 and lost, and then announced his political obituary—the liberal press "won't have Nixon to kick around anymore." But of course Nixon made another of his patented comebacks, and so they got to kick him around for at least another decade.

Nixon's critical step was to reverse the enormous population movement to California and migrate instead to New York. There in the mid-1960s he cultivated Wall Street contacts, the Council on Foreign Relations, the Atlantic Council, and a host of other Atlanticist outlets, and made peace with Nelson Rockefeller and many others in the eastern wing of the party. Nixon polished his internationalist credentials by drawing close to Harvard's Henry Kissinger, Rockefeller's key foreign policy advisor. Nixon turned his back on

Orange County fantasies about the American role in the world (which he never believed in the first place) and instead told Kissinger that he wanted to open up Communist China. This stunning démarche has now become a cliché for politicians changing their color ("Nixon goes to China"), but the records of the National Security Council in the 1950s show that Nixon had an excellent foreign policy mind. Council meetings went on for hours, and many of Nixon's later policies are prefigured in his astute comments, including bringing China out of its isolation.[18]

A Critical Election

If the opening to China reorganized the Pacific, with consequences still unfolding before our eyes, Nixon also helped to change his political party and its relationship to the world at large. The early postwar period was transformative not just of the American state and its relation to the world, but of partisan politics in the United States. The principled fiscal conservatism of the Taft wing of the Republican Party gave way to an uneasy coalition between eastern Republicans (e.g., the Dulles brothers and Nelson Rockefeller) and a newly rising western Republicanism (Nixon, Goldwater, Reagan) that had a large hole in its fiscal theory, caused by immense defense spending that founded one western industry after another. In the 1950s and 1960s the eastern wing was dominant, in part because it came together in the middle of the political spectrum with internationalist Democrats. But the subsequent rise of western Republicanism is inexplicable apart from the history of American national security since 1941 and the deluge of federal spending that it brought.

Nixon demonstrated twice that a California politician could win the presidency, but 1952 was more important than his victories in 1968 or 1972. Eisenhower and Nixon were *both* clearly of the West: Eisenhower, born in Denison, Texas (oil country) and reared in the railhead junction at the end of the Chisholm Trail, Abilene; Nixon, born in a small town in the northeast corner of Orange County (Yorba Linda). The 1952 election was not about splits between the eastern and western wings of the party, of course; Eisenhower might well have run as a Democrat, and anyway Republicans were ready for anybody but a pale, ineffective, even effete easterner like Thomas Dewey (who had lost in 1944 and 1948). What was important about 1952 is what evaporated then, never to return: Taftism in the Midwest and elsewhere, combining westward-leaning, nationalist, and isolationist constituencies with a principled position on federal spending, *including* a limited defense budget. Spending had quadrupled under Truman and was the fuel for a huge standing army, a national security state, and a massive military-industrial complex. At $50 billion (the 1952 figure), defense was over 50 percent of the federal budget; meanwhile the entire federal expenditure from 1787 to 1917 had been a bit under $30 billion.[19] Senator Robert A. Taft had 500 delegates locked up by the time he got to the Conrad Hilton Hotel in Chicago, but a well-oiled Eisenhower campaign assured that he got no more: Ike took 595 delegates to Taft's 500 before states started switching to give Eisenhower a landslide.[20] Taft was dominant through the middle of the continent but fatally weak on the coasts.

Taft was primarily a conservative champion of small and medium business and an opponent of federal spending and regulation (although he supported federal education, housing and health programs). Highly intelligent and respected for his integrity, he was never terribly interested in foreign affairs (like most of his countrymen) but nonetheless embodied principles that went back to Washington's Farewell Address. He consistently argued that American security could never be fully guaranteed and that to seek this would end up creating a garrison state and a permanent war economy. European quarrels would never end; the United States should stay out of them. America was isolated by geography, even in the age of airpower, and that was a good thing. A seventy-group air force, a formidable navy that did not duplicate the air force's strategic mission, and a small atomic arsenal would provide a sufficient and relatively inexpensive defense, he thought; a large standing army was anathema to the American experience, but the navy had a venerable tradition and airpower was a high-technology gift that would allow America to stand apart from Europe, as it always had. It might once have been the case that foreign enemies would take a modestly armed America lightly, Taft believed, but the spectacle of an immensely productive power creating a world-beating military machine in a matter of months after Pearl Harbor would not be lost on anyone.[21]

It is, of course, impossible to imagine what a president like Bob Taft would have done about the wars in Korea and Vietnam, or the challenge from the Soviet Union and China. The point is that his voice was stilled, and that voice was as old as the United States itself, had been dominant just a decade earlier, and reached a particular height of sophistication in the work—the very popular work—of historian Charles Beard. In 1952 a large Republican constituency was cut adrift from its own history and never found a coherent stance on America's relationship to the world thereafter. For the next half-century a bipartisan internationalist coalition, committed to the cold war and high defense budgets, dominated American foreign policy, and almost anyone who

dissented seriously from their basic tenets was tarred with the brush of isolationism, pro-communism, or simply Neanderthal thinking. Cranks like Patrick Buchanan and Ross Perot sought to appeal to Taft's historic constituency
on foreign policy grounds in the 1990s, with Buchanan harking back to 1930s
nationalist themes and getting nowhere, while Perot (a know-nothing on
world affairs) was instrumental in handing the White House to Clinton in
1992. His "big sucking sound" (jobs going to Mexico or China) now has an
important constituency, but this borderline southerner/Texan from Texar-
kana could never be elected president. But after 1952 Americans had no
trouble electing westerners.

General Eisenhower came from Abilene, firmly in the mythic West;
he won two terms. Richard Nixon was a Southern Californian with a new
strategy—to join the western and southwestern Sunbelt to the Deep South;
he also won two terms (even if he squandered the second one). Ronald
Reagan was another Southern Californian but also an iconic celluloid cowboy: he won two terms. George H. W. Bush lived in Texas, worked in the oil
industry, and occasionally wore a cowboy hat. But no one mistook him for a
Texan; good breeding in his home town of Greenwich, Connecticut, got
much too far under his skin. He merited only one term. Along comes the son,
George W. Bush, a Texan through and through (no doubt to the consterna-
tion of his aristocratic parents): two terms.

The rise of western politicians thus makes the 1952 election a critical one.
It realigned the outward stance of the Republican Party, silencing the foreign
policy positions of a huge midwestern and western constituency (because of
cotton the South was part of the free trade coalition, and was in any case
solidly Democratic until a different issue appeared and realigned it—race and
civil rights). More broadly, 1952 realigned both parties regarding the new-new
thing that came along in World War II, the military-industrial complex.
After a brief decline, the Korean War revived the military-industrial coalition, led to historically unprecedented peacetime defense budgets and a large
standing army, and turned the host of new industries that got going under
Roosevelt—primarily ones in the West, and especially California—into permanent institutions. These enormously influential forces were supported
thereafter on an entirely bipartisan basis: to champion serious cuts in the
defense budget was (and still is) a ticket to political oblivion.

The year 1952 simultaneously involved the silencing of a principled Republican fiscal conservatism, the rise of western Republicans of national stature, the emergence of a bipartisan cold war coalition that put serious cuts in
defense spending out of the question for the long term, and the emergence of

a Democratic Party forced to play a weak foreign policy hand in which it could easily be trumped: as "soft on communism," "weak on defense," unable to conclude wars that they got the country into (Korea and Vietnam), or afraid to run risks like opening relations with China (Kennedy wanted to, but Nixon did it). The Republicans have never stopped playing the defense and security card, while never acknowledging the major hole in their theory of a minimal state (or small federal government) caused by massive defense spending. Barry Goldwater was the Republican most ideologically committed to minimalism and general hatred of federal programs, but that never stopped him from championing another air base or defense factory for Arizona. Nixon, Reagan, and George W. Bush were more characteristic, though, in presiding over enormous hemorrhages of defense dollars while pretending to be opponents of federal spending. Nixon was truly a Keynesian in his expansion of all kinds of federal programs, including a big boost to environmentalism; massive increases in defense spending were unlikely as the Vietnam War wound down, and détente with the Soviet momentarily slowed the arms race. Reagan, however, quickly boosted defense spending over $450 billion in current dollars, and Bush's "war on terror," combining wars abroad and "homeland security," pushed it past the $650 billion mark in 2006. They were military Keynesians, like Truman and Acheson.

Walter Dean Burnham's "ideal typical" realigning election involves, first, "short-lived but very intense disruptions of traditional patterns of voting behavior." Majority parties become minorities and large blocks of the electorate shift their allegiances. Second, these elections show "abnormally high intensity," which spills over into party nominations, ideological polarization (within or between parties), "highly salient issue-clusters," and usually, high voter turnout. Burnham also found a uniform periodicity—the Republican ascendancy after 1896, the New Deal in 1932, establishing a new and durable Democratic coalition, or Nixon and Reagan doing the same by exploiting a "southern strategy" that demolished Democratic Party hegemony in the South.[22] The election of 1952 was not particularly intense, but the fight between Taft and Eisenhower supporters was very intense. Even so, extinguishing the foreign policy voice that Taft represented did not send a lot of Republicans scampering into the Democratic Party (in fact they had nowhere to go), and the defense budget was not a highly salient issue because of the Korean War and the widespread perception of a dire Soviet threat. Voter turnout at 76 percent was the highest in the 1950s and back to 1936, but the turnout for the 1960 election was about the same. Eisenhower was an essentially nonpartisan figure, a war hero of indeterminate politics presiding affably over a boom economy; Stalin died and the Korean War ended within months of his inauguration, which also made foreign policy less salient. But when you see the vehemence with which his treasury secretary, George M. Humphrey, intervened time and again in NSC meetings to demand sharp reductions in defense spending (getting little satisfaction),[23] you see the critical issue of fiscal conservatism disappearing in Senator Taft's rearview mirror.

The realignment that began in 1952 was of a different, less easily specifiable quality than Burnham's conception, more along the lines of V. O. Key's classic formulation of a realignment that "seems to persist for several succeeding elections," in this case a new foreign stance that slowly but surely eliminated Taft's ideas and his national standing. We see it best in C. Wright Mills's portrait in 1956 of "the perfect candidate" for the presidency—a man born on a modest farm in Ohio, law degree, Rotary Club stalwart, Episcopalian: William Howard Taft, in other words. But his son Bob Taft? No Ohioan has gotten anywhere near the presidency in the half-century since Mills wrote that, but many had before.[24] And we see it in the seamless bipartisan backing for the Pentagon and its archipelago of empire ever since.

The 1952 departure is still underappreciated, to say the least. Aristide Zolberg recently wrote that the "imperial transformation" and the rise of the national security state in the early postwar years "did not affect the components of the political process most grounded in American society, that is, parties and interest groups." David R. Mayhew criticizes the literature on realigning elections, but when he gets to the period 1948–72 there is no mention of the West, the rise of Barry Goldwater and Ronald Reagan, and least of all the attacks that western, conservative Republicans launched on the eastern wing of the party, especially against Nelson Rockefeller. He argues that 1948 through 1956 may constitute an important "juncture" if not a realignment, but unmentioned is the Korean War, the permanent national security state, or the evaporation of Taft and the isolationists after 1952.[25]

The election of 1952 realigned the historic Republican relationship to the world, but not domestic policy (where the terrain of conflict was race and the New Deal legacy). It shaped a politics in which no Democrat won two terms for half a century, until Clinton's victory in 1996. Truman had the right to run again in 1952 but chose not to because the highly unpopular Korean War had "demolished" his administration, in the words of Dean Acheson. John Kennedy won a close election in 1960 but was assassinated in 1963. The next year Lyndon Johnson, a Texan, cleaned the clock of another westerner, Barry Goldwater. But he also chose not to run again because the Vietnam War was demolishing his administration in 1968. Jimmy Carter, a southerner, defeated

Gerald Ford in 1976, a victory shaped primarily by the debacle of Watergate and Nixon's disgrace. Ronald Reagan booted him out in a landslide in 1980. George H. W. Bush might be a counterfeit Texan, but by 1988 he did not represent the old eastern wing of the Republican Party—he rode to victory on the back of Ronald Reagan's mastery of American politics and an appallingly inept Democratic campaign. Bill Clinton, another southerner, won in 1992 and 1996: the first Democrat since Roosevelt to be reelected. Al Gore—yet another southerner—won the popular vote in 2000 but not the Electoral College. John Kerry, from the Northeast, needed about 70,000 more votes in Ohio to win the Electoral College in 2004 but lost the popular vote by more than one and a half million. Republicans were the dominant force in presidential elections from 1952 until 2008—all of them westerners, and all but one of them (Goldwater) a victor.

An Orange—and a Red—County

In spite of an enormous influx of new residents, Southern California has had a conservative and usually Republican tendency from the 1890s down to the present. It has far more displaced midwestern Protestants—Taft flatlanders— than northern California, which attracted many immigrant Catholics (and always had a strong labor movement). But in the region, Orange County's conservatism has been the most intense. Orange County went for Roosevelt twice, in 1932 and 1936—an aberration brought on by the Depression—and never again voted Democratic. This brand of Republicanism had an important impact in the rise of Richard Nixon, but it never had a national impact before the Goldwater campaign. Even then, Orange County only gave 56 percent to Goldwater, while giving 72 percent to Reagan in 1966 (in the governor's race) and 63 percent to Nixon in 1968. Thus its significance in 1964 was primarily negative: it helped Goldwater get nominated, but the prominence of the John Birch Society, Knott's Berry Farm, and other forms of extremism in the campaign killed Goldwater's chances in the general election.

With the New Deal coalition still intact nationally, the Great Society being born, and liberals still self-confident, it was child's play to tar Goldwater (a classic western politician) as an extremist—and to do so was entirely mainstream: in its Republican convention issue, *Newsweek* pictured Goldwater on the cover in a pose recalling Hitler. The critical moment at the convention was the booing and shouting down of New York governor Nelson Rockefeller, a harbinger of the decline of the Wall Street internationalism and the modest liberalism that had long characterized the eastern wing of the party. Still, Orange County extremism seemed to epitomize everything that sent Goldwater and the party down to a crushing defeat. Its domestic mantras assaulted reigning New Deal verities, and it completely lacked a serious philosophy of foreign affairs: Birch Society conspiracy theories bespoke a catastrophic flatlander inability to understand a world entirely recalcitrant to their imaginings.

About America they knew more, but all of their pitches were to white men of a certain class and a certain removal from midwestern verities—or to women who would stand up and say, I will stay in the kitchen (in her long career Phyllis Schlafly epitomized this appeal). Orange grove conservatism, honed over decades before the war, might explain this political phenomenon. But Knott's theme park probably gets us closer, because conservatism ripened in the quarter-century after 1945 just as the groves dwindled, washed away in an ocean of concrete. The machine of suburbanization ate through them just like Chicago ate up Frederick Jackson Turner's Arcadia, leaving only the option of grasping one's fond hopes and ideals more tightly to the bosom with his "faith and courage, and creative zeal"—in this case recuperating and preserving, like Knott's boysenberry jam, the evaporated aura of gentlemen in cravat and bowler inspecting the thin skins and thick albedos of cadmium-bright citrus. Then something happened that might suggest that no one ever goes broke in America by invoking lost pasts.

Within a short few years Kevin Phillips had detected the beginnings of middle-class revolt in "the Sun country, and Southern California in particular"; Nixon's vaunted and highly effective "Southern strategy" was equally a *southwestern* strategy, returning to his root politics in Orange County. The civil rights movement and the extraordinary turmoil of urban ghettos in the late 1960s enabled the party of Lincoln to turn toward open—more often subliminal—appeals to frightened whites, then cascading into new suburbs for which lily-white Orange County provided a perfect model: never really urban, it became an instant symbol of postwar suburbanization. Indeed, the first gated community in the country opened there in 1960, with an all too literal name—the "Walled City of Rossmoor." Soon they covered Southern California like the orange groves once did and spread across the nation—and now private security forces vastly outnumber the official police.[26]

Orange County appeared to reach the apex of its national influence when one of its all-time favorites, Ronald Reagan, was elected president in 1980— but that was just the beginning. A westerner like Nixon and Goldwater (although originally a midwesterner, like so many Californians), he won a landslide a mere six years after Nixon resigned in disgrace. Clips from John Wayne films introduced the story of Ronald Reagan's life at the 1984 Republican Convention, and Reagan's second inaugural recalled the Alamo and the pioneers: "A settler pushes west and sings his song, and the song echoes out forever and fills the unknowing air. It is the American sound: It is hopeful, big-hearted, idealistic—daring, decent and fair."[27] Reagan was discovered and hoisted to prominence by Hollywood, living almost all of his adult life in and through the movies, and his ascendancy in the 1980s spoke less of Hollywood's influence than the effects of nearly half the population living in suburbs, the western imaginary, and the entire country's obsession with celebrity and imagery. Reagan's brilliance came from honing his mastery of the camera's eye in the 1940s and 1950s, his studied embodiment of the national image of what a president or a movie star should look like (a cowboy), and the consummate skill with which he delivered the lines handed to him by his aides.

Even if Orange County were just about orange groves, it would be conservative but would never have had a national impact. The war brought in El Toro Marine Base, Seal Beach Naval Ammunition Depot, the Naval Air Station at Los Alamitos, and the Santa Ana Army Air Base—which the city fathers obtained by offering the War Department a one-dollar-a-year lease on a big berry ranch. By 1950 "the military was thoroughly entrenched" and Korean War defense contracts poured into the county. A decade later defense industries employed 31,000 workers in firms like Hughes Aircraft, Ford Aeronautics, Nortronics and Autonetics; as the last two names imply, the county was already making a transition to high-tech enterprises that thoroughly blurred the distinction between Defense Department contracts and private industry.[28] So here, too, big defense budgets never got in the way of chatter about the minimal state.

When the cold war ended in 1989 Orange County's economy topped $60 billion, big enough to rank it among the top thirty countries in the world, alongside Argentina and Austria. It still produced oranges, too: but now the county ranked twelfth in the state by value, compared to fourth in 1940 and second in 1930.[29] Much more important, two terms of Ronald Reagan, the rise of the pro-family and anti-abortion movements, the Moral Majority, Howard Jarvis's Proposition 13, Pat Robertson's 700 Club, Focus on the Family, Pat Buchanan's "culture war," and especially the astonishing collapse of the Soviet Union and western communism seemed to fulfill the worldview that Walter Knott and his friends had long advocated—and to bring to national prominence just the kind of people whom they had long supported.

In sharply divided presidential elections in 2000 and 2004, the red states appeared to embrace many of the values that were first voiced in Orange County. Christian fundamentalist morality, fear of the darker races, antipathy toward unions, nostalgia for a lost past that few really knew, and hostility toward big government (except for the Pentagon)—these habits of mind correspond to the lily-white suburbia that Orange County pioneered.

The red state coalition also embodied what Richard White calls "plain folks Americanism," a contemporary version of 1920s flatlander thinking, also rooted in fundamentalist religion; for them hard work was the great equalizer, while welfare and the poor (usually viewed in racial terms) were anathema. During the 1960s turmoil of the civil rights and antiwar movements, protesting and frolicking college students, hippies and flower children, rioting ghettoes and wasteful bureaucrats—they could all be seen as a threat to white lower-middle-class values. Reagan hearkened to these nascent feelings of white victimization and lined these folks up "like ducks in a shooting gallery" in White's words.[30] The plain folks weren't running things, however: "Conservative 'businessmen's governments' had characterized local politics in the West for decades. Their agendas were heavily laden with economic restructuring, big capital projects promoting irrigation, freeway construction, airports, urban renewal, convention centers, and sports and office complexes. The full force of taxpayer financing was put behind the continued growth of urban empires."[31]

Powerful Republicans also benefited from the failures of the Democratic Party, which was never well organized in Southern California, unlike in the north and San Francisco; Hollywood and intellectual elites may have been Democrats, but the white masses weren't. Southern California was already suburban before the war, and Republicans appealed to the individualism and automobile lifestyle of suburbia. As for the great city-state itself, it had no politics: the Progressive Era in L.A. introduced reforms designed to prevent the emergence of big-city machines, putting power in the hands of the nonpartisan city council. No formal party structure emerged that could remotely be compared to eastern cities, and without it, "retail politics is impossible," in William Fulton's words: "Metropolitan Los Angeles sometimes looks as though it was deliberately designed to be ungovernable." Before the 1960s the oligarchy ran the city, keeping mayors like pets; after the accommodation between blacks and Jews, the real estate "growth machine" still ran things— with less direct influence, of course. Their power came from funding the huge media campaigns necessary to reach the people and get elected in this dispersed city. Almost everybody had an interest in keeping the growth machine rolling, including labor unions whose members' jobs depended on it. A general distrust of government throughout the region combined with vast decentralization to hamstring city and county administrations; inefficient or incompetent rule (Orange County went bankrupt in 1994) was preferable to a strong government that knows what it's doing.[32] The result is a hugely apolitical and (now) hugely diverse region called Southern California, underpinned by business interests and especially the real estate growth machine. It just happens to have been the original source of western and "red state" Republicanism.

Rise—and Decline?

The apogee of the California dream appeared to arrive in the early 1960s—the time when its promise was fulfilled, when the vitality of the state was at its height—Wallace Stegner's California, "unformed, innovative, ahistorical, hedonistic, acquisitive and energetic," with its "Good Life" increasingly imitated elsewhere.[33] Thanks to Korea and then the cold war, the post–Pearl Harbor boom continued on for a quarter of a century, with tax money flowing into government coffers and flowing out in stupendous public spending on everything, and especially highways—$10.5 billion for 12,500 miles of new freeways in the 1950s and 1960s; $1.75 billion for the California Water Project, the largest in history with sixteen dams and eighteen pumping stations, plus aqueducts, canals, and levees; a bunch of new campuses for the state university system (San Diego, Irvine, Santa Cruz). Much of this was accomplished under the leadership of Governor Edmund "Pat" Brown, but it all seemed to come to a crashing end with the 1964 Berkeley protests, the 1965 Watts riots, and Brown's defeat in 1966 by Ronald Reagan.[34]

The Watts riots started on the evening of Wednesday, August 11, 1965, and lasted a mere three or four days, but they shook the nation to its roots and were the harbinger of much more to come in Detroit and Newark, and then in virtually every inner-city ghetto after Martin Luther King was murdered in April 1968. Within three days, nearly 14,000 National Guardsmen were on the streets of Watts and ultimately thirty-four people had died. A few months later the Commission on the Los Angeles Riots issued its final report: "While the Negro districts of Los Angeles are not urban gems, neither are they slums. Watts, for example, is a community consisting mostly of one- and two-story houses, a third of which are owned by the occupants. In the riot area, most streets are wide and usually quite clean; there are trees, parks, and playgrounds. A Negro in Los Angeles has long been able to sit where he wants in a bus or movie house, to shop where he wishes, to vote, and to use public facilities without discrimination. The opportunity to succeed is probably unequalled in any other major American city." As David Wyatt wrote, the commission "concerned itself more with explaining why the riot should not have happened than with why it did."[35]

In the summer of 1965 the civil rights movement was at its height, Lyndon Johnson's War on Poverty was just beginning, the Vietnam War was heating up, and Berkeley students were worried about First Amendment rights of free speech rather than overthrowing the system. Watts had many meanings, but one is the retrospective judgment that it and subsequent urban uprisings stuck a dagger in the heart of American liberalism and idealism just when it appeared to be at its pinnacle, and that this was a peak it would never climb again. In the next nine years, culminating in Nixon's resignation in August 1974, no honest person could witness the cascading, tumultuous events—riots, assassinations, mass protests, hundreds of young men dying every week in a war with no end, a Nixon administration apparently capable of anything— and not think that something was deeply wrong with the country, that the surface affluence belied a troubling pathology. Watts suggested that blacks had known this all along.

If 1962 was the postwar high point of the California dream, 1992 was probably the nadir. When recessions hit the rest of the country in the past, California experienced only modest downturns if anything at all; corporate profit rates in all the Pacific states ran two or three times higher than those of eastern firms. Only when the cold war ended did the state suffer the lost jobs and dislocations that had been standard in the Rustbelt for decades. Suddenly the national media were full of dark fears and dire predictions about the state's future. The *New York Times* seemed secretly to enjoy California's travails, publishing dozens of stories in the early 1990s with titles like "Nature Humbles a State of Mind" and "Building on Sand: Pain Repays Reckless California." The attenuation of the defense industries, massive layoffs, earthquakes, floods, fires, mudslides, droughts, "eye-stinging smog, despoiled landscapes, [and] polluted beaches" (in the words of a *Time* magazine story), the 1992 uprising in South Central Los Angeles—it all added up to the conclusion that maybe no one should have built an urban civilization here in the first place.[36]

The eruption of South Central in April 1992, following the acquittal of Los Angeles Police Department officers in the videotaped beating of Rodney King, was much worse than Watts—or indeed anything since the 1863 draft riots in New York. Fifty people died, 500 buildings were burned, and three-quarters of a billion dollars in property was lost.[37] Here was the culmination of all the calamities that spelled the end of the California dream and the harbinger of worse to come. Except it wasn't: reports of California's demise were much exaggerated. True, when the cold war ended and the Soviet Union collapsed the bottom appeared to fall out of California's love affair with defense spending. (See map on page 332.) In the 1980s California still got nearly half of all NASA funding and led the nation with one-quarter of all Defense Department contracts. But in one year, July 1990 to July 1991, 75,000 defense jobs disappeared, and by 1993, 820,000 jobs were gone—and about 40 percent of these were in defense-related industries. Military bases folded like bad poker hands: Fort Orde on the Monterey Peninsula, with 16,500 jobs lost; Norton and George Air Force bases in San Bernardino County, with more than 12,000 jobs lost; also Moffett Field in Sunnyvale, bases at the Presidio and Hunters Point in San Francisco, Treasure Island Naval Air Station, Mare Island Naval Shipyard, Alameda Air Station—all gone. Nationwide, California lost 70 percent of all jobs eliminated through base closures (under the Defense Base Closure and Realignment Act of 1990). Aerospace factories closed down one after another, and unemployment hit 9.4 percent in 1993, highest in the nation. For the first time in its history California had significant out-migration: 600,000 people headed out between 1991 and 1994, mostly for the mountain states of the West. But if many blue-collar jobs disappeared, Southern California remained the center of aerospace research and development. Furthermore, just as this region hit its unemployment nadir, Silicon Valley became the leading sector of the entire world economy. Net in-migration began again in 1995 and boomed for the rest of the decade.[38] Today 1992 looks like a singularly bad year, but an orphan in a state known for having so few.

Water, Power, and the Genteel Tradition

North of the Monterey *Cupressus macrocarpa* you don't find a lot of Orange County conservatism or red-staters. The thinly populated Inland Empire has plenty, of course, but running up the coast you have to go all the way to Fort Bragg to find a reactionary town. Instead, affluent northern California joins Portland and Seattle in a region that epitomizes early twenty-first-century liberalism. Across the country liberals live in gated communities like other people, of course, but even better is to have an entire county with no gates that is still lily-white: superaffluent and arch-liberal Marin County has the lowest percentage of nonwhites in the state. The liberal epicenter, perhaps, locates in a place most people have never heard of—and when they do, they can't find it.

Bolinas is twenty miles up the coast from San Francisco, but you need to crane your neck watching for an unmarked road crossing to know where to turn. Epidermally you would think it's like Mendocino (a pure sixties redoubt), with peace signs on barns, tie-dyed and dreadlocked five-year-olds, the Bolinas People's Store, and the ubiquitous aroma of hemp. But if it were Mendocino, you wouldn't die of thirst: Bolinas's clever "gate" is the $310,000 it will cost you to get a water meter. There are 571 meters hooked up to the Bolinas water supply, a spring-fed creek called the Arroyo Honda—the same number when the town froze permits for new ones in 1971.

Here is a perfect genteel monopoly: the hoi polloi kept at bay, real estate prices steadily appreciating (a cottage on one-fifth of an acre cost $920,000 in 2005, a falling-down barn on three acres sold for $1.2 million), and time standing still. Residents include Susie Tompkins Buell, billionaire founder of the Esprit clothing line; Berkeley dean Orville Schell, whose farm supplies organically grown beef to Chez Panisse; and many other wealthy folks who prefer to remain hidden. But some residents just got lucky: they came to clean the feathers of loons, cormorants, grebes, and other birds that got slicked by an oil spill in 1971 and decided to stay—just in time to get water meters the old-fashioned way. Someone tried to sue the town over its water monopoly in 1982, charging that it violated individual property rights, but Bolinas unified to a man and defeated the suit on the grounds that "water was scarce" in California.[39] The old guard of the genteel tradition would have approved.

In Silicon Valley, too, nouveau riches got what they deserved. Steve Jobs crashed into the haute Woodside thicket in 1983, getting the bulldozers ready to go against a dilapidated "red-tile-and-stucco albatross." That would be the Daniel Jackling estate, whose architect was George Washington Smith, who created the "Santa Barbara look" in the 1920s (and it doesn't get more genteel than that). Jackling was an Anaconda Copper baron, once called "the Henry Ford of minerals," and he coppered his home abundantly—roof, gutters, downspouts, even copper hot water pipes to keep his bougainvillea warm in the winter. Jobs claimed the house was "poorly built," but the Woodside elders retorted, George Washington (Smith) built it, don't you know? He had studied architecture, Jobs said, but never heard of the guy. It's a teardown, Jobs insisted. Two decades later he's still insisting. Jackling's moldering-green home still abides, and to fill its vacant confines Jobs used to let Secret Service personnel stay there when Bill and Hillary Clinton were in town to raise money or visit their daughter at Stanford.[40]

Daniel Jackling made his money by pioneering the open-pit copper strip mine, his publicists said. Actually he just redirected toward the Montana garden the machine that demolished American River hillsides: heavy-artillery water. In the dry bottoms of the Blackfoot and Clark Fork rivers lie the bright green bones of dead cattle; even the riverbeds themselves are green from copper mined a hundred miles upstream, a color hiding the cadmium and arsenic and other mine waste backed up behind the Milltown Dam east of Missoula—all 6 million cubic yards of it. Milltown is where the waste flow backed up; arsenic seeped down into the aquifer, contaminating the water. Engineers hope these venerable rivers will begin to flow again once a $100-million project to remove the dam and the mountain of detritus piled up behind it is complete. Anaconda Copper (now part of Atlantic-Richfield) will pay $80 million to clean up its mess.[41] Norman Maclean made the Blackfoot famous in *A River Runs Through It.* Until the dam disappears in 2009, it won't.

The Return of the Natives

For decades the millions of emigrants to the West Coast "voting with their wheels" mimicked the flatlanders and the Okies: most of the arrivals were white people hoping lateral flight would mean upward mobility. The war brought millions of blacks to the West Coast, as we have seen, but this was still a mere dollop dropped on the blanketed whiteness that marked California, Oregon, and Washington. The Los Angeles oligarchy remained ensconced until the 1960s, when California's version of the civil rights movement brought a pact between South Central blacks and West Side Jews that finally overthrew a century of faux-WASP hegemony.[42] Then the new immigration law in 1965 unleashed another floodgate of migration, recalling the tens of thousands of Chinese who flocked to the gold mines and the railroads. But this time Asians crossed the Pacific by the millions, just as more millions of Mexicans returned to every part of their lost territory. By the 1980s about 400,000 immigrants flocked into California every year, most of them Asian or Hispanic. In 2000, 35 million people lived in California, of whom only 52 percent were white; Hispanics had grown to 30 percent, blacks were 7 percent, and the rest (11 percent) were Chinese, Koreans, Filipinos, Cambodians, Vietnamese, Hmong, and Samoans, most of them recent immigrants. Orange County's citrus groves and white purity completely gave way in the 1980s and 1990s; Santa Ana, which grew from 31,000 in 1940 to 300,000 today, is 70 percent Hispanic, and the Orange County phone book now has more people named Nguyen than Smith.[43] This darkening of the citizenry inspires laments about California's presumed decline and the demise of white dominance, but you probably need to sneak inside a gated community to hear

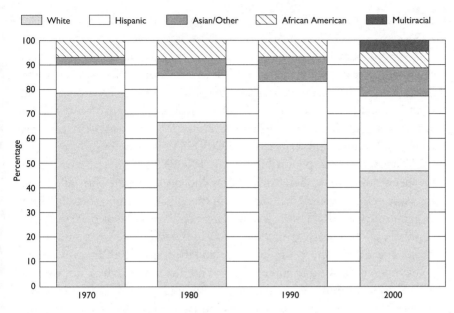

| White | Hispanic | Asian/Other | African American | Multiracial |

California, population by race and ethnicity, 1970–2000.
United States Census Bureau.

it said. Today Los Angeles is a Latino city, Silicon Valley is a Sino-Indian redoubt, Asian-Americans and especially Koreans fill up to half of the entering classes at the best public universities, Vietnamese do nails and noodles, Cambodians do donuts, and the daydream of a white Eden clings onto Portland and Seattle with white knuckles and cracked fingernails.

Like Silicon Valley, the Orange County economy is now rooted in high technology and defense spending, and especially state subsidies to high-tech firms funneled through the Pentagon (although Santa Clara County typically has 30 percent of its employment in high technology, twice as much as Orange County's 15 percent). The county was always lily-white until the 1980s, except for Mexican field hands and domestics; in 1970 it was less than 1 percent African-Americans. A decade later, however, about 15 percent of the population was Hispanic, Asian-Americans grew 371 percent to nearly 5 percent, and blacks had increased 140 percent.[44]

Meanwhile, Los Angeles is now a polyglot mosaic with a Hispanic majority. The 2000 census found that Latinos counted for 47 percent of the population in the city and 45 percent in Los Angeles County; Asians and African-Americans hovered around 10 percent in both places. Anglos—the oligarchy and the folks—who once had seamless dominance in the city, now constitute about 30 percent in the city and the county. In the six-county Los Angeles region, projections suggest that nearly 75 percent of the population will soon be nonwhite. The Asian-American population is both urban and suburban; Koreans, Vietnamese, and Chinese-Americans live downtown and in suburbs like Monterey Park, Alhambra, Garden Grove, Westminster, and what is sometimes called "Little Saigon" in Orange County.[45] As it did a century earlier, California mirrors the future for the rest of the country: whites will be in the minority nationally within a few decades.

When California's population surpassed New York's in 1962, nearly 16 million people inhabited the state. Only 1.3 million were foreign-born, and about the same number were nonwhite; most of those born abroad were from Great Britain and Canada. Three decades later California doubled New York's population. With nearly 37 million people in the fifth largest economy in the world, one in eight Americans live there, and the Census Bureau says Californians can look forward to approaching 50 million residents by 2030, when it will easily be the most diverse state in the contiguous forty-eight. Right-wing politics has utterly collapsed amid this human mosaic. As its verdant citrus towns turned into crowded cities, the blanketed whiteness of this county got drowned by a flood of polyglot newcomers, but paradoxically its conservative heritage popped up elsewhere in the nation like toadstools after a rain.

CHAPTER FOURTEEN

In California's Shadow:
The Rest of the West in the Postwar Era

The three states on the western rim of the nation comprise a new citadel of power.

—*Kiplinger Magazine,* 1948

A fter World War II Texas, Washington, Alaska, and Hawaii all charged ahead, building on the momentum of wartime industries and the new populations that arrived to work in them. The postwar West benefited from Pentagon spending, whether it was military bases, airfields, missile silos, or defense industries. Washington, Alaska, Hawaii, Utah, and Colorado all got more than a quarter of their income from defense in the 1950s. Aircraft production was centered almost entirely in the West—Los Angeles, Seattle, San Diego, Dallas–Fort Worth, and Wichita accounted for nearly all of it. Each state was a regional variant of the defense-driven boom in California. But each of them also prospered for additional, idiosyncratic reasons. In Texas the key ingredient behind the state's continuous population growth was a cool invention that finally made the state livable amid its torrid summer temperatures: the first air conditioners were used in theaters and department stores in the 1920s, but the invention of Freon in 1930 brought the price down and, after the Depression finally ended, home air-conditioning began to saturate the South and Southwest.[1] Several presidents were also nurtured in the soil of the Lone Star State, including a political dynasty that ran the White House for twelve years. In Hawaii the climate itself was air-conditioned, but it still got hit by a tempest—the whirlwind of tourists inundating the islands after transcontinental air travel boomed in the 1950s. In Washington a great firm built the finest commercial jetliner, the 707, and Boeing dominated the state's economy for most of the postwar era, while its home, Seattle, went from a somewhat provincial "most livable" city in the 1970s to a wealthy high-tech node in the world economy. Portland also grabbed hold of a new-new trend: political correctness, which it raised to the nth degree as it also became one of the most livable cities in the country, but one ever vigilant against "Californication." Less obvious were a multitude of nondescript boxes: they glide by on trucks with names like Hanjin pasted on their sides, they stack up by the hundreds at ports, they sit on flatbed ocean liners like so many Legos, sometimes itinerant folks commandeer them for ersatz homes, there may be 300 million of them in the world, but we barely notice them. Yet the unprepossessing container has truly showed the way toward circumambulating the globe.

Working for the Boeings

Seattle wasn't the obvious place to locate an airplane company, given the overcast skies and the distance from eastern markets, but William Boeing was born into wealth there and liked to fly planes—and that was that. In the middle of World War I he convinced the University of Washington to develop a specialty in aeronautical engineering, which resulted in the arrival in 1916 of Claire Egtvedt and Philip Johnson, engineering students, and the next year the university established a chair in aeronautics. As soon as Egtvedt and Johnson finished up, Boeing hired them, and by 1939 one was running the company and the other was chairman of the board.[2] It was still a small enterprise, though, barely known outside the Pacific Northwest. Three Bs— the B-17, the B-29, and the B-52—changed all that. During World War II and the cold war Boeing was like the Silicon Valley firms, sheltered from market forces and the need to advertise and sell, so it could build truly awesome high-tech bombers—especially the B-52—to exacting specifications no commercial company could meet.

But Boeing also did better than other firms in riding the new postwar wave of commercial air travel, producing a host of excellent airliners escalating through the 700s from the innovative 707 to the workhorse 727 and the 737, the behemoth 747, and the sleek 787 "Dreamliner" coming online in the new century. The 707 was conceived in 1952 when Korean War profits were pouring in, but if you discount the government contracts, it still amounted to a big gamble—because very few people flew around America at the time, and when they did, it was usually in Lockheed Constellations with their four-propeller engines. When the 707 appeared in 1959 with its sleek looks and jet engines hanging under swept-back wings, it seemed a generation ahead—and it was. Orders came flowing in, and within a year Boeing's defense business was smaller than its commercial returns; the success of the 747 jumbo jet in the 1970s meant defense production accounted for less than 20 percent of its business. Other wartime manufacturing industries in the Pacific Northwest, however, could not sustain their growth (shipbuilding, for example). Shortly after the war about one in five people in the King County labor force worked for Boeing; a decade later it was every other one.[3] For four decades after the war Boeing was everything to Seattle—a "company city" with a satellite company town in nearby Everett.

Two long-serving and powerful senators, Henry "Scoop" Jackson and Warren Magnuson, were past masters at funneling federal money from Washington to Washington. Jackson, often called "the senator from Boeing," was particularly close to the Pentagon. But Magnuson was, if anything, a bigger spillway for taxpayers' money—into all kinds of public works, hospitals, university contracts, and state-of-the-art facilities, like the cancer treatment center at the University of Washington. A legendary figure in the Senate for his skill with the pork barrel, his malapropisms, and the lovely women on his arm, he wasn't well known outside it. John Kennedy once remarked that Magnuson spoke so quietly on the Senate floor that few could hear him: "He sends a message up to the chair and everyone says, 'What was it?' and Maggie says, 'It's nothing important.' And the Grand Coulee Dam is built."[4]

Boeing benefited as much as any corporation from the "Star Wars" program, with defense-related work accounting for 70 percent of its profits in the mid-1980s. Together with the University of Washington and the Battelle Institute, Boeing completely dominated local high-tech employment: aerospace engineers, physicists, computer and software technicians—a pool that fledgling Microsoft first drew upon and then vastly expanded. Today Boeing has but one commercial competitor, the European Airbus consortium, and for decades has been a barely challenged exporter of the best airplanes. The largest aircraft manufacturer in the world, it is the second-ranking American exporter.[5]

The top people at Boeing are still almost all engineers, focused like a laser on the latest aerospace technologies, and even though the firm has done well in both the open and the sheltered market, it is the immense flow of Pentagon wealth that enables them to operate at the horizon of new technologies and advanced engineering without worrying too much about costs. It is thus an insular company full of insular people. This is one reason why the relations between this great firm and the people of the Pacific Northwest were always strained, arms-length, uneasy; strikes and layoffs were the major part, but many had the sense that Boeing was in the region but not of it—or they just had no idea how its great birds got off the ground, and Boeing didn't help much by being so secretive. Apart from a stadium full of jobs, Boeing didn't give back much to the community and most of its leaders were unknown to most people. Unlike other high-tech firms, however, Boeing was always unionized. During the war Boeing diversified to Wichita for security reasons, after the war it opened other plants in Cape Kennedy and Huntsville, Alabama, but whatever people thought about the firm they always thought its base was in Seattle.[6] That turned out to be wrong when Boeing removed its headquarters to Chicago in 2000 (even if aircraft production remained centered in the Pacific Northwest).

China has become such a huge customer that Deng Xiaoping and Hu Jintao have both visited Boeing's capacious assembly plant in Everett. When President Hu showed up in 2006, he stuck a Boeing baseball cap on his head while his entourage sampled airplane-shaped cookies and images flickered overhead of Chinese pilots announcing their admiration for the company: "Optimism! Brilliant! Vision!" (in translation). The reason why Boeing bows down to Chinese leaders isn't hard to locate: the People's Republic of China has bought 678 planes since 1972, at a cost of nearly $40 billion. Boeing's reach and reputation are so great that when I first visited North Korea in 1981, my guides asked me how long it took me to fly from Seattle to Beijing, how big the 747 was, how many people it could hold, how fast it could fly. Emerald City denizen that I was, I supplied the answers to gasps and breathless note-taking. In the new century Boeing has another 747-like gamble on the table: the 787 Dreamliner. Its unitary carbon-fiber fuselage eliminated 1,200 sheets of aluminum and 40,000 rivets, cutting its weight dramatically, while its engines require 20 percent less fuel than comparable airliners. Costs were lowered further by farming out subcontracting work to firms in Japan, France, Italy, and elsewhere. China is already on tap for 60 Dreamliners at $7.2 billion, once they start rolling off the line; President Hu also dropped off a current purchase order for 150 midsize 737s. Boeing will either smash its Airbus competitor, or both will simply continue as the Coke and Pepsi of commercial aviation.[7]

Not Working for the Boeings

From World War I through the early 1970s, Washington's basic economy had changed little: wheat, lumber, fish—and Boeing in Seattle. No other big American city was so dependent on one major industry. Even as Microsoft emerged in the late 1980s, Boeing still employed more than 100,000 people, twice its World War II level. More revealing of its dominance was the general absence of significant growth in other fields: Seattle's population was nearly

468,000 in 1950, 558,000 in 1960, but only 494,000 in 1980. The "Boeing bust" from 1968 into the early 1970s revealed the firm's centrality, as more than 60,000 jobs disappeared, throwing Seattle, Everett, and the surrounding region into a devastating tailspin. Unemployment jumped from 4.9 percent to 13.6 percent, and many experts thought the era of Pacific Northwest growth was over.[8] Cuts in spending for the Vietnam War, lower demand for commercial aircraft, Senate cancellation of the Supersonic Transport, and enormous start-up expenses for the 747 airliner all combined to demolish the lives of thousands of workers. But they were the least educated and experienced of Boeing's employees; skilled specialists took pay cuts or found other jobs, so the bust did not drain Seattle's formidable pool of talent. Instead it demonstrated that people liked the city and didn't want to leave. The national joke—"will the last person leaving Seattle please turn out the lights"—was really about waiting for the lights to come back on.

In the middle of the bust Boeing brought out a porpoise-shaped behemoth numbered 747: introduced in 1971, it wiped the floor with the world competition for the next two decades. Like so much else in the West, the 747 jumbo had its origins in a Pentagon contract calling for a mammoth plane twice the size of a Boeing 707 with three times the power of its engines—an unheard of 40,000 pounds of thrust. Three aircraft companies bid on it and Lockheed got the contract (resulting in the C-5A cargo plane), but to Boeing went the spoils: devastated by the loss of their bid in August 1965, Boeing's management decided in the same month to put 100 engineers to work under Joseph Sutter's leadership on a commercial airliner of similar size and power—it was a huge risk, but it changed the face of transcontinental air travel.[9]

World-Class Seattle, Politically Correct Portland

Seattle's broad middle class had few problems during the Boeing bust, and some people didn't even seem to notice the travails: in 1975 *Harper's* deemed Seattle America's "most livable city." *Seattle Magazine* also appeared, charged with the goal of enlightening the citizenry. It saw the light of day because one of the remaining scions (or dinosaurs) of the genteel tradition, Stimson Bullitt, put a bit of his fortune into it. Head of the dominant KING radio and television network, Bullitt embodied the venerable Seattle establishment all by himself (in part because it was so small). Stimson Bullitt sounded like a secretary of state, but other Seattle elite names like Brewster Denny didn't—they just got there early.

A lifelong liberal Democrat, Bullitt had a Yale education and always endeavored to draw the locals out of their provincial inanition. In 1964 he brought an easterner, Peter Bunzel, to edit the new magazine. Bullitt and Bunzel were going to shake Seattle out of its torpor and make it a big league city—and not like Minneapolis, either: like New York or San Francisco. But as Roger Sale pointed out, Bunzel could never figure out whether he was educating the citizens or looking down his nose at them. Seattle struck him the way it would have H. L. Mencken: his modal reader "was local, a booster, a complacent provincial who liked the World's Fair and the new downtown buildings, who was a hearty or a frightened know-nothing about blacks, who loved Husky football and freeways and hydroplane races and who believed in everything most destructive about progress. Bunzel treated this reader or target like a hick. He was always looking for a way . . . to imply that even the best in Seattle wasn't very good, or good enough."[10] Bunzel was no Mencken, but he succeeded in upsetting the *boobeoisie* anyway, and probably Bullitt as well; the magazine folded within six years.

Seattle also hoped it would "arrive" with its World's Fair in 1962, designed to make it "the gateway to the Orient," but in the end had little to show for it—mainly the dubious landmark called the "Space Needle" (which many residents thought looked like a clamming contraption). As late as 1991 four prominent political economists wrote that Seattle "remains a classic example of an ossified single-sector economy" and was still a cultural backwater. They noticed that the downtown emptied at 5:00 p.m., that the city lacked flair, that the people were courteous but unengaged in the life of the city and more likely to prefer hiking in the mountains.[11] They echoed a theme more than a century old. But 1991 was not 1962: this was just about the point at which Microsoft emerged with a monopoly every bit as global and as lucrative as John D. Rockefeller's a century earlier, as Starbucks coffee shops began proliferating around the country and then the world, and a few years later, as Amazon became one of the largest global retailers and Nintendo commanded the multibillion-dollar video game industry.

Suddenly the downtown hummed after working hours, haute-bourgeois shops like Gucci and Tiffany opened up, and chic new restaurants proliferated everywhere. But little has changed in easterners' assessments: when the Seahawks made it to the Super Bowl in 2006, one commentator after another discovered that there was this big city (half a million in Seattle, 3 million in the metropolitan area) way off in the upper Northwest, it had more than just Bill Gates, it could even field a good football team. Seattle hardly has an ossified economy, even if culturally the critics may still have a point. But if we define "culture" as writing books on screens with flawless graphics and automatic footnoting, or reading for hours (for free) in a coffee shop easy chair, or buying any book new or used at the touch of an Amazon button, then Seattle has given unstintingly to the national culture, because now we can do all these things in Kankakee or Keokuk.

Seattle will never have the protean energy of New York or Los Angeles, but that also makes it—well, livable and beautiful. An enormous state university with an Olmsted Brothers campus lies just across the junction of two shimmering freshwater lakes; the city itself, manageable and au courant, wraps around Elliott Bay with its houseboats and seaplanes, connected through locks to Puget Sound—easily the prettiest body of water in North America; great snow-capped mountains sparkle in the distance. One can be in the city, at the lake, sailing in fresh or salt water, and taking in the mountains more or less in the same mental moment. An hour's drive takes you east to the Cascade Range for skiing or west to the great rain forests of the Olympic Peninsula for hiking, beyond which the Pacific Ocean beckons. Fleets of marvelous ferries cruise across the sound to islands big and small (Vashon, Whidbey, the San Juans), fully the match of any setting in Cape Cod or along the Maine coast. The original WASP ascendancy long ago gave way to a remarkable diversity, and a population schooled in the participatory ethics of grassroots democracy. If it can be too politically correct (a waitress once denied a glass of wine to a pregnant woman, and that was only her first), it possesses an urbane tranquility largely unmatched in any other American city.

In the end, though, it wasn't the departed and unlamented Boeing or necessarily Amazon or Starbucks or even Microsoft that finally turned Seattle into the high-tech emerald of the Pacific. It was the growing sophistication of its people; the rise of a broad middle-class black community; the arrival of hundreds of thousands of Asian-Americans; the city's tolerance for a large gay community that demands the best of the city's restaurants, galleries, museums, and theaters—these groups supplied the "missing ingredient" with which so many writers ended their stories about Seattle, the complaint that the city fell short of its potential. Roger Sale supplied one reason why, which brings us back to Louis Hartz—low class difference: "Bourgeois from its first breath, Seattle has to struggle with finding out what that means."[12] But the leavening of white-bread Seattle with so much *difference* is not a Hartzian story; it is the American story. Seattle long had an insulation and an isolation that was different from, say, Omaha, and it didn't spawn simple narrow-mindedness. For all the early troubles, whites have lived with Indians in relative peace, and with tremendous influence returning from Indian culture (just as Chief Sealth said it would). It has always been a more tolerant city than most; one might say it can afford to be, but the timing of the new ethnic influx was beneficial or pacific because it came after the civil rights revolution. Seattle was already a twenty-first-century city before the millennium, and it will do nothing but prosper in a new era of Pacific civilization.

Seattle and Portland both call up Edward Banfield's question: "anybody in charge?"[13] Seattle has such self-effacing and mild-mannered mayors that it's hard to remember their names, or which party—if any—they belonged to (it's a nonpartisan office, whereas in Chicago any mayor is fine as long as he's a Democrat—and preferably named Daley). Some activity takes place in the city council and occasionally the mayor's office, but few citizens appeared to pay much attention. My favorite governor was Dixie Lee Ray, not a stripper but a former lifetime associate professor at the University of Washington who enjoyed naming her pigs after deans and inquisitive reporters she didn't like. From 1984 to 1992 Portland had a cheery mayor named E. "Bud" Clark who favored Jimmy Carter cardigans and whose chief claim to fame was riding around town on his bike, yelling out "Whoop-Whoop!" to passersby. By the 1990s both cities became so politically correct that mundane vices made you self-conscious; if you walked down the street smoking a cigar, people would cross to the other side. Police actually wrote tickets for jaywalking. Seattle's Chinatown is called the "International District." In 1993 Portland announced its desire to add another "green city" to the Northwest: through strong programs to curb greenhouse gases, it got its current levels back to what they were in 1990 (nationally they were up 16 percent). In mid-2007 new standards required significant percentages of biodiesel and ethanol in all fuel sold in the city. Thousands of commuters bike to work.[14] These are major achievements —the fact is Portland, Seattle, and California are the vanguard of highway environmentalism in our time: whoop-whoop!

Oregon has maintained its New England–style independence. Postwar trade through the port of Seattle overwhelmed Portland, putting that century-old rivalry in the shade; that and the absence of much heavy industry made this the last of the Pacific states to have its garden ground under by industry or by the federal government's nature remaking—in fact it never really happened: most World War II industry was limited to the Portland area, and it didn't conjure up big successors. Few newcomers came to the state after the war, in contrast to the other Pacific states, and its economy remained grounded in lumber and agriculture; it was but a minor participant in the defense spending bonanza in California and Washington. Senator Wayne

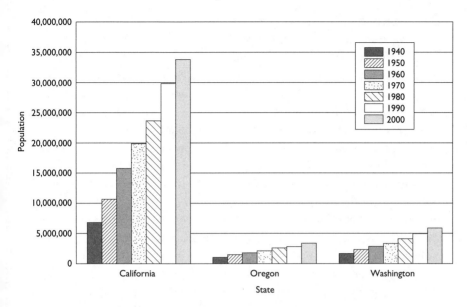

Population change in California, Oregon, and Washington, 1940–2000.
United States Census Bureau, California Department of Finance.

Morse, a former dean at the University of Oregon and the most independent senator of his time, was better known for hammering the Pentagon than sticking his palm out. (Morse and Ernest Gruening of Alaska were the only senators to vote against the Tonkin Gulf Resolution in 1964, the enabling legislation for prosecuting the Vietnam War.) Until the 1990s Oregonians tended to judge their economic health by the "sawdust empire"—by the well-being of the lumber industry—reliant on "rolling blankets of Douglas fir laid across the land, some of the trees as high as 280 feet." By and large Oregonians liked it this way: "What really worries us is California," one remarked in 1963; "We live in constant dread of Californians' falling in love with Oregon. It will be a sad day when those people come up here and decide to stay."[15]

Oregon's reputation for civic virtue and political correctness is old, perhaps as old as its faux–New England roots. It was clear under Governor Thomas McCall, who inaugurated the cliché in 1971 of telling tourists to come but asking them not to stay too long—especially their neighbors to the south: Oregonians feared getting "Californicated." Under McCall's long tenure (1967–75) he helped pass the first law in the country to outlaw pull-tab cans and nonreturnable bottles, he drove a Volkswagen rather than Detroit's "Belchfire Eights" and "Gas Glutton Supremes," and he liked to call Lincoln

City (a town along the coast) "a model of strip city grotesque." McCall chose Los Angeles to deliver a dictum that might sum up his home state: "Oregon has not been an over-eager lap-dog to the economic master. Oregon has been wary of smokestacks and suspicious of rattle and bang. Oregon has not camped, cup in hand, at anyone's affluent doorstep. Oregon has wanted industry only when that industry was willing to want what Oregon is." In our time it is worth noting that McCall was a Republican.[16]

Oregon's economic goals are still reasonably close to McCall's dictum: don't Californicate the state. It has world-class designer industries like Nike, for example, but most of its shoes are made in third world countries (and in sweatshops for decades, until a major protest movement forced changes). A small firm in 1980, Nike made two brilliant moves that catapulted it into global dominance in sportswear: it signed Michael Jordan in 1984 (after Adidas passed up the opportunity), and it put its highly imaginative, minimalist logo—the "swoosh" (almost on a par with Mercedes' star)—on every top athlete in sight. With Nike's 1985 "Air Jordan" sneakers, Jordan himself took off as one of the world's most recognizable logos: called the "jumpman," it extended his airborne highness's body as a slightly tilted X with a small head and a big basketball in the right hand. With sales of $12 billion in 2005, Nike's lead was so long that it was Snow White to Reebok, Adidas, and Puma's "three dwarves."[17]

Texas Oil, Texas Politics

The rise of the oil industry before the war did nothing to alter the image of the "typical Texan." The defender of the Alamo and the cowboy or gunman of the nineteenth century were little different from the free play of the oil wildcatter, made memorable by James Dean in *Giant* and Jack Nicholson in *Five Easy Pieces*. He (it was always a he) was a tall, strong, rugged frontiersman, cowpuncher, or wildcatter, "mobile, aggressive, and adaptive," glorying in the challenges of making a new state, driving longhorns north to the railhead or taming oil wells. Frontier conditions, exigencies, and beliefs had a longer life in this state than almost anywhere else, and bequeathed a personality that shows strong peculiarities in social science inventories: optimistic, egalitarian, individualistic, volatile, chauvinistic, ethnocentric, provincial, accepting of routine violence but not of government attentiveness, admiring of material wealth however obtained, with ethics hinged to a strict Protestant fundamentalism often honored in the breach.[18]

In his sprawling history, the proud Texan T. R. Fehrenbach painted the following portrait of the state in the late 1960s. "Most of Texas' industry, with the exception of the aero-space complex around Dallas and a few other scattered enterprises, was based on the processing of agricultural products and the extraction and processing of raw materials." It was more "a vast agricultural-mining complex" than a true industrial state. Two great universities emerged, Rice and the University of Texas, but most Texans cared more about high school and college football than having a first-class education: "Instinctively, the majority of Texans tended to admire or envy a family that owned 100,000 acres more than one that produced two great surgeons, a fine musician, or a new theory of relativity" (for novelist Larry McMurtry, Texas was like "writing into a rather stiff wind"). The big educational system produced fine trial lawyers, canny politicians, respected military officers, courageous soldiers (Audie Murphy of World War II fame was a cotton farmer from—Farmland), world-class oil engineers, and good businessmen, but few scholars and scientists. Even the burgeoning cities attracted mostly natives; 70 percent of Texans, when they moved, only moved a few miles and rarely out of state. Forty years ago, Fehrenbach believed that the essential culture of the state, rooted in the dominance of white Protestant Scotch-Irish ("Anglo-Celts") had not changed substantially in the previous century.[19] He may be wrong, but if he isn't his generalizations encompass the entire history of the state of Texas up to the Nixon era.

The crucial difference from California arose in the nature of most Texas wealth: it came from primary production—cotton, cattle, timber, and oil—and remained in a colonial status with eastern and foreign banks and markets for many decades. (The rich sank their money into real estate and mining but abjured Wall Street stocks and bonds—tending to distrust them.) The baronial cotton and cattle empires of Texas resembled the latifundia of California, where huge farm machines or thousands of cattle were handled by a scant cohort of workers; "a small, relatively rich landowning group accounted for most production," Fehrenbach wrote, and they usually controlled mercantile interests in the towns.[20] Oil was another industry with a relatively small and scattered labor force, and when a much smaller rate of migration to the state from outside is added to this mix, the Texan middle class was small and beleaguered from above and below, quite unlike California. But oil made the echelon of big land owners fabulously wealthy; suddenly cotton and cattle were much less important than the black gold underneath the soil.

More aggravating, everything about which Texas could boast, California could too: cotton, produced by the latest mechanized methods in the absence of slave and sharecropper holdovers; fine cattle and a little-noticed but leading dairy industry ranking behind only Wisconsin; timber by the millions of acres—and oil galore. California's narrative remains one of constant reinvention, an ever-changing future, dreams yet to come, but Texas's hold on the nation is in the frozen image of the man of action: the heroes of the Alamo, the lonesome longhorn drive, the wildcat taming black gold, and the eternal grip on the American mind of the Hollywood cowboy. Enclaves in Texas are now at the cutting edge of high-tech production, but people tend to forget or overlook them. We might divide California into north and south—northerners would like to—but Texas is a state of many disparate parts united by history, primary production, and mythology.

The Bush Dynasty

Midland and Odessa were small West Texas towns about twenty miles apart when oil discoveries in the nearby Permian Basin remade them into cities of 150,000, both almost exclusively concerned with oil—Midland being an administrative and financial center and Odessa housing refineries. This took place in what D. W. Meinig called the "purest example" in Texas of the "native white Anglo-Saxon Protestant" world, one largely bereft of blacks and with a Hispanic population mostly relegated to menial jobs, living in small enclaves on the outskirts of towns. Local preachers applauded the "pure-blooded, homogeneous" WASP character of their parishioners, many with ancestries in the backwoods of the South but now mostly middle class and often wealthy from cattle, cotton, or oil. The politics of the region mixed provincial folk fundamentalism with the "strongly ideological economic conservatism" of the nouveau riche, people who voted for Goldwater or Reagan even if they were Democrats, people suspicious of government, trade unions, and foreign involvements, and particularly the United Nations.[21]

George W. Bush grew up in Midland. He is a Texan, but also an aristocrat born into one of the most influential and wealthy dynasties in America. James Smith Bush was the first family member to attend Yale (in the 1850s) and became a prominent minister in the leading faith of the American establishment, Episcopalianism. His son, Samuel Prescott Bush, made the family's first fortune a century ago in Ohio industry (manufacturing steel castings for railway cars), and formed a marriage alliance with an even wealthier midwestern industrialist, George Herbert Walker. A buyer and seller of railways, Walker was close to Union Pacific head E. H. Harriman and his son, Averell, and to Robert S. Lovett, who took over management of the Union Pacific after the senior Harriman died in 1909. After World War I, Averell Harriman hired Walker to run his new Wall Street investment firm, W. A. Harriman and Company. Throughout the 1920s Walker ran this company and directed various investment vehicles for Harriman—one of the richest men in America. But Walker himself was no slouch, owning homes in Kennebunkport, Maine, Santa Barbara, Long Island, South Carolina, and a fabulous residence at 1 Sutton Place in Manhattan. In 1921 his eldest and favorite child, Dorothy, married Prescott Bush.[22]

Walker's son-in-law epitomized the Anglophile eastern establishment: Yale education, tapped by Skull and Bones, affecting British styles in clothing and speech, building the family mansion on Grove Lane in Greenwich, Connecticut, rising to the top of his father-in-law's firm—which by then had become Brown Brothers Harriman (for decades the largest investment bank in the United States). Later on Prescott Bush got elected to the Senate and had a wide network of friends in business, government, diplomatic and intelligence services, and needless to say, a host of all the right clubs. He and George Herbert Walker Jr. ("Uncle Herbie" to George H. W. Bush) exemplified what Washington insider Joseph Alsop "rightly called the 'WASP Ascendancy.'" Success in college sports was almost as important as one's subsequent career; the Bush trifecta in getting grandfather, son, and grandson into Skull and Bones and all three onto the Yale baseball team was remarkable, especially when recalling Franklin D. Roosevelt's failure to get into Harvard's Porcellian Club (where Theodore Roosevelt had been a member), which dogged him the rest of his life. In effect college never ended for the Bushes; Prescott donned a raccoon coat to introduce presidential candidate Dwight Eisenhower at Yale in 1952, and his son and grandson never outgrew their love of college pranks.[23]

This is hardly a typical Texas story, but it nonetheless became a Texas story when George H. W. Bush moved to Midland in 1948 and began a succession of independent oil ventures, funded by $50,000 from his father and $850,000 from Uncle Herbie. One of them was the Zapata Petroleum Corporation, a drilling outfit that got its name when Bush saw Marlon Brando in *Viva Zapata!* Bush was hardly the only Ivy Leaguer in Midland— many millionaires lived along Harvard or Princeton streets, and this budding if still small city had Harvard, Yale, and Princeton clubs.[24] But it was the rare oilman who had a senator from Greenwich for a father, a stalwart of an eastern Republicanism which barely existed in Texas—and after the 1952 defeat of Taft at the convention, Texas was increasingly moving toward a new, western Republicanism. George Bush senior wanted to bridge these two wings of his party and ultimately succeeded enough to win the presidency on his own. But his son George truly did bridge this gap, to forge successive administrations based in the so-called red states. And unlike his father, he went Texan with a vengeance.

George W. Bush is the epitome of Santayana's lapsed (or simply forgotten) genteel tradition, the victorious and blameless American. He may have gone through Andover, Yale, and Skull and Bones, but he also went to San Jacinto Junior High School instead of Greenwich Country Day, spoke Texan, walked Texan, and after conquering alcoholism, remade himself in the image of a God-fearing, Bible-thumping, gun-toting rancher. If Reagan had decades of Hollywood practice at feigning the cowboy role, Bush's Texas imprint made him seem like the real thing, uniting Republicans not in the old Northeast, but throughout the sun drenched, air-conditioned South and Southwest (where so many Americans had moved since the war) and in the underpopulated central and western states of the interior. George Bush showed that with these red states plus Florida and Texas, you could write off the Atlantic and Pacific coasts and still become president.

Eden's Archipelago: Niseis Win, Haoles Lose, the Pentagon Triumphs

If World War II moved America from isolation to global involvement, it transformed Hawaii from colony to modernity: it "cracked the spine of sugar feudalism, opened up a contracting economy and an immobile society, shattered forever the pleasant but formidable colonial world in which a handful of families controlled everything Hawaii did," in Joan Didion's cogent words.[25] Actually, the U.S. Army cracked the spine of planter dominance by declaring martial law on December 7, 1941, and keeping it in place for four years. Army officers ran courts, newspapers, hospitals, food production, utilities, and labor organizations; they made a quick accommodation with the oligarchy, putting many into top positions, and of course business did well during the war. Once the war ended several new forces made it impossible for the oligarchy to sustain its nearly seamless power (except in business, where it continued apace down to recent times): Nisei war heroes, a huge influx of soldiers who stayed on to live in the islands, the GI Bill opening higher education to all veterans, labor-saving machinery that began to empty the sugar fields, and electoral victories that ultimately gave the Democratic Party a stranglehold on power for decades to come.

Among the maimed of the decorated Nisei 442nd Regimental Combat Team was Daniel K. Inouye, who like his close friend Bob Dole of Kansas embodied the bloody sacrifices of American GIs and filled every room he entered with his presence and an unimpeachable, mute dignity—left hand extended, right sleeve in a coat pocket. In 1954 he, Spark Matsunaga, and hundreds of other new faces captured the territorial legislature and inaugurated a Democratic hegemony that has yet to end. Eight years later Mr. Inouye defeated a scion of the old oligarchy, Ben Dillingham, in a landslide vote that brought him a Senate seat in perpetuity. This outcome, too, had an interesting provenance: Jack Burns was a pioneer in racial harmony, having recruited several Asian-Americans who spoke Japanese to do secret investigations of the Japanese community before Pearl Harbor, which convinced him, the police, and eventually the FBI that the community was completely loyal. Burns backed Inouye and many others like him and dominated Hawaiian politics from 1954 until his death in 1975, winning three terms as governor—and then his protégé George Ariyoshi succeeded him for one term after another.[26] Among the Pacific states Hawaii has the most interesting politics—California takes the cake for the bizarre and unimaginable (Jerry Brown, Arnold Schwarzenegger), of course, but Hawaii has had serious, well-organized party politics: Republican dominance from the 1890s through the war, Democratic hegemony ever since.

The U.S. military was also a big winner in Hawaii because the war (and especially the cold war) made it the largest single employer on the islands—its expenditures quickly exceeded the total value of all Hawaii's exports. During the war more than 400,000 military personnel were stationed in or recuperating in Hawaii, and it remained a major rest and recreation point during the wars in Korea and Vietnam. By 1959 when statehood was achieved (over the objection of southern congressmen who thought the population was insufficiently white), military personnel and their dependents made up one-sixth of the population, a quarter of the citizens depended directly on defense spending, and over the years 16 to 25 percent of the land was owned or controlled by the military. The Pentagon employed 1 in every 7 people in Hawaii by 1980, and in 1990 military personnel and their dependents numbered 117,216 of a total population of 1.1 million, with an overwhelming concentration on the island of O'ahu (Hawaii's total area is 6,423 square miles, but O'ahu is less than one-tenth of that). The end of the cold war brought their numbers down to around 78,000 by 2000, but nearly 16,000 civilians also worked for the military, 112,000 veterans lived in the islands, and the military still owned or controlled 239,000 acres, compared to 63,000 acres given over to sugarcane, and 15,500 for pineapples; defense expenditures were 10 percent of the gross state product in 2000, second only to tourism, and both left the declining sugar sector far behind.[27] Edenic Hawaii, in other words, was and is the most militarized state in the union.

In the post–cold war era the military persists as a large employer in Hawaii and a large gobbler of real estate. The sterling courage of a Daniel Inouye and the heroism symbolized by the sands of Iwo Jima have given way, however, to a long slog through the perilous hills and dales, lurking water hazards, dangerous traps and concrete-fast greens of the marines' Klipper Golf Course, the Fort Shafter links, and the five other Pentagon-run golf courses on O'ahu (the Defense Department runs 234 golf courses worldwide). Military music may be an oxymoron, but the Pentagon loves its bands so much that (as David J. Kilcullen points out) they have more members than the entire Foreign Service. Senator Inouye, meanwhile, is one of the Pentagon's best friends in Congress, channeling billions of dollars of pork into the Hawaiian barrel for new submarine facilities, missile ranges, optical space tracking stations, a new National Guard medevac group, housing upgrades at various bases, not to mention $1 million to make sure the brown tree snake doesn't inadvertently slither aboard a stateside military aircraft and find a new habitat in Hawaii.[28]

In their leisure, American forces in Hawaii carry on the century-old tradition of the Pacific Army, which had its own prophylaxis clinic or "pro shop" as early as 1914 and licensed and inspected a dozen brothels by the 1930s. Eventually the military set up a huge administrative apparatus to regulate a trade in which women routinely had sex with as many as 100 men each day. Soldier-athletes joined semi-professional baseball, basketball, and football teams or boxed for their units. Commanders would "draft" recruits known for their athletic skills, and no base was more noted for this than the Schofield Barracks, which had a 10,000-seat "Boxing Bowl."[29] (When Montgomery Clift takes on the big bruiser and knocks him out in *From Here to Eternity*, James Jones knew whereof he spoke.) The military has been a remarkable venue for upward mobility, into the manifold plebian delights that the Pacific Army might offer enlisted men or officers—a chance to live the life of wealthy colons. William H. Whyte once likened suburbs to "a lay version of Army post life," a brilliant observation, and all the more so as suburbs became gated communities employing private policing forces. On O'ahu it is the reverse: as you drive around the bases and through the nicer suburbs, almost all of them are inhabited by the military, a Pentagon version of suburban life (with guard posts courtesy of the American taxpayer). As a nine-year-old told the *Honolulu Star-Bulletin*, "I love this housing because it is very safe. We don't need to worry about thieves, kidnappers or murderers."[30]

The indulgent good life reached its nadir in February 2001 when the captain of the USS *Greeneville* took his nuclear attack submarine out for "maneuvers" off Waikiki Beach to give several wealthy civilian supporters of the navy a boat ride.[31] As these guests milled around and playacted at the controls, the captain ordered the submarine to leap to the surface in attack mode, just in time to capsize the *Ehime Maru* and kill nine Japanese tourists, four of them high school students. If this accident mingled tragedy and farce in an absurd mix, with the feckless Prime Minister Mori Yoshirō getting the news on the golf course and deciding to play out his round, it was an accident waiting to happen and all too symbolic of how the hugely expensive American military machine searches for a function since the Soviet Union collapsed.

Gidget Goes Hawaiian

The advent of commercial jet travel in the late 1950s brought an enormous new force field of humanity down upon the islands: tourists. Waikiki Beach, now almost invisible amid a forest of high-rise buildings, had but three hotels before Pearl Harbor—even if one of them, the Royal Hawaiian, was a pink stucco paean to art deco splendor (its persimmon and obsidian marble lobby is still a wonder to behold). Opened in 1927, it offered high-speed elevators, badminton and croquet, its own white-sand beach, and native boys who climbed coconut trees and other things for tips. Before the war a grand total of some 500 air travelers arrived annually on Pan Am Clippers, most of them rich; Hollywood stars like Bob Hope and Mary Pickford joined the Rockefellers in well-publicized (by the sugar barons) celebrity cruises to Honolulu. Then commercial jet travel opened the floodgates: in the 1950s tourist spending grew by 350 percent, by 1960 half a million tourists had arrived by commercial airliner, and that was a mere down payment on a trade that ballooned beyond anyone's imagination—5 million tourists by 1985, 7 million by 2000, of which nearly 2 million came from Japan (and what tourists they were; the Japanese spent an average of $586 a day, compared to $119 a day from mainlanders). Right in the middle of this postwar explosion was World War II magnate Henry J. Kaiser, who saw the tourist hordes coming from many miles away and built the Hawaiian Village Hotel on top of slums and a swamp. Soon he also had a cement plant, a hospital, a TV station, and the ticket for what to do with obsolescent sugar plantations: turn them into real estate subdivisions and resorts (like the 14,000-home Koko Head resort city). Good New Deal industrialist that he was, Kaiser also brought low-cost comprehensive health care to Hawaii. Castle and Cooke, however, still looked only at the bottom line—and went into macadamia nuts and tuna fish. Meanwhile the Royal Hawaiian still had a starring role: in *Gidget Goes Hawaiian* (1961), Sandra Dee stays there with her parents, surfs, does the hula, and contemplates losing her virginity (that is, her character's virginity) under the paradisal "spell" of lovely Waikiki.[32]

Ultimately so much wealth has been produced in or showered on these islands—the military, tourists, successive real estate booms—that the postwar Democratic establishment could join the elite, prosper for themselves, and still confer generous welfare benefits on the people. Democratic hegemony coinciding with a long, even perennial, economic boom: this may be as good as it gets in America. This accommodation, so well analyzed by George Cooper and Gavan Daws,[33] meant many things: an osmotic disinclination to attack concentrated wealth or break up the venerable landholdings of the old caciques, the flip side of everybody making money in all manner of "development," and the resultant perduring of the Big Five down to the present, if in altered form; an astonishingly interlocked elite, if now encompassing missionary offspring, the upwardly mobile Japanese-Americans, and multiethnic hoi polloi; a bipartisan welcome mat rolled out to all things military and all things Japanese; booms one after another—tourist booms, defense booms, resort and condo booms, high-tech booms—all concentrated around the hottest real estate market in America; eternally rising living standards and home sale windfalls; endless hogwash about the manifold importance of the Pacific Rim and Hawaii's place in it; and one of the truly multiracial, multicultural societies in the nation—with many natives now wanting to take back their islands, and their sovereignty.[34] The venerable Punahou School is known now not for its doting succor to the planters' offspring, but for its most illustrious graduate: the multiethnic-in-one-person politician known as Barack Obama (who "eastered" from Hawaii to Occidental College to Harvard, thence to the White House). Somehow it seems appropriate that the austere, astringent Calvinist interlopers from Maine, driven nearly insane by the joie de vivre of the Hawaiians, should find themselves dissolving away in a wealthy sea of polyglot humanity.

A Cold Cold-War Bastion

Alaska's proximity to Japan and the Soviet Union gave it an overriding importance in World War II and the cold war, and so defense billions came pouring in there, too. In the late 1940s the Pentagon built Eielson Air Force Base near Fairbanks, designed for long-range bombers; when it opened it was the largest air field in the world. World War II bases like Fort Richardson and Elmendorf Air Force Base got refurbished and improved, and other bases emerged on the islands of St. Lawrence, Kodiak, Shemya, and Adak. St. Lawrence, where soldiers monitored Soviet radio transmissions a scant fifty miles away from Siberia, might be the worst posting in the world with freezing temperatures ten months of the year, no daylight in the dead of winter, and arctic winds howling outside the fifteen Quonset huts making up this listening post, sending temperatures to minus 60 degrees. Governor Ernest Gruening, later a strong opponent of the Vietnam War as a senator, campaigned for a comprehensive radar network in Alaska to give early warning of Soviet attack—later known as the Distant Early Warning or DEW line. Three thousand miles long, it was built over four years by American and Canadian construction crews totaling 23,000. Punctuated by fifty radar stations each with massive gold domes, the DEW line was operational by 1957 and connected up to the North American Defense Command (NORAD) in Colorado Springs. It was supposed to monitor Soviet Tu-16 Badger long-range bombers introduced in 1955, with 4,250-mile range. Soon, however, it scanned the heavens for intercontinental ballistic missiles arcing toward the continental United States, their supersonic speed leaving a scant twenty minutes of warning time.[35]

Postwar Alaska, like the Pentagon, lives comfortably amid acronyms—but really just two: ANCSA and ANILCA. The first is the Alaska Native Claims Settlement Act of 1971, and the second is the Alaska National Interest Lands Conservation Act of 1980, which would appear to have two unnecessary words—but they refer to ANILCA's place in American environmental history. The act denied 28 percent of Alaskan land to "development," and when added to the existing 12 percent already removed, close to half (42 percent) of the entire state was environmentally protected. ANILCA also set aside 104 million acres for conservation (and put 50 million acres of that into the wilderness category), thereby doubling the nation's total exempt land (thus the two odd words: "national interest"), while allowing Indians access to fish, game, and other resources on the same land (called "subsistence provisions"). Sixty percent of Alaskan land, an area twice the size of California, is thus reserved by the federal government; ANILCA is probably the best legislative victory for the environment in U.S. history.

Development interests supported by the majority of the settler population launched a protracted struggle against ANILCA, delaying implementation through the state legislature of its subsistence provisions until Washington mounted a takeover of fish and game management in 1998–99. This would be surprising if we imagine the average Alaskan off in the wilderness shooting grizzlies, but most whites live in urban settings, like their counterparts in the lower forty-eight; Anchorage, in particular, which began as a collectivity of tents in 1914, is every bit as undistinguished a city as Reno or Tampa. Meanwhile most Indians (16 percent of Alaska's population) actually live out the myths of the frontier—fishing, hunting, living off the land.[36]

These rugged individuals include Eskimos and Aleuts, two non-Indian aboriginal groups, and Pacific Northwest Coast and Athabaskan Indians, about 100,000 strong all tolled. They were the beneficiaries of ANCSA, "perhaps the most generous settlement ever between the federal government and American Natives," in the words of Stephen Haycox. They got fee simple title to 40 million acres of land in and around their villages; in recompense for relinquishing title claims to Alaska's remaining 330 million acres, the tribes received nearly $1 billion, which was used to capitalize twelve regional development centers and to support village corporations, most of which have proved successful over the years. Perhaps most important, over succeeding decades contempt for Alaska's native peoples, which had been ubiquitous, "disappeared from the press and from common discourse"—it was "a civil rights triumph." The oil companies also benefited from ANCSA because natives would never have agreed to pipelines if their claims had not been settled.[37]

Alaskans appear to be interested in Alaska but not much in the lower forty-eight: John McPhee called it "a foreign country significantly populated with Americans." They take the pre-Microsoft provincialism of Seattle and the measured pace of Oregon and quadruple both, into a world of *our* wilderness, our salmon, our bears, our mountains, our strawberries (Susitnas, Talkeetnas, and Matareds are just three of their strawberry varieties). Alaskan pride is stirred by cabbages the size of medicine balls, zucchinis like Trident submarines, elongated rhubarbs and bulbous cauliflower—it all grows there, not to mention eight-foot high-clover. The state motto might be, "never put restrictions on an individual," and let's not even mention that awful federal government, which used to own 99 percent of this state and now—a mere 60 percent. Alaskans love their winter silence, like softly falling snow in a vast natural chamber with no resonance; their aloneness is more complete than the "We Three" of the memorable Ink Spots song: they have themselves and their shadow—but no echo. Imagine there were only twenty-five people in New Jersey, McPhee wrote, as he tried to fathom a wilderness experience like no other (in Alaska, one person per square mile; in New Jersey, more than a thousand per square mile, ranking first among the states). A very slow pace comes to a glacial halt as the freezes descend. Families hunt through September and then subsist through the dark winter months on moose meatloaf, ground moose with Spanish rice, "spaghetti with mooseburger," and "Swiss moosesteak." Sometimes the monotony is broken with fresh shoulders of grizzly—a burgundy-colored cut, "more flavorful than any wild meat," including muskrat, weasel and . . . moose.[38]

Black Gold Again

Statehood deliberations coincided with the first oil discoveries in 1957 on the Kenai National Moose Range, managed by the Fish and Wildlife Service. The service had approved some exploration licenses two years earlier, and when big wells turned up Alaskans decided they didn't like moose that much after all. A decade later Atlantic Richfield found a deposit forty-five miles long and eighteen miles wide at Prudhoe Bay, a vast pool promising 15 billion barrels of oil and billions more cubic feet of natural gas—the biggest field ever found in the United States, which happened to sit between two federal land withdrawals: the largest wildlife area in the country and a strategic petroleum reserve. The battle was joined instantly between the oil developers (supported by most settlers) and the environmentalists. We know who won, of course. Alaska did not simply have an oil boom: after oil got funneled through the notorious permafrost pipeline, it remade the state. Oil provided more than 40 percent of the state's income, another 35 percent came from the federal government, and both towered over other private sector activities. Oil created more than 33,000 jobs (fully 28,000 workers were needed to build the pipeline, which ultimately cost nearly $8 billion). State tax coffers swelled by $50 billion from the 1970s to 2000 as oil accounted for 85 percent of revenue and literally spilled over, in that Alaskan residents got new high schools wherever there were at least fifteen students and annual dividend checks for everybody —$800 in 1982, rising to over $1,000 per resident in recent years. The pipeline has never had a serious leak, vindicating the developers.[39] No, Alaska didn't suffer leaks—just an 11-million-gallon cataract.

In 1899 E. H. Harriman's entourage cruised around Prince William Sound, as we have seen, flabbergasted by its natural beauty, its fjords (one of them got named Harriman Fjord), its soaring bald eagles, elephant seals and killer whales, its glaciers (four of which they named Smith, Bryn Mawr, Vassar, and Wellesley in hopes of planting a frosty New England here, too). In 1989 another ship entered the same sound, piloted by a drunken captain; it was three football fields long and filled with the equivalent of 1.26 million barrels of oil. It left its filling station at Valdez on the evening of March 27, skirted around some icebergs, and then "fetched up" on a reef just past midnight—it was now Good Friday. After Bligh Reef breached its holding tanks the *Exxon Valdez* kept going another 600 feet, disgorging nearly 11 million gallons of petroleum into the pristine sound. Then a spring storm lashed the area, making the deployment of containment booms impossible. The biggest oil spill in American history slicked 1,300 miles of shoreline and 200 miles of beaches and killed in the neighborhood of 22 killer whales, 250 bald eagles, 300 seals, 2,800 otters, and 250,000 seabirds of all varieties. Eventually the federal and state governments fined Exxon $150 million, later reduced to $25 million—not to let Exxon off the hook but in recognition of the $2.1 billion it paid out to clean up its own mess (a quarter of what it cost to build the Trans-Alaska Pipeline).[40]

A Containment Policy

They glide by on trucks and railcars with names like Hanjin pasted on their sides, they sit piled up on docks: what are they? Containers seemed to sneak up on us, starting up slowly and unnoticed in April 1956 when a reconfigured World War II tanker ferried fifty-eight aluminum truck bodies (wheels removed) from Newark to Houston. A North Carolinian named Malcolm P. McLean was sick and tired of Northeast Corridor transportation bottlenecks and dreamed of driving his company's trucks right onto surplus cargo ships and sending them up and down the coast. It turned out to be smarter to leave the undercarriage and take the truck box; then you could stack them one on top of another. When his business began, people paid $5.83 per ton to load cargo by the usual methods; it was less than 16 cents per ton when they did it McLean's way.[41] The sea-to-sea continent paid immeasurable dividends as ocean shippers stuffed cargo into the boxes, stacked them up, and offloaded them to waiting trains and 18-wheelers with almost no human labor. Another American invention, containers: a little-noticed but crucial contributor to the time-and-space of world commerce, this simple technology did more to circumambulate the globe than the steamship or the railways. Remember the difference between St. Louis stevedores loading individual bags of grain onto Mississippi barges and Chicago's grain elevators: now the elevated cranes are everywhere, but they deploy nondescript boxes. Containers are like Chicago's pigs or Swift's refrigerated cars, except they don't carry a river of corn or oranges: they carry everything.

What was good for Mr. McLean on the East Coast was far better for a planet covered two-thirds by water: it revived the oldest American transportation method, the riparian, at unheard of distances and economies of scale. A fully loaded, seemingly endless coal train is an awesome artifact of every midwesterner's childhood and ferries the heaviest weights across terra firma (some 23,000 tons); a big container ship carries three or four times that weight. A ship with 3,000 containers can be sent around the world with a crew of twenty, and it takes a mere ninety seconds for a giant crane to unload each box. A container leaving Malaysia arrives in Seattle in nine days, hops on a train to Chicago the next day, gets offloaded to a truck and arrives in Cincinnati twenty-two days after it left Penang. The gains from containers were revolutionary: if Mr. McLean drove his costs down by a factor of 37, shipping costs almost evaporated. In 1961 shipping constituted 12 percent of the value of all U.S. exports and remained relatively high through the late 1970s; although estimating these costs is very tricky, they are probably less than 5 percent today.[42]

With container shipping Pacific Coast ports were perfectly poised as entrepôts for the takeoff of the American West Coast and the East Asian economies, displacing the old centers and the old methods, like New York and San Francisco where tens of thousands of dockworkers clustered in the early postwar period—gantry cranes digging heavy pallets out of the hold, longshoremen unpacking the cargo, unions making the rules, the Mafia exacting surcharges, people darting here and there pilfering goods, Marlon Brando failing to become a contender. Container shipping turned the port of Seattle into James J. Hill's dream (a century late), making a rapid land bridge of the continent for shipments going back and forth between Asia, the United States, and Europe; depending on the year, either Seattle or San Jose leads all exporting cities in the country. Seattle was always closer (by a day's shipping) to Japan, Korea, and north China than any other Pacific port, but the container land bridge drastically reduced shipping costs with high-tech apparatuses that cluster like whooping cranes along the shore; lifting a container off a ship and depositing it on a train is almost automatic. In 1972 Portland and Seattle had about the same value of exports ($348 million for Seattle, $388 million for Portland), but by 1986 Seattle had $4.2 billion, Portland about $2 billion, and thereafter Seattle's trade just dwarfed its Oregon neighbor.[43]

Today Southern California is clearly the epicenter of the American container trade because it handles the exports of the workshop of the world: China, which fills more than a quarter of all existing containers. Indeed, it is impossible to imagine China's leap into the forefront of export-led development in the past thirty years without container shipping; Hong Kong and nearby Shenzhen handled 23 million twenty-foot containers in 2001, compared to 10 million in Los Angeles/Long Beach and a paltry 3.3 million in New York/Newark. Among world container ports, Los Angeles and San Pedro together ranked third in 2001, and Southern California ranked first when Long Beach was added. Oakland (another massive container entrepôt) completely displaced San Francisco, just as McLean's Sea-Land company in Newark devastated New York ports (the New York metropolitan area ranked fourteenth, but that was mostly Newark). By 2003 Los Angeles ranked eighth in the world by itself, Long Beach thirteenth, and Seattle was twenty-eighth (more telling, of the twenty largest container ports in the world, thirteen were on the Pacific Rim).[44]

I fear the reader may anticipate the next sentence, but even here the Pentagon was important. If the provenance of this invention was entirely in the open market, Sea-Land solved an enormous logistical problem for American forces as the rapid Vietnam buildup got going in 1965, by turning Cam Ranh Bay into a busy containerport. Since the ships had little to bring back, the same containers headed north to pick up exports in Japan, which touched off the ubiquitous container trade soon visible in any East Asian port. The business is now so refined that floating mega-platforms with 5,000—and soon 10,000—containers ply the Pacific, riding low in the water and taking their time, because the ships generate tremendous momentum and so "fuel consumption does not increase in proportion to tonnage," in Witold Rybczynski's words, yielding economies of scale like the riverine barges of the eighteenth century but with a planet to roam, thereby slashing even the miniscule costs of container transport a decade ago by 40 and 50 percent.[45] Your Nike sneaker, or anything else with parts hailing from ten or twelve countries, is inexplicable apart from the commodity chain made possible by dirt cheap shipping in containers. Cargo: finally this odd word has fulfilled its telos.

The Pacific Bridal Couch

The first Asian-Americans walked here over the Aleutian Island land bridge thousands of years ago. Today they have returned to populate all walks of life in this country, even if many whites remain clueless. Congressman Norman Mineta, a Nisei with ten terms in the House under his belt, got complemented on his good English by a General Motors executive, who then asked, "How long have you been in this country?" Senator Sam Brownback enjoyed faking a Chinese accent while lambasting Asian-American fundraising for President Clinton: "no raise money, no get bonus." Self-consciously Irish journalist Jimmy Breslin, outraged about reporter Ji-Yeon Yuh writing in *Newsday* that one of his columns was "sexist," bellowed out to the whole newsroom that "The fucking bitch doesn't know her place. She's a little dog, a little cur . . . a yellow cur. Let's make it racial." And just to show how off base Yuh's allegation was, for good measure he called her "a slant-eyed cunt."[46] Dr. Yuh's place is now in the Northwestern University History Department; she's a friend of mine, as is her brother. He told me about playing high school basketball in Georgia and hearing "chink" and "Jap" and "slope" as he ran down the court (he's Korean-American). When Asian-Americans finally achieve political clout commensurate with their wealth, education, and professional status in the country (they are nowhere near that position yet), this crude but usually visceral and unthinking abuse will move out of the public domain and into the quiet of private homes.

Science is still catching up to reality, too. In 1931 anatomy professor Robert Bennett Bean predictably determined that "the brain of the White Race is large," that of "the Yellow-Brown race" only "medium human in size"—but here's the good news: that makes Asians "less subject to cares and worries." It seems laughable, but in the 1990s psychologist J. Philippe Rushton sized up racial brains yet again, finding Professor Bean to be in error: "Oriental" brains are quite as large as white brains. But Rushton also assayed a second part of the anatomy to determine personality type and behavior. The more intelligent a person is, he discovered, the bigger the brain and the smaller his (and her?) genitalia and vice versa. "The racial gradient of Oriental-white-black occurs on multifariously complex dimensions," to be sure, but judging from "brain size, intelligence, and personality to law abidingness, social organization, and reproductive morphology, Africans and Asians average at opposite ends of the continuum, with Caucasian populations falling intermediately." Dr. Rushton's scientific inquiry also found that Orientals tend to be passive, but then people with larger brains tend to be that way, he explained.[47] Like the subtle alterations in Faye Dunaway's countenance as *Chinatown* progressed, America is looking more and more Asian—but still not thinking much about the likely consequences.

CHAPTER FIFTEEN

Archipelago of Empire: An American Grid for the Global Garden

We have been compelled to create a permanent armaments industry of vast proportions. . . . We annually spend on military security more than the net income of all United States corporations. The conjunction of an immense military establishment and a large arms industry is new to the American experience. The total influence—economic, political, even spiritual—is felt in every city, every Statehouse, every office of the Federal Government. We recognize the imperative need for this development. Yet we must not fail to comprehend its grave implications.

—President Dwight Eisenhower, January 17, 1961

Academe unfortunately turns up few practitioners of the occult art of maintaining internal combustion engines. But one venerable figure used to hop on his motorcycle in Nyack, a lovely Hudson River town, and roar down to Columbia University with leather saddlebags flying in the wind. He often said sociology was easy, tuning up a Harley was difficult. Somewhat like President Eisenhower, C. Wright Mills took a look around in the 1950s and discerned something entirely new in American life: a military-industrial complex. More than that, a "power elite" made most of the important decisions: a tripartite group of corporate leaders, executive branch administrators, and military brass had a virtual monopoly on key choices, industrial production, and the use of force. They talked to each other, exchanged jobs, sat on the same corporate boards, played golf together, and occupied the top portion of a pyramid of power (which suspiciously resembled the Masonic symbol on the back of your dollar bill). Just beneath the top were "the middle levels of power," which corresponded to the democratic and pluralist theories about how the country works that people imbibed from first grade through their PhD programs. Below that was a "mass society" filling two-thirds of the pyramid and containing most Americans, who were mostly clueless about elite practices.

For Mills, the idea that public opinion guided public affairs was a mere fairy tale. He couldn't figure out how this elite made its decisions—since there was so little evidence—but he knew all of them had prospered in the context of "an 'emergency' without a foreseeable end," that being not World War II but the turning point of 1950 and NSC-68, inaugurating an unprecedented era in American life. When the emergency ended in 1991, along came another one, just as Mills would have predicted, and his tripartite power elite is far more influential today than it was 50 years ago.[1]

Becoming Hegemonic

The United States basked in its own hemisphere for 150 years, rolling around like an Atlantic and Pacific great whale in the free national security afforded by its continental breadth and isolation, the absence of any credible threat, and the shelter of oceans on which the friendly British navy was dominant. World War II began for Americans in the Pacific, and that remained the primary theater (if not the main priority) of American warfare until D-Day in June 1944. If the allies bore the brunt of the fighting against the Nazis, especially the Russians, the United States was preeminent in the Pacific fighting and proceeded to organize a unilateral occupation of Japan and a general reorganization of postwar East Asian international relations. But in the years immediately after the end of the war, American power was tentative and unformed; under different leadership, it might well have receded back to continental isolation. It was not until 1947 that internationalist elites in Washington established a clear line and direction for America's position in the postwar world—to fulfill John Hay's prescience in 1900 and inherit Britain's hegemonic role at long last.

The baton of world leadership finally and definitively passed from London to Washington on February 21, 1947, when a British Embassy official informed Dean Acheson that England could not give Greece and Turkey $250 million in military and economic aid; by implication, it could no longer defend the Mediterranean and the newly found chasms of Middle Eastern petroleum. A few days later Acheson walked off to lunch with a friend, remarking that "there are only two powers in the world now," the United States and the Soviet Union. Acheson did not mean that an era of bipolarity had dawned, although he meant that as well; he meant something much deeper—the substitution of American for British leadership. Acheson was present at this creation and did not mistake the opportunities and perils of America's new position in the world.[2] His problem was to be pregnant with an idea that he could not articulate, lest Harry Truman lose the next election (for example, by announcing that the United States had now become the power of last resort for the world). To put it differently, the internationalist forces in American politics lacked a strong domestic base, particularly in the Congress. George Kennan provided the solution to this dilemma with an elegant metaphor: containment. Imagine, for an America to march outward and inherit Britain's role, and you mark it up for the defense. Imagine, a doctrine defining hegemony by what it opposes, obviating the necessity to explain to the American people what it is and what its consequences would be for them. But it worked: the decisions taken in the late 1940s shaped the world for the rest of the century.

Acheson knew almost nothing about military power. For him and other American statesmen, the defeat of Japan and Germany and the struggle with communism were but one part, and the secondary part, of an American project to revive the world economy from the devastation of global depression and world war. Acheson was an internationalist in his bones, looking to Europe and especially Britain for support and guidance, just like Henry Cabot Lodge, and seeking multilateral solutions to postwar problems. At first the problem of restoring the world economy seemed to be solved with the Bretton Woods mechanisms elaborated in 1944 (the World Bank and the International Monetary Fund). When by 1947 they had not worked to revive the advanced industrial states, the Marshall Plan arrived in Europe and the "reverse course" in Japan, removing controls on heavy industries in the defeated powers. When by 1950 the allied economies were still not growing sufficiently, NSC-68, written mostly by Paul Nitze but guided by the thinking of Acheson (by then President Truman's secretary of state), hit upon military Keynesianism as a device that did, finally, prime the pump of the advanced industrial economies (and especially Japan). The Korean War was the crisis that built the American national security state and pushed through the money to pay for it, and with victory in the war to reestablish the South (containment) and defeat in the war to topple the North (regime change), this war transformed and stabilized Kennan's doctrine. It also finally got the Japanese and West German economies growing strongly. From June to December 1950 the defense budget quadrupled, from $13 to $56 billion (or from $151 to $650 billion in constant 2007 dollars) or 14 percent of GNP, a high point never again reached during the cold war or even the dual wars in Iraq and Afghanistan.[3]

In the special partnership with Britain from 1900 to 1947, Americans learned how to pursue national interests through multilateral mechanisms and close relations with European allies, how to shape an intelligence function that was primarily civilian and academic, and ultimately how to take England's role upon itself. The American internationalists like Stimson or Acheson sought a hegemony defined as first among equals, through many-sided cooperation with Europe. They did not challenge European colonies but hoped to get an American foot in the door—through the "open door."[4] They were Atlanticists. If they had towering influence after 1941, they were never very influential before that. Then the bipolar rivalry with Moscow welded the United States to Western Europe in a way that might not have happened without the Soviet threat. After the cold war ended and the Soviet Union collapsed, the influence of the internationalists waned marginally in the 1990s—and then in the new century, dramatically. As the cold war recedes into history, so the American commitment to internationalism may as well. The westward-moving tradition of expansionism, unilateralism, the back turned to Europe, a belief in the efficacy of military force to forge political solutions, and violent confrontation with alien peoples came to life again in the new century. Atlanticist internationalism may be recuperated by new leaders coming to power in 2009, of course, but the iron necessity that forged it from 1941 to 1991 no longer exists. Meanwhile the military's heritage from World War II and Korea persists as if nothing had happened, as if Mills's "crisis" remained a vital threat to the nation.

Most postwar internationalists had little experience with or interest in the use of military force, an attribute they shared with John Hay and Henry Cabot Lodge. The seizure of Hawaii and the Philippines, the proclamation of the Open Door, and the intervention in the Boxer Rebellion marked a new outward advance, a thrust fully embodied in Teddy Roosevelt—it *was* empire, and it all happened in the Pacific. William Appleman Williams, following Charles Beard, memorably argued that this empire grew out of an agreement on expansion proposed by the agrarian South and West (cotton and wheat) and accepted by the industrial East.[5] The argument of this book has been different: empire grew out of the western thrust across the continent by expansionists who disdained Europe, its power politics, and its colonies, desiring instead maximum, unhindered American freedom in the world. Wall Street and the industrial East opposed the war with Spain, and if they weren't averse to taking the Philippines or sending troops time and time again to protect business interests in Central America, their preferred international model remained England, and particularly its hegemonic role as power of last resort in the long peace between 1815 and 1914. They were internationalist, multilateralist Atlanticists, and their heyday lasted sixty years, from 1941 to 2001. Since 1950, however, the American realm in the world has been

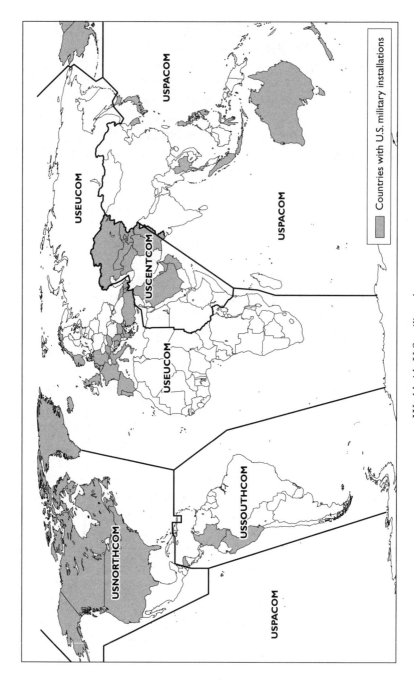

Worldwide U.S. military bases.

Map by Bill Nelson, based on maps done by the Peace Pledge Union and the U.S. Defense Department.

guaranteed by military forces who relate much more easily to the expansionist tendency. Empires need territory, and these folks live and work on an archipelago that is the clearest expression of the American empire.*

The Archipelago

In the second half of the twentieth century an entirely new phenomenon emerged in American history, namely, the permanent stationing of soldiers in a myriad of foreign bases across the face of the planet, connected to an enormous domestic complex of defense industries. For the first time in modern history the leading power maintained an extensive network of bases on the territory of its allies and economic competitors—Japan, Germany, Britain, Italy, South Korea, all the industrial powers save France and Russia—marking a radical break with the European balance of power and the operation of realpolitik and a radical departure in American history: an archipelago of empire.[6] The military structure of the British Empire was a globe-girdling chain of strategic naval bases, like the one at Singapore; no one in his right mind imagined British army bases perched on the soil of competing industrial nations.[7] The maritime dominance of the American archipelago is far greater than the United Kingdom's ever was, yet it also has vastly superior global air and land forces—and has bases almost everywhere.

This is an American realm with no name, a territorial presence with little if any standing in the literature of international affairs. The preferred strategy since Hay's Open Door was nonterritorial, whether in gaining access to imperial concessions in China a century ago, or in the postwar hegemony connoting a first-among-equals multilateralism: American preponderance but not dominance, a usage of hegemony consistent with its original Greek meaning in Thucydides or the ancient Roman *imperium* that also connoted nonterritorial power.[8] But hegemony and imperium sound equally inappropriate to most Americans: they sound like we run a colonial empire, as if we were England or Japan seventy years ago. We don't. But we do run a territorial empire—the archipelago of somewhere between 737 and 860 overseas military installations around the world, with American military personnel operating in 153 countries, which most Americans know little if anything about—a kind of stealth empire, "hidden in plain sight" as Kathy Ferguson and Phyllis Turnbull put it,[9] one part of which can occasionally be closed down (like U.S. bases in the Philippines in 1992) but which persists because it is politically and culturally invisible, at least to Americans.

---

* I first used the term "archipelago of empire" in Cumings (1993).

The postwar order took shape through positive policy and through the establishment of distinct outer limits, the transgression of which was rare or even inconceivable, provoking immediate crisis—the orientation of West Berlin toward the Soviet bloc, for example. That's what the bases were put there for, to defend our allies but also to limit their choices—a light hold on the jugular, which might sound too strong until Americans ask themselves, what would we think of myriad foreign bases on our soil? The typical experience of this hegemony, however, was a mundane, benign, and mostly unremarked daily life of subtle constraint, in which the United States kept allied nations on defense, resource, and, for many years, financial dependencies. This penetration was clearest in the frontline cold war semi-sovereign states like Japan, West Germany, and South Korea, and it was conceived by people like Kennan as an indirect, outer-limit control on the worst outcome, namely, orientation to the other side—what John McMurtry calls "determination by constraint": it simultaneously constrains and leaves a significant degree of autonomy.[10] The aggressors in World War II, Japan and Germany, were tied down by American bases, and they remain so: in the seventh decade after the war we still don't know what either nation would look like if it were truly independent. We aren't going to find out anytime soon, either.

In an important interpretation Robert Latham calls this structure the American "external state" and views it as a central element of liberal world-order building. The "free world" connoted a realm of liberal democracies and authoritarian client states. It was Acheson's liberal order, *and* it also led to a vast global militarization (by the 1960s encompassing 1.5 million American troops stationed in hundreds of bases in thirty-five countries, with formal security commitments to forty-three countries, the training and equipping of military forces in seventy countries), a phenomenon often treated as an unfortunate result of the bipolar confrontation with Moscow.[11] In another sense our troops in Japan and Germany are also *their* external state because without the bases they would have to rearm dramatically.

This permanent transnational military structure has not gone from victory to victory. Since 1950 the United States has fought four major wars—Korea, Vietnam, the Persian Gulf, and Iraq—and has only won one of them (at this writing). But outcomes have little impact on the archipelago's permanency. Win, lose, or draw, the wars end but the military no longer deflates and the troops no longer come home (with the exception of Vietnam: and had we been able to stabilize South Vietnam, they would still be there). The United States won a decisive victory in 1945, but the troops did not come home then, either: some 100,000 troops remain in Japan and Germany, just as the stalemate in Korea left 30,000 to 40,000 there.

The Korean War was the occasion for building a permanent standing military and a national security state where none had existed before, as containing communism became an open-ended, global proposition. A mere decade later President Eisenhower could say that "we have been compelled to create a permanent armaments industry of vast proportions," employing 3.5 million people in the defense establishment and spending more than "the net income of all United States corporations." That was from his farewell address; less remembered is Ike's final news conference where he sounded just like Mills by remarking that the armaments industry was so pervasive that it affected "almost an insidious penetration of our own minds," making Americans think that the only thing the country does is produce weapons and missiles.[12] When Western communism collapsed it appeared for a few years that a serious reduction in the permanent military might occur, but "rogue states" kept it going and then the "war on terror" provided another amorphous, open-ended global commitment.

This archipelago is the clearest territorial (and therefore imperial) element in the American position in the world, and it has its domestic counterpart in a host of home military bases and industries that serve defense needs, and in a highly lucrative revolving door where generals retire to become defense industry executives and industry executives take furloughs to run Washington agencies. (In 2001, for example, George W. Bush appointed Peter Teets, chief operating officer of Lockheed Martin, to run the National Reconnaissance Office—by far the best-funded intelligence agency; meanwhile the former NRO director, Jeff Harris, took a job with Lockheed Space Systems.)[13] Yet this archipelago is one of the most unstudied phenomena in American life. Although millions of Americans have inhabited these bases, their global landscape is so commonly unknown that its full dimensions almost always come as a surprise to the uninitiated (or to the initiates themselves: according to two eyewitnesses, when he arrived at the Pentagon in 2001 Secretary of Defense Donald Rumsfeld was surprised to learn that Korea still held 40,000 American troops).

There is a military-industrial complex, and certain firms are closely identified with this archipelago because they helped to build it: Bechtel for example. But it is difficult for outsiders to assess how things work, as Mills suggested, and easy to overestimate their influence. When the Bechtel Group sent Caspar Weinberger and George Shultz to serve in the Reagan administration, it was hard not to see a California conspiracy in the works: presumably power was now shifting radically west. In fact, Bechtel happily slurped at the federal trough for decades on a thoroughly bipartisan basis; John McCone, after all, was Kennedy's CIA chief, and Bechtel's candidate in 1980 was not Reagan but Texas Democrat John Connally. Furthermore, George Shultz had no respect for Weinberger going back to the Nixon administration when Shultz ran the Office of Management and Budget and Weinberger was his deputy; Shultz routinely bypassed Weinberger to get advice from Arnold R. Weber, a former colleague from the University of Chicago. Shultz was a savvy and unpretentious Henry Kissinger for one Republican administration or corporation after another, leaving Washington in May 1974 to run Bechtel as Nixon's imminent impeachment loomed, then coming back when Reagan asked him to be secretary of state.[14]

Long before George Shultz shifted from Washington to Bechtel and back, John McCone was an individual paradigm of the nexus between national security and industry—linking high position in Washington with Bechtel, defense firms, major oil companies, and vast construction projects in the Persian Gulf. He was one of the first westerners to join the establishment, and he was a charter member of the military-industrial complex with extraordinary staying power. After getting an engineering degree from Berkeley, he moved up to executive authority at Llewellyn Iron Works in Los Angeles, which provided steel fittings for the Boulder Dam. In 1937 he formed B-M-P in Los Angeles, specializing in the design and construction of petroleum refineries and power plants for installation throughout the United States, South America, and the Persian Gulf. After the war began his company built and managed the air force's modification center in Birmingham where B-24 and B-29 bombers were fitted out for combat, and through an affiliate called Pacific Tankers, he operated an extensive fleet of oil tankers for the U.S. Navy. By the 1950s a very wealthy man, he was the second largest shareholder in Standard Oil of California. During the cold war he held one sensitive post after another. He was a special assistant to then Secretary of Defense James Forrestal in 1948, undersecretary of the air force in 1950, head of the Atomic Energy Commission (AEC), and subsequently director of the CIA under both Eisenhower and Kennedy. Just at the time McCone became director of the AEC (a position that led Dwight Eisenhower to include him in the National Security Council), his friend Kenneth Davis left his position as director of reactor development at the AEC to go to work for Bechtel.[15] Bechtel, Shultz, Weinberger, and McCone are about a structure of state and corporate interests and a conservative Republican style of politics and business, a rightward-leaning ostensibly laissez-faire industrialism that hews closely to the state: but that has been true since the Six Companies built the Hoover Dam. And then there are all the Democrats who are part of the same elite, with liberal inflections.

A Waxing and Waning Military

Until 1950 Americans never supported a large standing army, and the military was a negligible factor in American history and culture, apart from its performance in wars. The Constitution itself "was constructed in fear of a powerful military establishment," the constituent states had their own independent militias, and only the navy seemed consonant with American conceptions of the uses of national military force. Americans loved victorious generals like Washington, Jackson, Taylor, Grant, and Eisenhower enough to make them presidents. But after the victory, the military blended back into the woodwork of American life. The army reached 50,000 during the war with Mexico, then dropped to about 10,000 soldiers, 90 percent of them arrayed against Indians in the trans-Mississippi West at seventy-nine posts and trailside forts. The military ballooned into millions of citizen-soldiers during the Civil War and the two world wars, but always the army withered within months and years of victory—to a 25,000-soldier constabulary in the late nineteenth century (at a time when France had half a million soldiers, Germany had 419,000, and continental-nation Russia had 766,000), a neglected force of 135,000 between the world wars, and a rapid (if temporary) shrinkage immediately after 1945. Likewise the navy declined quickly after the Civil War in spite of American prowess in ship technology, with the Asiatic Squadron retaining only five or six dilapidated gunboats. A permanent gain followed each war, but until 1941 the American military remained modest in size compared to other great powers, not well funded, not very influential, and indeed not really a respected profession. Military spending was less than 1 percent of GNP throughout the nineteenth century and well into the twentieth.[16]

The nineteenth-century American military was hardly a negligible fighting force. It was small but effective, flexible, worthy to its main task—fighting Indians—and capable of almost immediate expansion because so many citizens were virtual automatic patriots and also adept with weapons. This was a democratic army drawn from a male population the vast majority of whom owned a rifle, a core strength that enabled it to inflate and deflate rapidly. It was posted around the country and along the frontiers in small forts, but its extraordinary decentralization was also an asset in fighting skirmishes and even guerrilla wars with Indians.[17]

Of course, the nineteenth-century army was configured to fight overmatched Indians and to defend a continent that no one was likely to attack; two oceans provided their own security. By the time Indians were pacified, most Americans couldn't figure out a further use for it: around the old army general of the 1890s "in his neatly disheveled blue uniform," C. Wright Mills wrote, "there hang wisps of gun smoke from the Civil War." A few officers sought to fashion a military that could be used to extend American power abroad—always to the west or across the Pacific, with afterthoughts about Central America but never Europe. Until the 1940s none succeeded. Captain Arthur MacArthur (Douglas MacArthur's father) authored his "Chinese Memorandum" in 1883, arguing that "a commanding and progressive nation" would only materialize when "we secure and maintain the soverignty [*sic*] of the Pacific," but his memo was unread by anyone except his underlings until discovered in the archives a hundred years later. For Army Chief of Staff Hugh L. Scott, the army was "little more than a national constabulary" before the war with Spain.[18]

McKinley-Roosevelt Secretary of War Elihu Root reorganized the army, raising its strength to 100,000, and in 1912, as we have seen, the War Department created a colonial army for the Philippines, Hawaii, and the Canal Zone, which, although often understaffed, lasted until World War II and created a "cadre of semipermanent colonials" (in Linn's words) with much Pacific experience. They volunteered for two years in the Philippines or three in Hawaii and often repeated their tours of duty. In 1903 Douglas MacArthur graduated from West Point—having finished first in his class for three of his four years and achieving a merit rating topped only by Robert E. Lee. Soon he arrived in the Philippines with the Third Engineer Battalion and after two years became aide-de-camp to his father, Arthur. Douglas had an epiphany on a 1905 tour of military installations in Asia: here in the Orient was "western civilization's last earth frontier"; he convinced himself that American destiny and indeed "the future" were "irrevocably entwined with Asia and its island outposts."[19] But MacArthur quickly settled into the unhurried, idyllic life of the Pacific Army. Then came Pearl Harbor and instantaneous national mobilization to over 8 million in uniform, but again Truman shrank the military: the army had 554,000 soldiers by 1948; the navy's budget of $50 billion in 1945 slipped to $6 billion, and the air force watched most of its contracts get cancelled (aircraft industry sales dropped from $16 billion in 1944 to $1.2 billion in 1947). Defense spending fell to $13 billion a year, or about $150 billion in current dollars.[20]

The American military was still not a significant factor in national life before NSC-68 announced the answer to how much "preparedness" the country needed, thus closing a long American debate: and in mainstream Washington, it has never returned. Isolationists, of course, got blamed for the lack of military preparation in 1941, but the debate about America's role in the

world and what kind of military it should have is as old as the country itself:
was it a republic or an empire? During the Korean War the United States was
spending $650 billion on defense in current dollars, and it reached that maxi-
mum point again in the early part of this new century—a sum greater than
the combined defense budgets of the next eighteen ranking military powers
in 2009.

A Pacificist Orientation to the World

Ever since General Douglas MacArthur issued General Order Number One
on 15 August, 1945, excluding Allied powers from the occupation of Japan
(except in fig-leaf form), dividing Korea at the 38th parallel and Vietnam at
the 16th parallel, and seeking to unify China under Chiang Kai-shek's rule
by requiring Japanese soldiers in China to surrender to Nationalist forces,
American decisions have shaped the basic structure of international relations
in the East Asian region. The only part of that military division that did not
hold was China, and after the Communists cleared the mainland in 1948–49 a
new division took place: that between Taiwan and the People's Republic of
China (PRC), as the Seventh Fleet moved into the Taiwan Strait. Mac-
Arthur ruled Japan as a benevolent emperor, while the Korean War resulted
in a vastly deepened division of Northeast Asia: a heavily fortified demilita-
rized zone replaced the 38th parallel and remains to this day a museum of the
defunct global cold war. For a generation China was excluded from the postwar global system by its own radicalism, and by American blockade and war
threats. The archipelago of bases was the coercive structure that locked in the
American position in the North Pacific, offering a diffuse but palpable lever-
age over allies. The United States had bases all over Western Europe, too; the
difference was that unlike Europe, no NATO existed nor any ally capable of
independent action. No one really cared whether the Japanese or Koreans or
Filipinos or Chinese on Taiwan supported such policies, Americans just went
ahead more or less as they pleased. The archipelago of empire in East Asia
completely neutered the Pacific rivalry between Japan and the United States
that occupied the half-century before Pearl Harbor. An outgrowth of World
War II and Korea, this extensive base structure now persists into the current
century as if nothing had changed.

In 1947 George Kennan and Dean Acheson developed a strategy for
Japan's revival: both understood that Japan was the only serious industrial
power in Asia and therefore the only serious military threat; Kennan wanted
it again to be a strong military nation, to re-create the turn-of-the-century

balance of power in East Asia, but Acheson was shrewder in shaping a Japan with its industry revived and integrated into the American realm, an engine of the world economy and an American-defined "economic animal"—but one shorn of its prewar military and political clout. This occurred coterminously with the emergence of the cold war and deepened dramatically as Japan benefited tremendously from America's wars in Korea and Vietnam. Successive administrations wanted Japan to "share burdens" in the defense of the Pacific, but because any enlargement would be done under the American security umbrella, Japan's leaders resisted all but foot-dragging and creeping rearmament, through incremental defense increases. Today the country still recalcitrantly spends less than 1 per cent of its GNP on defense, and it is still impossible to imagine another Admiral Tōgō building great aircraft carriers or another Admiral Yamamoto putting nuclear submarines in the water. Japan remains entirely open to the permanent stationing of American "land, air, and sea forces in and about Japan," in the words of the United States– Japan Security Treaty; the treaty also gave the United States the right to use the armed forces it stations in Japan in any way of its choosing—and it did so in Korea and Vietnam.[21]

The long-term result of this American unilateralism in East Asia may be summarized as follows: it was an asymmetrical hub-and-spokes system in which the noncommunist countries of the region tended to communicate with each other *through the United States,* a vertical regime solidified by bilateral defense treaties (with Japan, South Korea, Taiwan, and the Philippines) and conducted by a State Department that towered over the foreign ministries of these four countries. The countries of the East Asian region might as well have been "hermit kingdoms" vis-à-vis each other, if not in relation to the United States: China didn't talk to Taiwan or South Korea; not even personal mail passed between the two Koreas; both Koreas hated Japan; and Japanese diplomacy looked to the United States, Europe, and Southeast Asia—but not to its near reaches. Each of them became semi-sovereign states, deeply penetrated by American military structures (operational control of the South Korean armed forces, U.S. Seventh Fleet patrolling of the Taiwan Strait, defense dependencies for all four countries, military bases on their territory), and incapable of anything resembling independent foreign policy or defense initiatives. The only serious breach in this system has been the rise of China, which put Taiwan in the shade of American concerns: but this change, too, owed as much to Richard Nixon's opening to China as to anything the Chinese leadership did; Nixon, Kissinger, and Carter unceremoniously dumped Taiwan and the American treaty commitment to it. Of course, Japanese leaders have contributed to the continuing divisions of the region by failing to reckon seriously with their aggression against their neighbors, quite in contrast to Germany. But that, too, was originally something encouraged by American policy, the Japanese leaders it supported, and the very soft peace Japan got in the late 1940s.

The postwar settlement thus remains the determining mechanism in explaining why East Asia, when compared to Europe, has so few multilateral institutions and mechanisms of cooperation and conciliation today, and even fewer through most of the postwar period. There was and is no NATO. There once was a SEATO (Southeast Asia Treaty Organization), but it never amounted to much, never spawned a NEATO, and died after two decades. There was a rump Marshall Plan (the ECA or Economic Cooperation Administration, which aided South Korea and Taiwan from 1947 onward). Like the Marshall Plan in Europe, the ECA was superseded by the revival of the advanced industrial economies—in this case the only one in the region, Japan. Nothing like the Conference on Security and Cooperation in Europe (CSCE) emerged, the Organization of Economic Cooperation and Development (OECD) was remote, and the theoretically all-inclusive United Nations was essentially an American operation in East Asia (as if anachronism, even atavism, were the name of the game, U.S. troops in Korea still sit under the blue flag of the 1950 United Nations Command). There is a modest alphabet soup of Southeast Asian international organizations—ASEAN, APEC, ARF—but none of these groups deploy the power and influence of a single American carrier task force, and even if they did, their tradition is one of mutual respect, never-ending consultation, and nonintervention in each other's affairs—even the affairs of a human rights nightmare like Burma. Even where you might expect to find multilateral organizations—in the financial, monetary, and economic realm, given the economic strength of the region— cooperation "remains extremely limited, at least by European standards."[22] Here too, the United States dominates.

China's turn outward since the 1970s expressed the way in which economic forces in the region have eroded and bypassed cold war boundaries, bringing former adversaries back into contact—but primarily through business contacts and pop culture, not through multilateral institutions. If the first phase of the cold war emphasized security considerations and divided the region, and the second phase exemplified the ascendancy of economic development and accelerated regional integration, it is important to remember that both these tendencies occurred primarily because of basic shifts in American foreign policy and the resulting pressures on East Asian states.

Contemporary obstacles to deeper integration in the region also trace back to Washington (although not only to Washington). Later we will have occasion to examine how contemporary American policy toward the entire world increasingly seems like a redirection of the Pacific pattern of unilateralism. But that very pattern was also the elaboration of a century-long practice of moving and facing West, with allies absent and little concern for what the people in the way of that advance had to say. (If there is a precedent it certainly isn't Atlanticism—Central American interventions bring us closer, but they were often part and parcel of Pacific expansionism.)[23] General Order Number One, the seven-year occupation of Japan, and the security structures that still hold sway in the new century were, in this sense, Douglas Mac-Arthur's way of paying homage to his father—Pacificism, American-style.

Touring the Archipelago

Okinawa functions as the "South Korea" of Japan, home to the only substantial marine contingent permanently stationed overseas (the Third Marine Expeditionary Force). New base construction in Japan took off with the Korean War, but unlike South Korea, Japanese and American elites were able to jam the vast majority (around 75 percent) of U.S. bases into this small island, keeping them conveniently out of sight to most Japanese. (Okinawa is halfway to Taiwan from Tokyo, a three-hour plane ride.) Japan provides about $5 billion a year in support of the seventy-three American bases on its territory, a bargain when compared to what Japan would have to spend to defend itself; meanwhile the United States spends $40 to $43 billion annually for its East Asian security commitments, the majority of which are directed toward Korea. The Third Marine Expeditionary Force has about 16,000 personnel and 100 aircraft, and the island houses another 10,000 personnel from the air force, army, and navy; an additional 22,434 dependents meant that in recent years some 50,000 Americans have resided on the island because of this expeditionary deployment. About 7,400 air force personnel and 100 aircraft are deployed at Kadena Air Force Base, including some 50 F-15 fighters of the air force's Eighteenth Tactical Fighter Wing, 15 KC-135 air-refueling tankers, and 2 E-3 AWACS airborne warning and control system planes; with dependents and civilian employees, the base population is almost 25,000. A former Japanese air force base, Kadena is mammoth, covering 14,000 acres with two runways of 3,650 meters, or nearly 4,000 yards; the largest air force base outside the United States, the full complex sits on 30,000 acres of prime land. The Defense Communications Detachment runs the largest direction-finding antenna in the world on Okinawa, surveilling all of Asia.

My visits to various bases in the summer of 2005 illustrated the beauty of Okinawa and the enormous chunks of it given over to the American military—often the most beautiful parts, like Camp Courtney on a shimmering peninsula. Captain Danny Chung had organized my schedule from the beginning, but by the time I got there he was off in Pakistan providing relief to earthquake victims. I told his counterpart that this was admirable—but why do American soldiers always have to do these things? "That's a great question," he replied, without further elaboration. I asked a marine commander if she thought sixty years was a long time to maintain bases on Okinawa: it is a long time, she agreed, but "we serve because we are ordered to serve." Logistical issues make it preferable for the marines to have forward bases, she said, and once you lose them you might not get them back—so what's the point of letting them go? Another marine officer whom I met sat beneath the object of his political attentions: a map marking off the sentiments of local mayors and town leaders throughout Okinawa: red for opponents of the bases, white for supporters, and yellow for wobblers in the middle. Marine officers admitted that they weren't quite sure what was behind Secretary of Defense Rumsfeld's plans for a "Revolution in Military Affairs" but doubted that they would have much immediate effect on Okinawa. During a discussion of "China's rise" with several officers, I again asked, why is that our problem? Why is it not a Japanese or Indian or Korean problem? They nodded, exchanged glances, didn't say much; I knew this question was "above their pay grade," in the best sense: marine officers follow orders, and ultimately civilians make the policies. Various people informed me that 75 percent of U.S. troops in Japan were not really in Okinawa, more like 50 percent; the United States contributed $771 million to the local economy in 2004; Americans were 4 percent of the Okinawa population but account for only 1 percent of island crimes—and so on.

Like Korea, this tight little island was always "good liberty" in soldiers' parlance, meaning women were easily available in the "Ville," a district full of saloons and whorehouses; one sailor remembered "a beautiful girl who danced naked with a huge python writhing around her" in a bar near Kadena's Gate Two. One humid evening in September 1995, Kendrick Ledet and Rodrico Harp, marine privates from Georgia, and their friend Marcus Gill, a sailor from Texas, got roaring drunk in the Ville, stopped by a shop on the Kadena base for duct tape, and then kidnapped a young girl who emerged from a stationery store in her standard-issue school uniform with its short skirt and thick white socks. They drove into a field where the sugarcane was tall and took turns raping this twelve-year-old before leaving her by the roadside, bleeding and in shock. An instant hue and cry erupted in Japan, made worse by the girl's tender age and the race of her assailants: African-American. The men were arrested by American military police two days later, who were under no obligation to turn them over to Japanese courts under the existing Status of Forces Agreement, which only fueled the rage over this incident. Walter Mondale, the U.S. ambassador to Japan, apologized profusely, but soon thousands of Okinawans were in the streets demanding that Americans simply get out and the bases be removed; by late October some 60,000 protesters mounted the largest demonstrations in Okinawan history. A few weeks later Admiral Richard C. Macke said the soldiers were not only wrong but stupid; they could have had a girl for the price of their rental car. He was forced into early retirement—but only for saying publicly what most officers thought in 1995 and had thought for the previous half-century.[24]

This nauseating rape was unusual only in the youth of the victim; otherwise American soldiers have continuously abused the people of Okinawa for six decades. The total of untoward incidents from one year alone (2002) amounted to 1 plane crash, 51 emergency landings, 12 brush fires, 81 criminal offenses (including "heinous" crimes), and 8 waste spills polluting the island's waters. The infamous Futenma Air Station arose on land that was forcibly confiscated from farmers in 1955, leaving them so bereft that most of them emigrated to Bolivia. Futenma has been the source of some 217 accidents and violent incidents since Okinawa reverted to Japanese control in 1972 and is scheduled to be moved to a new facility, a floating base on reclaimed coastal land—some time around 2020. (When I visited Okinawan bases I was told repeatedly that the air force had been asked to move Futenma's functions onto the Kadena base but had refused because that would require sacrificing two holes from its eighteen-hole golf course; the military also runs two other eighteen-hole courses on the island.) As the Okinawan population grew to over 1.3 million and towns turned into cities, this small, narrow island (seventy-seven miles in length and two to sixteen miles in width), resembling an anchovy, has gotten too crowded for an enormous military presence occupying about 20 percent of the main island's area. Bases cover 36 percent of Okinawa City, 45 percent of Yomitan, and 57 percent of Chatan; this land and much else, of course, was unilaterally appropriated by the United States after the war. The most dangerous crowding is in the city of Ginowan, where the Futenma Air Station is located. In August 2004 a mammoth CH-53D helicopter from Futenma crashed and burned on the campus of Okinawa International University, and a year later another American helicopter crashed on the grounds of a secondary school; luckily no Okinawans died in either incident.[25]

The biggest problem that the Okinawans have, of course, is their vulnerability to having their island completely obliterated, again, should a war erupt in Taiwan or Korea. (In 1945 it was the utterly demolished site of the bloodiest fighting in the Pacific campaign; as many as 130,000 civilians died.) A recent RAND study concluded that Kadena-based F-15s would give the Taiwan air force "at least a fifty-fifty chance of success against even an extremely robust Chinese force"; left unsaid is what China might do to Kadena —and all of Okinawa—should the United States join the battle for Taiwan. A report drawn up under the leadership of Richard Armitage (later Colin Powell's deputy in the State Department) in October 2000 reinforced the Pentagon's desire to stay forever in Okinawa. It argued vigorously for maintaining a heavy presence of U.S. forces in Japan along with appropriate "footprint reductions" to deal with untoward incidents, because Okinawa was the key to American security in East Asia: "In matters of security, distance matters. Okinawa is positioned at the intersection of the East China Sea and the Pacific Ocean—only about one hour's flying time from Korea, Taiwan, and the South China Sea." The Armitage Report also regarded Article 9 of the Japanese Constitution (forsaking the use of force as an instrument of state policy) as an unfortunate "constraint on alliance cooperation," and basically advocated getting rid of it ("lifting this prohibition would allow for closer and more efficient security cooperation")—something which the right wing in Japan has sought for many years. Thus a Japanese Constitution written by Americans in 1947 is now said to be deficient—according to Americans, if not to a Japanese public that continues overwhelmingly to support Article 9.[26]

In the camp towns around American bases in Korea the atmosphere is often malevolent, with an air of resentment and cold stares—a clear pathology. Okinawa may be jammed to the gills with foreign bases, but that atmosphere is much less obvious than it used to be, and relations between American soldiers and Okinawans are usually friendly. Ruth Ann Keyso's recent book recounts interviews with local women, young and old, who may or may not wish the bases were gone but show much appreciation for the Americans they meet—for their generosity, friendliness, and sincerity. Particularly for young women, American soldiers offer a kind of pleasant liberation from the culture of Japanese patriarchy. One young woman ran into serial sexual harassment in a Japanese company but felt no discrimination working on an American base: "People there are so serious. I mean, they do their jobs without bothering anyone else. I like that. And the men there have good manners." The black soldier whom she dated, in particular, was "a truly beautiful person." Okinawan women who date Americans, she thought, "are the ultra-independent females in this society."[27]

Korea: No Exit

Unbeknownst to most Americans, the first American combat troops arrived in Seoul in September 1945, not in 1950; they set up a full military government and plunged into the thicket of Korean politics and culture—and have yet to find a way out. By now the antique U.S. presence is almost a parody of Schumpeter's notion of empire as atavism. Recently I visited P'anmunjom again, the singular meeting point between the American and North Korean military since 1953, this time courtesy of the U.S. Army. As you enter the American area you see a mural from the days of the "Manchu Batallion" that helped put down the Boxer Rebellion in 1900. Our hosts gave us the army's construction of the history of the Korean War (a version that could not have changed since 1953) and a luncheon of rib-eye steak and French-fried potatoes of similar vintage, offered in a café that had a country music poster on the wall advertising Hank Williams's tour of Atlanta—in 1952. Our waitress was a pretty Korean woman in a 1970s-era miniskirt and 1950s-era makeup, complete with Marilyn Monroe–red lipstick; in the lobby was an oily Korean man offering cheap souvenirs and trinkets in a pidgin English indelibly associated with the long decades of the U.S. presence in Korea: two Koreans constructed in the image of the American military. North Korea has been locked into this struggle for more than six decades, too, and has its own highly developed type of atavism. ABC's Diane Sawyer visited Pyongyang in 2007 and interviewed, among other people, General Yi Ch'an-bok, the commander of the northern side of the DMZ. How long have you been commander, she asked innocently. "Forty years," he replied.

The Department of Defense counts 101 separate American military installations in Korea, but the gigantic Yongsan base in the middle of Seoul is the most famous—home to the Eighth U.S. Army and the United Nations Command, as well as the American-Korean Combined Forces Command. I have traversed its grounds going back to the late 1960s, looking for home-style food or a first-run Hollywood film. This sprawling base had the gated suburban ambience that Southern California popularized: high fences to keep Koreans out (who had to have a purpose and show identification to get through the gates); ranch houses with two-car garages for the officers; and an eighteen-hole golf course, three swimming pools, two gymnasiums, and a thirty-two-lane bowling alley.[28] First occupied by Yüan Shih-kai and his Chinese commandery in the late 1880s, Yongsan passed to the Japanese after the Chinese defeat in 1895, and then to the United States in 1945; American commanders use the same underground command bunkers that the Japanese built. The base looks about the same today, except that the golf course has been relocated to Sungnam, south of Seoul, and protesters are outside the gates almost every day. After President Roh Moo Hyun strongly demanded it in 2003, the Pentagon finally agreed to vacate Yongsan and to relocate well south of Seoul. That remove will unquestionably help the sad state of Korean-American relations, but it won't be completed until perhaps 2016.

Do American bases ever close and come home? The answer is that they do close, but they don't usually come home. In 1992 volcanic Mount Pinatubo erupted and inundated Clark Air Force Base in the Philippines. That act of God combined with the recent democratic revolution to force the United States out of the Philippines, where it deployed many bases for almost a century (although most of them dated to World War II). New technologies had shortened global distances by this time, however, so the Pentagon merely had to retreat a few hundred miles east to (also volcanic) Guam, which has now become a "lily pad" or "power projection hub" on the edge of Asia. "We don't want to be somewhere where they don't want us, where they can throw us out," an American diplomat said. The 160,000 residents of Guam are unlikely to do that, since the island is American territory—nor were they ever asked if they wanted to be a "power projection hub." B-52 and B-1 bombers are deployed at Anderson Air Force Base, the navy moved many ships and submarines out to Guam (cutting five days off the Pacific crossing from Pearl Harbor), the marines use this 209-square-mile island for urban and rural (or jungle) warfare exercises, and some sixty "igloos" store massive amounts of weaponry and ammunition.[29]

A Conservative Military?

The expeditionary American military has a corporate culture that is not easy to describe in a few words. Their job—putting their bodies on the line—breeds a strong patriotism and sense of sacrifice. In some respects, the military changes at a much slower pace than the broader society, and in others, like ethnic diversity, it is far ahead. Meeting military people often recalls the midwestern culture of the 1950s that I grew up in: friendly, solid, straightforward, guileless people who quite sincerely believe in West Point's watchwords:

duty, honor, country. The "high-and-tight" male haircut, shaved on the sides and a crew cut on top, reinforces the 1950s imagery. A McDonald's sits a half-block from Gate Two outside Kadena Air Force Base; it has an antique jukebox full of 45 rpm records from the fifties, a nickel for one play, a dime for two, six for a quarter: Bobby Darin, "Beyond the Sea," "Maybelline" by Chuck Berry, Danny and the Juniors, Pat Boone, Frankie Lymon and the Teenagers, Dion and the Belmonts, the Shirelles. The atmosphere mingled nostalgia with anachronism, but on the bases life was entirely professional.

To the extent that the career military is conservative and votes Republican (upwards of 70 percent in recent elections; a soldier is eight times more likely to come from Texas than New York), part of it may be small-town America held in suspended animation for decades on this global archipelago. It is as if the American military wished to parenthesize the 1960s, moving back and forth between the present and the 1950s, as if the decade of civil rights, Vietnam, sex, drugs, and rock 'n' roll didn't exist. A funeral service for a soldier killed in Afghanistan in 2003 included the 23rd Psalm, followed by "The Ballad of the Green Berets" from the John Wayne film of the same name. This sense is reinforced by bizarre practices, like the ubiquitous and pathological hatred of Jane Fonda: her photo is on military urinals (aim here). In a common ritual, after the lights are out a plebe at the U.S. Naval Academy yells out "Goodnight Jane Fonda!" and the whole company responds, "Goodnight bitch!" Tales of her selling out American POWs in Hanoi circulate easily, quite untouched by the actual facts of her visit. Carol Burke suggests that all this functions "to stabilize and punish the dangerous female."[30] Insular Americans operating abroad develop their own habits of cognition (or incognition). Commanding officers around the globe operate on "Zulu time," their own version of Greenwich Mean Time that keeps every base synchronized to the same minute. Soldiers posted to SOUTHCOM (Central America, Colombia, etc.) call it "the *cucaracha* circuit." The Green Berets fighting Muslim insurgents in the Philippines agree with their now-departed army and air force counterparts that there is no better duty elsewhere: "This is the only country in the world where the main tourist attraction squirms up and down on your lap," one soldier put it; "an Eden without rival for American males," as Robert Kaplan put it.[31]

Yet so much has changed in the last half-century, and it shows up in the military as much or more than in any American institution. When I visited marine bases on Okinawa in 2005, I met officers who were black, Hispanic, Asian-American, and white. The commander was a fifty-one-year-old woman, attractive and funny and clearly accustomed to command. The U.S.

military is a much more integrated institution than most, including our universities. (Blacks account for 22 percent of enlisted people, but only 8.5 percent of officers, which is not equality—but outside of professional sports, I can't think of another profession where nearly 9 percent of the leading figures are black.) Women command men, fly attack aircraft, and participate in combat. But men still impose their hegemony through initiation rituals, sartorial styles (the high-and-tight haircut), a special language enshrining the hallowed F word (as in snafus and figmos—fuck it, got my orders), and off-base carousing—all of which leave military women out and often degrade nonmilitary women (as the infamous Tailhook Convention illustrated).[32] Nothing happened with the various officers whom I met to alter my view that these are excellent Americans, loyal, professional, competent, disciplined, and orderly as a military organization should be. Nothing happened to change my decades-old sense that military bases are islands of America in foreign lands, with little real interaction with local cultures and peoples. Everything also emphasized how institutionalized American bases are in Okinawa, with new people arriving to inherit a predecessor's task and no one asking where these bases came from or whether their contemporary purposes were justified.

Sasebo is a small naval base with a big reputation. A nicely protected harbor on Japan's southeast coast not far from Nagasaki, it was first noticed by Admiral Tōgō Heihachiro in 1889 when he was still a lowly officer, and the navy quickly developed it. It played an important role in the Russo-Japanese War, World War II, and Korea—MacArthur's ship left from Sasebo to direct the Inchon landing. It is an unobtrusive base, you have to look for it in this small city; the surrounding hilly terrain and several large outlying islands shroud and guard its flanks. It is a Pacific Fleet liberty port, but the once-rowdy Ville has almost disappeared, and the few bars and clubs catering to sailors are side-by-side with a vigorous commercial area where it is rare to see an American. When I visited in 2005 security seemed almost casual; early in the morning I was able to walk right onto the base through a public park, an open gate, and a football field. A Japanese naval base is next to the American one, but I was told there was not a lot of contact between sailors from the two navies.

Yokosuka is the oldest and most famous naval base in Japan. Originally an iron works, the Meiji government took it over in 1868 and turned it into a shipbuilding and naval base, with much French assistance. It continued to be the home of the Imperial Navy until the United States took it over in 1945; it was bombed in the Doolittle raid in 1942, but was not destroyed in 1944–45 because the United States expected to take it over (one theory), or it might be given as reparations to a local American ally (another theory). Yokosuka was also the center of Japanese naval aviation and had some of the world's largest dry docks capable of harboring ships of up to 80,000 tons (so did Sasebo).[33] As the largest American naval base in East Asia at 500 acres and home to the carrier *Kitty Hawk* and eight other Seventh Fleet vessels, it is more obtrusive than Sasebo. But it still manages to remain fairly well hidden behind walls in a densely populated city. When I visited in 2005 I learned that the United States has done little to change its basic configuration over the decades—in part because it could accommodate Japan's largest aircraft carrier, the 68,000-ton *Shinano*, which was launched here in 1944 (and sunk by American forces a month later).[34] Around this base, too, the Ville seems a shadow of its former self: some desultory bars, dingy old shops selling Bowie knives, "Anytime Baby" T-shirts, Zippo lighters, guns and bullets, samurai swords, and camouflage jackets. Paunchy navy lifers shuffled along with their wives and girlfriends, but it had little vitality even of a tawdry sort. My guide and interlocutor reported that town-gown relations are fine; you might see a few protesters, but the locals want Americans to stay. (So does everybody else between Diego Garcia and Pearl Harbor, he seemed to think.)

Kadena Air Force Base's Gate Two reminded me not of bases I visited in Japan proper, but of Korean bases: the major interests were girls, beer, rock, sports, and tailoring. The Tomcat bar, Last Shot saloon, Blackjack nightclub, a House of Kimono with Chinese sarongs, "custom" tailors up and down the road, pawnshops, hip-hop outfits, sexy lingerie for your girlfriend or missus. This tawdry and notorious street, epicenter of what used to be a thriving Ville offering just about anything, is now barely a memory of its former self. It has rows of tasteless shops catering to two types of soldiers: those recuperating the 1950s and early 1960s, and the hip-hop generation of our time. Los Angeles Lakers basketball shirts compete with the Hawaiian designs that noncommissioned lifers love to wear. You hear Pat Boone here and 50 Cent there. At night a few bars open up with amusements that a late adolescent from Keokuk might find racy; prostitutes aren't very visible but the locals can direct soldiers to them; almost all of them are now foreign-born. (First in Japan, then in South Korea, and now in Okinawa, as the economy developed native prostitutes disappeared, so they were imported from the Philippines, Russia, and elsewhere.)[35] American soldiers drove by in customized Toyotas with loud mufflers. It was vulgar, dingy, rundown, and depressing—a complete contrast with the Japanese mainland. The locals look at Americans, when they look, with a sharp meeting of the eyes that says, you know and I know what's going on here (this is also a staple of human interaction near bases in Korea).

I stayed at a small hotel just outside Gate Two. Two large middle-aged Americans held forth in the dining room: one retired air force lifer who kept wangling free beer from the waitress and now worked for General Dynamics; he dined with a rotund man from Houston who came in from Travis Air Force Base via Anchorage on a 747 carrying freight for the U.S. forces. They carried on a desultory conversation, discovering that they both liked the same fishing spot in Arizona. "Mama-san" was their word for any native woman; neither seemed to know a thing about the local culture, nor could they pronounce a single Japanese syllable properly. They were dislocated, displaced, depressed men, deeply bored with Okinawa and probably with everything else in their lives.

I returned to my room after dinner and switched on Armed Forces TV. Don Rumsfeld was saying that the war in Iraq is not lost, we are not in a quagmire. More news, sports, then a "commercial" break for off-base activities: learn the tea ceremony, how to eat sushi, study Japanese—salutary suggestions for getting along with the natives. It's admirable, but I saw the same thing in Korea with no noticeable result over decades. Along comes a powerful clip showing a man taking a sledgehammer and shattering a large female sculpture with one blow, illustrating the effects of sexual abuse and assault. Another break applauds "America's melting pot: kiss me I'm Polish." The Armed Forces TV staff is indeed very diverse. But the evening schedule lists several stateside sitcoms, and I turn it off to listen to music and peruse the daily schedule for Armed Forces Radio: Paul Harvey at 7:07 a.m., Paul Harvey at 12:07, Paul Harvey at 4:12, and Rush Limbaugh at 8:00 p.m. No other news or talk shows, except for National Public Radio's *Talk of the Nation*—at four in the morning. It is hard to say that the Gate Two milieu offers anything edifying; it caters to adolescent minds aged eighteen to sixty caught in a couple of different time warps, and it is slowly dying. The general impression a traveler gets is that Americans have corroded the local culture and don't appear to have one themselves.

Ordo Templi Orientis: Smart Weapons and Brilliant People

The archipelago of empire doesn't just contain a multitude of military bases at home and abroad. Its domestic expression also has industries operating at the cutting edge of innovation and design, under the auspices of the central state. It sounds fated: Southern California as the inevitable home of the American aerospace industry. But it was anything but predictable; indeed, California rocket science had one of the oddest provenances in American history—yet one that conformed to the American tale of the tinkering individual and the "Silicon Valley way." "Rocket scientist" has become a popular metaphor for a real brain, but before World War II rockets were uninteresting to well-trained engineers and thought to be the province of science fiction or crackpots who wanted to fly to the moon; most physicists believed it was impossible for rockets to operate in the vacuum of outer space. When Cal Tech's Theodore von Kármán told an MIT physicist that he was working on rockets, the latter called it a "Buck Rogers' job" and said he preferred his current project: deicing bomber windshields. So when Cal Tech inventors began to show that rockets could work, they substituted the word "jet" to avoid the impugning connotations—as in Jet Propulsion Laboratory, which became the central organization in America's missile program.[36] If snotty physicists weren't interested, the air force was, and so Cal Tech became an integral part of the global archipelago.

John Whiteside Parsons was a slim man of Hollywood good looks. From one angle he looked like a cross between Bob Hope and Jack Nicholson, from another, a young Orson Welles. An only child born in 1914 into a considerable fortune, he grew up with his father absent and his mother present (and dominant in his life) at 537 Orange Grove Avenue in Pasadena, a great Italian-style villa with leather-lined walls right next to the exclusive Valley Hunt Club and down the street from the Wrigleys, Anheuser-Busches, the widow of James A. Garfield, and a host of other rich and famous people. As a child Parsons loved to read science fiction, and by his twenty-second birthday he and his "Suicide Squad" friends were experimenting with rocket motors in the Arroyo Seco in Pasadena—wild, arid gulches near the Devil's Gate Dam. He and his Cal Tech friend Frank Malina chose Halloween 1936 to try out a new rocket engine formed of magnesium, copper, and duralumin. The rocket blew up, sending flames shooting toward the small group. A month later they got the engine to fire for a full twenty seconds, however, a major success.[37]

In 1938 General "Hap" Arnold arranged a $1,000 grant to the Cal Tech group to work on jet-assisted takeoff devices, a seemingly minuscule sum that was a fortune to these indefatigable inventors (it was more than twice the annual salary of technicians); soon Robert Millikan arranged another $10,000 from the National Academy of Sciences. By mid-1941 Parsons had perfected a small jet-assisted rocket (or JATO) that used compressed gunpowder, that is, amide black powder mixed with corn starch and ammonium nitrate, "the whole mixture bound together with LePage's all-purpose stationery glue," in Pendle's words. In August his team strapped six JATOs under the wings of a small (753 pounds) plane piloted by Lt. Homer Boushey, a former student of von Kármán's who was game to fly just about anything. The Cal Tech team, including von Kármán, watched as the plane taxied down the runway, triggered the JATOs, and then catapulted into the sky ahead of shimmering white jet trails—the first jet-assisted takeoff in the United States. Soon the National Academy of Sciences had forked over another $125,000.[38]

The central problem in using solid fuel for a rocket was getting a steady, slow burn. Parsons's early JATOs had an unfortunate tendency to blow up at all the wrong moments, so he experimented with all kinds of fuels, burning up one rocket after another, with no success. Then one day he observed some men applying hot asphalt to a roof, and like Edward Doheny watching Mexican tar carts, Parsons had an epiphany; he already knew about "Greek fire," a fuel of pitch and other unknown elements which the ancient Greeks used to fashion terrifying flaming projectiles (Sparta used them as early as 429 BC). In 1942 Parsons blended a new rocket fuel using asphalt and an oxidizer that burned evenly for the length of the rocket tube; it was also inertly stable and could be stored for long periods at any extreme of temperature without igniting. He learned how to insert and cast this heated mixture (later called GALCIT-53) inside the rocket chamber until it cooled and hardened into a stable solid. Parsons thus perfected a solid-fuel JATO resembling a pipe bomb with an attitude, a round canister about 2 feet long and 5 inches in diameter with a single spark plug sitting atop its rear end (used for conduction rather than ignition) that could deliver 200 pounds of thrust for eight seconds. In April 1942 Parsons and Malina strapped the new JATOs to a 20,000-pound Douglas A20-A bomber and launched it into the air with ease; this prototype JATO, a small rocket easy to mass produce which proved invaluable in World War II for jet-assisted takeoffs from aircraft carriers and short runways, is now on display at the Smithsonian. But the GALCIT-53 fuel "caused a paradigm shift" in rocketry, according to George Pendle, becoming the favored solid fuel (in plasticized form) for the Polaris and Minuteman missiles. Meanwhile Parsons, Malina, and Martin Summerfield also went on to pioneer liquid fuels (mixtures of methyl alcohol and gaseous oxygen), and Malina led the Aerojet team that built the WAC Corporal, a liquid-fuel rocket—"the first rocket to escape the earth's atmosphere," in M. G. Lord's words. It was 16 feet long, weighed 665 pounds, and lifted 25 pounds of payload to an altitude of 235,000 feet in 1945. The Germans, of course, were the first to launch long-range rockets (the V-1 and V-2), but after the war ended the Cal Tech team inspected them and learned nothing they didn't already know.[39]

This unlikely group also invented a business prototype, a company all of their own that would profit from their originality—but also from a host of government and private grants and Cal Tech's sponsorship of the whole rocketry effort in the first place. It was a "rather incestuous" business, as Pendle put it, and Millikan opposed the idea on ethical grounds, but it became an early version of a formula that would later manufacture many billionaires in Silicon Valley. The company was called Aerojet Engineering (later Aerojet General); founded in early 1942 and housed in a former "Vita-Juice" plant, von Kármán was its first president, Malina its treasurer, with Parsons, Summerfield, and others as vice presidents and fellow stockholders. They each invested $250 to get it going. Like subsequent start-ups they had trouble getting established engineers to join them, so they relied on young people just out of graduate school; profits from one order paid for the work on the next. Most of the partners sold their stock early on, but Malina, who ran afoul of McCarthyism and moved to Paris to work for the United Nations, had the last laugh: his stock was worth $400,000 by 1953 and just kept going up, enabling him to quit his job and devote himself to his first love, painting.[40]

Another member of the "suicide squad" was Tsien Hsüeh-shen, a child prodigy born in Shanghai who came to MIT for his PhD and impressed others as a polymath who seemed to know everything. Von Kármán called Tsien "the undisputed genius" of high-speed aerodynamics and jet propulsion (indeed he was so brilliant that one of von Kármán's Jewish colleagues thought he must have Jewish blood). In 1943 Tsien wrote a paper showing that a 10,000-pound liquid rocket could reach 75 miles in altitude, a theory that the German V-2 rockets soon proved true. Tsien also did the first paper on nuclear-powered rocketry, now a classic in the field, and helped Malina develop the first American missile, the WAC Corporal. In 1949 this same rocket was launched off the nose of a reconstructed German V-2 and became the first rocket to enter extraterrestrial space, at a height of 244 miles.

In the 1940s the Jet Propulsion Laboratory developed basic concepts for long-range missiles and space satellites that much later became the "smart" weapons of our era, and Tsien was in the middle of it. As early as 1945 Tsien believed that current technologies could build a 6,000-mile ballistic missile, that it was already feasible to send up an artificial satellite, and that in time such satellites could guide rockets on their post-apogee, unguided descent down to a target. In 1945 the navy formed the Committee for Evaluating the

Feasibility of Space Rocketry (CEFSR) and contracted with Caltech's Guggenheim Aeronautical Laboratory to fund research on rocket and satellite development. The navy and the army air force (AAF) competed with each other; Curtis LeMay was the director of R & D for the AAF in 1946 and backed a "crash effort" to catch up with the navy. An AAF report in 1946 said the wars of the future would be fought largely by "high speed pilotless missiles" and satellites would play a vital role in bringing missiles down on their targets—and would also be critical to reconnaissance, communications, attack assessment, and weather forecasting. After much squabbling and skepticism about the feasibility of all this, the air force and RAND subsequently became the only service authorized to work with satellites; as early as mid-1949 RAND scientists also theorized that photographic and television equipment could be put on satellites.

By 1949 Tsien Hsüeh-shen headed Cal Tech's Guggenheim Jet Propulsion Center as the Goddard Professor of Jet Propulsion. In that same year the Chinese Communists took power in Beijing and sought to entice Tsien back to his homeland with claims that his father was ailing and wanted to see him. Tsien decided instead to apply for American citizenship. In the late 1930s, like many other professors and intellectuals, Cal Tech's rocket team had participated in evening political discussions—which turned out to have been infiltrated by the Los Angeles Police Department's "Red Squad." Tsien was never a communist or even very political and had the highest security clearances in the 1940s; but Sidney Weinbaum, another member of the group, certainly was political. In 1949 Weinbaum was tried on a perjury charge in Pasadena involving alleged communist ties, and Tsien, whose friendship with Weinbaum mainly involved their mutual interest in classical music, refused to testify against him. Shortly before the Korean War broke out in June 1950 Tsien was accused of being a communist; the FBI took away his security clearance, seized his library, and placed him under house arrest. He was refused a passport until 1955, when the government figured that the knowledge in his head was now obsolete. His preference had been to naturalize and remain in the United States, but his career was ruined and so he returned to China.[41]

Jack Parsons, meanwhile, continued to indulge his other lifelong passions: magic, spiritualism, radical metaphysics, expanding the mind's horizons, moving to the other side, otherwise known as séances, humbug, witchcraft, weird sex, and deviltry—a strange brew that seemed to distill Southern California's "great circus without a tent," in Carey McWilliams's words, of "clairvoyants, palm readers, Hindu frauds, crazy cults, fake healers." A druggist named Theodor Reuss got together with a fellow occultist, Franz Hartmann, in 1896 and founded the Theosophical Society of Germany, an offshoot of Freemason and Illuminati groups; in 1901 they were joined by a metallurgist named Karl Kellner in organizing the Ordo Templi Orientis (Order of the Temple of the Orient, OTO). In 1912 Reuss bestowed upon Aleister Crowley the "9th degree" of this order, and he later named Crowley to be his successor as outer head of the OTO.[42] Crowley, of course, went on to become perhaps the most famous of twentieth-century occult charlatans, notorious in a dozen countries for his eccentricity and haute mumbo jumbo, "tantric" exercises always accompanied by polymorphous sex (what he called "sex magick"), all of it accompanied by drugs (Crowley was a heroin addict). In the 1930s he became a frequent visitor to the Agape Lodge of the OTO in Pasadena, led by Jack Parsons; "agape" means love in Greek, and there was a lot of love to be had at Parsons's "lodge." "Do what thou wilt" was Crowley's law, an early version of "do your own thing"; indeed that was "the whole of the law." (Crowley later became the darling of Dr. Timothy Leary and other sixties gurus and can be seen staring out of the Beatles' *Sgt. Pepper's Lonely Hearts Club Band* album cover.)[43]

Jack Parsons ran his OTO outfit out of the family mansion on Orange Grove Avenue. A strong disciple of Crowley, who visited many times, Parsons attracted a heterodox crowd of revelers who rented rooms in the mansion and engaged in drunken, drug-filled orgies according to tabloid claims—and certainly devoted themselves to transcending the realm of the ordinary senses. Parsons's published poetry was not inclined to endear the Agape Lodge to the authorities: the opening line of one poem read, "I height Don Quixote, I live on Peyote, marihuana, morphine and cocaine." He showed up at parties with a long cobra draped around his neck and worked himself up into fits of ecstasy while reciting poetry or donning a black robe to call out otherworldly spirits through an ever-changing mix of hocus-pocus—chants, pentagrams, flourishes of a shiny chalice. Shortly after the war ended L. Ron Hubbard moved in with Parsons and his wife, Betty, and slowly started dominating the OTO Lodge; Hubbard had Parsons under his spell quickly, and almost as quickly had relieved Parsons of both Betty and the better part of his fortune. (The Church of Scientology, of course, denies that this ever happened.) Like Tsien, Parsons lost his security clearances as the cold war developed and retreated into a pained obscurity.[44]

On June 17, 1952, Jack Parsons was working in his garage, mixing up a rush-order chemical brew for a Hollywood pyrotechnic display, when he died in an explosion. Although many assumed foul play, he apparently dropped a can of fulminate of mercury by accident and it instantly exploded. Upon getting this news his mother Ruth committed suicide, saying she could not live without him; among his personal effects was reputed to be a film of him having sex with her. On the dark side of the moon, at 37 degrees north latitude and 171 degrees west longitude, sits Parsons Crater—named in honor of this authentic rocket pioneer. In the lobby of the central library at Jiaotong University in Xi'an, the ancient Tang capital in China's western interior, is a gigantic statue of Tsien Hsüeh-shen—a tribute to his commanding role as the father of China's intercontinental ballistic missile program.[45]

In reflecting back on this strange experience, it is worth asking if something like this could ever have happened at Yale or Harvard. The answer is no, in my view, because of traditions militating against business spin-offs, Pentagon contracts, or unlettered amateurs like Parsons in a place surrounded by entrenched local corporations with bureaucratized procedures standing in the way of the zany improvisations of the "suicide squad." Instead Parsons was a quirky and offbeat precursor of other inventors who would cluster around a different university: Stanford.

Skunks inside the Circus Tent

If the archipelago could accommodate an eccentric like Jack Parsons, it also embraced madcap rocket science at the other end of the political spectrum. German jet fighters streaked across Europe's skies for the first time in 1943, when American jet propulsion was limited to the Parsons-Malina JATOs. Soon another handful of characters with munificent Pentagon funds began experimenting in a California "garage"—only in this case it was not the Arroyo Seco but a circus tent. The War Department put a thirty-three-year-old Lockheed engineer named Clarence "Kelly" Johnson, a brilliant aerodynamicist who had designed the P-38 Lightning (the best propeller-driven fighter in the war) and the Lockheed Electra transport, in charge of a super-secret program to built a jet fighter prototype—and gave him six months to do it. The Lockheed complex was overflowing with work in 1943, so Johnson hoisted a circus tent and got busy with about fifty design engineers and mechanics. Al Capp's *L'il Abner* comic strip had a backyard moonshine apparatus turning out "kickapoo joy juice" called "the skonk works." That was the origin of Lockheed's "Skunk Works," which turned out the P-80 Shooting Star a month ahead of schedule; an excellent jet fighter, it saw its main action in the Korean War.[46]

Kelly Johnson dominated the Skunk Works for the next four decades as it turned out the F-104 Starfighter (America's first supersonic jet fighter), the

U-2 espionage plane of Gary Powers fame, the SR-71 Blackbird, and the "stealth" technology behind the F-117A fighter and the B-2 bomber. The Blackbird, now retired, was an amazing plane: not only sensuously aerodynamic and capable of streaking through the skies at 80,000 feet, at 2,092 mph, it was literally faster than a speeding bullet. It had side-look, high-resolution cameras that could, for example, cross the southern edge of the DMZ in ten minutes and photograph most of North Korea. (It located the *Pueblo* spy ship in Wonsan harbor shortly after it was seized in 1968.) Johnson and friends did all this on the Parsons-Malina model of shirtsleeves and open collars, informal teamwork, workaholic male camaraderie, disgust for paperwork and bureaucracy, dangerous experimentation and risk taking, and an open spigot of secret government money (which conferred autonomy). Hothouse innovation in the Arroyo Seco and the circus tent was thus an important forerunner of Silicon Valley work methods that became famous decades later.

Here was the "sheltered" market raised to the nth degree, as Johnson and his crew soon got ensconced in a highly secret two-story windowless concrete bunker in beautiful downtown Burbank, with electronics-proof walls and blanketed security. If "Big Blue" was later Apple's nemesis, for this free-wheeling crowd it was the "Blue Suits," the air force bureaucrats who wanted things done their impossibly dense and red-taped way. Luckily the Skunk Works had a hard-as-nails leader in Johnson, who could make self-important Pentagon generals wet their pants, and more powerful patrons in the Pentagon's Advanced Research Projects Agency (ARPA) and the CIA, which showered money on their unofficial "toy maker." A technically brilliant engineer as well as hands-on aircraft mechanic, Johnson ran his crew hard as they sought original solutions to seemingly insoluble problems.

The rare metal titanium, for example, could withstand jet exhaust heat and the tremendous pressures of supersonic speed and high altitudes, but the United States had limited supplies. So the CIA mounted a global search and found its best source in—the Soviet Union. The CIA bought the metal from the Russians through fronts and dummy companies, and then Johnson's people had to figure out how to work it; simply drilling holes into this superhard metal took months of intense experimentation. Apart from the overweening frat-boy macho culture reflected in Skunk Works lingo—"two-fisted fighter jocks," "that sucker was built," "the French [got] their butts kicked by Uncle Ho," and people actually named "Buzz Hello"—the Skunk Works was little different from Silicon Valley. Indeed, Clinton Defense Secretary William J.

Perry was heavily involved with the Skunk Works and later was a Valley venture capitalist.[47]

The Jet Propulsion Laboratory became the General Motors of rocketry, eventually employing 34,000 people. Fifteen years after the war ended, the Pacific Coast was the epicenter of missile production, accounting for two-thirds of total value, largely at the expense of East Coast firms.[48] The Skunk Works kept going into the 1990s, when it was finally closed—and sold to Disney to make a theme park. Rockets, jet fighters, spy planes, computers, satellites, precision-guided weapons (all operational or envisioned by the late 1940s)—these were just the things to fire the minds of energetic young men, cavorting in a perfect year-round climate without the overhang of old industries and factories, an open spigot of funds from a far-off central government negating visits to stodgy old bankers, willing universities and ebullient city fathers urging you on, here was the point at which risk, intelligence, fun, and glamour met: rather like Hollywood, as Howard Hughes was the first to discover. Here was yet another motor of continuous innovation, bringing flyers, engineers, physicists, managers, and technicians running from around the country. For decades Southern California was a key high-tech center in the country, and when it went into momentary eclipse after the end of the cold war, Silicon Valley picked up all the slack and then some.

A Militarized West

The archipelago of empire has its domestic expression not just in Southern California, but throughout the West. The Pacific Coast's development during the war had its counterpart in Denver, Houston, Albuquerque, and many smaller towns like Hanford and Los Alamos. Historian Roger Lotchin lists many western cities "structured around war and defense"; several others exist, of course, in New England and the Carolinas, but the predominance of the West and especially the Pacific Coast cities is remarkable. If it all started during the war, it got much bigger after it: the West had 13 percent of all prime military contracts in 1950, 24 percent in 1959, and the Kennedy administration directed nearly half of all Defense Department contracts for research and development to the Pacific Coast. By the early sixties one in three workers in Los Angeles and Long Beach depended on defense contracts.[49]

The rise of the Sunbelt and the Gunbelt during and after World War II usually involved a mutually beneficial relationship between the military in Washington and urban boosters: "no city was under compulsion to become a garrison town," Lotchin wrote; instead they competed to get the best facilities and contracts. This was a countrywide phenomenon, but California seemed to go out of its way, time and again; by the mid-1970s more than 3.6 million Californians worked in defense industries, and San Diego and Los Angeles joined San Antonio and Colorado Springs in boosting military spending and providing comfortable havens for retired military leaders. The absence of a highly developed industrial base and entrenched unions also directed military spending toward western cities, while the Midwest, so important to war production in World War II, seemed to drop off the map.[50]

In Texas, Lyndon Johnson secured the National Aeronautic and Space Administration's (NASA) Manned Spacecraft Center for Houston in 1961, aircraft industry or defense contracts formed the core of Fort Worth's economy, while San Antonio was heavily dependent on nearby military bases. The North American Aerospace Defense Command (NORAD) in Colorado is less a command post than "a vast underground city, a multi-level maze of rooms and corridors carved into the solid granite core of Cheyenne Mountain," in Reagan aide Martin Anderson's words, a city protected by steel doors several feet thick with a command center several stories deep, a room dominated by a huge display screen of the continental United States and clusters of young people monitoring computer screens that can instantly pinpoint a missile launch in Russia or China. (It was the model for the war room in *Dr. Strangelove;* when Ronald Reagan wanted to visit this Cheyenne redoubt in 1979, a Hollywood producer arranged it.)[51]

In Hawaii CINCPAC is not just the centerpiece of American military might on O'ahu: it is the core of the nation's global power. The commander runs "PACOM," or the Pacific Command, which has responsibility for the entire Pacific Ocean—and for Japan, Korea, Southeast Asia, China, and India as well (half the earth's surface). The PACOM logo is a fierce eagle spreading its wings over the cap—Perry's cocked hat—of the North Pacific, with one talon hovering above Beijing. But there are so many other commands that CINCPAC himself probably can't remember them all. This admiral (it is almost always an admiral) commands two Pacific fleets (CINCPACFLT), air force and army operations (CINCPACAF, CINCWESTCOM), the U.S. Eighth Army in Korea (EUSA—which means he also commands the 650,000-strong South Korean army—plus six or seven other Korean commands like COMUSKOREA), COMFMFPAC (Marine Fleet Forces), CINCUNC (the United Nations Command in Korea, begun in 1950), and the not-to-be-sneered-at CINCPACREPSWPAC, the admiral's man who runs the Southwestern Pacific. CINCPAC also deploys an armada of ships, planes, and weapons of all types, enough to blow up the planet several times; just one of them, the TAK-6 Ballistic Missile Resupply Ship, has enough to do it once all by itself. All together the admiral sits at his Mission-style headquarters, just off Ford Island at Pearl Harbor, directing about 220 ships, a multitude of alphabet-soup commands, and 362,000 people spread from one end of the Pacific to the other. Here is "the largest unified command in the world" as former CINCPAC commander Charles Larson proudly put it, with an area of responsibility stretching "over 100 million square miles, about 52 percent of the Earth's surface that encompasses two-thirds of the Earth's population."[52]

Along the picture-perfect O'ahu coast huge swaths of turf are still off-limits to local citizens. The military uses some 7,200 acres of land, seized under martial law in 1941, for target practice and mock battles. The scene of many protests over the years, things came to a head in 1997 when the military proposed to land 700 marines on Mâkua Beach and march inland for maneuvers, days after the ashes of a prominent advocate of Hawaiian autonomy had been scattered over the same spot. After more turmoil, in due course the military decided to land the marines elsewhere. In 1940 the navy seized the smallest of the eight islands in Hawaii, Kaho'olawe, and used it for bombing practice for half a century; in 1994 Congress allocated funds to restore the island and its farmlands.[53]

Conclusion: An Archipelago in Perpetuity

For Joseph Schumpeter imperialism was an atavism. Originally a strategy or policy called into action for expansionist reasons, it becomes a perpetual motion machine long after losing sight of its purpose: imperialism is "the objectless disposition on the part of a state to unlimited forcible expansion" (see appendix). There is an almost laughable discourse in the daily papers about whether American troops will leave Iraq tomorrow, next year, or in five years: laughable because post-1945 history teaches clearly that they never come home (except in the errant cases where we lose a war outright, as in Vietnam, or when a Mount Pinatubo erupts and dumps tons of ash on Clark Air Force Base). In June 2006 President Bush indicated that roughly 50,000 American troops would remain in Iraq indefinitely, analogous to the commitment to Korea. The United States now has more than 100 bases in Iraq, ranging from huge to middling to tiny, including several "superbases" like Balad Air Base (the largest one in the country). Balad has a miniature golf course, a Pizza Hut, Popeye's, Starbucks, and an open-all-the-time Burger

King to complement its 225 aircraft. Air-conditioned boxes like shipping containers house 20,000 troops. The Pentagon says it has no permanent plans to stay in Iraq and the troops are there at the invitation of the Iraqi government, but they have said that everywhere else since 1945, too; meanwhile high officials privately say they want at least four bases in Iraq for "the long haul"— but they will not announce that publicly.[54]

The global archipelago came into being not with the languishing, almost forgotten emplacements of pre-1941 Hawaii and the Philippines, nor with World War II, but with the transformation of a limited containment doctrine into a global anticommunist crusade in the four years from 1947 to 1951. Pearl Harbor was the tipping point and world war the necessary enabling element, but neither was sufficient for empire: the troops might have come home if Roosevelt had lived a normal life span. Kennan's 1947 strategy—five advanced industrial structures exist in the world, we have four, Moscow has one, containment means keeping things that way—might have sufficed to achieve the critical goal of reviving Western and Japanese industry (Kennan often said that by 1950 he thought enough had been done).[55] NSC-68 defined the new global strategy, but it was really NSC-48, signed by Truman at the end of 1949, that cast the Pacific die. The United States would now do something utterly unimagined at the end of World War II: it would prepare to intervene militarily against anticolonial movements in East Asia—first Korea, then Vietnam, with the Chinese revolution as the towering backdrop. The complexities of this turning point have been plumbed and documented by a number of historians, but they remain largely unplumbed, even today, among experts on foreign affairs, political scientists, journalists, and pundits, because their work places far too much weight on realpolitik and the bipolar rivalry with Moscow and relegates the two biggest wars of the period to the shadows of global concerns.[56]

This empire had to take on a military cast: first of all because by 1950 the problem was defined militarily (unlike Kennan's emphasis on economic aid, military advice, and the United Nations). Second, the United States had nothing remotely resembling an imperial civil service. Before the 1950s the Foreign Service was a microcosm of the Ivy League and the genteel tradition, operating outside the sight lines of most Americans and without a whole lot to do. It produced exemplary individuals like George Kennan, but it never had a strong constituency at home. It is well known that McCarthy's assault on officers in the China service ruined American expertise on East Asia for a generation, but Nixon's attack on Alger Hiss may have had worse consequences: anyone in pinstripes became suspect, people seen as internal foreigners, and the State Department was fatally weakened. In the 1960s came the academic specialists—McGeorge Bundy, Walt Rostow, Henry Kissinger, Zbigniew Brzezinski—Svengalis who would tutor the president in the occult science of foreign affairs. They also warred upon the State Department, appropriating its responsibilities while ignoring it, thus diluting its influence even more. The State Department often seems to be a foreign office with no clear constituency, but the 700-plus military installations around the world persist and perdure; they have an eternal writ all of their own. The permanence of our foreign military bases is as predictable and seemingly ineradicable as the phalanx of lobbyists on K Street. Nearly four decades ago the Senate Foreign Relations Committee paraphrased Schumpeter when it wrote: "Once an American overseas base is established it takes on a life of its own. Original missions may become outdated but new missions are developed, not only with the intention of keeping the facility going, but often to actually enlarge it."[57] Whether this far-flung archipelago is necessary in a world where American military power towers over any potential rival—and can hit any enemy from the continental homeland—is beside the point: it exists, therefore it persists.

CHAPTER SIXTEEN

Silicon Valley:
A New World at the Edge of the Sea

The actual realization of the astonishing fact, that instantaneous personal conversation can be held between persons hundreds of miles apart, can only be fully attained by witnessing the wonderful fact itself.

In the spring of 2000 I was searching for leave-year housing and driving my boys, one second-grader and one sixth-grader, over to a town called Mountain View. They spied a white building on the highway: "Look, Dad, there's Google!" "What's Google?" (They both laughed at my appalling ignorance.) Now I use Google's global satellite imagery to examine North Korean nuclear reactors as if I were in the National Security Agency, and this company has become something approximating another Microsoft by figuring out how to sell advertising effectively on the free Web (as people did in the 1920s for free radio—maybe it's another RCA). Just off the old Spanish road, El Camino Real, sat a Wal-Mart–like emporium and techie hangout devoted solely to electronics—Fry's—and this was merely one of several branch stores around the Bay Area. Fry's had every computer, video game, and cell phone accessory known to man, huge bins full of incomprehensible tiny objects, a kind of machine-and-spare-parts emporium for geeks. People who resembled undergraduate students pulled into the parking lot in Ferraris and Lamborghinis. The chic restaurants downtown (Café Verona, Il Fornaio) were booked solid for weeks. Draeger's carried $2,000 wines and $1,500 bottles of balsamic vinegar; I watched a kid who appeared to be about eighteen pull up out front in a $125,000 BMW Z-8 roadster.

Palo Alto's ubiquitous middle- and working-class bungalows and ranches were now mere "scrapes," knock-downs awaiting the next McMansion. Valley moguls put up 25,000-square-foot palaces with twenty-car underground garages. Oracle founder Larry Ellison, enamored of things Japanese except when it comes to their small-is-beautiful conceptions of size and taste, built a 192-foot yacht called *Sakura* (cherry blossom), with five decks of aluminum and teak; his $40 million Woodside home used traditional Japanese-style wooden pegs instead of nails, yielding a feng shui balance (in his words) of "Air, Earth, Time, Water, and Wood." He wears five-figure kimonos to stroll among his koi ponds and bonsai plants, and his airplane hangar has space enough for the Russian MiG-29 that he wants to buy if Washington will let him.

After a quarter-century of relative stagnation, productivity grew steeply from late 1996 to 2000, leading central banker Alan Greenspan to hail a "new economy" of continuous productivity growth. Books appeared one after another extolling "a technological revolution" that would affect all our lives, "a Long Boom, a vast economic expansion that could go for decades, spreading prosperity around the world and lifting billions into middle class lifestyles." After many years of instant billionaires and continuous stock market rallies, in the spring of 2000 it was hard not to believe it all; Valley firms had a total market capitalization of nearly $750 billion, compared to Wall Street's $514 billion, the auto industry's $136 billion, and Hollywood's $76 billion; Cisco Systems alone was valued at $146 billion by New Year's Eve 1999. During that same year one-third of all venture capital in the country went into the Valley.[1]

Soon, however, the slow hissing sound of a punctured bubble was almost audible in Palo Alto. In retrospect, the key date was March 10, 2000, when the Nasdaq hit its historic high of 5,048.62, fell, came back two weeks later almost to 5,000, and then never came back again (the nadir of 1,200 came in late 2002, by which time it had lost $6.5 billion of wealth or 78 percent of its peak value; it hovers around 1,500 at this writing). It took a while for people to understand that the party was over, of course, but as the months passed the Ferraris and Lamborghinis slowly vanished from the streets. By the fall Il Fornaio and Café Verona were half-empty. A bungled vote count stretched the presidential election out for six weeks, until five judges brought to power a man who seemed to embody the bad karma of a souring era. Companies worth hundreds of millions one day were worthless the next; companies worth billions like Enron and WorldCom turned out to have been run by carnival barkers, albeit with inferior ethics. Catholic parishioners searched the eyes of their priest to see if he, too, was a pedophile. Business potentates, politicians, priests, and hawkers of Silicon Valley miracles were all laid low as central institutions in American life got badly tarnished. A year after the Nasdaq hit 5,000, even the electricity was out in California, and then September 11 issued another coup de grace to the eternal American desire to escape history.

In retrospect it is difficult—and much too early—to determine what the remains of the halcyon days are for Silicon Valley. The 1990s were not "the greatest period of wealth creation in the history of the world." Silicon Valley technology has not "impacted [*sic*] the world more than any other occurrence since the Renaissance."[2] Clearly this was another episode—and one of the biggest—in California's longstanding tendency to lead the nation in great leaps forward, in sudden lurches and spasms that spin wealth seemingly out of thin air. But the silicon-chip revolution unquestionably created a new threshold in modern life, worthy of the steam engine or the automobile. By that revolution I mean the incessant innovation in transistors, integrated circuits, microprocessors, and applications like wireless circuits and the Internet, such that we now have in sight the knowledge of the world reduced to a stream delivered instantly to a $400 computer sitting in this office or that Starbucks (if Google can be believed). At some indefinable point a series of incremental innovations combined to create utterly unexpected qualitative explosions in the purest Schumpeterian fashion and led to the practical revolution that we all experience: cars that no longer fall apart after 60,000 miles, missiles that unerringly home in on targets halfway around the world, Toyota just-in-time inventories, Wal-Mart computer-driven warehouse merchandising that brought wholesaling crashing into retailing, cell phones that call Maine from Mt. McKinley, computers powerful enough to test nuclear weapons without an explosion, an Internet that seems to encompass the entire globe and every service that human beings can imagine, and a blogosphere that offers something for everyone while liberating every ill-informed, untutored, and tiresome opinion.

Was it a revolution in *kind* or merely one of *degree*—pitching everything we used to do up to warp speed? Everything is at my fingertips: so what? What can be done now that could not be done before with telephones, typewriters, stereos, newspapers, encyclopedias, atlases, and a good library, however longer it may take? Will my comprehension of Nietzsche improve because I have instant access to his works? Isn't it still a question of Thoreau's "improved means toward an unimproved end"? Speed and replicability (faxes, file sharing, DVDs, etc.) of course make a big difference, but not the difference that the telegraph made. For Manuel Castells the "annihilation of space and time by electronic means" is critical, but as we have seen that was perhaps the most common trope—if nicely poetic (Heine said it first in 1843)—about the railroad and the telegraph.[3] With one critical exception, then it was a revolution of degree, less important in history than the invention of the telegraph. But the exception may be enough to call it an authentic revolution, because the silicon era brought a 100 percent, works-all-the-time *reliability* to the affairs of the modern world, and in the end that will inevitably reengineer human relations across the globe.

The information age miraculously speeds up almost every act of human communication except the face-to-face, but this is a quantitative leap in degree from the invention of the telegraph, which shrank the globe to more or less instant communications for the first time in human history. What is transformative about the new technologies, I think, is to replace a host of modern technologies that worked until they wore out (a few hundred hours for radio tubes, a few thousand hours for TV picture tubes, a vacuum tube popping every minute or two in the 18,000 inhabiting the first ENIAC mainframe computer), with technologies that never wear out—even at unimaginably high speeds: products that have validity (they work) and ultimate reliability (they never quit), whereas for 200 years through steam, railroads, and autos they had only certain validity. The Pentagon grasped this fact fifty years ago and offered a critical wager: a predictable, nearly permanent sheltered market in return for standards of absolute reliability way beyond what the commercial market required—silicon wafers automatically governing Mach-2 jet fighters, ICBMs, and nuclear warheads. Put reliability into smaller and smaller packages as the technology systematically minimizes, and you can put a missile down a chimney in Russia or bomb anyplace in the world from Omaha, with the crew never touching terra firma (and back home by the next day).

Japan's Pacific Century?

The discourse on American decline assumed that Japan was killing the United States competitively because it effectively adapted new technologies (often ones invented in the United States) for the "exposed" or consumer market, from Sony's first transistor radio to VCRs, automobiles, and compact disc players, whereas American new technologies appeared in the "sheltered" market of Pentagon contracts. An entire literature emerged probing the reasons for Japanese success and American decline, especially the long stagnation in American productivity going back to the late 1960s. Influential authors claimed not only that Japan was ahead technologically, but it was about to become the hegemonic power of the globe (if it wasn't already).[4] A 1986 book, *The Pacific Century*, spoke of a looming transfer of global power to Japan, to which had already migrated "dynamism," "vigor," "spectacular growth," "entrepreneurship"(?), and a host of similar things that used to be housed in

America. In the face of this looming "threat," Americans could no longer rest on their laurels: "staleness is not tolerable" and neither is "stagnation," the author concluded. Even in the mid-1990s experts still harped on the mantra that "technological progress in electronics has shifted away from the U.S., in particular towards Japan," and that Japanese external assets had made it "the largest empire on earth."[5] The next century was going to be the Pacific Century, with Japan in the lead.

I never believed that Japan was significantly or irreversibly ahead of the United States in any important technology, let alone verging on hegemonic transfer (Japan is going hegemonic while American military bases still plaster its territory?), but I relied on a scholar's knowledge of Japan and had little expertise in the technologies. Productivity grew at a snail's pace after 1970, and it was reasonable for many to assume that it would never really outpace Japan again. Still, at the height of worries about American decline in the late 1980s, U.S. productivity was the highest in the world across an entire range of industries, from early sectors like agriculture, textiles, stone and glass products, or mining and oil drilling, to high-tech sectors like transportation and communications, machinery and scientific instruments. Japan was predictably more productive in automobile and steel manufacture (old industries in the United States, but newly rebuilt after 1945 in Japan) and chemicals (always a Japanese specialty given their lack of natural resources). In only one field was Japan threatening American dominance, but it happened to be the most important one: the advancing field of electronic equipment. There its productivity was a bit more than 10 percent higher than America's. In retrospect, though, there never was a real decline: the United States accounted for 30.52 percent of the world's GDP in 1971, and 30.74 percent in 2006,[6] and the main reason lay not in the ferment of market competition but in the shelter of a five-sided building in Washington.

In a prescient 1990 book Jean-Claude Derian expressed concern about America's technological lead in several areas, like semiconductors, super-computers, gigaflop processors, and high-definition television, but he was generally optimistic that the United States would retain or regain the global technological lead because of critical Japanese weaknesses in the sheltered culture of technology—whereas the United States operated effectively in both the open and the sheltered market. Japan, Inc. has a weak scientific tradition, with few Nobel Prize winners (Britain, for example, has hundreds more) and significantly lower absolute levels of research and development expenditure when compared to the United States. Japan had unquestionably done well in the exposed technological market, where the key is acquisition and product innovation rather than discovery of new technologies. But the United States held two trump cards that Japan did not: the first was its prowess in both the sheltered and the exposed culture, a result in part of enormous American military-related spending, and the second was its hegemonic birthright: the privileged position of the dollar as "the cornerstone of the world monetary system."[7]

Japanese firms had cornered just over half of the global chip and chip-making market by 1989, but within five years American computers were again the fastest in the world, American chips like Intel's Pentium were better than Japan's chips, U.S. firms had 46 percent of the chip market to Japan's 30 percent and 54 percent of the chip-making equipment. By 2000, experts estimated that Japan was four or five years behind the United States in information technology, and by 2006 it had just 23 percent of the semiconductor market and only three of its firms made the Top 10 list, as South Korea ate sharply into its chip position.[8] In software (which after all is the brains of a computer), the United States had and has retained a gigantic lead—and a flagship monopoly every bit as good as Standard Oil or U.S. Steel in 1900, namely, Microsoft. So much for Japan's Pacific Century.

The evidence of a productivity revolution that hardly anyone anticipated is also clear. In the early 1990s the question was how America could avoid falling further behind Japan, amid stagnant productivity growth for the previous thirty years. But by 1995 the results of huge investment in new technologies over four decades began to make themselves felt throughout the economy, and productivity rose at an average annual rate of about 2.5 percent through 2000, compared to a rate of 1.4 percent from 1972 to 1995; in short spurts, like the second quarter of 2000, it leapt ahead by as much as 6 percent. In 2001 the bursting bubble punctured high-tech stocks and the very idea that there was a "new economy," but it did not slow down productivity growth—instead it increased, averaging about 3.5 percent from 2001 through 2004. In spite of 9/11, productivity growth was an amazing 4.8 percent from July 2001 to June 2002. It hit 5.4 percent in the third quarter of 2005 and averaged 3.5 percent in the previous three years. Much of this growth owes to continued high rates of research and development; the United States accounts for about 40 percent of all R & D spending in the world. The "Global Competitiveness Report" ranked the United States second in 2005—behind high-tech Finland.[9]

Harvard economist Dale Jorgenson estimated that about half the productivity growth in the late 1990s came from information technology, but he and others have shown that in recent years rapid productivity growth comes also from service industries and the application of the digital revolution to them; they are the vast majority of industries in the United States, but economists had long thought that ginning up productivity was much harder in services than in manufacturing. The elephants in the room are Wal-Mart, using a variety of new methods to manage supply chains and logistics, warehousing and merchandising, or Seattle's Amazon, with its many innovations in computerized warehousing, instant cyberspace shopping, and (not-quite-so instant) shipping. Information processing occupies a huge chunk of the service sector: in 1960 the average cost of processing information was $75 per million operations; it was less than one-hundredth of a penny by 1990. However destructive this wave of creation and destruction has been (it gobbles millions of good jobs, replacing them with fewer and usually lower-paying jobs), it has forced the competition to adopt the methods Wal-Mart pioneered through the application of new information technologies to handling supplies, shipping, inventories, and sales.[10]

The Sheltered Revolution

Think about, say, the computing requirements of the National Security Agency, which monitors every global communication that it wants to sweep into its net, working with friendly agencies in Europe on programs like "Echelon" or George Bush's "Total Information Awareness" program (which died in 2002 and then reemerged surreptitiously) which are presumably capable of monitoring every phone or e-mail exchange in Europe and America; think of what it takes to surveill every square foot of China or to vacuum up its secret and open Internet traffic? The nation's nuclear engineers moved out of the dirty business of actually testing nuclear weapons because highly classified supercomputers can simulate the tests all by themselves—how powerful must such computers be? For every commercial and individual computer use that someone might think up, there is a corresponding government need to have the same thing only *much* better—and perhaps to monitor what you're doing with your own inferior technology. Thus about 70 percent of all university research in computers, semiconductors, telecommunications, and electronic engineering comes from Uncle Sam—and that doesn't count government contracts with private firms.[11]

Silicon Valley operated for decades in the sheltered culture of government contracts before people like Bill Gates and Steve Jobs showed their entrepreneurial prowess in the exposed, consumer market. Valley denizens with the right security clearances began using the Net long ago, in 1969—that is, the

ARPANET, run out of the very successful R & D Pentagon vehicle called the Advanced Research Projects Agency (ARPA) that was founded after the Sputnik scare of 1957. This network was meant to be a decentralized communications system that would be resistant to an all-out nuclear strike, operating through various nodal stations and switches, using information packets that could funnel millions of messages from one place to another. The first four "nodes" were all in the West—Stanford, UCLA, UC–Santa Barbara, and the University of Utah.

Bob Taylor was the Pentagon's team leader on ARPANET in the 1960s, spending years on the auspicious third floor, down the hall from Bob McNamara in the geometrically hallowed D-ring, ensconced in the most prestigious agency, Advanced Research Projects, inhabiting an office worthy of a three-star general—and these folks take rank seriously; even your ashtray bespoke your importance. Taylor, a Texan, administered the largest budget for computer research in the world, most of it plowed into fifteen to twenty projects at universities and firms throughout the country; perhaps the only person in the Pentagon who didn't worry about rank, he cut out the hierarchy and red tape by having everyone at ARPA report directly to him. He had two teletype terminals near his desk, a Model 33 and a Model 35. These machines were the cutting edge of the 1960s transition from punching out don't-spindle-or-mutilate cards and handing them to someone who stuck them in a mainframe, to doing your own computing—because with an archaic "modem" (a telephone handset) and BASIC (Beginner's All-Purpose Symbolic Instruction Code, invented in 1964), a teletype could be your very own rudimentary but real-time computer. Taylor's Model 33 was hooked up to UC–Berkeley, while Model 35 linked to a bulky Strategic Air Command mainframe in Santa Monica—probably at RAND, although its location still appears to be classified. This is how the ARPANET got going, on machines that were modest improvements on Morse's telegraph a century earlier. Of course, some new jiggering and upgrades were necessary to get the IMP, an "Interface Message Processor," up and running ("bring out the IMP"); the first one got installed at UCLA in September 1969, the second at Stanford Research Institute a month later, just as Taylor made a partial continental remove to the University of Utah—and soon enough Utah had an IMP, too, the third node in the four-node granddaddy of the Internet.[12]

Bob Taylor had soured on the mess in Vietnam, which had punctured ARPA's "academic" autonomy with demands for better methods of processing Vietcong body counts, but he didn't appear to be too enamored of Salt Lake City, either, so in 1970 he removed once again to Silicon Valley, to manage Xerox's computer laboratory at the Palo Alto Research Center, or PARC. (The genteel tradition was still alive and well at Yale, where snobs had told Xerox's Jack Goldman to take his proposed research facility somewhere else, so Stanford achieved another coup.) PARC director George Pake set himself up at Rickey's Hyatt House (a motel on motel-ridden El Camino Real) to recruit the best and the brightest. Tom Wolfe memorably imagined how they would have done it back East: "Some fifty-five-year-old biggie with his jowls swelling up smoothly from out of his F. R. Tripeler modified-spread white collar and silk jacquard print necktie would call up from GE or RCA and say, 'This is Harold B. Thatchwaite.'" By contrast Pake and his friends gathered at Rickey's or the Wagon Wheel where they would "trade war stories about phase jitters, phantom circuits, bubble memories, pulse trains, bounceless contacts, burst modes, leapfrog tests, p-n junctions, sleeping sickness modes, slow-death episodes, RAMs, NAKs, MOSes, PCMs, PROMs, PROM blowers, PROM blasters, and teramagnitudes." PARC employees were sheltered from Yale- and GE-like hierarchies, presumptions, and dress codes; about the only question was, can you do the work? Like Hewlett-Packard, PARC fostered an atmosphere of unpretentious informality and workaholic seriousness, "casual collegiality" and egalitarianism, lunchtime volleyball breaks, scruffy jeans, and mosh-pit offices. (In 1972 *Rolling Stone* called the brilliant Alan Kay, who helped invent the Alto PC and was one of Pake's most important acquisitions, a "computer bum" and compared him to a hot-rodder.)[13]

The research center at Palo Alto was a different kind of sheltered market: Xerox provided lots of R & D funds and paid little attention to what was going on—to their subsequent chagrin. Within two years Taylor's engineers had built the first prototype personal computer, the "Alto," which could display animated features—like Cookie Monster rolling across the screen. IBM was still the master of electric typewriters and mainframe computers, Bill Gates was applying to Harvard, and Steve Jobs was roaming India in search of good karma, but Bob Taylor and his friends were using e-mail, inventing the mouse, and reinventing the @ sign. In the seventies PARC produced one innovation after another from its headquarters at 3333 Coyote Hill Road, near Stanford University: word processing, interactive video conferencing, the computer mouse (originally a block of wood with two wheels), Ethernet transmission, three-dimensional computer graphics, pop-up windows, and the laser printer. Many of these inventions grew out of a set of seminal papers completed at PARC in 1971, anticipating a future office with electronic mail, computer and disk storage replacing rows of file cabinets, "smart" appliances run by integrated circuits, digital photo optics and sound, and a host of other ideas popping up as smart people envisioned the long-range implications of the rapidly increasing density of semiconductors. Xerox missed the boat on adapting most of these new-new things to consumer use (although not the laser printer, on which it earned billions), but like the Pentagon it showered "a seemingly limitless cascade of cash" on PARC just at the time when the hard chips were getting smaller and smaller and their capacity bigger and bigger—enough to write software directly onto them.[14]

These two apposite institutions—the Pentagon and Xerox—funded one discovery after another over the next thirty years, inventions that lay at the heart of the connected world we see today. The father of the Internet was not Al Gore, but certainly among the multiple parents was Vincent Cerf, a Stanford professor who used ARPA funds to invent TCP/IP (transmission-control protocol/Internet protocol) messaging in 1973, allowing computers using different software languages to communicate with each other and across different kinds of networks. Suddenly the twenty-odd nodes connected to the ARPANET could in theory communicate with any computer on any network.[15] Defense Department funds created the Stanford University Network, a UNIX-based system for powerful workstations which soon became Sun Microsystems. The Mosaic/Netscape Internet browser came out of an ARPA program in supercomputers. We will find many similar examples.

The Sheltered Market Nurtures the Open Market

Xerox made a world-historic mistake in August 1977 when it passed up the chance to build and market the first personal computer, preferring instead to offer to its capacious existing market the "Xerox 850," essentially an electric typewriter with a small screen and an even smaller memory, enough to hold three or four pages for a secretary to work over. Xerox and IBM and AT&T sunk their costs into mainframe computers, office machines well beyond the buying capacity of the individual consumer, communication trunk lines and all kinds of proprietary technologies, and then hoped to keep those structures in place for decades and provide the follow-on sales and customer services—a daisy chain of rental, maintenance, and upgrade contracts—all by themselves. It worked when they sold to the Internal Revenue Service or the FBI or any number of big corporations, who got locked in from the 1950s to the 1990s with programs to process tax returns or Social Security checks or monthly payrolls; Robert Cringely estimated in 1992 that there was $50 billion in mainframe software imbedded in the country for which the source codes no longer existed (because nobody would build them again).[16] You still see it all the time: walk into an auto parts store, for example, and there is likely to be a grungy twenty-year-old computer spewing fan-paper out of an ancient dot-matrix printer. That's why Xerox missed the boat.

In 1977 PARC experts traveled to a Xerox "futures day" in Boca Raton and showed off PCs, word processing, and graphic interfaces to a dazzled (and baffled) Xerox sales force, word got around, and soon Steve Jobs and Bill Gates were dropping by PARC to have a look. The Jobs legend states that he walked into PARC and walked off with the windows technology for the Macintosh. Michael Hiltzik, the best historian of PARC, shows that like most legends this is partly true and partly false. Xerox had invested about a million dollars in Apple, and the quid pro quo was a serious tour through PARC. Jobs arrived with a small entourage in November 1979 and saw the Alto with its mouse, keyboard, Bravo word processing, and a new graphics application called "Smalltalk." Later he found out how much he didn't see (Xerox had given him the public relations tour) and came back again. Jobs told (that is, shrieked at) the head of PARC that he was developing a new PC, called "Lisa," and had a right to see everything, since Xerox owned part of Apple. PARC capitulated and arranged the "confidential tour" which included the multiple, overlapping screens they had developed (think Windows) and the "GUI" (graphical user interface); nervous PARC scientists watched as the eyes of Apple engineers nearly popped out of their skulls. It wasn't so much that Apple stole PARC technology, it was more like the Soviets learning of a mushroom cloud over Hiroshima: now they knew that what they were working on—worked. It was "knowing it could be done," Apple's Bill Atkinson said, that empowered him to find a way to do it (he is the father of the consumer-friendly GUI that, along with its shape, made the Mac famous).[17]

Of course, everyone stole from everyone else. When Microsoft announced their new "Windows" interface in 1983, Jobs "went ballistic": get Gates down here immediately, he barked at his staff. Gates dutifully arrived the next afternoon, all by himself. "You're ripping us off!" Jobs screamed, while ten or fifteen Apple staffers crowded around Gates. Well, not quite, Gates responded coolly, "I think it's more like we both had this rich neighbor named Xerox and I broke into his house to steal the TV set only to find that you had already stolen it." But Jobs didn't steal Charles Simonyi, so Gates was able to hire him away from PARC—the inventor of Bravo, the WYSIWYG (what you see is what you get) technology that printed what you saw on the screen and inaugurated desktop publishing, and all-round tutor of Gates on operating systems, e-mail, spreadsheets, and word processing. Simonyi started out as a teenage computer hacker like so many others—except that he hacked the Soviet Ural II main-frame in Budapest, where he was the teenage night watchman in this most sheltered of all markets, thanks to his father's pull; by 1967 he was a computer science student at UC–Berkeley. He arrived in Seattle to run product development just after Gates had licensed his MS-DOS software platform to the Chess personal computer—code name for IBM's PC, an inferior machine in Steve Jobs's eyes, but then he didn't have the capability to place it in every office in the world, an opportunity Bill Gates did not miss. Somehow Big Blue accomplished the biggest rip-off of all: pulling the rug out from under arch-competitor Xerox by spiriting away much of what PARC had learned, only to make an inferior product—which sold by the millions in the 1980s.[18]

Beginnings?

Just like economists, Silicon Valley boosters try to interpret this revolution with dates and numbers: it all began in 1954, or 1965, or 1980 (and in 2000 it all did *what?*). The authors of *The Long Boom* brought their book out just as the bubble burst and sent them straight to the remainder table. For them everything began around 1980—the long boom, that is. Two aerospace engineers, T. J. Gordon and A. L. Shef, claimed that "the technological status of the world as a whole advances at a roughly constant exponential rate, doubling every twenty years, or in effect, every generation." But their home state didn't fit that generalization, they noticed; California was off the charts, ahead of any nation or place, and ahead of the rest of the United States by a good fifteen years ever since 1920: "What caused this is a matter worthy of future study," they wrote (indeed).[19]

The early management styles of "the HP Way" or Robert Noyce and Gordon Moore at Intel have led many analysts to assert that Silicon Valley is unique in its entrepreneurship and innovative style, the living-and-breathing American exceptionalism of our time. Chong-Moon Lee divided this phenomenon into four styles of entrepreneurship: long-term vision (Jerry Yang and David Filo of Yahoo!), acquisition entrepreneurs (Cisco Systems), transformational entrepreneurs (Scott McNealy at Sun Microsystems), and serial entrepreneurs (Jim Clark of Netscape fame). Lee has a detailed comparison between "traditional" entrepreneurs and Valley geniuses: the latter possess a "revolutionary mindset," they "try to control market rather than company," they envision future success and go after it, they are highly motivated, highly skilled, "multicultural"; they believe its "OK to talk to competitors, OK to move to another company, OK to fail," and so on.[20] The Valley is multicultural now but wasn't through most of its history, and it isn't clear that this has anything to do with entrepreneurship; all of Lee's other characteristics were true of Thomas Edison or Henry Ford. Talking to competitors ceases the nanosecond a Clark or a Jobs corners a "killer-ap" technology; for them, paranoia about the competition is the daily rule. Closer to the mark is Christophe Lécuyer, who shows that tightly-knit groups (rather than heroic entrepreneurs) that sought to meet reliability and performance standards set by the Defense Department, usually funded by that same department, account for many of the Valley's new technologies. No need to raise capital or do market research, just get to work on the contract. (San Jose often outranked even Washington, D.C., as the most defense budget-dependent city in America.)[21]

Maybe something happened in the vaunted 1960s? Some Silicon Valley boosters argue that the sixties counterculture had something to do with the entrepreneurial burst of energy that led to one invention and firm after another. The authors of *The Long Boom,* for example, applaud Tom Wolfe's *Electric Kool-Aid Acid Test* (1968) for capturing "the essence of the northern California ideology of extreme openness and creative exploration by telling the story of the countercultural heyday. . . . That somewhat [*sic*] moderated mentality partly accounts for the region's high-tech success today." Manuel Castells is closer to the mark in linking a host of movements (feminism, human rights, multiculturalism) to a core libertarianism that probably has something to do with the productivity and flexibility of Silicon Valley firms.[22] When a reader peruses photos of Silicon Valley leaders and entrepreneurs,[23] one could just as easily conclude that the Valley reinvented the 1950s; they are almost all male WASPs in suits, and the concerns of the 1960s—race, gender, class, war, and the university—are notable for their absence. Thomas Alva Edison demonstrated how many new-new things could be discovered through a combination of practical science, brilliant imagination, and indefatigable effort in a new place—his private industrial laboratory, perhaps the world's first, in Menlo Park (unfortunately for our story, the one in New Jersey). Edison had his lesser-known counterparts in Silicon Valley, but *when*— in 1980, or 1965, or 1954? As it happened, the Valley was a hothouse incubator of high-tech innovation for the past century, with an unbroken genealogy of electronic innovation beginning around 1909.

Radio Beginnings

We have forgotten what a revolutionary thing radio was: RCA's Victrola might bring you the Great Caruso, but radio brought you Bing Crosby, the Yankees, the latest news, and Roosevelt by the fireside. Ham radio enthusiasts made for a rambunctious community of young people like Steve Jobs's "Home Brew Computer Club." And radio was free, too, just like the Internet —if you call putting up with advertisements free. It was so important that a central scholarly book in the modernization literature of the 1950s focused on how many Turkish villages had radios. Americans did not invent it (Guglielmo Marconi did) but quickly pioneered its uses. Station KQW chose an interesting place to experiment with this new-new thing: San Jose.

The "Wireless Laboratories" at KQW began as the brainstorm of Charles D. Herrold, a Stanford graduate who had 11,000 feet of wire running between two seven-story buildings in 1909, connected to a rudimentary arc transmitter. Soon he was broadcasting songs, even tunes plunked on the ukulele by local high school kids; listeners included young men named Herbert Hoover Jr. and Frederick Terman, who captured broadcasts with the "spark set" they fabricated. In 1912 Herrold got the first government license in America for "radio telephony," and the next year he set a world record for long-distance radio transmission when the *Sherman*, an army transport, picked up his signal nearly 1,000 miles away. Herrold, who would be the "father of American radio" except for a string of misfortunes that left him working as a school janitor, also began experimenting in 1912 with Audion tube "cascade" amplifiers—not in San Jose, but in Palo Alto. His successes in amplifying radio signals led directly to the Magnavox loudspeaker—developed not in Palo Alto but in Oakland; this speaker perfected the moving coil in a magnetic field that became the basic technology of standard-issue consumer radios. Once the technology was in place, California also pioneered much of the "software" for radio—popular entertaining like KFRC's *Blue Monday Jamboree* or KGO's *One Man's Family* that became templates for the entire industry.[24]

Also in Palo Alto in 1909 was Stanford graduate Cyril Elwell, who got Stanford president David Starr Jordan and the university's Civil Engineering Department interested in his wireless telephone and telegraph outfit; they succeeded in getting the Crocker family and others to finance a start-up called the Federal Telegraph Corporation (FTC), which soon had wireless arc transmitters in the Pacific Mail Steamship fleet, and then hit the jackpot when the navy ordered ten 30-kilowatt arc transmitters for its ships. In World War I, FTC became known as "the navy's darling." For good measure, Elwell installed 100-kilowatt units linking the Panama Canal Zone with the Philippines and other Pacific posts. The FTC was perhaps the original example of the nexus of university/venture capital/private firm/protected military market. And like future Valley firms, the Bay Area was far enough off the beaten track to be relatively invisible to the dominant industrial centers back east—no one was looking when Philo Farnsworth began experimenting with television in San Francisco and transmitted his first television image in 1927 and patented his system in 1930.[25]

When World War I began the navy had wireless stations (carrying code, not voices) in Virginia, San Diego, the Canal Zone, Hawaii, Guam, and the Philippines (note the Pacific dominance), and during the war Woodrow Wilson maximized his penchant for speechifying through the radio—which he believed to be "the means for beaming truth directly to the people." On January 8, 1918, he beamed himself up to the entire world, transmitting his Fourteen Points address to Europe, East Asia, and Latin America. Later Wilson used his influence to suggest that General Electric create a radio monopoly: the Radio Corporation of America (RCA), formed out of GE, American Marconi, American Telephone and Telegraph, Western Electric, and—a nice touch—United Fruit. Soon Americans controlled radio in both western hemispheres through various consortia; Japan blocked similar arrangements in the Far East, but RCA expanded there anyway all through the 1920s, dominating transpacific radio. Meanwhile David Sarnoff was the Bill Gates of his era, building a virtual monopoly in radio for RCA.[26]

Charles Litton graduated from Stanford in 1928 and operated a ham radio operation out of his parents' home; soon he was experimenting with vacuum tubes and especially the intricacies of manufacturing their glass envelopes. In 1932 he established Litton Engineering Laboratories, built a shop on his parents' property in Redwood City to manufacture glass vacuum tube blanks, and invented an ingenious glass working lathe that could "simultaneously form a complex glass envelope and seal it to the tube's elements," in Christophe Lécuyer's words; Litton had bested RCA, in spite of its 250 patents on tube design and manufacture. By 1940 Litton's "magnetron" vacuum tubes for radar systems were being gobbled up by the U.S. military.[27] And by this time the ur-garage start-up was already off and running in Palo Alto.

Microwave Beginnings

In his childhood, David Packard, like Jack Parsons, was fascinated by explosives—but also by ham radio and football. At six-foot-five he made a good tight end on the Stanford football team, but an even better student of Frederick Terman, who let him into his graduate class in radio engineering when he was still a junior. Bill Hewlett fooled around with explosives as a kid, too, and had a mangled thumb to show for it. He and Packard hit it off in Terman's electrical engineering program. In 1937 Hewlett rented a bungalow for $45 a month in "professorville" in old Palo Alto, and the two young men gathered up $538 thus to began their collaboration in the garage at 367 Addison Avenue: ur-garage of all the start-ups to come. It was a mere twelve-feet-by-eighteen-feet, one-car, one-story garage with a ham radio, a nice Sears-Roebuck drill press, and not much else. Two years later they were selling a "Model 2000A" audio oscillator, which turned into the eight Model 2000Bs that Walt Disney bought for his classic animated film *Fantasia*—the hit musical of 1940, which Steve Jobs and other sixties denizens watched in the dark of old theaters while experimenting on their brain chemistry. Soon the war came and HP instruments for measuring radio frequencies were much in demand; by 1945 they had 100 employees and nearly $1 million in sales.[28]

Russell Varian learned about vacuum tubes from Charles Litton and together with a Stanford physicist, William Hansen, built "klystrons" that were both vacuum tubes and electronic circuits, the first devices that could operate in the microwave range, a quite amazing technology now sitting in everyone's kitchen. Using Litton's glass-working lathe, they began turning out klystrons for Sperry Gyroscope in 1938, then for French radar systems, and after Pearl Harbor Varian was the main producer of microwave tubes to the military. But if Litton and Hewlett and Packard were typical chips off the Palo Alto block, the Varians were from another world. Born into a chiropractor's family in the socialist-theosophist community of Halcyon on the Big Sur coast where property was held in common, they had strong socialist principles and contempt for big business. In 1948 they got together with some Stanford professors and an engineer named Myrl Stearns, most of whom were New Dealers or socialists living in a housing cooperative called Ladera in the hills above Stanford, to form Varian Associates. The whole idea was to build a firm that was a cooperative, lacking hierarchies—"an association of equals" with extensive employee ownership.[29]

Many in the group had justified working for the government by the threat of the Third Reich, but they got more than what they bargained for: during the early years of the cold war Varian won a highly secret contract from a federal ordnance fuse laboratory to develop the R-1, "an exotic reflex klystron." Stuck into the nose of an aerial bomb, it could monitor the distance to a target continuously so that the explosion could go off just at the right time. It had to be highly reliable and immune to shocks and vibrations. The R-1 had a specific purpose: it would detonate an atomic airburst at a specified distance above a target. The distance from Halcyon to Armageddon had been short and quick, but Russell and Sigurd Varian soon came to regret their work on atomic bombs, and by the late 1950s Sigurd had developed mental problems that ended his work. But they had few qualms about defense work in general, it seems: during the Korean War, Varian's sales grew more than tenfold (from $461,000 to $5,197,000), and their firm expanded from 75 to 600 employees. This war boosted Varian into a big business, and in 1957 the brothers took their company public—making them both wealthy beyond imagination. (Likewise Korea allowed Litton to expand from making magnetrons to a full panoply of electronic products in what became Litton Industries; its sales increased tenfold during the war—and its profits were astounding: $1.2 million on sales of $3 million.) Varian continued to be a major Pentagon supplier, with contracts for Ballistic Missile Early Warning Systems and a host of other programs.[30]

More central to the history of the Valley, though, was "the HP way": trusting and respecting employees, first-name informality, profit-sharing, retrenchment for everyone in hard times rather than firing workers, and "management by walking around." Hewlett and Packard were on the work floor all the time, interacting with their employees; Bill Hewlett hated hierarchies and wouldn't even sit at the head of the table during staff meetings. Many scholars and practitioners (like John Seely Brown, a former director of Xerox PARC) believe that the social organization of work in the Valley may have been more important than the high technology itself in realizing sharp productivity gains.[31] The *way* also meant maintaining close ties to Stanford—to Terman and his students and programs, and to the development office, which they eventually showered with hundreds of millions of dollars—plus it was a sophisticated way to ward off labor unions, strongly entrenched in the Bay Area. But by now this is a well-known story.

Another "way" was to put one or two questionably-attired young men in a room and put them to work "for a hundred days without a break, often sleeping on the floor" and ingesting a diet that would turn the nose of a goat, thus to solve a problem: in this case radar antennas for aircraft. Alexander Poniatoff arrived in San Francisco via Moscow and Shanghai, working as a research engineer for Pacific Gas and Electric. In 1934 he hooked up with Tim Moseley, who owned a machine shop; a decade later the navy asked if they could make radar antennas to exacting specifications: and that's when their hundred-day epic began. When they were done, their prototypes beat out Westinghouse and GE, and they got the contract. By the end of the war their firm, Dalmo Victor, was the leading manufacturer of airborne radar antennas, and by 1966 it provided 90 percent of the navy's submarine antennas, too.[32]

Semiconductor Beginnings

The semiconductor is a type of transistor, and the transistor came into the world through the unlikely vehicle of William Shockley: direct descendant of *Mayflower* Puritans, the only child of an engineer, he grew up wealthy in Palo Alto, went "back east" to get his doctorate at MIT, and then took a job at Bell Labs, AT&T's renowned think tank located at the time in another protean neighborhood—Greenwich Village. After the war Bell was in New Jersey, trying to get rid of the ubiquitous glass vacuum tube, which powered radios and all kinds of other devices but had the bad habit of getting hot, burning out, or blowing up. Everyone who opened the back of a radio knew this, but the thirty-ton ENIAC had 18,000 vacuum tubes blowing out so often that special assistants stood by at the ready to replace them. Moths flitted around the hot bulbs causing short circuits (you wondered why they were called "computer bugs"?). Bell put Shockley in charge of a team focused on "semiconductors," so named because crystalline materials like silicon or germanium could be either insulators or conductors—best of all *both*, by switching from negative to positive currents. At the end of 1947, two young men on Shockley's team, John Bardeen and Walter Brattain, invented the first working semiconductor, which was much more powerful than a vacuum tube at amplifying electricity. Soon the invention was called a transistor (short for transfer resistor, "a semiconductor device which can amplify electrical signals . . . composed entirely of cold, solid substances"), but it was a combination amplifier and electric switch in one tiny package. By 1954 almost a million of them were sold by various companies; a year later a small Dallas firm named Texas Instruments began making pocket transistor radios. Rockets whose vacuum tubes needed to be warmed up before takeoff now had instantaneous ignition—and a thousand other applications that the Pentagon began disgorging billions to discover. By 1957 nearly 5 million transistors were produced in the United States.[33]

Shockley made important contributions to this invention, but his real strength was in grasping its commercial promise. A man with great taste in cars if not much else, he bought a British racing-green XK-120 roadster and drove it home cross-country, back to his Silicon Valley roots. With the support of Professor Terman, in 1956 he began a research lab in an old apricot storage shed on San Antonio Road in Mountain View. He soon hired a Philco physicist named Robert Noyce and a twenty-seven-year-old Cal Tech chemist named Gordon E. Moore. (Like Jack Parsons, as a child Moore had almost burned down his neighbor's house in Pescadero—on the coast near

Palo Alto—with a homemade rocket.) Shockley had a brilliant eye for young talent and brain-dead ways of managing it, like posting everyone's salary on the bulletin board. He administered lie detector tests to his employees, and like Captain Queeg in *The Caine Mutiny*, launched intrusive investigations over trifling incidents. He essentially operated in three speeds: mean and ornery, rank and nasty, paranoid and volcanic; soon his lab resembled "a big psychiatric institute." As the world later learned, this Nobel Prize winner (shared with Bardeen and Brattain in 1956) also had eccentric ideas about what made white people so great: sure enough, and true to his *Mayflower* roots, Anglo-Saxon genes were the ticket to greatness, just as crummy genes made people of color stupid, necessitating birth control (Shockley set up a sperm bank for geniuses and stipulated that his sperm could only go to women with Mensa IQs).[34]

Within a year Noyce, Moore, and six other "traitors" left Shockley to his bizarre theories and set up Fairchild Electronics, another ur-Valley firm, and of course by 1968 Noyce, Moore, Jean Hoerni, and András Gróf—a young Hungarian otherwise known as Andy Grove—had set up Intel (short for Integrated Electronics), still the world's best semiconductor firm. Noyce died a rich man in 1992, but Intel made Moore richer than any other Californian, including Steven Spielberg and George Lucas. Meanwhile two other Fairchild leaders, Jerry Sanders and John Carey, founded Advanced Micro Devices. Some perspicacious individuals noticed the quiet triumphs in the Valley at this particular beginning: the poet and critic Kenneth Rexroth wrote in 1967 that the Pacific Coast was in "the front rank of a world revolution"; the obvious part of it was the cultural revolution then unfolding on a global scale, with San Francisco at the pinnacle during "the summer of love," but the real motive force in this revolution, and the secret of the difference between West Coast culture and the rest of the United States, he thought, was "the new technological society," a dawning electronic age that unfolded into the future.[35] He was right.

The transistor began this program of maximal reliability, of course, but until the 1970s these devices might be guaranteed 99 percent reliable, but the Pentagon needed 100 percent—it needed perfection and set much higher standards than would a commercial firm (who wants to market an appliance that never breaks?). The air force, in particular, poured billions of dollars into digital electronics because some aspect of its analog-based avionics systems (an electron tube, a navigation instrument) failed on the average of once every seventy hours—a bit of a problem at 30,000 feet. Even tapping transistors with a pencil could destabilize their voltage. So the Pentagon placed impossibly high reliability requirements on its contracts for things like the Minuteman missile, which only goaded the engineers at Fairchild Electronics to work harder. The 1959 NPN transistor had a failure rate of 0.1 per cent per thousand hours, but the transistors for the Minuteman when it became operational averaged less than one failure in ten millennia—once every 10,000 years.

Here is the moment when semiconductor engineers created a revolution in reliability, which they carried over to Intel's microprocessor, the first "computer on a chip," combining solid-state electronics with programmable software (what Intel called "frozen software"). Instead of configuring individual chips dedicated to a particular function on a board, this microprocessor could be programmed and reprogrammed. It was all in the dip—the acid dip, that is. Technicians were getting only two working chips per manufactured silicon wafer and no matter what they did—including posting a rubber chicken as a good luck charm—it didn't get better. Then toward the end of 1969 someone mixed a new dip formula and produced a yield of twenty-five silicon wafers instead of two. Intel moved out of the sheltered market, into the free market—and everybody made money, including the "traitorous eight" and other Fairchild people, who founded nearly all of some twenty-six silicon-chip firms started up in the 1960s. But the sheltered market came running, too; Lockheed moved its Missiles and Space Division from Burbank to Sunnyvale, building Polaris missiles at nearby Moffett Field.[36] The microprocessor was easily an invention ranking in importance with the steam engine, if not the telegraph. It soon powered everything from A-bomb simulations to toasters, and it never quit.

Robert Noyce was coinventor of the microchip, and at Fairchild and Intel he helped to pioneer an informal, laid-back, genteel form of work that would have warmed the hearts of Palo Alto's founders—nondirective, nonhierarchical, collegial, interactive, graduate-student-like work with open collars, khakis, and moccasins (it was the fifties), and long hours but many compensations in the insights of colleagues and the joys of discovery. Intel's early employees could get 10 percent of their salary in stock at the special price of $5 a share; Intel went public in October 1971 at $23.50 a share and split five times just in the 1970s. Anyone who held onto the stock became a millionaire—and Noyce eventually became one of the richest men in the Valley. But he may also have been the nicest, a truly likeable and admirable man. He located one Intel fabricating plant on a Navajo reservation. He showered the excellent small college that educated him, Grinnell, with endowments and scholarships. When he was worth $100 million he would still walk extra blocks to find a set of colored pencils that wasn't overpriced. When one of his children asked if her skills or his status and money were behind her success, he replied, "Do you think I could do what I've done if I had been black or a woman?" Like anyone he wasn't without faults; the youth movement of the sixties nauseated him and estranged him from one or two of his children, who themselves got caught up in drugs—hardly an unusual family story.[37] But if anyone ought to have set up a Silicon Valley sperm bank . . .

Intel makes chips in factories all over the world, but its headquarters sits in Santa Clara and its soul is pure Silicon Valley. The presence of Noyce and Moore at most of the Valley's early creations and their combination of scientific knowledge and intuition made them the Valley's twin early gurus; Moore famously observed in *Electronics Magazine* in April 1965 that the capacity of semiconductors had been doubling every year and probably would continue to do so for another decade—annually packing more power into tinier and tinier spaces while the price of the chips fell systematically. When later stretched to eighteen months to two years this rule turned out to be about right—accurate enough to be called "Moore's Law." Moore called Intel's first programmable chip, the 4004 microprocessor of 1971 with 2,300 transistors etched into its architecture, "one of the most revolutionary products in the history of mankind." (Two teenagers in Seattle named Bill Gates and Paul Allen bought the second-generation 8008 in 1972 and built a meter for measuring traffic and then immediately formed a company called Traf-O-Data—which quickly collapsed.) In 1974 Intel brought out the 8080 chip, five times faster than the 8008, and their business took off, with their payroll jumping from 42 to 3,100, and their sales leaping to $135 million. But even Gordon Moore couldn't anticipate nano-technologies that would come online to sustain his law-like insights. In 2006 IBM and JSR Micro of San Jose announced that they had etched the thinnest lines yet drawn on a chip using deep ultraviolet lithography, each line being 29.9 nanometers in width (a nanometer is a billionth of a meter). Within a few years memory chips might store 64 billion bits of information, compared to the then current maximum of 4 billion bits.[38] Here is the world's avatar of reliability, and a tiny engine of such capacity as to put the knowledge of the whole world through the eye of a needle.

A Flexible Coupling Called Stanford

Stanford established itself as a very different university from the Ivy League giants back East. Fred Terman was at the budding nexus of university, government, and corporation back in the 1930s, when Stanford was one of the few elite private universities to accept federal aid. Harvard, Princeton, and Yale had set an example by arguing that private universities were the only "true havens" where scholars and scientists could seek the truth "free of all possible political influence," in the words of Rebecca Lowen. Public universities had to listen to taxpayers and state legislatures, and by taking government money, private universities would put themselves in a similar position. Harold Dodds, president of Princeton, believed that federal funds would inevitably taint the private university: "Let us be sure not to barter [our freedom] away to any external control in a moment of fright," he said. Many faculty members at Stanford agreed, but Terman was undeterred and soon he had established Stanford's model of open and unabashed ties with government and business and corporate spinoffs for faculty. In 1937 he got the board of trustees to agree that the university should own any patents achieved by its researchers, opened the physics lab to the Varian brothers, and began banking royalties from Sperry Gyroscope for Varians' klystrons.[39]

Stanford's finances were still shaky a few years later, however, when the president of the board of trustees, Donald Tressider, invited Terman and his father, Lewis, along with some other professors and wealthy alums to spend a weekend at the Ahwahnee Hotel in Yosemite Valley to figure out new ways to finance the university. Pearl Harbor interrupted their retreat but quickly solved Stanford's financial problems. Terman was at the center of the university's transformation into a client for government and business, arguing that Stanford was like a factory, dealing with "raw materials and with thought processes," yielding degrees that were also products "bought and paid for by the consuming public." He urged the president to centralize administrative control and rely on deans, so that departments and faculty would find their (previously substantial) power diminished, to set up institutes and research outlets in new fields or in ways independent of the departments, and to become a "service" institution for government and the corporations (especially those in the Bay Area).[40]

In so doing, the worst fears of the Ivy League presidents and several notable Stanford faculty were realized: not only did Stanford faculty in all the sciences and even in psychology and philosophy end up doing classified research, but Terman and others let the federal government and private corporations determine research agendas in one field after another—from the beginning: "Only by promising to undertake research of specific interest to aircraft companies," board of trustees head Tressider insisted in 1944, could Stanford engineers "hope to attract financial support from the industry." (In 1947 he was more explicit: "The hand which holds the purse strings sways the throne.") Stanford flourished during the war (Tressider worked in chemical warfare), and just after it ended Washington provided funds for the Stanford Research Institute; aided also by Stephen Bechtel and Henry J. Kaiser, it became one of the largest corporate-government think tanks in the country. Defense spending often accounted for more than half of the institute's budget as it helped the Pentagon with laser radars, ballistic missile defenses, and methods to defeat the Vietcong. (The Bechtel Group has always been closely involved in its activities.)[41]

Like so much else in the California defense industry, it was the Korean War that set this pattern in stone: Stanford Industrial Park opened in 1951, a self-described model for the future, synchronizing the university, research, government contracts, and industry. Laid out like a college campus, it was a featured exhibit at the 1958 Brussels World's Fair. Stanford also celebrated "a new academic type," in Rebecca Lowen's words—"a professor devoted to research and strongly connected to the world outside the university, an entrepreneur in search of research funds upon which his career, and the university's financial well-being and reputation, depended." Faculty deemed likely to dissent from the new arrangements were denied tenure, and as secret contracts proliferated, armed guards materialized outside the doors to Stanford's laboratories. But it was Stanford, not Harvard or Princeton, that was prescient: by the end of the 1950s federal funds supported more than 60 percent of research budgets at almost all the leading universities.[42]

The Korean War also brought into existence the Electronics Defense Laboratory (EDL), originally a division of Sylvania in Mountain View, which obtained a Signal Corps contract in 1953 to develop electronic countermeasures to protect (and bring down) missiles. EDL had extensive ties with Stanford's engineering departments, grew rapidly, and by the mid-1960s had 1,300 employees and additional projects in satellite detection and microwave physics. But the director of EDL, William Perry (subsequently defense secretary under Clinton), chafed under Sylvania's aegis and bolted in 1964 with six other engineers and managers to found ESL: Electronic Systems Laboratories, a direct competitor of EDL. By that time Santa Clara County was "the microwave capital" of the world, building microwave devices for missile countermeasures, reconnaissance, and communications. "We are continually demanding microwave tube performance beyond the state of the art," Perry wrote, but he might have added that the sheltered market of defense contracts was pushing just as hard—and guaranteed that the tubes would find a buyer: the military was the biggest and often the only customer for microwave tubes and semiconductors.[43]

So it didn't all start in 1980: by that time the Valley was miles ahead of the competition, with a well-oiled model for government-university-business collaboration, assured sales, advanced research in both the sheltered and the open market, and ways to make everyone rich. One detailed study in 1977 found that California had almost twice as many high-tech jobs (641,000) as its nearest competitors, Illinois (360,000) and New York (337,000); Massachusetts had 205,000, fewer than Texas. Those jobs were located both in Silicon Valley and Southern California, of course, but whereas other firms dispersed their production to subsidiaries elsewhere (often across the country), high-tech firms in the Valley did almost all their research and development at home, and over 70 percent of their manufacturing and assembly was either in the Valley or in the Pacific Northwest or Southern California. These intensive networks and associations were another critical element in the peninsula's success.[44]

The Garden of Apple

The products that Steve Jobs and Bill Gates pioneered are the reason most people think the digital revolution began in 1980—because that's when we began to have personal computers, word processing, fax machines, VCRs, and a host of other new-new consumer items. Steve Jobs is that rare Schumpeterian thing, both an innovator and an entrepreneur, doodling and thinking all by himself over his morning coffee at Il Fornaio on Cowper Street, stamping his company with an inimitable sensibility. When it first appeared nothing compared to the elegant iPod Nano, about the size of a small cream-filled wafer but formidable in its weight and gravity in your hand while holding a thousand songs, or the slightly larger iPhone, a dazzling pocket computer and Web surfer. Apple cultivated a sense of style found only in a few other places on earth (mostly in Italy and Japan), a sensual blend of form and function that is simply unmatched, a small-is-beautiful sensibility that is sweeping the world as I write. The logo should have told us from the beginning: Apple takes us back to the human origin and to California's permanent trope—to the garden, to Eden—and takes Eve's fateful bite for granted: let's have some fun. The colors of the rainbow drape the Apple, not the hackneyed red, white, and blue—but they're upside down to recall the sixties.

Jobs is also irascible, arrogant, boorish, ruthless, his enemies say he's crazy; like the late Jerry Rubin, he parodied his generation through the decades: rock and roll, Indian gurus, communes, and "fruitarian" diets in your twenties; veggies and workouts and bulimia to keep your figure as forty beckons, while monitoring the stock ticker; in late middle age Armani suits, a Gulfstream V private jet, helipad, Zen Buddhism, mega-mansion, blanketed security, an all-round master of the universe.[45] In this duo Steve Wozniak was clearly the computer wizard and the decent man, but Jobs could motivate, agitate, sell the product, and envision a future—not *the* future, but a more chic, stylish, worldly and ease-of-use future than anyone else envisioned, and then risk everything to make it happen. People who have mastered various programs on a computer have no idea how it all works and if you told them they wouldn't understand, but more important, they don't want to know—they want something good looking that does what it's told. Apple accomplished that time and again, while Microsoft still thinks it's cool to sell you a new computer with maniacal and indestructible pop-ups, telling you every day or two that the machine you bought last month needs an update.

Most boomers in the Valley claim to have been hippies or activists or druggies, but Jobs and Wozniak were the real thing. Wozniak's father was a Lockheed engineer who spawned a tinkerer in the best American tradition; Steve was already an electronic wizard at Homestead (yes, Homestead) High School in Cupertino, the 1960s equivalent of a ham radio buff except his métier was computers. He and Bill Fernandez built their first computer from spare parts in the latter's garage (where else?) at 2066 Crist Drive in Los Altos—the "Cream Soda Computer" after what they drank all the time (in the garage at least). Soon Fernandez took him to meet Steve Jobs, another Homestead alum who at the age of twelve impressed his teachers by calling Bill Hewlett at his home to chat him up for a part-time job—and getting it. In 1971 the two Steves began selling their "blue box" in college dormitories for $150: its electronic tones mimicked Ma Bell's, so you could phone anywhere in the world. As Owen Linzmayer tells it, Wozniak used the box and his Henry Kissinger accent to call the Vatican and say Henry wanted to speak with Pope Paul VI; he was told politely that the pope was sleeping but would get back to him soon. A photo from the time shows the two of them in full sixties-seventies regalia—long hair, beards, jeans.[46] Like Jack Parsons, they make the point that creativity often originates in rebellion, or is an act of rebellion itself.

Jobs and Wozniak borrowed another garage in Menlo Park (California, not New Jersey) in 1975 to house their Homebrew Computer Club, until dozens had joined and it moved to the Stanford Linear Accelerator Center auditorium. Wozniak was the best of all of them. He took a new MOS Technology 502 microprocessor that he got for a mere $20, BASIC language, a standard QWERTY keyboard, and an ordinary TV monitor and made his first computer. Club members were well impressed, but Jobs wanted to sell it. Wozniak was making a nice living working at HP, however, and tried to sell his bosses on marketing his computer—but nobody was interested. So Jobs sold his beloved Volkswagen bus and Wozniak his HP calculator to start their company. What to call it? Jobs had been up to the All-One commune in Oregon, which had a lot of apple trees (although later it became Adam and Eve or even Sir Isaac Newton who spawned the name). Apple Computer Company opened on April Fools' Day, 1975. Jobs walked barefoot into Jay Terrel's Byte Shop on El Camino Real and sold him fifty computers at $500 each. But no knock-downs: Terrel wanted them fully assembled. So Jobs and Wozniak brought in a couple of more people, worked like hell, and soon had the Apple 1 in the Byte Shop window for $666.66 (the Mark of the Beast), and Apple had its first profit of $8,000.[47]

This success was enough to interest Don Valentine of Sequoia Capital (not yet a Sand Hill Road legend), although he was less than impressed by Jobs's bare feet and torn jeans: "Why did you send me this renegade from the human race?" But his colleague Mike Markkula took a shine to these hippie tinkerers, put up $92,000 of his own money, got a quarter-million-dollar loan from Bank of America, and brought in an adult (Michael Scott) to run things. Apple was incorporated, flush, and off and running. Jobs was already a brassy countercultural guru in blue jeans, beard, and black turtleneck, but it was Wozniak who assembled the Apple II almost single-handedly—in his garage (he also figured out how to hook up a color monitor to it because he wanted to play the game "Breakout" in Technicolor). The two Steves then mass produced the Apple II with less than forty employees at their shop in Cupertino, a marvelous personal computer when it first appeared in 1977. Smaller than an electric typewriter, the Apple II was the first PC most people had ever laid eyes on, including many computer scientists; it put everything on a single board, interacted seamlessly with a TV monitor, had programming in the random-access memory and color graphics—all for the first time in one small package. It sold for the unheard of price of $1,250 (no monitor) and caused a sensation—even in the Pentagon; soon every tactical nuke team in Europe used Apple IIs for targeting.

After this success Apple went public in 1980, and Jobs began pushing the Macintosh very hard—hard enough so that Wozniak left the firm. He could afford to: Apple was the biggest opening on Wall Street since the Ford Motor Company. A genuine blithe spirit who met his first wife through the Dial-A-Joke operation he ran out of his Sunnyvale apartment, Wozniak worked with Bill Graham on early-1980s three-day rock concerts that sought to

Steve Jobs demonstrating the Apple II prototype, May 1977.
Photo by Bill Kelley.

rekindle the Woodstock spirit (in the Reagan years . . .), and returned to his first love: teaching elementary school.[48] Today, of course, Apple is still a superlative firm, but the old days are long gone: its research and development facility at One Infinite Loop in Cupertino is run with such blanketed security it might as well be the National Security Agency West.

The success of the Apple II enabled the firm to open an automated factory in Fremont in 1981, where labor counted for exactly 1 percent of costs, and to begin working on the Macintosh (Mac). Jobs and designer Jerrold C. Manock wanted something that looked like a Cuisinart, the new-new kitchen accessory then, so suddenly the computer was in an upright case, a small monitor imbedded in the top, with a detached keyboard. Most of the activity consisted of clicking on icons with a mouse, moving things around the high-resolution graphics screen, playing games, and drawing pictures; the memory was so capacious that the Mac needed a brand-new 3.5-inch disc from Sony, instead of the ubiquitous 5.25-inch floppies. The new factory meant the Mac cost only $500 to build, but a $15 million advertising blitz—including the fabled Super Bowl commercial attacking IBM not just as Big Blue, but as the realization of Orwell's *1984* (in January of that year)—bid up costs. So the Mac came out very high at $2,495—and sold 72,000 in the first 100 days.[49] It was that rarest of consumer products—entirely novel, does what it says, way ahead of the field, and thus capable of creating its own cult of worshippers. As in: "There are occasionally short windows in time when incredibly important things get invented that shape the lives of humans for hundreds of years": the Macintosh "was one of these events" (Steve Wozniak talking).[50]

Also-Ran Billionaires

Larry Ellison's big break came from a CIA-funded database management project code-named Oracle at a company called Ampex. It never got off the ground, so Ellison left Ampex in 1977 with two other employees, started a company, and bid on another CIA contract to build a "specialized" (to say the least) database. The new company, founded in Santa Clara, was dubbed Software Development Labs. Its grubstake was small (Ellison put in $1,200 for a 60 percent stake, and his two friends put up $400 each), but the most sheltered market of all was waiting with baited breath in Langley, Virginia. They began working furiously on "relational database" technologies that IBM had pioneered and which had been around for several years, trying to make them fast, reliable, crash-proof, and small enough for minicomputers. As Ellison's firm developed newer and better ways to make this software "portable"—able to interact with any hardware or operating system—the business took off. Ellison purloined the CIA's code name and became chairman and CEO of Oracle in 1982; sales doubled annually in the 1980s, but when Oracle went public in 1986 the stock price increased only 45 percent—because Microsoft went public on the same day (March 12). Ellison kept his hands on every share he could grab, however, and soon became the most flamboyant and profligate billionaire in the Valley—and as a notorious recluse and martinet, the one with the least interest in "the HP way." What the CIA did for Ellison is clear: it subsidized Ellison's first commercial project for relational database software in 1979. No information is available on what he did for the CIA, but the CIA, the National Security Agency, Navy Intelligence, and the air force kept his work going (Ellison had only twenty-five customers in 1981), buying database management packages at $48,000 a crack.[51]

We have seen that the wizards running Xerox passed on commercializing many of the innovations developed at PARC, but one of their biggest hallucinations came when senior staffers irritated DARPA (ARPA had changed its name, adding Defense) by setting too high a price on the many PARC Alto workstations it wanted to buy, so DARPA found out about Stanford University Network (otherwise known as SUN) workstations and sought to buy those instead—but Stanford wasn't selling. Other companies like IBM and 3Com couldn't or wouldn't fill the order. So with two other Stanford grad students, Vinod Khosla and Scott McNealy (the latter a Stanford MBA recruited at a McDonald's in Palo Alto), plus Bill Joy from Berkeley, Andy Bechtolsheim founded Sun Microsystems in 1982 to build workstations, using off-the-shelf hardware and the Berkeley UNIX system that Joy had helped to develop, and began selling them to DARPA. Sun gave away much of its software, like Network Filing Systems, which then became the industry standard—whereupon Sun would have hardware built to the new standard and license it out. Conscious that he was in a business with maddeningly short product cycles, Bechtolsheim relied on a myriad of small Silicon Valley suppliers to keep making Sun machines better. With constant improvements to RISC (reduced instruction set computing) and SPARC processors, Sun kept ahead of giants like IBM and DEC from the mid-1980s into the late 1990s, by which time it was a flagship Silicon Valley behemoth.[52]

Jim Clark was born in Plainfield, Texas, and studied computer science at Utah before moving to Stanford. He always loved airplanes and was mesmerized by figuring out how they could be displayed using three-dimensional graphics. In the summer of 1979 he moved in next door to Lynn Conway's office at PARC, took graphics technology that she and others had developed, combined it with what he and his students had been doing on an ARPA contract, worked like a dog for four months, and came up with the "Geometry Engine," a 3-D graphics chip that became the core technology of his start-up, Silicon Graphics.[53] But it was Netscape that made him a billionaire— or more particularly, Marc Andreessen and six other students at the University of Illinois.

The technology for Internet browsers now in such wide use barely existed in 1992, when Andreessen was a twenty-one-year-old Illinois student working at its federally funded (that is, ARPA-funded) National Center for Supercomputing Applications (NCSA), writing UNIX code for $6.85 an hour. His older buddy Eric Bina, a programmer at this center, thought Andreessen's rudimentary ideas for a browser were good enough to take off three months so they could both work night and day amid empty Mountain Dew bottles and Skittles wrappers, until they had written 9,000 lines of code for a simple graphical program that would overlay the World Wide Web, display photos and other multimedia, and have commands anyone could master: they called it Mosaic and offered it to Web users for free. I still remember the day in 1994 when I watched a colleague download it and begin using it. Mosaic was an instant sensation, doing for the Internet "what Vatican II did for Roman Catholics," in David Kaplan's words, by putting UNIX into general vernacular usage. Now anyone could point a mouse toward an icon and click and connect to "a universal, boundless library of information," without paying someone, getting government permission, or requiring any knowledge of the quarter-century of hard- and software development making it possible.[54] Soon Andreessen was off to Silicon Valley where Jim Clark had bright ideas about how to commercialize Mosaic's success.

At the peak of the bubble Clark was the genius-protagonist of Michael Lewis's best-selling *The New New Thing* (Clark had "a new form of power," he wrote—Clark-power: "if anyone was going to predict the future it was him"), but more interesting is how he became a billionaire by taking the brains and the money to be found at the Stanford-Pentagon-business nexus and running away with it, with no apologies and no look back; most interesting of all, he can't keep his mouth shut when he clearly would be advised to do so, because he has an ego the size of Alaska ("only Alaska?" he would say). Clark was a smart computer scientist in the right spot at the right time, "chance favoring the prepared mind," as the saying goes, and little more. But to hear him tell it, it was all his genius and anyone who disagrees is an idiot. He convinced Michael Lewis and many others that any number of other people's inventions and ideas were his. In fact Clark founded both Silicon Graphics and Netscape by grabbing other people's ideas and taking credit for everything. At Silicon Graphics he was "the technology visionary, business leader, organizer, and founder," according to him; at Netscape he went one better, he was everything—"the monarch."[55]

Clark's first prophetic vision came to him on an ARPA contract to develop "tools for computer-aided design." He set several doctoral students to work on the project, and soon he and one of them, Marc Hannah, had created the Geometry Engine—with a lot of help from PARC and Lynn Conway (but neither merits the slightest mention in the book Clark wrote). Of course he wanted to take his chip "public," and Stanford—being Stanford—was entirely accommodative: "If you did the thinking, you deserved the credit," the university believed; "If you started a company, you deserved a profit." Stanford unquestionably benefited mightily from its many accommodations, since Valley billionaires know how to give back.[56] But the system seems to be this: you get a secret contract from ARPA and put students (funded by Stanford or themselves) to work, migrate over to PARC to see what's going on at Xerox's expense, pick brains and codevelop a new-new thing, and then take off with barely a thank you: Clark's self-described "revolutionary" discovery abruptly "ended my academic career and began my business career," where he was soon producing "dazzling machines." To paraphrase Mel Brooks, it's good to parlay a Stanford professorship and a top-secret Pentagon contract into becoming a wealthy monarch—or Lawrence of Arabia meets the Valley, or Alexander Graham Bell, take your pick from his book.[57]

When Clark departed Stanford and PARC with his "Geometry Engine" under his wing to found Silicon Graphics, he became an instant millionaire. But he nonetheless felt that Sand Hill venture capitalists had screwed him, taking the lion's share of the income—so now he wanted to found his own company with his own capital. In early 1994 he had yet to hear of Mosaic (it appears that I learned about it before he did) and ultimately made no technological contribution to it, but a young employee told him about it, and about Andreessen. "I knew a good thing when I saw it," Clark wrote, and so he decided to bankroll a "Mosaic-killer." Andreessen felt he hadn't gotten enough credit for his work at Illinois, so he and Clark flew to Champaign-Urbana amid a snowstorm and made pitches to six others in the Mosaic group. Clark offered salaries of about $65,000 to $80,000 each and a quite generous 1 percent of the company's stock—but by then he didn't have to worry about "vulture capitalists" (he also called them "velociraptors") controlling things. Instead he went over to Sand Hill Road and made offers most of them could refuse: put up $5 million and get a quarter of Netscape, which Clark valued at $20 million (when it had three employees), about three times what Clark had put up: but the canny John Doerr bit and soon watched his $5 million turn into $765 million. There was the trifling problem that Illinois owned the rights to Mosaic, which the group got around (or so they say) by writing all new code from scratch in another shambling night-and-day mosh pit of crushed soda cans, crumpled candy wrappers, and dirty underwear. Mosaic—renamed Netscape—launched one of the great stock openings in American history in August 1995. The underwriters expected to sell 5 million shares for twelve to fourteen bucks each, but interest was so high that it opened at $28 on August 9 and quickly hit nearly $75 before settling back to $58—and making Clark half a billionaire overnight.[58]

There you have it, again: Illinois's National Center for Supercomputing

Applications was yet another ARPA project, Mosaic was a new-new thing built there and teleported to Palo Alto where it was re-created "from scratch" and then taken public with a reward of billions. True, Andreessen and his cohort created Mosaic in the first place: "created it" by taking three months to add graphics and user-friendly items to an existing Web browser invented in Geneva, Switzerland, by Tim Berners-Lee, who gave it away free. The University of Illinois gave it away free, too, providing fantastically expensive Cray supercomputers on taxpayers' money so students like Andreessen could use them (virtually for free) at a great public university that always has given enormous value to Illinois and the nation. Larry Smarr, director of NCSA, had the antediluvian idea that since the university had provided the expensive framework and paid for the work, it owned Mosaic.[59]

Clark says that "armies of the young" have made this revolution, just like teenage combat marines fight the great battles: stamina, "near-trancelike focus," a mild insanity combined with a belief that you'll live forever, working in the present but thinking only about the future—"the future, Mr. Gitts." It is true, but then it's also true of millions of other teenagers fanatically flailing away at computer games, who resemble Bob Newhart's infinite number of monkeys banging on an infinite number of typewriters (who will eventually write all the world's great books). The laser-like focus gets us closer to the kind of method Einstein touted, which is to work on a problem with as much concentration as one can muster over a long enough period of time, waiting for an intuition to appear out of nowhere—accidentally, blindly, like a natural mutation. But all Einstein needed was chalk and a blackboard, not a Cray supercomputer. So maybe Larry Smarr had a point? The Pentagon's ARPA and the ARPANET cost taxpayers a lot, too, as did the CIA's Oracle project, but Clark sees it all as free goods, wrapped up with "sixties altruism" about giving things away for free. The University of Illinois had the gall to imagine profiting by "producing software with public money": "I didn't want them dead," Clark wrote, but he certainly wanted the profits from Mosaic in his own pocket—and of course, altruist that he is, the pockets of Andreessen and his group. After an intellectual property lawsuit, in the end Clark and the university reached a still-secret settlement that cost Netscape $3 million.[60]

Clark also thought the sunny Valley had a lot to do with his Mosaic coup: it barely took him a day to tire of Champaign-Urbana, the lousy University Inn, the "typically mediocre" Italian food with "Chianti-in-a-basket," and snowy Illinois more generally. Vast reaches of the Middle Border no longer attracted chic masters of the universe born in Plainfield, Texas. "Mosaic glinted like gold in the stream at Urbana's very own Sutter's Mill," and this pathetic university expected the profit to come to it, rather than to "the best and brightest of the university's students who had done the work." In the relative nano-moment between Netscape going public and getting sold to America Online, Jim Clark was the master of the Silicon Universe. Venture capitalists flocked around him like Labrador retrievers, according to Lewis, and one of them, Glenn Mueller, even committed suicide when he couldn't get in on a particular deal.[61] Jim Clark was a classic entrepreneur in Schumpeter's sense: building firms based on others' innovations. Soon, however, he was just another Valley billionaire.

While Clark was romancing Andreessen, Jerry Chih-Yuan Yang was working on a doctorate in electrical engineering at Stanford and beginning to make inroads into the WASP leadership of Silicon Valley that soon became a flood, as Asian-Americans made up between 30 and 40 percent of the Valley population in the late 1990s and about a quarter of Valley executives.[62] Yang, who came to California from Taiwan at age ten and was raised by his widowed mother in San Jose, spent his elastic quota of grad-student spare time in an office trailer with his friend and fellow grad student with nothing better to do, David Filo, playing fantasy basketball—and winning the league. Mosaic, however, had turned them into that new-new thing, Web addicts: they put up their personal Web sites, searched the Web for outlandish oddities, tracked sports scores and sumo wrestling tournaments, subsisted amid category 5 Katrina-style offal, and gradually began to work up a subject list of interesting sites—accumulating "hyperlinks" as they are known. The categories: news, sports, science, recreation. Soon (late 1994) they had a Yellow Pages all their own, "Jerry and David's Guide to the World Wide Web." Timing was everything; before Mosaic there wasn't much of a Web, but now it was growing like topsy so someone had to try and put another "overlay" on the overlay of Mosaic: a search engine. Yellow for yellow pages (and the Asian explosion?) became the color, but what would be the name? Well, it wouldn't be Yet Another Hierarchical Officious Oracle, this new company, so let's just call it Yahoo! It was another brilliant Valley triumph over the way things were done everywhere else, juvenile all the way to the bank; Yang and Filo captured in five letters the vitality and verve of the exploding Internet era, where brand name was suddenly everything (Yahoo or Webcrawler? Google or Lycos?). In 1995 Yang and Filo offered Sequoia Capital a 25 percent stake for $1 million; that turned into almost $8 billion in 1999, and by the end of that year Wall Street valued Yahoo at $91 billion.[63] Today workers fill the myriad purple cubicles in its Sunnyvale campus trying to find ways to stay abreast of Google.

A Googol Here, a Googol There—
Pretty Soon It Runs into Real Money

In the mid-1990s the Internet was clearly the next new thing, but the question was how to make serious money off it. Michael Wolff tells of a 1996 visit to the Basking Ridge (New Jersey) headquarters of former mega-monopoly AT&T—"the kind of structure that might be erected in an oil-rich one-party state"—where self-important moguls sat around trying to figure out how to turn the Web into a cash cow. If someone could create "the ultimate navigational system" for the Internet and then "create a product that can habituate the customer" so that you make just a penny a day off AT&T's 80 million customers, voilà, a horn of plenty.[64] But they didn't do it, and neither did anyone else; no one could figure out how to "habituate the customer" and start real money cascading through the Internet. The Web was just another catalog business, however easy and convenient—Sears Roebuck on steroids. Maybe the Internet was nothing more than a communications system, Wolff thought—a hyperfast take on the culture itself, and not a very good one: "contentwise [*sic*] it's 99 percent dross," a bunch of fads and trends mixing with larger forces (like history and society) about which it remained clueless.[65] Beyond catalog shopping, no one was making serious cash. Most amazing of all, Microsoft's geniuses couldn't figure it out, either, they were behind the curve all through the 1990s and at this writing, they still are. Then Google came along—or was it TREC that came along, in an unlikely place?

Page and Brin superseded Yang and Filo as famous Stanford grad students-cum-entrepreneurial stars, starting Google up in (you guessed it) a rented garage at 232 Santa Margarita Avenue in Menlo Park, but "search" began in the singular town that magically channels all the worst winter weather through its portals—Ithaca, New York (doubtless down there with Urbana on Jim Clark's Chianti-in-a-basket list). Around the time that the ARPANET flashed into being, so did SMART—Salton's Magical Automatic Reviewer of Text. Gerard Salton, a Cornell computer scientist, came up with seminal ideas like "concept identification based on statistical weighting and relevance algorithms based on feedback from queries." So began another long technological slog through the decades, often via the annual Text Retrieval Conferences (TREC) that Salton's work inspired and that heralded the newest state-of-the-art techniques. TRECkies weren't very interested in the Web, but Larry Page and Sergey Brin were; their first "pitch" of Google in 1996 ran something like this: "The primary benchmark for information retrieval, the Text Retrieval Conference (TREC 96) uses a . . . 'Very Large Corpus' benchmark [of] only 20GB compared to the 147GB from our crawl of 24 million Web pages. Things that work well on TREC often do not produce good results on the Web."[66] If you can understand that, you can begin to understand that twenty gigabytes is a flea-flicker's notion of capacity, a flyspeck on Google's terabytes today.

Soon this dynamic duo had a crawler called BackRub that not only collected millions of sites but ranked them as well, through algorithms that they understand and I don't—and neither do you. Google algorithms are the best in the business, and as closely guarded as Bill Gates's operating systems; instead of searching for acne ointments and getting the Web site of a teenage werewolf in Dubuque, your friendly algorithm locates those sites judged best (or most popular) by everyone else looking for the same thing. BackRub thus returned robust results, while AltaVista and Excite gave you trivia. Best of all, as John Battelle put it, this search engine would scale as the Web scaled, that is, "the bigger the Web got, the better their engine would be." So they changed BackRub to Google after *googol,* the name mathematicians give to a 1 followed by 100 zeroes. The first version of Google was on Stanford's Web site in August 1996. Trouble was, it required such mind-boggling capacity that it took up nearly half of the university network's bandwidth. Within a year or so, however, Valley moguls were starting to cough up a lot of money (Brin and Page celebrated their first $100,000 at Burger King), along came John Doerr again, and by 2000 Google was sitting alongside the hailstorm of traffic on Highway 101 in Mountain View, with about 150 employees.[67]

Google's motto is "do no evil." What does it mean? It might just be another iteration of "Valley uniqueness," or graduate student innocence, or good public relations; the firm has the requisite sloppy dress codes and lunch volleyball—but PARC had that forty years ago. Page and Brin validated their motto when they took Google public in August 2004: Wall Street had to stand aside and witness one of the first stock offerings in American history where insiders and dominant firms had not cornered most of the value already. In a complicated Internet auction, anyone with a hundred dollar bill was able to make a bid, and basically if you bid above $85 you ended up with a share—or many shares. Wall Street clairvoyants had valued the stock at anywhere between $20 and $90, but it settled around $85 and then passed $700 in 2007. As the stock escalated, Google also resisted the urge to split it, the sleight of hand Wall Street uses to fool the incognoscenti.

In the first years of the new century Brin and Page showed everyone how to sell advertising profitably on the Internet, just like on the radio in the 1920s, while keeping ads to a relative minimum (text boxes rather than irritating pop-ups). Through AdWords anyone with a credit card could post an ad on Google, through AdRank the most popular ones went to the top of the heap, and then after much experimentation, Brin and Page figured out how to charge customers only when someone actually *clicked* on their ad. It seems counterintuitive; people may only click on one out of a thousand ads. But the *googol*s are so wildly humongous (AT&T was right about that), and the incentive to post free ads until someone notices them so overpowering, that Google can make a ton of money.[68]

Valley Outliers: FYIFV Seattle and Austin

Beyond the Valley there are two other places where you find successful high-tech firms in the West: the Northwest (mostly Seattle, but also Portland) and Texas (mostly Austin). Across the lake from Seattle is Redmond, the lair of Jim Clark's hydra-headed monster Microsoft, run by an "utterly ruthless" tyrant and a couple of other "badly dressed geeks"—arch-monopolist Bill Gates and his friends, who built their Evil Empire in "misty, mossy Seattle (of all places)." Or maybe he's the Kim Il Sung of Bellevue, surrounded by a cult of personality and craving his daily hit of hero worship.[69] Or he might just be a competitive son of the WASP bourgeoisie and their nonostentatious genteel tradition, transplanted to misty-mossy Seattle: home in Laurelhurst, summers in the mountains, private school at Lakeside, Harvard education, corporate career, a man of bland ambition about whom cultish folks might ask, what personality? Well, that was more or less Bill's father (except that he didn't go to Harvard)—corporate lawyer, pillar of the community, board member of charities and universities, and entirely typical of the public-spirited upper crust of a city having none: no Brahmins, few Irish or blacks or Hispanics or Jews, just God-fearing white folks who got there *first*, a mere hundred years before Bill Gates was born.

William Henry Gates Jr. wasn't quite that early, arriving in the 1880s and then quickly departing for Nome during the Alaska gold rush. He returned to found a secondhand furniture business in Bremerton, across Puget Sound from Seattle, prospered in "dry goods" and soon belonged to "virtually every civic organization and social club in the area." William Henry Gates III was born in 1925, served in the army in World War II, studied not at Harvard but at the University of Washington, and made his best move when he spied a Kappa Kappa Gamma girl called "Giggles," Mary Maxwell, "vivacious so-cial dynamo" on campus but more important perhaps, granddaughter of the founder of the National City Bank of Seattle. Grampa died in 1951, just when

Bill and Giggles got married, remembering to leave an estate worth half a million dollars.[70]

Bill Gates and Mary Maxwell lived well but modestly in the View Ridge neighborhood, where their son—William Henry Gates IV, inexplicably called Gates III like his father, ergo his nickname "Trey"—was born in 1955, and where he went to grade school. It wasn't ostentatious, but Bill and Mary knew everyone, including people like Dan Evans (as in Governor Evans) or Brock Adams (as in Senator Adams), and Bill Sr. became famous for his role in an antitrust case against the whitest white of them all, Wonder Bread. Like the Kennedys, they exhausted themselves competing against each other in outdoor sports, swimming, skiing, races, games, and puzzles. Nor did the unostentation last long; by fourth grade the family was in a large home in swank Laurelhurst, with a much-coveted panoramic view of Lake Washington. Thence it was Bill to Lakeside, Bill to Harvard, and Bill to MS-DOS immortality.

A friend of mine spent most of her career working at Lakeside, and over dinners I would hear one story after another about the latest rowdy exploits of the egregiously spoiled brats at this all-male school and the hovering, wincing, cowering teachers-cum-therapists who gently sought to cajole the boys to stop vomiting on each other or blowing up the toilets. But it was Seattle's most exclusive prep school with a lovely transplanted New England campus, *and* it was rich enough to have an ASR-33 Teletype machine, not too different from what Bill Taylor had in the D-Ring at the Pentagon—except that ARPA wasn't paying for it (for once) so it cost $8 an hour, with additional bucks for storing your data. The Lakeside Mothers Club rode to the rescue by making the ASR-33 their worthy cause of the year 1968 and piled up enough cash so that "a runty freckle-faced eighth grader" could proceed to hog it for hours on end. If that wasn't enough, the university had just installed Seattle's first state-of-the-art Digital Equipment Corporation PDP-10 computer, a "minicomputer" compared to IBM mainframes but still very powerful, and was selling time on it to Boeing and other local firms. A staffer at the computer center had a son at Lakeside, and he thought it might be nice to let him and his friends have some free time on it to see if they could get "bugs" out of it or even try to "crash" it—which they did every Saturday morning. Bill Gates whiled away his Saturdays learning BASIC, FORTRAN, and DDT-10 ("Dynamic Debugging Technique"). Then he met Paul G. Allen, who could exhaust his university librarian father's computer-time account, and the free hours on the PDP-10 just kept on expanding. Soon DEC itself was asking the kids to try and crash newer and newer programs, and they routinely obliged.[71] It was

Bill Gates in his salad days at the Lakeside School.
Courtesy of Lakeside School Archives.

something like being Henry Ford's test-driver and handyman in 1910, careening around Dearborn in Model Ts to see if they break down or crash.

In 1972 Gates and Allen did the same thing Jobs and Wozniak did: they built their own computer, using the 8008 chip that all the computer geeks coveted. Paul Gilbert in the university physics lab knew hardware (Gates and Allen were and always have been strictly software experts), and together they built the vaunted Traf-O-Data to automatically count cars in Seattle's mostly empty streets (thanks to the Boeing bust). But Bill had also busted out his SATs with a perfect 800 in math, so it was a normal Laurelhurst story after all: off he went to Harvard, in fact to the ever-popular Wigglesworth Hall, where he roomed with one black and one Jew, as if someone had thought it all up in advance to give a Seattle boy some broadening. He didn't date and he got a C here and there, but at least he was out of the suite most of the time (more than one acquaintance found him obnoxious) because he was now mesmerized by a video game called Breakout—which happened to have been developed for Atari by Jobs and Wozniak.[72] And in his second year he got to know someone who could pass in any Seattle country club.

Steve Ballmer doesn't quite come off as a nerdy geek or even a nasty guy— rather an outgoing, good-natured, strapping would-be jock who grew up in a Detroit suburb, the son of a Ford executive who aced so many math and science tests that he got into Cal Tech and MIT but went to Harvard, where he inadvertently hit the jackpot when he walked into Currier House in his sophomore year and found that Bill Gates was his new roommate. Gates soon dropped out to join the computer revolution; Ballmer graduated, but by 1980 he was helping Gates run Microsoft's finances, and he was instrumental in the somewhat notorious deal that purchased a program called "86-DOS" (also known as QDOS for "quick and dirty operating system") for $50,000 from Tim Paterson of soon-to-be-history Seattle Computer Products, and the even more notorious (to Steve Jobs and Jim Clark) deal with IBM that followed on its heels to put "86-DOS," excuse me, MS-DOS, into every IBM personal computer—and all the clones, too—which meant into nearly every office in America and soon, most of the world. The next month (August 1981) IBM unveiled its personal computer, and within a decade there were 50 million IBM-compatible PCs on American desktops.[73]

Selling the computers or the clones, however, was much less valuable then selling the MS-DOS operating system because profit margins on it ran to around 90 percent—and then came the real ringer: once the IRS or the FBI or your "health care provider" teaches millions of employees how to use the program, wild horses won't make them change. It's like telling a baseball player the pitcher now gets to stand fifty feet away, or you can use your hands in soccer because that's how they do it in basketball. It's the principle of the QWERTY keyboard: it may not be the best arrangement, but it's been around for over a century and rearranging the keys would cause a general panic, so it persevered into the computer age. Change won't happen, you will just upgrade when Bill says it's time. Nearly 1 billion computers worldwide ran Microsoft operating systems in 2009.

In Seattle if not the Valley, Microsoft was the gentle lamb to Boeing's rough beast, the city adored it, and the city fathers all knew Bill's dad. They also loved its sensational stock opening in 1986. Before the public offering, local newspapers said anyone could buy shares at $18 a pop. The stock hit almost $28 on its first day, and anyone who held onto a thousand shares at $18 until the late 1990s became a millionaire several times over (the stock lost about 50 percent of its value when the bubble burst, and some unwise souls wrote the company off).[74] When Microsoft moved to its Redmond campus, that is, to 400 wooded acres called Evergreen Place next to a development called Sherwood Forest, it was accompanied by a choreographed reiteration of Silicon Valley customs: no pecking orders, no obvious management privileges, no clocks on the walls to encourage workaholism, volleyball nets and basketball hoops for breaks, the earliest birds into the parking lots got the best spots, and it didn't matter if they wore shorts and sandals, and cafeterias offered everything from burgers to tacos to veggie to Thai.[75] (As always, keeping labor unions at bay was also in the mix.) It looked like a college campus (or a minimum security prison), and the people in it looked like college kids; some called it testimony to the flat leading the bland. But at least in the early years there was an admirable esprit de corps and absolute dedication to one's work, so it is hard to know why so many people hate the new Big Blue; Silicon Valley with its up-to-the-gills saturation in secret Pentagon contracts, user-friendly Stanford pliability and Ellison/Clark/Jobs-style megalomania rarely attracts invective like the Evil Empire: "a fraternity of rich eggheads"; "softies" with their FYIFV buttons ("fuck you, I'm fully vested"); callow, white people who've never worked anywhere else; profanity (no!); a "supremely aggressive" and intensely smug and insular culture; "slavish fealty" and "zombielike [*sic*] devotion to the Maximum Leader" (and that's just one author).[76] Perhaps a certain WASP-strikes-back element excites this anger—but again, why not in Silicon Valley, too?

Bill Gates moved on to a more distant relationship to Microsoft and to Rockefeller-like philanthropy as America's perennial richest man, but Paul Allen used his software billions to truly remake himself as an incident to remaking Portland and Seattle. Famously reticent and sequestered (a reporter likened public glimpses of Allen to "Big Foot sightings"), he bought the Portland Trail Blazers (basketball), the Seattle Seahawks (football) and, some say, much of both cities. In 2006 one of his companies, Vulcan, was promoting an eco-friendly "New Urbanism" by constructing a 10-million-square-foot biotech hub in the drab and seedy industrial district south of Lake Union (that is, downtown Seattle), including a dozen or more fifty-story condo towers that will house 10,000 workers, while another $100 million went into the "Allen Brain Atlas," a project hoping to chart the entire neuro-anatomy of the human brain, not to mention $240 million for a rock-and-roll emporium in tribute to Seattle legend Jimi Hendrix. Meanwhile Allen lurks about in his own private submarine and works out of Captain Kirk's *Star Trek* chair, leading some to wonder if he's squandering his $20 billion nest egg on realizing childhood fantasies.[77]

Texans Can Do High-Tech, Too

Texas Instruments had a provenance just like Hewlett-Packard and Varian. It originated in the 1930s as a small seismograph producer for the oil industry called Geophysical Services, but during the war this Dallas company expanded dramatically by producing electronic devices for the military, like airborne radar systems and submarine detectors. The firm changed its name in 1951, and a year later, after coughing up $25,000 for a license, it began producing transistors, mainly for the Pentagon during the Korean War. Silicon was much harder to work with than germanium but infinitely available (on the beaches of the world among other places), and after Texas Instruments (TI) hired Gordon Teal away from Bell Labs, in 1954 his team mastered the art of making chips with high-purity silicon. In May he attended the National Conference on Airborne Electronics in Dayton, Ohio, and heard one speaker after another talk about how impossibly hard it was to make transistors from silicon. When Teal's turn came he mounted a podium, gave his scheduled talk about TI's recent research, and then closed by telling his audience that TI had already made silicon transistors—"I happen to have a few of them here in my pocket." TI's Pentagon business had dropped by two-thirds after the Korean War ended, so the firm went commercial by making cheap transistors for the world's first pocket radio, originally priced at $49.95. It sold 100,000 units in 1955—and sold out all over the country. But TI wasn't making a decent profit on the radio because its four transistors were too expensive, so they got out of pocket radios and settled on producing transistors for what clearly was a high-volume market for this new-new thing.[78]

Akio Morita and Masaru Ibuka got to know each other in 1945 when they were desperately trying to build heat-seeking missiles to take down American B-29s blasting Japan's cities. Ibuka, an electrical engineer and by 1952 the president of Tokyo Tsushin Kogyo (Tokyo Electronic Industries), visited New York and told Morita that the enemy nation, America, was actually rather fantastic: "Buildings are brightly lit until late at night. Streets are jammed with automobiles. This is a stunning country!" Like Texas Instruments, the two men forked over $25,000 (a fortune in war-ravaged Japan) for a license to produce transistors. Soon they had a prototype radio, a few months after TI's portable hit the stores. But would Americans buy a radio from a company whose name they couldn't pronounce? The two friends found the Latin for "sound" in a dictionary—*sonus*. But *sonus* was not mellifluous, so after more cogitation they got it right—and Tokyo Tsushin Kogyo became Sony.[79]

If Sony quickly cornered the market that TI had created, a six-foot-six Kansan named Jack Kilby wandered the empty halls of Texas Instruments during its mandated July vacation time in 1958 (as a new hire he had no vacation days), wondering how the army's "Micro-Module" program, which stacked silicon wafers together like poker chips, could be made to work more simply. How about putting everything—resistors, capacitors, transistors, and diodes—on a single silicon chip? Within two months TI had fabricated the vaunted "monolithic chip" that everyone else had been trying to make. Almost at the same time, Robert Noyce and Jean Hoerni at Fairchild Semiconductor hit on a similar chip that wrapped the silicon wafers in oxide layers, drastically reducing impurities and thus creating "planar" surfaces. Once oxide-sealed, these chips were impervious to external jolts or shocks and seemed to last forever. Unfortunately for Kilby, Noyce landed the patent for the integrated circuit. (It was just what the air force was looking for, but Texas has congressmen, too, so the air force also bought TI's new chip.) Then John F. Kennedy's plan to put a man on the moon combined with the ever-present cold war struggle to keep a ravenous (if sheltered) market growing wildly for Fairchild, TI, and other Sunbelt firms all through the 1960s (in 1962 the government bought every single integrated circuit made in America). Meanwhile more established companies like AT&T hesitated to disrupt their existing markets, machines, and networks with these miniaturized marvels—elaborations of what Bell Labs had first invented but for which they had little immediate need.[80]

Another prominent Texas high-tech firm, Tandy, became the largest mass retailer of electronic goods and made 40 percent of all personal computers sold in 1980. It worked closely with Microsoft to bring out the Model 2000 three years later—a more powerful version of the PC which could run an early version of Windows (which was so powerful it made IBM PCs grind to a halt) and would have a built-in market: nearly 8,000 RadioShack stores around the country distributed Tandy products. The first Windows computer! But as Robert Cringely put it, the brains behind RadioShack back in their Fort Worth headquarters thought of their trusty customers "as Albanians who would loyally shop at the Albanian Computer Store" regardless of what other stores might be selling. The Model 2000 was a total flop—except at RadioShack stores, which each got one to keep inventories whether they liked it or not.[81]

It got better for Texas after three Texas Instruments engineers—Rod Canion, Jim Harris, and Bill Murto—got together at a House of Pies in Houston and used a placemat to lay out the architecture of an IBM clone.

It would be 100 percent compatible with the IBM PC but, with artful corner cutting, about $800 cheaper. Compaq PCs first appeared in Sears and ComputerLand stores in 1982, and then took off like Don Garlits: 47,000 computers worth $111 million sold in its first year. It got even better when an eighteen-year-old University of Texas undergraduate started clearing as much as $30,000 a month by selling "gray market" PCs from his dormitory room and went on to found Austin's Dell Computer, as in Michael Dell.[82] But when all was said and done this was cloning, not creation. Compaq and Dell possessed mass marketing genius (and Dell still does); these firms helped contribute to Texas's position as the leading state in merchandise exports in 2005 (California was second, New York third, and Washington fourth). Except for Texas Instruments,[83] though, technological virtuosity still resided in Silicon Valley.

Perhaps hoping to remedy this imbalance, in 1988 fourteen firms funded a semiconductor research and manufacturing consortium in Austin called Sematech, into which the Pentagon plowed $100 million a year. The idea was to share the costs of early product development and think and plan for the long term thus to compete with the Japanese, who were thought not only to be dumping chips unfairly, but to be state-guided visionaries who planned for the distant future. Robert Noyce came out of Silicon Valley and retirement to run it. Sematech had a complex and checkered history, but it validated Austin and the University of Texas as the winning candidate for "Silicon Elsewhere," as thousands of high-tech jobs were created in the 1980s and branches of Intel, IBM, Advanced Micro Devices, National Semiconductor, and other firms sprouted nearby, and home-grown Dell became the world's leading merchant of personal computers. But running Sematech meant very long and draining working hours for Bob Noyce, and within two years he died from a massive heart attack. This towering figure in American high-technology history was a mere sixty-two years old.[84]

Texas was hardly bereft when it came to government contracts. Politicians, preeminently Lyndon Baines Johnson, made sure that a lot of federal pork detoured through Texas before heading out to the coast. We have seen that NASA's Manned Space Center started up southeast of Houston in 1961 (it is now the Lyndon Baines Johnson Space Center), a Pentagon-subsidized aircraft industry was the core of Fort Worth's economy, and San Antonio remains dependent on several nearby military bases. After a succession of accidents and calamities, however, NASA was closer to a national embarrassment than the high-tech center of the future, and many called for simply shutting it down. Austin remains the high-tech nexus of the state, but it is a mere shadow of Silicon Valley.

Conclusions: Daily Life at Warp Speed and the American Position in the World

Silicon Valley had a long, dilated beginning from the day that Charles D. Herrold began stringing his radio wires in San Jose, flying under the radar of the nation until Bill Gates and Steve Jobs made most Americans an offer they couldn't refuse: a computer all of their very own with magical and maddening qualities, which ordinary beings contemplated like Cro-Magnon man staring at fire. If steel mills couldn't be hidden from the day they started belching smoke, the silicon chip was a perfect, unobtrusive machine to infiltrate the Valley's garden. It remains the most important research corridor in the country—and the world. The Valley was clearly the most productive node in the American economy in the 1990s, but it probably was since the 1950s, in value-added per employee—where Valley productivity is not only very high compared to other sectors but even higher across *its own* industries compared to the same industries in the rest of the country. By the mid-1990s the Valley produced more than a third of California's exports, making San Jose the leading exporting city in the United States; even after the bubble burst it was still ranked second in 2006 (behind Seattle).[85]

There is unquestionably something startling about Silicon Valley and its Pacific Coast rival Seattle—you can read book after book on semiconductors and computers and barely find a mention of Route 128 or MIT (well, Shockley) or Harvard (OK, Lotus 1-2-3) or Yale (?). What makes the difference? AnnaLee Saxenian's definitive study attributes the decline of Route 128 to a host of weaknesses: confrontational politics, a difficult labor market, weak social networks, companies too large to change, Harvard not being a flexible coupling like Stanford, Puritan heritage, hierarchy and authority instead of an egalitarian and democratic working culture, all combining to explain the absence of the kind of synergy so obvious in Silicon Valley. She adds that Stanford had a very different relationship to Washington than did MIT: both were up to their ears in open and secret contracts, but Stanford was far and MIT near, so people ran up and down the Bosh-Wash corridor spending many fruitless hours cultivating policy networks.[86] I would add that the Valley and Microsoft were also a continent away from the prestige and power of the elite corporations and universities of the Northeast quadrant, providing a

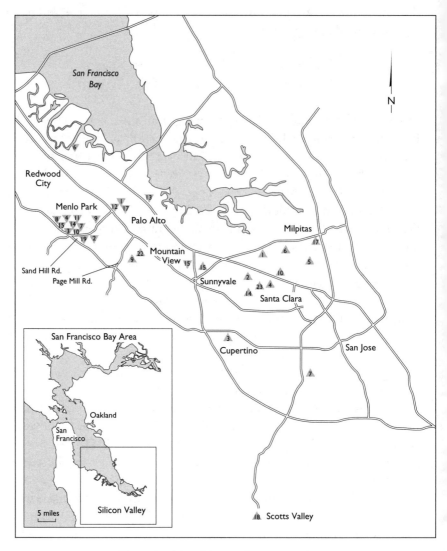

The geography of firms in Silicon Valley.
Map by Bill Nelson.

realm of freedom for experimentation, particularly for young people like Bill
Gates or Steve Jobs who clearly couldn't care less about the prestige or postur-
ings of IBM and AT&T, Harvard and Yale.

Doug Henton found four cycles in the technological development of
what he aptly calls "Innovation Valley" in the last half-century: (1) a "defense"

wave starting in World War II but taking off during the Korean War; (2) an integrated circuit wave in the 1970s; (3) a personal computer wave in the 1980s; and (4) an Internet wave in the 1990s.[87] I would add a radio wave a century ago, a Stanford-Varian-HP (micro)wave in the late 1930s, a transistor wave from 1947 to 1970, and a defense wave that started in the late 1930s and has never quit, with military procurement acquiring almost all transistors and integrated circuits until the consumer wave began in the 1980s, and with Washington agencies either buying high-tech products or sponsoring research leading to electronic mail, the Web, 3-D graphics, Web browsers, and many other technologies. In other words, this was a direct continuation of the profound role of the central state in the development of the Pacific Coast, and probably the most important of all in its impact on cutting-edge technology and American leadership in the world. This industry has been the avatar of American technological prowess, the essential basis of its awesome military reach, and the critical reason why the American position vis-à-vis its industrial rivals has barely changed since they reestablished themselves after World War II.

However it happened, it is a fact that it happened on a particular crust of the earth on the edge of the Pacific, and no other nation has such a sprawling realm of advanced industries up and down one lengthy, protean coast. Across the Pacific are East Asian counterparts of the Valley, in Japan, Korea, Taiwan, and now China; in high technology the North Pacific is already a Braudelian Mediterranean. Absent a distant and wide-open West Coast, it is entirely questionable whether the same thing could have emerged in the industrially crowded Northeast or Midwest. Relying on its comparative advantages, from the late 1930s onward Silicon Valley grabbed Noah Cross's "future," that ingrained California thing, and ran away with it—occupying the horizon of advanced industry, where it remains today.

The history of government, business, and university collaboration makes it difficult to really call the Valley a unique "habitat for innovation and entrepreneurship."[88] Elsewhere in the world important innovations and efficient production have not required start-ups and "synergy" in a valley distant from the core—they have gone on in centralized megacities and even old industrial centers like Paris-Sud, London's M-4 corridor, and the megalopolises of Tokyo and Seoul. Valley innovation has been non-stop, and visionary entrepreneurs like Steve Jobs exist, but most of the crucial innovations have come from a massive river of cash generated on the other side of the continent in Washington, the energetic labors and self-exploitation of smart young people, and the vision of early leaders like Terman, Hewlett and Packard, Noyce and Moore, who founded a new and eminently questionable relationship between secret work for the Pentagon and the CIA, the ostensibly open university, and the profit-oriented corporation. It is not a question here of judging this,[89] but of saying, this is what happened, and absent state funding and an accommodating university, it probably wouldn't have.

In the 1990s California got a new kind of farming to add to the good old days of wheat and citrus—"server farms"—because of another huge comparative advantage that it shares with the Pacific Northwest: an abundance of cheap electricity. In 1995, 20,000 server farms existed, and six years later, 6 million; Google's are the biggest and best. Contrary to popular opinion, they gobble gargantuan amounts of electricity: in recent years a single server farm typically used as much electric power as the Twin Towers in New York. Even your wireless Palm Pilot requires the electricity of a heavy-duty refrigerator, but you don't see the stream of power because the guts of the industry are sitting in unobtrusive but hugely expensive air-conditioned buildings, housing servers, routers, fiber-optic cables, and the immeasurable stored-up human and mental labor that runs the system.[90]

Google has a thirty-acre server complex along the banks of the hydro-electrically bountiful Columbia River in The Dalles, historic terminus of the Oregon Trail and the site for Henry Coke's elegiac tribute to wide rivers, high mountains, and tall pines. Google's ever-deepening algorithms are wonderful if you're looking for an old girlfriend or a new plastic surgeon or a hotel in Delhi lacking bedbugs—or perhaps you just want free e-mail. As always, however, your democratic government was way ahead of you. Under the Patriot Act of 2001 the National Security Agency got the right to riffle through all your e-mail messages and searches on Google, Yahoo!, and anything else in cyberspace. Naïve Americans thought this couldn't be done without a judge's warrant, but right after September 11 the Bush administration began secretly tapping into the massive communications junctions that now unite all of us. The NSA requires Google or Sun or Verizon or any other company to place security traps and trace devices along its junctions and circuits in the United States and around the world.[91] So it isn't clear if we're in the realm of Silicon Valley free play or we're realizing Kubrick's *2001* dystopia.

CHAPTER SEVENTEEN

Conclusion:
The American Ascendancy

Once we cease to distract ourselves with lifeless arguments about isolationism, we shall be amazed to discover that there is already an immense American internationalism. American jazz, Hollywood movies, American slang, American machines and patented products, are in fact the only things that every community in the world, from Zanzibar to Hamburg, recognizes in common.
— HENRY LUCE, 1941

An immense democracy, mostly ignorant, and completely secluded from foreign influence . . . with great contempt for history and experience, finds itself in possession of enormous power and is eager to use it in brutal fashion against anyone who comes along, *without knowing how to do it,* and is therefore constantly on the brink of some frightful catastrophe.
— E. L. GODKIN, 1895

Beneath the immense bleached sky, the Pacific states form the earthly margin where we run out of continent—where "things had better work out," as Joan Didion wrote, because there was no place else to go. By and large, all things considered, they have: the American Pacific Rim is more than a facsimile of the hopes and dreams of nineteenth-century leaders and prophets. The pot of gold at the end of the rainbow materialized immediately, before the ink was dry on the treaty ending the war with Spain, but the built environment of today, from the Puget Sound down to Coronado Bay, would flabbergast visionaries from that time, even full-throated believers in Manifest Destiny like Thomas Hart Benton. Sparkling cities—Seattle, San Francisco, San Diego—punctuate the coastline with three different paradigms of flourishing, urbane civil society. The highly productive continental economy remains the standard by which all other countries define themselves. For all its problems, the United States is still a recognizable contemporary version of the hopes of people like Benton 150 years ago.

The North Pacific can now be circumambulated in eight hours on a

Boeing 787 from Seattle to Tokyo. A couple of hours on, and you're in Shang-hai—a contemporary version of Chicago rising on the prairie, or Los Angeles bringing the city to the valley and the valley to the city. Shanghai distills the talent flowing out of two grand river valleys, just as China deploys an enor-mous market for the world economy, for the first time in world history. There's "no place else to go" for the Pacific states but to China—and vice versa. Americans are again turning around to face West: will that face be martial or pacific, comprehending or unworldly? Today Americans show two faces to the world: an arbitrary, nationalist, militarized face, and the heritage of Atlanticist internationalism, predicated on a first-among-equals sharing of a common democratic heritage. In the new century American leaders com-mitted every imaginable sin in John Quincy Adams's book of foreign policy calamities. A catastrophic failure to understand the real sources of American strength and the uses and limits of military force propelled the world toward a darkening horizon and drove anti-Americanism to unprecedented heights on all continents. Paradoxically, however, Henry Luce's prophecy on the eve of Pearl Harbor still offered a dream for everyman, and a hope that the country would return to its ideals. "The mark of a living civilization is that it is capable of exporting itself, of spreading its culture to distant places" Braudel wrote,[1] and America still held a very long lead over any competitor in doing just that.

A Pacific Coast Still Facing East

One hundred and fifty years ago the United States dismembered Mexico on the way to making a continental union, which immediately brought Pacific influences pouring into the country—Mexicans and Indians in the South-west, and tens of thousands of Chinese laborers to dig out the gold and build the railroads. The gold rush was the catalyst for an instant and diverse peo-pling of California, and for sending new waves of technology and innovation washing over the state ever since. It also stimulated movement across the Pacific, symbolized by Perry's mission. But did this create a new Pacific culture? Oregon and Washington quickly achieved a settled system that is a manifest extension of the New England pattern. Texas and California created new versions of American culture, but not new cultures. F. Scott Fitzgerald's *The Great Gatsby* is probably the best example of an American genre that we might call "the eastern": someone out of the Midwest or West tries to make good in the citadel of wealth and culture, New York or Boston or Cambridge, and fails. In facing East it discloses an inferiority complex. After so many years have passed, has the Pacific West (or at least California) established a self-confident alternative cultural sphere?

For Kevin Starr the "coast of dreams" had truly become an East-meets-West reality by the early years of the new century, which he called "Zen California." At its foundation was "a feeling of integration, of mind-body well-being," drummed into the soul through a thousand purveyors of Asian-derived practices: guru incantation, tortuous yoga postures, mind and body detoxification, Shiatsu and friction massages, Ayurvedic potions, anointing with oils (*shirodhara*) and hot towels (*abhyanga*), "Bliss Facials," gourmet vegetarian meals, holistic childbirth, and career/lifestyle assessments with your Chopra counselor—and this is just the regimen at one spa, the Chopra Center for Well-Being in La Jolla. Starr also surveyed the rapid growth of Eastern religious influence, like the Novice Buddhist Academy in Long Beach, poet Gary Snyder's works (which Starr thinks infuse the California landscape with Zen meaning), and "the most trendy" new-new thing, un-named Tibetan fetishes popular in Hollywood. If Edmund Wilson's "void of the vast Pacific" was ever true, it isn't now: "Pacific Rim Culture, of California as of Asia, dominates the demography and consciousness" of our time.[2]

If we examine "Zen California" demographically, no doubt California is America's most Asianized state among the contiguous forty-eight. Thirty percent of the population in Silicon Valley is Asian, about half a million Koreans live in a transformed central Los Angeles community west of the Harbor Freeway called Koreatown, then we have Chinese in Monterey Park, Vietnamese in Orange County's "Little Saigon," Cambodians in Long Beach, Laotians in Santa Ana, Samoans in Compton and San Pedro, Little Manila in Daly City just south of San Francisco, Hmongs in the Central Valley, and Asian Indians who grew to 314,819 in the state by 2001.[3] But in what sense beyond the aesthetic, the exotic, and the demographic has Pacific Coast culture come to dominate or even influence European and Atlantic civilization? Isn't this just a predictable evolution from the Theosophists' Raja Yoga School in San Diego a century ago or Barry Goldwater's first cousin, Julius Goldwater, who was ordained as a Zen priest in the 1930s?

Zen California encompasses New Age baby boomers and their offspring looking for something out of the ordinary. But it remains another *choice* in the vast consumer inventory, another means of coping with advanced industrial society—often a mere affectation, an epidermal addition; it doesn't remotely have the impact on individuals or the nation that, for example, Southern California Christian fundamentalism has had, and when it tries to influence national politics it instantly prepares its own defeat (witness Governor Moonbeam, Jerry Brown). The New Right is unquestionably a western phenomenon, beginning with Barry Goldwater and gaining its lasting momentum with Ronald Reagan. But in the end that, too, is a reaction to the cultural and political dominance of eastern liberals, recuperating the virtues of the frontier and small town America.

Today "facing West" is for the unilateral extension of American military power, for trade and for exotica, all running on entirely separate tracks. CINCPAC looks after the whole, widgets crisscross the Pacific in containers, and Asian exotica excites the curiosity of adults with disposable income. Buddhism in the Big Sur, a Noguchi lamp for the study, yet another sushi restaurant on Geary Avenue, L.A. Laker basketball coach Phil Jackson's "Zen" hocus-pocus, Oracle-founder Larry Ellison's full-tilt Japanoiserie at his "Sanbashi" mansion in Atherton. "The Orient has repeatedly offered a line of flight" from the banality of American daily life,[4] but it is usually no more than that—a temporary flight of the spirit, an aesthetic touch, a penchant for unthreatening Orientalia.

The intellectual traffic across the continent and the Pacific is still mostly one way: an enormous American literature—best sellers, novels, history books, social science texts, biographies, self-help guides—continues to be produced in the East and consumed in the West; it gets translated into Japanese, Korean, and Chinese, but traffic the other way is slight. The words of Henry Kissinger, Samuel Huntington, or Francis Fukuyama are dissected in East Asian capitals, while specialists on foreign affairs in East Asia use American theories to understand the world.[5] The very best literature from East Asia gets translated (sooner or later), but the bulk of what the reading public consumes there does not; in a field like history, hardly anything from East Asia reaches the general reading public until it is translated into English and published here—and since that reading audience is small to begin with, little gets translated. Asians see nearly all our films; we view a mere handful of theirs, mostly in the dwindling stock of repertory and art cinemas around the country. Films with Asian themes that do big business usually traffic in exotica: Quentin Tarantino's excellent *Kill Bill* is a highly stylized kung fu movie. *Memoirs of a Geisha*—both the blockbuster book and the less-watched movie—offered Orientalia, but it enters a place in the American mind scarcely different from Pearl Buck's *The Good Earth*.

Our newspaper of record, the *New York Times*, covers East Asia much less than Europe or the Middle East. The second largest economy in the world gets attention in the business pages, but otherwise articles about Japan appear when another typhoon or earthquake strikes, or when a new prime minister comes along, or when another cultural oddity gets unearthed (new and voluminous stipulations for recycling garbage in Tokyo, people lining up around the block to get into a noodle house that seats eight people, etc.). China gets attention mainly for its unfortunate human rights situation, its booming economy, and its "looming threat," but when Jiang Zemin was China's president, the *Times* twice referred to him as "President Zemin." North Korea hogs almost all the press from that peninsula, so long as a "nuclear crisis" endures and Kim Jong Il provides such good copy, but major events in South Korea easily pass unnoticed here.

A friend of mine taught at the Naval War College and was amazed to find that few officers read the op-ed page of the *New York Times* or had even heard of its columnists. Why? Because it is impossible to follow policy debates in the Bosh-Wash corridor without reading it, and this paper of record remains the daily national arbiter of what's what in culture, the arts, books, theater, films, fashion, real estate, food; only the *Wall Street Journal* beats it for business news—and it's also in New York. Across the continent, intellectuals strain to pay attention to the *Times*. But what do you say about the premier Pacific Coast newspaper putting its editorial and opinion pages in the hands of the same Bosh-Wash elite? In 2005 East Coast transplants were managing and deputy managing editors of the *Los Angeles Times,* New Yorkers ran the editorial page and the op-ed columns, and they reported to Michael Kinsley, former editor of the *New Republic* and *Harper's*. The whole paper was "looking east for direction."[6] Apart from local news and issues, there really is no counterpart to the eastern papers, so they dominate elite circuits.

America has continuously shaped and been shaped by its Atlantic and Pacific dimensions, but the Atlantic influences remain dominant—something that owes as much to inertia as to any other force, to a longstanding mobilization of Atlanticist bias that overwhelms most of our institutions. Our secretaries of state spend nearly half their time visiting Europe (41 percent of foreign trips in 1977–85, 44 percent in 1997–2004) compared to about 12 percent for East Asia, even though our trade with East Asia surpassed trade with Europe by 1980 and towers over it today (in 2000, United States imports from East Asia alone were higher than our total trade with Europe).[7] In polls taken in the 1990s more people in Japan than in the United States could name *our* secretary of state, and the average American cannot name the Japanese prime minister—and in truth, can barely tell the difference between Japan, China, and Korea. As usual, though, it is the educators who most need educating. High schools still persist in teaching French and Spanish, and if you're lucky to be in a good one, German. University curricula make room for the serious study of East Asia, but when compared to the settled academic ballast of Europe—the "West" of Allan Bloom's or Samuel Huntington's imagination —there is no comparison.

The neglect of America's Pacific history manifests itself inadvertently, in general books on a given subject that make no mention of a state—usually California—that distinguished itself in that same subject: thus a history of electricity fails to mention that the first large-capacity power line opened in California, or that Los Angeles was the first fully electrified American city; a fine history of the Ford Motor Company forgets about the pioneering role of the near-saturated Southern California market in the 1920s; a recent economic history of the United States focuses on California only for the gold rush. David Igler is right to say that the industrial history of the Far West has yet to be integrated into American economic history. Even William Appleman Williams, who sprinkled his book with the "frontier-expansionist theory of history," barely mentions the Pacific states and the continentalism that brought them about.[8] By the first decades of the new century, Pacific Americans had not come close to repositioning the cultural center of the country; the East Coast was still Kris Fresonke's "American cultural headquarters."

Decline and Apocalypse?

In the 1970s and 1980s we had "power shifts" to the Sunbelt (as in Kirkpatrick Sale's book by that title) and a general "Pacific Rim" discourse that frequently ended with Japan emerging as the dominant power of a coming "Pacific Century." It is remarkable that as recently as 1993 an American historian could still write about "the white man retreat[ing] from the North Pacific" with the torch passing to the Japanese—to "a third type" of political economy, a "corporatist developmental economy." Once nine of the world's top ten banks were American; "now eight of ten are Japanese." Suddenly the Japanese seemed to be buying everything—Rockefeller Center, Hollywood studios, Pebble Beach golf links, hotels, and mountains of individual and corporate real estate. All in all, he thought, we confront "the military, economic, and demographic retreat of (1) the United States, (2) American business, and (3) white people."[9]

Where is that retreat? In fact, Japan's standing in the world recalls an observation that a friend once made about Isamu Noguchi: "He always stepped on the accelerator and the brake at the same time."[10] If its economy seemed to grow unstoppably for several decades, its security position remained remarkably stable: resting ultimately on American guarantees, taking one step forward, then another inevitable step back. Washington began prodding Tokyo to do more for the defense of the Pacific and "share burdens" during the Kennedy administration and has never let up, but Japan ineffably stays at or below the 1 percent of GNP ceiling for defense expenditures—half a century later. Andre Gunder Frank published a remarkably contrarian "declinist" book before he died, *ReOrient*, in which he argued that Asian economies were at the center of the world economy from 1400 onward, that Europe had a brief spurt of development beginning around 1800 that temporarily gave it a leg up (by "climbing up on Asian shoulders," along with a few technical inventions), and now we are back in an Asian-centered world economy. If Europe's leadership lasted for a full century (1815–1914), the American Century "lasted only twenty years," from 1945 to 1965.[11]

This is nonsense. The American Century began in 1941 (Henry Luce spoke in the future tense in his famous essay) and continues apace. By the time the industrial powers rebuilt themselves after the war, the American share of world GNP quite predictably dropped to 35 percent by 1960 and 30 percent by 1970; the decline of industries in the rust belt and the loss of the war in Vietnam made it appear that America's share would continue to fall. But it still stands at 30 percent today. Even in manufacturing, the American share today is essentially the same as it was in 1900: one-fifth of what the world produces; and in manufacturing value-added, California and Texas lead all other states by a large margin. East Asia's share of global GNP grew from 13 percent in 1960 to 26 percent in 2000, but that came mostly at the expense of Western Europe, which dropped from 41 percent in 1960 to 32 percent in 2000. China's growth has been rapid, but it still mimics Japan's growth from the Korean War through the 1980s, or Korea and Taiwan from the mid-1960s to the mid-1990s—its leading exports are toys, textiles, light electronics, and (slowly but surely) steel and autos, and it has a miniscule high-tech presence. Its share of worldwide manufacturing in 2004 was a little under 9 percent, barely double South Korea's share, a country that now has a major high-tech presence.[12] It is China that faces a world-historical predicament of figuring out how to accommodate itself to American power, not vice versa; the world and the American ascendancy are shaking China, not the reverse.

In September 2008 the worst economic crisis since the Great Depression revealed itself. Few had seen it coming, and even fewer appeared able to chart a way out of it. It started in the United States, but hegemony also means transferring your crises to others, and quickly much of the world was engulfed. Thus this calamity did not appear to alter the global hierarchy; it just made everyone poorer. Fundamental power has not shifted to East Asia or even to the Sunbelt. Central political, financial, and cultural influence still runs from Washington up through New York to Cambridge. You see it in many ways, but one index might be that if you have three national newspapers in one region (the *Wall Street Journal, New York Times,* and *Washington Post*) and just one in the West (the *Los Angeles Times*), power discloses itself. Likewise a good technological rule of thumb disclosing the hierarchy of power in the world is the global dispersal of supercomputers: the United States was way ahead in 2006, owning 61 percent of all of them, claiming the four fastest supercomputers in the world and six of the top ten, while Japan had just two in the top ten (and its top machine was in seventh place); France had one supercomputer ranked fifth, and Germany's machine ranked eighth. Now and then Japan builds a faster computer giving it a temporary lead (in 2002 for example), but the speed record in 2006 was held by the "BlueGene" at Livermore, a joint project of the Department of Energy and IBM which in 2006 was the only computer ever to achieve 280 teraflops (a teraflop = trillions of calculations per second), and no competing machine had even reached 100 teraflops. South Korea ranked twenty-second and China thirty-fifth, but the former has an American Cray machine and the latter an IBM, and both are limited to meteorological work. (The entire African continent has no super-computer in the top 500 list.)[13]

If the dour vision of American decline proved wrong, any number of writers, culminating with Mike Davis, have produced a more convincing noir vision of California so replete with catastrophic imagery—fire, flood, drought, mudslides, urban riots, freeway gridlock, freeway collapses, freeway snipers, spectacular forty-vehicle fogged-in pile-ups, and the ultimate metaphor, earthquake (the big one)—that you wonder why the place still exists, why a San Andreas rupture hasn't turned California into the island of Bartolomé de las Casas's dreams, why it hasn't fallen back into the Pacific where it existed in the Jurassic. In the early 1990s one writer after another wrote off California— its defense industries were closing, the Los Angeles ghetto was erupting, earthquakes shook the L.A. Basin, man-made and natural calamities had come together to fulfill an apocalyptic vision and write its epitaph. An earthquake hit San Francisco during the 1989 World Series, two years later a raging wildfire burned through the Oakland hills, along came the South Central riots in 1992, and the Northridge earthquake in 1994. Is this new?

Apocalyptic prophecies shadowed the Los Angeles Basin since Americans first showed up. In the depths of the Depression Myron Brinig, a writer for the *New Yorker,* published a novel, *The Flutter of an Eyelid,* that upset a small coterie of writers and intellectuals usually known as poet Jake Zeitlin's circle (Zeitlin pioneered book-selling and highbrow commentary in Los Angeles and sat more or less at the center of bohemia there, such as it was).

Brinig spent some time with this circle and then caricatured it mercilessly in his novel, which ends with an earthquake that throws Los Angeles—and California—into the ocean.[14] The San Andreas fault may open up tomorrow and fulfill Brinig's nightmare (although for him it was probably a wish); a Santa Ana wind-whipped inferno may wipe Malibu from the face of the map; fans driven wild by Tom Cruise or mad by Joan Rivers may crash through the velvet ropes and trample a hundred Academy Award winners. But think about it: does anyone talk about Oregon or Washington this way?

If the reader laughs at that comparison, no one really talks about any place north of Santa Barbara this way, either. The San Andreas fault runs through Big Sur, a paradise of natural grace and repose. Palo Altans go down to the sea through Arcadian foothills where winemakers bring out a product that matches Sonoma's best; it is mildly arid to the east and rain- and fog-drenched to the west, just before getting to Half Moon Bay. The fault runs right through those hills, but it's hard to imagine anything untoward happening there, ever. The Marin and Mendocino coastlines north of San Francisco look like they would topple right into the ocean if the San Andreas ruptured, so close is it to the shore, but you could hardly find a more relaxed, placid, bucolic part of California—special herds of cattle in Bolinas marbling up red meat for Alice's restaurant; farmers raising fifty kinds of goat cheese on contract to *Whole Foods;* hippies long in the tooth growing pot in Mendocino.

The scribes of the California apocalypse should be a bit more comparative and a bit less American, and take a look at Japan. The entire country is perched on an intricate hatchwork of geological faults and fissures, earthquakes go off all the time at all magnitudes, and the Pacific, so placid a vista off Southern California that it never blasts the shore with hurricanes or even dangerous tempests, rakes Japan with typhoons for months on end—and then there's that indispensable word of Japanese etymology, "tsunami." The summer of 2004 seemed to be one continuous typhoon, with torrential rains and continuous floods and mudslides; one storm after another caused hundreds of deaths and billions of dollars of damage. A global view of "earthquake risk" shows *all* of Japan to be in equal or greater danger than Los Angeles (only Indonesia has a comparable threat; we remember that it yielded 220,000 deaths on Sumatra alone from the 2004 earthquake/tsunami).[15]

The vast urban agglomeration named Tokyo, where one-third of the population of Japan (40 million people) lives and which makes Los Angeles seem underpopulated, has already been flattened by a massive temblor at the cost of 143,000 lives (1923), once again by Curtis Lemay's firestorms (80,000 dead in one 1945 night), and another cataclysm could happen any day of the week. No visit to Tokyo is complete without the earth rumbling and glasses tinkling on the shelf—it happens all the time, which is why Japan (which could fit into the Great Central Valley) has more seismographs than California. So why aren't yoga gurus, vegan fanatics, rapture ascenders, Pentacostal con men, conspiracy paranoiacs, sky-is-falling crackpots, peyote-chewing clairvoyants, Turkish palm readers, and Hindu fakirs running amok in the streets of Tokyo? Why, when we lived there, did I never have a qualm about my eight-year-old riding the labyrinthine subway from one end of the city to another by himself, or worry about the beer vending machines all over the city when my older son entered his teens? If Angelenos suffered 143,000 deaths, we would never hear the end of it. Meanwhile after the 1923 cataclysm Japanese planners hired historian Charles Beard to help them lay out the new Tokyo,[16] and got on with their lives.

I much prefer Carey McWilliams: "God has always smiled on Southern California; a special halo encircled this island on the land." He declared himself to be "as devoted to the region as a native son" and ended his great book with a paean of praise to the beauties of the region, the matchless climate, and the people. He could do without "the swamis, the realtors, the motion-picture tycoons, the fakirs, the fat widows," of course, but the City of Angels was like no place else: "Here the American people were erupting, like lava from a volcano; here, indeed, was the place for me—a ringside seat at the circus." They were building "the great city of the Pacific, the most fantastic city in the world."[17] A progressive man of the left and an optimist and idealist in the best American grain, McWilliams always gave credit where credit was due—enough to fall in love with an island on the land, warmed by the Pacific.

The Exterminating Havoc Redux: The Bush Foreign Policy

Ultimately what the two decades after the fall of the Berlin Wall brought was not American decline or Japanese advance but a subtle, imperceptible decoupling of that relationship so critical to Atlanticism: the American relationship with continental Europe. George Kennan wrote in 1948, "The older cultural centers of Europe . . . are meteorological centers in which much of the climate of international life is produced."[18] That judgment had been valid for centuries, but cultural ballast shifted to the United States in the postwar era, for better or worse, and remains there today—increasingly cut free from intimate association with its European roots. Likewise American foreign policy ranges the world, no longer tied to a European base or close relations with its traditional allies (save England). This is one way in which the west-facing expansionists won a victory long after their enterprise seemed to disappear in the wake of the internationalist triumph during World War II. Then an entirely unpredictable provenance revived much of their program in the new century.

The first years of the twenty-first century produced a burst of American nationalism, unilateralism, aggression, and sovereign absolutism, all wrapped up in a program of solipsistic idealism so self-defeating as to suggest a country or at least a leadership gone haywire. This culminated in the invasion of Iraq, prefaced by a new National Security strategy tabled in September 2002 that famously enshrined preemptive attacks, but had a deeper meaning in the assumption that American sovereignty was inviolable—but nobody else's was. Santayana asked long ago whether Arabs and Chinese, Latins and Slavs, "if they were not benighted in mind and degenerate in body," would want to be "model Anglo-Americans." Can it be that "all nations are expected gladly to exchange their religion and their customs for the Protestant genteel tradition"?[19] As George W. Bush cast about retrospectively for a reason why he invaded Iraq in 2003, no weapons of mass destruction having turned up, he alighted upon the oldest of American shibboleths: mission. This president, the personification of Santayana's Americans who fly the genteel coop (trying to remember what it was they long ago forgot), would democratize Iraq as prelude to freeing the entire Middle East. This was not the first time such tendencies have inhabited American behavior in the world, as this book has sought to illustrate; indeed, the Bush Doctrine was in many ways a return—but a return to what? To Polk instigating war with Mexico or McKinley seizing the Philippines, to a movement away from "old Europe" toward a new American destiny? Or to a kind of harebrained Wilsonianism? It was all of the above—except that this American left office neither victorious nor blameless.

The American ascendancy has dual Atlantic and Pacific dimensions, with different orientations toward the broader world embedded in each. Going back to the turn of the last century, the Atlantic dimension defined an American relationship to the world for internationalists, for an eastern foreign policy establishment that may have changed its inner composition over time but remains deeply imbued with commitments to cooperation with Europe, collective security, and a world under law. A seamless consensus on free trade, multilateral consultation, an alphabet-soup of international organizations, and an alliance of democracies—in short, Atlanticism—defined the American orientation to the world from 1941 to 2001, as world war and cold war bound America to Europe. There was little ballast behind this worldview in American history, and occasional departures into unilateralism happened under

Kennedy and Johnson in Vietnam and under Reagan in Central America, but these were exceptions, widely criticized after a time. The truly serious departure came with the arrival of George W. Bush, his vice president, Dick Cheney, and his defense chief, Donald Rumsfeld—boosted by assorted and mostly anonymous "neoconservative" acolytes supplying a madcap form of "idealism." Here was both a departure from Atlanticism and a *return* to the modus operandi of westward expansion and Pacific imperialism; it was a reorientation and redirection to the world of the historic American unilateralism that has always characterized our relations with East Asia, an elaboration of a century-long practice of facing and moving west, with allies absent and little if any concern for the people in the path of that advance.

The first principle—no one standing in the way—really needs to be taken seriously. Second, a solipsistic conviction that you know best, your critics are ideologues, and allies should just get in line. Third, faith in the efficacy of military force (now quite carried away with the breathtaking "smart" capability to hit a needle in any global haystack) to effect political solutions. Fourth, regardless of success or failure, the professional military takes control and turns any base or operation into a permanent perpetual-motion machine. Last and most disastrous, stumbling yet again into a foreign political, cultural, and historical thicket with half-baked plans for "democracy" *without knowing how to do it.* The people we know not turn out to have dignity and resourcefulness; they are willing to die for their beliefs; faith-based ideology meets a real world recalcitrant to American imaginings; smart technologies destroy the infrastructure but can't find low-tech "improvised explosive devices"; another quagmire with no exit emerges; finally, the very ideas of American mission, freedom and democracy get dragged through the mud yet again—but "each detail was for the best."

Always described by its advocates as coherent, logical, part of a master strategy, Bushism also revived the ad hoc, improvised, spasmodic, eclectic, and absent-minded imperialism of a century ago: a quick victory in ousting the Taliban from Afghanistan masked the fumblebum failure to capture top Al Qaeda or Taliban leaders, soon funds for the effort were cut, the war was forgotten, and then it turned out we had successfully secured Kabul and little else. A tragedy occurs in New York, Bin Laden was its author, and so we attack Saddam Hussein, a secular dictator with no use for believers like Osama: it's as if a batter gets beaned by the pitcher and runs into the stands to slug the beer vendor. Much ink has been spilled about this imperialism mingling tragedy with farce, carnage with pratfalls, obsessive scrutiny with dumbfounding inattention, rank disregard for the Constitution amid senseless fiascos like Guantánamo, but few connect it to American history before Pearl Harbor—perhaps because they are so intent on holding onto the verities of Atlanticism, now fading into the distance.

The critical tradition in studies of U.S. foreign relations often attributes a farseeing sagacity to American leaders, and if that means John Quincy Adams, John Hay, or Theodore and Franklin Roosevelt, it is right; but when it speaks of McKinley, or Johnson, or George W. Bush, it is wrong. Instead we are returned to Henry Adams's judgment, in *The Education,* that "those who ought to know what they are doing, since they are the ones in charge . . . have in fact no idea whatsoever of what they are doing."[20] That is a more daunting thought, because it makes of three devastating wars since 1945 and the millions of lives lost a mere coda to human folly. Americans barging into the middle of ancient civilizations about which they know nothing. Americans here, there, and everywhere on their civilizing mission—and you mark it up in the lost column. "The difficulty many Americans have in understanding that their power in the world is not unlimited—a difficulty shared by no other people," Richard Hofstadter wrote forty years ago, "was created by a long history that encouraged our belief that we have an almost magical capacity to have our way in the world."[21]

For the past century, the sequence of expansion typically follows this pattern: the president announces that vital interests of national security are at stake and we must use force. He is greeted by near-universal acclamation, among elite opinionmakers and the public alike. Things go well and then do not go well. The dead and the sacrifices begin to mount. The first questions are heard about the mission itself. Years go by, an impasse negates victory, a stalemate results, military bases need to protect the stalemate, so they have to remain in place. Amid laments, regrets, and lapses of memory, the Pentagon locks in the institutional gain of more foreign bases (meaning more places for officers to earn medals). Galloping in across the horizon is the winner, the fifth horseman of the Apocalypse: forgetting. And the troops never come home. The one exception to these rules is the one war that truly threatened our vital interests: World War II. (And even then, the troops remain.) Add to all this the venerable American suspicion of anyone who lived abroad, spoke a foreign language, or "put on airs," and their love of direct men of action, and you end up with our situation under the unlikely Texan, George W. Bush: everyone, it seemed, even the president, had to talk tough and flex muscles to get a hearing. The State Department was freely described as the foreign office of some other country. Everyone was required to "support our troops." Indeed we must, since they are scattered across the face of the globe. But a fact remains: military force is rarely the solution to any serious problem. And then there is this: military officers know how to run bases and they may know how to fight wars, but they don't know how to run an empire.

The wars in Afghanistan and Iraq vividly illustrate this persistent pattern. The Taliban were quickly displaced in comparatively minor fighting, but the result was a major extension of the military's footprint: American bases are all over the Middle East and Central and South Asia—Afghanistan, Uzbekistan, Kyrgyzstan, Pakistan (secretly)—often occupying former Soviet facilities like Bagram Air Force Base, which was the main staging center for the Russian war in Afghanistan. The war in Iraq ground on for years without success— except in the construction of American military bases: like Al-Asad, a giant base in the western desert holding 17,000 soldiers and working staff, fed by Pizza Hut and Burger King outlets; Balad Air Base (also known as Anaconda), with 2 million cubic feet of concrete housing 120 helicopters, a host of huge C-5 transports, and a local Baskin-Robbins ice cream store; Ali Air Base at Tallil, surrounded by a double perimeter security fence and a moat (or "vehicle entrapment ditch with berm" in Pentagonese), plus dozens of other Iraqi bases, big and small—Washington proposed to spend nearly $1 billion on Iraq military construction in 2005–6 alone. "I think we'll be here forever," an airman stationed at Balad told reporters.[22] Pentagon planners also hope to get more bases in Senegal, Mali, and Ghana, in the now critical oil-producing region of West Africa, and even Mongolia is in play, for its uses in containing China.

In other words, the U.S. military is trying to stabilize the most unstable region in the world: the belt of populous and mostly Muslim countries stretching westward from Indonesia all the way to Algeria, southward along the African coast, and northward into Central Asia, into the former Soviet republics and the Muslim populations of China's western reaches—into a region which has never been central to American strategy but one where the interests of four nuclear powers intersect (China, Russia, Pakistan, and India). "Here I am in a nation I had never heard of," Brigadier General Jared Kennish, a troop commander in Kyrgyzstan told a reporter, "couldn't pronounce and couldn't find on a map six months ago." Vice Admiral Lyle Bien told the same reporter, "We're developing a force that makes it almost too easy to intervene. I am concerned about America pounding herself out." Meanwhile pundits like Robert Kaplan write with equanimity about the American military having "appropriated the entire earth."[23] At minimum, the long-term result of both wars is likely to be a more or less permanent extension of the archipelago of empire to the Middle East, Central Asia, and the most unstable and/or oil-rich parts of Africa.

The essential counterpart of this post-1950 archipelago was a new kind of mechanism at home: a national security state. NSC-68 built the global structure but was perhaps more influential in transforming the American political economy from one where the professional military and the armaments industry had minor influence (1789 to 1941) to one of dominant influence ever since. In the 1990s the collapse of the Soviet Union led to incremental but ultimately steep declines in the defense budget and the industries that supply it—perhaps making of the half-century after 1941 an unusual parenthesis in American history. But now with a commitment to global war against a shadowy, unseen adversary, the military-industrial complex has the best of all possible worlds: it needs everything imaginable to fight the enemy because you can't find him, so the project is utterly open-ended—and you will never know when you have won. Readers may disagree with this analysis, but first they should examine the fortunes of the following firms since 9/11: Lockheed Martin, Boeing, Northrop Grumman, Raytheon, General Dynamics, and United Technologies—just for starters. General Dynamics got $8.2 billion in prime Pentagon contracts in fiscal 2003, Northrop Grumman got $11 billion worth, and Boeing nailed down $17.3 billion. But Lockheed Martin was the hands-down winner of Pentagon contracts in 2003, netting nearly $22 billion (and almost matching its total sales in 2001 of $24 billion). ("It's impossible to tell where the government ends and Lockheed begins," a Pentagon-watcher told *New York Times* reporter Tim Weiner.)[24]

The ubiquitous nature of the terrorist threat vastly compounds the problem of Hartzian America in a threatening world. The communists, who were so visible abroad and so invisible at home (thus the necessity to *look* for them), gave way to an inchoate enemy who might be here, there, and everywhere: in Yemen or Kyrgyz or your corner convenience store. If Americans did not fathom the historical roots of foreign communist movements, how much less could they understand an operator like Osama Bin Laden (if they could find him)? "There is always an imbalance between the nationalist outcry and the reality of the threat which it meets," Hartz wrote, but after a thousand treason trials and congressional investigations, "the Martian remains"—and through his invisibility "he keeps coming closer all the time." Today the Martian is a nihilistic terrorist, he's closer all the time, and he knows what he's doing: "All we have to do," Bin Laden said in 2004, "is to send two mujahedeen to the farthest point east to raise a piece of cloth on which is written Al Qaeda, in order to make the generals race there to cause America to suffer human, economic, and political losses."[25] This critical imbalance poses a dire threat to the free institutions of this country because everybody and everything can be a suspect in somebody's tableau—as the generals stretch American power across the globe to the breaking point.

A New American Relationship to the World

When I began this project in the late 1990s I had no inkling of this turn in American foreign relations. I had argued in a number of papers and articles that the collapse of Western communism, the rise of the European Union, and the wide-ranging multilateralism of the Clinton years represented the culmination of the world order that statesmen like Stimson and Acheson had hoped for and helped to build during and after World War II, a *redirection* of Atlanticism toward the rest of the world, and particularly toward East Asia which seemed poised to develop a host of multilateral institutions and new relationships. I wanted to show how radically different our policies had been in that region, and how that past could now be overcome in a wide-ranging accommodation with our historic antagonists since 1945—China, North Korea, and Vietnam. I was particularly interested in internationalist mechanisms that would deepen American engagement with China and enmesh it in a Pacific and world order that would avoid the confrontation that so many saw coming between America and China—to do for China what John Hay had wanted to do for Great Britain, to slowly bring it into an American-defined system in which the United States would be a collegial first among equals.

It also never occurred to me that George W. Bush, a Texas governor with few accomplishments he could call his own, would depart so completely from the internationalism bred into the bones of his father and grandfather. Bush's invasion of Iraq and the failures that followed brought into being the broadest coalition among Atlanticists and Europeans since the Marshall Plan, and an almost seamless opposition in the leading organs of internationalist opinion. Bush also combined unilateralism and confidence in the efficacy of force with a Cotton Mather–like belief in good and evil[26] and the messianic idealism of a Woodrow Wilson running amok at the confluence of the Tigris and the Euphrates—except that Wilson was as notable for compromising his doctrine of democracy and self-determination (regarding all the colonies, for example) as for promoting it in the first place. With its designation of "Islamic fascism" as the global enemy, Bush's foreign policy became a parody of Robert Taft's critique: "No one has ever suggested before that a single nation should range over the world, like a knight-errant, protect democracy and ideals of good faith, and tilt, like Don Quixote, against the windmills of fascism."[27] Historically, however, American unilateralism was associated with different ideas: no foreign entanglements; no encumbering alliances; the salutary shelter of two great oceans; no lurches outward in search of dragons to slay. I am quite certain that if a leader emerged who took God away from the Republican Party and said here was His real plan—to remove North America from a world foolishly recalcitrant to its ministrations and make of it a shining example—that much of the party's Christian fundamentalist constituency would come along. Atlanticists would call it isolationism: but who would win the day?

As the Iraq War ground on, centrist elites were indeed warning about a new isolationism, already showing up prominently in public opinion polls; if isolationism is forced on the internationalist elite by the American people, there will be hell to pay. But if leaders were to emerge who had the courage to say we don't need 725 foreign military bases, we don't need to go abroad in search of monsters to destroy (and we don't do it very well when we try), that the nation remains a continental behemoth sheltered by two oceans that aren't going away any time soon, that our advanced technology makes any potential attacker aware that we can strike back anywhere in the world from our homeland, and that the most effective leadership is by example rather than by forcing our way of life down other people's throats, we might be able to have a serious national debate for the first time since the sixties about our relationship to the world.[28]

Of course the attacks on 9/11 and the Iraq War did lead to a big, bubbling, spreading debate, but for the most part it consisted of liberals who either opposed the war and found confirmation in its catastrophic aftermath, or liberals who had initially supported the war but thought the occupation was conducted badly (probably a majority); and on the other side conservatives, almost all of whom had supported the invasion but who later divided over how bad things had gotten and who was to blame. Andrew Bacevich's 2005 critique cut deeper and coincided with my own sense that the magnitude of our crisis requires a complete rethinking of America's relationship to the world. Professor Bacevich, a former military officer whose son died fighting in Iraq, presented a number of principles, the first of which was to "heed the intentions of the founders." Nothing in the Constitution, he argued, "commits or even encourages the United States to employ military power to save the rest of humankind or remake the world in its own image." He went on to argue for Congress to reassert its constitutional obligations in foreign affairs, "to view force as a last resort," to limit American dependence on foreign resources, to organize U.S. forces for national defense rather than power projection, and finally, to reconcile the professional military with the realities of American society. These principles, which I share, would call for a full rethinking of the many American garrisons abroad (the military archipelago) and truly significant reductions in defense spending—so we can bring ourselves into consonance with what all our advanced industrial allies spend.[29]

It is utterly forgotten that the five sides, five stories, five rings, and seventeen and a half miles of corridors making up the Pentagon (for which ground was broken on September 11, 1941, exactly sixty years before 9/11) were to revert to civilian uses after the war. It is forgotten that Franklin Roosevelt wanted a postwar peace in which America would be primus inter pares in Europe, in pursuit of two goals. First, "a radical reduction in the weight of Europe, in effect to preside over its indefinite retirement from the international scene," in John Lamberton Harper's words; these arrangements would have to be "drastic and definitive enough" to realize the second—and more important—goal: "to allow the United States to return to its natural Western Hemisphere and Pacific habitat and preoccupations—but with one eye cocked toward Europe and able to exercise long-range striking power . . . to be able to arbitrate from afar."[30] The first arrangement turned into a host of American military bases and American-dominated multilateral organizations, which did effectively retire West Germany, Italy, England, and Japan as "normal" or prewar big powers—but FDR did not have a permanent archipelago of bases in mind. FDR's second point seems radical in our context, but it summarized 150 years of foreign policy conducted according to the principles of George Washington and John Quincy Adams. Then Roosevelt died young, and the cold war and the hot wars in Korea, Vietnam, and Iraq built a far different system: precisely the intensive close-up "arbitration" and gross overextension that Taft and Charles Beard warned about just as the Truman Doctrine came into view. As Beard put it, Washington had now "set out on an unlimited program of underwriting, by money and military 'advice,' poverty-stricken, feeble and instable [*sic*] governments around the edges of the gigantic and aggressive Slavic Empire." In this way, "the domestic affairs of the American people became appendages to an aleatory expedition in the management of the world." Beard counseled "a prudent recognition and calculation of the limits on power," lest the United States suffer "a terrible defeat in a war"—like the "wrecks of overextended empires scattered through the centuries."[31]

War with China?

Many critics of the invasion of Iraq were "realists" like Zbigniew Brzezinski or John Mearsheimer who thought it diverted and squandered American resources against a peripheral enemy. For them, a different and more consequential adversary looms on the horizon: China. Likewise many analysts believe China is the real reason for the enormous military spending of recent years, the new bases in central Asia, and a direct intervention in the Middle East at a time when the United States and China compete worldwide for petroleum supplies. The Pentagon began preparing for a coming contest with China almost as soon as the Soviet Union collapsed; if one examines long-range planning documents or "POMs" (Program Objective Memorandums) from the early 1990s, "you will see China looming throughout as the dominant planning assumption." Secretary of Defense Donald Rumsfeld's "Revolution in Military Affairs," promising a lean, mobile, high-tech striking force, rested heavily on the doctrines of longtime Pentagon gadfly Andy Marshall, who first tabled his ideas for this "revolution" in 1992, and who envisioned China as the most likely American enemy in the twenty-first century.[32] Mearsheimer and Huntington, both in the Atlanticist and realist tradition, ended their recent books with predictions about a Sino-American war in the twenty-first century, an upcoming cataclysm presented in an almost casual, offhand way, as if anyone would understand the likelihood of this eventuality. They are more sophisticated than Homer Lea's scenarios for war with Japan a century ago, but like him their rash and irresponsible prognostications rarely seem to get criticized or even countered in the mainstream press.

For Mearsheimer the casual presentation is a given, since he believes that war between the big powers every now and then is inevitable. For him great powers are those that can field a conventional army capable of conducting all-out war and that have a survivable nuclear deterrent, they perpetually seek to maximize their share of world power in a zero-sum struggle with other powers doing the same thing, and their ultimate aim is to be the hegemon— "the only great power in the system." Anarchy reigns in the international system, the guy with the biggest gun wins ("the strongest power is the state with the strongest army"), it's a dog-eat-dog world, when you get into trouble there's no 911 to call, and a cruel fate awaits us all because for every human neck, "there are two hands to choke it."[33]

This approach is called "realism," and it has a venerable tradition in

Europe and the United States, even if Mearsheimer applies a ruthless logic to wring every warlike possibility out of it. But is this realpolitik? China has a survivable deterrent—usually called a second-strike capability—in its submarine-launched missiles. Its huge population also gives it a macabre "survivability" that Americans could never sustain. When General Xiong Guangkai remarked rather unkindly that Americans like Los Angeles better than Taiwan,[34] he reminded Washington of the PRC's longstanding deterrent policy: not the overkill signified by the Pentagon's thousands of nukes, but enough to tear an arm off the bear. Mearsheimer's doctrine has centuries of history behind it, but not an iota of evidence that it operates in a nuclear world; in more than sixty years no great power wars have occurred, precisely because of the Mexican standoff that nuclear deterrence creates. Meanwhile, millennia of Chinese history, going back at least to Sun Tzu, testify to the myriad strategies available to both sides once a military stalemate arises— like beating your pants off in a competition to educate your people and create wealth.

Samuel Huntington's influential attempt to recast world politics in cultural and civilizational terms seemed to explain more about the nature of post–cold war conflict, because of the reappearance of old ethnic conflicts in the former Yugoslavia along a presumed East-West divide going all the way back to the division of the Roman Empire into western and eastern parts, and then September 11 appeared to bring this theory to life; one would be hard put to find in those terrorist attacks an end to history or an example of "realism" in action, but they did seem to portend a new and darkening horizon for the "clash of civilizations." Unlike Francis Fukuyama's celebration of the victory of "the West," Huntington found an Atlanticist civilization embracing Western Europe and North America in decline, with its primary competition coming from a rising East Asia. Like Mearsheimer's book, Huntington's comes to an end with a scenario for "civilizational war" between the United States and China.

"Assume the year is 2010," he begins. American troops are out of Korea and only small contingents remain in Japan. The navy's carrier task forces have been so decimated by spending cuts that they barely have a single one to send to the South China Sea when China invades Vietnam (presumably this is not a "civilizational" war to start with, Vietnam being part of Huntington's "Sinic" sphere). China and the United States initially approach each other warily—the United States because the "Hispanic-dominated states of the southwestern U.S." don't want war. India uses the crisis to attack Pakistan.

Japan decides Washington is unreliable so it "bandwagons" with China. The American and Japanese navies clash in the Pacific. Washington does its best to mobilize its Western allies (including Russia). The Islamic states join up with China. Just at the moment where we are dying to know the answer to the ultimate question—who wins?—Huntington backs off and demurs: this war might destroy the world or it might lead to a cold war–style peace. At home, however, the people blame "the narrow Western orientation of WASP elites" and so "Hispanic leaders come to power." Huntington admitted that his scenario may be a "wildly implausible fantasy," but he used it to warn against the dangers of American intervention in the affairs of "other civilizations" (to my surprise).[35]

Each sentence implies its own refutation: 2010 beckons—and? The only diminution of American troops in Korea and Japan came when 9,000 soldiers in Korea were diverted to the Iraq War; 30,000 remain there, 50,000 in Japan. China invaded Vietnam once already (in 1979) and got whipped. The United States has new carrier task forces to add to the existing ones and the defense budget is above the historic high reached during the Korean War. India attacks Pakistan: and both destroy each other with nuclear weapons. The "Japanese Navy" clashes with the U.S. Navy: in the American lake called the Pacific, which the CINCPAC command in Honolulu dominates like no world ocean has ever been dominated? Russia is part of Western civilization? (It would like to be.) Islamic states ally with China—why? To detach China's Muslim-dominated western provinces? The saddest part of the book is to see this Boston Brahmin, blessed with a chair at Harvard for four decades, holding such unreconstructed views of Hispanics as some unreliable, un-American "other." It's embarrassing, and he should have been ashamed of himself—but don't expect that from remnant New Englanders who can still write about Atlantic civilization as if it were white, male, Protestant, and Atlanticist.

Prelude to a Pacific Civilization: Sino-American Affinities

The late Michael Rogin wrote that "a genuine American exceptionalism" would not separate America from Europe but would place the United States within the European world order—as "a European fragment whose history was formed by the encounter between Europeans and peoples of color" (those already here, or brought to America).[36] This is a Hartzian point, but it improves on Hartz because he saw the American liberal fragment spinning out its telos in a vacuum, whereas Rogin (and preeminently Richard Slotkin) recognized the determining impact of peoples of color on the white fragment —overwhelming in the case of African-Americans, significant regarding Native Americans, Hispanics, Chinese, and other Asians.[37]

Here is the shaping point of difference between Atlanticism and Pacificism: in the first case, a direct, acknowledged, admired, and welcomed European and especially British influence; in the second, a direct, often unacknowledged, repressed, unwelcome, (and for much of its history) extremely violent encounter with non-Europeans. As I argued in an earlier book, the stalemate in Korea, the lost war in Vietnam, and the unwillingness to confront China militarily in the 1960s spelled an end to westward expansion, to the dominating trope of virgin emptiness, and to the legend of invincible and regenerative violence as Americans encountered and failed to defeat what was ultimately a civilizational challenge. Or as the Vietnam War's best writer, Michael Herr, put it, we "might as well say that Vietnam was where the Trail of Tears was headed all along, the turnaround point where it would touch and come back to form a containing perimeter." Going directly against George Kennan's conviction about China's relatively modest weight in global politics, the United States fought two Asian wars with the goal of containing the Chinese revolution. Rough peasant armies, Chinese and North Korean, fought our troops to a standstill in Korea; another rough peasant army, led by a man named Ho Chi Minh who showed Deng Xiaoping where to find the best croissants in Paris back in the 1920s, defeated us outright.[38] Together both wars left millions of Koreans and Vietnamese and nearly 100,000 Americans dead for our efforts, and now Mearsheimer and Huntington blithely predict that it will happen again, against a China armed with nuclear-tipped ICBMs that can reach the American heartland.

Whether China is Mearsheimer's rising great power, Huntington's wounded and fundamentally alien civilization, or a nation that operates within its own historical paths and continuities, is something that only time will tell. History tells us that China has been a singular country, confining its expansion to its near reaches and putting self-constraint on its choice of military means (like its modest nuclear deterrent); some of its neighbors like it (Koreans in North and South), and some do not (Vietnam, Mongolia). But everyone in the neighborhood likes it better than Japan, which has to go all the way to Burma to find a friend who has been steady since the World War II era. When China used force since 1949, it did so within its historic region and more than once it did so judiciously and effectively. Chinese leaders may still proclaim the inherent superiority of their culture, but that heritage also teaches them the ultimate weakness of a power that only expresses itself militarily. Nor can military force solve China's deepest problem, which is the continuing predominance of the West. The answer to that challenge is civilizational, not military.

Americans cannot recognize a victory when they see one. In three decades of peace since 1975, Vietnam has become the country we always wanted it to be: pro-American, opening to the world market, a buyer of American goods. China has moved in the same direction, to a depth inconceivable in 1975, and even moat-builder North Korea now wants entry to the only game in town. They all just happen still to be led by communists. Furthermore, in the new century China is falling all over itself to assure Americans that it has no difficulty accommodating to a unipolar world run out of Washington; its leaders feared provoking the worst instincts of the Bush administration like every other country, but with added emphasis given China's vulnerability to American military might: they sought by all means to modify "China's rise" to say "China's peaceful rise" (and in 2006 they dropped "rise"; the new slogan was "peace and development"). Here is Premier Wen Jiabao in New York at the end of 2003: "The Chinese nation has always cherished peace and harmony. The rise of China is peaceful. It relies on itself for progress. . . . China will never seek hegemony and expansion, even when it becomes fully developed."[39] There is an important message here: Beijing is saying that it wants a partnership with the hegemonic power to shape its own development and to slowly incorporate itself into a world system managed by Washington and its allies. This is analogous to the British-American approach to the rising power of the United States a century ago, creating a partnership that lasted through two world wars and finally (in the late 1940s) led to a peaceful transfer of hegemonic responsibilities.

Long inured to either Atlanticist presumptions about the importance of Europe or alarmist claims about the rise to power of Japan or China, Americans in recent years have lived through the eclipse of any potential rival in Europe or East Asia. What is now clear is the towering predominance of the United States for the foreseeable future. How can that influence be retained? One way is by thinking through American affinities with other peoples— especially the Chinese who, like Californians, shower their great river valleys with multitudes of human talent. Over the past two centuries the United States and China essentially developed in isolation from each other; now, however, economic ties have thrown them together—and it seems safe to say that they must sink or swim together in this century. What if we asked the heretical question, what makes China and America alike, rather than different?

China and the United States are both continental nations, of geographically similar size. Both have experienced prolonged periods of noninvolvement with the rest of the world—China through centuries in which the Han majority expanded on the continent, almost by accretion, with only a brief heyday of world trade in the eleventh century; America through nearly two centuries (the 1780s to the 1940s) of relative isolation and indifference to events abroad. With a couple of exceptions like Tibet, most neighbors lived at peace with China and to varying degrees (Korea and Vietnam a lot, Japan less so) emulated its arts and letters, philosophy, statecraft, and social institutions. Meanwhile American borders have been peaceful for 150 years, if entirely permeable by Mexicans. China's legendary self-absorption and self-sufficiency, compounded by its solipsistic (or at least Sino-centric) sense of cultural superiority and civilizational centrality as the Middle Kingdom, nonetheless led to a kind of benign neglect of its near neighbors. America's provincialism and self-absorption are harder to detect because they are so organic to the majority of the people that they are not matters for reflection—not really worth talking about. (In a single generation three foreign-born people were the most important national security advisors to their presidents: Kissinger, Brzezinski, and Madeleine Albright—how often does this happen in any other country?)

In the United States the end of the cold war appeared to have spawned the strongest resurgence of indifference toward the rest of the world, if not necessarily isolationism, since 1941. Two years before 9/11 a major opinion poll asked Americans to name the two or three most important foreign policy issues facing the United States: fully 21 percent of the public couldn't think of one (they answered "don't know"), and a mere 7 percent listed foreign policy concerns among problems that were important to the country. The attacks on the Twin Towers disrupted that somnolent apathy, but with the manifest failures of the Iraq War, contemporary polls show a growing isolationism again.[40] In the late 1980s an officially sponsored and greatly popular television documentary series, *Elegy for the Yellow River,* castigated China's ingrown, navel-contemplating, sedentary, and land-bound culture and argued that China would have to join with Western civilization or risk disintegration and oblivion.[41] The United States could use criticism along the same lines. So, a curious isolationist affinity may be one of the deepest historical and cultural elements between the two peoples, paradoxically undergirding the chances for Sino-American peace. If so, it is one among many other affinities.

Both China and America have had world-influencing revolutions and in many ways have been revolutionary societies. Both have weak military traditions and strong principles of civil governance and civilian supremacy. Both experience profound tensions between governmental centralization and decentralization. Both have long histories of prowess in small business and petty capitalism. Both strike foreign observers as highly egalitarian societies, just as both contain heterogeneous ethnicities, especially when compared to Japan, Korea, or Germany. Both produced large diasporas—except the American diaspora is within, through vast immigration, and the Chinese diaspora is without, through historic emigration. Both have ideals of the independent, hardworking pioneer: in the Chinese case, the myriad Chinese families living alone for generations in American small towns, running a restaurant or a laundry.

Isn't it interesting to imagine the many ways in which America and China, so often conceived as diametrically opposite in civilization, customs, values, and practices (especially political ones) are actually similar? Given the complex difficulties of Sino-American relations, we need many more telling reversals of common presuppositions—for example, during Premier Zhu Rongji's visit to the United States, Bill Clinton asked Americans who worry about China's rise not to forget about "the risks of a weak China, beset by internal conflicts, social dislocation and criminal activity, becoming a vast zone of instability in Asia."[42] For the century and a half following on its first defeat at the hands of the West in the Opium Wars, China was exactly that— a vast zone of instability.

In this century, a Pacific civilization is finally ending this placid ocean's isolation from intense human activity, turning it into the expansive scene of an infinite variety of interactions. An ocean is no more important to humans than a lake or a forest, until people use it, shape it, and reshape it: "The wheel of human fortune has determined the destiny of the sea,"[43] Braudel wrote, and now the whole of the Pacific is in human hands, really for the first time. To shape Pacific civilization requires a radical redirection toward the Pacific of the best in the Atlanticist tradition: collective security, consensual international law, open systems, a panoply of multilateral institutions, and especially, respect for the dignity of the billions of people who ring this ocean. Europe knew civil war and catastrophe from 1914 to 1945, and it has known peace and tranquility since then by forswearing the obsolescent doctrines of realism and *machtpolitik;* both doctrines are integral to the Atlanticist tradition, but one path led to the inferno—to the exterminating havoc—and the other to an admirable modern civilization at peace with itself, culminating in the transnational democratic modalities of the European Union. The United States—still the least experienced of the great powers even today—has not learned the same lesson, because warfare has not raged across its territory in 150 years. Pacific civilization is inevitable, it will grow through war or through peaceful exchange or both. The United States and China have much in common, and leaders can choose to emphasize those affinities. The alternative is to bring into being the very enemy that some national security professionals think they already see (and perhaps need).

A demographic contest is also underway between the growing diversity of Americans themselves, with a sharp Asian-American inflection in the professions and on the Pacific Coast, and the slow demise of whiteness as an index of American elite *difference*. You can find far more human variety in a Mountain View noodle shop than exists, even today, at the Chicago or Harvard faculty clubs, but the actuarial tables will inevitably carry away the Huntingtonian conception of WASP ascendancy with its centuries-old ties to Atlanticism. The 2000 census found whites in the minority in California and a distinct minority in Los Angeles County: 31 percent, compared to Hispanics at 45 percent, Asians at 12, and blacks at 9 percent. In half a century the blanketed whiteness of this county (90 percent white in 1950, 5 percent each for Hispanics and blacks) had disappeared. Asian-Americans constituted 12 percent of California's population, but they were heavily concentrated in places that count: 29 percent in San Jose, 27 percent in San Francisco and nearby suburbs, 54 percent in Daly City, and 40 percent in Fremont, with huge overrepresentation in Berkeley, UCLA, Stanford, and Cal Tech—and in Santa Clara County, high-tech epicenter, Asian-Americans were more than 30 percent. The population of Americans claiming mixed racial backgrounds also grew very rapidly, to 5 percent of the state's population and more than 15 percent of Silicon Valley's.[44] Maybe California's cities and valleys will continue to diversify enough to recognize their shared humanity and destiny with the cities and valleys of China. But a different and more difficult contest exists within the Pacific frontiers of the American mind, beginning with the overwhelming ballast of Eurocentrism in the leading universities, newspapers, publishing houses, and the arts, ultimately yielding the eastward-leaning intellectual terrain of the entire continent.

My four decades of involvement in East Asian studies has taught me how little most of my colleagues in other fields know about this region of the world. Unless it is newly exotic or growing rapidly, it isn't interesting. It is still seen whole, as "China," or "Japan," or the Orient. Against all manner of disavowal, it remains true that many of the best minds retain a kind of Jungian archetype of an organic totality in the East. As Martin Buber put it in 1967 (in "The Spirit of the Orient and Judaism"): "The great complex of Oriental nations can be shown to be one entity, an organism whose members, no matter how functionally different, have a similar structure and a similar vitality." Buber's definition of "the Oriental type of human being" as a man "of pronounced motor faculties" (compared to the Occidental "sensory man") is a restatement of the shibboleth, indolent Orient versus dynamic Occident, made ridiculous by East Asian industrial prowess if nothing else (not to mention by Jews, whom he thought were especially illustrative of Oriental "motor faculties").[45] A generation ago Buber was the saint to whom one philosophy and religion professor after another bowed down; perhaps this happens rarely today. But the master trope of unfathomable individual sameness remains in the subterranean shadows of the American intellectual mind, making it very difficult to find allies when Washington identifies Tokyo or Beijing or Kim Jong Il as the enemy, and making it correspondingly easy to stampede the American people. Recent history—the trade wars of the 1980s, the McCarthyite fantasies of the 1999 Cox Report, the demonization of North Korea, the astonishingly thin opposition to Bush's preventive war in Iraq before it happened, the inordinate obsession with "the rise of China" today—teaches that this still can happen overnight. War with China? It can easily happen in our lifetime. But if that awful eventuality should come to pass, unlike the old Soviet Union Americans will finally have rendezvoused with a formidable adversary.

What American Ascendancy Really Means

E. L. Godkin articulated a hard truth that has been valid for over a century: we try to remake countries but we don't know how to do it. Japan and Germany came out well not because of our ministrations, but because they had democratic revolutions beginning in the late nineteenth century and decades of experience with parliamentary democracy aborted by Hitler and Tōjō (and because our military bases on their soil hedge against another such abortion). It was Asia-firster Henry Luce who trumped the Atlanticists and understood the real truth about American power: it's in the lifestyle. He wanted to "Coca-colonize" the world because he knew the world wanted Coca-Cola—"from Zanzibar to Hamburg." A while ago I retrieved the February 17, 1941, issue of *Life* that carried Henry Luce's original essay, "The American Century." My faith in college students' probity and tender concern for their peers was requited when I found the speech ripped out of the University of Chicago library's lone copy. So I contented myself with perusing what remained of the magazine. This single issue displayed, by quick count, 447 white people, 46 blacks, 1 Hispanic, and no Asians (not counting the evanescent pages 61 to 66, where Henry Luce once held forth). Nineteen of the blacks come from a scene in *Cabin in the Sky*, a Broadway musical with an all-black cast. A singular black face also inhabited a photo of the Art Students League of New York.

The remaining blacks were residents of Whale Cay in the Bahamas, a private island owned by Betty Carstairs, an heiress of the Standard Oil Bostwick family. Photos show Ms. Carstairs guiding the Duke and Duchess of Windsor around the island, directing a construction gang of blacks engaged in building roads, and commanding the rank-and-file members of the 87th Bahamas Regiment, her private army made up mostly of current and former Boy Scouts. As reported by *Life,* Ms. Carstairs runs the island with "a firm and feudal hand" and has done wonders for the natives, all of whom work for her: "She makes them eat more vegetables, forbids them anything stronger than beer, prohibits voodoo practices, and takes holidays away from the whole island if there is any mass bad behavior." Such bad behavior might include eating white rice, since the owner had directed that only brown rice should be served on Whale Cay. What does this mean? That the genteel tradition held sway on Whale Cay and that the "third world" of people of color, most of them in internal or external colonies in 1941, did not exist for *Life Magazine*— and did not exist for the white majority of Americans. They were invisible, people without history, people with a future only through the civilizing appurtenance of white leadership.

When we turn to the blonde-haired, blue-eyed, fresh-scrubbed publisher himself and his celebrated essay (a pristine copy of which I found in a local public library), you see what a great salesman Henry Luce was; "The American Century" was a wonderful logo for this eternal optimist to merchandise the American dream, but his ideas did not go beyond vexation about creeping "national socialism" in America (read New Deal); the bankruptcy of an isolationism that still could not grasp why Americans should fight and die for "dear old Danzig or dear old Dong Dang"; and the recommendation that the consumptive paradise that had arisen in the 1920s, when American industry perfected both mass production and the means to digest the same goods en masse ("the abundant life," as Luce called it), is or should be available "for all mankind" once they wake up to "America's vision." This program, of course, should not march forward just with an overflow of consumer durables, but under the banner of American idealism: "It must be a sharing with all peoples of our Bill of Rights, our Declaration of Independence, our Constitution, our magnificent industrial products, our technical skills. It must be an internationalism of the people, by the people and for the people."

Amid much frothy rhetoric like this ("We must undertake now to be the Good Samaritan of the entire world"), Luce held out to underdeveloped peoples the chance to escape their problems by becoming American—an absurd proposition in 1941. But he put his finger on a truth, the same one an American officer in Stanley Kubrick's *Full Metal Jacket* fingered when he answered Private Joker's weighty question—"Why are we in Vietnam?"— with this: "Inside every Vietcong is an American trying to get out." Or as Luce put it, "Once we cease to distract ourselves with lifeless arguments about isolationism, we shall be amazed to discover that there is already an immense American internationalism. American jazz, Hollywood movies, American slang, American machines and patented products, are in fact the only things that every community in the world, from Zanzibar to Hamburg, recognizes in common."

Our ideals work at home, but our *things* work everywhere: an imperium with the look of a great emporium. However much radicals may lament this, ever since Angelenos showed the consumptive way in the 1920s, people everywhere want our *stuff*: every father wants his TV, every mother wants her washing machine, and every teenager hankers after a nice car. The Soviet people wanted what we had, not what they had: the first human to descend from outer space, Yuri Gagarin, paraded through Moscow in 1961 waving from a chrome-laden Zil four-door convertible with tailfins and wide white-walls set off by iridescent green paint. Like Luce's vision, the American dream lived in California was a very white one, symbolized by blonde surfers, blonde hot-rodders, blonde beach babes and weight lifters, and the very blonde Beach Boys. That did not staunch the desire to go there, to be there, to act out the dream, to live the "endless summer" (the title of a superb surfing film) from welling up across the country and in people from Azerbaijan to Zambia.

Shortly before the Berlin Wall fell Michael Arlen visited a small, distant village in Soviet Armenia where the young people had a name for the City of Angels: "Los." That's where they all wanted to go—*Los*: "When I get to Los, I will have a house and a red BMW."[46] *I want to go to Los*: here is the essence of what links America to the world, and a profound source of its continuing global power and influence: the idea that anyone can go to California (or America) and realize their fondest hopes and dreams, because it is open, egalitarian—and rich. Atlanticists of the genteel tradition moping around Cambridge can and do deplore all this, but *Los* is not an either-or proposition: millions of American lives show that you can love Mozart *and* the Beach Boys, James Baldwin *and* Big Slice's Snoop Devilles, Ingmar Bergman *and* David Lynch (not to mention chocolate milkshakes at Bob's Big Boy). The island on the land also leads by example: forcing your ideas down other people's unwilling throats never works and it leads to endless mischief—when you could be cruising down Whittier Boulevard in the warm glow of the Pacific sun.

Appendix

A Hungarian émigré scholar named Imre Boba who taught at the University of Washington had the habit on Friday afternoons of inviting friends in to see his "dissertation"—a small liquor cabinet masquerading as a bulky thesis. He kept a poster on his wall stating, "Ideas have consequences." John Maynard Keynes remarked that those who care nothing for theory are usually the mental slaves of some dead economist. This book, like my other work, involved a constant back-and-forth dialectic between initial assumptions and conceptions, the evidence, reconnoitering my ideas and those of others, more evidence, theory, back to the evidence, and finally, consequential interpretation. Theory has to be "interpenetrated" by data in Schumpeter's formulation, or by practice in Marx's. The United States is often seen as all practice and no theory, or theory handed down from the misty past (Americans "huddled around the Lockean center"), but no facts and no practice exist apart from theory. Nietzsche wrote that there are no facts, only interpretations; he was of course not talking about biology but about philosophy and history. His statement is too strong, but it makes a point. Here I want to briefly sketch the ideas that underpin this book.

The reigning doctrines of American economics offer little help in understanding the rapidity of America's rise to global industrial and technological dominance, the remarkable leaps forward of cities like Chicago or Los Angeles, or the simultaneous concurrence of several revolutions in California's development. Economists are taught to think abstractly and incrementally, so they have trouble conceptualizing change, especially qualitative change; they and economic historians have produced an enormous literature on technological development, but rarely can they explain how and why it happens—perhaps because, as Joel Mokyr argues, technological progress is itself a kind of exceptionalism. Economists' ideas have to be expressed in models, and change is hard to model except as increments against a known base. Why did "most economists between 1820 and 1970" represent the economy as "a set of perfectly competitive markets"? Because they knew how to build models of perfectly competitive markets, wrote Paul Krugman.[1] Economists are not taught to think critically about language, and so they freely mingle quantitative data with vocabulary assumed to be uniform and transparent in meaning when it is not—like the "new slabs of resources" opened up by the frontier (what are "slabs"?). The long tenure of American central banker Alan Greenspan is another good example, where Wall Street rose and fell on every nuance of his take on the state of the economy—from "irrational exuberance" to "middle-term concerns" about deflation or inflation to "froth" (but not a "bubble") in the real estate market. Economists postulate nonexistent "equilibrium conditions" (like perfect competition or full employment) that get "disturbed" by "exogenous factors" like technology, whereupon a new equilibrium is realized—but we are no closer to understanding the effect of a qualitative change like the telegraph or the semiconductor on the economy. Political economy has ceased to exist in most American universities, residing if at all mostly in political science departments; economic history has all but disappeared from the economics profession and is no longer a prominent field in most history departments. The giants of a distant era are more help in understanding the transformation of a continent by leaps and bounds.

Technology

Perhaps because this country is the world's preeminent example of continuous technological transformation, Americans are loath to pay attention to the shaping effects of new technologies on people, society, the economy, and the country. Technique is for use, it isn't for contemplation. Any discussion of it barely proceeds before someone says "determinism," because, as G. A. Cohen points out, a focus on technology is considered demeaning to humanity. Or Marx's name comes up. But what Marx said is that "technology discloses man's mode of dealing with nature" and the process of production "by which he sustains his life." Technology enriches people in their labor; it doesn't dehumanize them. Cohen goes on to say, in the most sophisticated analysis of Marx's thought on this subject that I have found, that for Marx, history "is the development of human power," and the development of human power finds its clearest expression in "the character of the productive forces." Cohen then asks some simple questions: When was the last time a society replaced superior productive forces—or technologies—with inferior ones? Is there an invariant human nature? Most Marxists answer no, and many people called conservatives say yes. Cohen then makes some points we can all agree on: We are mammals. We have a brain enabling us to transform

ourselves and our environment. He then advances three tentative propositions: People are "somewhat rational." They live in conditions of scarcity.
Human intelligence enables us to improve our situation. Taken together,
these tentative facts suggest that when given the opportunity of expanding
productive power, people "will tend to take it, for not to do so would be
irrational." Cohen concludes that there is "a perennial tendency to productive
progress, arising out of rationality and intelligence in the context of the
inclemency [scarcity] of nature," and that this human tendency tends to be
more pronounced in capitalist society. Capitalism, more than any previous
form, rewards technical innovation—and protects it, through patents and
other means.[2]

In this book we have seen a protean Midwest give way to the dominance
of the coasts, except perhaps for the continuing sway of Chicago. I remarked
that in Henry Commager's *The American Mind* that Middle Border was
understood without any condescension or sense of loss, because when he
wrote the book in 1950 there was no hint that the region was on the cusp of
decline. To ask another Cohen-type simple question, is there no relationship
between the preeminence of the midwestern industrial base a century ago and
the once-dominant work of three great historians, Turner, Beard, and Parrington? They have a peer today in William Cronon, but he has excavated the
concerns of a new generation (like the environment) in the heyday of Chicago's dominance as the first city of the West (not the Midwest). Turner
grabbed hold of American history and ripped it away from New England
scribes who sought every American precedent in English experience and for
whom the frontier or forest was the habitat of brilliant Teutonic forebears.
But that is the same thing the Midwest's industrial might did to New England textiles.

"Joseph Schumpeter (1883–1950) is the most influential single writer on
technical change. He saw innovation—of which technical innovation is the
main, but not the only, variety—as the engine of economic development."[3] So
wrote Jon Elster, not a Marxist but a scholar interested in his doctrines, just as
Schumpeter was. But Marx also bored Schumpeter with his desire to etch in
stone a grand philosophy of human society, for all times and all places, and so
Schumpeter merely jumped off from the point that Cohen articulated many
decades later. Still, Elster's formulation needs to be expanded because neither
technology nor the innovator go far enough—Schumpeter thought the most
important force in modern life was history, especially economic history, and
even more so *industrial* history. If technique and innovation provide the
drive, industrial history is the outcome and the motive force for explain-

ing prosperity and depression, wealth and poverty, having work or not having it, in other words, the *business cycles* that drive advanced industrial capitalism.[4] Schumpeter specified several cycles—Kitchins, Juglars, Kondratieffs—that need not concern us here, but again, ask a simple question: is the New Deal political coalition that dominated American life for half a century explicable apart from the Great Depression? In cycles of economic development lasting decades, Schumpeter sought to isolate a *leading sector*—cotton textiles in the first phase of industry, railroads in the second, electricity in the third, and so on—as the basic engine of growth (or the exhaustion of growth, through decline, obsolescence, foreign competition, collapse of demand for whatever reason). New energy sources were also part of his theory: steam, electricity, or petroleum cascade through the economy, destroying old forms of energy (like coal) and vastly cheapening industrial and commercial endeavors. Mokyr thinks that "increases in the stock of human knowledge," including technological progress and institutional change, summarize much of Schumpeter's meaning, quite apart from material forces.[5]

Eduard März takes Schumpeter's general insights right back to Cohen: what Marx and Schumpeter share is the idea that "the ultimate cause of social developments" is to be found in the "productive combinations" for the latter, the "productive forces" for the former. Marx's unit of history was social class, Schumpeter's was the creative individual or organization, but both took industrial development to be the most important cause of qualitative leaps and transformations in modern life, particularly in the form of "the application of machinery by still greater application of machinery," in Marx's words, or "the introduction of machinery," in Schumpeter's, which he saw as "a special case of all changes in the productive process": getting from carriages and stagecoaches to trains and automobiles, which infuses capitalism with an enormous energy and transformative intensity, well beyond any previous social formation. If Marx sought to explain transitions from one social formation to another—feudalism to capitalism—Schumpeter was concerned with qualitative leaps from stagecoach to railroad, or electricity to atomic energy. If we wonder why Marx has any business being invoked in a discussion of Schumpeter, it is because Schumpeter "never failed to pay the deepest respect to the dynamic overall conception of Marx."[6]

Creative Destruction

Schumpeter took on a central element of modern economic thought, the idea of equilibrium and incremental changes that migrate until equilibrium is thrown off and a new equilibrium emerges, and argued that you cannot get there from there: "Add successively as many mail coaches as you please, you will never get a railway thereby."[7] Equilibrium did not move somehow to disequilibrium, progress was not smooth and harmonious only to develop inexplicable disharmonies, instead change is "lopsided, discontinuous, disharmonious by nature." The history of capitalism is replete with "violent bursts and catastrophes which do not accord well with the alternative hypothesis we herewith discard . . . evolution is a disturbance of existing structures and more like a series of explosions than a gentle, though incessant, transformation." Some changes are small and incremental; they can be measured by the existing methods. Other changes disrupt the existing economy and move it in novel directions: "dynamics" was his original word for these sharp changes (he later dropped it), which often take the form of innovation; that may mean a new technique, but it could also be a new product, new forms of organizing production, newly created wants (Madison Avenue also makes innovations), or bringing new locations—markets—into the economy (like California).

Innovators and entrepreneurs were central to Schumpeter, or more specifically, the innovator invents something and the entrepreneur makes it work commercially or industrially; they are usually two different processes and two different individuals. But the entrepreneurial function could also be performed by groups, organizations, even state institutions (like the Ministry of Trade and Industry in Japan). Capitalism "is incessantly being revolutionized *from within*," he wrote, "by new enterprise, i.e., by the intrusion of new commodities or new methods of production or new commercial opportunities into the industrial structure." New combinations suddenly appear as swarms, moving furiously on the "jerky," disturbed surface of a new enterprise or industry, and a boom unfolds, setting the business cycle in motion. Schumpeter was also fascinated by another innovation, which we call *credit*—how a person walks into a bank, walks out with a fortune, and founds a new line of business. It is almost magical how bankers create money out of thin air, redeploying depositors' funds to give oxygen to an entrepreneur, or for an agency like Korea's Economic Planning Board to direct rapid industrialization by diverting credit to industrial sectors it wanted to see grow. By such means people "carry out new combinations" and employ new productive forces; the banker is thus "the ephor of the exchange economy."[8]

Schumpeter's work on business cycles is both his best work and his most difficult. Without going into the many different phases of business ups and downs that fascinated him, we can listen to him discuss "those long waves" of economic activity that reveal "the nature and mechanism of the capitalist process better than anything else": "Each of them consists of an 'industrial revolution' and the absorption of its effects. For instance we are able to observe . . . the rise of such a long wave toward the end of the 1780's, its culmination around 1800, its downward sweep and then a sort of recovery ending at the beginning of the 1840s. This was the Industrial Revolution dear to the heart of textbook writers. Upon its heels, however, came another such revolution producing another long wave. . . . These revolutions periodically reshape the existing structure of industry by introducing new methods of production . . . new commodities . . . new forms of organization . . . new sources of supply." And here he goes on to a long list—from the mechanized factory, to automobiles, big mergers, and Katanga copper. He famously called this "the perennial gale of creative destruction," resembling a man tumbling down a mountaintop in an avalanche, growing with each tumble, dumped into this or that snow bank and then out again, emerging at the bottom like Hercules—and looking for the next mountain to scale. Except that in business one man's tumble is another's gain, in incessant competition. The next new thing can never be predicted *ex ante,* but everyone understands it *ex post:* capitalism is like life itself, a never-ending dialectic of bursting (innovation) and confining (patents, or trade secrets like Google's algorithms). For him, creative destruction was "the essential fact about capitalism," striking again and again not at the margins but at the foundation of enterprise, and giving it a truly revolutionary momentum.[9] What he could not have imagined was the role that the American state would play after 1941 in founding new industries, providing guaranteed markets, and funding a sheltered technological regime that would take away most of the risks of innovation (destroying existing product lines, "free rider" costs of others using the new technology, and the like), and then disappearing while the protagonist becomes a billionaire.

Time

If economics had trouble explaining Schumpeter's spurts of growth and leaps forward, *time* has also been a difficult concept for neoclassical economics—so it got left out of econometric models. Alexander Gerschenkron succeeded Schumpeter as the most illustrious economic historian at Harvard and introduced new conceptions of time—he became famous for his theory of "late" development. When you actually turn to the theory, however, he didn't say much. Or what he had to say, he said in a spectacular twenty-five-page paper, "Economic Backwardness in Historical Perspective," which he presented first at the University of Chicago in 1951. In broad strokes he sketched an argument that no two industrializations are the same, every episode is idiosyncratic, because they follow each other in world time and every nation is different: "Imitation of the evolution in advanced countries appears in combination with different, indigenously determined elements." A common-place to the historian, perhaps, this idea aimed squarely at an American developmental economics claiming that all nations can grow if they just get their prices right and lead from their comparative advantage. Gerschenkron argued that England had a luxury of time that no one else did, because it was there first; the United States combined early and late characteristics because it was across the Atlantic and had a continent to work with (Gerschenkron never made this latter point—he wasn't much interested in the United States); but on the Continent, France and Germany had to industrialize with the British breathing down their necks, occupying key markets and parlaying long leads in industry and technology, so they mobilized key resources and substitutions at the center, through investment banks and the state.

The Soviet Union was really Gerschenkron's primary subject. He came from a wealthy family that left Russia after the Bolsheviks took power, and he saw in Stalin's five-year plans a complete manufactory for modern industry—state control and investment, creating factories but also a proletariat and a cadre of experts that didn't exist, and the quick, brutal transformation of sedentary, subsistence peasants into workers and soldiers; he also saw in Stalinist development the jerky, sporadic, and military-dominated Russian growth pattern that had emerged with tsarist industrialization. The Soviet government, he pointed out to Americans enthralled with the theory of totalitarianism, was "a product of the country's economic backwardness." William Lockwood extended his analysis to Japan's late industrialization, Alexander Eckstein found it useful for China, and David Landes became a lifelong disciple. Indeed, Gerschenkron was a profound influence on economic historians and political economists well into the 1980s.[10]

Gerschenkron's analysis of "backwardness" argued for obvious liabilities but also unseen advantages accruing to the late-coming nation. It can borrow or copy advanced technology; banks or the state can accumulate, centralize, and direct scattered wealth; the state and its experts can substitute for entre-preneurs; a nation may have latent assets like a tradition of strong central power or a mass of disciplined people (like Prussian peasants) to deploy; it may or may not have a strong class of landowners standing in the way (or they may be quickly cleared out, Bolshevik- or Chinese-style); it may marry banks with particular industries (as Germany did); or it may draw on a feudal background to marry state, bank, industry, and corporation (as Japan did). Some stages of industry may be easier to develop than others (light industries like textiles), other stages may bring forth concatenated change across a nation that only a strong state can manage (heavy industries like railroads). Late-coming breeds resentments that can turn into a nationalism salutary for development, as with Germany and Japan. Gerschenkron shared with Schumpeter the idea that industrial development can be "sudden, eruptive," and therefore revolutionary; great leaps forward went hand in hand with decay, decline, and great leaps backward. Gerschenkron concluded his most influential essay with the thought that "there are no four-lane highways through the parks of industrial progress."[11] Had he examined American continental development more closely, he might have amended this statement.

Space and
Long-Distance Trade

For Adam Smith, economic exchange and the division of labor were limited or expanded by the *extent* of the market, by which he meant both its human depth and its geographic expanse. In his time water carriage was so much more expedient than land carriage that markets quickly developed along seacoasts and riverbanks, with the smooth and unperturbed Mediterranean being his best example of how water facilitates commerce. But the discovery of America and the passage to Asia around the Cape of Good Hope were, for him, "the two greatest and most important events recorded in the history of mankind," because they united the most distant parts of the world and prepared the way for the most extensive commerce "growing still greater and greater every day"—a world market, in other words.[12]

It is symptomatic of the glacial pace at which economists allow the real world to intrude into their econometric models that it was only in 1990 that Paul Romer surprised the profession with his paper "Endogenous Technological Change." For economists, new technologies were exogenous miracles, "manna from heaven," qualitative changes that they could not explain— so they didn't try to. Somewhat like a primitive man smelling food and wandering into a kitchen to discover refrigerators, stoves, and Cuisinarts, Romer found that the government subsidies hated by the Chicago School might actually work (rather than waste money) if they subsidized new technologies, new plants—and more broadly, new knowledge. Government was particularly helpful in absorbing the fixed costs of producing new knowledge that ongoing businesses might resist. There is much more to his argument, but Romer insisted on coining neologisms like "nonrival goods" that could be translated into mathematics, and thus he remained chained to the prison house of language in which economists try to hold words still with a singular meaning, when the instability, migration, and volatility of words and concepts makes them always a moving target. Other innovative papers followed, like "Schumpeter Might Be Right" by Robert King and Ross Levine, looking at the relationship of finance to growth. Then some economists discovered William Cronon's *Nature's Metropolis* and the importance of "the distribution of settlements over the landscape," otherwise known as the frontier disappearing over the horizons of the West. Paul Krugman's work on geography and trade has also been essential in this revisionist literature. Ultimately, of course, this new direction in economics arrived because of the overwhelming evidence of new ideas and technologies producing a new economy in Silicon Valley: as Warsh put it, "The models that included intellectual property and entrepreneurs and technology policy no longer could be resisted."[13]

In the postwar period the very essence of American growth in the West and Southwest reflected Cronon's understanding of space; Gerschenkron's of the state and comparative time; and Schumpeter's insistence on the creation of new goods and technologies, the miraculous way in which money (finance) interacted with entrepreneurial genius, and the stimulative role that the government can play.

Fernand Braudel was not impressed by Schumpeter's entrepreneur, Marx's class struggle, or Max Weber's Protestant ethic; capitalists are people, too, they are human, "and like other human beings, they behaved in various ways. Some were calculating, others ready to take risks, some were mean, others prodigal, some had a touch of genius, others were 'lucky' at best." (It is a judgment readers might make about the dramatis personae in this book.) Instead, for Braudel long-distance trade was critical to the emergence and development of capitalism. Long-distance trade organized production and created new social structures at both ends of the commodity chain—sugar plantations in Hawaii and sugar mills in San Francisco, for example. Risks were high, but the profits were higher—almost unavailable in settled domestic production. English merchants caught otters in the Pacific Northwest and sold the furs in Canton, picking up money "by the shovelful"—it is just another example of a kind of trade that was "an unrivalled machine for the rapid reproduction and increase of capital." For Braudel, capitalism is not about markets but monopolies, and long-distance trade was one of the best routes to monopoly. Markets have always existed, he wrote, but superprofits come from extinguishing market competition, supply and demand, through control. But capitalism is also about change—"the essential characteristic of capitalism was its capacity to slip at a moment's notice from one form or sector to another." Meanwhile the essential characteristic of this historian was to bring space and human structures together: "Geography . . . helps us to rediscover the slow unfolding of structural realities, to see things in the perspective of the very long term." His definitive work, of course, was on the great trading areas of the inland sea separating Casablanca and the Riviera, situated first around the geography and distinctive and usually lovely climate of the Mediterranean, then around the stormy, moody Atlantic. To read his account of how peoples as diverse as the human rainbow created a Mediterranean world without discovering any new land is a memento for how the Pacific will serve as the site of an infinity of transactions in the twenty-first century.[14]

Empire

The most familiar and least convincing theory of imperialism is about "the pressure of capital for more profitable investment than could be ensured at home" (and that goes double for the United States, with its vast continental market; protectionist tariffs at home were real guarantees of superprofits,[15] compared to exports abroad). More convincing is the search for markets, with the China market always uppermost in the minds of businessmen and diplomats; more convincing still is great power rivalry over markets and competition between national economies, where the strongest prefer an "open door" but lesser powers want to carve out their own private, exclusive, well-protected zones of activity, otherwise called colonies. For Karl Polanyi, colonies were a kind of external protectionism, pound and franc and yen blocs masquerading as projects of native uplift. But the rivalry among the powers makes it difficult to separate economic from political motives.[16] In the case of the United States, its internal colony—the continent, the national market—was so huge as to generate much less thrust toward empire than among the European powers, and its industrial and technological prowess in the late nineteenth century propelled it toward seeking foreign *access,* not control, because it was competitive in almost every product. To want access and to want trade to operate under commonly understood rules is not the same as imperialism or zero-sum expansionism. It is internationalism, and Hay's Open Door was an early version of the internationalism that would describe American strategy after World War II.

Bill Williams attributed the war with Spain to a general American desire for overseas expansion, and particularly to agrarian interests who wanted new export markets. LaFeber placed more emphasis on business interests, their friends in the State Department, and their common search for markets; McCormick on the reality and the chimera of the China market; Marilyn Young on the rhetoric of empire; and still other historians on geostrategic concerns like coaling stations and bases in the Pacific. Kristin Hoganson in an important recent interpretation disagrees, locating the origins of the war in a culture of "manliness" and male aggrandizement that reached an apogee in Teddy Roosevelt's somewhat frantic efforts to express his manhood.[17] For my purposes this causality is overdetermined: markets, strategic calculation, and a culture of manliness marked continental expansion from the 1840s onward; meanwhile no single expansionist episode had a determined quality. If many Americans questioned armed expansion, hardly anyone questioned commercial expansion.[18]

Schumpeterian thought helps us also to understand empire, and particularly the American empire conceived as an archipelago of military bases. His understanding of imperialism departed entirely from Lenin's theory, or from any iron necessity linking capital and empire. Empires existed long before capitalism (indeed he thought they were largely antithetical to commerce), and they have their own dynamic—which is akin to a perpetual-motion machine, or George Kennan's famous metaphor of the Soviet empire as a wind-up mechanical toy car, which expanded in one direction until blocked, then flipped around and went off in another direction. Empire is also atavistic: forces set in motion for one purpose (say, war) become routinized just as they lose sight of their goals. For Schumpeter, imperialism "is the objectless disposition on the part of a state to unlimited forcible expansion"; a class of professional warriors forms to carry out expansion, and once in place, they tend to continue in place. Elsewhere he refers to imperialism as a *policy,* that is, a choice, which when called into action keeps going long after the policy disappears or can even be remembered. It quickly becomes an atavism ("the survival of interest"), or something impelled by atavistic forces in a nation, like Prussian Junkers who outlive their agrarian usefulness and opt for imperial aggression. Or a policy decision taken in the "dim past" simply becomes the immanent but invisible and forgotten rationale for system maintenance, around which cluster a host of military and political interests and large numbers of people dependent on the continued functioning of specific parts of the system, with no one envisioning the whole.[19] Thus American forces arrive in South Korea in September 1945 and remain there today, with next to no contemporary understanding of how or why they got there in the first place; or in 2005 every bigwig and thousands of ordinary people in Hawaii wrap their hopes and fears around a single aspect of a now-preeminent base that the United States put next to no effort into for over half a century, simply because Congress threatened to close a small part of Pearl Harbor's vast operations, and that will cost jobs (Congress lost, of course). Empire thus grows not in the soil of capitalism but in the daily grinding of bureaucratic gears and the military's beloved "standard operating procedures." Like Hartz, Schumpeter understood that America was the nation "least burdened with precapitalist [*sic*] elements, survivals, reminiscences"[20] (and we have argued that California was the least burdened of all), but he did not reckon with the permanency and career utility of several hundred foreign bases.

Hegemony

The work that brings all of these concerns together is Karl Polanyi's *Great Transformation*, which develops the role of technology and industry in commodifying land and labor and vastly intensifying upheavals and business cycles into a theory of production for profit in the ever-widening gyre of the world market, beginning (as with Braudel) with the emergence of modern long-distance trade in the sixteenth century. Polanyi merges the national with the international to explain the transformation of the European balance of power that prevailed for a century after 1815; that world system necessitated a hegemonic power (England), whose minimum function required a night watchman–like concern for the free flow of trade and convertible currencies, a lender and power of last resort who would keep the system together.

In place of the conventional narrative that sees World War I terminating the European balance of power, Polanyi argues that 1933 was the critical year—"the snapping of the golden thread brought a world revolution." When Great Britain went off the gold standard it signaled that it was no longer the power of last resort, the force holding the world economy together. London could no longer lead, and Washington was not yet ready. In the wake of global economic collapse each industrial nation withdrew from the system in its own idiosyncratic way—a New Order in Germany, a New Deal in America—followed by another world war and the rise to hegemony of the United States. Nothing remotely comparable to the effect of 1914, 1933, and 1939 on Great Britain has happened to threaten the continued global leadership of the United States today, which is why the American Century continues apace.

The hegemonic power bursts forth initially with comprehensive superiority in those things that count, like advanced technology, productivity, and finance, which gives it an awesome but brief period of complete dominance—perhaps for twenty-five years (the United Kingdom, 1815–40, the United States, 1945–70). It then has a much longer run as primus inter pares. It does not dominate like an empire: it leads as first among equals, preferably with a broad, multinational, consensual mandate. It writes the rules of the game, but collegially. It influences others through its authority, its goods, its example, its vision (every hegemonic power seeks to foster or impose its own domestic revolution), and through consultation, consensus, indirection, and the establishment of distinct outer limits on the behavior of its allies, its adversaries—and itself. It has the burdens of last resort in the world economy. Hegemonic powers are militarily dominant at the beginning of their careers, and superior force locks in their advantages for the long term. But in normal times military force is a last resort, and its use is almost always a sign of some earlier failure. The question for the hegemonic power is how to establish and maintain legitimate global leadership.

Notes

Preface

1. Chirot (1986), 224. (Daniel Chirot calls this the fourth revolution, the third being chemicals and electricity. I think textiles, iron, steel and railways, and autos and mass production all had more transformative impact than chemicals and electricity, but I can see his point.) Willa Cather quoted in Commager (1950), 153–54.

2. *Weekly Variety,* March 18, 1996, p. 123.

3. For my critique of these terms see Cumings, "Rimspeak; or, the Discourse of the 'Pacific Rim,'" in Dirlik (1993), 29–50; see also Alexander Woodside, "The Asia-Pacific Idea as a Mobilization Myth," in Dirlik (1993), 13–28; also McEvedy (1998), ix.

4. I published nothing related to this book until 1999, when I did a long paper on "the American ascendancy" which appeared the following year in the *British Journal of International Studies* and in a shorter version in the *Nation.* These articles show that I did not anticipate the recrudescence of unilateralism; my views about internationalism and expansionism had actually developed in the Reagan years, which involved what now seems to be a mild return to American nationalism and unilateralism. For another account predicting that the world was moving toward a broad multilateralism—even "governance without government"—see Hardt and Negri (2000), 13–14.

5. Gene Balsley (1950) in Rhodes (1999), 193–94.

6. Schrag (1999), 27. George B. Leonard, later a leader of the Esalen Institute, wrote in 1962 of the "migrating millions who vote with their wheels for California." Quoted in Schrag (1999), 28.

7. "Just like the title," Evans said, the script "was pure Chinese—nobody, I mean nobody, understood it." Evans in *The Kid Stays in the Picture* (Los Angeles: Woodland Films, 2002).

Chapter 1. The Machine in the Garden

1. Nugent (2001), 7; Fresonke (2003), 1. About half of western historians think the West begins at the Mississippi or the Missouri, according to a recent survey, but the others say it starts from the eastern Great Plains or the foothills of the Rockies. Hine and Faragher (2000), 10.

2. Fenton and Lawrence quoted in McWilliams (1946), 181, 269; Wilson (1950), 45–47; Wilson, "The Boys in the Back Room" (1940) quoted in Starr (1997), 287.

3. For this last point I am indebted to Kris Fresonke's masterful little book, *West of Emerson.*

4. Menand (2001), 6.

5. Bailyn, "Preface," Armitage and Braddick, "Introduction," and Armitage, "Three Concepts of Atlantic History," in Armitage and Braddick (2002), xvii–xix, 3, 11–15, 18.

6. Huntington (2004), xvii, 42–45.

7. Ibid., 305–8, 311.

8. Foucault (1972), 210.

9. Hodgson (1976), 113–14, 116–17; Mills (1956), 206–7.

10. LaFeber (1989), 9; Goetzmann (1966b), 94; Bryant (1947), 109–12; Tchen (1999), 29; Pletcher (2001), 9, 17; Varg (1983), 154–55.

11. Tchen (1999), 46–49, 56; Fairbank (1953), 226–27; Varg (1983), 156; Pletcher (2001), 15.

12. In Digby Baltzell's words, around 1900 these patricians "held the vast majority of positions at the very heart of national power, and set the styles in arts and letters." Baltzell (1964), 12.

13. Menand (2001), 7.

14. Quoted in Hunt (1987), 46.

15. Santayana (1967), 40–43, 59, 64; the point about forgetting is in a 1918 essay: Santayana (1967), 103. Dickens quoted in Varg (1983), 216; Commager (1950), 101. For a broader discussion of pragmatism see Louis Menand's excellent account (2001).

16. Hartz (1964), 9.

17. Hofstadter (1968), 447–48; Hartz (1964), 6, 9–10, 10n, 13.

18. Hartz (1964), 3–22.

19. Hietala (1985), 1–2; Tocqueville (1840), 1:193, 432.

20. MacIntyre (1981), 2–3.

21. Santayana (1967), 128.

22. Wilde quoted in Seidensticker (2006), 202.

23. Arcadia was an isolated mountain kingdom in ancient Greece, and the Roman poet Virgil was probably the first to romanticize the agrarian life, as opposed to the city. Hanson (1996), ix–x.

24. Real estate boosters quoted in Brown (1995), 140.

25. Smith (1950), 123–24.

26. Reverend Smith quoted in Smith (1950), 132; Varg (1983), 220–22.

27. Williams (1973), 44, 142–64, 216; James quoted in Marx (1964), 353.

28. Tocqueville (1840), 1:21; DeVoto (1952), 408. Pages 406–11 amount to a beautiful geographic poetry delineating the national space of the United States.

29. An unnamed Connecticut observer quoted by West in Milner et al. (1994), 131; Meinig (1993), 269–72.

30. Webb calls the 98th meridian "an institutional *fault* . . . running from middle Texas to Illinois or Dakota"; and "practically every institution that was carried across it was either broken or remade or else greatly altered." Webb (1931), 8, 18. Others agreed that Turner's "frontier" thesis did not extend to the West but chose the 100th meridian instead—see Stegner (1953), xviii and Reisner (1993), 107.

31. Lawrence, *Studies in Classic American Literature,* quoted in Marx (1964), 145.

32. Marx (1964), 13–15, 29, 69, 246–48.

33. Cronon (1991), xvi, 9–12.

34. Ibid., 111–13.

35. Mailer (1968), 88; Cronon (1991), 208–11, 226–30.

36. Cronon (1991), 90–93, 307, 310; Frank Norris, *The Pit* (1903), quoted in Cronon (1991), 3.

37. U.S. Census data available at www.experts.about.com/e/m/ma/Madison (and the same, for Granville).

38. McMurtry (1997), 699.

39. William Morris Davis's 1915 map distinguished the Allegheny Plateau from the prairies and plains, in Meinig (1998), 311; on the Western Reserve and Granville, see Meinig (1993), 225, 228.

40. Elliott West, "American Frontier," in Milner et al. (1994), 124–25; Linklater (2002), 72–73, 160–66.

41. Rogin (1975), 103; Linklater (2002), 72–73, 160–66, 175.

42. Hine and Faragher (2000), 333.

43. Stegner (1953), 220–21; Smith (1950), 190; Slotkin (1992), 30; Limerick (1987), 125.

44. Nugent (2001), 131–32; Hine and Faragher (2000), 334–36; Linklater (2002), 228; Weigley (1967), 267. The 160-acre limit was finally dumped in 1982 for a standard six times higher. See Limerick (1987), 136.

45. Jehlen (1986), 9, 92, 131, 235.

46. Hine and Faragher (2000), 27; Thornton (1987), 23–32, 36–37; Braudel (1995), 1:394–96. Russell Thornton's work contains close and careful comparisons of various estimates, and the reasoning behind his own. He interpolates his figures from scholars at odds over how many natives existed in North America above the Rio Grande at the time of the first encounters with whites, with estimates ranging widely between 900,000 and 56 million (the high figure is from Sale [1990], 315); see also Stannard (1992), 10–11; Nugent (2001), 23–24; Berger (1991), 28–9; and Todorov (1982), 133. The most recent discussion of these numbers that I have found is in Mann (2005), 92–94, 130–33, who notes how much disagreement on the numbers remains among experts.

47. Stannard (1992), 33; Hine and Faragher (2000), 27; Kicza (2003), 176; Thornton (1987), 71–76; Karl W. Butzer in Conzen (1994), 45; Painter (1987), 163; Mather quoted, p. 75. If scholars differ over how many Indians existed in what became the United States around 1492, they don't differ much over how few remained just a century ago: 250,000 according to Hine and Faragher (25–27), 300,000 according to Nugent (23–24); Lowitt (1984) listed 246,834 Indians on reservations in 1891 (p. 122).

48. West in Milner et al. (1994), 125–26; on Michigan see Kolodny (1984), 131, 150, 154; Winthrop and Massasoit quoted in Linklater (2002), 28–30, 44. Linklater points out that settlers in Australia, New Zealand, and South Africa also declared that natives did not have any legal claim to land (p. 210).

49. West in in Milner et al. (1994), 130.

50. Meinig (1998), 160–61.

51. Taylor (2006), ch. 1 and passim; Raines quoted in Heizer (1971), 30; Limerick (1987), 188. The quarter-million figure is for overland transit before the Civil War and the railroads, and the number of Indian murders (362) is for 1840–60. In the same period whites killed 426 Indians. See Unruh (1979), xv, 9, 160, 179, 185. For a sensitive essay on Olmsted's views, see Dawson and Brechin (1999), 183–85.

52. DeVoto (1942), 363–64; Brown in Milner et al. (1994), 416; Mitchell (1981), 243–44.

53. Webb (1931), 138; Brown (1995), 87, 91.

54. Webb (1931), 67–68, 169–71, 177–79; Brown (1995), 97, 119, 373; Weigley (1967), 268.

55. DeVoto (1942), 249–50, 305, 506–7n. In a subsequent book, however, DeVoto was almost pioneering in finding a "tendency to write American history as if it were a function of white culture only," with "a dismaying amount . . . written without regard to the Indians . . . [and] their diverse and always changing societies." See DeVoto (1952), xv.

56. White (1991), 5, 170, 497, 501–2.

57. The United States is always far out in front of any other advanced industrial nation in murders per capita. When compared with Japan, the disparities become chasms. In 1998–2000, the United States had .04 murders per 1,000 people, ranking it with Uruguay and Bulgaria; England, France, Germany, and Italy were at 0.1 per thousand; in Japan the figure was 0.0, that is, statistically insignificant. (United Nations figures cited at www.nationmaster.com/cat/cri-crime.) Of course, no episode in American history, including the elimination or removal of Indians, compares to the German destruction of European Jewry or the massacres of Armenians by Turks.

58. D. H. Lawrence, *Studies in Classic American Literature,* quoted in Slotkin (1973), 2.

59. Slotkin (1973), 5, 18, 42–43, 52.

60. Ibid., 162; Slotkin (1985), 53–54; Elliott (1970), 44; Todorov (1982), 49–50, 53.

61. Todorov (1982), 144.

62. Remington quoted in White (1968), 109; Townshend (1869), 106, 148–49.

63. Goldberg (1993), 150.

64. Baudet quoted in Rogin (1975), 8; Goldberg (1993), 150; *New York World,* January 18, 1874, quoted in Slotkin (1992), 41.

65. Rogin (1975), 11; Francis X. Holbrook, "Come, Papillangi, Our Fires Are Lighted," in Barrow (1973), 112–25.

66. See David Grann, "The Lost City of Z," *New Yorker* (September 19, 2005), pp. 56–81; also McNeill (1983), 39; Mann (2005), 4–5.

67. Parrington quoted in Hofstadter (1968), 361n, 364.

68. "The Middle West," first published in 1901, in Turner (1920), 127–57; see also "Contributions of the West to American Democracy," first published in 1903, in Turner (1920), 235; "The West and American Ideals," first published in 1914, in Turner (1920), 274–75.

69. To paraphrase Raymond Chandler in *Farewell, My Lovely* (1939), 103.

70. For example, Harvard political theorist Michael Sandel recently offered a return to Jeffersonian republicanism as a cure for the ills of American civil society. See Michael J. Sandel, *Democracy's Discontent: America in Search of a Public Philosophy* (Cambridge: Harvard University Press, 1996), 3–7, 124–33, 351.

71. George G. S. Murphy and Arnold Zellner, "Sequential Growth, the Labor Safety-Valve Doctrine, and the Development of American Unionism," in Hofstadter and Lipset (1968), 207–9; Mokyr (1990), 4.

72. Nordlinger (1995), 51; Washington's address quoted, 50–51.

Chapter 2. "The Remote beyond Compare"

1. McPhee (1993), 18, 21–22, 105; see also the excellent historical maps in McEvedy (1998).

2. Arif Dirlik in Dirlik (1993), 5; Evelyn Hu-Dehart in Dirlik (1993), 252; Wolf (1982), 153.

3. David J. Weber, "The Spanish-Mexican Rim," in Milner et al. (1994), 47; Mc-Evedy (1998), 40, 54.

4. Quoted in Polk (1991), 47; see also Wolf (1982), 131.

5. Bean (1968), 18; Starr (1990), 232. "California" is a word no one has nailed etymologically, but Carey McWilliams thought that it appeared first in the *Song of Roland* as "Californe" and probably comes from the Persian term *Kari-i-farn*, "mountain of paradise." McWilliams (1949), 3

6. Philbrick (2003), 3, 12; Weber in Milner et al. (1994), 49; McEvedy (1998), 34; Winchester (1991), 83–91. According to the *Oxford English Dictionary* the first written usage of "Pacific Ocean" came in 1555: "The sayde sea cauled *Pacificum.*" In 1568 another author linked "the sea pacifick" to "the sea of Magellan."

7. Polk (1991), 122, 254.

8. Dashiell Hammett, *The Maltese Falcon* (New York: Vintage Books, [1929] 1989).

9. Bean (1968), 20; Starr (1973), 10; Morgan (1967), 34; McEvedy (1998), 56.

10. Heckrotte and Sweetkind (1999), 20–28, 50; Polk (1991), 289–90, 326; Starr (1985), 11; Stegner (1953), 275, 423.

11. DeVoto (1952), 279, 282, 284.

12. Ibid., 538; Philbrick (2003), 4–5.

13. Bean (1968), 37–39, 43.

14. Ibid., 46, 50; Pomeroy (1965), 12.

15. Bean (1968), 27.

16. Johnson (1992), 16–19; Weber in Milner et al. (1994), 65–67; Bean (1968), 72; Reisner (2004), 7–8; White (1993), 33; Royce (1886), 28. Royce put the non-Indian population at 5,780 in 1840 (p. 17).

17. DeVoto (1952), 9–21, 38–39, 290; Cabeza de Vaca quoted in Todorov (1982), 197.

18. Howard (1998), 15–16; Bean (1968), 77–78; Bancroft (1886), 152–60.

19. Bean (1968), 87.

20. Howard (1998), 6–9; Federal Writers Project (1939), 15. Hornbeck locates the emergence of the Sierra Nevada in the Jurassic, Cretaceous, and Triassic periods. Hornbeck (1983), 6.

21. Dawson (1933), 33, 38, 39, 42, 133–34.

Chapter 3. A Continent in Five Easy Pieces

Epigraph quoted in Smith (1950), 10.

1. According to John Adams's *Works*, quoted in Royce (1886), 215. See also De Voto (1952), 59.

2. Smith (1950), 15; Goetzmann and Goetzmann (1986), 110; Jefferson quoted in Linklater (2002), 56.

3. DeVoto (1952), 390–91, 397; Wilentz (2005), 109–10; Hine and Faragher (2000), 136; Goetzmann (1966b), 6–9; Linklater (2002), 156–57.

4. Turner (1920), 165; Meinig (1993), 4, 11–12.

5. "Westering," I learned from Howard R. Lamar, is a fourteenth-century Middle English word, used memorably by John Steinbeck in *The Red Pony*. Lamar, "Westering in the Twenty-First Century: Speculations on the Future of the Western Past," in Cronon et al. (1992), 257.

6. Cotton quoted in Sanford (1974), 16; Turner (1920), 261; Mill quoted in Saxton (1971), 103; Tocqueville (1840), 1:26.

7. LaFeber (1965), 18–22, 39–41; also Varg (1983), 93.

8. Nugent (2001), 45.

9. DeVoto (1952), 430; De Voto (1948), 4–5; Lewis and Clark (1953), 287.

10. Goetzmann (1966a), 3–4; Adams quoted in Johansen and Gates (1967), 113.

11. Onuf (2000), 2, 57–8; Jefferson quoted, 15, 45; Stephanson (1995), 21; Merk (1963), 3; Bemis quoted in Hietala (1985), 259.

12. LaFeber (1989), 72–75; Clark (1981), 182; Goetzmann (1966b), 1–2; see also Drinnon (1980), 113. Paul Kramer argues that "expansionism" was a term that "starkly separated" American intervention in the Philippines and elsewhere from European imperialism, but that hardly characterizes the Wisconsin school (Williams, LaFeber, McCormick, Gardner, and others) or Drinnon's work. See Kramer (2006), 15.

13. LaFeber (1965), 96.

14. John L. O'Sullivan, "Annexation," unsigned article, *United States Magazine and Democratic Review* 17 (July–August 1845): 5–10, reprinted in Sanford (1974), 26–32. "Manifest Destiny" achieved a wider fame with O'Sullivan's presentation in the *New York Morning News*, December 17, 1845. The swatch of rhetoric here is quoted in Stephanson (1995), 39–40.

15. Quoted in Wilenz (2005), 563. Sean Wilenz emphasizes Manifest Destiny's impulse to spread American democratic values, perhaps with an eye cast on the early years of this century (pp. 562–64).

16. Quoted in Hofstadter (1968), 56–57.

17. DeVoto (1942), 194; Horgan (1984), 757; Goetzmann (1966b), 54; Wilentz (2005), 604. Goetzmann called it "America's 'forgotten war'" in 1966 (p. 116), when there was "no extended study" of the Mexican War, but that was soon remedied by the scholarship of K. Jack Bauer, Gene Martin Brack, Paul Bergeron, Sam Haynes, Myra Jehlen, Robert W. Johannsen, Robert Leckie, James McCaffrey, David Pletcher, and John H. Schroeder, among others.

18. For a a fuller discussion, see Cumings (1990), ch. 13.

19. Haynes (1997a), 11, 62, 73, 116; DeVoto (1942), 7–8; Wilenz (2005), 570–73; Norman A. Graebner, "Polk," in Dudden (2004), 107.

20. Brewer (1990), xix.

21. Elliott (2006), 272; Weber in Milner et al. (1994), 59; Meinig (1969), 39; Fehrenbach (1968), 269.

22. Horgan (1984), 605–7, 661–65, 670–71, 705; Weigley (1967), 173; Meinig (1993), 151; Haynes (1997a), 130; DeVoto (1942), 16; Graebner (1955), 153–54; White (1993), 77–78; Wilenz (2005), 581–82.

23. Pletcher (1973), 374–77, 384–86.

24. Merk seemed to think hardly any Americans died (Merk [1963], 113), but DeVoto notes one battle in Mexico that left 900 Americans dead or disabled (DeVoto [1942], 294) and Hine and Faragher (2000), give the 13,000 figure for Americans killed (p. 206).

25. "Brave, benignant, stupid, as common as your Uncle Bill." DeVoto (1942), 193, 284.

26. Hitchcock and Thoreau quoted in DeVoto (1942), 110, 213; see also 14–15, 488; Hietala (1985), 156–57, 172; Grant quoted in Hine and Faragher (2000), 205. See also McPhee (1993), 51.

27. Haynes (1997a), 11, 62, 73, 116, 193; DeVoto (1942), 7–8; Hietala (1985), 121; Weigley (1967), 182; Meinig (1993), 159, 209, 222.

28. Fresonke (2003), 73; Wilentz (2005), 287.

29. Quoted in Dudden (2004), xxii.

30. Quoted in Van Alstyne (1960), 152; Pletcher (1973), 386.

31. Benton quoted in Horsman (1981), 90; Fresonke (2003), 76; Lebergott (1984), 178; Townshend (1869), 83. For the full text of Berkeley's famous poem, see LaFeber (1989), 6–7.

32. Smith (1950), 23–25; quoting Benton, 28–29, 32–33. Turner thought that Benton was "the man of widest views of the destiny of the West." Turner (1920), 30.

33. Stegner (1953), 2; Karnes (1970), 14–15.

34. Gilpin, *Mission of the North American People* (1874), quoted in Smith (1950), 37, and Karnes (1970), 136; see also Karnes pp. 96–98. I have taken some liberties with the quotation to pull out the bullets.

35. Gilpin quoted in Smith (1950), 39, and Robbins (1994), 175. A world map of this zodiac is in Karnes (1970), 151. See also Slotkin (1985), 220–21; Goetzmann and Goetzmann (1986), 331; Graebner (1955), 97–98, 221. One can still find historians who think that Americans occupy boundaries of latitude wherein "humans are at their most energetic" (Martin [1992], 31).

36. Quoted in Smith (1950), 45–47, and Foley (1997), 21.

37. Hietala (1985), 58–62, 92–93; Fairbank (1969), 195–96.

38. Merk (1963), 261, 266.

39. Benton's 1855 speech is reproduced in Dana (1861), 364, 384, 386–87, 389, 392. See also the discussion of Benton and Guyot in Hine and Faragher (2000), 280; Whitney quoted in Bain (1999), 9, 29; Gilpin's position is in Karnes (1970), 227; see also Russel (1948), 11–12; Clark (1981), 11.

40. Graebner (1955), xiv, 2, 218; *San Francisco Daily Alta California,* quoted in Pletcher (2001), 1.

41. DeVoto (1942), listing all these technologies and many more, 216–21; see also Kasson (1976), 41; Bain (1999), 6; Meinig (1993), 385–86, 398; Paskoff (1989), xviii–xx.

42. George G. S. Murphy and Arnold Zellner, "Sequential Growth, the Labor Safety-Valve Doctrine, and the Development of American Unionism," in Hofstadter and Lipset (1968), 202 (emphasis in original); Schumpeter (1942), 109; Braudel (1966), 1:23. Paul Krugman recently wrote that economic geography "is almost completely absent from the standard corpus of economic theory" (Krugman [1995], viii).

43. Prown et al. (1992), 96–97.

44. For a delightful and thoroughly researched study of early global news agencies, see Alex Coyne-Nalbach, "The Ring Combination: Information, Power, and the World News Agency Cartel, 1856–1914," Ph.D. diss., University of Chicago (1999). See also Braudel (1995), 1:355–94.

45. Goetzmann and Goetzmann (1986), 91; on the telegraph see Standage (1998), viii, 29–30, 48, 197; also Gordon (2004), 153; Mokyr (1990), 124.

46. Hine and Faragher (2000), 487.

47. Quoted in Goetzmann and Goetzmann (1986), 192.

48. Hietala (1985), 84; DeVoto (1942), 47–48; Howard (1998), 28–30; Goetzmann and Goetzmann (1986), 168–73.

49. White (1993), 80; DeVoto (1942), 223–25; Lavender (1972), 133–34; Royce (1886), 46–48; Meinig (1993), 130, 137. "Comic opera" is from Starr (1973), 5.

50. DeVoto (1942), 199–200, 223–25, 229–30, 471; Royce (1886), 49; Philbrick (2003), 341; Bean (1968), 92–94; Hietala (1985), 76. The 49th parallel was established in June 1846 with the Buchanan-Pakenham Treaty.

51. Ken Pomeranz uses this term to describe the impact of Atlantic trade on the United Kingdom and Europe. Pomeranz (2000), 23.

52. Bryant (1947), 236–38, 248, 267–69.

53. Ibid., 275, 277; Wiley (1990), 46; Perry (1856), 5, 75.

54. Bryant (1947), 277–79; Perry (1856), 235, 238; LaFeber (1997), 12. Adas (2006), 2–5; Beasley (1995), 46–47; Thompson (2001), 23–29; Goetzmann and Goetzmann (1986), 344–45. The "jingoistic American Geographical and Statistical Society of New York" was also a big lobby for Perry's mission, according to Goetzmann and Goetzmann (1986), 343. Hiroshi Mitani's excellent book lets us see how Perry looked from the Japanese side, including his threats of war. Mitani (2006), 187–89.

55. Whitman quoted in LaFeber (1997), 24; Perry (1856).

56. Adams (1907), 90–91; Pletcher (2001), 39; LaFeber (1989), 157; LaFeber (1993), 17; Dudden (1992), 24; Seward quoted, 61.

57. There are several accounts of this incident, but the most interesting is the one taken down firsthand by Gale (1972, 310–11) from an old hermit of Pyongyang.

58. Shufeldt quoted in Drake (1984), 107; Kim (1980), 56–61. The best study of this war (by far) is Chang (2003).

59. Kim (1980), 56–61; Griffis (1888), 412–18; Low and King Kojong quoted in Chang (2003), 1355, 1360.

60. Drake (1984), 292.

61. Ibid., 296–98.

62. Quoted in ibid., 115–16.

63. See Weinberg (1935) for the nationalist argument, Williams (1959) for the imperialist argument, and a general treatment in Merk (1963). Merk got mesmerized by Americans who wanted to take over all of Mexico after Polk's war began in 1846, devoting much of the second half of his book to this inconsequential sideshow (see pp. 107–201).

64. Thoreau and Whitman quoted in Fresonke (2003), 128, 134, 154; Whitman quoted in DeVoto (1942), 26, 38.

65. Smith (1950), 187; Brockett quoted in Smith, 186.

66. Royce (1886), 119; Horgan (1984), 619.

67. Mathiessen (1941), xv.

68. Stanley W. Trimble in Conzen (1994), 9; Bryce quoted in Meinig (1998), 29.

69. Charles F. Lummis, "The Right Hand of the Continent," *Out West* (June 1902–July 1903), quoted in Gordon (1972), 195–96.

Chapter 4. Manifest Destiny's Offspring

1. Rawls, "Introduction," in Rawls and Orsi (1999), 3; Bean (1968), 16.

2. Quoted in McPhee (1993), 50; see also Bean (1968), 109, and "James Marshall's Own Account of the Discovery of Gold in California," in Bari (1931), 69. "Thou common whore" is from Shakespeare, *Timon of Athens.*

3. Bean (1968), 83–84; Jackson (1970), 16–17; McPhee (1993), 49.

4. Bean (1968), III; McPhee (1993), 51; Lavender (1972), 155.

5. Engels quoted in Hobsbawm (1979), 63; Marx (1857–58), 174–80, 225.

6. Bean (1968), 113–14, 117; Gordon (2004), 180; McPhee (1993), 55–56; Federal Writers Project (1939), 30; Dawson (1933), 74. McWilliams put the total size of the mining area at nearly 300 miles long and 40 to 100 miles in width. McWilliams (1949), 27.

7. Agricola quoted in McPhee (1993), 60; see also pp. 43, 62, 65; Lavender (1972), 152–53; Royce (1886), 224; Gordon (2004), 182.

8. Jackson reported individual hauls of $26,000, $76,000, and $80,000 (Jackson [1970], 24). See also McPhee (1993), 42–43, 55–56; McWilliams (1949), 26–28; Lavender (1972), 157.

9. Quoted in McWilliams (1949), 55. See also Lavender (1972), 158–59; Taylor (1998), 87.

10. Lincoln quoted in DeVoto (1952), 401–2; see also Pomeroy (1965), 76–77. Henry Adams has a brilliant account of Gladstone's and Lord Palmerston's consistent strategy of seeking two American nations, in Adams (1907), 131–53.

11. McEntire (1946), 74–75; Pomeroy (1965), 264.

12. Freaner quoted in Johnson (1992), 26.

13. Taylor quoted in McWilliams (1949), 37; Rexroth quoted in Brook et al. (1998), viii.

14. Bryce, *The American Commonwealth* (1891), quoted in Pomeroy (1965), 125.

15. Brechin (1999), 54; Cumings (1990), 99–100, 142–44; Schweikart, Larry and Lynne Pierson Doti, "From Hard Money to Branch Banking: California Banking in the Gold-Rush Economy," in Rawls and Orsi (1999), 215.

16. McWilliams (1949), 31; Bruchey (1988), 73; Brechin (1999), 221; Cumings (1990), 801n; research by Charles L. Schwartz cited in Brechin (1999), 355n.

17. McPhee (1993), 43, 65; Gordon (2004), 182.

18. De Quille quoted in Jon Christensen, "The Silver Legacy: San Francisco and the Comstock Lode," in Brook et al. (1998), 95.

19. De Voto (1947), 147–48; Pomeroy (1965), 10; Federal Writers Project (1939), 34–35; Brown (1995), 247–54; McWilliams (1946), 26. A mild corrective to the characteristic image of the "Diggers" can be found in Phillips (1975).

20. Hine and Faragher (2000), 249–50; Brands (2002), 316; Kroeber (1961), 43–47.

21. Starr (1997), 332, 341; Kroeber (1961).

22. McPhee (1993), 58; Hine and Faragher (2000), 283–85; Deverell (1994), 13; Brands (2002), 341; Bain (1999), 91–92; Peirce (1972), 105.

23. Huntington quoted in Hine and Faragher (2000), 285; see also 283–85; Bain (1999), 92–93; Bean (1968), 210–12; Brands (2002), 341; Pomeroy (1965), 96–97; Birmingham (1980), 52–53.

24. Hine and Faragher (2000), 286–89; Bain (1999), 209, 222, 239; Birmingham (1980), 54; Pomeroy (1965), 101; Misa (1995), 1–4.

25. Bain (1999), 707.

26. Ibid., 709–11; Lavender (1972), 278; Sackman (2005), 42; Huntington quoted in Hine and Faragher (2000), 417.

27. McDougall (1993), 372; Adas (2006), 112–13.

28. See Kolko (1965).

29. Kolko (1963), 1–5; Lebergott (1984), 282; Hine and Faragher (2000), 281–82; White (1993), 146; LaFeber (1989), 149.

30. Ripley and Emerson quoted in Marx (1964), 199–200, 234; Kasson (1976), 122–23, 146, 155, Whitman quoted, pp. 172, 178; Rigal (1998), 183–85.

31. Gordon (2004), 151; Heine quoted in Schivelbush (1986), 37.

32. Schivelbush (1986), 92.

33. Schivelbush (1986), 100–11; Woodward (1951), 125.

34. d'Eramo (2002), 18.

35. McMurtry (1968), 11, 94; McMurtry (2001), xi; Rhodes (1999), 115.

36. Meinig (1969), 23; Caro (1983), 5–6, 11–14, 52. A dog-run cabin means two separated cabins or rooms connected under a continuous roof. See Caro (1983), 17.

37. Webb (1931), 161; White (1993), 65–69; Anderson and Cayton (2005), 247–48, 267–68; Meinig (1969), 41; Fehrenbach (1968), 275; Caro (1983), 5.

38. De Beauvoir (1954), 202; also Wolfe (1989), 30.

39. Bruchey (1988), 48–51; Lewis quoted in Foley (1997), 2; Fehrenbach (1968), 563; see also the map of Texas settlement by whites from the Deep South, p. 597.

40. Webb (1931), 209, 216–17, 230, 313–14; Foley (1997), 28; Caro (1983), x.

41. Joan Didion on Wayne in Didion (1968), 31; Kramer (1977), 17, 56; on Kissinger's interview with Oriana Fallacci, see her obituary, *New York Times* (September 16, 2006), p. A16.

42. Webb (1931), 245; Jennings quoted in Webb, p. 494n.

43. Wills (1997), 11, 17, 21, Mast quoted, p. 147; harrisinteractive.com/harris—poll/ index.asp?PID=631; Johnson (2004), 59. Wayne traipsed through Honolulu "hunting commies" for the House Committee on Un-American Activities in the 1952 film, *Big Jim McLain.* See Wood (1999), 107.

44. Webb (1931), 477; Wills (1997), 13.

45. Nicholas Lemann argued that when Bush was growing up he never quite mastered Texas masculinity; like his father and Dick Cheney, he "hunts doves and quail but not deer." Instead he stands in awe of strong, silent, laconic types like fireballer Nolan Ryan and was in the stands on August 4, 1993, when Ryan beaned Robin Ventura, who charged the mound and caught six short, sharp blows to the face from Ryan (then forty-six years old). "It was a fantastic experience for the Texas Rangers fans," Bush said. And, as a Texan would say, Ryan was only acting in self-defense. Lemann, "Remember the Alamo," *New Yorker* (October 18, 2004), p. 18.

46. Webb (1931), 497.

47. Ibid., 167; Brown (1991), 5, 17, 156; Ngai (2004), 68.

48. Larry McMurtry, "Texas: The Death of the Natives," *New York Review of Books* (September 21, 2006), p. 64.

49. Brown (1975), viii.

50. Ibid., 273, 276; Anderson (2005), 172–94, 345–77.

51. See the excellent discussion in Foley (1997), 2–12, 44, also citing research by historian David Roediger; Holmes quoted in Palumbo-Liu (1999), 29; Meinig (1998), 212, 223; Fehrenbach (1968), 670.

52. Walker (2004), 283; Edward J. M. Rhoads, "The Chinese in Texas," in Dirlik (2001), 166; Brady (2004), 9, 42–43, 63.

53. Foley (1997), 120.

54. David Uhler, "The Gusher That Changed the World," *San Antonio Express-News,* carried in *San Francisco Chronicle* (January 10, 2001), p. 5; Fehrenbach (1968), 666–68; Brown (1995), 158–59.

55. Leslie Wayne, "Perry R. Bass, 91, Patriarch of Famed Oil Texas Family," *New York Times* (June 2, 2006), nytimes.com.

56. Wolfe (1989), 78.

57. Rick Lyman and Anne E. Kornblut, "The Ranch Where Politicians Roam," *New York Times* (February 19, 2006), nytimes.com.

58. McWilliams (1949), 25.

Chapter 5. Abroad in Search of Monsters to Destroy

1. Musicant (1998), 117, 125, 137–40, 144; Weigley (1967), 290–91, 568. For an excellent account of McKinley's decision-making that nonetheless places too much weight on his strategy and leadership, see McCormick (1967), 108–11, 116–17.

2. Williams cited in LaFeber (1989), 161.

3. Shafter quoted in Anderson and Cayton (2005), 336; Drinnon (1980), 313; Okihiro (1994), 56–57; Linn (1989), 7, 139, 157; Root quoted in Linn (1989), 23. Brian Linn is at pains to show that the insurgents employed "terrorism" and seems to imply that this justified harsh U.S. countermeasures—an argument with a contemporary ring a century later (Linn [1989], 18–19, 161).

4. Stephanson (1995), 75–78; Musicant (1998), 210, 250–51; Trask (1981), xii–xiii; Anderson and Cayton (2005), 318, 327–37; Gould (1980), 20, 35, 110; Dallek (1983), 22; Meinig (1998), 354.

5. Especially Iriye (1972), viii, 26–27, and passim.

6. Field quoted in Iriye (1972), 13–14.

7. Royce (1886), 23, 42; Chisholm (1990), 4.

8. Wiebe (1967), 225–27. On Wall Street's shift toward war, see LaFeber (1963), 392. Walter LaFeber has shown in several books (especially *The New Empire*) how small and critically placed elites expanded American power in Central America and the Pacific in the nineteenth century, but most Americans were unaware of these excursions, and speaking broadly, until 1898 they were incidents and they were policies, but they were discrete rather than connected in a pattern (beyond the westward expansion which involved almost everyone) and lacked significant impact on the country—even if trade policies were closely watched by cotton, wheat, and other exporters. The agency charged with foreign affairs, the State Department, was a weak, stodgy, and fractious place throughout the nineteenth century. Visionary secretaries of state—John Quincy Adams, William Seward—were certainly important, they were avatars of empire, but they did not sway the nation like Woodrow Wilson or Franklin Roosevelt did in the next century. Perhaps the forgotten hero, James Polk, is the closest analogy to strong or "imperial" twentieth-century presidents. LaFeber leans toward this position in his later work, in my reading. See in particular LaFeber (1993), 234–39.

9. Rosenberg (1982), 4–7, 16, 21; Mokyr (1990), 142–44.

10. Adams (1907), 287–88, 319, 492n.

11. Hoganson (1998), 5–6, 68; Linderman (1974), 34; Linn (1997), 10; Trask (1981), 99–101; Gould (1980), 1, 12–14, 60–61; Beale (1956), 6; Musicant (1998), 220–21, 226.

12. Hoganson (1998), 6–7; Ngai (2004), 99; Musicant (1998), 591, 604; Linn (1997), 16. These sources differ slightly in the number of Filipinos and Americans who died. The civilian toll varies widely, with the largest figure coming from Adas (2006), 134.

13. Healy (1970), 62–65; Roosevelt quoted in LaFeber (1989), 190; see also LaFeber (1963), 400–402; LaFeber (1993), 159.

14. Linn (1997), 12–14, 20, 28–29, 83.

15. Brechin (1999), 136, quoting General Smith; Smith's words vary slightly in the quotation given in Morris (2002), 100; see also pp. 101–2, and Hoganson (1998), 135; and Linn (1997), 14.

16. Twain's essay reprinted in Shaw and Francia (2002), 57–68; Young (1968), 193–94; Linn (1997), 21; James in Robert Beisner's paraphrase, Beisner (1968), xxii–xxiii, 45, 165.

17. Godkin quoted in Healy (1970), 218; emphasis in original. Godkin was the editor of the *Nation*.

18. Morris (2002), 3–4.

19. Beale (1956), 28.

20. Roosevelt quoted in Beale (1956), 40, 57.

21. Roosevelt quoted in Beale (1956), 81, 159.

22. Slotkin (1992), 36–40; Linderman (1974), 106.

23. Slotkin (1992), 106–7, 109–11; Adas (2006), 88.

24. Wiebe (1967), 254; McCormick (1967), 60–63, 125, and passim; Tom McCormick's *China Market* and Marilyn Young's *Rhetoric of Empire* are the best books on the Open Door and America's China policy at the turn of the century. See also Bryant (1947), 382.

25. Young (1968), 6; Iriye (1967), 80–82.

26. LaFeber (1963), 316.

27. Adams (1907), 303, 351; Osborne (1998), 130; LaFeber (1963), 313–14; Hay quoted in Healy (1970), 33, also McCormick (1967), 158.

28. Quoted in Healy (1970), 174.

29. Anderson and Cayton (2005), 344–46; Katz (1981), 195–202.

30. McDougall (1993), 379.

31. Adas (2006), 8; Sumida (1989), 37, 362; Evans and Peattie (1997), 152–53.

32. Limerick (1987), 271; Saxton (1971), 254–55.

33. Reckner (1988), xi, 6, 56–7, 89, 107; Linn (1997), 86–87; Sherry (1987), 103. Stimson sent a handful of B-17 bombers to the Philippines in September 1941, but they couldn't function effectively without other support services. See Sherry (1987), 106.

34. Bryant (1947), 391; Esthus (1966), 263; Evans and Peattie (1997), 12, 60, 147.

35. Reckner (1988), 113–14, 119; Dickinson (1999), 27–28, 73; Beasley (1995), 51, 152; Evans and Peattie (1997), 153, 194–95, 201. For a detailed discussion of Japan's plans for war with the United States from 1907 onward, see Evans and Peattie (1997), 187–89.

36. I discuss this pattern at length in Cumings (1998), ch. 1.

37. Charles E. Neu, "1906–1913," in May and Thomson (1972), 155–72; Hunt (1985), 211–14; Iriye (1967), 123; Sklar (1992), 78–82. "Orange plans" for war with Japan went back to the late 1890s, and the Army War College had mounted Orange vs. Blue war games for years (Linn [1997], 88–89).

38. Todd (1921), 1:vx–xvi, 31–32.

39. *Inscriptions at the Panama-Pacific International Exposition* (1915), 12, 15–16. Goethe's statement came in a conversation with M. Soret in 1827.

40. *Blue Book* (1915), 46–49, 292.

41. Todd (1921), 2:302.

42. Ibid., 3:95. A "Chinaficationist" appears to be a person who favors peace, because

in his speech Roosevelt had denounced "professional pacifists" who wanted to "Chinafy this country."

43. *Blue Book* (1915), 48–9.

44. Todd (1921), 3:210–16, 376; 4:128.

45. Reckner (1988), x, 8, 15; LaFeber (1993), 227; McCormick (1967), 72–73; Young (1968), 34, 123; Rockhill quoted in Young, p. 228. (In trade with Japan, by contrast, the United States exported $53 million and imported $81 million.) See Iriye (1972), 223; Iriye (1969), 36; also Linn (1997), 113, 115–21, 128–29, 145–46.

46. Weigley (1967), 400–403, 567–68. U.S. troop strength expanded in 1940–41 to 10,569 in the Philippines and 42,857 in Hawaii.

47. Linn (1997), 245, 253–54.

48. Marilyn Blatt Young, "American Expansion, 1870–1900: The Far East," in Bernstein (1967), 180–81, 187; LaFeber (1997), 76–77; McCormick (1967), 193–94.

49. Adams (1907), 10; see also 301–4.

50. Bryant (1947), 377, 388; Pletcher (2001), 80, 82; Drinnon (1980), 273; Lodge quoted in Dallek (1983), 29; Adams (1903), xv.

51. Turner (1920), 228, 271, 289.

52. Williams (2nd ed., 1972), 11, 29–30, 171, 31; McCormick (1967), 128; Seward quoted in Paolino (1973), 11, 25, 29.

53. The full address is available in LaFeber (1965), 42–46; emphasis in original.

Chapter 6. East of Eden

Epigraph from Coke (1852), 317. Coke was a visiting Englishman.

1. Schwantes (1996), 22–23, 49–51.

2. Kelley (1971), 49, 273; Chris Dixon, "A Coast Less Traveled," *New York Times* (April 29, 2005).

3. Philbrick (2003), 260, 264; Pomeroy (1965), 56; Wilkes quoted in White (1995), 5; Johansen and Gates (1967), 200.

4. Nugent (2001), 78.

5. Ibid., 156–57.

6. Vancouver quoted in Robbins et al. (1983), 205.

7. Heilemann (2001), 161.

8. The "sweet Arcadian valley of the Willamette" was a constant trope in settler imaginings. See Bunting (1995), 415–16.

9. Crawford (1898), 73.

10. MacColl (1998), 2; White (1993), 72.

11. Hine and Faragher (2000), 184; Webb (1931), 149; MacColl (1998), 108–9; Unruh (1979), 119; Johansen and Gates (1967), 284, 297; Drinnon (1980), 233; Meinig (1998), 70.

12. Johnson (1992), 8–9, 42–43, 142, Williams quoted, p. 181. See also Peirce (1972), 223; Samuel Thurston quoted, pp. 159–60. Also MacColl (1998), 3–4, 91–92, 167; Unruh (1979), 93; Johansen and Gates (1967), 339; Morgan (1967), 86.

13. Oral histories cited in Nugent (2001), 213.

14. Pomeroy (1965), 254.

15. White (1993), 101–2; Schwantes (1996), 28–29, 38–39, 144–53.

16. J. H. Beadle, quoted in Johnson (1992), 269.

17. Pomeroy (1965), 146; Lewis and Clark (1953), 285, 295, 312. I saw the Maharaj Ji's outburst on television at the time; he did allow, however, that in Oregon he had discovered the best drink in the world: Canada Dry ginger ale (unfortunately, an import from across the border).

18. MacColl (1998), xv.

19. Peirce (1972), 190; DeVoto (1942), 372; Pomeroy (1965), 136; Johansen and Gates (1967), 564; Morgan (1967), 17, 122; Schwantes (1996), 267; Freeman Tilden, "Portland, Oregon: Yankee Prudence on the West Coast," *World's Work*, October 1931, pp. 34–40, cited in Nugent (2001), 230–31. The lawyer is quoted in MacColl (1979), 3; see also p. 655.

20. Johnson (1992), 275–78, 312; Pomeroy (1965), 101, 137–38; Lavender (1956), 362; Johansen and Gates (1967), 310–13, 406, 410; Nordhoff (1874), 213; Meinig (1998), 75–77.

21. Edith Feldenheimer oral history, quoted in Nugent (2001), 210.

22. Taylor (1998), 82; Katz (1996), 73–77; Ficken and LeWarne (1988), 21–23; Mac-Donald (1987), 3, 7, 13; Meinig (1998), 81; Sealth quoted in Sale (1976), 27–28. Many writers have said the chief's prose seems rather too polished, but these ideas were certainly his.

23. MacDonald (1987), 35; Lavender (1956), 409; Hidy et al. (1988), 73.

24. Schwantes (1996), 50, 308. The ship canal and the Montlake cut were constructed from 1885 to 1917.

25. Adams quoted in Pomeroy (1965), 345; see also 98–100; Martin (1976), 7, 26, 35, 51, 389.

26. Rosenberg (1982), 16–18; Johansen and Gates (1967), 313–16; Hidy et al. (1988), 123; Martin (1976), 396–97, 430, 545, 613; Pomeroy (1965), 255.

27. Carlos A. Schwantes, "Wage Earners and Wealth Makers," in Milner et al. (1994), 435–36; Pomeroy (1965), 118; Johansen and Gates (1967), 400–402; Lavender (1956), 353, 411–12; Peirce (1972), 223; d'Eramo (2002), 87; Schwantes (1996), 221; Sale (1976), 115–16.

28. Johansen and Gates (1967), 482, 621; MacDonald (1987), 60; Sale (1976), xi; Pomeroy (1965), 147, 153.

29. Meinig (1968), 5, 435, 511; Johansen and Gates (1967), 370, 375–76; Peirce (1972), 268n; Royce (1886), 35.

30. Pomeroy (1965), 216; MacColl (1979), 7. Johansen and Gates (1967) say only that Pierce had open Klan support (p. 496).

31. MacColl (1979), 476–77, 483–85; Schwantes (1996), 384–85. Kubrick used the mountain vistas and exterior of the Timberline Lodge and the interior of a resort in Colorado.

32. Johansen and Gates (1967), 481, 485–87; Schwantes (1979), 219–20; Ficken and LeWarne (1988), 95.

33. Sale (1976), 153.

Chapter 7. Edens Lush and Frigid

1. Landauer (1999), 1, 10.

2. Wood (1999), 30; McEvedy (1998), 64; Schwantes (1996), 20. One of Cook's men had also killed a chief on the same day, before Cook's death. On Cook inventing the Pacific, or our Pacific, see Arif Dirlik in Dirlik (1993), 5; also Dirlik in Dirlik (1998), 353.

3. Twain quoted in Peirce (1972), 314; Schmitt (2002), 69, 91, 95.

4. Burns quoted in Peirce (1972), 32; see also p. 336; Landauer (1999), 217; Meinig (1993), 166.

5. Parrington quoted in Hofstadter (1968), 414; Royce (1886), 28; Young (1968), 143.

6. Twain (1872), 392; Merry (2000), 230, 236, quoting Lyman; Stewart quoted in Wood (1999), 38; Trask in Dirlik (1998), 358–59; on Tahitian women, see Sherry (1994), 312–13. A phalanx of British missionaries arrived in 1797 and proceeded to quash as much fun as they could there, too (p. 411).

7. See Gananath Obeyesekere's 1992 critique of Marshall Sahlins, and Sahlins's retort, in Sahlins (1995).

8. Quoted in Obeyesekere (1992), 162; see also Landauer (1999), 52.

9. Lippmann quoted in Susman (1973), 47; Cook quoted in Wood (1999), 103.

10. Fuchs (1961), 38, 84; Sahlins (1985), 1–4, 105; Merry (2000), 156–57, 174; Schmitt (2002), 1.

11. Fuchs (1961), 12–13, 68.

12. Merry (2000), 40; Fuchs (1961), 16–19, 21–22, 54, 113, 246–47, 250; Peirce (1972), 338; Coffman (2003), 9, 209; Pletcher (2001), 47.

13. Victoria Wyatt, "Alaska and Hawai'i," in Milner et al. (1994), 582–83; Merry (2000), 128–29; Fuchs (1961), 24–25, 55, 90–91; Coffman (2003), 16–18.

14. Dole (2004), 7.

15. Ibid., 22, 25, 30, 33, 36, 43, 58, 60, 65.

16. Ibid., 73, 75, 97–98; Fuchs (1961), 242.

17. Dole (2004), 82–83. Maybe the past tense isn't appropriate since all this was written in a 2004 book.

18. Examples can be found in Bruggencate (2004), 126. In this book we learn that the pineapple and sugar plantations are responsible for the "modern transformations in the Islands," while providing "for virtually every need of their employees"—housing, health care, retail stores—they even "hired police and meted out justice" (p. vi).

19. Sklar (1988), 83; Katznelson (1996), 140.

20. Landauer (1999), 195.

21. Merk (1963), 233–34.

22. McDougall (1993), 380–81; Fuchs (1961), 3–4, 30–33; Landauer (1999), 144–45, 149; McKinley quoted in Gould (1980), 14; Beale (1956), 65; Sahlins (1995), 102; Coffman (2003), 12; Cooper and Daws (1990), 3.

23. Landauer (1999), 153–54, 158; Osborne (1998), 124. "Half-way house" was the favorite term of Ohio Congressman Charles H. Grosvenor, a good friend of McKinley's and a leading proponent of annexation. On Nagasawa, see Iriye (1972), 41–43. Iriye saw the *Naniwa* incident providing "the final impetus" to American annexation (p. 51).

24. Meinig (1993), 164; Philbrick (2003), 233, 242; Goetzmann (1966a), 102–3; Fuchs (1961), 20–21; Jones (2002), 65, 107; Bryant (1947), 353; Landauer (1999), 7, 131.

25. Landauer (1999), 116–18; Coffman (2003), 8; Linn (1997), 6; Seiden (2001), 10.

26. Landauer (1999), 179–180, 194; Mokyr (1990), 129.

27. Landauer (1999), 201, 205, 249, 254–55, 262.

28. Peirce (1972), 324; Jones (2002), 14, 19; Seiden (2001), 65.

29. Mead quoted in Fuchs (1961), 153; also 179; Coffman (2003), 13.

30. The U.S. government's own term. See LaFeber (1997), 219.

31. Fuchs (1961), 306.

32. Peirce (1972), 337–38, 345–49; Fuchs (1961), 237. Masayo Duus has a full, gripping account of the 1920 strike and the astonishing hypocrisy and violence of the authorities (Duus 1999). See also Cooper and Daws (1990), 171, 185.

33. Fuchs (1961), 290, 297–98, 397–99.

34. Haycox (2002), x–xi; McPhee (1977), 17–18.

35. Ritter (1993), 92–99; Borneman (2003), 16; McPhee (1977), 22, 103, 142; Lang in Haycox (2002), vi.

36. Haycox (2002), 20, 36, 41–43; Borneman (2003), 173–75, 200–203; McPhee (1977), 224–26. Haycox spells the name "Carmacks," Borneman and McPhee have it as "Carmack."

37. Haycox (2002), 61, 68–69, 72; Nalty (1999), 92–93; Borneman (2003), 337–41, 350–52, 364–66.

Chapter 8. Pacific Crossings

1. Dirlik (2001), xxi; research by Ching-Hwang Yen and Persia C. Campbell cited in Okihiro (1994), 41–42; Nugent (2001), 214; Starr (1997), 136.

2. The 1852 quote is from Brott (1982), 9; St. David J. Clair, "The Gold Rush and the Beginnings of California Industry," in Rawls and Orsi (1999), 187; Jackson (1970), 213; McWilliams (1949), 59, 66–67; Bancroft (1886), 699, 708; Royce (1886), 168–69. "Long-time Californ'" is the title of Victor and Brett de Bary Nee's fine book: Nee and Nee (1972).

3. Nee and Nee (1972), 49–52; Saxton (1971), 63; Takaki (1979), 215–49.

4. The *California Farmer* quoted in Worster (1985), 219; Hine and Faragher (2000), 359, citing scholarship by Sucheng Chan and Ronald Tagaki; Hale (1851), 40.

5. Saxton (1971), 8, 149; Igler (2001), 129–30; Nee and Nee (1972), 67; Smith quoted in Stoll (1998), 149. For a laudatory account of "the Chinatown Squad" that might have been written in 1920, see Flamm (1978), 84–94. On contemporary *tong* criminality see Kwong (1996), 120–22.

6. Saxton (1971), 7, 170; Atherton (1945), 154; Starr (1997), 137; Nee and Nee (1972), 15.

7. Rusling (1877), 38, 56, 250, 269, 301, 305.

8. Ibid., 310, 317–18, 320.

9. Dirlik (2001), xxiv, xxxii; Saxton (1971), 202–3; David H. Stratton, "The Snake River Massacre of Chinese Miners, 1887," in Dirlik (2001), 215, 220, 226.

10. Saxton (1971), 205–9, 263; MacDonald (1987), 24–25; Sale (1976), 37–49. (Sale has a detailed account of the Seattle expulsion.) For a long list of Chinese exclusion laws see the appendix in Nee and Nee (1972).

11. McPhee (1966), 90; Klein (1997), 58–60.

12. Wyatt (1997), 7, 112; Genthe quoted in James Lee, "Another View of Chinatown: Yun Gee and the Chinese Revolutionary Artists' Club," in Brook et al. (1998), 166; Wilde quoted in Hine and Faragher (2000), 422; Irwin in Genthe (1912), 27–8.

13. See Henry Yu's excellent discussion of Siu's research, Yu (2001), 133–36, 168.

14. Yu (2001), 172; Chin quoted in Nee and Nee (1972), 377–89.

15. Azuma (2005), 23, 29; Starr (1990), 146–47; Starr (1997), 162; Starr (2002), 55.

16. McWilliams (1945), 39–46; McWilliams (1949), 140–41; Pomeroy (1965), 272; Heizer and Almquist (1971), 160, 165, 181; Modell (1977), 99, 105–7.

17. Starr (2002), 47, 49–50; Iriye (1972), 126–41.

18. Stoddard (1920), vi–vii, xiv, xxxi, 50, 196. The great Franz Boas had already

established, through his "cephalic index," that the various races were equal in mental capacity (Menand [2001], 383–85). For his efforts Boas was denounced as "a radical environmentalist and a Jew" by Harvard anthropologist Ernest Hooten (in Willinsky [1998], 168).

19. Lye (2005), 16, 25, 30, 40–41. Meredith Jung-en Woo first brought "The Unparalleled Invasion" to my attention. On Professor Adams, see George L. Henderson's brilliant dissection: Henderson (1998), 91–96.

20. Ngai (2004), 3, 8, 40, emphasis in original; Heizer and Almquist (1971), 189–90; Henderson (1998), 89; Beard (1935), 193–95; Palumbo-Liu (1999), 39. Ngai notes that many American liberals still remain ambivalent about immigration from the third world (p. 246).

21. Palumbo-Liu (1999), 40; Clements quoted in McWilliams (1939), 139.

22. Lea (1909), 269, 307; Bywater (1925), 97; Modell (1977), 35, 64; Starr (2002), 51–55; Honan (1991); Sackman (2005), 125, 143–58, 295.

23. Bywater (1925), 97. On Yamagata's racial views, see Dickinson (1999), 43–44

24. Duus (2004), 13–31, 162–64, 168–69; Wyatt (1997), 185–89; Noguchi's unpublished manuscript, quoted in Duus (2004), 164.

25. Walker (2004), 81; Clark quoted in Nash (1985), 150; Lotchin (2003), 105.

26. Nugent (2001), 234–37.

27. Ngai (2004), 155–56; Walker (2004), 72–73.

28. Sale (1976), 176–77.

29. MacDonald (1987), 151–53; Sale (1976), 177–78; LaFeber (1997), 221.

30. Tchen (1999), 22; Starr (1973), 406–07; Starr (1990), 7–8.

31. Especially the Los Padres Forest, one of the largest national preserves.

32. Starr (1997), 53–54.

33. Ibid., 99–102.

34. Starr (1990), 336–37.

35. Ibid., 365.

36. Ibid., 190–91; Starr (2002), 56.

37. Kwong (1996), 101; the Korean activities come from the author's experience in Seattle and Chicago. The Korean autonomous area in China has the largest diaspora, a much older population just across the North Korean border.

38. The entering class in 2006 at Berkeley was 46 percent Asian, 56 percent at UC-Irvine, and 43 percent at UCLA. See Timothy Egan, "Little Asia on the Hill," *New York Times Education Life* (January 27, 2007), pp. 24–26.

Chapter 9. A Garden Cornucopia

1. Kelley (1971), 37, 47–48, 165; Stoll (1998), 3; Williams (1997), 14–15.

2. McPhee (1993), 17–18; Federal Writers Project (1939), 18; Lowitt (1984), 196; Peirce (1972), 81–82.

3. Didion quoted in Dawson and Brechin (1999), xiv; Dasmann, "Foreword," in Dawson and Brechin (1999), xi.

4. Frémont and James quoted in Starr (1973), 375, 418.

5. Here I draw on Cumings (1998); see also Kelley (1971), 201–8.

6. Lummis (1892), 269; Davis (1992), 25; Gordon (1972), 99.

7. Walker (2004), 1–3, 32, 51, 88–89, 110. California produced about 2.1 billion pounds of cheese in 2006, compared to Wisconsin's 2.4 billion. See Monica Davey, "Wisconsin's

Crown of Cheese Lies within California's Reach," *New York Times* (September 30, 2006), pp. A1, A13.

8. Hanson (1996), x. Hanson also refers to "present-day legislation and tax codes" that have evolved into "support of *latifundia*" (p. 280). But that happened in the 1880s in California.

9. Theodore W. Fuller, *San Diego Originals*, San Diego Historical Society, www .sandiegohistory.org/bio/Haraszthy/Haraszthy htm.

10. Bean (1968), 152; Ellison (1927), 7–8; McWilliams (1939), gives a figure of 8 million acres owned by 800 grantees (p. 13).

11. McWilliams (1939), 12–14; Johnson (1992), 19–21, 241, and Lavender (1972), 107–9.

12. Fogelson (1967), 15.

13. Ibid., 17; Worster (1985), 103; Pisani (1996), 86–87; Nugent (2001), 87.

14. Kahrl (1982), 28; Igler (2001), 4–5, 13; Starr (1985), 164; Lawrence James Jelinek, "'Property of Every Kind': Ranching and Farming during the Gold-Rush Era," in Rawls and Orsi (1999), 241; McWilliams (1939), 30–31.

15. McWilliams (1949), 101, 157, 169.

16. Williams (1997), 31–33; Walker (2004), 164–66; McWilliams (1939), 51, 60–61; Worster (1985), 99; Daniel (1981), 33. Meinig (1968) says the first combine in eastern Washington probably came from California in 1888 (pp. 394, 499).

17. Arax and Wartzman (2003), 3–6, 21, 97, 338–39; Reisner (1993), 181.

18. McWilliams (1939), 51, 60–61; Worster (1985), 99; Daniel (1981), 33.

19. Pisani (1996), 101.

20. Starr (1985), 135; Vaught (1999), 14–15, 23.

21. McPhee (1966), 11, 63.

22. Ibid., 9–13; Sackman (2005), 5–7; Walker (2004), 24, 114; David Karp, "Lemons, Yes, but Please! Don't Squeeze," *New York Times* (February 2, 2005), pp. D1, D6.

23. Henderson (1998), 64–67; McWilliams (1939), 63; McWilliams (1946), 211–12; Starr (1985), 133, 141; Pomeroy (1965), 110–11; Sackman (2005), 42–43. George Hammond invented a refrigerated car ("an icebox on wheels") in 1868, and a decade later Swift improved it with venting that sent icy air flowing over the whole carload of meat. Cronon (1991), 233–34.

24. Williams (1997), 14–15.

25. McWilliams (1946), 150.

26. McPhee (1966), 23, 98; Pomeroy (1965), 106–8; Stoll (1998), 36–37.

27. Tyrrell (1999), 56–60. As early as 1874 California already had a million eucalyptus trees.

28. Starr (1985), 142–43; Nugent (2001), 90. On the almond as "an instrument of civility," see Vaught (1999), 39.

29. Sackman (2005), 23, 34; McWilliams (1946), 152–53.

30. Stoll (1998), 45, 175.

31. Brunner (1922), 31, 46, 65.

32. Ibid., 24–27; Henderson (1998), 12–13, 64–67; McWilliams (1946), 211–12.

33. Vaught (1999), 53; Vaught emphasizes the progressive virtues of orchard cultivation, which may have been true in the 1890s but not in the twentieth century.

34. Starr (1985), 101.

35. McWilliams (1949), 325; McWilliams (1946), 152; McClung (2000), 92; Smythe (1899), 97, 100, 102–3.

36. Starr (1985), 86.

37. Ibid., 143.

38. McWilliams (1946), 375–78.

39. Ibid., 220.

40. McPhee (1966), 54–57, quoting an orange picker; Henderson (1998), 87, citing research by Gregory Woirol.

41. Sackman (2005), 127, 132; Hine and Faragher (2000), 390; McWilliams (1939), 67–68, 71–75.

42. Sackman (2005), 132–33; Nagle quoted in McWilliams (1939), 107, also 108.

43. Hine and Faragher (2000), 394; Walker (2004), 95, citing research by Masakazu Iwata; Starr (1996), 62–63; McWilliams (1939), 108–13; McWilliams (1949), 114; Vaught (1999), 189.

44. McWilliams (1939), 129, 305.

45. Stoll (1998), 127–31.

46. McGirr (2001), 32, 36, 54, 60; Peirce (1972), 170–72.

47. Ibid., 31.

48. Ibid., 98–104, 135.

49. Quoted in Lieven (2004), 16.

50. Mike Davis wrote that this "real-life Garden of Eden" was drowned by "an estimated three billion tons of concrete (250 pounds per inhabitant)." Davis (1992), 80; see also Sackman (2005), 295.

51. Sackman (2005), 25, 262.

Chapter 10. "There It Is. Take It"

1. Walton (1992), 232.

2. Kahrl (1982), 12–15, 47–48; Starr (1990), 47, 49; Bean (1968), 350; Fogelson (1967), 95. "Top drawer" is in Mulholland (2000), 29.

3. Reisner (1993), 73; Hoffman (1981), 12.

4. Kahrl (1982), 49; Starr (1990), 53; Wyatt (1997), 142. On the drought and the drained city reservoirs, see Kahrl (1982), 489n, who finds no evidence of drought (true) and no evidence that Mulholland drained reservoirs (other experts disagree, e.g., Reisner [1993], 78). Lots of water was clearly draining out into the Pacific, as much as 5 million gallons a day, but Mulholland's granddaughter says it was the result of old, leaky sewers. Mulholland (2000), 103. See also the authoritative account in Hoffman (1981), 96–98; Mulholland may not have been running water into the Pacific, but he was happy to use "warnings of an imminent water famine" to advertise the aqueduct: "We must have it."

5. Hoffman (1981), xiii.

6. Starr (1990), 51. *Beyond Chinatown* is animated by a belief that if someone says two or more people got together to bamboozle the public, this constitutes "conspiracy theory." The book talks of "water conspiracy theory," "overplotted" conspiracies, "shadow" conspiracies, skullduggery done "Chinatown fashion," and the like, while never laying a hand on Kahrl and other historians. See Erie (2006), 42, 45, 49, 53.

7. Robert Towne later said that he "didn't base a single character in *Chinatown* on any person I read about in the Owens Valley episode" (Wyatt [1997], 147). But Mulwray's character draws heavily on Mulholland's life and character, especially his love of the river and his ethical qualities—with the caveat that "he has to swim in the same water we all do."

8. Kahrl (1982), 18–21, 232.

9. Quoted in Reisner (1993), 85–86.

10. Kahrl (1982), 230–31, 312–13; Wyatt (1997), 137, 141; Starr (1990), 162–63; Birmingham (1980), 109–10; McWilliams (1946), 195.

11. Kahrl (1982), 437.

12. Mulholland (2000), xv.

13. Kahrl (1982), 96, 186–88, 227; Hoffman (1981), 125–27; Wyatt (1997), 145; Starr (1990), 54; Fogelson (1967), 86–87. Mulholland's granddaughter responds to claims of syndicate chicanery with the comment, "Certainly no one was forced to sell his land"; the same could be said of a person who innocently sells quartz to a jeweler who knows it to be gold. See Mulholland (2000), 123.

14. Starr (1990), 56; Kahrl (1982), 158.

15. Starr (1990), 97, 110; Fulton (1997), 7–9.

16. Kahrl (1982), 201–02; Starr (1990), 59.

17. Kahrl (1982), 133; Starr (1990), 60–61, 391; Starr (1997), 159.

18. Erie (2004), 61.

19. Starr (1990), 26–27, 43; Morgan (1967), 58.

20. Starr (1996), 276.

21. Ibid., 279–80.

22. Starr (1990), 12–13, 48, 60–61; Starr (1996), 280, 287.

23. Starr (1990), 46.

24. Worster (1985), 4–5, 193.

25. Ibid., 6–7.

26. Ibid., 15, 50, 303.

27. Walker (2004), 125–28, 175–76.

28. McWilliams (1946), 154–56; Starr (1990), 16.

29. Starr (1990), 30–32; see also Fiege (2000), 11, 115.

30. Walton (1992), 150–52; Morris (2002), 115; Worster (1985), 130–31; Roosevelt quoted in Nye (2004), 237.

31. Kelley (1971), 244; Worster calls the 1902 Reclamation Act "the most important single piece of legislation in the history of the West, overshadowing even the Homestead Act" (130–31).

32. Starr (1990), 20; Reisner (1993), 120–21.

33. Starr (1996), 294; Wiley and Gottlieb (1982), 5.

34. Starr (1996), 297; Reisner (1993), 126; Wiley and Gottlieb (1982), 4–5.

35. Starr (1996), 297–300.

36. Priestley quoted in Starr (1996), 302–3.

37. Fulton (1997), 101–2, 109. For an interpretation emphasizing democratic control of Southern California water, see Erie (2006).

38. McClung (2000), 17, 80.

39. Smythe (1899), 152, 200; MacColl (1979), 553; Roosevelt quoted in Sackman (2005), 287; Johansen and Gates (1967), 240–41; Woody Guthrie, "Walking Columbia," quoted in White (1995), 62; Didion (1979), 62.

40. Walker (2004), 150; McClung (2000), 32.

41. Quoted in Pomeroy (1965), 391. On the continuing virtual obsession with Turner's frontier thesis among historians of the West, see Steiner (1995).

Chapter 11. Southern California

1. Kraft and Leventhal (2002), 224–25, 230; Stevenson quoted in Neuenburg (1946), 190.

2. Starr (1973), quoting Chase's 1913 book, *California Coast Trails.*

3. McWilliams (1946), 4–7, 103.

4. McWilliams (1946), 91–92; Starr (1985), 13, 42–43; Jordan quoted in Pomeroy (1965), 141.

5. Nugent and Ridge (1999), 93; McWilliams (1946), 119, 133; McClung (2000), 33.

6. Starr (1985), 70; Jackson (1985), 250; Fogelson (1967), 89; Kahrl (1982), 93.

7. Starr (1985), 55.

8. Nugent (2001), 92–93; Brechin (1999), 257; Tygiel (1994), 21; Birmingham (1980), 23–24; Gerald White, "California Oil Boom of the 1860s: The Ordeal of Benjamin Silliman, Jr.," in Gressley (1966), 2–3.

9. Starr (1985), 124; Nugent (2001), 210–12; Williams (1997), 6–7, 127, 130.

10. Williams (1997), 176, 195, 202–4, 216–17, 227, 272; Hobsbawm (1987), 347.

11. Jonnes (2004), 367; Meinig (2004), 49; Walker (2004), 99; Gordon (2004), 308; Lebergott (1984), 352, 424; Lotchin (2003), 61.

12. De Grazia (2005), 3.

13. Susman (1973), "Introduction"; 126–28.

14. Bureau of the Census figures cited in Fogelson (1967), 78; McWilliams (1946), 113–14; Verge (1993), 1–3; Starr (1997), 182.

15. Kahrl (1982), 260; Adams quoted in McWilliams (1946), 135; Starr (1990), 71–72, 81; Blevin quoted in Starr (1990), 70, 177.

16. Pomeroy (1965), 396; Longstreth (1998), xv, 110, 152–53; Fogelson (1967), 143–45, 157; Williams (1997), 157; Fulton (1997), 72; Mumford quoted in Fulton (1997), 339.

17. Cohen (2004), 20–22; Leach (1993), xiii.

18. Leach (1993), 16–17, 22, 189.

19. Leach (1993), 340; Bruchey (1988), 144, 147; Judt (2005), 338.

20. Marx (1964), 363, quoting Fitzgerald's *The Great Gatsby.*

21. Sachs (1992), 3–12, quoting various people and car advertisements; the quote at the paragraph's end is from Otto Julius Bierbaum, who authored the first German-language book devoted to auto travel.

22. Dirlik (2001), xii.

23. Bottles (1987), 93; Brilliant (1989), 202; Nugent (2001), 22, 225; Bean (1968), 378; Starr (1990), 79–80; d'Eramo (2002), 113; Brinkley (2003), 370; Jackson (1985), 161–63.

24. R. L. Duffus quoted in Pomeroy (1965), 365.

25. Gordon (2004), 298; Susman (1973), 133–37; Ford quoted, p. 136; Schumpeter (1939), 262–70.

26. Hobsbawm (1969), 255.

27. Sachs (1992), 27, 42–45, 47–50.

28. Ross (1995), 21–27, 37–38, 46.

29. Harootunian (2000), 44, 47–50, 258, 382.

30. McClung (2000), 195.

31. Quoted in ibid. 196.

32. Kathleen Karapondo, "Frank Lloyd Wright, Arizona Car Guy," *Sports Car*

Market (April 2005), p. 28. Lynch didn't miss a daily milkshake from 1998 to 2005, according to Jenn McKee, "Filmmaker David Lynch to Discuss Meditation and the Creative Process," *Ann Arbor News* (September 24, 2005), pp. 1, 12. Art critics call Bob's Big Boy "a stunning example of 'Googie' architecture," apparently referring to "1950s modernism." See Patricia Leigh Brown, "California Revisited: How Googie Was My Valley," *New York Times* (November 26, 2000), News of the Week in Review, p. 10.

33. Brilliant (1989), 36–37; Cumings (1997), 174.

34. Longstreth (1999), xv–xvi, 54, 57–59, 81, 111, 130–31; Judt (2005), 338. Victoria de Grazia places her discussion of American self-service supermarkets—"the most important invention in retailing over the previous two decades"—in the mid-1930s (de Grazia [2005], 381). The earliest counterpart to the L.A. supermarket opened in Flushing, Queens, in 1930. Longstreth (1999), 111.

35. Jackson (1985), 263–64; Longstreth (1999), 28–29; Starr (1997), 5–6;

36. Malcolm Gladwell, "The Trouble with Fries," *New Yorker* (March 5, 2001), pp. 52–54, reviewing Eric Schlosser's *Fast Food Nation.*

37. Huxley (1939), 6–12, 15–17, 38–39.

38. Danny Hakim, "Spinning the Wheels of Snoop Dogg's Fleet," *New York Times* (October 28, 2004), pp. B1, B8. On the army's collaboration with the National Hot Rod Association, see Johnson (2004), 98.

39. Klein (1997), 35; Federal Writers Project (1939), 121–22; Adam Goodheart, "Ten Days That Changed History," *New York Times* (July 2, 2006), sec. 4, pp. 1, 3.

40. De Grazia (2005), 294; Starr (1985), 313, 315; Friedrich (1986), 14.

41. McWilliams (1946), 333, 348; Davis (1992), 102; Bean (1968), 384; Starr (1997), 126, 268.

42. Rosenberg (1982), 100–2; Balázs quoted in Rogin (1987), 13; de Grazia (2005), 305; Paul Virilio, *War and Cinema: The Logistics of Perception,* trans. Patrick Camiller (New York: Verso, 1989), 13.

43. De Grazia (2005), 288, 302, 333.

44. Friedrich (1986), 95–96, 273, 330–31; Mann quoted in Nash (1985), 188–89.

45. *Taiwan News,* August 27, 2006, p. 9.

46. McWilliams (1946), 274; Reisner (2004), 31.

47. Starr (1990), 102–3.

48. Starr (1985), 72–74.

49. Kahrl (1982), 175, 178.

50. Quoted in Reisner (1993), 72.

51. Zelinsky (1992), 27.

52. Graves (1930), 27, 122–23, 131, 259, 263, 287, 292, 301.

53. Peirce (1972), 158; Kotkin and Grabowicz (1982), 50–53, 61; Wiley and Gottlieb (1982), 81.

54. Starr (1990), 144; Taylor (1998), 17; Mosley (1990), 34; McWilliams (1946), 85, 321, 324; Starr (1997), 96; Nugent (2001), 166–68; Hine and Faragher (2000), 426–27.

55. McWilliams (1946), 168, 179.

56. Ibid., 157; Wright quoted, pp. 157–58.

57. Adamic quoted in Fogelson (1967), 74; Rand quoted in McClung (2000), 208.

58. Starr (1990), 121–32, quoting Bliven and Adamic.

59. Williams (1997), 295–96, 297–304, 320–21; Jacobs quoted, p. 346.

60. Kennan (1989), 148–50.

Chapter 12. The State as Pretense of Itself

1. Dean Acheson, "An American Attitude toward Foreign Affairs," November 28, 1939, in *Morning and Noon* (Boston: Houghton Mifflin, 1965), 267–75; see also Acheson's reflections on the speech, pp. 216–17.

2. Federal policy had a huge impact on the South as well; like the industrialization of the West it was an impact mostly neglected in the literature until Bruce Shulman's *From Cottonbelt to Sunbelt* (1994).

3. Markusen et al. (1991), 8–9.

4. Reisner (1993), 119–21, 146; Wiley and Gottlieb (1982), 3.

5. Worster (1985), 52–56.

6. White (1995), 73–82; and Stuart Chase, "A Vision in Kilowatts," *Fortune* (April 1933), quoted in White (1995), 58; Reisner (1993), 155, 158, 161–66. See also Worster (1985), 269–71; Schwantes (1996), 13.

7. Starr (1996), 318–19, 323.

8. Nugent (2001), 251; Carl Abbott, "The Federal Presence," in Milner et al. (1994), 482; Jackson (1985), 139.

9. Weigley (1967), 419, 435; Sherry (1987), 22, 60. Sparrow (1996), 227, 244. I use "air force" to designate the Army Air Corps (1926–41), the Army Air Forces of World War II, and the subsequent U.S. Air Force.

10. Bryant (1947), 419–23, 432–34, 440–41; Davis, Mayhew, and Miller (2003), 13; Langer and Gleason (1952), 549.

11. Langer and Gleason (1952), 588; Evans and Peattie (1997), 373–80, 475.

12. Landauer (1999), 264–66, 271; Seiden (2001), 41; LaFeber (1997), 211; Evans and Peattie (1997), xix, 304–14, 344–46; McComas (1991), passim.

13. Ienaga (1978), 33; Gordon Prange, *At Dawn We Slept: The Untold Story of Pearl Harbor* (New York: Penguin Books, 1981), 539; McComas (1991), 95; Jones (2002), 27. The casualty figures in Prange and Jones differ slightly; some sources say as many as 65 civilians died.

14. Quoted in Charles Beard, *President Roosevelt and the Coming of the War, 1941: A Study in Appearances and Realities* (New Haven: Yale University Press, 1948), 244–45, 418, 519, 526–27. See also Richard N. Current, "How Stimson Meant to 'Maneuver' the Japanese," *Mississippi Valley Historical Review* 40:1 (1953): 67–74. Michael Sherry has a cogent discussion of Roosevelt's and Stimson's thinking, and concludes that Roosevelt did not want or expect general war with Japan, but may have reasoned that an undeclared war would help him mobilize the country more. See Sherry (1987), 114. On the perfect metaphor of the "slipknot," see LaFeber (1997), 182–90.

15. McComas (1991), 107.

16. Bean (1968), 425–26; Nash (1985), 19; Starr (2002), viii; McWilliams (1949), 233. Discrepancies in the aggregate totals derive from Nash, the standard source, using the years 1941 to 1945, while others use 1940–46.

17. Nash (1985), 5, citing research by Leonard J. Arrington; White (1993), 496–97; Taft quoted in White (1980), 17. See also p. vii.

18. Nash (1985), 19–20; Heiner (1991), 170–76; White (1980), 18; Wiley and Gottlieb (1982), 21–23; DeVoto quoted, 19. Kaiser helped to build the Hoover, Grand Coulee, and Shasta dams (although he only supplied cement for Shasta) (Heiner, p. 267).

19. White (1980), 48–49, 67–71, 74, 81; Gordon (2004), 353; Johansen and Gates

(1967), 523; Ficken and LeWarne (1988), 131; Fehrenbach (1968), 654; Taylor and Wright (1947), 175.

20. Lotchin (1992), 65, 73, 184, 231; Sherry (1987), 193; Arthur C. Verge in Nugent and Ridge (1999), 244–45.

21. Johnson (1993), 79–80, 127; Starr (2002), 147–49.

22. Starr (2004), 357; Pomeroy (1965), 129; Johnson (1993), 14, 18–19, 24.

23. Nash (1985), 26–29, 69; Johnson (1993), 33, 53; Heiner (1991), 119–22, 134–35, 151; Starr (2002), 68, 74–76, 146; Pomeroy (1965), 297; Abbott (1993), 4.

24. Johnson (1993), 62–63; Wollenberg (1990), 10–11.

25. Starr (2002), 147–48; Cumings (1997), 323–24.

26. Heiner (1991), 110–12; Nash (1985), 27–29.

27. Heiner (1991), 159.

28. Wollenberg (1990), 7–9; McCartney (1988), 12, 50–53, 208.

29. Nash (1985), 74; Wollenberg (1990), viii, 29–31, 39, 53, 90–91, 102–3; McCartney (1988), 66.

30. Starr (1997), 94–97, 105–8.

31. Ibid., 109–14.

32. Davis, "The Next Little Dollar: The Private Governments of San Diego," in Davis, Mayhew, and Miller (2003), 28–29, 46–47; Starr (1997), 90–93.

33. Starr (1990), 91–92; Starr (1997), 102–5; Lotchin (1992), 37–38, 43.

34. Starr (1997), 90–93; Starr (2002), 144; Davis, Mayhew, and Miller (2003), 7.

35. See Nash (1985), 59, 63, 67; he lists many navy bases and naval air stations, and army bases in Los Angeles and San Francisco; also Cragg (2000), 25–32; Starr (2002), 77; Abbott (1993), 9; Davis, "The Next Little Dollar: The Private Governments of San Diego," in Davis, Mayhew, and Miller (2003), 60–61.

36. Johnson (1993), 2; McWilliams (1949), 9; Nash (1985), 38, 58.

37. *Fortune* quoted in Pomeroy (1965), 297; Lotchin (2003), 13, 56; Starr (2002), 135, 151; Nash (1985), 64.

38. Himes quoted in Starr (2002), 112, 115; McWilliams (1946), 324; Nugent (2001), 266–67; Nash (1985), 91–92, 99–100; MacColl (1979), 580–623.

39. Nugent (2001), 270–71.

40. Cayton (1963), 1–3, 34–35, 44–47.

41. Rae (1968), vii, 2–3, 8–10, 71; Starr (1990), 116–17.

42. Rae (1968), 30–31, 66; Starr (1990), 265–67; Lotchin (1992), 117–18.

43. Hise (1997), 117.

44. Lotchin (1992), 93–95, 100, 103; Starr (1997), 64; Starr (2002), 136; Sherry (1987), 187.

45. Rae (1968), 95–96, 104–8.

46. Ibid., 113–114, 139, 149–51; Lotchin (1992), 179–80.

47. McWilliams (1949), 14–15.

48. Starr (2002), 124–25, 138–39; Nash (1985), 92.

49. Abbott (1993), 21; Bird and Sherwin (2006), 206; Nash (1985), 154–55.

50. Nash (1985), 28–29; Schwantes (1996), 422–23; Sale (1976), 137, 180–83; Rhodes (1986), 584.

51. MacDonald (1987), 144–46; Nugent (2001), 257–59; Nash (1985), 62, 75, 77, 79; Pomeroy (1965), 288; Kesselman (1990), 2, 13; Johansen and Gates (1967), 529; MacColl

(1979), 571–84; White (1993), 499; Lotchin (2003), 10; Ficken and LeWarne (1988), 138–40; Stanley Goldberg in Hevly and Findlay (1998), 65.

52. Hevly and Findlay (1998), 64–65; Schwantes (1996), 425.

53. U.S. Census data, cited in Nash (1985), 218; White (1993), 501. Brown and Root was central to the rise of Lyndon Johnson in Texas, illustrating the bipartisan nature of the military-industrial complex. See Caro (1983), xv. Now called Kellogg, Brown and Root, it has mastered "the instant American military base," well described in Kaplan (2005), 197.

54. First table in Nash (1985), 217–19, from the 1953 *Statistical Abstract;* second table in Nash (1985), 7, from U.S. Census, County Data Book, 1947.

55. Starr (2002), 153.

56. McWilliams (1949), 233, 236; Starr (2002), 207; Starr (2004), 310.

57. Lotchin (2003), 175–77.

Chapter 13. Postwar California and the Rise of Western Republicanism

1. McWilliams (1946), 371–74.

2. Bean (1968), 493.

3. De Beauvoir (1954), 112, 129–30.

4. In an important but highly technical book on location and "space-economy" published six years before California's population surpassed New York's, Harvard's Walter Isard reproduced a 1940 "population potential" map that showed California's population density along the coast at the same level as Nebraska's and its interior population as equivalent to Utah's; Isard then commented that California's population potentials were actually "of considerably smaller value" than the other two states. See Isard (1956), 66–67.

5. Robbins (1994), 187; Nash (1985), 38; Hornbeck (1983), 76; Fulton (1997), 258; Pomeroy (1965), 308–9; Kling, Olin, and Poster (1991), 15, 22.

6. Friedrich (1986), 343; Kotkin and Grabowicz (1982), 121–23; see also White (1993), 613.

7. Davis, "The Next Little Dollar: The Private Governments of San Diego," in Davis, Mayhew, and Miller (2003), 65; Bryant (1947), 552–53.

8. See Cumings (1990), for a full discussion; also Markusen et al. (1991), 10, citing Council of Economic Advisors data.

9. Davis, "Next Little Dollar," 66–67, 78; White (1993), 541; Lotchin (1992), 65, 73, 184, 231; Sherry (1987), 193.

10. Peirce (1972), 165–69.

11. *Statistical Abstract of the United States* figures, cited in White (1993), 609–10; U.S. Department of Defense, *Prime Contract Awards by Region and State,* cited in Markusen et al. (1991), 13, 18–19, 33–36; also Markusen et al. (1991), 231, 267.

12. Markusen et al. (1991), 82; Johnson (2004), 63.

13. Brown quoted in Kotkin and Grabowicz (1982), 5, 235; and in Winchester (1991), 25.

14. Wills (1969), 151.

15. Mitchell (1998), 43; Starr (2002), 284.

16. Kyle Palmer wrote this in the *Los Angeles Times,* May 18, 1950, quoted in Mitchell (1998), 4; see also 17–26; Bush is quoted on p. 66.

17. Mitchell (1998), 47–48, 97–98, 154–56, 228–30, 244; Harriman quoted on p. 249.

18. The voluminous NSC records held at the Eisenhower Presidential Library,

Abilene, Kansas, are primarily in the Whitman file. At the 193rd meeting of the NSC on April 13, 1954, for example, Nixon noted the chances of influencing the regime's direction, were the United States to open trade with China. Roger Morris, Nixon's best biographer, wrote that Kissinger was flabbergasted after his first meeting with Nixon in December 1969 at the Pierre Hotel when he learned that Nixon wanted "to reorganize China." See Morris, *Uncertain Greatness: Henry Kissinger and American Foreign Policy* (New York: Harper and Row, 1977), 203.

19. Mills (1956), 212n.

20. Patterson (1972), 558–60.

21. For a good summary of Taft's views see Hogan (1998), 99–101, 141–43, 394–96; also Patterson (1972), 196–99. His views were much more nuanced than his critics thought; he was, for example, a strong supporter of the creation of Israel.

22. Burnham (1970), 6–10, 142–43.

23. Whitman file, Eisenhower Presidential Library, Abilene, Kans.

24. Key quoted in Rogin and Shover (1970), xiii, 19–20; Mills (1956), 225.

25. Zolberg in Katznelson and Shefter (2002), 44; Mayhew (2002), 40–41. Mayhew does mention Korean War spending on p. 123, but without further development.

26. Phillips (1969), 435; McGirr (2001), 41; Rogin and Shover (1970), 153–57, 173. In the 1990s the United States had some 800,000 security guards, compared to about half a million police. See McRae (1994), 35.

27. Reagan quoted in Limerick (1987), 324.

28. McGirr (2001), 24–27, 33.

29. Kling, Olin, and Poster (1991), 1; Walker (2004), 58–59, 254.

30. White (1993), 601–7.

31. Hine and Faragher (2000), 528

32. Fulton (1997), 46–47, 153–54.

33. Stegner quoted in Schrag (1999), 30.

34. Schrag (1999), 33–35, 47; Lotchin (1992), 315.

35. Quoted in Wyatt (1997), 211.

36. Schrag (1999), 54–55.

37. Robert Fishman, "Foreword," in Fogelson (1967, 1993), xxv. For an excellent account of the disturbances and the "black-Korean conflict" see Nancy Ablemann and John Lie, *Blue Dreams: Korean Americans and the Los Angeles Riots* (Cambridge: Harvard University Press, 1997).

38. Starr (2004), 238–41, 261–62; Kotkin and Grabowicz (1982), 9; 250–51, 257; Schrag (1999), 53.

39. Fred A. Bernstein, "One Town Stops Time by Turning off the Water," *New York Times* (October 8, 2005), Real Estate section, p. 16.

40. Patricia Leigh Brown, "Bringing down the House, California Style," *New York Times,* carried by the *International Herald-Tribune* (July 21, 2004), p. 9.

41. Jim Robbins, "Dam and Waste Will Go, Freeing Two Rivers," *New York Times* (August 4, 2005), p. A12.

42. Davis (1992), 124–30.

43. Schrag (1999), 57–60.

44. M. Gottdiener and George Kephart, "The Multinucleated Metropolitan Region: A Comparative Analysis," in Kling, Olin, and Poster (1991), 45.

45. Gottlieb et al. (2005), 78–9; Allen and Turner (2002), 10–11, 35, 40, 47.

Chapter 14. In California's Shadow

1. Gordon (2004), 374.
2. Sale (1976), 180–82; Markusen et al. (1991), 165–66.
3. Sale (1976), 185–88.
4. Upper Left at upper-left.blogspot.com/2003—11—16—upper-left—archive.html.
5. Markusen et al. (1991), 156–57; MacDonald (1987), 182–83.
6. Sale (1976), 184–85.
7. Leslie Wayne, "Boeing Bets the House," *New York Times* (May 7, 2006), pp. 3–1, 3–7.
8. MacDonald (1987), 155, 173; Robbins et al. (1983), 217.
9. Winchester (1991), 317–18.
10. Sale (1976), 214.
11. Markusen et al. (1991), 161.
12. Sale (1976), 248.
13. Edward Banfield, *Big City Politics: A Comparative Guide to the Political Systems of Atlanta, Boston, Detroit, El Paso, Los Angeles, Miami, Philadelphia, St. Louis, Seattle* (New York: Random House, 1965), 132–33.
14. Clark entry, Wikipedia.com; Nicholas D. Kristof, "Another Small Step for Earth," *New York Times*, News of the Week in Review (July 30, 2006), p. 13.
15. Peirce (1972), 210; Nugent (2001), 389.
16. Schwantes (1996), 402–6.
17. Mark Landler, "Two Brands Running as a Team to Overtake Nike," *New York Times* (August 4, 2005), p. C4.
18. Meinig (1969), 88–89.
19. Fehrenbach (1968), 82–92, 654, 671–73, 707, 711; McMurtry (1968), 18.
20. Fehrenbach (1968), 666.
21. Meinig (1969), 104–6.
22. Phillips (2004), 3–8, 20–24.
23. Ibid., 24–29.
24. Ibid., 42–43.
25. Didion (1968), 198.
26. Coffman (2003), 52, 341.
27. Fuchs (1961), 379; Schmitt (2002), 10, 283; Merry (2000), 123. The U.S. military says it owns or controls 16 percent of the land, but other sources put the figure at 25 percent. See Ferguson and Turnbull (1999), 1.
28. Johnson (2004), 5; Ferguson and Turnbull (1999), 163; David J. Kilcullen, "New Paradigms for 21st Century Conflict," *eJournalUSA* (May 2007), usinfo.state.gov/journals/itps/ijpe/kilcullen.htm.
29. Brian Linn has a superb recounting of Pacific Army life between the wars in Linn (1997), 115–21; also 128–29. See also Ferguson and Turnbull (1999), 53.
30. William H. Whyte, *The Organization Man* (New York: Simon and Schuster: 1956), 280; Ferguson and Turnbull (1999), 81.
31. Reporting subsequent to the event showed that the ship was not on routine maneuvers but went out only because the navy didn't want to disappoint the civilians.
32. Fuchs (1961), 380, 383–87; Schmitt (2002), 105, 111; Brown et al. (1982), 98–99; Coffman (2003), 276; Wood (1999), 48.

33. Cooper and Daws (1990), passim.

34. See Trask (1993).

35. Borneman (2003), 388–94.

36. Haycox (2002), 2–3, 8, 10, 101; Borneman (2003), 502–13; McPhee (1977), 130–31. McPhee didn't take to Anchorage: he called it "the northern rim of Trenton," "wild as Yonkers," "an American spore."

37. Haycox (2002), 8, 97–100.

38. McPhee (1977), 126, 171, 198, 271, 297, 419–21, 436; Schwantes (1996), 525, giving population density figures for 1990.

39. Haycox (2002), 9, 16, 80–84, 107, 125–27.

40. Ibid., 140–42; Borneman (2003), 200–4. It was never proved that the pilot was intoxicated, but most experts believe that he was.

41. Witold Rybczynski, "Shipping News," *New York Review of Books* (August 10, 2006), pp. 22–25.

42. Rybczynski, "Shipping News"; Levinson (2006), 4, 7–9, 254–63, 284n.

43. Levinson (2006), 195–97.

44. Ibid., 237, 273; Meinig (2004), 87, 262–63; Erie (2004), 14; Keith Bradsher, "China's Growth Creates a Boom for Cargo Ships," *New York Times* (August 28, 2003), p. A1, C6; also Bradsher, "At the Beating Heart of an Export Machine," *New York Times* (January 26, 2003), sec. 3, pp. 1, 13

45. Rybczynski, "Shipping News"; Levinson (2006), 275.

46. See these episodes in Zia (2000), 24, 98–99, 297.

47. Palumbo-Liu (1999), 151, 153–54.

Chapter 15. Archipelago of Empire

1. Mills (1956); I also draw on an appreciative essay by John H. Summers, "The Deciders," *New York Times Book Review* (May 14, 2006), p. 39. David Gibbs has noted how concerns about high defense spending materialized again in the late 1970s and in the early 1990s, only to disappear with the "war on terror." See Gibbs (2004).

2. Acheson (1969), 7.

3. Spending went above the $400 billion point in 1968 (Vietnam) and during the 1983–88 Reagan buildup. Michael E. O'Hanlon, "Limiting the Growth of the U.S. Defense Budget," Brookings Institution *Policy Brief* no. 95 (March 2002); also table, "National Defense Outlays," *Statistical Abstract of the United States, 2004–2005* (Washington, D.C.: Government Printing Office, 2006), p. 326. It stood at about $622 billion in constant dollars for fiscal year 2008, or approximately 4 percent of GNP. (David S. Cloud, "Record $622 Billion Budget Requested for the Pentagon," *New York Times* [February 3, 2007], p. A11.) For an excellent and succinct account of how from 1947 to 1952 American planners linked Northeast Asia and Western Europe together in a productivist growth coalition and then primed global economic pumps through military Keynesianism, see Borden (1984), 3–17.

4. See my longer discussion in Cumings (1990), 26–27.

5. Williams (1959), 20–26.

6. In May 1966 de Gaulle said he wanted "full sovereignty [over] French territory" and so asked Washington to take American forces and bases home. See Johnson (2004), 194.

7. I am indebted to Patrick Karl O'Brien for discussion on these points, and for his paper, "The Pax Brittannica and the International Order, 1688–1914," presented at the Osaka University of Foreign Studies Workshop on Global History, November 22–23, 1999.

8. Katzenstein (2005), 2.

9. The number changes frequently; these are Defense Department figures in Johnson (2004), 4–5, and Johnson (2006), 5–6. See also Ferguson and Turnbull (1999), xiii.

10. McMurtry quoted in Little (1986), 53–54; see also p. 58.

11. Latham (1997). Marx referred to nineteenth-century colonies as "the state externally." See Marx (1857–58), 264.

12. Eisenhower quoted in Sherry (1995), 233–35.

13. Johnson (2004), 79–80.

14. McCartney (1988), 167–68, 170, 177, 178–79, 213–14.

15. U.S. Senate, Committee on Armed Services, 87th Congress, January 18, 1962, "Nominations of McCone, Korth, and Harlan" (Washington, D.C.: Government Printing Office,1962), p. 35; Joint Committee on Atomic Energy, U.S. Senate, 85th Congress, July 2, 1958, "Nomination of John A. McCone to be a Member of the Atomic Energy Commision" (Washington, D.C.: Government Printing Office, 1958), pp. 2–18, 56. I am indebted to Meredith Jung-en Woo for these sources.

16. Mills (1956), 175–76; Unruh (1979), 201, 210; Cunliffe (1968), ch. 1; Pletcher (2001), 119; Hobsbawm (1987), 351; Sherry (1995), 5.

17. LaFeber (1989), 11; Katznelson in Katznelson and Shefter (2002), 90–92, 98–99.

18. Mills (1956), 179; Linn (1997), 6, 52.

19. Linn (1997), 53, 62–65; Anderson and Cayton (2005), 342–43.

20. Weigley (1967), 475, 486, 568; White (1980), 1–2.

21. Schonberger (1989), 259, 269; Cumings (1990), 45–58.

22. Katzenstein (2005), 35, 136–37, 219–20.

23. Greg Grandin is right to locate some of the roots of George W. Bush's unilateralism in Reagan administration interventions in Nicaragua and Guatemala, with John Negroponte, John Bolton, Elliott Abrams, and other neoconservatives playing important roles. See Grandin (2006), 5–6. But these interventions were little different from the multitude of similar episodes going back to the war with Spain, and all of them were subordinate to the more important Pacific and East Asian involvements.

24. Millard (2001), 18–24.

25. Tsuneo Oshiro, Kazuhisa Ogawa, and Koji Murata in Hashimoto, Mochizuki, and Takara (2005), 53, 57–58, 70–72, 115, 121; Cragg (2000), 364–67; Kozy K. Amemiya in Johnson (1999), 54.

26. Casualty totals for Okinawa can never be accurate because so many civilians simply disappeared in battle or threw themselves into the ocean. Masahide Ota estimates 130,000 civilians "killed in action," which includes 107,539 counted and 23,764 estimated (Ota [1981], 95). The Armitage Report represented the views of a sixteen-member study group; Democrat Joseph Nye was a member but the majority were Republicans. The report was issued on October 11, 2000.

27. Keyso (2000), 99, 102, 108.

28. Cragg (2000), 360.

29. James Brooke, "Looking for Friendly Overseas Base, Pentagon Finds It Already Has One," *New York Times* (April 4, 2004), p. A15.

30. Burke (2004), 177–86; Kaplan (2005), 56n, 247.

31. Kaplan (2005), 44, 161, 174, 197.

32. Burke (2004), xiv–xv, 19, 21.

33. Evans and Peattie (1997), 5, 303, 373.

34. Cragg (2000), 349–52; Eric Talmadge, "Kitty Hawk Still Has a Few Lives before the Moth Balls," *Japan Times* (July 23, 2004), p. 3.

35. Neferti Xina M. Tadiar, "Sexual Economies in the Asia-Pacific Community," in Dirlik (1993), 201.

36. Pendle (2005), 157–58.

37. Ibid., 32–33, 101–3; Lee (1992). On how arroyos are created by nature, see Davis (1998), 11.

38. Lord (2005), 84, 86–87; Pendle (2005), 157, 177, 180, 185.

39. See the JATO photo in Carter (2004), 46; see also Lee (1992); Carter (2004), 72–3; Lord (2005), 69, 89–91, 95; Pendle (2005), 199–201. Pendle notes that the roof tar story might be apocryphal.

40. Lord (2005), 88–89, 111; Pendle (2005), 194–96.

41. Lee (1992).

42. Wilson in Carter (2004), 6.

43. Carter (2004), 42; Lee (1992).

44. Lee (1992); Pendle (2005), 217–59.

45. Carter (2004), 192; Pendle (2005), 6–8, 299–307; Lee (1992); Chang (1996), 143–50, 188. A nuclear physicist at Berkeley, Wang Ganchang, also went back to China and became a central figure in the PRC's atomic bomb project. See Chalmers Johnson, "Big Bucks, Big Bangs," *London Review of Books* (20 July 2006), p. 21. Wang went home in 1949, and I do not know if security problems in the United States had anything to do with his return.

46. Rich and Janos (1994), 111–12.

47. Ibid., 7, 24, 107, 185, 203, 214, 245, 308, 347.

48. Markusen et al. (1991), 90–92, 97.

49. Lotchin (1992), 320, 353; Pomeroy (1965), 302.

50. Lotchin (1992), 1, 4–5; Markusen et al. (1991), 39, 43, 51–53.

51. FitzGerald (2000), 20; Peirce (1972), 280, 286; Carroll (2006), 486.

52. Winchester (1991), 196–200; I tried to improve on Winchester's characterization of CINCPAC but couldn't. See also Larson quoted in Ferguson and Turnbull (1999), 79–80, and Kaplan (2005), 134–35.

53. Ferguson and Turnbull (1999), 103–4.

54. David E. Sanger and James Glanz, "U.S. Seeking New Strategy for Buttressing Iraq's Government," *New York Times* (June 11, 2006), nytimes.com; Tom Englehart, "Can You Say 'Permanent Bases'?" *Nation* (March 27, 2006), pp. 28–29.

55. Kennan wrote in 1994 that containment, to him, was "primarily a diplomatic and political task, though not wholly without military implications." Once the Soviets were convinced that more expansionism would not help them, "then the moment would have come for serious talks with them about the future of Europe." After the Marshall Plan, the Berlin blockade, and other measures, he thought that moment had arrived by 1950. However, "it was one of the great disappointments of my life to discover that neither our Government nor our Western European allies had any interest in entering into such discussions at all. What they and the others wanted from Moscow, with respect to the future of Europe, was essentially 'unconditional surrender.' They were prepared to wait for

it. And this was the beginning of the 40 years of Cold War." *New York Times* (March 14, 1994), op-ed page.

56. For a fuller discussion see Cumings (2003), ch. 1.

57. A 1970 Foreign Relations Committee statement quoted in Johnson (2004), 152.

Chapter 16. Silicon Valley

Epigraph from a Rochester New York newspaper article in 1846 about the telegraph, quoted in Seidensticker (2006), 154.

1. Schwartz, Leyden, and Hyatt (2000), v; Kaplan (1999), 9–10, 120–21; Lee, Miller, Hancock, and Rowen (2000), 2, 43; Nevens in Lee, Miller, Hancock, and Rowen (2000), 81, 83; Deutschman (2000), 182–83. Bureau of Labor Statistics data show that productivity rose 12.3 percent from the last quarter of 1996 to the third quarter of 2000, or about 3 percent a year. See "Productivity of Workers Increases, as Do Labor Costs," *New York Times* (November 3, 2000), p. C4.

2. Gordon (2004), 417; Winslow (1995), xiii.

3. Castells offers a contrary view that I find fascinating but unconvincing. He writes that the information revolution transformed how we communicate, trade, consume, and make war, which I think is true. But it has not transformed "the way we think" or the way "we live, we die," and least of all has it transformed the way "we make love," Americans still being many miles behind the *Kama Sutra* or the *Thousand Nights and a Night*. See Castells (1998), 2; also 343.

4. Clyde Prestowitz wrote as if Japan were already hegemonic and claimed that the United States "had effectively lost its consumer electronics industry by the mid-1970s" and faced a "crisis" in the semiconductor industry in 1985. See *Trading Places* (New York: Basic Books, 1989), 92–93, and Cumings (1998), ch. 1.

5. Linder (1986), 1–3, 118; McRae (1994), 33, 213, 251.

6. Research by Edward N. Wolff, cited in Sylvia Nasar, "Cars and VCRs Aren't Necessarily the First Domino," *New York Times* (May 3, 1992), p. E6; also data from the McKinsey Global Institute cited in David Brooks, "The Nation of the Future," *New York Times* (February 2, 2006), p. A25.

7. Derian (1990), 5–6, 175, 267, 285.

8. In September 1996 Sandia Labs announced that it had built a Janus parallel supercomputer with teraflop (1 trillion calculations per second) capability, by far the fastest computer in the world. See also Martin Fackler, "Japan's Chip Makers Search for a Strategy," *New York Times* (January 2, 2006), p. C5.

9. Bureau of Labor Statistics cited in *New York Times* (November 3, 2000), p. C4, and in Martin Crutsinger, "Productivity Gains Slowed a Lot in 2005," Associated Press story carried in *Ann Arbor News* (February 3, 2006), p. 4. See also Jeff Madrick "Economic Scene," *New York Times* (January 24, 2002), p. C2; Richard W. Stevenson, "Greenspan Hails Output Gains in Sluggish Economy," *New York Times* (October 24, 2002), nytimes .com; and Austan Goolsbee, "How the U.S. Has Kept the Productivity Playing Field Tilted to Its Advantage," *New York Times* (June 21, 2007), p. C3. Other figures come from David Brooks, "The Nation of the Future," *New York Times* (February 2, 2006), p. A25; and from Hal R. Varian, "American Companies Show an Edge in Putting Information to Work," *New York Times* (January 12, 2006), p. C3.

10. Daniel Gross "Economic View," *New York Times* (December 25, 2005), sec. 3, p. 3, citing Dale Jorgenson and his collaborators. See also Castells (1996), 45.

11. Rowen in Lee, Miller, Hancock, and Rowen (2000), 191.

12. Hafner and Lyon (1996), 12, 151–52; Cringely (1992), 86–87.

13. Hiltzik (1999), 17, 37, 48, 58, 150–51, 155–57; Wolfe (1983).

14. Hiltzik (1999), xiii–xv; xxi–xxvi, 45–48, 65, 122–23, 144; Hafner and Lyon (1996), 151–52, 189.

15. Hafner and Lyon (1996), 223–27.

16. Cringely (1992), 304.

17. Hiltsik (1999), 264, 311–12, 329, 332–33, 340–42, 358–60, 368–59; Linzmayer (2004), 75; Cringely (1992), 105–06.

18. Hertzfeld (2005), 192; Hiltsik (1999), 195–96.

19. Schwartz, Leyden and Hyatt (2000); Moore in Rhodes (1999), 243; Gordon and Shef in Rhodes (1999), 279–81.

20. Lee in Lee, Miller, Hancock, and Rowen (2000), 94–123.

21. Lécuyer in Lee, Miller, Hancock, and Rowen (2000), 159, 166. San Jose ranked first and Washington second in 1989, for example, as a "defense-dependent community." See Mia Gray, Elyse Golob, Ann R. Markusen, and Sam Ock Park, "The Four Faces of Silicon Valley," in Markusen (1999), 295.

22. Schwartz, Leyden, and Hyatt (2000), 316; Castells (1998), 339–40.

23. For example, Winslow (1995).

24. Federal Writers Project (1939), 117–18.

25. Timothy J. Sturgeon in Kenney (2000), 19–21, 28, 30, 35.

26. Rosenberg (1982), 92–96; Chandler (2001), 17.

27. Timothy J. Sturgeon in Kenney (2000), 27, 30–33; Lécuyer (2006), 15, 19, 25–28, 30, 49.

28. Kaplan (1999), 33–37, 44; Lavender (1972), 442; Lécuyer (2006), 53–55, 77, 83; Damon Darlin, "A Shrine to Time Spent Tinkering in a Modest Garage," *New York Times* (December 4, 2005), p. N37. Darlin points out that Walt Disney started his business in a garage, too—in 1922.

29. Lécuyer (2006), 55–59, 92–98,

30. Ibid., 101–4, 116–17, 122, 124.

31. Steve Lohr, "New Economy," *New York Times* (February 2, 2004), p. C6.

32. Timothy J. Sturgeon in Kenney (2000), 42–43, 52.

33. Riordan and Hoddeson (1997), 1–4, 6–7, 202–4, 254; Berlin (2005), 53; Kaplan (1999), 38–9, 40–46. The quotation is from the June 30, 1948, news conference when Bell Labs announced the discovery, which got reported on page 46 of the *New York Times* the next day (Riordan and Hoddeson, 164–65).

34. Riordan and Hoddeson (1997), 225, 234–39; Kaplan (1999), 45–47; Berlin (2005), 5, 26, 70, 87; Cringely (1992), 37.

35. Quoted in Morgan (1967), 7. Meanwhile Alfred Chandler Jr. defined IBM as the "path definer" for the industry from the 1950s into the 1990s, another good example of Eastern blinkers. Chandler (2001), 82.

36. Berlin (2005), 182–86; Lécuyer in Lee, Miller, Hancock, and Rowen (2000), 167, 177–83; Winslow (1995), 30; the best discussion of ultra-reliability is in Lécuyer (2006), 148–61.

37. Berlin (2005), 210–13.

38. Kaplan (1999), 45–49, 68–69; Berlin (2005), 217; John Markoff, "I.B.M. Researchers Find a Way to Keep Moore's Law on Pace," *New York Times* (February 20, 2006), nytimes.com.

39. Lowen (1997), 31–33, 37–38.

40. Ibid., 69–72.

41. Hornbeck (1983), 95; McCartney (1988), 78n.

42. Lowen (1997), 78, 89, 115, 120–21, 137. David Packard took a personal interest in a professor named John Bunzel, said to be "anti-nuclear." In 1962 Packard asked Stanford's president to "flag" his file. The Political Science Department voted unanimously for Bunzel's promotion, but he was denied tenure (Lowen, p. 219).

43. Stuart J. Leslie in Kenney (2000), 60–61, 63; Lécuyer (2006), 7.

44. Markusen et al. (1986), 78, 99.

45. Deutschman (2000), 33, 287.

46. Linzmayer (2004), 1–2; Mokyr (1990), viii.

47. Linzmayer (2004), 5–8.

48. Ibid., 10–12, 18, 23, 27–33, 45; Lécuyer (2006), 1.

49. Linzmayer (2004), 94–98.

50. Wozniak in Hertzfeld (2005), xv.

51. Kaplan (1999), 134–35, 138–42; Winslow (1995), 68; Symonds (2003), 59–63, 412–13. Ellison acknowledges that he first heard about relational databases "at a meeting with the CIA." Symonds (2003), 59.

52. Cringely (1992), 298–303; Annalee Saxenian in Kenney (2000), 143.

53. Hiltzik (1999), 264, 311–12.

54. Kaplan (1999), 226–29.

55. Lewis (2000), 27–54, 75, and passim; Clark (1999), 7, 34.

56. By the time Bill Hewlett passed away in 2001, he and David Packard had dropped more than $300 million on the university, an amount equivalent to Leland Stanford's original endowment. Obituary, "He Led the 'HP Way,'" *San Francisco Chronicle* (January 13, 2001), p. A15.

57. Clark (1999), 22–25, 32; Clark quoted in Kaplan (1999), 232.

58. Kaplan (1999), 234–37, 241–43, 249–51; Clark (1999), 7. Clark told Lewis he wanted $18 million for Mosaic when he had seven employees—the Illinois seven. See Lewis (2000), 71.

59. Clark (1999), 38–40, 49. Berners-Lee is remarkably equable about his pioneering work being turned into Silicon Valley fortunes and, like Clark, tends to censure NCSA. See Berners-Lee (2000), 69–71, 82–83.

60. Clark (1999), 67, 73, 84, 190–91; Berners-Lee (2000), 93; Mokyr (1990), 276–78. Dr. Smarr's career and his new position were featured in *New York Times Business Section* (December 10, 2000), pp. 1, 16.

61. Clark (1999), 54–56, 60: Lewis (2000), 72–3, 121–22.

62. The percentage of Asian-American professionals depends on the method for counting them. By counting Asian surnames, one study found that 24 percent of technology firms in Silicon Valley were run by Asians in 1998, and that they founded 26 to 29 percent of start-ups from 1990 to 1998. See Saxenian (2000), 7–9.

63. Kaplan (1999), 303–6, 312; Battelle (2005), 57–58; Saxenian in Lee, Miller, Hancock, and Rowen (2000), 252. Kaplan says Sequoia provided $1 million, Battelle says $2 million. The Asian-American population is about 30 percent both in San Jose and in Santa Clara County, according to 2005 Census Bureau estimates.

64. Wolff (1998), 78.

65. Ibid., 245, 252, 265.

66. Battelle (2005), 33–34.

67. Ibid., 65–68, 75–78, 85, 89, 130.

68. Ibid., 124, 142.

69. Clark (1999), 79, 224–25, 230; Cringely (1992) calls him Kim Il Sung, p. 114.

70. Manes and Andrews (1994), 11–13,

71. Ibid., 15–19, 25–34, 47.

72. Ibid., 50–52, 57, 62.

73. Andrews (1999), 41–46; Cringely (1992), 132–33, 144, 149; Manes and Andrews (1994), 157–62. At first Gates paid an upfront fee of $10,000 to Seattle Computer to license 86-DOS, and then in July 1981 he bought it outright for $50,000. Manes and Andrews don't know exactly how much Gates got from IBM for each usage of MS-DOS; some people say $1, others $10 or $15.

74. For example, Heilemann (2001) subtitled "The End of the Microsoft Era."

75. Manes and Andrews (1994), 308–9; Heilemann (2001), 48–49.

76. Heilemann (2001), 48–49, 53.

77. Timothy Egan, "Seahawks Rise, as Does Seattle, in Tycoon's Eyes," *New York Times* (January 21, 2006), pp. A1, A9.

78. Riordan and Hoddeson (1997), 209, 210–13.

79. Ibid., 213–16.

80. Ibid., 256–62, 271; Berlin (2005), 137; Lécuyer in Lee, Miller, Hancock, and Rowen (2000), 173.

81. Chandler (2001), 135; Cringely (1992), 168–69.

82. Cringely (1992), 168–69, 171–75.

83. TI's revenues increased sharply in recent years, from $8 billion in 2001 to an estimated $15 billion in 2006, as it made alliances with Mokia and Samsung. Damon Darlin, "Cashing in Its Chips," *New York Times* (July 9, 2006), sec. 3, pp. 1, 7.

84. Berlin (2005), 281–86, 304. (Berlin has an excellent account of Sematech.) See also Lécuyer in Lee, Miller, Hancock, and Rowen (2000), 173–79.

85. City export data is available at ita.doc.gov/td/industry/otea/state—reports.

86. Saxenian (1994), 11–12, and passim; her tables on pp. 108–9 chart the systematic rise of Silicon Valley and decline of Route 128 from the 1940s to the 1990s.

87. Henton in Lee, Miller, Hancock, and Rowen (2000), 46–49, 51–53.

88. Lee, Miller, Hancock, and Rowen (2000), v.

89. For a completely rosy view of these relationships by a Stanford engineering dean, see Gibbons in Lee, Miller, Hancock, and Rowen (2000), 200–217.

90. Roger Anderson, "Wattage Where It's Needed," *New York Times* (June 6, 2001), op-ed page.

91. Battelle (2005), 14–15, 197–200.

Chapter 17. Conclusion

Epigraph from Godkin quoted in Healy (1970), 218; Godkin was the editor of the *Nation*.

1. Braudel (1995), 2:763.

2. Starr (2004), 10, 23–25; Starr (1997), 288.

3. Starr (2004), 156–69.

4. Eperjesi (2005), 14.

5. See, for example, Takashi Inoguchi, "Why Is There No Asian Theory of International Relations? The Case of Japan," July 12, 2005, paper provided to me by Professor Inoguchi.

6. Jamie Court, "Eastie Editors Are Colonizing L.A.," *Los Angeles Times* (April 24, 2005), p. M2.

7. Katzenstein (2005), 234.

8. Jonnes (2004); Brinkley (2003); Gordon (2004); Igler (2001), 8–9, 181; Williams (1961).

9. McDougall (1993), 11, 699, 703.

10. Duus (2004), 7.

11. Frank (1998), 277, 319.

12. Arrighi et al. (2003), 303; Katzenstein (2005), 209; Louis Uchitelle, "If You Can Make It Here," *New York Times* (September 4, 2005), nytimes.com; *Statistical Abstract of the United States, 2004–2005* (Washington, D.C.: Government Printing Office, 2006), 505, 977.

13. "Top 500 Supercomputing Sites," www.top500.org. Japan had a temporary breakthrough in 2002 when a government-financed program brought forth the fastest machine in the world, a HNSX supercomputer, but HNSX is a unit of a NEC subsidiary based in Littleton, Colorado. John Markoff, "Japanese Computer Is World's Fastest, as U.S. Falls Back," *New York Times* (April 20, 2002), nytimes.com.

14. Starr (1990), 305, 327–28.

15. "Earthquake Risk: A Gobal View," *National Geographic* 209, no. 4 (April 2006), map supplement.

16. I was ignorant of this fact until a former student, Ken Kawashima, pointed it out to me.

17. McWilliams (1946), 339, 376–77.

18. Quoted in Connelly (2002), 279.

19. Santayana (1967), 194.

20. Adams's thoughts rendered in Carolyn Porter's apt words, in Porter (1981), 188–89.

21. Slotkin (1985), 163; Hofstadter (1965), 132.

22. Charles J. Hanley, "Huge Bases Portend Long Iraq Stay," Associated Press report reprinted in *Ann Arbor News* (March 22, 2006), p. A3.

23. Eric Schmitt and James Dao, "U.S. Is Building Up Its Military Bases in Afghan Region," *New York Times* (January 9, 2002), p. A1; Kennish and Bien quoted in Greg Jaffe, "Pentagon Prepares to Scatter Soldiers in Remote Corners," *Wall Street Journal* (May 27, 2003), pp. A1, A6; Michael Klare, "Imperial Reach: The Pentagon's New Basing Strategy," *Nation* (April 25, 2005), 13–18. See also Phillips (2006), 84–85; Kaplan (2005), 3–4, 92.

24. V. Dion Haynes and Vincent J. Schodolski, "Crisis Creates Case for Defense,"

Chicago Tribune (September 20, 2001), sec. 5, p. 1; also Tim Weiner, "Lockheed and the Future of Warfare," *New York Times Business Section* (November 28, 2004), pp. 1, 4. We have examined Boeing and Lockheed. Northrop makes missiles, naval vessels, radar systems, and the B-2 bomber; Raytheon makes missiles and targeting optics; General Dynamics makes tanks, assault vehicles, and artillery systems; United Technologies produces various military helicopters among other things.

25. Hartz (1964), 13, 22; Bin Laden quoted in *New York Times* (September 12, 2006), p. A25.

26. "One of the things that's most striking to me is how much [Americans] hate questioning themselves and the world as it is. They need to believe that Good and Evil are clearly divided categories and that Good is or will be brought about easily." Simone de Beauvoir (1954), 382.

27. Quoted in Patterson (1972), 198.

28. The late Eric Nordlinger tried to start this conversation with his excellent 1995 book, *Isolationism Reconfigured*, which is particularly good on America's historic and geographical immunities, on leading by example, and the follies of "a vaulting idealism" (p. 7).

29. Bacevich (2005), 208–21.

30. Harper (1996), 79; Carroll (2006), ix–xi, 1.

31. Beard (1948), 580, 592–93, 597.

32. Barnett (2004), 115; Peter J. Boyer, "Downfall: How Donald Rumsfeld Reformed the Army and Lost Iraq," *New Yorker* (November 20, 2006), p. 59.

33. Mearsheimer (2001), 2–3, 31–34, 84.

34. See Mann (2000), 334. In the same year another Chinese official, Qiao Shi, said Beijing would take out New York City if Washington attacked it with nuclear weapons (ibid.).

35. Huntington (1996), 312–16.

36. Rogin (1987), 277–78.

37. Slotkin (1985), 12.

38. Cumings (1990), 772–74; Michael Herr, *Dispatches* (New York: Vintage Books, 1968), 49. In 1949, when Mao was coming to power, Kennan convened a group of East Asian experts at the State Department; after listening a while, he told them "China doesn't matter very much. It's not very important. It's never going to be powerful." China had no integrated industrial base, which Kennan thought basic to any serious capacity for warfare, merely an industrial fringe stitched along its coasts by the imperial powers; thus China should not be included in his containment strategy. Japan did have such a base and was therefore the key to postwar American policy in East Asia. Quoted in Cumings (1990), 55.

39. Quoted in Sutter (2005), 265. See also Fei-ling Wang in Deng and Wang (2005), 22.

40. John C. Reilly, ed., *American Public Opinion and U.S. Foreign Policy, 1999* (Chicago: Chicago Council on Foreign Relations), 8, 37; Andrew Kohut, "Speak Softly and Carry a Smaller Stick," *New York Times* (March 24, 2006), p. A19.

41. Nathan and Ross (1997), 33.

42. Clinton's speech of April 7, 1999, reproduced in the NAPSNet Daily Report of April 8, 1999, on the Nautilis.org Web site.

43. Braudel (1995), 1:170.

44. Bureau of the Census figures cited in *New York Times* (March 30, 2001), p. A16, and in John Hubner, "Data Shows Mixed-Race Population in Bay Area Twice National Average," *San Jose Mercury News* (March 30, 2001), p. A21.

45. Quoted in Lambropoulos (1993), 305–6.

46. Michael Arlen, "An Armenian Journal: Faucet Sales and Crash Syndrome," *Nation* 248, no. 16 (April 24, 1989): 22.

Appendix

1. Mokyr (1990), 7, 16; Krugman (1995), 73.

2. Marx (1887), 372n; Cohen (1978), 146–55; Little (1986), 89, 147–48.

3. Elster (1983), 113.

4. Schumpeter (1939), 7; Swedberg (1991), 130–31.

5. Mokyr (1990), 6.

6. März (1991), 4, 9, 58; Schumpeter (1934), 133; part 1 of his best-known book begins with five chapters on Marx: Schumpeter (1942). Daniel Little also has an excellent discussion on productive forces in Marx's theories, Little (1986), 49–50.

7. Schumpeter (1934), 64n; Schumpeter (1939), 62–77.

8. Schumpeter (1934), 61n, 64n, 73–74, 98, 231; Schumpeter (1939), 76–77, 85; Schumpeter (1942), 31; März (1991), 5–7, 13, 20; Swedberg (1991), 29–35, 173; Lebergott (1984), 62; Mokyr (1990), 287–94, 299. Schumpeter visited Japan for lectures in 1931 and fell in love with the country, which reciprocated. On credit and the state in South Korea, see Woo (1991).

9. Schumpeter (1942), 67–68, 83–84; Schumpeter (1934), 407, 411.

10. Gerschenkron (1962), 1–30; Dawidoff (2002), 176.

11. Gerschenkron (1962), 8–30.

12. Smith (1776), 27–30, 793–95. On space and its absence from neoclassical economics, see also Chisholm (1990), 83, 95–96.

13. Warsh (2006), xv, 25, 212, 292, 315, 372, 379. Margaret Somers has an excellent discussion of the culture, historicity, and symbolic construction of social science concepts in "Narrating and Naturalizing Civil Society and Citizenship Theory: The Place of Political Culture and the Public Sphere," *Sociological Theory* 13, no. 3 (November 1995): 232.

14. Braudel (1992), 402–408, 416, 433; Braudel (1995), 1:23.

15. Andrew Carnegie later said the 1870 tariff was a major reason why he entered the steel industry, since it added between $7 and $25 million each year to steel industry profits. See LaFeber (1993), 32. Of course the ideal was to corner the home market *and* export abroad, which Carnegie, Standard Oil, Singer, and other companies did after 1890.

16. Hobsbawm (1987), 65–67; Polanyi (1944), 212–15. The Bush foreign policy stimulated an enormous new literature on empire: Ronald Steel reviewed thirteen new books in "Totem and Taboo," *Nation* (September 20, 2004), pp. 29–36. Readers can judge whether this new literature made a big breakthrough in studies of empire; I have not found that it did, but a cogent discussion of empire can be found in Maier (2005).

17. Williams (1959), 41–43; LaFeber (1963), 370; McCormick (1967); Young (1968); see also the discussion of Williams and LaFeber in Hoganson (1998), 210–13n.

18. Whitman and Jackson quoted in Williams (1961), 270.

19. Schumpeter, "The Sociology of Imperialisms," in Schumpeter (1991), 141–219; Swedberg (1991), 98–102; März (1991), 64.

20. Schumpeter (1934), 193.

Bibliography

Abbott, Carl (1983). *Portland: Planning, Politics and Growth in a Twentieth Century City.* Lincoln: University of Nebraska Press.

———. (1993). *The Metropolitan Frontier: Cities in the Modern American West.* Tucson: University of Arizona Press.

Acheson, Dean (1969). *Present at the Creation: My Years in the State Department.* New York: W. W. Norton.

Adams, Brooks (1903, 2003). *The New Empire.* Honolulu: University Press of the Pacific.

Adams, Henry (1907, 1999). *The Education of Henry Adams.* Ed. and intro. Ira A. Nadel. New York: Oxford University Press.

Adas, Michael (2001). "From Settler Colony to Global Hegemon: Integrating the Exceptionalist Narrative of the American Experience into World History." *American Historical Review* (December): 1692–1720.

———. (2006). *Dominance by Design: Technological Imperatives and America's Civilizing Mission.* Cambridge: Harvard University Press.

Allen, James P., and Eugene Turner (2002). *Changing Faces, Changing Places: Mapping Southern Californians.* Northridge: Center for Geographical Studies, California State University.

Almaguer, Tomás (1994). *Racial Fault Lines: The Historical Origins of White Supremacy in California.* Berkeley: University of California Press.

Anderson, Fred, and Andrew Cayton (2005). *The Dominion of War: Empire and Liberty in North America, 1500–2000.* New York: Viking.

Anderson, Gary Clayton (2005). *The Conquest of Texas: Ethnic Cleansing in the Promised Land, 1820–1875.* Norman: University of Oklahoma Press.

Andreano, Ralph (1970). "The Structure of the California Petroleum Industry, 1895–1911." *Pacific Historical Review* 39 (May): 171–92.

Andrews, Paul (1999). *How the Web Was Won: How Bill Gates and His Internet Idealists Transformed the Microsoft Empire.* New York: Broadway Books.

Arax, Mark, and Rick Wartzman (2003). *The King of California: J. G. Boswell and the Making of a Secret American Empire.* New York: PublicAffairs.

Armitage, David, and Michael J. Braddick, eds. (2002). *The British Atlantic World, 1500–1800.* New York: Palgrave Macmillan.

Arrighi, Giovanni (1994). *The Long Twentieth Century: Money, Power, and the Origins of Our Times.* New York: Verso.

Arrighi, Giovanni, Takeshi Hamashita, and Mark Selden, eds. (2003). *The Resurgence of East Asia: 500, 150 and 50 Year Perspectives.* New York: Routledge.

Arrington, Leonard (1969). "The New Deal in the West: A Preliminary Statistical Inquiry." *Pacific Historical Review* 38 (August): 331–36.

——. (1983). "The Sagebrush Revolution: New Deal Expenditures in the Western States, 1933–39." *Pacific Historical Review* 52 (February): 1–16.

Atherton, Gertrude (1945). *Golden Gate Country.* Ed. Erskine Caldwell. New York: Duell, Sloan and Pearce.

Augsberger, Michael (2004). *An Economy of Abundant Beauty: Fortune Magazine and Depression America.* Ithaca: Cornell University Press.

Azuma, Eiichiro (2005). *Between Two Empires: Race, History, and Transnationalism in Japanese America.* New York: Oxford University Press.

Bacevich, Andrew J. (2005). *The New American Militarism: How Americans Are Seduced by War.* New York: Oxford University Press.

Bain, David Haward (1999). *Empire Express: Building the First Transcontinental Railroad.* New York: Penguin Books.

Baldassare, Mark (2000). *California in the New Millennium: The Changing Social and Political Landscape.* Berkeley: University of California Press.

Baltzell, E. Digby (1964). *The Protestant Establishment.* New York: Random House.

Bancroft, Hubert Howe (1886, 1966). *The Works of Hubert Howe Bancroft: History of California.* Vol. 3, *1825–1840.* Santa Barbara: Wallace Hebberd facsimile.

Bari, Valeska, ed. (1931). *The Course of Empire: First Hand Accounts of California in the Days of the Gold Rush of '49.* New York: Coward-McCann.

Barlett, Donald L., and James B. Steele (1979). *Howard Hughes: His Life and Madness.* New York: W. W. Norton.

Barnett, Thomas P. M. (2004). *The Pentagon's New Map: War and Peace in the 21st Century.* New York: G. P. Putnam's Sons.

Barrow, Clayton R., Jr., ed. (1973). *America Spreads Her Sails: U.S. Seapower in the 19th Century.* Annapolis: Naval Institute Press.

Battelle, John (2005). *The Search: How Google and Its Rivals Rewrote the Rules of Business and Transformed Our Culture.* New York: Penguin Books.

Baudet, Henri (1959, 1988). *Paradise on Earth: Some Thoughts on European Images of Non-European Man.* Trans. Elizabeth Wentholt. Middletown, Conn.: Wesleyan University Press.

Bauer, K. Jack (1974). *The Mexican War, 1846–1848.* New York: Macmillan.

Beach, Walter G. (1932). *Oriental Crime in California: A Study of Offenses Committed by Orientals in That State, 1900–1927.* Stanford: Stanford University Press.

Beale, Howard (1956). *Theodore Roosevelt and the Rise of America to World Power.* Baltimore: Johns Hopkins University Press.

Bean, Walton (1968). *California: An Interpretive History.* New York: McGraw-Hill.

Beard, Charles A. (1935). *The Open Door at Home: A Trial Philosophy of National Interest.* With the collaboration of G. H. E. Smith. New York: Macmillan.

——. (1948). *Roosevelt and the Coming of the War, 1941: A Study in Appearances and Realities.* New Haven: Yale University Press.

Beasley, W. G. (1995). *Japan Encounters the Barbarian: Japanese Travellers in America and Europe.* New Haven: Yale University Press.

Beisner, Robert L. (1968, 1992). *Twelve against Empire: The Anti-Imperialists, 1898–1900.* Chicago: Imprint Publications.

Bennett, James (1906, 1987). *Overland Journey to California.* Fairfield, Wash.: Ye Galleon Press.

Benton, Thomas Hart (1885, 2005). *Thirty Years' View.* New York: Kessenger Publishing.

Berger, Thomas R. (1991). *A Long and Terrible Shadow: White Values, Native Rights in the Americas Since 1492.* Seattle: University of Washington Press.

Bergeron, Paul H. (1987). *The Presidency of James K. Polk.* Lawrence: University of Kansas Press.

Berlin, Leslie (2005). *The Man behind the Microchip: Robert Noyce and the Invention of Silicon Valley.* New York: Oxford University Press.

Berman, Milton (1961). *John Fiske: The Evolution of a Popularizer.* Cambridge: Harvard University Press.

Berners-Lee, Tim, with Mark Fischetti (2000). *Weaving the Web: The Original Design and Ultimate Destiny of the World Wide Web and Its Inventor.* New York: HarperBusiness.

Bernstein, Barton, ed. (1967). *Towards a New Past: Dissenting Essays in American History.* New York: Vintage Books.

Billington, Ray Allen (1938). *The Protestant Crusade, 1800–1860: A Study of the Origins of American Nativism.* New York: Macmillan.

Bird, Kai, and Martin J. Sherwin (2006). *American Prometheus: The Triumph and Tragedy of J. Robert Oppenheimer.* New York: Vintage Books.

Birmingham, Stephen (1980). *CaliforniaRich.* New York: Simon and Schuster.

Blaut, J. M. (1993). *The Colonizer's Model of the World: Geographical Diffusionism and Eurocentric History.* New York: Guilford Press.

Blodgett, Peter J. (1999). *Land of Golden Dreams: California in the Gold Rush Decade, 1848–1858.* San Marino, Calif.: Huntington Library.

Blue Book (1915). *The Blue Book: A Comprehensive Official Souvenir View Book of*

The Panama-Pacific International Exposition at San Francisco. San Francisco: Robert A. Reid View Books.

Bobbitt, Philip (2003). *The Shield of Achilles: War, Peace, and the Course of History.* New York: Alfred A. Knopf.

Bode, William Walter (1896). *Lights and Shadows of Chinatown.* n.p.

Bolton, Roger (1966). *Defense Purchases and Regional Growth in America.* Washington, D.C.: Brookings Institution.

Boorstin, Daniel (1976). *The Exploring Spirit: America and the New World, Then and Now.* New York: Random House.

Booth, Mary Lyman (1915). *Visions and Memories: California Nineteen Hundred and Fifteen.* San Francisco: John J. Newbegin.

Borden, William S. (1984). *The Pacific Alliance: United States Foreign Economic Policy and Japanese Trade Recovery, 1947–1955.* Madison: University of Wisconsin Press.

Borneman, Walter R. (2003). *Alaska: Saga of a Bold Land.* New York: Harper-Collins.

Bottles, Scott L. (1987). *Los Angeles and the Automobile: The Making of a Modern City.* Berkeley: University of California Press.

Bowen, William A. (1978). *The Willamette Valley: Migration and Settlement on the Oregon Frontier.* Seattle: University of Washington Press.

Bradford, James C., ed. (1988). *Command under Sail: Makers of the American Naval Tradition, 1775–1850.* Annapolis: Naval Institute Press.

Bradley, Harold Whitman (1942). *The American Frontier in Hawaii: The Pioneers, 1789–1843.* Stanford: Stanford University Press.

Brady, Marilyn Dell (2004). *The Asian Texans.* College Station: Texas A & M University Press.

Braisted, William Reynolds (1968). *The United States Navy in the Pacific, 1897–1909.* Austin: University of Texas Press.

———. (1971). *The United States Navy in the Pacific, 1909–1922.* Austin: University of Texas Press.

Brands, H. W. (2002). *The Age of Gold: The California Gold Rush and the New American Dream.* New York: Doubleday.

Braudel, Fernand (1966, 1995). *The Mediterranean and the Mediterranean World in the Age of Philip II.* Vols. 1 and 2. Trans. by Siân Reynolds. Berkeley: University of California Press.

———. (1992). *Civilization and Capitalism, 15th–18th Century.* Vol. 1, *The Wheels of Commerce.* Trans. Siân Reynolds. Berkeley: University of California Press.

Brechin, Gray (1999). *Imperial San Francisco.* Berkeley: University of California Press.

Brewer, John (1990). *The Sinews of Power: War, Money and the English State, 1688–1783.* Cambridge: Harvard University Press.

Brilliant, Ashleigh (1989). *The Great Car Craze: How Southern California Collided with the Automobile in the 1920's.* Santa Barbara, Calif.: Woodbridge Press.

Brinkley, Douglas (2003). *Wheels for the World: Henry Ford, His Company, and a Century of Progress, 1903–2003.* New York: Viking Penguin.

Brook, James, Chris Carlsson, and Nancy J. Peters (1998). *Reclaiming San Francisco: History, Politics, and Culture.* San Francisco: City Lights Books.

Brookhiser, Richard (2002). *America's First Dynasty: The Adamses, 1735–1918.* New York: Free Press.

Brooks, Elisha (1922). *A Pioneer Mother of California.* San Francisco: Harr Wagner Publishing.

Brott, Clark W. (1982). *Moon Lee One: Life in Old Chinatown, Weaverville, California.* Redding, Calif.: Great Basin Foundation.

Broussard, Anthony (1993). *Black San Francisco.* Lawrence: University Press of Kansas.

Brown, Dee (1970). *Bury My Heart at Wounded Knee.* New York: Henry Holt.

———. (1995). *The American West.* New York: Touchstone Books.

Brown, DeSoto, Anne Ellett, and Gary Giemza (1982). *Hawaii Recalls: Selling Romance to America.* Honolulu: Editions Limited.

Brown, Peter Harry, and Pat H. Broeske (1996). *Howard Hughes: The Untold Story.* New York: Dutton.

Brown, Richard Maxwell (1975). *Strain of Violence: Historical Studies of American Violence and Vigilantism.* New York: Oxford University Press.

———. (1991). *No Duty to Retreat: Violence and Values in American History and Society.* Norman: University of Oklahoma Press.

Bruchey, Stuart (1988). *The Wealth of the Nation: An Economic History of the United States.* New York: Harper and Row.

Bruggencate, Jan K. Ten (2004). *Hawai'i's Pineapple Century: A History of the Crowned Fruit in the Hawaiian Islands.* Honolulu: Mutual Publishing.

Brunner, Edmund de Schweinitz, and Mary V. Brunner (1922). *Irrigation and Religion: A Study of Religious and Social Conditions in Two California Counties.* New York: George H. Doran.

Bryant, Samuel W. (1947). *The Sea and the States: A Maritime History of the American People.* New York: Thomas Y. Crowell.

Buchanan, Patrick J. (2002). *The Death of the West: How Dying Populations and Immigrant Invasions Imperil Our Country and Civilization.* New York: St. Martin's Press.

Bunting, Robert (1995). "The Environment and Settler Society in Western Oregon." *Pacific Historical Review* 64, no.3 (August): 413–32.

Burke, Carol (2004). *Camp All-American, Hanoi Jane, and the High-and-Tight: Gender, Folklore, and Changing Military Culture.* Boston: Beacon Press.

Burnham, Walter D. (1965). "The Changing Shape of the American Political Universe." *American Political Science Review* 59, pp. 7–28.

———. (1970). *Critical Elections and the Mainsprings of American Politics.* New York: W. W. Norton.

Bywater, Hector (1921). *Sea Power in the Pacific: A Study of the American-Japanese Naval Problem*. New York: Houghton Mifflin.

——. (1925). *The Great Pacific War: A History of the American-Japanese Campaign of 1931–1933*. Bedford, Mass.: Applewood Books, n. d.

Caro, Robert A. (1983). *The Years of Lyndon Johnson: The Path to Power*. New York: Alfred A. Knopf.

Carrier, James G., ed. (1995). *Occidentalism: Images of the West*. Oxford: Oxford University Press.

Carroll, James (2006). *House of War: The Pentagon and the Disastrous Rise of American Power*. New York: Houghton Mifflin.

Carter, John (2004). *Sex and Rockets: The Occult World of Jack Parsons*. Intro. Robert Anton Wilson. Los Angeles: Feral House.

Castells, Manuel (1996). *The Information Age: Economy, Society and Culture*. Vol. 1, *The Rise of the Network Society*. Malden, Mass.: Blackwell.

——. (1998). *The Information Age: Economy, Society and Culture*. Vol. 3, *End of Millennium*. Malden, Mass.: Blackwell.

Caughey, John Walton (1948). *Gold Is the Cornerstone*. Berkeley: University of California Press.

Cayton, Andrew R. L. (1986). *Frontier Republic: Ideology and Politics in the Ohio Country, 1780–1825*. Kent, Ohio: Kent State University Press.

Cayton, Horace R. (1963). *Long Old Road: An Autobiography*. Seattle: University of Washington Press.

Chambers, William Nisbet (1956). *Old Bullion Benton: Senator from the New West*. Boston: Little, Brown.

Chandler, Alfred D., Jr. (2001). *Inventing the Electronic Century: The Epic Story of the Consumer Electronics and Computer Industries*. New York: Free Press.

Chandler, Raymond (1940, 1988). *Farewell, My Lovely*. New York: Vintage Books.

Chang, Gordon H. (2003). "Whose 'Barbarism'? Whose 'Treachery'? Race and Civilization in the Unknown United States–Korea War of 1871." *Journal of American History* (March): 1331–65.

Chang, Iris (1996). *Thread of the Silkworm*. New York: Basic Books.

Chen, Xiangming (2005). *As Borders Bend: Transnational Spaces on the Pacific Rim*. New York: Rowman and Littlefield.

Chen, Xiaomei (1992). "Occidentalism as Counterdiscourse: *He Shang* in Post-Mao China." *Critical Inquiry* 18:686–712.

Chinn, Thomas W. (1989). *Bridging the Pacific: San Francisco Chinatown and Its People*. San Francisco: Chinese Historical Society of America.

Chirot, Daniel (1986). *Social Change in the Modern Era*. New York: Harcourt Brace Jovanovich.

Chisholm, Michael (1975). *Human Geography: Evolution or Revolution?* New York: Penguin Books.

——. (1990). *Regions in Recession and Resurgence*. London: Unwin Hyman.

Clark, Frank M. (1994). *Sandpapers: The Lives and Letters of Eugene Manlove*

Rhodes and Charles Fletcher Lummis. Foreword by Keith Lummis. Santa Fe: Sunstone Press.

Clark, Jim (1999). *Netscape Time: The Making of the Billion-Dollar Start-Up That Took On Microsoft*. With Owen Edwards. New York: St. Martin's Press.

Clark, Malcolm (1981). *Eden Seekers: The Settlement of Oregon, 1818–1862*. Boston: Houghton Mifflin.

Clark, Sterling B. F. (1929). *How Many Miles from St. Jo? The Log of Sterling B. F. Clark, A Forty-Niner*. San Francisco: privately printed.

Cochran, Thomas C. (1981). *Frontiers of Change: Early Industrialism in America*. New York: Oxford University Press.

Coffman, Tom (2003). *The Island Edge of America: A Political History of Hawai'i*. Honolulu: University of Hawaii Press.

Cohen, G. A. (1978). *Karl Marx's Theory of History: A Defence*. Princeton: Princeton University Press.

Cohen, Lizabeth (2004). *A Consumer's Republic: The Politics of Consumption in Postwar America*. New York: Vintage Books.

Cohen, Warren I. (2000). *East Asia at the Center: Four Thousand Years of Engaagement with the World*. New York: Columbia University Press.

Coke, Henry J. (1852). *A Ride over the Rocky Mountains for Oregon and California*. London: Richard Bentley.

Commager, Henry Steele (1950). *The American Mind: An Interpretation of American Thought and Character Since the 1880's*. New Haven: Yale University Press.

Connelly, Matthew (2002). *A Diplomatic Revolution: Algeria's Fight for Independence and the Origins of the Post–Cold War Era*. New York: Oxford University Press.

Connery, Christopher (1994). "Pacific Rim Discourse: The U.S. Global Imaginary in the Late Cold War Years." *Boundary 2*, vol. 21, no. 1, pp. 30–56.

Conzen, Michael P., ed. (1994). *The Making of the American Landscape*. New York: Routledge.

Coodley, Lauren, ed. (2004). *The Land of Orange Groves and Jails: Upton Sinclair's California*. Berkeley: Heyday Books.

Cook, Warren L. (1973). *Flood Tide of Empire: Spain and the Pacific Northwest, 1543–1819*. New Haven: Yale University Press.

Coons, Arthur G., and Arjay R. Miller (1941). *An Economic and Industrial Survey of the Los Angeles and San Diego Areas*. Sacramento: California State Planning Board.

Cooper, George, and Gavan Daws (1990). *Land and Power in Hawaii: The Democratic Years*. Honolulu: University of Hawaii Press.

Cragg, Dan (2000). *Guide to Military Installations*. 6th ed. Mechanicsburg, Pa.: Stackpole Books.

Crawford, C. H. (1898). *Scenes of Earlier Days in Crossing the Plains to Oregon*. Petaluma, Calif.: J. T. Studdert.

Cringely, Robert X. (1992). *Accidental Empires: How the Boys of Silicon Valley*

Make Their Millions, Battle Competition, and Still Can't Get a Date. New York: Addison-Wesley.

Cronon, William (1991). *Nature's Metropolis: Chicago and the Great West.* New York: W. W. Norton.

Cronon, William, George Miles, and Jay Gitlin, eds. (1992). *Under an Open Sky: Rethinking America's Western Past.* New York: W. W. Norton.

Cumings, Bruce (1990). *The Origins of the Korean War, II: The Roaring of the Cataract, 1947–1950.* Princeton: Princeton University Press.

——. (1993). "Global Realm with No Limit, Global Realm with No Name." *Radical History Review.*

——. (1997). *Korea's Place in the Sun: A Modern History.* New York: W. W. Norton.

——. (1998, 2002). *Parallax Visions: Making Sense of American–East Asian Relations.* Durham: Duke University Press.

——. (2003). *North Korea: Another Country.* New York: New Press.

Cunliffe, Marcus (1968). *Soldiers and Civilians: The Martial Spirit in America, 1775–1865.* Boston: Little, Brown.

Dallek, Robert (1983). *The American Style of Foreign Policy: Cultural Politics and Foreign Affairs.* New York: Oxford University Press.

Dana, C. W. (1861). *The Great West or the Garden of the World; Its History, Its Wealth, Its Natural Advantages, and Its Future.* Boston: Thayer and Elderidge.

Daniel, Cletus E. (1981). *Bitter Harvest: A History of California Farmworkers, 1870–1941.* Berkeley: University of California Press.

Davis, Edward J. P. (1955). *The United States Navy and U.S. Marine Corps at San Diego.* San Diego: Pioneer.

Davis, Mike (1992). *City of Quartz: Excavating the Future in Los Angeles.* New York: Vintage Books.

——. (1998). *Ecology of Fear: Los Angeles and the Imagination of Disaster.* New York: Metropolitan Books.

Davis, Mike, Kelly Mayhew, and Jim Miller (2003). *Under the Perfect Sun: The San Diego Tourists Never See.* New York: New Press.

Dawidoff, Nicholas (2002). *The Fly Swatter: Portrait of an Exceptional Character.* New York: Vintage Books.

Dawidoff, Robert (1992). *The Genteel Tradition and the Sacred Rage: High Culture vs. Democracy in Adams, James, and Santayana.* Chapel Hill: University of North Carolina Press.

Dawson, Nicholas (1933). *Narrative of Nicholas "Cheyenne" Dawson.* Intro. Charles L. Camp. San Francisco: Grabhorn Press.

Dawson, Robert, and Gray Brechin (1999). *Farewell, Promised Land: Waking From the California Dream.* Berkeley: University of California Press.

de Beauvoir, Simone (1954, 1999). *America Day by Day.* Trans. Carol Cosman. Foreword by Douglas Brinkley. Berkeley: University of California Press.

De Graaf, Lawrence (1970). "The City of Black Angels: Emergence of the Los Angeles Ghetto, 1890–1960." *Pacific Historical Review* 39 (March): 323–52.

de Grazia, Victoria (2005). *Irresistible Empire: America's Advance through Twentieth-Century Europe.* Cambridge: Harvard University Press.

Deloria, Vine, Jr. (1977). *Indians of the Pacific Northwest.* Garden City: Doubleday.

———. (1984). *The Nations Within: The Past and Future of American Indian Sovereignty.* New York: Pantheon Books.

Deng, Yang, and Fei-ling Wang, eds. (2005). *China Rising: Power and Motivation in Chinese Foreign Policy.* Lanham, Md.: Rowman and Littlefield.

Dent, Harry S., Jr. (1999). *The Roaring 2000s: Building the Wealth and Lifestyle You Desire in the Greatest Boom in History.* New York: Simon and Schuster.

d'Eramo, Marco (2002). *The Pig and the Skyscraper: Chicago: A History of Our Future.* Trans. Graeme Thomson. Foreword by Mike Davis. New York: Verso.

Derian, Jean-Claude (1990). *America's Struggle for Leadership in Technology.* Trans. Severen Schaeffer. Cambridge: MIT Press.

Dertouzos, Michael L. (1997). *What Will Be: How the New World of Information Will Change Our Lives.* San Francisco: HarperSanFrancisco.

Deutschman, Alan (2000). *The Second Coming of Steve Jobs.* New York: Broadway Books.

Deverell, William (1994). *Railroad Crossing: Californians and the Railroad, 1850–1910.* Berkeley: University of California Press.

De Voto, Bernard (1942, 2000). *The Year of Decision 1846.* New York: Truman Talley Books.

———. (1944). "Geopolitics with the Dew on It." *Harper's Magazine* 188 (March): 313–23.

———. (1948, 1998). *Across the Wide Missouri.* New York: Houghton Mifflin.

———. (1952, 1983). *The Course of Empire.* Lincoln: University of Nebraska Press.

Dickinson, Frederick R. (1999). *War and National Reinvention: Japan in the Great War, 1914–1919.* Cambridge: Harvard University Press.

Didion, Joan (1968). *Slouching Towards Bethlehem.* New York: Farrar, Straus and Giroux.

———. (1979). *The White Album.* New York: Farrar, Straus and Giroux.

Dietrich, William (1995). *Northwest Passage: The Great Columbia River.* New York: Simon and Schuster.

Dillon, Richard (1976). *Images of Chinatown: Louis J. Stellman's Chinatown Photographs.* San Francisco: Book Club of California.

Dingman, Roger (1976). *Power in the Pacific: The Origins of Naval Arms Limitation.* Chicago: University of Chicago Press.

Dippie, Brian W. (1982). *The Vanishing American: White Attitudes and U.S. Indian Policy.* Lawrence: University Press of Kansas.

Dirlik, Arif, ed. (1993). *What Is in a Rim? Critical Perspectives on the Pacific Region Idea.* Boulder, Colo.: Westview Press.

———. (1998). *What Is in a Rim? Critical Perspectives on the Pacific Region Idea.* 2nd ed. New York: Rowman and Littlefield.

———. (2001). *Chinese on the American Frontier.* New York: Rowman and Littlefield.

Dole, Richard, and Elizabeth Dole Porteus (2004). *The Story of James Dole.* Waipahu, Hawaii: Island Heritage Publishing.

Drago, Harry Sinclair (1968). *Roads to Empire: The Dramatic Conquest of the American West.* New York: Dodd, Mead.

Drake, Frederick C. (1984). *The Empire of the Seas: A Biography of Rear Admiral Robert Wilson Shufeldt, USN.* Honolulu: University of Hawaii Press.

Drinnon, Richard (1980). *Facing West: The Metaphysics of Indian-Hating and Empire-Building.* New York: New American Library.

Dubofsky, Melvyn (1969). *We Shall Be All: A History of the Industrial Workers of the World.* Chicago: Quadrangle Books.

Dudden, Arthur Powell (1992). *The American Pacific: From the Old China Trade to the Present.* New York: Oxford University Press.

———, ed. (2004). *American Empire in the Pacific: From Trade to Strategic Balance, 1700–1922.* Burlington, Vt.: Ashgate Publishing.

Dudziak, Mary L. (2000). *Cold War Civil Rights: Race and the Image of American Democracy, Politics and Society in Twentieth-Century America.* Princeton: Princeton University Press.

Dulles, Foster (1932). *America in the Pacific.* Boston: Houghton Mifflin.

Duus, Masayo (1999). *The Japanese Conspiracy: The Oahu Sugar Strike of 1920.* Berkeley: University of California Press.

———. (2004). *The Life of Isamu Noguchi: Journey without Borders.* Princeton: Princeton University Press.

Dyson, Esther (1998). *Release 2.1: A Design for Living in the Digital Age.* New York: Broadway Books.

Elliott, J. H. (1970). *The Old World and the New, 1492–1650.* New York: Cambridge University Press.

———. (2006). *Empires of the Atlantic World: Britain and Spain in America, 1492–1830.* New Haven: Yale University Press.

Ellison, Joseph (1927, 1969). *California and the Nation, 1850–1869: A Study of the Relations of a Frontier Community with the Federal Government.* New York: Da Capo Press.

Elster, Jon (1983). *Explaining Technical Change: A Case Study in the Philosophy of Science.* New York: Cambridge University Press.

Englehardt, Tom (1995). *The End of Victory Culture: Cold War America and the Disillusioning of a Generation.* New York: Basic Books.

Eperjesi, John R. (2005). *The Imperialist Imaginary: Visions of Asia and the Pacific in American Culture.* Foreword by Donald E. Pease. Hanover, N.H.: Dartmouth College Press.

Erie, Steven P. (2004). *Globalizing L.A.: Trade, Infrastructure, and Regional Development.* Stanford: Stanford University Press.

———. (2006). *Beyond Chinatown: The Metropolitan Water District, Growth, and the Environment in Southern California.* Stanford: Stanford University Press.

Espiritu, Augusto Fauni (2005). *Five Faces of Exile: The Nation and Filipino American Intellectuals.* Stanford: Stanford University Press.

Esthus, Raymond A. (1966). *Theodore Roosevelt and Japan.* Seattle: University of Washington Press.

Evans, Daniel C., and Mark R. Peattie (1997). *Kaigun: Strategy, Tactics, and Technology in the Imperial Japanese Navy, 1887–1941.* Annapolis: Naval Institute Press.

Fahey, John (1986). *The Inland Empire: Unfolding Years, 1879–1929.* Seattle: University of Washington Press.

Fairbank, John King (1953, 1969). *Trade and Diplomacy on the China Coast: The Opening of the Treaty Ports, 1842–1854.* Stanford: Stanford University Press.

Federal Writers Project (1939). *California: A Guide to the Golden State.* New York: Hastings House.

Fehrenbach, T. R. (1968, 1983). *Lone Star: A History of Texas and the Texans.* New York: American Legacy Press.

Ferguson, Kathy E., and Phyllis Turnbull (1999). *Oh, Say, Can You See? The Semiotics of the Military in Hawai'i.* Minneapolis: University of Minnesota Press.

Ferguson, Niall (2003). *Empire: The Rise and Demise of the British World Order and the Lessons for Global Power.* New York: Basic Books.

Ficken, Robert E. (1995). *Rufus Woods, the Columbia River, and the Building of Modern Washington.* Pullman: Washington State University Press.

Ficken, Robert E., and Charles P. LeWarne (1988). *Washington: A Centennial History.* Seattle: University of Washington Press.

Fiege, Mark (2000). *Irrigated Eden: The Making of an Agricultural Landscape in the American West.* Foreword by William Cronon. Seattle: University of Washington Press.

Field, James A. (1978). "American Imperialism: The Worst Chapter in Almost Any Book." *American Historical Review* 83 (June): 644–68.

FitzGerald, Frances (1972). *Fire in the Lake: The Vietnamese and the Americans in Vietnam.* Boston: Atlantic Monthly Press.

———. (2000). *Way Out There in the Blue: Reagan, Star Wars and the End of the Cold War.* New York: Simon and Schuster.

Flamm, Jerry (1978). *Good Life in Hard Times: San Francisco's '20s and '30s.* San Francisco: Chronicle Books.

Flannery, Tim (2001). *The Eternal Frontier: An Ecological History of North America and Its People.* New York: Atlantic Monthly Press.

Fogelson, Robert M. (1967, 1993). *The Fragmented Metropolis: Los Angeles, 1850–1930.* Foreword by Robert Fishman. Berkeley: University of California Press.

Foley, Neal (1997). *The White Scourge: Mexicans, Blacks, and Poor Whites in Texas Cotton Culture.* Berkeley: University of California Press.

Foster, Mark S. (1989). *Henry Kaiser: Builder in the Modern American West.* Austin: University of Texas Press.

Foucault, Michel (1972). *The Archaeology of Knowledge and the Discourse on Language.* Trans. A. M. Sheridan. New York: Harper.

Frank, Andre Gunder (1998). *ReOrient: Global Economy in the Asian Age.* Berkeley: University of California Press.

Fresonke, Kris (2003). *West of Emerson: The Design of Manifest Destiny*. Berkeley: University of California Press.

Friedheim, Robert L. (1964). *The Seattle General Strike*. Seattle: University of Washington Press.

Friedrich, Otto (1986) *City of Nets: A Portrait of Hollywood in the 1940's*. New York: Harper and Row.

Friis, Herman R., ed. (1967). *The Pacific Basin: A History of its Geographical Exploration*. New York: American Geographical Society.

Fuchs, Lawrence H. (1961). *Hawaii Pono: A Social History*. New York: Harcourt Brace Jovanovich.

Fulton, William (1997). *The Reluctant Metropolis: The Politics of Urban Growth in Los Angeles*. Baltimore: Johns Hopkins University Press.

Gale, James Scarth (1972). *History of the Korean People*. Annotated and introduced by Richard Rutt. Seoul: Royal Asiatic Society.

Garreau, Joel (1992). *Edge City: Life on the New Frontier*. New York: Anchor Books.

Genthe, Arnold (1912). *Old Chinatown*. Text by Will Irwin. New York: Mitchell Kennerley.

Gerschenkron, Alexander (1962). *Economic Backwardness in Historical Perspective*. New York: Belknap Press.

Gibbs, David N. (2004). "Pretexts and U.S. Foreign Policy: The War on Terrorism in Historical Perspective." *New Political Science*, 26, no. 3.

Glisan, Rodney (1874). *Journal of Army Life*. San Francisco: A. L. Bancroft.

Goetzmann, William H. (1966a). *Exploration and Empire: The Explorer and the Scientist in the Winning of the American West*. New York: Alfred A. Knopf.

——. (1966b, 1999). *When the Eagle Screamed: The Romantic Horizon in American Expansionism, 1800–1860*. Norman: University of Oklahoma Press.

——. (1987). *New Lands, New Men: America and the Second Great Age of Discovery*. New York: Penguin Books.

Goetzmann, William H., and William N. Goetzmann (1986). *The West of the Imagination*. New York: W. W. Norton.

Goldberg, David Theo (1993). *Racist Culture: Philosophy and the Politics of Meaning*. Cambridge, Mass.: Blackwell.

Gordon, Dudley (1972). *Charles F. Lummis: Crusader in Corduroy*. Los Angeles: Cultural Assets Press.

Gordon, John Steele (2004). *An Empire of Wealth: The Epic History of American Economic Power*. New York: HarperCollins.

Gottlieb, Robert (1988). *A Life of Its Own: The Politics and Power of Water*. San Diego: Harcourt Brace Jovanovich.

Gottlieb, Robert, Mark Vallianatos, Regina M. Freer, and Peter Dreier (2005). *The Next Los Angeles: The Struggle for a Livable City*. Berkeley: University of California Press.

Gould, Lewis L. (1980). *The Spanish-American War and President McKinley*. Lawrence: University Press of Kansas.

Graebner, Norman A. (1955, 1989). *Empire on the Pacific: A Study in American Continental Expansion.* 2nd reprint ed. Claremont, Calif.: Regina Books.

———. ed. (1968). *Manifest Destiny.* New York: Bobbs-Merrill.

———. (1980). "The Mexican War: A Study in Causation." *Pacific Historical Review* 49 (August): 405–26.

Grandin, Greg (2006). *Empire's Workshop: Latin America, the United States, and the Rise of the New Imperialism.* New York: Metropolitan Books.

Graves, Jackson A. (1930). *California Memories, 1857–1930.* Los Angeles: Times-Mirror Press.

Greenblatt, Stephen (1991). *Marvelous Possession: The Wonder of the New World.* Chicago: University of Chicago Press.

Gressley, Gene M., ed. (1966). *The American West: A Reorientation.* University of Wyoming Publications, vol. 32.

———. ed. (1994). *Old West/New West.* Norman: University of Oklahoma Press.

Griffis, William Elliot (1888). *Corea: The Hermit Nation.* New York: Charles Scribner's Sons.

Gulick, Sidney L. (1914). *The American Japanese Problem: A Study of the Racial Relations of the East and the West.* New York: Scribner's Sons.

Guyatt, Nicholas (2003). *Another American Century? The United States and the World since 9/11.* New York: Zed Books.

Haas, Lisbeth (1995). *Conquests and Historical Identities in California, 1769–1936.* Berkeley: University of California Press.

Hafner, Katie, and Matthew Lyon (1996). *Where Wizards Stay Up Late: The Origins of the Internet.* New York: Simon and Schuster.

Hale, John (1851, 1954). *California as It Is.* Privately printed.

Hamashita, Takeshi (1990). *China-Centered World Order in Modern Times.* Tokyo: University of Tokyo Press.

Hanlon, David, and Geoffrey M. White, eds. (2000). *Voyaging through the Contemporary Pacific.* New York: Rowman and Littlefield.

Hanson, Victor Davis (1996). *Fields without Dreams: Defending the Agrarian Idea.* New York: Free Press.

Hardt, Michael, and Antonio Negri (2000). *Empire.* Harvard University Press.

Harootunian, Harry (2000). *Overcome by Modernity: History, Culture, and Community in Interwar Japan.* Princeton: Princeton University Press.

Harper, John Lamberton (1996). *American Visions of Europe: Franklin D. Roosevelt, George F. Kennan, and Dean G. Acheson.* New York: Cambridge University Press.

Hartz, Louis (1955). *The Liberal Tradition in America.* New York: Simon and Schuster.

———. (1964). *The Founding of New Societies: Studies in the History of the United States, Latin America, South Africa, Canada, and Australia.* With contributions by Kenneth D. McRae, Richard M. Morse, Richard N. Rosecrance, Leonard M. Thompson. New York: Harcourt, Brace and World.

Harvey, Mark W. T. (1994). *A Symbol of Wilderness: Echo Park and the American*

Conservation Movement. Foreword by William Cronon. Seattle: University of Washington Press.

Hashimoto, Akikazu, Mike Mochizuki, and Kurayoshi Takara, eds. (2005). *The Okinawa Question and the U.S.–Japanese Alliance.* Washington, D.C.: Elliott School of International Affairs.

Haycox, Stephen (2002). *Frigid Embrace: Politics, Economics, and Environment in Alaska.* Corvallis, Ore.: Oregon State University Press.

Haynes, Sam W. (1997a). *James K. Polk and the Expansionist Impulse.* New York: Longman Press.

———. (1997b). *Manifest Destiny and Empire: American Antebellum Expansionism.* College Station: Texas A & M University Press.

Healy, David (1970). *U.S. Expansionism: The Imperialist Urge in the 1890s.* Madison: University of Wisconsin Press.

Heckrotte, Warren, and Julie Sweetkind, eds. (1999). *California 49: Forty-nine Maps of California from the Sixteenth Century to the Present.* San Francisco: California Map Society, Occasional Paper No. 6.

Heilemann, John (2001). *Pride before the Fall: The Trials of Bill Gates and the End of the Microsoft Era.* New York: HarperCollins.

Heiner, Albert P. (1991). *Henry J. Kaiser: Western Colossus.* San Francisco: Halo Books.

Heizer, Robert F., and Alan J. Almquist (1971). *The Other Californians: Prejudice and Discrimination under Spain, Mexico, and the United States to 1920.* Berkeley: University of California Press.

Henderson, George L. (1998). *California and the Fictions of Capital.* Philadelphia: Temple University Press.

Hereniko, Vilsoni, and Rob Wilson, eds. (1999). *Inside Out: Literature, Cultural Politics, and Identity in the New Pacific.* New York: Rowman and Littlefield.

Hertzfeld, Andy, et al. (2005). *Revolution in the Valley: The Insanely Great Story of How the Mac Was Made.* Sebastopol, Calif.: O'Reilly Media.

Hevly, Bruce, and John M. Findlay, eds. (1998). *The Atomic West.* Seattle: University of Washington Press.

Hidy, Ralph W., Muriel E. Hidy, Roy V. Scott, and Don L. Hofsommer (1988, 2004). *The Great Northern Railway: A History.* Minneapolis: University of Minnesota Press.

Hietala, Thomas R. (1985). *Manifest Design: Anxious Aggrandizement in Late Jacksonian America.* Ithaca: Cornell University Press.

Higham, Charles (1993). *Howard Hughes: The Secret Life.* New York: St. Martin's Press.

Hiltzik, Michael (1999). *Dealers of Lightning: Xerox PARC and the Dawn of the Computer Age.* New York: HarperCollins.

Hine, Robert V., and John Mack Faragher (2000). *The American West: A New Interpretive History.* New Haven: Yale University Press.

Hise, Greg (1997). *Magnetic Los Angeles: Planning the Twentieth-Century Metropolis.* Baltimore: Johns Hopkins University Press.

Hobsbawm, E. J. (1969). *Industry and Empire: From 1750 to the Present Day.* New York: Penguin Books.

———. (1979). *The Age of Capital, 1848–1875.* New York: New American Library.

———. (1987). *The Age of Empire, 1875–1914.* New York: Pantheon Books.

Hodgson, Godfrey (1976). *America in Our Time, from World War II to Nixon: What Happened and Why.* New York: Doubleday.

Hoffman, Abraham (1981). *Vision or Villainy: Origins of the Owens Valley–Los Angeles Water Controversy.* College Station: Texas A & M University Press.

Hofstadter, Richard (1965, 1996). *The Paranoid Style in American Politics.* Cambridge: Harvard University Press.

———. (1968). *The Progressive Historians: Turner, Beard, Parrington.* New York: Alfred A. Knopf.

Hofstadter, Richard, and Seymour Martin Lipset, eds. (1968). *Turner and the Sociology of the Frontier.* New York: Basic Books.

Hogan, Michael J. (1998). *A Cross of Iron: Harry S. Truman and the Origins of the National Security State, 1945–1954.* New York: Cambridge University Press.

Hoganson, Kristin L. (1998). *Fighting for American Manhood: How Gender Politics Provoked the Spanish-American and Philippine-American Wars.* New Haven: Yale University Press.

Honan, William H. (1991). *Visions of Infamy: The Untold Story of How Journalist Hector C. Bywater Devised the Plans that Led to Pearl Harbor.* New York: St. Martin's Press.

Hooks, Gregory (1994). "Regional Processes in the Hegemonic Nation: Political, Economic, and Military Influences on the Use of Geographic Space." *American Sociological Review* 59 (October): 746–72.

Hooks, Gregory, and Leonard E. Bloomquist (1992). "The Legacy of World War II for Regional Growth and Decline: The Cumulative Effects of Wartime Investments on U.S. Manufacturing, 1947–1972." *Social Forces* 72, no. 2 (December): 303–37.

Horgan, Paul (1984). *Great River: The Rio Grande in North American History.* Middletown, Conn.: Wesleyan University Press.

Horkheimer, Max, and Theodor W. Adorno (1944, 1969). *Dialectic of Enlightenment.* Trans. John Cumming. New York: Continuum.

Hornbeck, David, et al. (1983). *California Patterns: A Geographic and Historical Atlas.* Palo Alto: Mayfield Publishing.

Horsman, Reginald (1981). *Race and Manifest Destiny: The Origins of American Racial Anglo-Saxonism.* Cambridge: Harvard University Press.

Horton, John (1995). *The Politics of Diversity: Immigration, Resistance, and Change in Monterey Park, California.* Philadelphia: Temple University Press.

Howard, Thomas Frederick (1998). *Sierra Crossing: First Roads to California.* Berkeley: University of California Press.

Hunt, Michael H. (1973). *Frontier Defense and the Open Door: Manchuria in Chinese-American Relations, 1895–1911.* New Haven: Yale University Press.

———. (1985). *The Making of a Special Relationship: The United States and China to 1914.* New York: Columbia University Press.

——. (1987). *Ideology and U.S. Foreign Policy.* New Haven: Yale University Press.

Huntington, Samuel (1996). *The Clash of Civilizations and the Remaking of World Order.* New York: Touchstone Books.

——. (2004). *Who Are We? The Challenges to America's National Identity.* New York: Simon and Schuster.

Hurtado, Albert L. (1988). *Indian Survival on the California Frontier.* New Haven: Yale University Press.

Huxley, Aldous (1939, 1993). *After Many a Summer Dies the Swan.* Chicago: Ivan R. Dee.

Ickes, Harold L. (1953). *The Secret Diary of Harold L. Ickes: The First Thousand Days, 1933–1936.* New York: Simon and Schuster.

Ienaga, Saburō (1978). *The Pacific War: World War II and the Japanese, 1931–1945.* New York: Pantheon Books.

Igler, David (2001). *Industrial Cowboys: Miller and Lux and the Transformation of the Far West, 1850–1920.* Berkeley: University of California Press.

Ingram, Robert L. (1968). *The Bechtel Story: Seventy Years of Accomplishment in Engineering and Construction.* San Francisco: Bechtel Corporation.

Inscriptions at the Panama-Pacific International Exposition, The (1915). San Francisco: San Francisco News.

Iriye, Akira (1967). *Across the Pacific: An Inner History of American–East Asian Relations.* New York: Harcourt, Brace and World.

——. (1969). *After Imperialism: The Search for a New Order in the Far East, 1921–1931.* New York: Atheneum.

——. (1972). *Pacific Estrangement: Japanese and American Expansion, 1897–1911.* Cambridge: Harvard University Press.

——. (1981). *Power and Culture: The Japanese-American War, 1941–1945.* Cambridge: Harvard University Press.

Isard, Walter (1956). *Location and Space-Economy: A General Theory Relating to Industrial Location, Market Areas, Land Use, Trade, and Urban Structure.* Cambridge: MIT Press.

Jackson, Joseph Henry (1970). *Anybody's Gold: The Story of California's Mining Towns.* Intro. Wallace Stegner. San Francisco: Chronicle Books.

——, ed. (1952). *The Western Gate: A San Francisco Reader.* New York: Farrar, Straus and Young.

Jackson, Kenneth T. (1985). *Crabgrass Frontier: The Suburbanization of the United States.* New York: Oxford University Press.

Jacobsen, Matthew Frye (2000). *Barbarian Virtues: The United States Encounters Foreign Peoples at Home and Abroad, 1876–1917.* New York: Hill and Wang.

Janeway, Eliot (1951). *The Struggle for Survival: A Chronicle of Economic Mobilization in World War II.* New Haven: Yale University Press.

Jehlen, Myra (1986). *American Incarnation: The Individual, the Nation, and the Continent.* Cambridge: Harvard University Press.

Jezek, George Ross, and John W. Westcott (2003). *Orange County: Past and Present.* San Diego: George Ross Jezek Photography and Publishing.

Johansen, Dorothy O., and Charles M. Gates (1967). *Empire of the Columbia: A History of the Pacific Northwest.* 2nd ed. New York: Harper and Row.

Johanssen, Robert W. (1985). *To the Halls of Montezuma: The Mexican War in the American Imagination.* New York: Oxford University Press.

Johnson, Chalmers, ed. (1999). *Okinawa: Cold War Island.* Cardiff, Calif.: Japan Policy Research Institute.

———. (2004). *The Sorrows of Empire: Militarism, Secrecy, and the End of the Republic.* New York: Henry Holt.

———. (2006). *Nemesis: The Last Days of the American Republic.* New York: Metropolitan Books.

Johnson, David Alan (1992). *Founding the Far West: California, Oregon, and Nevada, 1840–1890.* Berkeley: University of California Press.

Johnson, Marilynn S. (1993). *The Second Gold Rush: Oakland and the East Bay in World War II.* Berkeley: University of California Press.

Jones, Charles A. (2002). *Hawai'i's World War II Military Sites: A Comprehensive Guide Focusing on O'ahu.* Foreword by Daniel A. Martinez. Honolulu: Mutual Publishing.

Jonnes, Jill (2004). *Empires of Light: Edison, Tesla, Westinghouse, and the Race to Electrify the World.* New York: Random House, 2004.

Judt, Tony (2005). *Postwar: A History of Europe since 1945.* New York: Penguin Books.

Kahrl, William L. (1982). *Water and Power: The Conflict over Los Angeles' Water Supply in the Owens Valley.* Berkeley: University of California Press.

Kajima, Morinosuke (1968). *The Emergence of Japan as a World Power.* Rutland, Vt.: Charles E. Tuttle.

Kaldor, Mary (1981). *The Baroque Arsenal.* New York: Hill and Wang.

Kaplan, Amy, and Donald E. Pease, eds. (1993). *Cultures of United States Imperialism.* Durham: Duke University Press.

Kaplan, David A. (1999). *The Silicon Boys and Their Valley of Dreams.* New York: HarperCollins.

Kaplan, Robert D. (2005). *Imperial Grunts: The American Military on the Ground.* New York: Random House.

Karnes, Thomas L. (1970). *William Gilpin: Western Nationalist.* Austin: University of Texas Press.

Kasson, John F. (1976, 1999). *Civilizing the Machine: Technology and Republican Values in America, 1776–1900.* New York: Hill and Wang.

Katz, Frederich (1981). *The Secret War in Mexico.* Chicago: University of Chicago Press.

Katz, William Loren (1996). *The Black West: A Documentary and Pictorial History of the African American Role in the Westward Expansion of the United States.* New York: Touchstone.

Katzenstein, Peter J. (2005). *A World of Regions: Asia and Europe in the American Imperium.* Ithaca: Cornell University Press.

Katznelson, Ira (1996). *Liberalism's Crooked Circle.* Princeton: Princeton University Press.

Katznelson, Ira, and Martin Shefter, eds. (2002). *Shaped by War and Trade: International Influences on American Political Development.* Princeton: Princeton University Press.

Kazin, Michael (1987). *Barons of Labor: The San Francisco Building Trades and Union Power in the Progressive Era.* Urbana: Illinois University Press.

Kelley, Don Greame (1971). *Edge of a Continent: The Pacific Coast from Alaska to Baja.* Palo Alto: American West Publishing.

Kelley, Robert (1989, 1998). *Battling the Inland Sea: Floods, Public Policy, and the Sacramento Valley.* Foreword by David N. Kennedy. Berkeley: University of California Press.

Kennan, George F. (1989). *Sketches From a Life.* New York: Pantheon Books.

Kenney, Martin, ed. (2000). *Understanding Silicon Valley: The Anatomy of an Entrepreneurial Region.* Stanford: Stanford University Press.

Kent, William (1929). *Reminiscences of Outdoor Life.* San Francisco: A. M. Robertson.

Kesselman, Amy (1990). *Fleeting Opportunities: Women Shipyard Workers in Portland and Vancouver During World War II and Reconversion.* Albany: State University of New York Press.

Keyso, Ruth Ann (2000). *Women of Okinawa: Nine Voices From a Garrison Island.* Ithaca: Cornell University Press.

Kicza, John E. (2003). *Resilient Cultures: America's Native Peoples Confront European Colonization, 1500–1800.* Upper Saddle River, N.J.: Prentice Hall.

Kim, Key-Hiuk (1980). *The Last Phase of the East Asian World Order.* Berkeley: University of California Press.

Kinzer, Stephen (2006). *Overthrow: America's Century of Regime Change From Hawaii to Iraq.* New York: Times Books.

Kipling, Rudyard (1949). *Rudyard Kipling's Letters From San Francisco.* San Francisco: Colt Press.

Klein, Norman M. (1997). *The History of Forgetting: Los Angeles and the Erasure of Memory.* London: Verso.

Kling, Rob, Spencer Olin, and Mark Poster, eds. (1991). *Postsuburban California: The Transformation of Orange County since World War II.* Berkeley: University of California Press.

Kolko, Gabriel (1963). *The Triumph of Conservatism: A Reinterpretation of American History, 1900–1916.* New York: Free Press.

——. (1965). *Railroads and Regulation, 1877–1916.* Princeton: Princeton University Press.

Kolodny, Annette (1984). *The Land Before Her: Fantasy and Experience of the American Frontiers, 1630–1860.* Chapel Hill: University of North Carolina Press.

Koshiro, Yukiko (1999). *Trans-Pacific Racisms and the U.S. Occupation of Japan.* New York: Columbia University Press.

Kotkin, Joel (2000). *The New Geography: How the Digital Revolution Is Reshaping the American Landscape.* New York: Random House.

Kotkin, Joel, and Paul Grabowicz (1982). *California, Inc.* New York: Avon Books.

Kraft, Jeff, and Aaron Leventhal (2002). *Footsteps in the Fog: Alfred Hitchcock's San Francisco.* Foreword by Patricia Hitchcock O'Connell. Santa Monica: Santa Monica Press LCC.

Kramer, Jane (1977). *The Last Cowboy.* New York: Harper and Row.

Kramer, Paul A. (2006). *The Blood of Government: Race, Empire, the United States, and the Philippines.* Chapel Hill: University of North Carolina Press.

Krauss, Ellis S., and T. J. Pempel, eds. (2004). *Beyond Bilateralism: U.S.–Japan Relations in the New Asia-Pacific.* Stanford: Stanford University Press.

Kroeber, Theodora (1961). *Ishi in Two Worlds: A Biography of the Last Wild Indian in North America.* Berkeley: University of California Press.

Krugman, Paul (1995). *Development, Geography, and Economic Theory.* Cambridge: MIT Press.

Kwong, Peter (1996). *The New Chinatown.* Rev. ed. New York: Hill and Wang.

LaFeber, Walter (1963). *The New Empire: An Interpretation of American Expansion, 1860–1898.* Ithaca: Cornell University Press.

——, ed. (1965). *John Quincy Adams and American Continental Empire: Letters, Papers and Speeches.* Chicago: Quadrangle Books.

——. (1989). *The American Age: United States Foreign Policy at Home and Abroad since 1750.* New York: W. W. Norton.

——. (1993). *The Cambridge History of American Foreign Relations.* Vol. 2, *The American Search for Opportunity, 1865–1913.* New York: Cambridge University Press.

——. (1997). *The Clash: A History of U.S.–Japan Relations.* New York: W. W. Norton.

Lamar, Howard, and Leonard Thompson, eds. (1981). *The Frontier in History: North America and Southern Africa Compared.* New Haven: Yale University Press.

Lambropoulos, Vassilis (1993). *The Rise of Eurocentrism: Anatomy of Interpretation.* Princeton: Princeton University Press.

Landauer, Lyndall, and Don Landauer (1999). *Pearl: The History of the United States Navy in Pearl Harbor.* Lake Tahoe, Calif.: Flying Cloud Press.

Langer, William L., and S. Everett Gleason (1952). *The Challenge to Isolation: The World Crisis of 1937–1940 and American Foreign Policy.* Vol. 2. New York: Harper and Row.

Latham, Robert (1997). *The Liberal Moment: Modernity, Security, and the Making of the Postwar International Order.* New York: Columbia University Press.

Lavender, David (1956, 2001). *Land of Giants: The Drive to the Pacific Northwest, 1750–1950.* Edison, N.J.: Castle Books.

——. (1972, 1987). *California: Land of New Beginnings*. Lincoln: University of Nebraska Press.

Lea, Homer (1909). *The Valor of Ignorance*. New York: Harper and Brothers.

Leach, William (1993). *Land of Desire: Merchants, Power, and the Rise of a New American Culture*. New York: Pantheon Books.

Lebergott, Stanley (1984). *The Americans: An Economic Record*. New York: W. W. Norton.

Lécuyer, Christophe (2006). *Making Silicon Valley: Innovation and the Growth of High Tech, 1930–1970*. Cambridge: MIT Press.

Lee, Chong-Moon, William F. Miller, Marguerite Gong Hancock, and Henry S. Rowen, eds. (2000). *The Silicon Valley Edge: A Habitat for Innovation and Entrepreneurship*. Stanford: Stanford University Press.

Lee, Doby (1992). "Scirocco." Unpub. novel in the author's possession, used with permission.

Lee, Mary Paik (1990). *Quiet Odyssey: A Pioneer Korean Woman in America*. Seattle: University of Washington Press.

Legacy of the Exposition: Interpretation of the Intellectual and Moral Heritage Left to Mankind by the World Celebration at San Francisco in 1915 (1916). San Francisco: Panama-Pacific International Exposition Company.

Lenihan, John H. (1980). *Showdown: Confronting Modern America in the Western Film*. Urbana: University of Illinois Press.

Leong, Kren J. (2005). *The China Mystique: Pearl S. Buck, Anna May Wong, Mayling Soong, and the Transformation of American Orientalism*. Berkeley: University of California Press.

Levinson, Marc (2006). *The Box: How the Shipping Container Made the World Smaller and the World Economy Bigger*. Princeton: Princeton University Press.

Lewis, Meriwether, and William Clark (1953, 1997). *The Journals of Lewis and Clark*. Ed. and intro. Bernard DeVoto, foreword, Stephen E. Ambrose. New York: Houghton Mifflin.

Lewis, Michael (2000). *The New New Thing: A Silicon Valley Story*. New York: Penguin Books.

Lieven, Anatol (2004). *America Right or Wrong: An Anatomy of American Nationalism*. New York: Oxford University Press.

Limerick, Patricia Nelson (1987). *The Legacy of Conquest: The Unbroken Past of the American West*. New York: W. W. Norton.

Limerick, Patricia Nelson, Clyde A. Milner II, and Charles E. Rankin, eds. (1991). *Trails: Toward a New Western History*. Lawrence: University Press of Kansas.

Linder, Staffan Burenstam (1986). *The Pacific Century: Economic and Political Consequences of Asian-Pacific Dynamism*. Stanford: Stanford University Press.

Linderman, Gerald F. (1974). *The Mirror of War: American Society and the Spanish-American War*. Ann Arbor: University of Michigan Press.

Linklater, Andro (2002). *Measuring America: How the United States Was Shaped by the Greatest Land Sale in History.* New York: HarperCollins.

Linn, Brian McAllister (1989). *The U.S. Army and Counterinsurgency in the Philippine War, 1899–1902.* Chapel Hill: University of North Carolina Press.

———. (1997). *Guardians of Empire: The U.S. Army and the Pacific, 1902–1940.* Chapel Hill: University of North Carolina Press.

Linzmayer, Owen D. (2004). *Apple Confidential 2.0: The Definitive History of the World's Most Colorful Company.* San Francisco: No Starch Press.

Lipset, Seymour Martin (1996). *American Exceptionalism: A Double-Edged Sword.* New York: W. W. Norton.

Little, Daniel (1986). *The Scientific Marx.* Minneapolis: University of Minnesota Press.

Lockhart, Charles (2003). *The Roots of American Exceptionalism: History, Institutions and Culture.* New York: Palgrave Macmillan.

Loeb, Paul (1982). *Nuclear Culture: Living and Working in the World's Largest Atomic Complex.* New York: Coward, McCann and Geoghegan.

Longstreth, Richard (1998). *City Center to Regional Mall: Architecture, the Automobile, and Retailing in Los Angeles, 1920–1950.* Cambridge: MIT Press.

———. (1999). *The Drive-In, the Supermarket, and the Transformation of Commercial Space in Los Angeles, 1914–1941.* Cambridge: MIT Press.

Lord, M. G. (2005). *Astro Turf: The Private Life of Rocket Science.* New York: Walker.

Lotchin, Roger W. (1974). *San Francisco, 1846–1856: From Hamlet to City.* New York: Oxford University Press.

———. (1992, 2002). *Fortress California, 1910–1961: From Warfare to Welfare.* Urbana, Ill.: University of Illinois Press.

———. (2003). *The Bad City in the Good War: San Francisco, Los Angeles, Oakland, and San Diego.* Bloomington: Indiana University Press.

Low, Victor (1982). *The Unimpressible Race: A Century of Educational Struggle by the Chinese in San Francisco.* San Francisco: East/West Publishing.

Lowen, Rebecca S. (1997). *Creating the Cold War University: The Transformation of Stanford.* Berkeley: University of California Press.

Lowitt, Richard (1984, 1992). *The New Deal and the West.* Norman: University of Oklahoma Press.

Lukes, Timothy, and Gary Okihiro (1985). *Japanese Legacy: Farming and Community Life in California's Santa Clara Valley.* Cupertino: California History Center.

Lummis, Charles F. (1892, 1982). *A Tramp across the Continent.* Intro. Robert E. Fleming. Lincoln: University of Nebraska Press.

Lye, Colleen (2005). *America's Asia: Racial Form and American Literature, 1893–1945.* Princeton: Princeton University Press.

MacColl, E. Kimbark (1979). *The Growth of a City: Power and Politics in Portland, 1915–1950.* Portland, Ore.: Georgian Press.

MacColl, E. Kimbark, with Harry H. Stein (1998). *Merchants, Money, and Power: The Portland Establishment, 1843–1913.* Portland: Georgian Press.

MacDonald, Norbert (1987). *Distant Neighbors: A Comparative History of Seattle and Vancouver.* Lincoln: University of Nebraska Press.

MacIntyre, Alasdaire (1981). *After Virtue: A Study in Moral Theory.* Notre Dame, Ind.: University of Notre Dame Press.

Madsen, Deborah L. (1998). *American Exceptionalism.* Jackson: University Press of Mississippi.

Mahan, Alfred Thayer (1897, 2008). *The Interest of America in Sea Power, Present and Future* n.p.: Tutis Digital Publishing Pvt. Ltd.

Maier, Charles S. (2006). *Among Empires: American Ascendancy and Its Predecessors.* Cambridge: Harvard University Press.

Mailer, Norman (1968). *Miami and the Siege of Chicago: An Informal History of the Republican and Democratic Conventions of 1968.* New York: New American Library.

Manes, Stephen, and Paul Andrews (1994). *Gates: How Microsoft's Mogul Reinvented an Industry and Made Himself the Richest Man in America.* New York: Simon and Schuster.

Mann, Charles C. (2005). *1491: New Revelations of the Americas before Columbus.* New York: Alfred A. Knopf.

Mann, James (2000). *About Face: A History of America's Curious Relationship with China, from Nixon to Clinton.* New York: Vintage Books.

———. (2004). *Rise of the Vulcans: The History of Bush's War Cabinet.* New York: Viking.

Markusen, Ann R., Scott Campbell, Peter Hall, and Sabina Deitrick (1991). *The Rise of the Gunbelt: The Military Remapping of Industrial America.* New York: Oxford University Press.

Markusen, Ann R., Peter Hall, and Amy Glasmeier (1986). *High-Tech America: The What, How, Where, and Why of Sunrise Industries.* Boston: Allen and Unwin.

Markusen, Ann R., Yong-Sook Lee, and Sean DiGiovanna, eds. (1999). *Second Tier Cities: Rapid Growth beyond the Metropolis.* Minneapolis: University of Minnesota Press.

Marshall, Jonathan (1995). *To Have and Have Not: Southeast Asian Raw Materials and the Origins of the Pacific War.* Berkeley: University of California Press.

Martin, Albro (1976, 1991). *James J. Hill and the Opening of the Northwest.* St. Paul: Minnesota Historical Society Press.

———. (1992). *Railroads Triumphant: The Growth, Rejection, and Rebirth of a Vital American Force.* New York: Oxford University Press.

Martin, Thomas S. (1975). *With Fremont: To California and the Southwest, 1845–1849.* Ed. and intro. Ferol Egan. Ashland, Calif.: Lewis Osborne.

Marx, Karl (1857–58, 1973). *Grundrisse: Foundations of the Critique of Political Economy.* Trans. and foreword by Martin Nicolaus. New York: Vintage Books.

——. (1887, 1967). *Capital: A Critique of Political Economy.* Vol. 1. Trans. Samuel Moore and Edward Aveling. New York: International Publishers.

Marx, Leo (1964). *The Machine in the Garden: Technology and the Pastoral Idea in America.* New York: Oxford University Press.

März, Eduard (1991). *Joseph Schumpeter: Scholar, Teacher and Politician.* New Haven: Yale University Press.

Mathiessen, F. O. (1941, 1968). *American Rennaissance: Art and Expression in the Age of Emerson and Whitman.* New York: Oxford University Press.

May, Ernest R., and James C. Thomson, Jr., eds. (1972). *American–East Asian Relations: A Survey.* Cambridge: Harvard University Press.

Mayhew, David (2002). *Electoral Realignments: A Critique of an American Genre.* New Haven: Yale University Press.

McCartney, Laton (1988). *Friends in High Places: The Bechtel Story: The Most Secret Corporation and How It Engineered the World.* New York: Ballantine Books.

McClung, William Alexander (2000). *Landscapes of Desire: Anglo Mythologies of Los Angeles.* Berkeley: University of California Press.

McComas, Terence (1991). *Pearl Harbor Fact and Reference Book.* Honolulu: Mutual Publishing.

McCormick, Thomas J. (1967). *China Market: America's Quest for Informal Empire, 1893–1901.* Chicago: Quadrangle Books.

——. (1989). *America's Half-Century: United States Foreign Policy in the Cold War.* Baltimore: Johns Hopkins University Press.

McDougall, Walter A. (1993). *Let the Sea Make a Noise . . . : A History of the North Pacific from Magellan to MacArthur.* New York: Basic Books.

McEntire, Davis (1946). *The Population of California.* San Francisco: Parker Printing.

McEvedy, Colin (1998). *The Penguin Historical Atlas of the Pacific.* New York: Penguin Books.

McGirr, Lisa (2001). *Suburban Warriors: The Origins of the New American Right.* Princeton: Princeton University Press.

McMurtry, Larry (1968, 2001). *In a Narrow Grave: Essays on Texas.* New York: Simon and Schuster.

——. (1997). *Comanche Moon.* New York: Pocket Books.

——. (1999). *Crazy Horse.* New York: Penguin Books.

——. (2001). *Sacagawea's Nickname: Essays on the American West.* New York: New York Review of Books.

McNeill, William H. (1983). *The Great Frontier: Freedom and Hierarchy in Modern Times.* Princeton: Princeton University Press.

McPhee, John (1966). *Oranges.* New York: Farrar, Straus and Giroux.

——. (1977). *Coming Into the Country.* New York: Farrar, Straus and Giroux.

——. (1993). *Assembling California.* New York: Farrar, Straus and Giroux.

McRae, Hamish (1994). *The World in 2020: Power, Culture and Prosperity.* Boston: Harvard Business School Press.

McWilliams, Carey (1939, 1999). *Factories in the Field: The Story of Migratory Farm Labor in California*. Berkeley: University of California Press.

——. (1945). *Prejudice: Japanese-Americans, Symbol of Racial Intolerance*. Boston: Little, Brown.

——. (1946, 1973). *Southern California: An Island on the Land*. Santa Barbara: Peregrine Smith.

——. (1949, 1999). *California: The Great Exception*. Berkeley: University of California Press.

Mearsheimer, John (2001). *The Tragedy of Great Power Politics*. New York: W. W. Norton.

Meinig, D. W. (1968, 1995). *The Great Columbia Plain: A Historical Geography 1805–1910*. Foreword by William Cronon. Seattle: University of Washington Press.

——. (1969). *Imperial Texas: An Interpretive Essay in Cultural Geography*. Austin: University of Texas Press.

——. (1993). *The Shaping of America: A Geographical Perspective on 500 Years of History*. Vol. 2, *Continental America, 1800–1867*. New Haven: Yale University Press.

——. (1998). *The Shaping of America: A Geographical Perspective on 500 Years of History*. Vol. 3, *Transcontinental America, 1850–1915*. New Haven: Yale University Press.

——. (2004). *The Shaping of America: A Geographical Perspective on 500 Years of History*. Vol. 4, *Global America, 1915–2000*. New Haven: Yale University Press.

Melzer, Arthur R., Jerry Weinberger, and M. Richard Zinman, eds. (1993). *Technology in the Western Political Tradition*. Ithaca: Cornell University Press.

Menand, Louis (2001). *The Metaphysical Club*. New York: Farrar, Strauss and Giroux.

Merk, Frederick (1963). *Manifest Destiny in American History*. New York: Vintage Books.

Merry, Sally Engle (2000). *Colonizing Hawai'i: The Cultural Power of Law*. Princeton: Princeton University Press.

Millard, Mike (2001). *Leaving Japan: Observations on the Dysfunctional U.S.–Japan Relationship*. Armonk, N.Y.: M. E. Sharpe.

Mills, C. Wright (1956). *The Power Elite*. New York: Oxford University Press.

Milner, Bart (2004). *Google and the Mission to Map Meaning and Make Money*. London: Electric Book.

Milner, Clyde A. II, Carol A. O'Connor, and Martha A. Sandweiss, eds. (1994). *The Oxford History of the American West*. New York: Oxford University Press.

Mintz, Sidney W. (1985). *Sweetness and Power: The Place of Sugar in Modern History*. New York: Penguin Books.

Misa, Thomas J. (1995). *A Nation of Steel: The Making of Modern America, 1865–1925*. Baltimore: John Hopkins University Press.

Mitani, Hiroshi (2006). *Escape from Impasse: The Decision to Open Japan.* Trans. David Noble. Tokyo: International House of Japan.

Mitchell, Don (1996). *The Lie of the Land: Migrant Workers and the California Landscape.* Minneapolis: University of Minnesota Press.

Mitchell, Greg (1998). *Tricky Dick and the Pink Lady.* New York: Random House.

Mitchell, Katharyne (2004). *Crossing the Neoliberal Line: Pacific Rim Migration and the Metropolis.* Philadelphia: Temple University Press.

Mitchell, Lee Clark (1981). *Witnesses to a Vanishing America: The Nineteenth-Century Reponse.* Princeton: Princeton University Press.

Modell, John (1977). *The Economics and Politics of Racial Accommodation: The Japanese of Los Angeles, 1900–1942.* Urbana: University of Illinois Press.

Mokyr, Joel (1990). *The Lever of Riches: Technological Creativity and Economic Progress.* New York: Oxford University Press.

——. (2002). *The Gifts of Athena: Historical Origins of the Knowledge Economy.* Princeton: Princeton University Press.

Morgan, Neil, and the Editors of Time-Life Books (1967). *The Pacific States: California, Oregon, Washington.* New York: Time Incorporated.

Morison, Samuel Eliot (1967). *"Old Bruin": Commodore Matthew C. Perry, 1794–1858.* Boston: Little, Brown.

Morris, Edmund (2002). *Theodore Rex.* New York: Modern Library.

Mosley, Walter (1990). *Devil in a Blue Dress.* New York: W. W. Norton.

Mulholland, Catherine (2000). *William Mulholland and the Rise of Los Angeles.* Berkeley: University of California Press.

Mullins, William H. (1991). *The Depression and the Urban West Coast, 1929–1933.* Bloomington: Indiana University Press.

Musicant, Ivan (1998). *Empire by Default: The Spanish-American War and the Dawn of the American Century.* New York: Henry Holt.

Myres, Sandra L., ed. (1980). *Women's Overland Diaries from the Huntington Library.* San Marino: Huntington Library.

Nalty, Bernard C., ed. (1999). *War in the Pacific: Pearl Harbor to Tokyo Bay.* Technical advisor Russ A. Pritchard. Norman: University of Oklahoma Press.

Nash, Gerald D. (1985). *The American West Transformed: The Impact of the Second World War.* Bloomington: Indiana University Press.

Nathan, Andrew J., and Robert S. Ross (1997). *The Great Wall and the Empty Fortress: China's Search for Security.* New York: Norton.

Nee, Victor G., and Brett de Bary Nee (1972). *Longtime Californ': A Documentary Study of an American Chinatown.* New York: Pantheon Books.

Neu, Charles (1967). *An Uncertain Friendship: Theodore Roosevelt and Japan, 1906–1909.* Cambridge: Harvard University Press.

Neuenburg, Evelyn (1946). *California Lure: The Golden State in Pictures.* Prologue and epilogue by Oscar Lewis. Pasadena: California Lure Publishers.

Ngai, Mae M. (2004). *Impossible Subjects: Illegal Aliens and the Making of Modern America.* Princeton: Princeton University Press.

Noble, David W. (1965). *Historians against History: The Frontier Thesis and the National Covenant in American Historical Writing since 1830.* Minneapolis: University of Minnesota Press.

———. (1985). *The End of American History: Democracy, Capitalism, and the Metaphor of Two Worlds in Anglo-American Historical Writing, 1880–1890.* Minneapolis: University of Minnesota Press.

Nordhoff, Charles (1874, 1974). *Northern California, Oregon, and the Sandwich Islands.* Berkeley: Ten Speed Press.

Nordlinger, Eric A. (1995). *Isolationism Reconfigured: American Foreign Policy for a New Century.* Princeton: Princeton University Press.

North, Douglass C. (1961). *The Economic Growth of the United States, 1790–1860.* Englewood Cliffs, N.J.: Prentice-Hall.

Nugent, Walter T. K. (1981). *Structures of American Social History.* Bloomington: Indiana University Press.

———. (2001). *Into the West: The Story of Its People.* New York: Vintage Books.

Nugent, Walter, and Martin Ridge, eds. (1999). *The American West: The Reader.* Bloomington: Indiana University Press.

Nye, David E. (1994). *American Technological Sublime.* Cambridge: MIT Press.

———. (1990). *Electrifying America.* Cambridge: MIT Press.

———. (2004). *America as Second Creation: Technology and Narratives of New Beginnings.* Cambridge: MIT Press.

Obeyesekere, Gananath (1992). *The Apotheosis of Captain Cook: European Mythmaking in the Pacific.* Princeton: Princeton University Press.

Okihiro, Gary (1994). *Margins and Mainstreams: Asians in American History and Culture.* Seattle: University of Washington Press.

Onuf, Peter S. (2000). *Jefferson's Empire: The Language of American Nationhood.* Charlottesville: University Press of Virginia.

Osborne, Thomas J. (1998). *Annexation Hawaii.* Waimanalo, Hawaii: Island Style Press.

Ostrander, Gilman M. (1970). *American Civilization in the First Machine Age, 1890–1940.* New York: Harper and Row.

Ota, Masahide (1981). *This Was the Battle of Okinawa.* Naha, Okinawa: Naha Publishing.

———. (2000). *Essays on Okinawa Problems.* Gushikawa City, Okinawa: Yui Shuppan.

Painter, Nell Irvin (1987). *Standing at Armageddon: The United States, 1877–1919.* New York: W. W. Norton.

Palat, Ravi Arvind, ed. (1993). *Pacific-Asia and the Future of the World-System.* Westport, Conn.: Greenwood Press.

Palumbo-Liu, David (1999). *Asian/American: Historical Crossings of a Racial Frontier.* Stanford: Stanford University Press.

Paolino, Ernest N. (1973). *The Foundations of the American Empire: William Henry Seward and U.S. Foreign Policy.* Ithaca: Cornell University Press.

Parkman, Francis. Jr. (1849, 1985). *The Oregon Trail.* Ed. and intro. David Levin. New York: Penguin Books.

Paskoff, Paul E., ed. (1989). *Encyclopedia of American Business History and Biography: Iron and Steel in the Nineteenth Century.* New York: Facts on File.

Patterson, James T. (1972). *Mr. Republican: A Biography of Robert A. Taft.* Boston: Houghton Mifflin.

Patterson, Tom (1971). *A Colony for California: Riverside.* Riverside, Calif.: Press Enterprise Company.

Peirce, Neal R. (1972). *The Pacific States of America: People, Politics, and Power in the Five Pacific Basin States.* New York: W. W. Norton.

Pempel, T. J., ed. (2005). *Remapping East Asia: The Construction of a Region.* Ithaca: Cornell University Press.

Pendle, George (2005). *Strange Angel: The Otherworldly Life of Rocket Scientist John Whiteside Parsons.* New York: Harcourt, Inc.

Perlstein, Rick (2001). *Before the Storm: Barry Goldwater and the Unmaking of the American Consensus.* New York: Hill and Wang.

Perry, Commodore M. C. (2000). *Narrative of the Expedition to the China Seas and Japan, 1852–1854.* Ed. Francis L. Hawks. Washington, D.C.: Congress of the United States, 1856; Dover Publications Reprint.

Philbrick, Nathaniel (2003). *Sea of Glory: America's Voyage of Discovery, The U.S. Exploring Expedition, 1838–1842.* New York: Penguin Viking.

Phillips, George Harwood (1975). *Chiefs and Challengers: Indian Resistance and Cooperation in Southern California.* Berkeley: University of California Press.

Phillips, Kevin P. (1969). *The Emerging Republican Majority.* New Rochelle, N.Y.: Arlington House.

———. (2004). *American Dynasty: Aristocracy, Fortune, and the Politics of Deceit in the House of Bush.* New York: Viking Penguin.

———. (2006). *American Theocracy: The Peril and Politics of Radical Religion, Oil, and Borrowed Money in the 21st Century.* New York: Viking Penguin.

Pisani, Donald J. (1984). *From the Family Farm to Agribusiness: The Irrigation Crusade in California and the West, 1850–1931.* Berkeley: University of California Press.

———. (1996). *Water, Land, and Law in the West: The Limits of Public Policy, 1850–1920.* Lawrence: University Press of Kansas.

Pitkin, Walter B. (1921). *Must We Fight Japan?* New York: Century Books.

Pletcher, David M. (1973). *The Diplomacy of Annexation: Texas, Oregon, and the Mexican War.* Columbia, Missouri: University of Missouri Press.

———. (2001). *The Diplomacy of Involvement: American Economic Expansion across the Pacific, 1784–1900.* Columbia: University of Missouri Press.

Polanyi, Karl (1944). *The Great Transformation.* New York: Beacon Books.

Polenberg, Richard (1972). *War and Society: The United States, 1941–1945.* Philadelphia: J. B. Lippincott.

Polk, Dora Beale (1991). *The Island of California: A History of the Myth.* Lincoln: University of Nebraska Press.

Pomeranz, Kenneth (2000). *The Great Divergence: China, Europe, and the Making of the Modern World Economy.* Princeton: Princeton University Press.

Pomeroy, Earl (1965, 1991). *The Pacific Slope: A History of California, Oregon, Washington, Idaho, Utah, and Nevada.* Reno and Las Vegas: University of Nevada Press.

Porter, Carolyn (1981). *Seeing and Being: The Plight of the Participant Observer in Emerson, James, Adams, and Faulkner.* Middletown, Conn.: Wesleyan University Press.

Potter, Elizabeth Gray, and Mabel Thayer Gray (1915). *The Lure of San Francisco: A Romance Amid Old Landmarks.* San Francisco: Paul Elder.

Powell, G. Harold (1990). *Letters from the Orange Empire.* Ed. Richard G. Lillard, afterword by Lawrence Clark Powell. Los Angeles: Historical Society of Southern California.

Powell, H. M. T. (1931). *The Santa Fe Trail to California, 1849–1852.* San Francisco: Book Club of California.

Prown, Jules David, et al. (1992). *Discovered Lands, Invented Pasts: Transforming Visions of the American West.* New Haven: Yale University Press.

Pyne, Stephen J. (1982). *Fire in America: A Cultural History of Wildland and Rural Fire.* Princeton: Princeton University Press.

Quinn, Thornton, J. (1855, 1945). *The California Tragedy.* Oakland: Biobooks.

Rae, John B. (1968). *Climb to Greatness: The American Aircraft Industry, 1920–1960.* Cambridge: MIT Press.

Rawls, James. J., and Richard J. Orsi, eds. (1999). *A Golden State: Mining and Economic Development in Gold Rush California.* Berkeley: University of California Press.

Reckner, James R. (1988). *Teddy Roosevelt's Great White Fleet.* Annapolis: Naval Institute Press.

Reisner, Marc (1993). *Cadillac Desert: The American West and Its Disappearing Water.* Rev. ed. New York: Penguin Books.

——. (2004). *A Dangerous Place: California's Unsettling Fate.* New York: Penguin Books.

Renshaw, Patrick (1967). *The Wobblies: The Story of Syndicalism in the United States.* Garden City: Doubleday.

Rhodes, Richard (1986). *The Making of the Atomic Bomb.* New York: Simon and Schuster.

——, ed. (1999). *Visions of Technology: A Century of Debate about Machines, Systems and the Human World.* New York: Simon and Schuster.

Rich, Ben R., and Leo Janos (1994). *Skunk Works: A Personal Memoir of My Years at Lockheed.* New York: Little, Brown.

Riesenberg, Felix (1940). *The Pacific Ocean.* New York: McGraw-Hill.

Rigal, Laura (1998). *The American Manufactory: Art, Labor, and the World of Things in the Early Republic.* Princeton: Princeton University Press.

Riordan, Michael, and Lillian Hoddeson (1997). *Crystal Fire: The Invention of the Transistor and the Birth of the Information Age.* New York: W. W. Norton.

Ritter, Harry (1993). *Alaska's History: The People, Land, and Events of the North Country.* Anchorage: Alaska Northwest Books.

Robertson, Douglas S. (1998). *The New Renaissance: Computers and the Next Level of Civilization.* New York: Oxford University Press.

Robbins, William G. (1994). *Colony and Empire: The Capitalist Transformation of the American West.* Lawrence: University Press of Kansas.

Robbins, William G., Robert J. Frank, and Richard E. Ross (1983). *Regionalism in the Pacific Northwest.* Corvallis: Oregon State University Press.

Rodgers, Daniel T. (1978). *The Work Ethic in Industrial America, 1850–1920.* Chicago: University of Chicago Press.

Rogin, Michael Paul (1975). *Fathers and Children: Andrew Jackson and the Subjugation of the American Indian.* New York: Alfred A. Knopf.

——. (1987). *Ronald Reagan, the Movie: and Other Episodes in Political Demonology.* Berkeley: University of California Press.

Rogin, Michael Paul, and John L. Shover (1970). *Political Change in California: Critical Elections and Social Movements, 1890–1966.* Westport, Conn.: Greenwood Publishing.

Rohrbough, Malcolm J. (1997). *Days of Gold: The California Gold Rush and the American Nation.* Berkeley: University of California Press.

Rolle, Andrew (1991). *John Charles Frémont: Character as Destiny.* Norman: University of Oklahoma Press.

Roosevelt, Theodore (1902, 1990). *The Rough Riders.* New York: Da Capo Press.

Rosenberg, Emily S. (1982). *Spreading the American Dream: American Economic and Cultural Expansion, 1890–1945.* New York: Hill and Wang.

Ross, Kristin (1995). *Fast Cars, Clean Bodies: Decolonization and the Reordering of French Society.* Cambridge: MIT Press.

Rothschild, Emma (1974). *Paradise Lost: The Decline of the Auto-Industrial Age.* New York: Vintage Books.

Royce, Josiah (1886, 2002). *California: A Study of American Character.* Berkeley: Heyday Books.

Ruiz, Vicki (1987). *Cannery Women, Cannery Lives: Mexican Women, Unionization and the California Food Processing Industry, 1930–1950.* Albuquerque: University of New Mexico Press.

Rusling, James F. (1877). *The Great West and the Pacific Coast.* New York: Sheldon.

Russel, Robert R. (1948). *Improvement of Communication with the Pacific Coast as an Issue in American Politics, 1783–1864.* Cedar Rapids, Iowa: Torch Press.

Sachs, Wolfgang (1992). *For Love of the Automobile: Looking Back into the History of Our Desires.* Trans. Don Reneau. Berkeley: University of California Press.

Sackman, Douglas Cazaux (2005). *Orange Empire: California and the Fruits of Eden.* Berkeley: University of California Press.

Sahlins, Marshall (1985). *Islands of History.* Chicago: University of Chicago Press.

——. (1995). *How "Natives" Think: About Captain Cook, For Example.* Chicago: University of Chicago Press.

Sale, Kirkpatrick (1990, 1991). *The Conquest of Paradise: Christopher Columbus and the Columbia Legacy.* New York: Penguin Books.

Sale, Roger (1976). *Seattle: Past to Present.* Seattle: University of Washington Press.

Sanford, Charles L., ed. (1974). *Manifest Destiny and the Imperialism Question.* New York: Wiley.

Santayana, George (1967, 1998). *The Genteel Tradition.* Ed. and intro. Douglas L. Wilson. Lincoln: University of Nebraska Press.

Saunders, Frances Stoner (1999). *The Cultural Cold War: The CIA and the World of Arts and Letters.* New York: New Press.

Sawyer, Richard (1996). *To Make a Spotless Orange: Biological Control in California.* Ames: Iowa State University Press.

Saxenian, AnnaLee (1994, 2000). *Regional Advantage: Culture and Competition in Silicon Valley and Route 128.* Cambridge: Harvard University Press.

——. (2000). "Silicon Valley's New Immigrant Entrepreneurs." Working Paper 15. University of California–San Diego, Center for Comparative Immigration Studies, May.

Saxton, Alexander (1971). *The Indispensable Enemy: Labor and the Anti-Chinese Movement in California.* Berkeley: University of California Press.

Schivelbusch, Wolfgang (1986). *The Railway Journey: The Industrialization of Time and Space in the 19th Century.* Berkeley: University of California Press.

Schmitt, Robert C., ed. (2002). *Hawaii Data Book.* Honolulu: Mutual Publishing.

Schonberger, Howard B. (1989). *Aftermath of War: Americans and the Remaking of Japan, 1945–1952.* Kent, Ohio: Kent State University Press.

Schrag, Peter (1999). *Paradise Lost: California's Experience, America's Future.* Berkeley: University of California Press.

Schroeder, John H. (1973). *Mr. Polk's War: American Opposition and Dissent, 1846–1848.* Madison: University of Wisconsin Press.

Schulman, Bruce J. (1994). *From Cotton Belt to Sunbelt: Federal Policy, Economic Development, and the Transformation of the South, 1938–1980.* Durham: Duke University Press.

Schumpeter, Joseph (1934, 1983). *The Theory of Economic Development.* Trans. Redvers Opie. Intro. John E. Elliott. New Brunswick, N.J.: Transaction Books.

——. (1939, 1989). *Business Cycles: A Theoretical, Historical and Statistical Analysis of the Capitalist Process.* Abr. ed. Intro. Rendig Fels. Philadelphia: Porcupine Press.

——. (1942, 1950). *Capitalism, Socialism and Democracy.* 3rd ed. New York: Harper and Row.

———. (1991). *The Economics and Sociology of Capitalism.* Ed. Richard Swedberg. Princeton: Princeton University Press.

Schwantes, Carlos A. (1979, 1994). *Radical Heritage: Labor, Socialism, and Reform in Washington and British Columbia, 1885–1917.* Boise: University of Idaho Press.

———. (1996). *The Pacific Northwest: An Interpretive History.* Rev. ed. Lincoln: University of Nebraska Press.

Schwartz, Peter, Peter Leyden, and Joel Hyatt (2000). *The Long Boom: A Vision for the Coming Age of Prosperity.* Cambridge, Mass.: Perseus Publishing.

Schwartz, Stephen (1998). *California and the Making of the American Mind.* New York: Free Press.

Seiden, Allan (2001). *From Fishponds to Warships: Pearl Harbor, A Complete Illustrated History.* Honolulu: Mutual Publishing.

Seidensticker, Bob (2006). *Futurehype: The Myths of Technology Change.* San Francisco: Berrett-Koehler.

Sellers, Charles G. (1966). *James K. Polk, Continentalist, 1843–1846.* Princeton: Princeton University Press.

Shaw, Angel Velasco, and Luis H. Francia, eds. (2002). *Vestiges of War: The Philippine-American War and the Aftermath of an Imperial Dream, 1899–1999.* New York: New York University Press.

Shepherd, Sandra Brubaker (1993). *California Heartland: A Pictorial History and Tour Guide of Eight Northern California Counties.* San Francisco: Scottwall Associates.

Sherry, Frank (1994). *Pacific Passions: The European Struggle for Power in the Great Ocean in the Age of Exploration.* New York: William Morrow.

Sherry, Michael S. (1987). *The Rise of American Air Power: The Creation of Armageddon.* New Haven: Yale University Press.

———. (1995). *In the Shadow of War: The United States since the 1930s.* New Haven: Yale University Press.

Sinclair, Upton (1926, 1997). *Oil!* Berkeley: University of California Press.

Sklar, Martin J. (1988). *The Corporate Reconstruction of American Capitalism, 1898–1916: The Market, the Law, and Politics.* Cambridge: Cambridge University Press.

———. (1992). *The United States as a Developing Country: Studies in U.S. History in the Progressive Era and the 1920s.* Cambridge: Cambridge University Press.

Slotkin, Richard (1973, 1996). *Regeneration Through Violence: The Mythology of the American Frontier, 1600–1860.* New York: HarperPerennial.

———. (1985, 1998). *The Fatal Environment: The Myth of the Frontier in the Age of Industrialization, 1800–1890.* Norman: University of Oklahoma Press.

———. (1992, 1998). *Gunfighter Nation: The Myth of the Frontier in Twentieth-Century America.* Norman: University of Oklahoma Press.

Smith, Adam (1776, 2003). *The Wealth of Nations.* Intro. Alan B. Krueger. New York: Bantam Dell.

Smith, Henry Nash (1950, 1978). *Virgin Land: The American West as Symbol and Myth.* Cambridge: Harvard University Press.

Smythe, William E. (1899, 1969). *The Conquest of Arid America.* Intro. Lawrence E. Bee. Seattle: University of Washington Press.

Snyder, Jack (1991). *Myths of Empire: Domestic Politics and International Ambition.* Ithaca: Cornell University Press.

Sparrow, Bartholomew H. (1996). *From the Outside In: World War II and the American State.* Princeton: Princeton University Press.

Sprout, Harold, and Margaret Sprout (1944). *The Rise of American Naval Power, 1776–1918.* Princeton: Princeton University Press.

Standage, Tom (1998). *The Victorian Internet: The Remarkable Story of the Telegraph and the Nineteenth Century's On-line Pioneers.* New York: Berkley Books.

Stannard, David (1992). *American Holocaust: Columbus and the Conquest of the New World.* New York: Oxford University Press.

Starr, Kevin (1973). *Americans and the California Dream, 1850–1915.* New York: Oxford University Press.

——. (1985). *Inventing the Dream: California through the Progressive Era.* New York: Oxford University Press.

——. (1990). *Material Dreams: Southern California through the 1920s.* New York: Oxford University Press.

——. (1996). *Endangered Dreams: The Great Depression in California.* New York: Oxford University Press.

——. (1997). *The Dream Endures: California Enters the 1940s.* New York: Oxford University Press.

——. (2002). *Embattled Dreams: California in War and Peace, 1940–1950.* New York: Oxford University Press.

——. (2004). *Coast of Dreams: California on the Edge, 1990–2003.* New York: Alfred A. Knopf.

Stegner, Wallace (1953, 1982). *Beyond the Hundredth Meridian: John Wesley Powell and the Second Opening of the West.* Lincoln: University of Nebraska Press.

Steinbeck, John (1936, 1972). *In Dubious Battle.* New York: Bantam Books.

Steiner, Michael (1995). "From Frontier to Region: Frederick Jackson Turner and the New Western History." *Pacific Historical Review* 64, no. 4 (November): 479–502.

Stephanson, Anders (1995). *Manifest Destiny: American Expansionism and the Empire of Right.* New York: Hill and Wang.

Sterling, George (1916). *The Evanescent City.* San Francisco: A. M. Robertson.

Stewart, Edgar I., ed. (1968). *Penny-an-Acre Empire in the West.* Norman: University of Oklahoma Press.

Stoddard, Lothrop (1920). *The Rising Tide of Colour against White World Supremacy.* Intro. Madison Grant. New York: Charles Scribner's Sons.

Stoler, Ann Laura, ed. (2006). *Haunted by Empire: Geographies of Intimacy in North American History.* Durham: Duke University Press.

Stoll, Steven (1998). *The Fruits of Natural Advantage: Making the Industrial Countryside in California.* Berkeley: University of California Press.

Strong, Josiah (1891). *Our Country: Its Possible Future and Its Present Crisis.* New York: Baker and Taylor for the American Home Missionary Society.

Sumida, Jon Tetsuro (1989). *In Defence of Naval Supremacy.* London: Routledge.

Susman, Warren I. (1973). *Culture as History: The Transformation of American Society in the Twentieth Century.* New York: Pantheon Books.

Sutter, Robert G. (2005). *China's Rise in Asia: Promises and Perils.* Lanham, Md.: Rowman and Littlefield.

Swedberg, Richard (1991). *Schumpeter: A Biography.* Princeton: Princeton University Press.

Symonds, Matthew (2003). *Softwar: An Intimate Portrait of Larry Ellison and Oracle.* New York: Simon and Schuster.

Takaki, Ronald D. (1979). *Iron Cages: Race and Culture in Nineteenth-Century America.* Seattle: University of Washington Press.

Taylor, Alan (2006). *The Divided Ground: Indians, Settlers, and the Northern Borderland of the American Revolution.* New York: Alfred A. Knopf.

Taylor, Frank, and Lawton Wright (1947). *Democracy's Air Arsenal.* New York: Duell, Sloan and Pearce.

Taylor, Paul S. (1928). *Mexican Labor in the United States Imperial Valley.* Berkeley: University of California Press.

Taylor, Quintard (1998). *In Search of the Racial Frontier: African Americans in the American West, 1528–1990.* New York: W. W. Norton.

Taylor, Sandra C. (1984). *Advocate of Understanding: Sidney Gulick and the Search for Peace with Japan.* Kent, Ohio: Kent State University Press.

Tchen, John Kuo Wei (1999). *New York before Chinatown: Orientalism and the Shaping of American Culture, 1776–1882.* Baltimore: Johns Hopkins University Press.

Thompson, Robert Smith (2001). *Empires on the Pacific: World War II and the Struggle for the Mastery of Asia.* New York: Basic Books.

Thornton, Russell (1987). *American Indian Holocaust and Survival: A Population History since 1492.* Norman: University of Oklahoma Press.

Tocqueville, Alexis de (1840, 1945). *Democracy in America.* Vol. 1. Henry Reeve text, rev. Francis Bowen, ed. and intro. Phillips Bradley. New York: Vintage Books.

Todd, Frank Martin (1921). *The Story of the Exposition.* 5 vols. New York: Knickerbocker Press.

Todorov, Tzvetan (1982, 1999). *The Conquest of America: The Question of the Other.* Trans. Richard Howard. Norman: University of Oklahoma Press.

Townshend, F. Trench (1869). *Ten Thousand Miles of Travel, Sport, and Adventure.* London: Hurst and Blackett.

Trachtenberg, Alan (1982). *The Incorporation of America: Culture and Society in the Gilded Age.* New York: Hill and Wang.

Trafzer, Clifford E., and Joel R. Hyer, eds. (1999). *"Exterminate Them": Written*

Accounts of Murder, Rape, and Slavery of Native Americans during the California Gold Rush, 1848–1868. East Lansing: Michigan State University Press.

Trask, David F. (1981, 1996). *The War with Spain in 1898.* Lincoln: University of Nebraska Press.

Trask, Haunani-Kay (1993). *From a Native Daughter: Colonialism and Sovereignty in Hawai'i.* Monroe, Maine: Common Courage Press.

Turner, Frederick Jackson (1920, 1977). *The Frontier in American History.* Franklin Center, Pa.: Franklin Library.

Turner, Frederick W. (1983). *Beyond Geography: The Western Spirit against the Wilderness.* New Brunswick, N.J.: Rutgers University Press.

Tutorow, Norman E. (1971). *Leland Stanford: Man of Many Careers.* Menlo Park, Calif.: Pacific Coast Publishers.

Twain, Mark (1872, 1962). *Roughing It.* New York: Penguin Books.

Tygiel, Jules (1994). *The Great Los Angeles Swindle: Oil, Stocks, and Scandal during the Roaring Twenties.* Berkeley: University of California Press.

Tyrrell, Ian (1999). *True Gardens of the Gods: Californian-Australian Environmental Reform, 1860–1930.* Berkeley: University of California Press.

Unruh, John D., Jr. (1979). *The Plains Across: The Overland Emigrants and the Trans-Mississippi West, 1840–60.* Urbana: University of Illinois Press.

Varg, Paul A. (1983). *New England and Foreign Relations, 1789–1850.* Hanover, N.H.: University Press of New England.

Van Alstyne, Richard W. (1960). *The Rising American Empire.* New York: Quadrangle Paperbacks.

Vaught, David (1999). *Cultivating California: Growers, Specialty Crops, and Labor, 1875–1920.* Baltimore: Johns Hopkins University Press.

Verge, Arthur C. (1993). *Paradise Transformed: Los Angeles during the Second World War.* Dubuque, Iowa: Kendall/Hunt Publishing.

Vevier, Charles (1959). "The Collins Overland Line and American Continentalism." *Pacific Historical Review* 28 (August): 237–53.

Wada, Michael (1994). *The Council on Foreign Relations and American Foreign Policy in the Early Cold War.* Providence, R.I.: Berghahn Books.

Walker, Richard A. (2004). *The Conquest of Bread: 150 Years of Agribusiness in California.* New York: New Press.

Wallerstein, Immanuel (2006). *European Universalism: The Rhetoric of Power.* New York: New Press.

Walton, John (1992). *Western Times and Water Wars: State, Culture, and Rebellion in California.* Berkeley: University of California Press.

Warsh, David (2006). *Knowledge and the Wealth of Nations: A Story of Economic Discovery.* New York: W. W. Norton.

Watkins, T. H., and R. R. Olmsted (1976). *Mirror of the Dream: An Illustrated History of San Francisco.* San Francisco: Scrimshaw Press.

Webb, Walter Prescott (1931, 1981). *The Great Plains.* Lincoln.: University of Nebraska Press.

Weber, David J. (1992). *The Spanish Frontier in North America.* New Haven: Yale University Press.

Weigley, Russell F. (1967). *History of the United States Army.* New York: Macmillan.

Weinberg, Albert K. (1935). *Manifest Destiny: A Study of Nationalist Expansionism in American History.* Baltimore: Johns Hopkins University Press.

Welch, Richard E., Jr. (1979). *Response to Imperialism: The United States and the Philippine-American War, 1899–1902.* Chapel Hill: University of North Carolina Press.

Wells, Miriam J. (1996). *Strawberry Fields: Politics, Class, and Work in California Agriculture.* Ithaca: Cornell University Press.

West, Nathaniel (1939, 1983). *The Day of the Locust.* New York: Signet Classics.

White, G. Edward (1968, 1989). *The Eastern Establishment and the Western Experience: The West of Fredric Remington, Theodore Roosevelt, and Owen Wister.* Austin: University of Texas Press.

White, Gerald T. (1980). *Billions for Defense: Government Financing by the Defense Plant Corporation during World War II.* University: University of Alabama Press.

White, Richard (1991). *The Middle Ground: Indians, Empires, and Republics in the Great Lakes Region, 1650–1815.* New York: Cambridge University Press.

——. (1993). *"It's Your Misfortune and None of My Own": A New History of the American West.* Norman: University of Oklahoma Press.

——. (1995). *The Organic Machine.* New York: Hill and Wang.

Whitman, Walt (1855, 1959). *Leaves of Grass.* Ed. and intro. Malcolm Cowley. New York: Penguin Books.

Wiebe, Robert H. (1967). *The Search for Order, 1877–1920.* New York: Hill and Wang.

Wilentz, Sean (2005). *The Rise of American Democracy: Jefferson to Lincoln.* New York: W. W. Norton.

Wiley, Peter Booth (1990). *Yankees in the Land of the Gods: Commodore Perry and the Opening of Japan.* New York: Viking.

Wiley, Peter, and Robert Gottlieb (1982). *Empires in the Sun: The Rise of the New American West.* Tucson: University of Arizona Press.

Wilford, John Noble (2000). *The Mapmakers: The Story of the Great Pioneers in Cartography—From Antiquity to the Space Age.* New York: Alfred A. Knopf.

Williams, James C. (1997). *Energy and the Making of Modern California.* Akron, Ohio: University of Akron Press.

Williams, Raymond (1973). *The Country and the City.* New York: Oxford University Press.

Williams, William Appleman (1959, 1972). *The Tragedy of American Diplomacy.* 2nd rev. ed. New York: Dell.

——. (1961, 1988). *The Contours of American History.* New York: W. W. Norton.

Willinsky, John (1998). *Learning to Divide the World: Education at Empire's End.* Minneapolis: University of Minnesota Press.

Wills, Gary (1969). *Nixon Agonistes: The Crisis of the Self-Made Man.* Boston: Houghton Mifflin.

——. (1997). *John Wayne's America.* New York: Simon and Schuster.

Wilson, Edmund (1950, 1962). *Classics and Commercials: A Literary Chronicle of the Forties.* New York: Vintage Books.

Wilson, Joan Hoff (1975, 1992). *Herbert Hoover: Forgotten Progressive.* Ed. Oscar Handlin. Prospect Heights, Ill.: Waveland Press.

Winchester, Simon (1991). *Pacific Rising: The Emergence of a New World Culture.* New York: Prentice-Hall.

Winslow, Carleton Monroe, et al. (1916). *The Architecture and the Gardens of the San Diego Exposition.* San Francisco: Paul Elder.

Winslow, Ward, ed. (1995). *The Making of Silicon Valley: A One Hundred Year Renaissance.* Palo Alto: Santa Clara Valley Historical Association.

Wolf, Eric R. (1982). *Europe and the People without History.* Berkeley: University of California Press.

Wolfe, Jane (1989). *The Murchisons: The Rise and Fall of a Texas Dynasty.* New York: St. Martin's Press.

Wolfe, Tom (1983). "The Tinkerings of Robert Noyce: How the Sun Rose on the Silicon Valley." *Esquire* (December): 346–74.

Wolff, Michael (1998). *Burn Rate: How I Survived the Gold Rush Years on the Internet.* New York: Simon and Schuster

Wollenberg, Charles (1990). *Marinship at War: Shipbuilding and Social Change in Wartime Sausalito.* Foreword by Jack Tracy. Berkeley: Western Heritage Press.

Woo, Jung-en (1991). *Race to the Swift: State, Finance, and Industrialization in South Korea.* New York: Columbia University Press.

Wood, Houston (1999). *Displacing Natives: The Rhetorical Production of Hawai'i.* New York: Rowman and Littlefield.

Woodward, C. Vann (1951, 1999). *Origins of the New South, 1877–1913.* Baton Rouge: Louisiana State University Press.

Worster, Donald (1985). *Rivers of Empire: Water, Aridity, and the Growth of the American West.* New York: Pantheon Books.

——. (1994). *An Unsettled Country: Changing Landscapes of the American West.* Albuquerque: University of New Mexico Press.

Wroth, Lawrence C. (2004). *The Early Cartography of the Pacific.* Mansfield Centre, Conn. Orig. pub. 1944.

Wyatt, David (1997). *Five Fires: Race, Catastrophe, and the Shaping of California.* Oxford: Oxford University Press.

Young, Marilyn Blatt (1968). *The Rhetoric of Empire: American China Policy, 1895–1901.* Cambridge: Harvard University Press.

Yu, Henry (2001). *Thinking Orientals: Migration, Contact, and Exoticism in Modern America.* New York: Oxford University Press.

Zelinsky, Wilbur (1992). *The Cultural Geography of the United States.* Rev. ed. Upper Saddle River, N.J.: Prentice-Hall.

Zia, Helen (2000). *Asian American Dreams: The Emergence of an American People.* New York: Farrar, Straus and Giroux.

Index

Page numbers in *italic* type indicate graphs, maps, or tables.